The Gathering Apocalypse And World Judgement

What It Brings - Even Now - And Why!

Charles S. Brown

THE GATHERING APOCALYPSE AND WORLD JUDGEMENT

What It Brings – Even Now – And Why!

Charles S. Brown

This Edition published in New Zealand by
Crystal Publishing. – www.crystalbooks.org
P.O. Box 60042, Titirangi, Waitakere City,
Auckland, **New Zealand**.

Second Edition 2012
First Published 2005

Copyright © 2005 – 2012 Charles S. Brown

All rights reserved. No part of this publication may be reproduced, stored in a retrieval system, or transmitted in any form, or by any means, electronic, mechanical, photocopying, recording or otherwise, without the prior permission of the publisher.

Moreover, this book is sold on the condition that it shall not, by way of trade or otherwise, be lent, re-sold, hired out or otherwise circulated without the publisher's prior consent in any form of binding or cover other than that in which it is published and without this condition being imposed on the subsequent purchaser.

ISBN 978-0-9582627-9-8

Dedication

With very deep gratitude, this book recognises and confesses *that* Higher guidance from Above which, in its **Eternal Beneficence**, **Grace** and **Power**, *ever* offers humankind the pure and genuine **Love**.

It is a guidance, moreover, which graciously led me to the recognition of Its concomitant Knowledge and therewith the necessary spiritual insights and clarification required to write this book.

Under the mantle of that **Perfect Love**, therefore, this work is offered as a bridge to lead the spiritually-open reader to *that complete Knowledge.* For only with that perfect and enlightened wisdom will we ever be able to fully clarify the reasons for the rapidly increasing uncertainty, fear and confusion now clearly facing humankind in every aspect of human life and endeavour.

Acknowledgements

I am extremely grateful to the many people who assisted in various ways with this work.

Special thanks to certain of those whose input was particularly helpful here:

Dr. Stephen Lampe (author of "The Christian and Reincarnation" and "Building Future Societies: The Spiritual Principles") for his very kind permission to use essential material from his publications, without which this work would have been deficient.

Dr. Kanayo Nwanze for reviewing a key part of the work.

Sally Green for her invaluable computer-savvy in tutoring skills which offered the greatest single aid for the writing of the book.

Mr. John Copas who has been a most valuable reviewer.

Ms. Hazel Morrissey (BA [Hon. MSc]) for both her support and her challenging critique of parts of this work.

And Mr. R. M. Duraisamy (BE Hons., author of "From India to the Truth: Towards a New Knowledge for the Reformation of Indian Spirituality") for his support and spiritual insights, and for applying the right amount of steady pressure to bring this work to completion. And, not least, for reviewing the final draft and converting it to the appropriate electronic medium in preparation for printing and publishing.

Contents

UN Warns of Apocalypse Now   10

Introduction   11

1   GOD: Omniscient - Omnipotent   27

2   God's Law, or Human Law?   35

3   The Spiritual Laws – The Necessary Knowledge   47
    3.1   The Nature of The Spiritual Principles 57
    3.2   Movement = Life 62
    3.3   Decisions Produce Consequences 66
         3.3.1   Faith Versus Works 66
         3.3.2   Attitude to the Suffering 80
    3.4   Like Attracts Like 82
         3.4.1   Spiritual Qualities as the First Consideration   87
         3.4.2   Families and Children 88
    3.5   Gravity – The Spiritual Dynamic 94
    3.6   Balance in Life – A Vital Necessity 97
         3.6.1   To Give, or to Take? 105
    3.7   Rebirth – Fact or Fiction? 111
    3.8   Grace – A Gift of Divine Love 119
    3.9   Conclusion 123

4   The Origins of Man – "Genesis" and Science Agree. 127
    4.1   Our Spiritual Origins 127

5   The Emergence of Language – The Legacy   173

6	**The First Death!**	**195**
6.1	"Death, the Great Leveller"	199
6.2	Jesus – "The Calling of the Dead to Life"	218
6.3	The Nature of Hell	225
6.4	The Ramifications of Loud Wailing	228
6.5	Death of a Soldier	231
7	**The Second Death**	**235**
7.1	One Life – or Many Lives?	241
7.2	Earthbound Souls	260
7.3	Hypnotism – a Spiritual Crime	265
7.4	The Danger of Leading Astray	267
8	**Elemental Lore of Nature**	**275**
8.1	The Circle of Life	276
8.2	Native American "Spirituality" – A European Philosopher's View	306
8.3	Excerpts from Chief Seattle's Address	310
8.4	The Elemental Connection to the Animal Kingdom	313
9	**Where to Now?**	**331**
9.1	Where to Now?	331
9.2	Recognition or Rejection?	336
10	**Humankind's Lost Potential**	**339**
11	**Jesus – His Birth, Death and Resurrection**	**353**
11.1	The "Virgin" Birth – The Immaculate Conception	355
11.2	Mission of the "Three Wise Men"	362
11.3	Resurrection and Ascension	364
11.4	The Revelation and The Holy Grail	378
11.5	Crucifixion of The Son Of God: Medical Forensics Speak	383
11.5.1	The Roman 'Flagrum': The 'Scourging' of "The Son Of God"	387
11.5.2	The 'Burden' of the Cross	389
11.6	The 'Murder' at Golgotha	390
11.6.1	The 'Nailing'	390
11.6.2	His Final Moments	393

12 The Two Sons of God!   407

    12.1 The Disciples' Confusion 415

    12.2 "He" Who Is "Enthroned"! 427

    12.3 Destruction by "Fire" 432

    12.4 The 'Rapture'? A Distortion of Bible Truth! 439

    12.5 THE PROCLAMATION! 442

13 The "Seven Churches in Asia" – The Revelation   445

14 Science supports the Judgement process!   469

    14.1 "The Inconceivable ... Here It Happens." 476

    14.2 The "Last Judgement." 477

    14.3 The "degeneration" of Matter 478

    14.4 The Human Spirit and Matter 480

    14.5 The Collapse 483

    14.6 The Separation from the Light 485

    14.7 The Absence of Differentiation 489

    14.8 "Torn apart and crushed..." 491

    14.9 The experience of time 492

    14.10 The End shall become the Beginning 494

    14.11 Conclusion 496

15 Right Bible/Wrong Bible   501

    15.1 The Number 666 of The Revelation 502

    15.2 Intellectual Volition versus Spiritual Volition 507

    15.3 Fenton's Translation of The Bible 512

Epilogue   **513**
Bibliography   **523**

UN Warns of Apocalypse Now

Earthquakes, floods and other natural disasters could kill millions in the world's mega-cities and time is running out to prevent such catastrophes, the United Nations warns. Mega-cities have 10 million or more people, many concentrated in slums. In Kobe, the Japanese city still nursing wounds from a deadly earthquake that struck a decade ago, UN emergency relief director Jan Egeland painted an apocalyptic picture.

"Perhaps the most frightening prospect would be to have a truly mega-disaster in a mega-city," Egeland told the World Disaster Prevention Conference. "Then we could have not only a tsunami-style casualty rate as we saw on Boxing Day, but one that's one hundred times that." He said "time is running out" to prevent such a catastrophe.

The greater Tokyo area, with a population of more than 35 million, tops the list of mega-cities, followed by Mexico City at 19 million, greater New York at 18.5 million and Bombay at 18.3 million. "Some mega-cities are earthquake prone, others are prone to flooding. We have to have city planning, we have to have development, and we have to have investment in poor areas because the poor people are the most vulnerable," Egeland said.

Tokyo, squatting on one of the world's most unstable foundations, is shaken by dozens of earthquakes a year and lives in fear of a repeat of the 1923 earthquake and tsunami that levelled the city and took 140,000 lives. But there are far worse scenarios. A magnitude 8 quake similar to that in 1923 could kill 150,000, destroy 2.6 million buildings, and leave 7.5 million people stranded.

Death and destruction from the quake would be followed by enormous financial repercussions for the rest of the world. Tokyo's economy is larger than Australia's and it houses the headquarters of some of the planet's largest banks and corporations. Experts say such a quake could trigger a world financial crisis.

Economist (January 2005)

Introduction

This book, prepared over a number of years, is written to explain *why* there must now be an apocalyptic outcome for present-day humanity. The UN's warning of apocalyptic-style catastrophes was surely seeded by the catastrophic effect of the relatively recent Indian Ocean tsunami tragedy. Ideas mooted at a World Disaster Prevention Conference shortly after to try to stave off such disasters – whilst admirable and even altruistic – will, unfortunately, ultimately prove fruitless. It is akin to shutting the stable door after the horse has bolted. In short, *it is far too late for that now!* The solution never rested in such things as better city planning or helping more of the world's poor anyway. Yes, it could go a long way to *reducing* death tolls in the short term, but the *fundamental reason is not at all addressed thereby*. Such tinkering would only be a "Band-Aid measure".

But if it is too late for humanity to prevent many more and far greater disasters from occurring now, it behoves the reader to at least *try* to understand *what* will come upon us but more especially the *why* of it! In order to grasp and assimilate the reasons for such impending disasters, the great questions of life also need to be looked at. For they hold vital keys to recognising *why* we have arrived at this critical point of final resolution in humanity's journey. This Work is therefore also offered to fill the gap in the long line of many books written to *seemingly* answer some of the greatest questions that mankind have puzzled over for millennia.

Always more and more questions and more and more theories. Rarely have we been gifted with absolute and definitive answers to the great questions of life. Some of those questions could not have been resolved prior to this time anyway, for they needed the input of certain aspects of scientific knowledge. However, they could not have been resolved *at all* without the complete and detailed knowledge inherently contained within **The Spiritual Laws of Creation**. That is a level of knowledge so comprehensive and far-reaching in its import that it was reserved for this latter and closing point in our evolutionary journey to be revealed.

Therefore, to *fully* understand *why* there *must* be an accompanying Judgement – *a Judgement that we must recognise as one that we have ultimately brought upon ourselves* – one needs to understand the subject matter of each individual Chapter. Whilst each one is more or less complete within itself, the reader should nevertheless read the Chapters sequentially. For, collectively, they all link together to provide a comprehensive overview to more completely explain the "**why**" of the impending event, through the outworking of *Immutable and Inviolable Laws*.

It is also most important for the reader to understand that precisely because the subject matter that this Work examines and explains is so controversial and contentious, it is very necessary to constantly reinforce the points raised. The repetitive aspect of the book's explanatory style around certain key subjects is thus vital for a greater understanding of concepts that stand well outside currently accepted scientific, religious and general educational parameters of the Western world.

This particular work, whilst deriving its validity from out of the knowledge inherent within those Laws to therewith clarify the great questions of life, is specifically impacted by the increasing uncertainty and unease about the future of humanity clearly permeating the world's peoples.

In the natural course of our evolutionary development, therefore, we should by now have developed a sufficient level of intelligence and spiritual maturity to be able, in the very first place, to *recognise* the clear fact that systems are failing in so many areas of human endeavour and influence *precisely because* certain "**Rules of Life**", certain precise and inviolable "**Universal Laws**", are being transgressed continually. And, moreover, have been for a very long time. The actual and explicit nature of such radical new knowledge, however, means that it must challenge the very fabric of the many and varied beliefs that humankind have believed to be so correct for so long, *yet are clearly so wrong in so many areas*.

In just one domain alone, that of the wonderful natural world of the many and varied eco-systems of the earth – *and a domain in which man must now face and accept full responsibility for the worst kind of stewardship possible* – the clear flouting of perfectly-intermeshed "Laws of Nature" has brought us to our present, perhaps now irreversible, "natural-world crisis". Thus the precise purpose of that "New Knowledge", *inherently contained within those "Laws of Creation"*, was to bring that clarifying enlightenment which would show us the pathway out of the mess we have created. And thereby garner at least *some* understanding of the mammoth and fundamental significance of them.

Whether or not we may believe an apocalyptic end to the planet, to the human race, or to the global system we have created is probable, possible, feasible, unlikely or ridiculous, it is nevertheless *a potential* that increasingly exercises the minds of more and more people. And not solely those of religious bent either. Along with numerous books, articles, television documentaries and varied opinions, even Time Magazine has quite recently featured the "apocalyptic view". The 'New Zealand Listener', a highly respected magazine, in its Dec. 4-10 2004 Edition, carried a lead feature about global warming, and on the cover, the words: "Global Meltdown – The Coming Climate Catastrophe".

Now, even such an august body as the United Nations has found the courage to use the A-word – **Apocalypse**. Clearly, the world has at last awakened to the fact that catastrophes far larger in scale and sheer area than has historically been the case, *are going to occur*.

The rise of global terrorism in all its viciously-deadly forms has produced international concern ranging from unease to almost paranoiac fear. The new and added dimension of bio-terrorism and the potential for nuclear blackmail exponentially increase the terror factor. And that is only human activity. If we add rapidly increasing natural disasters to that volatile mix, like a "Global Meltdown" to name just one, then we do begin to see the possibility of catastrophic events able to produce even millions of deaths in a single-event episode in crowded areas of human habitation, particularly. A multiple-event occurrence clearly cannot be ruled out either.

The latest fears to haunt global humanity – though they have been waiting in the wings developing and mutating for some time now – are the increasing number of virulent viruses and associated, easily transmissible, infectious horrors. Will it be a case of: From mad-cow disease and BSE potential – which did jump the species barrier – to Avian bird-flu potential, also now known to have mutated to the same degree. And both directly related to farming activities. Yet, while BSE is basically contracted by *eating* infected meat, latest research indicates that Avian bird-flu may have mutated to such a degree that it may now possess *more* than *airborne* transmitted terror-potential. What will that do for world business and aviation should it suddenly erupt into a pandemic? For should it crest the optimum threshold level of infectious spread in any given country, it will "go global" in an instant. SARS was surely a wake-up call. But with a death rate of 70% for Avian bird-flu, the *potential* for widespread death – and panic of course – might just be the worst *so far*.

Another potential horror perhaps "waiting for its time" is the "neapa virus" which emerged on pig farms in Malaysia in the mid 1990's. The emergency necessitated the slaughtering of over a million pigs in that country. The virus attacked the lungs and the animals developed a severe cough which infected the farmers. Since pigs are "organically" similar to humans, the death rate of those farmers and farm workers infected by the "airborne droplets" was very high. The particular problem associated with this particular virus is its insidious ability to become "fully-blown" and exceptionally virulent in its human host for days before the signs of infection become evident. By then, the human host is close to death and has already spread the virus.

Eventually contained in Malaysia, similar outbreaks have unfortunately occurred in Sri Lanka and other places in the region. It, too, has the potential to literally become globally airborne simply by an apparently healthy person taking it on board a commercial aircraft. We should not forget the re-emergence of TB either. What has emerged here, however, is a mutated strain which is becoming increasingly difficult to treat. Though outbreak are spasmodic, when they do occur they infect and kill more people. It, too, is an "infected droplet" horror.

Whilst the idea of an Apocalyptic-style Judgement has been mainly a religious-fringe idea up to relatively recent times, the possibility of an apocalyptic event in its own right has worked its way into the thinking of the scientific community now, too. So much so, that one eminent scientist, Cambridge University Professor Martin Rees, (and Britain's honorary astronomer royal) has now calculated Apocalypse odds at 50-50. His recent book sub-titled "A scientists warning. How terror, error, and environmental disaster threaten humankind's future in this century - on Earth and beyond", details many and varied possibilities for such odds to be realised.

The truly fascinating aspect of an apocalyptic potential from perhaps a scientific position is that it is akin to a "better late than never" realisation. For if that particular realisation is the point we have *now finally reached*, "scientifically", then there may yet be *the further and key recognition* that perhaps, just perhaps, the Prophets of old who stated that such things **would** come to pass **did actually know**. Not just know, moreover, but know *why*, exactly! Therein lies the key. **Why!**

As stated at the beginning, that is one of the reasons for which this book was written; to examine **the why**! To do that effectively, however, we need to go beyond the standard academic mindset and address this issue from the co-joined and synthesised perspectives of religion, science, philosophy and, most importantly, Spiritual Law in its absolute inviolability. This book thus offers a markedly different outlook from most others on why the problems of the world are here in the first place, and how they need to be addressed if there is to be any meaningful change for the better. That is, of course, if there is sufficient time left to institute such changes for at least *some* of the earth's population.

The quite recent and rapid development of the mathematical phenomenon known as "The Bible Code" – not in any way influential in this work, however – nevertheless offers a puzzling and intriguing dimension to the whole matrix of source-material citing end-time scenarios. Quietly waiting for the time when computing power would sufficiently develop to *reveal* this "Code", the growing number of books on the subject written by highly qualified and respected men in their field, virtually by the day, adds more weight to what *will* come to pass. Whilst many of the researchers quite rightly point out that the future is not fixed by ordination – by virtue of the fact that we possess free will – the future, unfortunately, *is now fixed for global humanity in the collective sense*.

As individuals, we can still *perhaps* exercise *some* degree of free will, but only to change ourselves, and perhaps our individual fate. The collective decisions for a beneficial return globally in this present (end-time) should have been seeded a very long time ago, but also in an ongoing way through recognising, understanding, and living by, the true Laws of Life. Laws Perfect and Inviolable, which drive *all* decisions to their subsequent and ultimately justified outcome.

Unfortunately that is not our historical reality. That being the case the *actual* seeding for thousands of years to come through our *free-will attribute* – thereby consequently producing the *reciprocal return* we are even now experiencing more strongly – has been that of blood, wars, slavery, and dark exploitation and destruction. And it is still ongoing today. Because certain code-findings resonate strongly with Revelation prophecy, "The Bible Code" may perhaps be viewed as part of the outworking of The Laws that govern life.

My conviction is that what is written within these pages will help the open-minded reader not only to a very different and more understandable view of certain prophetic and key pronouncements from The Bible for this time, but also to a far more expansive overview of exactly **"the why"** of the seemingly insurmountable problems facing the many and varied peoples and their religions in collective humanity today. In particular, the rapidly increasing religious and ethnic polarisation and hatred arising in more and more previously stable communities.

This book should ***not*** be regarded as a religious work, however. As explained further on, religions, in essence, are humankind's current, end-excrescence of those great Truths given to the earth's people by enlightened men and Prophets who were Called for that purpose. Now, however, Teachings greatly altered in form and meaning. Evident in the many different *religions* today is the clear and unequivocal reality that what those men of God were Called to give can no longer be regarded as the clear Truth which they had once disseminated and explained.

Thus: *The Light Above gives the Truth to men, and men then convert it to just religions. Religions of diverse and often conflicting interpretations.*

If, however, in place of just religion one seeks, instead, to embrace the **collective essence of *all* the great Teachings**, then we may perhaps aver that that might provide the foundation for most of The Truth. To thereby provide key pointers as to where such spiritual understanding and inner security *can* be found. Therewith lies the *primary* purpose of the book.

Prior to the so-called Age of Enlightenment there at least existed then a far stronger acceptance of a Creator and some form of long-reaching justice that no one could escape. In other words, Inviolable Law. And few under the yoke of the Church questioned it or, indeed, even dared to. What do we see today, however! Books, probably numbering in the thousands, which question the existence and/or validity of a Creator and inviolable Laws. Or whether Jesus existed, and whether He was Divine, a man, or both.

Of course, it is certainly not wrong to question. That is why we have a questioning mind. And some truly contentious publications provide very valuable information about the historical and religious framework that existed at the time, and equally valuable research into the machinations, intrigue and religious power-politics that subsequently derive from such significant events as the life of Jesus.

One such publication is *"The Holy Blood and the Holy Grail"*, a thoroughly researched document offering the reader a broad and fascinating grand sweep of history with very much valuable information exactly about the machinations of those holding religious power. Associated with that, the calculating manipulation of The Books of The Bible and of The Bible overall.

However, since The Holy Grail is not linked with the primary reason for which this book is written, why the naming of It in the opening pages? A strange side of the human condition is that *it prefers mystery to truth*. With a mystery men are free to indulge their fantasies unchecked. With the Truth of a particular thing, however, *that is no longer possible*. For the Truth simply Is, and all men must *ultimately* bow to It! As so many writers and researchers have concluded that The Holy Grail is somehow associated with Jesus, we believe it necessary to dispel the many wrong conceptions centred around the whole idea. Towards the end of Chapter 11, from a logical analysis of Bible Scripture, the reader will discover the exact quote from The Revelation which states precisely what It is.

The hypothesis about Jesus and The Holy Grail postulated by the co-authors of "The Holy Blood and the Holy Grail" is therefore effectively redressed by that revelation. In any case, the fact that so much effort has been expended by so many well-meaning writers and researchers to try to locate it – without success – surely warrants resolution.

Very appropriately, however, on pages 437-438 of that work the co-authors suggest their reasons why their particular premise might possess some validity and offer the "right" solution for a more equitable global society than will ever be realised through the present, inferior and flawed systems of societal governance. It is a general view with which we concur for it offers some of the reasons why radical change *will* be *forcibly thrust* upon humankind. It is thus our absolute conviction that the premise offered in *this* work will ultimately be recognised – unfortunately through very hard experiencing now – to be that which provides the key solution to our mega-problems. It is probably that which the authors of the following excerpt are perhaps *actually* seeking.

> The political systems and ideologies which, in the early years of our century, seemed to promise so much have virtually all displayed a degree of bankruptcy. Communism, socialism,

capitalism, Western-style democracy have all, in one way or another, betrayed their promise, jaundiced their adherents and failed to fulfil the dreams they engendered. Because of their small-mindedness, lack of perspective and abuse of office, politicians no longer inspire confidence, only distrust. In the West today there is increasing cynicism, dissatisfaction and disillusion. There is increasing psychic distress, anxiety and despair. But there is also an intensifying quest for meaning, for emotional fulfilment, for a spiritual dimension to our lives, for something in which genuinely to believe. There is a longing for a renewed sense of the sacred that amounts in effect, to a full-scale religious revival – exemplified by the proliferation of sects and cults, for example, and the swelling tide of fundamentalism in the United States. There is also, increasingly, a desire for a true 'leader' – not a Fuhrer, but a species of wise and benign spiritual figure, a 'priest-king' in whom mankind can safely repose its trust. Our civilisation has sated itself with materialism and in the process become aware of a more profound hunger. It is now beginning to look elsewhere, seeking the fulfilment of emotional, psychological and spiritual needs. There are many devout Christians who do not hesitate to interpret the Apocalypse as nuclear holocaust. How might the advent of Jesus's lineal descendant be interpreted? To a receptive audience, it might be a kind of Second Coming.

Whilst we agree with the overall message in the above text and applaud the co-authors' bid to seed some measure of spiritual awakening in the general populace, and similarly agree with their axiom regarding the necessity for a true Spiritual Leader we, however, do not agree with their seeming conclusion; that he will arise from out of a postulated bloodline from The Son of God.[1]

The once authoritative view of a nuclear holocaust ending civilisation probably holds much less credence today than it previously did. Bearing that in mind, what other possibilities do we have; what kind of "primary-force" could generate destruction on an apocalyptic scale? Some years ago the book, "The Helmet and the Cross", was published. A few extracts from the Postscript make interesting reading.

> A small earth tremor shook his glass on the side table and made the ice tinkle briefly. Potts ignored it.

---

[1]The meaning of the word Son should not be taken as that which is universally accepted. For "Son of God", *in this case,* ultimately means **"Part of God"**.

"Oh my God, John, look there!" She was pointing out and away, towards the ocean, or to where the ocean should have been. It was not there any longer.

"Tsunami," Potts said tersely. "There's going to be one hell of a tidal wave."

Then the music died. The radio was a Worldmaster, and a voice began to speak excitedly in Dutch... And then the voice itself was cut off. - - - -

"Find a local station," Helen told him. "Be quick!"

But there was no time, for time was running out at last.

The process began in the Great Rift Valley by the west shore of the Dead Sea with an earthquake that flattened every high-rise building in Israel; then the Rift sundered itself apart from Syria to East Africa. But that was only a local effect. Unprecedented transfers of heat energy were taking place deep within the earth: changes of state. Molten crustal material welled up through every volcano in the world in a devastating series of eruptions and explosions. Simultaneously every earthquake focus was activated as the plate boundaries ruptured across the globe, decillions of tons of rock uplifted and fractured. The plates lost their form: Arabian, Antarctic, Indian, Nazca, African, Philippine, Caribbean, Eurasian, Pacific, South American, Cocos, North American. The energy transfers involved were enough to make global thermonuclear war look like a child's fireworks display. The skies conformed as the oceans of the world roared in tsunami, and billions of people died in the first minute.

The tidal wave which hit the Los Angeles Basin was three hundred and thirty feet high, travelling at five hundred and eighty miles an hour when it struck the Pacific Palisades.

The P-wave of the first shock had thrown them to ground as it went through at five miles a second, rippling the earth and jolting the rocks as it went...; the San Andreas [fault] could hold no longer, and half of California was on its way into collision with the tidal wave.

After the jolting shock of the P-wave came the wrenching, twisting shock of the S-wave, moving at only two and three-quarter miles a second, but still five times faster than a high-velocity shell.

Noise was in the air, the earth, inside himself. Fire and steam and thunder immeasurably multiplied, a mesh of red-hot wires screaming in his skull from high-frequency sound, the bellowing of a million bulls as a ground-bass.

Potts thought he could hear a voice in his head or outside it – he could not tell which – that said, 'So things are concluding;...

A chasm sixty feet wide opened up, John and Helen Potts were falling.

He felt strangely removed, time and subjectivity altering as he fell. From the first millennium head cases had predicted the end of the world; he remembered them in London proclaiming its imminence on sandwich boards. But the world had turned upside-down and bade fair to turn inside-out now; and the time had come for the head-cases to be right.

And the mountains broke like glass. The enclosing ranges shattered round the cities of the plain of eighteen hundred square miles: the Tehachapis, the San Gabriels, the Santa Monicas, the San Bernadinos, the Santa Anas. The Palos Verdes had already vanished. And still Potts fell.

He had time for thought. His eyes were open, but his mind was racing free in the darkening fissure. Sodom and Gomorrah were infant playschools compared to the world he had lived in.

The West. Take the money and run. Do as thou wilt shall be the whole of the Law. And the drugs internationals and the gambling internationals; environmental destruction in the name of progress; the sexual morality of the mole-rat with attendant plagues; the weapons of mass murder. And only a few men and women had paused to consider that certain behaviour patterns might be wrong.

The East. Genocide and subjection of peoples; the Gulag; the perversion of medicine into the State drug racket that kept its dissidents in mental hospital prisons; lack of the basic freedoms and any sense of the value of the individual. Uncountable loss, the abomination of desolation; a system geared only to keeping an elite in power, making the Roman Empire seem avuncularly caring by comparison. The weapons of mass murder.

East and West conspiring to hold down the Third World, helped by its own massive corruption. It had all been *wrong*.

The author paints a very descriptive but rather frightening scenario. So could global destruction on such a scale be possible, do we think? Probably feasible from a purely geological perspective. Perhaps a sufficiently large jolt or earth movement where two or more Tectonic Plates intersect might be enough to trigger a monstrous subterranean ripple in a "knock-on" effect thereby also initiating multiple volcanic eruptions around the globe.

Geologists are very much aware of earthquakes *overdue* in various regions of the world. The region encompassing the Tokyo Prefecture with its tens of millions of close-packed residents is one. Should the San Andreas Fault "let go" to its full length of "catch-up-travel", the resulting destruction will be on a scale presently unimaginable. In the classic conundrum of "not if but when" Civic authorities in California once explored the idea of relocating the whole infrastructure and population mass presently within the danger zone of the San Andreas fault – basically San Francisco and Los Angeles – to another location. The projected estimates of cost for relocation and rebuilding elsewhere were so prohibitive it was determined that even the massive destruction that *is* one day going to occur might prove less costly than complete relocation. Clearly, that is an "unknown", however.

Geologists have issued a statement to the Turkish Government warning that the very active Anatolian Fault will generate a large earthquake centred on or near Istanbul. Because the majority of the city's buildings are not quake-proof, the shock will produce huge damage with perhaps considerable loss of life. Basically, much of the city may simply collapse into a pile of rubble.

Large, active volcanoes adjacent to major population centres, such as Popocatepetl right next door to Mexico City on the earthquake-prone central plateau, are virtual disasters waiting to happen. Though currently monitored round the clock, with the wind in the right direction during a full-scale eruption and pyroclastic cloud discharge, millions of residents could conceivably die there in a matter of minutes.

And for America, the super-volcano centred in Yellowstone National Park erupts, geologically speaking, to a precise cyclical timetable. It is now due. Geologist are presently monitoring increasing activity over the vast area that is the mega-caldera. When it erupts, for it is not an if, it will almost certainly bring the USA to its knees. The super widespread destruction resulting from it will financially cripple the country.

Even in relatively small population centres, one perfectly timed and directed eruption can simply destroy all infrastructure to the point where rebuilding would be untenable. On the 8th May, 1902, the town of St. Pierre on the island of Martinique was destroyed by the massive eruption of Mt Pele, the largest mountain on the island. Virtually the entire population of 30,000 were killed in just a few seconds; the time it took for the super-heated mass to blast into St Pierre when the side of the volcano facing the town blew out. Though badly burned, one man in the town's thick-walled jail survived. Reports state that all buildings in the town were destroyed.

Do we see here what might be termed the "capricious nature" of Mother Nature? Volcanoes are obviously very large roundish objects encompassing 360 degrees. Yet the full force of the pent-up energy which exploded from the rent in the side of the volcano struck the town. Most deaths were caused by seared lungs and/or asphyxiation from poisonous volcanic fumes.

The horrific swathe of death and destruction in the countries bordering the Indian Ocean, produced by an exceptionally powerful earthquake generating associated tsunami, in an instant brought the stupendous power of Nature to the riveting attention of the whole world by the sheer, mind-numbing scale of it. What was perhaps so startling was not so much the *size* of the tsunami waves, which were "relatively" small by ocean standards – the world's top surfers surf giants measuring up to 80ft off Hawaii – *but the incredible power they possessed*; able to drive a roiling mass of debris up to four kilometres inland in some places. Given the huge amount of destruction and desolation they caused, what credence might we then place on a wave topping three hundred and thirty feet high, as in the foregoing narrative describing the destruction of California?

Dr. Brian Atwater's recent discoveries of the salt-water drowning of once large cedar forests inland on the Pacific Northwest coast of the USA have forced geologists to accept that only "mega-tsunami" could have caused that amount of devastation. Subsequent to that conclusion, the search was on for the origin of that particular episode. It was caused by an earthquake close to the coast. It lowered the land and sent a tsunami across the Pacific to Japan, killing coastal dwellers around the impact site. A search for any other location world-wide that could generate a similar event has identified one prime site on the volcanically active island of La Palma in the Canary Islands off the west coast of North Africa.

Research by Dr Duncan Copp has highlighted a truly nightmarish potential for the Americas' there. An eruption from the Cumbrevieja volcano in 1949 opened up a very long trench on its western flank, dropping it around 3 to 4 metres. The currently fractured fault-line is clearly evident. Should magma rise to the surface, huge volumes of trapped rain-water *inside the volcano* would super-heat in an instant pressurising the whole volcano far more than would be the case with just magma being erupted. This potential "double effect" could cause the whole western side of Cumbrevieja to "slab off" into very deep water, thereby sending a mega-tsunami towards the Eastern Seaboard of the Americas'. This particular volcano erupts unpredictably. Sometimes, however, every decade.

Affecting an area from Greenland to South America, the main focus would be on the US coastline. Projected height of the wave on impact? Anything from 50 metres to 650 metres depending on how much land slips and with what force and speed. *If* the currently-fractured, unstable land area of the volcano suddenly "lets go" in one single, monumental splash – an estimated 600 billion tons of rock – then it is projected that the subsequent tsunami will tend toward the greater figure in terms of height-on-impact. Travelling at a speed of 720 km per hour, it would take just 8 hours to cross the Atlantic, not anywhere near enough time to evacuate the cities and coastline. The ground on which the mega-city of New York stands, along with all other cities on the Eastern Seaboard, would be virtually wiped clean with a wave of that size.

Not only that, but the large rivers that empty into the Atlantic offer perfect pathways for such a wave to maintain height and power to travel very far inland also taking out all infrastructure along the way. The same event would produce tsunami waves of 7 to 10 metres on the south coast of the United Kingdom and, of course, on the coastline of Africa. In short, a truly apocalyptic nightmare. Prof. Costas Synolakis of the Tsunami Research Centre at the University of California, has commented that a wave of 50 metres from this potential would cause incalculable devastation. A 500 to 600 metre wave generated from an erupting Cumbrevieja volcano was simply too scary to think about.

Evidence of huge tsunami generated by large land-slips has been catalogued in Lituya Bay in Southern Alaska. Oil-exploration geologists have noted cliff-faces, recently forest-covered, wiped clean to heights of 450ft. and 520 ***metres*** in 1953 and 1958 respectively.[2] Though only travelling a relatively short distance, the same effect would have occurred over longer distances, because it is the *energy* of the event that ultimately produces the rearing-wave on impact.

The grand-daddy of all tsunami, however, must surely have been that triggered by a landslide from the island of Oahu a few million years ago. Oceanographer Prof. Gary McMurtry has estimated the volume at around 3,000 cubic kilometres. The wave

---

[2]Source: Discovery Channel Documentary – "The Next Wave".

may have been a few kilometres high, and would have absolutely devastated the US Pacific coast.

Bible Prophecy, which we examine in some detail in later Chapters, states that such destruction *will* take place. Three are worth noting here. One from the great Prophet, Isaiah, one from The Revelation and one from Jesus. From Isaiah 24, 19-20. (Fenton)

> For windows from on high are opened,
> And the earth's foundations shake!
> And the land with crashing crashes,
> And the land with breaches breaks!
> Tottering land meets ground that totters,
> Staggering earth like drunkard staggers,
> And flapping, quivers like a tent;
> And her crimes are heavy on her,
> She will fall, nor rise again!

Many will be aware of the prophecy in The Revelation that states an Angel will hurl a large stone into the oceans destroying a third of the ships and sailors on the sea. Clearly, this equates to an earth-crossing meteor. Given when the Disciples of Jesus asked Him what signs will indicate "the completion of the age", part-verses 21-22 from The Book of Matthew also offer a sobering insight into, now, near-future events.

> "...for there shall then be wide-spread affliction, such as has not been known since the beginning of the world until now, no, nor will ever be known again. And if those times were not cut short, not a man would be saved."

Will the world and humanity awaken sufficiently to fully recognise the true meaning and import of the Indian Ocean tsunami tragedy? For that was just *one* of the "signs" prophesied about this time – the "end-time". Or will we give very generously on the one hand, and yet continue to "break all the rules" and then be shocked and bewildered all over again when the next natural yet *lawful* catastrophe strikes.

Senator Al Gore's long crusade to bring to the attention of formerly sceptical scientists and politicians the developing crisis of "global warming", has certainly borne powerful fruit in 2007. Millions of people are now much more enlightened as a result of Al Gore's incontrovertible and more than timely documentary, *"An*

Inconvenient Truth". Supported by excellent science, the documentary, in one brilliant presentation, illustrated both the seriousness of the situation and the stupidity and ignorance of global humanity.

Many Hollywood celebrities are now actively involved in supporting environmental issues too. Leonardo DiCaprio, converted by Al Gore almost a decade ago in a kind of personal version of *An Inconvenient Truth*, has put his earnings and backing to the cause. With his production company he has, for the past three years, been developing a full-length feature film on the subject. Titled *11th Hour*, he describes it as "16 environmental scientists and Nobel laureates and people like Stephen Hawking and Gorbachev talking about global warming".

At the close of January, 2007, a major international report by the world's leading climate scientists has emerged. Issuing their strongest statement yet, they warn that human activities are heating the planet. Global warming will bring more severe rains, melting glaciers, droughts and heatwaves and a rise in sea levels. That, of course, will mean more frequent and increasingly catastrophic storm systems.

What is so very interesting about the regular scientific pronouncements around this growing problem is the exponential factor evident in projections about global temperature rise and its generation of associated disaster-scenarios by all the *experts*. The pronouncements are constantly being reviewed upward. That clearly means that current projections are already rendered incorrect by the speed of change which, in itself, is absolutely exponential, for it cannot be anything else but from now on.

In concert with what we are just as strongly stating, what are the very self-evident ramifications for global humanity from that consensual, scientific statement? Well, it is this: That the pre-millennial period must be filled with suffering and not joy is solely the fault of a blind and intransigent humanity, for we have seriously transgressed the very Laws of Life. Ultimately, that is the actual reason for, and true cause of, all humanity's problems. It is not simply that there are "too many people" on earth to accelerate an already rapidly deteriorating situation, it is about the necessary knowledge of The Law – to which we and our individual and collective, global activities are absolutely subject!

The Chapter headings and sub-headings listed in the Table of Contents address key themes of contentious import. The explanations clarifying them starkly show why there simply cannot be any other outcome for human global societies but destruction! This work should not therefore be dismissed out of hand as just one more religiously-inclined, superficial book without a thorough and objective analysis.

It is an unfortunate reality of life that sometimes the very things we push aside are, on later reflection, recognised as being exactly that which was needed most. To that end, therefore, the ultimate extrapolation of the outworking of The Spiritual Laws in the affairs of humankind – *under the* **Ordination of the Living Light** *at this critical time in our history* – permits us our book title.

Because both the Title and Contents of this book are obviously highly contentious, the decision to write it was not taken lightly. Years of preparatory composition and research clearly showed an earth deteriorating more and more rapidly. An "apocalyptic potential", therefore, at least needs to be aired. Given the gravity of the subject matter, I believe that this essay is written with spiritual clarity and honesty. A fair and objective examination of this work will thus offer the reader a very different and challenging view of some of the greater questions to life. Even though uncompromisingly direct at times, I further believe that it also embodies the virtues of sincerity and compassion and respect toward others under the inviolable aegis of **THE LAW!** For only with that precise knowledge will the reader fully understand that we do – **even now** – actually stand in the time of **The World Judgement! It is here!**

Chapter 1

GOD: Omniscient - Omnipotent

> "First and foremost thank you to the Almighty God, Creator of all."
>
> (Acknowledgements, "Pacific Rhythm" music CD, EK Music Entertainment, 2002)
>
> "Only a few natural laws apply to the whole universe which, of itself, testifies to the existence of a great and Almighty God."
>
> (Sir Isaac Newton's stated conviction.)

When events in the world are forcing many to voice doubts about the existence of God – with past publications sporting Titles like: "Does God Exist?", or asking, "Is God Dead?", or stating, "God is Dead" – thus forcing a rethink in personal beliefs, why do we so emphatically state our absolutely unequivocal acceptance of a God Omniscient and Omnipotent? Would such a sure standpoint derive from simple Faith, or might there be far stronger reasons for a clearly stated conviction of that kind?

Many Pacific Island peoples accept the existence of God – an acceptance derived from very strong faith – and strong enough to be the very first acknowledgement on *a Pacific-culture music CD*. Primarily derived from revelatory insights in mathematics and astronomy Newton, a towering giant of the scientific world, by his very own words certainly believed in the existence of God.

We know that GOD is Omniscient and Omnipotent – All-knowing and All-powerful – The Creator of all the worlds. Would such a God visit an Apocalypse and World-Judgement upon us? The Bible certainly says an Apocalypse and Judgement will take place. Religious works from other main faiths also say it will happen. If we were of the standard Christian mind-set we would probably say that since He is The Creator of the worlds, only He *could* bring about a World-Judgement. Not only that but would carry out the actual judging of each individual Himself. After all, it is His Creation, and He is its Owner!

Why should we believe that as a matter of course, however? For we would probably also say that God is Love and therefore would not wish believers in Him to perish. And we would probably further state that He loved us all *so* much that "He sent His only begotten Son to die for our sins". So, not just an All-powerful and All-knowing God, but One determined to save us from our own folly too. In short, a God for all seasons and reasons. What about a God of Justice and Law, though? The three major monotheistic religions, all of which name Abraham as their founding Patriarch have, as their very foundation, primary books of "God's Law". Where, then, stands man in transgression of those Laws? For The Laws of The Creator must surely be Perfect, and we certainly would not want to have our personalised God imperfect.

Such a strange relationship so many humans have with their God. Everyone wants Him to be on *their* side. Everyone wants Him to destroy *their* enemies. Yet opposing sides of the same faith have often prayed to the same God for victory over the other. The First World War produced one of the most remarkable wartime episodes ever, when opposing British and German Units simply stopped fighting and joined together to exchange Christmas greetings and gifts and sing the time-honoured Christmas Carols. Technically, it was a mutinous act by both groups of soldiers and the British High Command soon put a stop to it by directing an artillery barrage toward that part of the "line".

Bob Dylan, troubadour, contemporary and often quite insightful, socially-influential bard and songwriter, over his career has produced lyrics that have literally changed perceptions and galvanised groups globally.

Perfectly tailored for this Chapter, his song, "With God on Our Side" exactly illustrates the strange relationship humans have with their God. Verse four:

> Oh the First World War, boys
> It closed out its fate
> The reason for fighting
> I never got straight
> But I learned to accept it
> Accept it with pride
> For you don't count the dead
> When God's on your side.

During the Second World War, major Units of the German Army carried, as part of their uniform, the engraving "Gott Mit Uns" (God with us.) on their belt buckle. Could a Just and Perfect God support something as horrific as Hitler's megalomanic rampage of death destruction? Surely only a distorted mind would think so. The compelling verse five from Dylan's same composition tells it succinctly.

> When the Second World War
> Came to an end
> We forgave the Germans
> And we were friends
> Though they murdered six million
> In the ovens they fried
> The Germans now too
> Have God on their side.

On a much smaller scale, what about the very many things in life that affect us so profoundly just on an individual basis. We often give thanks to a Deity for good things that come our way, but may rail against the fates and the same Deity when we suffer tragedy. Does this indicate that we expect that *only* good things *should* come from the God we choose to thank? Surely such a mindset would be akin to childish pettiness. Or does it show that, for the most part, humanity on earth have little or no understanding of the God we feel to pray to in times of great distress, particularly.

Even when praying to our God, we invariably assume we are offering Him Worship. It rarely crosses our mind that during *prayer* we are actually not always offering Worship at all. Very often we are *asking Him* for something that *we* personally want or need. That is *not* worship, it is *petition*. So prayer and petition produce two fundamentally different kinds of "forms", even though both are presented under the general guise of "prayer". A very simple summary to this point thus reveals that we human beings have next to no understanding of the very Power that, in the final analysis, permitted us conscious life and a beautiful earth upon which to live out physical life.

It is hardly surprising, then, that from time to time questions arise about whether Creation came about by accident or Divine Plan. Associated with that is invariably the question of God's existence, and/or that perhaps there is no God after all. Unfathomable disasters often trigger such debates, as in the case of the recent Indian Ocean tsunami tragedy. Where, then, lies absolute faith and belief? For if one is *genuinely* true to one's stated belief that one has "found Truth", then such terrible tragedies should produce **compassionate understanding** of it, *not* non-understanding. Deriving from the inherent truth of that perception, one of the strangest ironies to emerge from that catastrophe was that the most senior clergyman of one of the world's major Christian denominations publicly questioned his own faith over the issue of so many tsunami deaths. All the training for the position, the very reason for being in the chosen church, must surely have presupposed the very strongest belief in God, or a God. Even if only to set an example in guiding and leading the flock.

To publicly state that such a tragedy "...should make all Christians question the existence of God" perfectly illustrates the opening "question and statement" dialogue regarding a "personalised God" Who only produces what *we* think He should. This preeminent clergyman's query, "How can you believe in a God who permits suffering on this scale?" perfectly portrays the classic assumptive question. On the one hand is the **totally unrealistic belief** that such things **should never ever happen**. On the other, the only reason that it did happen is because **God let it.** "What other reason could there possibly be", seems to be the dangerously fundamentalist mindset here. It is almost medieval in its particular brand of reasoning. Paradoxically, both views reveal the clear fact, also stated by him: "...*most of the stock Christian answers to human suffering do not go very far in helping us*, one week on, with the intolerable grief and devastation in front of us." (Italics mine.)

And therein lies the true answer. Religions – all religions – whilst professing to understand The Laws of God, stand uncomprehending before disasters of this magnitude. If the followers of the various religions were to be brutally honest about it they would admit that such questions are asked at times of great tragedy simply because they possess no real answers. Just the same old tired, standard phrases. So we must never question the obvious in the case of the recent tsunami, i.e. the logical fact that waves clearly cannot distinguish between adults and children. Or coral reefs and animals.

Affecting millions in various religions over a relatively large portion of the globe, the most devastating natural disaster to hit the world in a long time would surely have tested the faith of the sufferers in a way not perhaps ever experienced before. The peoples bordering the Indian Ocean are mainly Hindus, Buddhists and Muslims; with some Countries supporting quite large Christian populations as well.

In its tsunami reporting of Wed. 05-01-05 The New Zealand Herald included a Newsweek Magazine breakdown of how the different religions of the area would generally regard the visitation of a major natural disaster upon them. A key observation; "No survivor of a disaster of this magnitude can long avoid asking the 'Job-like' questions, 'Why us, why here, why now?' "

Hindus: Hard-hit by the tsunami, Hindu fishing communities along the coast of south India relate strongly to various local deities who exert a powerful influence on their everyday life. "Local deities possess the power to create or destroy". "The ocean itself is a terrible god who eats people and boats, but also provides fish as food." According to Richard Davis, "a specialist in South Asian Hinduism at Bard College in New York", "Hindus explain happenings like the tsunami as destructive acts by the gods". The key explanation from our perspective is this statement: "Relating to the local deity and cooling her anger through propitiation is more important than thinking about personal or collective guilt for what has happened."

Buddhists: Donald Lopez, professor of Buddhist studies at the University of Michigan, states: "Buddhists will look to the idea of karma and ask what they did, individually and collectively, that a tragedy like this happened." Generating good merit to transfer to the deceased as a positive force in their next lifetime would be a primary concern. Monks would be employed to act as intermediaries in the transfer of merit.

Muslims: The Muslim view – as explained in this particular source – is especially revealing. "Like the Bible, the Koran recognises no natural laws independent of God's will. All that happens is Allah's doing, and nature itself – wind, rain, storms, – constitute signs of his mercy and compassion. Even the destructive tsunami, therefore, must have some hidden, positive purpose". According to Akbar Ahmed, chair of Islamic Studies at American University: "Ninety per cent of Muslims will understand a tragedy like this in this way. On the individual level they also have this notion that God is testing them by taking away a child or a spouse. Will you lose your faith, or will you continue to believe?" Ahmed says this idea of testing, and the patience it requires, gives an "inbuilt psychological cushion which allows Muslims to absorb a tragedy of this scale."

Christians: Christians in the affected area had to try to make sense of it all too. "Although the acceptance of suffering is embedded in the Christian world view, the death of so many innocent children alone was an excruciating test of the Christian belief that their God is a God of Love." Little wonder that from Sumatra to Madagascar, voices cry out to God.

The closing observation is one that many more than just those affected might also wonder at. "The miracle, if there is one, may be that so many still believe". Perhaps the greater degree of understanding, however, was that voiced by Syed Abdullah, "a local imam of Nagapattinam", a port where Muslims, Hindus and Christians have lived together for centuries. "In this kind of tragedy there is no religion", he said. "Let the dead be buried together. They died together in the sea. Let their souls get peace together."

Four *different* religions espousing four *dissimilar* views. Which of the four, if any, correctly describes the why of the tragedy? Obviously, each will avow that it has the answer. Logically, however, without agreement or consensus uncertainty remains. Yet could all of the stated views hold at least *some* measure of truth, even if to varying degrees about the why? If so, could all those truthful elements be culled and somehow combined to give a more comprehensive answer than the subsequent fragmented anguish? And what if the actual reason why such an event occurred on the scale that it did were to have some degree of resonance and answer in *all* of the main religions, as should be considered? Could the powerful, controlling, Christian West, in its drive to democratise other nations, accept the possibility that perhaps other religions might offer at least some element of the ultimate reason why? In the present climate of global power-politics and fragmenting world religions, probably not.

In the tsunami aftermath, former US Presidents, George Bush Snr. and Bill Clinton, interviewed on CNN's "Larry King Live", offered insights from their own personal-faith aspect. Bill Clinton, however, presented an understanding that really explained it more simply and truthfully than perhaps any other commentator from the main global news players over the two weeks of intensive coverage. His simple but profoundly truthful observation resonates well with the whole tone and message of this work. The sense of his statement was, basically: "We are not in charge here. The earth is an organism that has its own [dynamics]. We have to remember that we are not in charge." Our acceptance of the view that "we are not in charge" certainly runs to the earth and the cosmos and beyond. In terms of *personal fate*, however, we would absolutely state that yes, we *are* in charge. The subsequent Chapters will explain both parts of that, perhaps *apparent*, quandary. Bill Clinton went on to say that rather than diminishing his faith, in the face of such adversity, the courage of the human spirit strengthened it.

In the final analysis what took place in the Indian Ocean, indeed, whatever transpires anywhere, does so under the outworking of inviolable Laws. The very nature of planet earth, in terms of its own "life-dynamics", means that what we call disasters and catastrophes must, and will, always continue to happen. An objective viewpoint, therefore, will logically note that "Mother Nature" is simply bringing about *necessary change* within the body of the earth – albeit huge changes from our perspective. Such events are **not** caused by some kind of all-powerful, vengeful finger coming out of the sky to *arbitrarily* destroy communities on a capricious whim. Were that the case it would mean that we are nothing more than puppets dangling on the end of a string at the constant mercy of a super-deity who possesses no logic, no love. What, then, would be the point of being on earth at all, if we could not determine our own fate? Only illogical superstition and human-religious belief systems could invent such pointless ideas.

The outworking of Perfect Law and Truth from a God Omniscient and Omnipotent could never do so.

Chapter 2

God's Law, or Human Law?

> "...to say that everything happens according to natural laws, and to say that everything is ordained by the decree and ordinance of God, is the same thing."
>
> (The Wisdom of Israel, The Wisdom of Spinoza, p 409)

The philosophical insights of the Jewish Philosopher, Spinoza, earned the admiration of giants such as Goethe, Hegel, Shelley and even Einstein. Some present-day commentators of his work believe Spinoza saw God as a kind of "perfected-distillation" of all the natural Laws. So, accepted by him as the Supreme entity but, evidently in his view, not quite a God *separate and far above* the materiality of earthly environs. As we examine the "natural laws of God" of Spinoza's insight, we will discover that while the core of his particular discernment is basically correct, the true picture is far more encompassing than Spinoza believed or, indeed, could ever have known in his lifetime.

    Individuals in crisis.
    Families in crisis.
    Races in crisis.
    Nations in crisis.
    Global humanity in crisis.

The facts bombard us continually; from TV, radio, newspapers and magazines. Endless conferences are held, national, international, economic, educational, religious, racial, defence, women's: all seeking solutions to so many problems. We see the planet degraded by pollution, poverty, disease, ethnic savagery, tribal butchery and increasing crime and human rights violations by fellow human beings. In short, ongoing lawlessness. With it more despair, more agony, more hopelessness, more apathy, more suicides – more questions desperately needing to be answered. And since each year that passes prepares the foundation for the next, what is the prognosis for the world in two years time, or five, or ten.

How long has the cry been heard: "It will be better tomorrow, next year, after the next conference?" The reality for many of the world's people is that it is simply a lie. This incredibly beautiful "blue planet" we call home has, for increasing numbers, simply become a hopeless hell.

Does this herald a "Gathering Apocalypse", then? An Apocalyptic Judgement? Most certainly one has been prophesied for a very long time, and not solely from Biblical sources either. The lifestyle of the contented wealthy, the "well-off" and perhaps the very healthy might offer a large degree of insulation against such an idea. As it also might for the non-religious and the non-believer. I would suggest, however, that underneath all those different human veneers there perhaps arises from time to time moments of acute unease about the worsening state of global humanity. More particularly when groups of eminent scientists and conservationists warn Governments and societies to recognise what is happening and institute appropriate changes.

But changes to what, and where - exactly? Clearly, correct answers will logically provide correct solutions and directions. Governments and politicians have not succeeded in providing them even though they continually promise to do so. And neither have the churches and religions of the world, nor rational science, nor intellectual sophistry and erudition. Small problem pockets *have* been given short-term solutions and, in some areas, there are genuinely sound ideas that offer possible answers in the long term. These, however, are often isolated and few and far between. Generally speaking, we travel down an increasingly bleak path. And the further we travel down this path, the fewer and fewer solutions there seem to be available to us to "turn it all around". We appear to have reached the point where we generally accept that some problems may simply be too overwhelming in scale to rectify.

So, *can* we know *what* to do, and *are* there *actually* answers? If we do not at least ask the question *why* with sufficient "forceful integrity", then it is unlikely that we will ever succeed in finding or *recognising* those correct answers and solutions we so desperately need. For it must surely be logical to accept that if we are able to *recognise* the **true** reasons *why*, then we must have our solutions? In knowing the *why* and thus *recognising* the *cause*, it would then require only a simple step to apply the *solution*. However, since our problems continue to multiply in both gravity and scale, it is glaringly obvious that we have *not yet recognised* the *why*, irrespective of all the "expert" answers. Until such time as this necessary *recognition* finally dawns there will not, and indeed there cannot, be any real and lasting *solutions*.

However, for this to happen mankind must first undergo a radical and fundamental change. Our way of being – for thousands of years – is the *cause* of today's horrendous problems. What we are currently experiencing is the culmination of so much wrong thinking and foolish decision-making over that long period of time in the belief that our way was always the right way. That belief is now so solidly entrenched that, on the surface at least, it is difficult to see *how* change can be brought about. So even if we have the *cause*, as a *global community* we do not yet *recognise* the precise mechanism of *either* the *how* or the *why*.

Major catastrophes such as the Indian Ocean tsunami, as unfortunate and devastating as they are, do present opportunities for major rethink and change. However, with regard to the religious-answer quandary it has presented and the associated donation and distribution of billions of dollars of aid to the affected peoples, a fascinating aspect arises in the aftermath of it. The unprecedented outpouring of aid donations and associated large mobilisation of Military Forces, particularly, has *primarily* sprung from the wealthier or more militarily-powerful Western Nations. This same major aid-donating bloc also generally subscribes to the Judeao/Christian ethos, upon which the same have built their basic societal Law and derived their main religious beliefs and tenets.

Seemingly reminiscent of the concept of Manifest Destiny which the founding Europeans of North America used to justify the subjugation of both the land and the Native people, "democratisation" of the world, as promoted by the USA and European Democracies, must ultimately also seek to influence the religion of the country or region of the world targeted. Even if religious freedom and tolerance is stated to be one of the prime reasons for promoting democracy in the first place, through various subtle and not so subtle influences, the underlying purpose would be to make the "democratised state" more amenable to the *purposes* of whomever wishes to do the "democratising".

For the very ethos of Western democratisation, particularly the brand promoted by the world's major superpower, simply cannot have religious views which differ so markedly from its own, that different religions become a threat in themselves. Religions perhaps too difficult to control or contain. The underlying reason for such devious religious and political machinations is surely continued access to oil. Any view to the contrary is simply hypocrisy.

The idea of democracy, while seeming to be the most just system of Government yet devised, actually *does not at all* accord with Divine Will. A society that genuinely strove to embrace The Divine Will and The Laws that inherently derive from it, however, would naturally produce the correct spiritual leader(s) for that particular people.

Therefore, in the change that mankind must undergo, this needs to be a personal one in the first instance. For each one individually. We cannot *change* anyone else, we can only *change* ourselves. Governments cannot enact legislation to "force" *change* in the citizenry either. Even totalitarian regimes are not able to do this. At best in such cases there is only a suppression of sorts, and only for a particular time until the pressure is released. And then often violently, thus producing further change. The new order is not necessarily that much better for the long term either, just different. That is the history of mankind on Earth. And this is because there is no widespread transition to the **true understanding** of the *why*.

Only in knowing the *why* can a nation or race become strong and remain so, and have the peace and prosperity that seems such an impossible dream for most at present. If such an understanding can become universally accepted within the state, the concomitant vision and goal can be attained. A new direction for all societies, religions and ethnic groups based precisely on the understanding and clarification of the *why* of all our problems would have solved all societal ills.

This crucial **why**, however, can only be found in the recognition of The LAW. We may well ask, "what law"? We already have laws. We have civil law, criminal law, religious law (the 10 Commandments, and Scriptures from many religions), military law, decrees and pronouncements etc. Laws constantly changing, continually being reviewed and reformulated, modernised for "today's thinking", and differing from country to country. In some countries, from state to state, in others from tribe to tribe. In short, a ludicrous situation. Is it any wonder that so little of any real and lasting import can be progressed collectively anywhere, anymore?

Some may assert that individual cultures and societies inherently possess the right to formulate their own laws and that such laws will therefore be correct and lawful for that group. And that no culture or society has the right to impose its set of laws or values on any other. Of course societies need to develop certain rules and guidelines in order to function more or less lawfully and harmoniously. However, the fact that increasingly complex societal laws, globally, constantly require review and reformulation, positively indicates that they are flawed from the outset. Only a Perfect Law needs no further change or refinement. Clearly, mankind is not capable of formulating laws sufficiently clear or fair in the dispensation of true justice as to *not need* this continual re-working process. Moreover, as there is an obvious need to have more than one law, each law should then smoothly intermesh with every other without contradiction or conflict, thereby producing an harmonious whole needing no further fine-tuning.

Since we are not able to do that either, is it not now time to search for the "right way", so that we might finally produce fair and decent societies for whatever time we may have left? The "right way" *is* available to us but such a vital recognition will require far greater inner strength and humility from those who *covet* or aspire to "leadership", particularly in the political, scientific and religious disciplines. Such "leaders", by their recognition and example, could then *more legitimately* lead the way, thus allowing all members of society to fulfil their full potential under the aegis of more correct laws than we currently have. For they are the people who are in authority, who hold temporal power, and who therefore set in place the *conditions* under which we all must abide and answer to.

The key point here, however, is that for such a radically far-reaching yet ultimately beneficial global societal change to ever occur, such recognition and understanding must firstly be a **Spiritual** one! For the very essence of The Laws about which we speak is that of Life Itself. They are Living Laws, as opposed to humankind's generally lifeless laws. In simple terms, in their *automatic operation* these **Spiritual Laws** *return to us the reciprocal effects of all our free-will decisions*. We have been gifted the attribute of free will to enable us to choose a personal path through life. With free will, however, comes responsibility. That means *spiritual* responsibility – for each decision made. But only the **decision** is free, the **consequences** are not!

In that short simple statement lies many an answer to so many *seemingly* unknowable questions. The simple recognition of this fact would unequivocally show us that we truly are masters of our own fate. The truth and correct meaning of the Biblical Scripture, "What a man sows, *that* **shall** he reap", (Gal. 6. 7) should thus be more readily understandable. In this Scripture lies a vital key to spiritual understanding of virtually all of humankind's problems! Unfortunately, however, the true ramifications of this particular Spiritual Law are not fully understood at all even though it is quoted enough – and invariably with great authority by the religiously inclined.

What is therefore vitally important to understand is that there is only **One LAW** for all men irrespective of race, colour, creed, or geographical location. *Any belief to the contrary is ultimately irrelevant.* For it is within the parameters of The Living Laws *only* that *all* events must take place. Thus the premise upon which this book is based – *and from which it derives its validity* – is that there **is** such a "Law". It is precisely this "One Law", designated as The Laws of Creation or The Eternal or Spiritual Laws, which is decisive for all of humankind to know about.

It is that "Law", moreover, which has brought the world into being, and humankind with it. This "Law", however, does not take into account the personal interpretations that men may place upon it in their belief that it should serve their every whim. For the "Eternal" or "Spiritual Laws of Creation" are Perfect, Inviolable, Immutable and, therefore, **Unalterable!** To them we must submit if we wish to have a better life than that which is currently the way of the world. Put bluntly, it is that way purely and simply because we will not live according to them. We continually choose to *"break the rules"* and thus suffer accordingly.

In order to explain certain aspects of The Laws, we will occasionally need to quote from various religious and philosophical works. This does not make it a religious work, however. Religion is utilised where it may have relevance to the subject matter of the moment. In any case, religion is *not* necessarily **Truth**. The structure of virtually all *religions* is simply that of man-made organisations, and is therefore the earthly form under which man establishes and promotes his many and varied ideas of worship. Neither are such doctrines, by virtue of their "status" as a religion, necessarily ordained or Divinely blessed from Above. History teaches that they were often put in place to perpetuate the power and influence of the group concerned with that particular set of doctrinal beliefs or cultural traditions. Is it any different today?

There is certainly no doubt that the world's major religions carry great and wonderful Truths within their teachings. However, because there are so many vastly differing interpretations within each "religion", it is eminently clear that not a single one of those "interpretations" can lay claim to being an absolute and definitive authority on all matters - either temporal or spiritual.

The unequivocal reciprocal outworking of The Laws of Creation on all human decisions and endeavours means that no one single ethos of religion, science, education, politics, economics, cultural traditions or belief system can alter this *one, single, immutable reality*. Therefore, either we voluntarily adjust ourselves to the true Laws and reap the associated benefits, or *continue* to oppose them and consequently *continue* to suffer for our intransigence. We are imbued with free will to choose whatever we wish; heaven or hell on earth, thus reinforcing the stark fact of The Law. Unfortunately for mankind, The Laws take no account of whether we are *even aware of them or not*.

Ultimately, therefore, the price of being permitted the gift of conscious life is the *spiritual responsibility* to seek out these Spiritual Laws and *live accordingly*. Thus, until lawmakers finally formulate their societal laws in accordance with that greater and more beneficial regime, and educators of all societies recognise and *teach* this also, there will never be any progress toward a truly equitable and harmonious society anywhere.

In utilising the knowledge contained within The Spiritual Laws of Truth, one is more able to objectively review the past, examine the present, and thereby project future probabilities. For what is not learned from the lessons of history will return to haunt us and perhaps be re-lived, until the lessons are learnt. All we need do is witness the current state of the world to see that!

The source of the information and the veracity of the explanations contained in this publication would certainly be of interest to the reader. And while the *source* will only be stated later on, the *veracity* will be shown more and more clearly in the continuing and further breakdown of **all** aspects of society, both nationally and globally – also especially in increasing natural disasters – **if** there is no acknowledgement and voluntary acceptance of the only regime left to humankind for at least a few to find their way out of the mess we have created. That regime, this "life-belt" for humanity, is the knowledge of **Spiritual Law**.

It is therefore vitally important to not assess the subject matter of this book from a purely intellectual point of view, for the aspiritual and earthly nature of the intellect can only permit a purely material analysis. Here, the intuitive faculty of the *spirit* is needed. However, it must be an open spirit, not a closed one. Neither does one's religion or race matter. The reader only needs to be open-minded and objective with *absolutely no preconceptions*, and must therefore be willing to suspend, at least for the duration of the study of this book, all the generally accepted teachings of religion and science.

For the knowledge of The Spiritual Laws provides the very benchmark we need in order to make sense of our world in both the visible and the non-visible aspects. The ever-growing demands of an increasingly complex society continually bombard us with conflicting ideas and messages. We struggle in the undergrowth with our eyes on the ground, seeing only our personal opinions, our precious ego and our pride, all the while believing that what we have is a clear vision to the horizon. We need to extend our vision beyond our immediate consumer, cultural or traditional wants, to find the light of an overriding message of Truth against which everything else can be measured. One which can offer a clear, uncluttered view to that horizon. Then we will have simple, coherent and unchanging guidelines for a more fulfilling life, and a greater understanding of the why of all of our present and increasing problems.

By utilising the distilled essence of man's collective seeking throughout his long march through history we may glimpse elements of the One Law from his analyses of the natural world, his perceptions and possible fears of the accepted but unseen worlds, his philosophic meanderings, his religions, his science and, latterly, the strange paradox of his increasing spiritual insights. From this distillation, we will more certainly arrive at a more logical view of our world, Creation and the unalterable Laws which govern it, than that which has been handed down from ancient times to present-day religions, cultures and societies.

Even that long period of often hard experiencing, however, still did not provide sufficient spiritual insight for humankind to *collectively* recognise the One Law with which this book is concerned with. Six hundred years before the birth of Christ, a new way of thinking began to evolve in Greece. Before this development people generally accepted that the answers to their questions could be found in their various religions. However, whilst they might be termed religious explanations, they were more the myths of the people handed down from generation to generation. Their myths sought to offer "rational" explanations about the activity of their "gods" which, in turn, made sense of their immediate world, as they believed it to be. Thus the Greek philosophers contributed immensely to the long history of man's quest for the ultimate answers to life, earnestly questioning all that was current in their society to begin with. This was not without some danger at the time, however.

One of the greatest philosophers, Socrates, (470-399 BC) accused of "introducing new gods" and "corrupting the youth", was sentenced to death by a jury of five hundred citizens of Athens. Forced to drink hemlock, he died surrounded by friends. By daring to continually question the status quo, he finally forfeited his life. His death profoundly affected Plato, (428-347 BC) one of his pupils. Also considered one of the greatest philosophers, Plato noted in the death of Socrates – whom he considered to be Athens most noble citizen – a striking example of the conflict that can exist *"between society as it really is and the true or ideal society"*.

We also ask serious questions about certain current beliefs, particularly in religious thinking. Hopefully, such questioning should not produce the same reaction now as it did in Athens then. Paradoxically, however, whilst the Greek philosophers were correct to move away from a purely mythical explanation of the world around them, their singular pursuit of answers from more the intellectual approach – notwithstanding their struggles to clarify the question of the duality of man, i.e. body and soul – they nevertheless moved away from one vital aspect concerning their particular "pantheon of gods". Full understanding of that very relevant point would have filled a particular and crucial gap in their knowledge.[1]

Thus, for many of our analyses, we will make use of the philosophies, religions and scientific findings of other races and cultures. A major source will be The Bible since the Western world, to a large extent, broadly uses Judaeo-Christian ideas for societal law-making and is therefore entirely appropriate for our purpose. We will also utilise the knowledge contained in Eastern religious thought. Despite the fact that the general sources indicated do provide the bulk of our material, the *unequivocal* conclusions arrived at are not ultimately derived from any kind of final, distillation process from them.

---

[1] We examine this most important point in the later Chapter on "Elemental Lore".

No, the key aspect of a more correct spiritual interpretation – which is the overriding principle of this book – is sourced from a relatively recent and *genuinely* Spiritual Work. A completely *new* insight into the age-old questions of our origins, the meaning of life, the process of death and the WHY of all our problems can thereby now be offered! It is the "NEW" which we need to recognise and know!

The path that man has embarked upon by choice since his arrival onto the earth plane clearly shows the unfortunate consequences of it. Therefore the vital need is to assess the question "why" from the *reciprocal outworking* of The Eternal Laws even though via this means certain matters examined herein cannot necessarily be "proven scientifically". It is a *reciprocal outworking*, nevertheless, that unequivocally reveals the current effects and consequences that mankind's decisions have brought to them. And obviously *differently* from that which the human view might once have espoused or expected.

There is a very appropriate saying which, incidentally, accords perfectly with the inviolable Laws of Truth, and it states:

The proof of the pudding is in the eating!

If the truth of this saying is applied to the content of this particular book, and reflected upon with a truly open and questing mind, free of any preconceptions or angry or emotive indignation, it is my sincere hope that the reader will find enlightening clarification within these pages. As previously stated, as well as offering "spiritual" explanations for the problems of humankind globally, more importantly it is a signpost *pointing the way* to where the complete understanding of the rapidly increasing problems that confront us today *may be found!* With that recognition there should arise a clarity of spiritual purpose and a greater measure of inner peace and sureness for all peoples irrespective of religious beliefs or cultural or ethnic connections.

In that sense, we may regard the whole thrust of this exercise as showing us more and more starkly, as we continue to travel down our self-chosen, increasingly precarious, collective path, what we must do to find the way out! "Waiting in the wings", however, and *irrespective* of whether or not a better, more spiritually enlightened direction has been embarked upon, lies the "eating of the pudding", of which we have already begun to taste! Thus, through "spiritually objective discernment", the uncertain or unhelpful flavours currently present in our global "human pudding" may bring about a necessary, beneficial and *timely* change of recipe!

Today, the dynamics of market forces, consumerism and technology affect virtually all races in the world no matter where they live, and the overriding goal seems to be the relentless drive toward crass materialism. Conversely, however, whilst spiritual values are in retreat everywhere, more and more individuals are looking to what little is left of the purely natural world for the harmony and integrity that human society has generally lost, and clearly needs once more.

In the final analysis, the subject matter is addressed to all humanity since we are all incarnated here together at this fateful point in planet earth's history and evolution. Our *collective* concern and purpose, therefore, should be to strive to become, in the first instance, true "spiritual stewards" of this beautiful "blue planet" which nurtures and protects us. In order to fulfil that purpose, however, our choices should reflect a concomitant acceptance and willingness to live according to the very Laws which have permitted us a spiritually conscious life here, in the clear recognition of the ultimate earthly gift from Above of a blessed and beautiful, bountiful earthly home.

Even though the title of this book may possibly be contentious, it should nevertheless act as a spur to seek out the why of it. For by examining more than these statements, the reader will discover concepts that have had no airing thus far but which, in their actual effect, impact upon each of us in no small measure. Since we are airing an apocalyptic viewpoint – the actuality of which has finally been brought about through humankind's continuing transgressions against the very Laws we were meant to obey – the question of Bible interpretation or, more precisely, incorrect Bible interpretation provides a vital key to global society's impending demise.

Correct Bible interpretation has clearly eluded the global Christian community historically. Were this not so we would not have so many diverse groups promoting their particular brand of Bible belief; sometimes at completely illogical variance to others. Of course, the same must be said of most religions and belief systems. Yet the reality of certain contentious so-called "religious events" which took place at certain points in history must nevertheless forever follow absolute and lawful criteria, as stated in Chapter 1. And therefore in the final analysis, cannot possibly be subject to so many differing human views under the guise of some kind of personal-truth "reality". The events occurred *as they actually did* – fact! Thus any interpretation of a given event or incident ultimately cannot be subject to human opinions or ideas but must "live" within absolutely strict and logical parameters of Spiritual Law, i.e. **"Inviolable Divine Law"**.

Chapter 3

The Spiritual Laws – The Necessary Knowledge

"Oh the Ancient Truth!
Ages upon ages past it was found,
And it bound together a Noble Brotherhood.
The Ancient Truth!
Hold fast to it!
"

(Johann Wolfgang von Goethe.)

"Without Revelation a Nation fades.
But it prospers by knowing the Law!"

(Proverbs 29:18)

This Chapter should be regarded as the key link to all the others, as the understanding of The Spiritual Laws is imperative for the complete understanding of the aim and purpose of this work. And that is **to know the Law**. As stated above – *"Without Revelation a Nation fades. But it prospers by knowing The Law!"*

Knowledge of The Law, which therefore permits us to know why the mainly dark and blood-thirsty actions of humankind over millennia **must** call forth a Judgement upon itself, is the primary purpose of this Chapter. It is a Judgement, however, perfectly

just in its application, for it will be exactly commensurate with the degree of good or evil that the various groups and races within humanity have visited upon each other over that period of time. The reader should therefore strive to understand the explanations that *interlink* the different Laws.

In the context of religious thinking and cultural tradition the word "spiritual" may mean any number of things. In its distilled essence and form, however, *it should mean only one thing*. By **"Spiritual"**, we should mean "of the spirit", i.e. that which is **not** of the material but which occupies the *higher level*. We should not use this word to attempt to describe things that are concerned solely with the mundane and earthly, including some aspects of traditional cultures. And we certainly should not debase the inherent noble power of the word by attempting to ascribe to it practices or beliefs such as those pertaining to occult or psychic activity, for example.

If we, however, describe this word as being more uplifting, more noble in its origin, and therefore in its application more able to offer those higher virtues capable of producing the best kind of society; and if it *is* that which originates from out of the Higher Spheres, are we not then talking of absolutes? Are we speaking, then, of possibly needing to apply "rules" to achieve this desired state? And are we, in the final analysis, stating that any such thing can only be possible under clear, uniform, strict and unchangeable "Laws" perhaps?

Our answer to all of the above is an unequivocal yes! We can, moreover, state these "guidelines" to be that perfection, alluded to in Chapter 2, which are naturally inherent within **"The Spiritual Laws"**. It is thus important to clarify this amorphous thing called "The Law" in order to give better understanding of some of the many *incorrect* interpretations of this vitally important life-word – **"Spiritual"**. And therewith strive to illustrate its true meaning, thereby separating the beneficial from the clearly unhelpful, and certainly from the dangerous.

Irrespective of the basic tenets of the various religions, The Law is invariably *perceived to have*, as its underlying foundation, a higher being or beings who are the guardians of this "Law", with those same beings watching over the people to whom they have supposedly given the knowledge of It! Throughout history many races have striven to base their societies upon the ideal of The Law, with the Jewish people perhaps possessing the strongest application of it in their long history. If one reads the Old Testament as an historical document rather than as a religious one, it is very clear that the ancient Israelites *only* prospered when they *obeyed* The Law. When they rejected it outright or even simply adopted the laws of the peoples around them, they invariably suffered invasion, enslavement and sometimes great slaughter.

By definition, the *customary law* of any race of people can *only* derive from the beliefs, customs and traditions which that particular group will have believed was correct for them at a particular time in their development. Unfortunately, however, the historical record for many ethnic groups and tribal societies reveal their particular law as being also strongly derived from their *fears and superstitions*. So whilst that "customary law" may have served well for a given time of development, if a race proceeds normally and naturally through the various stages of "spiritual" growth and development, certain factors of that law should clearly change as greater insights hopefully lead away from the fear and superstitious aspects perhaps previously present within that group.

The nature of The Spiritual Laws or Principles therefore decree that they are the only model on which to base any society today because, **by their very constitution**, they are absolutely inviolable and unchangeable. Since these absolute parameters logically further decree that such Laws unequivocally transcend humankind's generally narrow views; in their clear perfection they are thus the ideal foundation for all societies and ethnic groups. Whilst we should certainly examine all laws which contribute to the sum total of all legislation that a given country or people might possess, only those aspects which accord with The Spiritual Laws should be retained. That which does not should be discarded as more correct laws are formulated to replace them.

This Chapter explains those Laws!

The English empiricist philosopher, John Locke, (1632-1704) notable for his "Two Treatises of Government" which justified the English Revolution of 1688 opposing the notion of the Divine Right of Kings, held the view that the idea of God was a "potential" of human reason. And that it was likely for human reason to know that God exists. Most of the Enlightenment philosophers also believed in the "reality" of a God, for the world was far too rational for that not to be the case, in their general view.

At times of human suffering, and given this seemingly inherent belief in God on the part of humankind, it is therefore not surprising to hear the anguished cries of: "If there is a God of Love, how can He let this happen?"; "How can there be a God of

Love when there is so much misery and suffering in the world?"; "How can it be?"; "Why him, her, them?"; "Why did they have to be taken?"; "I don't understand it!" etc.. Very great puzzlement is also evinced at the seemingly unfair and untimely death of "good" people or young children, or in the birth of the handicapped. Yet whilst there may not generally be clear understanding of the reasons for such "hard fate", the very fact that many people ask why "God" should allow it appears to bear out the Enlightenment philosophers belief of a probable knowing within man of the existence of a great and All Mighty "Creator".

Therein lies our conundrum, our non-understanding! We feel great pain and anguish during times of deep sorrow because the ultimate reason *why* is often difficult to understand. Words of solace and condolence are offered but, whilst they are comforting, they may not provide answers. What is then left? An experience that *can* serve to bring people together, but also an event – if deeply traumatic – with the potential to shatter lives and split families apart. And, moreover, it can unfortunately also reduce the quality of life of those affected because the nature of the event itself and the ongoing memory of it may not *appear* to offer any logical reasons as to why. The resultant legacy may well be the inability to ever find reasons or answers, thus resulting in ongoing and unresolved heartache.

Yet to be faced with seemingly unfair "blows of fate" should act as the *strongest* impetus to ask the key question – "why"? The Enlightenment philosophers encouraged rational enquiry about God by rejecting any mysterious doctrines and maintaining that the existence of God could be arrived at by introspection and human experience. However, it would be unhelpful if we became so absorbed in our enquiry or search that much else that is worthwhile and valuable in life is excluded. Therefore, in the continuation of one's life, one should adjust one's thinking and perhaps one's lifestyle to support the aim of finding that reason why. In order to find such answers, however, there must logically be some rational mechanism whereby this can be achieved.

The premise postulated here is that only with the knowledge of The Spiritual Laws of Creation can sense ever be made of our existence and our reason for being. Only a thorough knowledge of The Spiritual Laws can provide a logical "thought-process mechanism" through which the question of apparently unfair or "hard blows of fate" can be answered. And thereby offer the potential for a more benign and enlightened global society than is currently the case. A brief introduction to just two points of "The Law" should suffice to illustrate why there is such an entrenched general refusal by humankind to acknowledge the existence of Spiritual Law - let alone the inviolability of it. The same two points will further demonstrate how beliefs which do not acknowledge The Spiritual Laws effectively prevent basic understanding of the why of life's tragedies anyway.

Firstly, it is probably reasonable to assume that most people accept the notion that we possess "free will", i.e. we can, and do, make decisions for ourselves virtually every minute of each day. And that personal decisions via this mechanism should allow us full command over our individual destinies. If this were not so, we would be forced to assume that what happens in our lives is determined by factors outside our control. If such an "arbitrary force" did actually exist, it might perhaps have to be regarded as a mischievous or even rogue one given that some people seem to suffer more setbacks than might reasonably be expected to occur in a "normal" life.

Secondly, the simple act of making a decision about anything must presuppose an outcome of some kind. Most students of religion, philosophy, or even home-spun logic will probably accept the concept that "what one sows one must, or shall, reap". Certainly for the general Christian community, this biblical directive is sacrosanct in its perceived truth. If that is so, there must logically be a just and lawful mechanism which produces the outcome or the reaction to every decision made. If it is reasonable to assume the first part of the equation – that there will be an outcome from a decision made – then it is surely equally reasonable to assume the second; that there will be a "return" – without fail! The premise here is that ultimately it is our own decisions that therefore determine all outcomes which affect us. Science, in essence, states this process thus: "For every action there is an equal and opposite reaction."

What happens, however, when these two cornerstones, i.e. the notion of *free will* and *we reap what we sow*, are brought together to try to make sense of tragedy and misfortune? For if each notion is true, (and this work accepts that truth) then any misfortune - and it is usually only misfortunes and tragedies that produce any kind of soul-searching for answers anyway - must have been set in place somewhere, sometime, ***by*** the "reaper". Therefore, if the essence of the two particular tenets are absolute, then the ***first absolute*** would naturally presuppose that the ***second one*** is also

– in terms of a logical and meaningful *connection* and *outcome*.

But because the *reasons* for misfortunes are not always *immediately* apparent – whereby the concept and logic of "free will" and its equally logical *connection* of "reaping the effects" is clearly *visible* and thus understandable – it becomes necessary to attempt to postulate some kind of *different* mechanism as an explanation. The clear contention stated in *this* particular equation is that if both tenets are absolute and sacrosanct as an inviolable Law, then we cannot possibly postulate other reasons which exclude or alter either one to simply fabricate such a connection between our *free-will decision-making ability*, and *reaping what we sow*. And we certainly should not try to make it conveniently fit a religious doctrine or dogma or, indeed, any personal faith or mode of belief.

Whilst we therefore possess the inherent freedom to make any kind of decision we may wish to, we must clearly recognise that we are absolutely *not free* to choose to *either accept or reject* the returning consequences! Under the inviolability of this absolute *equation of life*, **consequences must always derive from decisions**. That is the clear and unequivocal reality.

Now, if the two tenets are *not* accepted as being absolute and thus lawfully connected, then searching outside these two sacrosanct positions to try to find an answer would *seemingly* provide "other" alternatives. However, if such an "answer" **denies** the inherently logical and thus lawful connection between a "free-will decision" and "reaping what one has sown" (i.e. accepting that there must naturally be a consequence from making a decision in the first place) then that particular position naturally refutes the inherent inviolability of any "lawful connection" to begin with. Yet the two inviolable "cornerstones" of this *"equation of life"* unequivocally state that they clearly *must be absolute*, both in essence and reality.

The inviolability of "inherent justice" naturally contained within The Spiritual Laws ensures that they will *always* provide correct answers. It is an infallible mechanism that not only does *not* compromise the absolute nature of the two "cornerstones" of our illustration, but positively strengthens the interlinking of all The Spiritual Laws to provide genuine solutions! Therefore, since the two "cornerstones" are absolute and lawfully connected, the clear contention here is that another law – equally as valid and sacrosanct – must be taken into account if one wishes to understand **all** connections. It is that *other* Law, not generally recognised and accepted, which provides the key. Unfortunately, it is the refusal to accept this factual Law which gives rise to so much confusion and anguish when needing to find answers – for major problems, particularly.

That "other Law" – **The Law of Rebirth** – is explained later in this Chapter under the sub-heading: **Rebirth – Fact or Fiction?**

The concept of reincarnation, whilst not generally accepted by most Western religions or the scientific community, is an absolute belief for hundreds of millions world-wide. Multiple earth lives provide the mechanism whereby the two "spiritually lawful" cornerstones of *"free will"* and *"reaping what one sows"* can be logically explained. More particularly where an earth-life does not offer sufficient time for certain categories of "reaping" to occur. It is not for nothing that Jesus stated quite emphatically, "Seek, and You Shall Find" (Matthew 7:7). By virtue of His Divine Origin, Jesus spoke always from the Knowledge of The Spiritual Laws of Creation! He was able to survey all happenings, both the small and the large, in their complete cycles from cause to effect. Therefore, if any answers are to give a true and comprehensive explanation, ***they must first explain it* spiritually**.

In contrast to the spiritual point of view taught by Jesus, a purely medical, scientific, religious, political or sociological explanation for a particular problem can only take in the material effect. Though the end *effect* may be seen or felt in the material, it is, nevertheless, the *result* of a "spiritually-willed" decision made somewhere, sometime by someone individually, or some group collectively. By virtue of its purely material application, earthly disciplines are therefore not able to give a complete overview for they are not always able to see the actual starting point of such outcomes, irrespective of views to the contrary from within the individual disciplines. This is not to decry the very great help that we can obviously obtain from disciplines concerned with empirical paradigms. However, where it is a question of finding the actual source of many of our problems, or the answers to life itself, earth-orientated practices are not able to supply this. Because only in Spiritual Law and Its Source can we find these ultimate answers!

Despite the superiority of the spiritual viewpoint over the materialistic one, the whole thrust of our much-vaunted, modern education system virtually denies the existence of anything other than what can be materially seen, heard, felt, or measured. Currently, the scientific and rationalist point of view reigns supreme. But there are other voices questioning the narrow strictures of such points of view. These voices are slowly swelling in volume and some are coming from within the scientific disciplines too. In essence, the realisation may be slowly dawning that all we have been taught to blindly accept through the education and religious systems may prove to be very different from the actual reality.

So, from where springs this irrational attitude and widespread defiance that seeks to deny man the knowledge of his true spiritual self, and therewith his actual origin? Should this not be the ultimate goal of the various disciplines rather than the present one of attempting to steer all away from this so-called "irrational and unscientific" view? Is there fear, then, of this unscientific, perhaps politically and even culturally incorrect word, – **SPIRITUAL?**

The obvious problem encountered when discussing "The Spiritual" is that the very word itself is generally lumped with whatever ideas humankind may determine it to encompass. Things that originate from, or are connected to, the actual Spiritual Realm, can be deemed to be truly spiritual. And because only the *truly* spiritual can *actually* be of "The Spiritual", what is of that Realm is therefore sacred and holy.

However, because the Realm of the so-called "beyond" is generally deemed as being "all spiritual", anything that is connected with, or derived from, it is also viewed similarly by some religions and cultures. Far too much is made of purely man-made icons being designated sacred and therefore regarded as spiritual in humankind's estimation. Thus there exists the farcical idea that everything that man *decides* is sacred must therefore be so. And, by extension, also spiritual and thus holy.

Nothing could be further from the truth!

In fact some aspects of various cultures, such as the meanings ascribed to grotesque carved images or in particular ancient practices to name two examples, are so aspiritual in both form and connection that it is difficult to even begin to understand how their supporters ever arrived at such a conclusion. The Spiritual Laws of Creation offer clear, objective solutions as to how a more open and correct mind-set can free cultural emotionalism or scientific rigidity from self-imposed and inculcated beliefs that stubbornly cling to a wrong understanding of this vitally important *life-word* – **SPIRITUAL!**

The greatest teacher humankind has ever had is history, and within its pages may be found the struggle of individuals who have been lone and lonely "voices in the wilderness". Boat-rockers, all of them! Voices that were raised in protest against blindness and often sheer stupidity. Voices of people who possessed the clarity of vision or perception to *know* that certain "official" teachings and views were gravely in error. Those same lonely voices were often stilled, silenced, to protect the ego and power base of those in authority who fought to maintain, *at all costs,* the "official" version.

In some cases the lone voices were able to convince the "authorities" of the correctness of their beliefs, though often after years of protest. Then, in an absolute farce, the "new knowledge" became the accepted norm. A norm or standard not only *accepted* by the ruling authority, but *promoted* by it as being correct and therefore suitable for the masses. Is it any different today? No, it is not. For mankind's collective ego has not yet humbled itself sufficiently to *voluntarily* recognise the very truth of what we assert here – that historically, the essence of truth has never lain with the masses – only with the few!

A classic example is that of the view of Ptolemy (ca 90-168 AD), a Graeco-Egyptian mathematician and geographer who believed that the earth was the centre of the universe and that the sun and planets revolved around it. In stating this view, he set in place a theory which remained unchallenged for about 1600 years. The main reason for such a long acceptance of a wrong belief was that it perfectly suited the egocentric interpretation of the Church. And no voice was raised against it until 1543 when Copernicus, (1473-1543) a Polish astronomer, found that only with the sun at the centre of the universe could the planetary system work. From that point on the Ptolemaic belief was rejected – at least by the newly-emerging sciences.

Unfortunately, this was not a belief shared by the Church and is graphically illustrated in the persecution of Galileo (1564-1642) by the Inquisition in 1633. Galileo, an Italian astronomer and mathematician, agreed with the claim of Copernicus that the sun was the centre of our universe. This "unacceptable view", however, led to his persecution. He recanted, but is said to have muttered under his breath: "But it [the Earth] does move."[1]

Another stark example was the debate between flat-earth theorists, led by the European Church, and the opposite belief that the earth was spherical, accepted by scholars in some monasteries. Accepted also by Columbus and other navigators as being the *prob-*

---

[1] It is interesting to note that Copernicus did not publish his theory until the year of his death at age 70. Perhaps it was a purposeful decision on his part to publish as late as was possible for him in an effort to escape the censure of the Church.

able truth. The latter purely by their logical observations of the curved and disappearing horizon. History records that the journey of Columbus forced an immediate change of view within "the establishment". Long before then, however, Greek mathematicians already understood the truth of a spherical earth.

What the teaching "authorities" should learn to accept is that the very nature of **Truth** guarantees that it cannot be stifled or suppressed forever. Far better, then, to keep a completely open mind to *all* "voices". The one constant that will determine the *validity* of any definition of "The Spiritual" will be whether or not it accords with the actual Spiritual Laws themselves, thereby separating the "superficial voices" from the "true ones". The lawful mechanism contained within The Living Law thus determines which "voices" will ultimately fail, and which will stand the test of time. This is the only true measure as these Laws are, themselves, eternal. And, within the life-path parameters given for humankind, it is we who must finally acknowledge and accept this fact, since our life, being and sustenance are given only via these Laws.

To glibly state that mankind is "not meant to understand the ways of The Creator" presupposes the requirement to submit to and accept all suffering in fatalistic ignorance. The Spiritual Laws decree that we actually **are** "masters of our own destiny", even if present events seem to suggest otherwise. It is our refusal to accept the Truth of The Law, *as it actually is*, that is the problem. The above historic examples together with the previously postulated premise that we are masters of our own destiny indicate that no one should be afraid to abandon dogma when it becomes apparent that it is clearly not true. We should especially beware of leaders who knowingly still maintain the old errors out of fear of a collapse of their authority and organisation.

On the relationship between science and religion, the scientific giant Albert Einstein observed:

> "Intelligence makes clear to us the interrelation of means and ends. But mere thinking cannot give us a sense of the ultimate and fundamental ends. To make clear these fundamental ends and valuations, and to set them fast in the emotional life of the individual, seems to me precisely the most important function which religion has to perform in the social life of man. And if one asks whence derives the authority of such fundamental ends, since they cannot be stated and justified merely by reason, one can only answer: they come into being not through demonstration *but*

through revelation, through the medium of powerful personalities. One must not attempt to justify them, but rather to sense their nature simply and clearly."

(Albert Einstein, *Ideas and Opinions*, p 42-43. Bonanza Books, New York, Italics mine.)

As we state unequivocally throughout this work and strongly illustrate in the next Chapter, there should be no contradiction between science and religious truth, and that science cannot supersede any such truths. Though noting the demarcation between science and religion, Einstein also understood the strong reciprocal relationships and dependencies between the two.

He stated:

"Though religion may be that which determines the goal, it has, nevertheless learned from science, in the broadest sense, what means will contribute to the attainment of the goals it has set up. *But science can only be created by those who are thoroughly imbued with the aspiration toward truth and understanding.*"

Einstein summarises his view of the relationship between science and religion in the famous words: *"Science without religion is lame, religion without science is blind."* (Italics mine.)

3.1 The Nature of The Spiritual Principles

"The Laws of Creation derive their eternal validity from the fact of God's Perfection. On account of God's Perfection, His Will is therefore perfect. Consequently, The Laws manifesting This Will are also necessarily perfect. They cannot be improved upon, and they remain absolutely unchangeable."

(*Building Future Societies: The Spiritual Principles*, p 23, Stephen Lampe. Millennium Press.)

This inviolable premise logically stipulates that God cannot act in an arbitrary manner and "do anything He wants". It may certainly be convenient to offer this sort of explanation to a difficult religious question thereby seeming to temporarily get rid of the problem, but it still, nonetheless, awaits a correct answer.

For if God is able to do "anything He wants" by virtue of the fact that He Is God, *where then lies His Perfection*? Since it **must** logically follow that if He Is Perfect and His Laws are Perfect and therefore unchangeable, then any belief that states otherwise *automatically* casts doubt on this accepted belief in **"A Perfect God"**. Quite simply, any attempt to change a *Perfect Law* naturally implies that The Law could not have been perfect in the first instance – if it then needed to be changed. *It is thus impossible to impute imperfection to a Perfect God!* Therefore the recognition of The Laws of Creation, *as they actually are in their inviolability*, will finally return to The Creator the Perfection that is His.

Two thousand years ago Jesus, arguably the greatest, most wonderful "boat rocker" of all, gave stern warning to the, then, leaders of the church. The fact that He did not support their practices is clearly apparent by virtue of His condemnation of them. The same lawful condemnation applies today to all teachings and disciplines which attempt to suppress the Truth.

> "Woe to you, play-acting professors and Pharisees! Because you lock up the Kingdom of Heaven in the face of mankind; while you yourselves neither enter, nor allow those arriving to go in."
>
> (Matthew 23:13, Fenton.)

In accordance with that clear message, it is our conviction that there are certain Spiritual Laws or principles that guide and determine the course of everything throughout Creation, including the destiny of man on Earth. These Laws are Eternal, i.e. they have existed from eternity. Everything in Creation, including humankind, came into being via the operation of these Laws, and our continued existence here depends on them also. The originator of these Laws is God, The Creator. Only what is inherent in His Laws of Creation can ever come to full blossom and be sustained in Creation. By extension, all else, i.e. activities not supported by those Laws, *must inevitably fail.*

Even though The Spiritual Laws allowed us the gift of conscious life, they have not always been clearly recognised. Throughout man's long and convoluted history, great and wise spiritual teachers arose at varying intervals to call attention to them. Teachers such as Krishna, Zoroaster, Lao-Tse, Moses and the Prophets, Buddha, Mohammed – and Jesus. At best, their Teachings were often not understood or sometimes misinterpreted. At worst, they were *knowingly* distorted.

Because The Laws *were* insufficiently understood, misinterpreted, taken out of context or knowingly distorted, it was not possible to consistently apply them beneficially. The origin of the present dangerous rise of religious fundamentalism can probably be traced to this problem of narrow, non-understanding. This unfortunate development, among many other increasing problems now facing us, may be seen as a direct correlation between **the immutability of The Spiritual Laws** and **our refusal to heed them**. The solutions to **all** our problems lie **solely** in a voluntary adjustment to them in a conscious, correct and consistent way.

Simply put, we have no choice but to understand and apply The Spiritual Laws to every facet of human life and not believe we can formulate better principles that are as effective. For it would be foolish to imagine that human beings can improve on The Will of The Creator, as we ourselves are only products of those Laws. Chaos and confusion will always be the result of attempting to deviate from them. No one can evade or change them, and The Laws apply equally to all in the same measure. To rich and poor, the powerful and the weak, the clever and the stupid, to kings and slaves. The effects are the same on those who know The Law as on those who do not, and ignorance of them does not keep their effects at bay!

If man's laws are compared with Spiritual Law, we find that earthly laws differ from society to society whereas The Laws of Creation remain the same everywhere and are Eternal. Our laws are constantly in a state of review, and can even be changed by public opinion or dictatorial decree, so what may have been perfectly legal yesterday may not be so today. By contrast, Spiritual Law is immutable and unchangeable, and will forever remain so.

The cost, complexity and duration of trials in earthly law courts indicate quite conclusively that our laws are not simple to understand, and require lawyers who have needed to spend years of study to become conversant with them. Even then, however, there can be much disagreement over individual points of law. By comparison, The Laws of Creation are clear, concise and simple. Moreover, they are few in number, easily understandable, and do not require years of laborious study. They are alluded to in all the major religions and philosophies of the world's peoples. Lawyers offices and judge's chambers will contain row upon row of books of laws and statutes. The Eternal Laws, however, can be contained in just *one publication*.

The Eternal Laws have, as their infallible foundation, Justice, Love and Purity, and are therefore perfect in the dispensation of justice. By virtue of our present level of spiritual *immaturity* we, on the other hand, do not have such a benchmark. Despite the fact that we have many laws, we do not always see justice done. So-called "legal technicalities" permit clever lawyers to exploit the present "justice system" to set free people who have *actually* committed crimes. By contrast no one escapes The Spiritual Laws. Their infallible, automatic outworking ensures that Justice and Love are meted out in perfect balance at all times, even though not always immediately, or even apparently so. But meted out they always are!

The incorruptible nature of The Eternal Laws ensures that they will reign supreme. This means that in the determination of innocence or guilt in an earthly court of law, man's laws do not always offer protection or absolution should an innocent person be wrongly condemned and sentenced. The responsibility for that miscarriage of justice, however, will fall back on all those who contributed to it – as it must in all things. To attempt to shelter behind a veil of "fulfilling one's duty" in the ostensible application of justice via the nation's laws matters not at all. We are all irrevocably tied to the consequences of our decisions, and a wrong conviction will eventually bring the inevitable reciprocal effect.

Judges and juries, then, have a particularly difficult task given the spiritually unhealthy state of our secular laws. Passing judgement according to such laws may satisfy the dictates of earthly society, but if the judgement is a transgression against The Laws of Creation, the judges are bound to reap the reciprocal effect of *their* spiritually-wrong decisions. For that reason, it should be in the interests of the judiciary to actively concern themselves with the knowledge of The Eternal Laws.

What should be understood is the fact that the material worlds are *presently* in transition between one phase and another. Literally everything is in transition and upheaval, man and nature. Consequently man is being strongly compelled to heed these Laws under the increasing spiritual pressure currently being applied to all things. The effect of this pressure is seen in the accelerating breakdown of our society and the increasing problems globally. In short, man's time of formulating his own policies is at an end. We will now be forced to adjust to The Laws of Creation, or perish. This increasing pressure actually strengthens both the good and the bad.

Thus the good – or that which *adjusts itself* to The Laws – *will flourish*. And the bad or wrong – that which *opposes* The Laws – *will collapse*. In this we have an infallible standard by which to measure events around us and to choose accordingly.

The **Spiritual Laws of Creation** are:

1. **The Law of Movement**

2. **The Law of Reciprocal Action**

3. **The Law of Attraction of Similar Species**

4. **The Law of Spiritual Gravity**

5. **The Law of Balance**

6. **The Law of Rebirth**

7. **Grace – A Gift of Divine Love**

The living dynamic of the above principles is that their *inviolable effects* are *felt* as Laws whenever we oppose them. They *cease* to be Laws, and therefore become *helps*, when we abide by them. So by examining each of The Laws named, it will be shown that everything in Creation is interlinked and interdependent. A brief explanation is also offered on the vital characteristic of **Grace**.[2]

How, then, should The Spiritual Laws be described? By examining philosophical, scientific, religious and spiritual works, clear and consistent reference to them can be found. Therefore they could be termed "Universal". Everyday observations of the natural world show this universality of The Laws in their working reality.

The philosopher Heraclitus (c.540-480 BC) of Ephesus in Asia Minor believed that this "universal reason" or "universal law" is something common to all and which guides not only every person but also everything that happens in nature. Yet he observed that instead of following this "higher guidance", most people lived by their individual beliefs. This "something", which was the source of everything, he called God or *logos* – meaning reason.

---

[2] It is a feature lawfully linked with the perfect intermeshing of The Eternal Laws, commensurate with those decisions which strive for, or are directed toward, spiritual ascent.

3.2 Movement = Life

The Law of Movement

Heraclitus also postulated a new concept – that of flux or change. He observed that everything flowed, everything is in constant flux and movement, nothing stands still. He expressed this concept of constant change by saying that "you cannot step twice into the same river." The river changes because "fresh waters are ever flowing in upon you." Heraclitus thought that this concept of flux "...must apply not only to rivers but to all things, including the soul of man. Rivers and men exhibit the fascinating fact of becoming different and yet remaining the same. We return to the 'same' river although fresh waters have flowed into it, and the man is still the same person as the boy." (*Philosophy History and Problems*, Third Edition, p 12-13.) Therefore, when we step into a river for the second time, neither we nor the river are the same.

Everything, literally everything, is in constant motion. Movement is the one activity that ensures the maintenance of life in all things. Without movement everything would become sluggish and eventually come to a complete standstill, a situation akin to death and disintegration. Therefore motion can be stated to be a most necessary principle throughout Creation. The higher and lighter the plane of Creation, the faster the motion. Conversely, therefore, the further away from The Source of life, as for example in the material planes, the more sluggish the motion. As "movement" is thus a vital principle, all other laws can be said to operate within the parameters of this most important Law. However, the movement must be of the *right* kind and in harmony with all else if it is to bring benefit.

Imagine life in the Universe and on earth without the elemental activity of the Forces of Nature bringing movement. We observe the rotation of the earth each day to give the necessary circadian rhythm of day and night. The earth rotates around the sun to provide the four seasons. These in turn produce the different weather patterns needed for planting and harvesting. The motion of the winds ensures freshness and change where there might otherwise be staleness. Consider the moon's rotation around the earth, offering its different phases and bringing the rise and fall of the tides. Consider, also, the great ocean currents that constantly mix the waters of our "blue planet", and the movement of the continents over the liquid core of the earth in plate tectonics, instrumental in the formation of new lands. Constant movement equals constant renewal. Further out into the incomprehensible vastness of the observable universe, galaxies of immense size, wheel and rotate their billions of suns to the same primordial rhythm.

Science has long discovered that individual cells, molecules and atoms, are "alive" with the constant movement of sub-particles, with each fitting perfectly into its ordained place to become part of the whole. And even in the microscopic sub-atomic world where the behaviour of quarks and neutrinos appears to circumvent all the known *scientific* laws they still, nevertheless, follow the dictates of Universal Law. It is our non-understanding of those laws that force us to declare our lack of knowledge about such behaviour. The rocks of the earth, even though appearing to be solid, dense and lifeless, are also awhirl with active movement. A crystal-clear glass of clean water gives no hint of the motion of electrons, protons and neutrons in the structure and composition of either the glass or the water. Animal and human bodies have the same basic activity in their molecular structure also, whether living and breathing, or dead and decomposing.

The physical body, with which we are all familiar, signals to us the need for constant movement in order to remain healthy. In breathing we quite automatically accept the rise and fall of the chest as the lungs inhale and exhale. The heart pumps blood in necessary circulation throughout the body. Exercise keeps the body healthy and strong, inactivity weakens it. The demands of the toilet call us to the process of the elimination of body wastes at various times during the day. Even in supposedly restful sleep there is still the need for the body to change its position more often than we might be aware of during the sleep state. Everything must obey The Law of Movement if it is to remain healthy and not stagnate.

Rivers and streams remain fresh and oxygenated through movement. The world's great river systems yearly transport millions of tons of silt to form large, fertile deltas at their mouths. In manmade lakes where dams block the normal river flow to the point where the amount of draw off prevents any natural spillage, the impounded body of water still has movement between the vertical layers of water.

In the world of birds and fishes, lack of the right kind of necessary movement has resulted in the loss of certain abilities that some once possessed. For example, there are fish that are no longer able to withstand the currents and must remain near the bottom. Many birds in various parts of the world have become flightless through not having used their wings over a long period of time. These examples showing the principle of adaptation, with which biological scientists are familiar, are a consequence of The Law of Movement.

To this point we have only examined the physical effect of this Law. In the first instance, however, it is a Spiritual Law. Therefore, in the case of the physical body, every movement must first be willed by the spirit, because the spirit is the animating force, the "power pack", within each of us. This *signal* between spirit and body happens so quickly as to be virtually simultaneous and imperceptible in its time-lapse aspect.[3]

The activity of the natural world demands that every creature and plant must strive to maintain its place or perish. Spiritual activity must produce the same, and more, if there is to be growth and ascent. Therefore, effort must be expended if we wish to achieve anything of lasting value. We cannot sit back and expect wonderful things to just happen. Whether applied to the physical, mental or spiritual, laziness in any one area is a transgression against this Eternal Law. Moreover, the different kinds of activities – spiritual, intellectual and physical – must always be kept in proper balance. Without spiritual activity as a necessary counterpoise, physical and intellectual expenditure of effort will ultimately be worthless. We can extrapolate from this that a genuinely spiritual goal will always have furthering values that will never change and, by definition, be far-reaching and beneficial.

Present trends allow people to eagerly anticipate retirement after a lifetime of work. The thought of the remaining years of life spent in blissful inactivity appeals to many. Yet this offends against The Law too. Of course the elderly could not be expected to maintain the same level of activity that a much younger person might. Nevertheless, for the older body to maintain reasonable health, movement of the right kind is still necessary. Fortunately, current directions now see more and more of the elderly pursuing this beneficial course. The "acceptance of change" that time and development naturally bring under The Law of Movement permits one phase of life to flow into the next, for movement is designed to bring about *further* development.

Conversely, "workaholics", some professional sports people, and others engaged in constant frenetic activity actually transgress this

---

[3]The "Spiritual Origins of humankind", thus that which pertains to the Origin and nature of the human spirit and soul, is addressed in the following Chapter.

Law and will eventually harm themselves. A sense of balance should be maintained in all that we do by adjusting our pace to a natural rhythm which is connected to The Law of Movement. Perhaps the latter day phrase, "Everything in moderation", is an unconscious reaction to the increasingly unnatural pace of modern society. In heeding The Law of Movement, we also need to obey The Law of Balance as well, for this Law is also a consequence of motion.

History's testament to the rise and fall of some of the great civilisations provides excellent examples of what occurs if the correct "spiritual" movement is not maintained. The rise to greatness can show the right kind of movement, whilst the disintegration process invariably indicates the opposite. The Law of Movement decrees that no one person, group or nation can simply stop and rest on past or even present glories. What has been achieved, if spiritually worthwhile, must be maintained or stagnation, retrogression and disintegration will quickly follow. In the same way, persons who have been publicly honoured by society should be required to maintain that position of honour.

The propensity of many to attempt to live in the past offends against The Law of Movement also. The current strong cultural trend in some ethnic communities to promote tribal links or a return to tribalism per se, clearly transgresses The Law of Movement in both the spiritual and material sense. The spiritual power and pressure inherent in this Law decrees that the tribal phase for any race is exactly that – just a phase. Consequently any beneficial outworking contained within the power of The Law of Movement for a people will be greatest when and where *correct movement* is undertaken. For certain ethnic groups, that would translate into leaving tribalism behind and moving toward becoming one nation, one people.

This does not mean that we should not assess history, or try to correct past wrongs. The Laws, however, require us, indeed command us, to *live in the present.* They further command us to strongly heed The Law of Movement – in the spiritual sense particularly – if there is not to be stagnation and retrogression.

Thus The Law of Movement decrees that absolutely nothing can stand still. Should a point of stagnation be reached, then a new impetus must be developed to prevent the possibility of retrogression. Any new idea, though, should have, as its foundation, the application of Spiritual Law so that only upward movement is generated. For this Law will drive either upwards or downwards equally powerfully, exactly in accordance with the kind of decision taken.

3.3 Decisions Produce Consequences

The Law of Reciprocal Action

> "Do not err; God cannot be deluded: for what a man sows, that he will also reap.
>
> If he sows for his sensuality, he will reap perdition; but sowing for the Spirit, from the Spirit, he will reap eternal life."
>
> (Galatians 6:7-8, Fenton.)

The key word in the above Scriptures is **"will"**. It is not a word such as *perhaps*, for example, or *might*, or *maybe*, or *possibly*. No, the texts are quite unequivocal. They clearly state that we **"will"** reap what we sow! Other Bibles use the word "shall" in this context, but the meaning is obviously still the same.

In eastern religions the word "karma" is generally used to describe the very same effect/outcome. This particular word, however, unfortunately produces negative reactions in many "Christians". Yet the very word perfectly represents the exact Law that Its Bringer, Jesus, taught.

Thus: *"A knowledge of the* **iron law of karma** *encourages the earnest seeker to find the way of final escape from its bonds."* (Paramahansa Yogananda, *Autobiography of a Yogi*, p 563, Italics mine.)

3.3.1 Faith Versus Works

The theological argument of *faith* versus *works* can best be clarified using this "iron Law" as a guide. Faith is that aspect of a belief which strongly accepts that a particular thing is so and which therefore stems from a confident belief in the truth, value or trustworthiness of it. It is a belief, moreover, which does not rest on logical proof or material evidence. Faith, therefore, can perhaps be stated to be an implicit belief and trust in God and in the doctrines expressed in the Scriptures or other sacred works. Faith, however, even though a noble virtue, is nevertheless amorphous in its nature for its *actual* essence cannot be seen or touched. The New Testament documents many cases where faith alone produced miraculous outcomes around the presence of Jesus. The woman who believed that all she had to do was touch His robes to be healed, and the ones who stated that He had only to "say the Word" and those for whom they sought healing *would* be healed. His acknowledgement: "Your faith has saved/healed you".

Faith in its sum and substance can therefore provide, and be, a powerful anchorage for one's religious beliefs, but it probably cannot be said to *be,* or *hold,* **absolute conviction** in the thing believed in. Faith, however, *should precede* **conviction** – that element of *sure and certain knowing* commonly derived from, but no longer *constrained by,* the faith paradigm itself.

Historically, great and wonderful works have been produced from and by faith, and the outworking of the great law of **Sowing and Reaping** will automatically bring the appropriate "return effect" to the instigators and builders of those works. So remarkable blessings can derive from good works produced by faith, alone.

If, however, works are undertaken out of **conviction** – clearly accepting that that very word presupposes an *absoluteness of knowing* – then the volition, the instigation and the building of the works proceeds with the concomitant sureness of knowing *exactly why* such a project is undertaken. The one, or the group, thus consciously *works* within the actual parameters of The Laws and their reciprocal outworking. Works produced through conviction, therefore, inherently carry within them a much stronger connection to the source of that particular certainty. Works produced by faith cannot inherently do so. One has the *sureness of knowing,* the other possesses the lesser value of simply *believing it knows.*

In terms of the outworking of The Law of Reciprocal Action, however, the absolute perfection of The Spiritual Laws will return the exact reciprocal effect to both kinds of "builders" – whether through faith or conviction. In the final analysis, though, the faith/belief paradigm, which many in the Christian world promote as the only standard necessary for spiritual ascent, clashes diametrically with that which their "Master" clearly stated, vis-a-vis:- "*By their* **works** *you shall* **know** *them.*" When told by His Disciples – whilst preaching in a synagogue – that His Mother and brothers were waiting outside for Him, Jesus declared, in essence: "Who is My mother, who is My brother? They are those who *carry out* **The Will** *of the* **Father!**"

The lament of Jesus over the little faith expressed by those of the race who were called to **support and follow Him** ring down through the centuries as an indictment on many today, i.e.: "O ye of little faith." Such paucity of faith during his life contrasted hugely with His great joy upon finding firm and unshakeable faith in Him and His Mission from people not of that chosen race, such as the Roman Centurion.

How, then, should one carry out such **works**? Through faith, or through conviction? Whose teachings should the well-meaning Christian follow? Paul the Apostle *taught* that faith, alone, was sufficient. Jesus, on the other hand, **demanded works.** His admonition to; "Take up the cross and follow Me" simply means that any believer in Him must *live The Laws* and not simply pay lip service to them.

The Pauline philosophy of "faith alone" has unfortunately now bequeathed to millions of Christians world-wide a spiritually dangerous mind-set that offers "believers" little more than the "broad easy path" Jesus warned against. To simply opt for faith, alone, without genuine works – even if only works to at least back up the faith aspect – fatally inculcates an acceptance that there is "no need to do any more". Unfortunately, such an attitude basically derives from the flawed belief of many Christians that "He died for us", "for our sins". In my view it is an element of, and an extrapolative excrescence that can clearly be derived from, the Pauline philosophy.

There is obviously no doubt that Jesus died *because* of us! But the unshakeable belief of many that He died "for us" being sufficient to secure "a place in heaven" for them, logically ensures that the perfect and inviolable outworking of The Law of Sowing and Reaping cannot possibly extend its Grace and Blessings to such believers – **if it *is* works that are demanded by Jesus, and thus by The Living Divine Laws**! Consequently it would seem to be a very intelligent thing to choose to heed the *admonitions* of Jesus over the *philosophy* of Paul.[4]

The necessary transition from faith to conviction – from faith to ***works*** – can only thus derive from, firstly, the *recognition* of The Spiritual Laws of Creation and, secondly, their *serious application* in one's life.

Now, since all The Spiritual Laws can be designated as Natural Laws – which outworking and fulfilment we observe and experience in the totality of our lives each day – then it is vital to understand that the *infallible mechanism* for that outworking is actually the

---

[4] Chapter 11 offers further clarification about this and other key theological questions around the life and death of Jesus.

inviolable perfection of The Laws themselves. They are Laws whose validity, authority, perfection, and therefore absolute inviolability, derive from The Divine Perfection of The Creator Himself, and are those Laws which, without flaw or deviation, return to us every nuance of every decision we make.

And because we sought conscious life and petitioned The Creator for it, The Spiritual Laws of Life, woven into the fabric of His Creation, are thus the Rules by which we must live. For by that very petition for conscious life we were irrevocably bound to the *living reality* that the gift of free will *automatically* imbued us with the *personal responsibility* to exercise that gift correctly by heeding His Laws and living accordingly. A key Law by which the effect of our free-will inheritance is most clearly revealed and experienced is "The Law of Reciprocal Action".

A prime example of the damage that can be wrought through transgressing this particular Law may be clearly observed in the relatively recent episode of "mad cow disease" in Britain. Shortcut economic practices in British agriculture resulted in the concomitant emergence of a human equivalent of the disease through the consumption of contaminated meat and meat products from infected animals. This resulted in the terrible but necessary slaughter of many thousands of infected beasts.

The Laws of Creation ordain that herbivores such as cows and beef cattle should not consume food derived from their own kind. Meat and meat products are the ordained, natural food of carnivores, and the farming industry cannot arbitrarily *force* such a radical change in the diet of captive animals without expecting severe consequences. A hard, "lawful" lesson for agricultural science.

Should this kind of animal husbandry practice be continued with, perhaps that "hard lesson" may still yet manifest in a globally devastating way. The discovery of "prions", the strange and potentially lethal "protein agent" perhaps implicated in the "brain-eating" diseases, CJD, BSE, sheep scrapie and "kuru" (from New Guinea), are now a great concern. Over the past few decades, American and Australian scientists observing and researching these diseases have noted the striking similarities between them. At the same time, they have also noted the increasing incidences of variants of the disease, particularly among the young.

The Book of Job (Ch.34:11), in succinct truth about this particular Law, perfectly states the consequential reality of such foolish "science" in just six blunt words.

"But man's actions return on himself."

Science notates the essence of this very Law thus: "For every action, there is an equal and opposite reaction." However, what is probably not accepted or even known is that there is not just simply an "*equal*, opposite reaction", but a reaction that is always "lawfully imbued" with *greater power **in the "return"***. Thus very much more than might be expected to result from the originating decision.

In the case of our example of the moment, the possibility that "mad cow disease" may have crossed the species barrier to infect humans, should be regarded as unequivocal proof that The Spiritual Laws, which ultimately manifest as physical Laws, cannot be transgressed without ***serious*** consequences. The full potential horror of "mad cow disease" resulting from this particularly foolish transgression may still be a little way off as the great uncertainty is whether or not there may be a large pool of infected people quietly moving through an unknown incubation period.

In fact, according to research published in the British Medical Journal around September 20th 2002, more than 7000 Britons could face an increased risk of contracting the human form of mad cow disease. In this example alone we can clearly note that The Law of Reciprocal Action, as with all The Spiritual Laws, necessarily supports every other Law as a part of all processes and outcomes.

But even with such obvious warning signs now clearly present, science, in its dangerously flawed mind-set that it can change the lawful processes of natural development against the Ordination of The Creator, are slowly taking this aberrant experimentation to what must be recognised and understood as being levels of actual insanity. The position adopted by this particular branch of science states that by inserting human genes into cows, milk will be produced that will ostensibly heal various kinds of diseases in human beings. Such a misguided view, however, fails to even *begin to understand* that if we desire better outcomes in *all areas* of life – *including health* – then we must heed the very Laws of Life. That is how we gift to ourselves optimum health.

Perhaps the greater danger, however, lies in the insidious nature of the seductive, emotional propaganda that is used to sell the whole idea. That emotionalism ultimately feeds on the fear of millions of the sick world-wide whom GE science claims could be saved from so-called premature death if these "life-saving" techniques were permitted. The other beguiling aspect is that not only are many political "leaders" hell-bent on supporting this branch of "science", but even within indigenous communities of the world there are those who have been seduced by this new and dangerous direction.

An interesting paradox arises here. The sophisticated technology of this particular branch of western scientific thinking – which regards the cow as solely a factory unit for the production of by-products to pamper people who, for the most part, have refused to live correctly healthily anyway – have absolutely no idea of *either* The Laws which govern all science and *ultimately constrain "wrong science"*, or the *life-force* present in all animals. In striking contrast to that position, many millions in India view cows in a totally different light. Even though wrongly revering them as sacred, they nevertheless understand that their value lies in the animal as it is *in its natural state* – as a giver of milk as food unadulterated by flawed science. At least, that is the general position at this time.

The one note of sanity in the West thankfully lies in the swelling volume of people and groups utterly and implacably opposed to any such aberrant deviation away from the complete naturalness of the Perfection of The Laws of GOD, the earthly expression of which we may note in The Laws of Nature. Or, to use a better understood term, the "Natural Laws"! And no earthly science can ever oppose them with arrogant impunity. Of course, there is always a period of time for such experimentation to run its particular course, for free will is never taken from us.

If the world's humanity were to truly spiritually awaken, then implacable opposition to all GE technology would be understood to be spiritually, and thus *scientifically*, correct. It would not be regarded as some kind of aberrant "green-fringe fanaticism" as it presently is. For we already have, among other disturbing incidents, the lessons of lower yields for GE crops, and the increasing spread of GE contamination away from original release points.

Gary Goldberg, when CEO of the American Corn Growers Association (ACGA), spoke about the harm GE technology has caused US farmers:

> **"This is a case of if we knew then what we know now, American farmers would not have been so easily convinced that GE crops were the way to go.** Our land has become contaminated with GE pollution that we cannot control or remove from our environment. Conventional farms are being contaminated, and we have no choice of GE or non-GE crops. **None of the promises have come true and it is time for farmers to under-**

stand that the promises that have been made and will continue to be made will not come true either. We are losing export markets. Those markets can be filled by [other] farmers."

(*Physicians and Scientists for Responsible Genetics.* Parentheses mine.)

But even facts such as those outlined here are still not yet sufficient to convince the proponents of this dangerously-flawed foolishness – the scientists, the politicians and those people who subscribe to it – that any kind of experimentation with the actual genome of humans and animals to try to bring about a genetic modification or mutation will be far more devastating than just simple plant modification.

For whilst each species of the plant kingdom has its own specific genetic code, which gives it its particular perfection of function and form, the plants themselves do not possess the same *kind of life force* that humans and animals have. And it is that *specific kind of inner animation* that has driven the development of humans and given the many and varied species of animals their unique place in the world. Without any input from human "science", the evolution and development of all life forms has proceeded in accordance with a plan that permits the absolute perfection of each. It is a plan that GE earth-sciences could not even begin to emulate, yet arrogantly believes it can improve upon.

Such a serious transgression is not at all difficult to prophesy against, for that will forever and always be the outcome of working against The Laws of life in any case. Therefore the final outcome will reveal itself in the reciprocal effects that each group – the supporters and the opposers – will one day subsequently receive. That, we can be sure, will be a devastating "return" for one side – that of its supporters.

At a more natural level, a brief examination of this effect in the natural world will clearly show even the most inexperienced gardener that if he wishes to harvest corn, he must plant corn, and if he wants to grow beans, he must plant beans. What would be the result if The Laws were inconsistent and we were always uncertain as to what the sown seed would produce? Total confusion. And there is no confusion in The Spiritual Laws of Creation. Therefore, as it reveals its absolute certainty in the garden, so can the same certainty be observed in all other kinds of "sowing".

Closely connected with this fact should be the realisation that we do not necessarily *"reap in the same season that we sow"*. Thus, whilst the time difference between sowing and reaping, or cause and effect, usually has set periods between the sowing and harvesting of seed for earthly food crops, no such set time-period can be determined for the sowing and harvesting of "spiritual" seed. The Spiritual Laws alone determine the precise time of such "returns".

Moreover, within the various races and religions of the world, the natural Laws take no account of a man's colour or belief. Rice sown by a white, brown or black man will produce exactly the same as for a yellow man. In the same way, wheat sown by a Jew, a Christian, a Buddhist, a Moslem, a Hindu, a Pagan, or an Atheist, will return only wheat at harvest time. As previously stated, this earthly effect well reflects the fact that this Law, along with all the other Spiritual Laws, grants no special bias or favour to any particular race or religion. Neither should it be expected to do so.

The perfection of The Laws absolutely guarantees that they cannot possibly do anything other than dispense Perfect Justice to all men. Thus, if an Atheist or a Pagan sows goodness, they are lawfully bound to receive goodness; as will a Christian Bishop, a Hindu Monk, a Moslem Imam, or a Native Shaman. Therefore it is not necessarily a man's belief or religion that determines whether he will *ascend* or not, it is **how he stands in his inner being**. It is the "spiritual volition" of his inner nature toward all that surrounds him, both the seen and unseen, that greatly determines this.

Spiritually then, it would be wrong to think that membership of a particular religion or sect would guarantee "good returns" or *reaping* – or even salvation. The purpose of all religion should be to help to correctly interpret The Will of God as expressed in The Laws of Creation, thus showing us how we are to carry out His Will. If it can do that, then it fulfils its place, for religion should be recognised as a means to an end and not ends in themselves. As previously noted, the dangerous rise of religious fundamentalism illustrates too narrow an interpretation of just earthly "religious law".

Since the current premise under the particular Law being discussed here is exactly that of "reaping what one has sown", but from the spiritual viewpoint overall, it is necessary to have a mechanism whereby this "spiritual" aspect also produces "physical reaping". Anecdotal evidence from American medical research has shown that concentrated thoughts directed to a sick patient can directly influence the healing process of that patient. Thus what spiritual and even philosophical thinking have been saying for a very long time actually happens. In simple terms, good thoughts directed to a patient can hasten the healing process whilst bad thoughts can lengthen it.

The best-selling "Sophie's World" offers a light-hearted insight regarding this quandary:

> A Russian astronaut and a Russian brain surgeon were once discussing religion. The brain surgeon was a Christian but the astronaut was not. The astronaut said, "I've been out in space many times but I've never seen God or angels." And the brain surgeon said, "And I've operated on many clever brains but I've never seen a single thought."
>
> (p 193)

Of course, neither view is able to conclusively prove that one or the other exists materially. And that is as it should be for neither God or angels nor thoughts are material in form. Nevertheless, in accordance with Spiritual Law, they do exist! Therefore, what might the foregoing anecdotes suggest to us?

That *despite* the invisible nature of thoughts, they *do* have the power to influence our lives, and produce visible effects. Our thoughts must thus have to be much more than empty vaporous things. To be able to influence in such a way, they must necessarily be imbued with some kind of inherent power. All the great Spiritual Teachings, even from ancient times, strongly advise to constantly strive to think good and pure thoughts. The emotive words of love, beauty, compassion and kindness automatically arouse in us vastly different feelings from words such as hate, selfishness, envy and bitterness. This small example, where the outworking of Spiritual Law is concerned, should serve to show that language alone is not the deciding factor here. The actual "volition" of the "producer" of the spoken word very strongly determines what is ultimately released *from* him into "the world".

Thus every thought we think, every word we speak produces a "form" which actually lives. The thought or word produces the actual form of it, i.e. thoughts or words of hate or bitterness will produce corresponding forms, ***irrespective of whatever language is used as the medium of production***. Forms of love and harmony are produced by the same mechanism. So just because such forms cannot always be seen does not mean that they do not exist, for they can certainly often be felt. Neither do they simply and conveniently disappear. No, the forms that we produce, that we have given birth to, live on until such time as they return to us under this iron Law of Reciprocal Action.[5]

We, as the individual originators, are the *owners* of them. They are ours. Moreover, our thoughts naturally affect our immediate environment, families and friends. We may note how refreshing it feels to enter the dwelling of a family who live a happy, balanced, harmonious life. Contrast that with a household racked by jealousy, hate and bitterness. A thoroughly unpleasant atmosphere, which is immediately perceived, pervades the place. The constant production of the corresponding *forms* "fills" the house. **It becomes their home too.**

This process, then, can be viewed as *spiritual sowing*. We "sow" through thoughts, words, volition, deeds and actions. Thus, by this simple mechanism, humankind *"forms and forms and forms"*. Indeed, through the inherent free will of our spiritual nature, we are ***unable*** to stop forming. Therefore, if our thoughts are always good, we must naturally receive good. If they are constantly evil, that is what will be eventually received. If our thoughts and actions change between good and evil, we will receive mixed fortunes incorporating both those aspects. In this infallible mechanism lies perfect justice!

The admonition, *"As you wish men to do to you, do the same to them"* (Luke 6:31, Fenton), was surely given for our benefit under the knowledge of this particular Law. Therefore the greater strength and benefit will always lie in doing good. The key to so many unsolved problems rests in the operation and understanding of this Law, for The Law of Reciprocal Action decrees that we cannot do anything other than continually "produce" our personal "works". Yet because we cannot "physically" see them, it is difficult to accept that such a process might be possible.

Since thoughts have the power to influence, in cases where people act differently to their actual intentions, i.e. as a "wolf in sheep's clothing" etc., The Law of Sowing and Reaping absolutely ensures that the "true" actions, including related thoughts and volition, are still all exactly weighed. The same inflexible process takes place with people who make donations to organisations for some kind of personal gain or publicity, but do not accept or share

---

[5]What happens to them whilst on their 'journey' will be explained later in this Chapter under the effects of "The Law of Attraction of Homogeneous Species"

their aims and ideals. This attitude is actually one of hypocrisy and is judged accordingly because of its base level of calculative premeditation.

The common Biblical quote, ***"Judge not, lest ye be judged!"*** (Matthew 7:1) is well known. Because so few people have the ability to clearly assess the true intentions of others, however, it is often difficult to know whether intuitive "gut feelings" are correct, simply because a person's appearance or actions may belie his true volition. And even whilst seeing his actions and hearing his words, we may still not know his real motives.

However, if the term "judge" *means* to "weigh" or "consider", then the points for and against any particular issue should *not* be seen as a transgression of the above Scripture. Clearly we are meant to utilise our reason, intelligence and intuition to consider whether a particular thing is good or not. Therefore judging the actions of a person or an issue is vastly different from *passing judgement* on the person or issue. In this light, the same Scripture from Fenton's translation of The Bible offers a clearer and better interpretation: ***"Condemn not****, so that you may not be **condemned**.*" (Matthew 7:1)

Whilst we have examined the mechanism that "produces our reaping", it is necessary to clarify the very important *reciprocal extension* of the process. The ostensibly enigmatic Scripture from The Book of Hosea actually offers perfect clarification:

> "And as they have sown only Wind, the Whirlwind alone shall they reap."
>
> (Hosea 8:7, Fenton.)

Thus, in the world of Nature, each seed that is planted produces a huge multiple of the same at maturation or harvest time. In some cases, in the millions. Some crops require only a few months between sowing and harvesting. In the forest industry, tree crops take many years to mature before felling. Depending on when planting took place, they may not be ready in a given lifetime. Even different varieties of the same kind of crop may mature at different intervals.

How should this be related to the great Spiritual Law of Sowing and Reaping? Quite simply, our spiritual sowing of either good or bad thoughts and deeds also returns a multiple of the same, in close association with another Eternal Law – The Law of Attraction of Similar Species. Hence the truth of "reaping the whirlwind" in the previous Biblical quote. The differences in the time frame of crop maturation also have their equivalent in the spiritual too, and apply equally to the thoughts, words, deeds, volition, and even prayers of people.

The outworking of all these factors provide the answer as to why sudden misfortune can visit itself on a "good person", or good fortune arrive to a well known "waster". That is also the reason why someone who is totally debased may not receive his "whirlwind" until very much later in life, or even after earthly death. Rest assured, though, it will come to him. Not, however, in the same measure as he meted out to others, but under the additional severity of the *"whirlwind constant"*.

Were this not the case, i.e. without any form of ultimate justice, there would be little point in bothering with the good. In the jungle that would develop, it would be easier to simply "take whatever one wanted". In this regard the Scripture, *"PUNISHMENT IS MINE, I WILL REPAY"* (Hebrews 10:30, Fenton) is more easily understood. Thus The Eternal Laws automatically keep track of all transgressors and, at the ordained time for that person, dispense the appropriate justice.

This does not mean, however, that we should not punish wrongdoers through our earthly justice system, otherwise there surely would be chaos. It simply means that nothing is missed in Creation, nothing can be hidden, and no individual can "get away" with any crime against The Spiritual Laws. The reciprocal effect, moreover, will always be greater than the strength of the original volition or deed under the outworking of the *whirlwind constant*. This process should offer some comfort as we observe more horrifying events and crimes that would have been unthinkable even a short while back, and which greatly increase in number and degree of brutality. Therefore the rule of law must be upheld at all times, as it should reflect our recognition of the "Higher Laws" along with a desire to build the right kind of society. Humankind's societal/religious "guidelines", however, need to fully accord with, and be adjusted to, those "Higher Laws".

It should also be a simple matter to deduce that we can only reap what we have *personally* sown. We cannot simply "sow" for someone else, or "reap" for them either, not even for a loved one. So a person constantly striving for good who receives bad experiences *apparently unfairly*, should understand that he will have given cause for it at some point in the past. As difficult a concept as this may be to accept, it *is* the causal reality of many of our problems. There is then nothing to be gained by bemoaning one's fate for this only increases the sense of burden and hardship. Recognition and acceptance of this lawful process, however, then connects us to the outworking of **Divine Grace**.[6]

In the global sense both our earthly home and the creatures upon it were given to humankind to nurture and protect, to take only what was required. But what of the earth today? The story is glaringly obvious. Poisoned and pillaged in a mind-set of rapacious, selfish greed under the name of progress and *"good economic strategy"*. Unfortunately, because such practices ultimately impact on all eco-systems, it is now time for global humanity to "pay the ferryman". Yet the price may prove to be well beyond our ability to pay. Learning the "Rules" and living by them may perhaps go some way toward lessening the cost. It will still be very high, however, as that cannot be changed now, though it can perhaps be reduced.

There must, however, be a truly genuine desire to want to change, to seek something better. Superficiality in this case will simply ensure not just more of the same, but increasingly severe "reaping". For, as with all of The Spiritual Laws, this particular Law operates from the smallest, even apparently insignificant individual happenings, to global decisions and events collectively made and subsequently "reaped".

Because the impact of "returning fate" may offer no apparent reason why, it is easy to rail against misfortune or bad luck, or to curse the fates and demand an end to hardship. And then, in times of deep pain with seemingly no way out, to desperately seek help in prayer. In my personal experience, *"when the chips are down"* virtually *everyone* calls out to some greater Power Above. There are few who will not seek help at such times. This inner recognition, most often brought about by painful experiences, should help us to understand that the reaping of bitter fruits once sown should be seen as the best possible *spiritual* reminder that *we have strayed from the path ordained by The Creator.*

If our understanding of The Eternal Laws and how we stand in relation to them is then examined honestly and in genuine humility, such an assessment can only help us to grow spiritually. By this process the lessons needing to be learned can be more readily identified. Consequently, as the necessary adjustments are made whereby only good seeds are sown, The Law of Sowing and Reaping

---

[6]The ramifications of this particular principle are examined later in this Chapter.

will ensure a good return at the ordained time.

Thus there should be less thought of hard, cruel, or undeserved fate. Yet neither should we be totally fatalistic about our lot in life. ***It is in our power to change it – at any time.*** Of course, change may not come overnight, but stubbornly refusing to change for the better will absolutely guarantee that *nothing* will change or, indeed, *can* change. The Laws of Creation actually do provide the means for happiness or misery. What is "Willed" from above for all human spirits is peace and happiness, through the understanding of Spiritual Law. What one receives, however, depends solely upon ***individual choice.***

The question or problem of the "evil within man" and how evil arose in the world – so long a point of debate – has its primary explanation within this Law. It is simply a free-will choice, which we all inherently make in any case. And irrespective of whether the particular choice is made consciously and intentionally, or in total ignorance of this law, The Law of Sowing and Reaping ***will***, nevertheless, always deliver the consequences.

In Cicero's "The Nature of the Gods", a simple and logically correct explanation is offered. In this particular discourse about the opposing views of Christianity and Stoicism, Thomas Godless asks Lactantius four questions on this subject.

> "My first difficulty," he said, "is that you do not seem to have been any better able than the Stoics to solve the problem of evil. How is the existence of pain and evil in the world compatible with your view that the world is under the care of an infinitely powerful and infinitely loving God?"
>
> To which Lactantius replied, "Thomas, I give you two answers. First, if Christianity offers men reconciliation with God, it is not required to solve every intellectual difficulty. But secondly, Christianity does provide a better answer to this age-old problem than Stoicism, because Stoicism is in principle deterministic, whereas the Christian God has given *freedom of choice to man...* He wants all things to serve him, not as automata but by free choice; but this gift of freedom involves the risk that man will *choose evil rather than good.* If God refrains from punishing the wicked in this world, that is a sign not of his powerlessness, but of his magnanimity. Epicurus insisted on human freedom, but at the expense of the gods' reality; the Stoics insisted on divine omnipotence, but at the expense of human freedom. Christianity allows for both."
>
> (Italics mine.)

Despite the *intellectual* brilliance with which the Greek and Roman philosophers were able to debate the pros and cons of major issues such as life and death and good and evil, without the knowledge of The Spiritual Laws of Creation to ultimately define the lawful processes under which all events have their beginning, life and end, all their philosophic meandering had to remain exactly that. For the final key to the puzzle was not available to them at *that* time. That notwithstanding, the long line of philosophic thought in many ways did provide the necessary step for the later entry and recognition – at least for some – of the **All** of Spiritual Truth and Law.

Thus, in this particular Law is fulfilled the fate or karma of humankind, and it offers solutions to the terrible tragedies which we witness today. Through the increasing spiritual power now entering the Material Part of Creation, all the deeds of thousands of years past are pressured to a quicker, final release, thereby also accelerating the **natural catastrophes**. This *relentless pressure* and its attendant global events will not cease until all past cycles have closed, the deeds returned to their owners to face, and all opposition to The Eternal Laws has been removed. Then a new era will be ushered in, a time of genuine peace and happiness. Only for those of the world's people, however, who have genuinely striven for the good.

Decisions Produce Consequences. That is the lawful effect of *The Law of Reciprocal Action!*

3.3.2 Attitude to the Suffering

Given the obvious ramifications of the previous Law, it might be thought that we advocate total disregard for the plight of those in desperate straits. If, as is stated, people do bring suffering on themselves through non-observance of The Laws and that they are solely responsible for their plight, should compassion be shown for them? Are they not simply reaping what they have sown in this earth-life, or perhaps an earlier one? And do they therefore deserve to be helped? The simple answer to virtually all aspects of the overall question is yes! Compassion and kindness are virtues which, if given selflessly, can only bring a good return to the giver. For The Law of Sowing and Reaping should clearly show the need to do good at all times.

"*Do unto others...*" should be one of the key factors governing our way of life. It is difficult to imagine that anyone would actually want others to visit harm or evil upon them. Yet there are so many who seem to have little compunction in wishing that on others. That is the coward's way of course, and clearly the way of much of today's world. It is not the way of nobleness, which is synonymous with true and genuine spirituality. Neither is it the way of **the genuine warrior**, for a true warrior will reflect those higher qualities and virtues. Employing genuine spirituality from out of the **true** knowledge as both his *primary* weapon and shield, he will fight for, and protect and defend, the weak, the helpless and the downtrodden.

Any good works we do, we do solely for ourselves since the fruits of our deeds return to us as multiples of our original sowing under the aegis of the *whirlwind constant*. The possibility of helping sufferers should therefore be regarded as an opportunity to do good, to "sow good seeds". The cause of the person's suffering should not be our concern. In short, we should not "pass judgement". Given the general nature of human beings, most judgements are based on externals anyway. And a superficial assessment may belie the true situation. However, help given should not be one-sided, for that will not help the sufferer in the long term.

In any case the perfection of The Laws automatically ensures that should a sufferer not deserve help, or should he need such experiencing to change his ways, then no one will cross that person's path who might be in a position to give help. Conversely, any necessary "crossing of paths" could mean that a connective origin might lie somewhere in the past e.g., as a "debt owed". In this case two opportunities are given for two different souls to expiate a possible past karmaic connection, sever it, and thus become free. If such an opportunity is not recognised, then, quite obviously, the debt and connection remain.

Under the inviolability of Spiritual Law, all human beings will necessarily have ties to many people, and some will be to other races. Yet all will need to be resolved, even if the individual has no knowledge of such connections, or proffers cynical disbelief at such an idea. For the justness of The Laws will ensure that individual paths will cross at the appropriate time for any such bonds to be severed. Given the increasing spiritual pressure being relentlessly applied to the earth and all the affairs of men in this time of final accounting, a superficial or cynical outlook or lifestyle will not be conducive to correct or timely recognition. Just as our past free-will decisions irrevocably bind us to the origin of all "returning karma" today so, too, are we offered the free choice to unbind ourselves from them when the opportunity arises. Conversely we are equally free to remain shackled.

"Free-will" allows us the choice of what we will sow in thought, word or deed. The outworking of The Law of Sowing and Reaping then returns to us a multiple harvest, in just accordance with the *whirlwind constant.*

3.4 Like Attracts Like

The Law of Attraction of Similar Species

This Law is aptly expressed in sayings such as, "Birds of a feather flock together". How strongly mankind even unconsciously lives this particular Law is illustrated in another saying: "You can tell a man by the company he keeps". In essence, we constantly live this Law at the everyday social and work level even though we may not be aware of it or its far reaching implications. Yet its effects can be readily observed around us every single day. Like-minded people gravitate toward certain occupations and professions. In our recreational time the same factors apply. A more striking example, however, may be found at large social gatherings where small groups will form themselves based on what they have in common. It may be their religion or spiritual beliefs, political leanings, profession, musical tastes, sports, language or race, a particular love of something, or even a shared hatred. It can be any number of things or varying combinations, but it will always be a reflection of "The Law of Attraction..." in operation.

Some ancient peoples were aware of the effect of this important Law and followed it unconsciously in that they separated out into occupational and educational classes, crafts and guilds. In that spiritually correct system, every member of society had the opportunity to live and develop to his fullest potential within each particular "level" attained to. Unfortunately societies gradually changed into divisions of upper, middle and lower classes. This development eventually embraced the full social spectrum of envy and hatred on the one hand, and conceit and arrogance on the other, until finally ending in class-conflict.

What is infinitely more beneficial, and clearly desirable, is that the various occupations and socio-economic groups in societies develop in such a way that they stand "side by side", thus offering the greatest possibility for "working together" harmoniously. Genuine self-esteem for every group could develop to its fullest potential then. And because the different sectors will possess abilities that the others might not have, each becomes a necessary link to every other, thus producing a sound whole. Anti-social problems should then gradually disappear as a better society develops under the correct recognition of this Law. The key consideration here, however, is *"Working Together, Side by Side!"*

In a completely different kind of example, gardening can show the extent of this Law quite graphically. In the practice of "companion-planting", one type of plant or group of plants assists the growth and development of others. An "inappropriate" plant, however, can actually prevent the "companion" from reaching full maturity or producing fruit. In the wild communities of plants this "Law of Attraction..." guarantees a natural balance of the various groupings. With the exception of a few species, the animal world operates under the same principle, as do the birds and fishes. The advantages of groupings are quite obvious. A greater protective umbrella and care of the offspring probably being the primary consideration. In working together, food supplies may be more secure and the group entity is better able to develop a higher social structure than lone individuals can.

"The Law of Attraction..." also guarantees that if a particular species is split, the split parts will seek to re-unite when given the opportunity. In terms of the attracting quality, whole species that are similar will attract, and split parts of the same species will also strive to re-unite. This Law is a fundamental necessity for everything seeking union in Creation.

What does this mean for us, the human species? And where do we place this powerful force of attraction between men and women? Because of its nature and place in Creation, the human being also carries, as an inherent quality within it, the desire for union. Sexual instinct aside, this basically explains the natural attraction between man and woman.

As previously stated, we possess the ability, by virtue of our spiritual nature, to produce the forms of our thoughts, words and deeds. What has not been stated, however, is the fact that these forms, which are our *works*, are *whole species*. Therefore, under the outworking of this particular Law they, in turn, attract *similar species*. Since man is unable to *stop forming*, what, then, do we have? What is thereby produced are extremely large groupings of correspondingly *similar* forms. These homogeneous groupings we can designate as "power centres".

This is an apt description as they *do* possess power. By utilising the power inherent in our "normal" everyday thought-processes we not only produced them in the first place, but automatically sustain – and thus maintain – all the many and varied "centres" now in existence: the dark, dangerous and evil, and the light, good and beneficial. And depending on our personal nature and volition, we therewith automatically connect to those with which we will have a respective affinity. We can, moreover, greatly increase the size and power of these "centres" by "feeding" them *greatly intensified* thoughts, particularly those of hate, envy and anger etc.

So, where do these "power centres" reside, and what is their function? They exist in their non-material state close to our physical environment. From there they are easily able to influence the affairs of men – *if men **choose** to attach themselves to*, and therefore *extract substance from*, the particular "power centres" of their choice. That is, the ones exactly corresponding to the nature of the thoughts at any given time. For each "centre" corresponds with, and attracts to itself, the *same kinds* of similar forms. Thus there are "power centres" of all the virtues and vices from the "works" of humankind. Simple use of our imagination can offer an indication of how some might look. Those of hate, jealousy and bitterness must be ugly to witness, whilst those of love and kindness would be havens of happiness and peace. A small illustration of how The Spiritual Laws intermesh and how the effect of these "power centres" on human beings can be so terribly devastating – *even if the recipient has absolutely no knowledge whatsoever of them* – can reveal how insidiously powerful they are.

We know that ignorance of The Laws does not *prevent* the dispensing of true justice. Marriage, and the family unit, by virtue of the closeness of the relationship, is invariably a place where much emotion – both beneficial and unhelpful – is generated. Should a situation develop where a breaking down of what might once have been a relatively happy unit degenerates into a difficult and perhaps bitter experience for one or both partners, the emotional pain will produce forms associated with that turmoil.

This will probably be compounded if there is a third party involved or if there are children to the marriage. If there can be no reconciliation or resolution and a breakdown is inevitable, the emotional pressures generated might be such that the normal strength of at least one of the partners is temporarily rendered far weaker than would otherwise be the case. With the ebbing of "spiritual strength" – this "strength" being at the same time also spiritual protection – in the belief that one's hopes and dreams are about to be dashed, there may arise in the mind of *the one most likely to suffer the greatest loss,* the wish to "do something about it". More particularly with the possible estrangement from everyday contact with much loved children.

This potential chain of events may only begin as just the emotion of hurt and then perhaps anger. If it stays at that level and is resolved relatively peacefully, nothing untoward should occur to bring about a dangerous situation. However, should it develop further to the point of one partner "wanting to get even", the forms generated by the powerful emotions of such a situation – i.e. those of hate and revenge – begin the process of attracting around that individual correspondingly similar forms from the relevant "power centre/s".

His developing volition for revenge is thus *strengthened* to a considerable degree under this Law of Attraction of Similar Species. If the individual cannot then generate sufficient spiritual strength to resist a rapidly weakening *former good volition*, and thus *change the forms around him*, it could well be that at the moment of greatest weakness, the pressure from the "attacking" similar forms *forces* the carrying out of a tragic deed.

How often do we hear comments evinced with great puzzlement; "How could he/she have done that?" "It is so totally out of character!" "I would never have believed that he/she could ever be capable of doing that!" In times of normalcy, it might never have happened. However, with the base volition at such a time vastly amplified by the other attracted forms, the receiver is rendered temporarily incapable of clear and logical reasoning. Other "forces" have "taken over". That lawful process offers a good explanation of the Biblical Scripture:

> *"Because our fight is **not** against blood and flesh; but against the sovereignties, against the powers, against the commanders of the darkness of this world..."*
>
> (Ephesians 6:12, Fenton.)

Unfortunately, however, it is a darkness that humankind have created. With the exception of true insanity – or in cases where the personal free-will volition of a person is temporarily rendered impotent by a stronger *occupying entity* – the perpetrator is, nonetheless, still spiritually responsible for his actions. Therefore, irrespective of the circumstances – or even possible provocation – it still rests with the individual whether or not he chooses a good volition or a dark one. It should never be forgotten that we are always subject to *the whirlwind constant.* We may believe we are only *"sowing the wind"*, but we **will** ***"reap the whirlwind"*** under Spiritual Law. The harvesting must always be greater than the sowing and this is equally true in good or bad. Neither can we escape the effects of our works at earthly death. The biblical saying, *"...and their works accompany them"* (Revelation 14:13, Fenton), means exactly that too.

Consequently, no one can escape spiritual justice purely because one conveniently dies an earthly death. No, the "works" spoken of here are composed of **all the forms** produced by our thoughts, our words, and our actions or deeds. Because we are the producers, the originators, of them, they are tied to us until such time as we finally undertake to expiate them, either upon their return to us as possible hard lessons or experiences, or we bring about a change in the nature of them by a corresponding change in our own personal attitude and spiritual volition. Thus, in strict accordance with The Laws of Justice, *what has not been dealt with and completely expiated on the earth* waits to be faced in the planes of what we loosely refer to as "the beyond". For we **cannot** escape "our works". *They follow us, purely and simply because they must* – ***because they are ours.***

The birth of Jesus into the Jewish race provides an excellent example of how "The Law of Attraction of Similar Species" operates in its inviolable way. As a people with strong religious convictions, the Israelites through their prophets divined the existence of the One Invisible God thus anchoring a channel of *knowing acceptance* of, and for, messages and events from that Highest Source. The strength of this exalted belief, even in times of hard persecution, was such that it reached upward to The Godhead Itself thus permitting the strongest possible *spiritual* connection to It at that time. The Jewish people, therefore, were able to provide the necessary "spiritual connection" for the birth of Jesus to take place. Hence the reason why Jesus, The Son of the Invisible God **could**, and **did**, incarnate into that particular race.

For only with such a sure conviction from the Jewish people could the appropriate connections be established for such an event to take place. Without this inner divining of the "Highest Heights", a necessary attracting quality for this happening was impossible. An incarnation by Jesus into any race other than one with the requisite spiritual belief of the Highest Spheres would mean a huge gulf of non-understanding, so is not possible under The Laws of

Creation. Quite logically, therefore, an incarnation into a savage tribe of idol worshippers would have been a rather pointless exercise for the entry of The Son of God onto the earth plane.

3.4.1 Spiritual Qualities as the First Consideration

Because we are inherently imbued with the nature and quality of The Spiritual, the potential to develop the correspondingly more ennobled characteristics *should* be the primary factor which determines to whom or to what we will be naturally attracted. Most people will have probably felt strongly drawn to certain persons for no *apparent* reason other than a feeling of an especially strong bond. Sometimes to our great surprise - though it should not be so under the effect of the "Law of Attraction..." - we may even discover that certain meetings quickly produce bonds that are far stronger than those we experience with some members of our own immediate family.

As previously alluded to earlier in this Chapter, a particular story in the life of Jesus illustrates this fact perfectly. When told that His mother and brothers were waiting to see Him, He replied:

> "Who is My mother? And who are My brothers?" Then, extending His hand in the direction of His disciples, He said, "Why, those are My mother and My brothers! For whosoever does The Will of My Father Who is in Heaven, he is My brother, and sister, and mother!"
>
> (Matthew 12:48-50, Fenton.)

Spiritual qualities, therefore, should be recognised as the correct thing to strive for in the first instance, even if it means breaking free from the sometimes cloying and often selfishly-emotional influence and demands that some family groups generate. The present generally low level of spiritual maturity exhibited by human societies today is clearly demonstrated by the fact that, for many people, only race and ethnicity are the main considerations in their relationships with others. This lack of understanding for the deeper and finer qualities ensures that this superficiality places outward appearances such as skin colour, race, physical looks, fashion and religion etc. foremost.

Spiritual knowledge, particularly the right knowledge of The Law of Rebirth, will show the relative unimportance of such things as a person's race or nationality. The basis for assessing the worth of a human being can then be made on character alone. The following Biblical quotation probably best encapsulates this:

> "A useful tree cannot produce bad fruit; nor can a worthless tree produce good fruit. Every tree not producing good fruit will be felled and used as firewood. Reject their produce; for by this you can recognise them."
>
> (Matthew 7:18-20, Fenton.)

3.4.2 Families and Children

The ramifications posed by the question of how and why particular souls incarnate into certain family groupings under the "Law of Attraction..." are so far reaching that if humanity were to ***truly know*** and ***live*** this Knowledge, much of society's ugly side could be made non-existent – in perhaps just a few generations. Whilst that may seem a very broad statement, an examination of the serious importance of it and the equally grave responsibility attached to it should become evident to the open-minded reader. More especially if one is a parent, or wishes to become one. Since procreation is very much the norm rather than the exception, the significance of our opening sentence should be of primary interest to this group particularly.

Who has not heard the statements at some time, often given as an emotional outburst: "I didn't ask to be born!" or: "I didn't choose my parents!" Unfortunately, not so! Notwithstanding that reality, it is nevertheless not an uncommon utterance. Particularly from the young who may be subject to spiritually-wrong family constraints at the time that natural development calls them to enter the phase of adulthood and independence. Random selection does not operate here, but under the determination of one's free-will, The Laws of "Attraction", "Reciprocal Action" and "Spiritual Gravity" most certainly do. These Laws basically determine the geographical location, the particular family of "lawful choice" and all other circumstances into which one is born. For an act of procreation simply provides *an opportunity* for *individual souls in the "beyond" to incarnate on earth.*

Since there are many souls awaiting such an opportunity, certain precise factors will finally bring the "correct one" to the prospective mother. As this determination is governed by Spiritual Law, the family *environment* and connections to the *pregnant mother,* particularly, will be crucial to the kind of soul that eventually incarnates. Strong similarities between the incoming soul and the mother or other members of the family may also have a bearing on *who* finally arrives. Or perhaps the prospective soul may have ties to a particular person or group of people that the prospective mother has close connections with. That potential can act as a powerful force of attraction for the souls surrounding her who are awaiting an opportunity to incarnate. Thus women, who are the providers of the "spiritual bridge" and are the primary link by which incoming souls are able to enter the earth plane, have a very great responsibility here.

Past life connections to various members of the family can be a strong determinant as well, and one which may later provide either harmonious relationships, or severely strained ones, depending on the circumstances of the past association. In all cases, however, the particular soul that finally inhabits the growing foetus will have been strictly determined according to Spiritual Law. And will thus possess all the necessary characteristics to be able to fulfil its particular role and purpose within the family grouping and in its own *personal* life-path as well.

The entry of the soul into the growing foetus, also determined by Law, takes place about the middle of pregnancy.[7] The seal of attraction is then complete and the soul takes full possession of its new home – the growing body in the mother's womb. The mother might well have mixed feelings, which may range from bliss to unease. This will depend on the nature of this *new stranger* she is *compelled to accept*.

The emotionally-charged issue of abortion takes on an entirely different hue when viewed from the perspective of Spiritual Law. According to The Eternal Laws by which we are granted life and sustenance, abortion is not the automatic right of any mother at any time during pregnancy. Of course, there will always occur certain life-threatening situations which may necessitate certain difficult decisions in this respect. But the strident cry of, "My body, my right!", does not remove the spiritual consequences of

---

[7]This entry time has been corroborated, **unknowingly**, by Dr. Robert Winston (of "The Human Body" fame). His statement to this effect was made in Part 1 of his *second series* which traces the birth, life and development of a group of new-born babies to adulthood. His observations of major changes around that time – which his narration outlined – indicated that much more happens in, and to, a growing foetus than just a continuation of normal physical development within the womb. Thus what Spiritual Law inviolably states, medical science has now noted – albeit unwittingly at this time.

unnecessary abortions by all involved – for there *is* "freedom of choice" here too. However, in both freedom of choice and the so-called *right* to "abortion on demand", the spiritual consequences nevertheless remain.

Even a purely foetal abortion – in the early stages of pregnancy before the entry of the soul – does not absolve the participants of the spiritual repercussions of such an act. From the waiting soul's point of view, all its hopes and aspirations for that particular earth life with its chosen parents, and the mutual opportunities of spiritual growth for both parties, is effectively lost. Whether or not a second opportunity for incarnation might present itself for the *same players* via another pregnancy could only be determined under the outworking of The Spiritual Laws.

Abortion after the entry of a soul into the growing foetus is similar to physical murder under The Spiritual Laws of Creation, ***regardless of what the medical profession, women's groups, or the lawmakers have determined for themselves***. It is a foolish delusion to believe that the act of ending the life of a human being as a purely "convenient solution" would not carry *serious spiritual consequences* for the perpetrators. Consequences, moreover, that impact upon *all* who *support* such practices.[8]

The birth of handicapped children is therefore not without purpose either, whether for the mother, the family or, not least, for the handicapped one. Because these events are strictly governed by Spiritual Law, it is only through the knowledge of them that full understanding can be gained as to why such an event will visit itself upon a family group. It is surely certain, however, that in caring for the handicapped one, the nature of the handicap will allow both family partners the necessary spiritual experiencing for which the birth was perhaps ordained. Permitted, moreover, through the *free-will decision of the parents for sexual union* thus leading to the ensuing procreative event. In this case, it is important to understand that it is only the physical body that is handicapped. The inner, animating core of the spirit, *the real person*, is never so!

---

[8]It is interesting to objectively observe the plight of certain peoples today whose *primary method* of birth control is abortion. The acceptance of this kind of birth-control regime, in the case of very populous countries, translates to hundreds of thousands, possibly millions, of destroyed lives over many years. The now more rapid reciprocal effect of all *spiritual* transgressions accelerates the consequences of this particular practice in such societies. The subsequent accelerating deterioration of the *material* and *social* environment of such nations is hardly surprising because the whole land becomes a vast, "reciprocal-reaping collective" for the particular peoples concerned.

In a similar vein, the infertility of certain couples is also not an arbitrary act. The inability to naturally produce offspring is likewise governed by "Spiritual Law". In other words, there will be a very good reason for this, even if not readily apparent. It may well have its origin in the long distant past, with its reciprocal effect translating into a deep desire to want children in the present, but not easily being able to, or possibly not at all, even with modern medical procedures. Infertile couples should thus determine whether or not it is within their ordained life-path to pursue parenthood. It could mean that having no children might allow them to fulfil a particular purpose more completely, whereas having children may make it much more difficult, or even impossible.

A more enlightened attitude would see couples planning for children solely from the *spiritual point of view*. Where no children are desired, conception would simply be avoided. The very nature of physical desire between couples, which should be viewed as both natural and special, means that the possibility of pregnancy is ever-present. With an understanding of the processes that determine the kind of new family addition that could arrive, however, future prospective parents will be better able to plan for the reception of children who will be more aware and enlightened than might otherwise be the case without this knowledge.

Just as the new soul will provide certain experiences and lessons for the family group into which it has incarnated, its new family and circumstances will offer similar provision for what it will need for its spiritual growth too. Viewed in this light, the wish to want a child should be more seriously considered because such a desire should be tempered by the acceptance of the responsibility to provide the correct upbringing for any offspring. Children are not ours to own and neither should we see them as arriving to us as a completely clean slate upon which we can write our own personal program for them.

With each act of procreation, the opportunity is offered for a soul to reside with us until such time as its ordained path or personal choices calls it to travel its own individual journey. If we have attracted spiritually and guided well, "offspring" should naturally develop the inner urge to make good decisions for themselves whenever cross-roads are reached. Hopefully, the decision made then will be in accordance with The Eternal Laws, thus ensuring a good return for those we have nurtured and set free.

Under the outworking of this "attracting-process" a family of noble people will generally attract noble souls. The arrival of a so-called "black sheep" might indicate that the pregnant woman may have allowed a less than honourable person into her immediate sphere of influence *around the time of the entry of the soul*. ***Under the outworking of The Eternal Laws, a darker soul seeking to incarnate onto the earth plane will always drive back a lighter, more noble soul seeking the same opportunity, so long as a hand is offered to it.***

This is purely the lawful effect of The Law of Attraction of Similar Species. Perhaps earlier generations intuitively understood this process in part, in determining pregnancy as a time, or term, "of confinement". Thus as a period of "protective separation" from detrimental influences of society. This custom would offer natural spiritual protection, more especially up to the entry of the soul into the foetus. It is unlikely, however, that "modern feminist views" would accept such an assertion. Nevertheless, these strict and lawful "spiritual" processes cannot be circumvented by so-called "modern, enlightened attitudes" – social or medical![9]

The effect of "The Law of Attraction..." on families and crime has produced some interesting statistics. Police records in many countries have recorded whole families – even generations of families – where crime in its myriad forms is regarded as the norm by such groups of wrong-thinking people. Sometimes, however, even in that kind of situation and against all the odds, a member of such a family may choose to follow a different path. Thus the more noble and spiritual characteristics of compassion, courage, inherent respect for justice and inner grace, for example, are **not** biologically inherited. The uglier traits of humankind are similarly not inherited either.

Nevertheless, it is still The Law of Attraction of Similar Species that primarily determines the make-up of families. Therefore, it should not be presumed that a soul with an innate propensity to live a less than noble existence on the earth must necessarily do so. Our inherent free-will factor gives such a person the opportunity to break free from any base propensities, no matter how strong, ***if it so chooses or wills for itself.***

Genetic processes, which are by no means accidental, are what give rise to the physical characteristics of parental offspring. The Law of Reciprocal Action ensures that in this situation only those

---

[9] We may note this spiritually-cleansing preparation-time around the incarnation of Jesus. There, the Annunciation by the Messenger to Mary helped her to *prepare* her spirit and body for the reception of His Divine Core during the pregnancy.

who have "sown the appropriate seeds" are incarnated into families and places where they are bound to enjoy genetic advantage or, conversely, suffer from hereditary handicap. By way of example, as a given disease is conquered in a particular part of the world, those souls whose karma *might* need the living experience of that disease will only be able to incarnate in a country where it still exists.

In the light of this knowledge, we should re-examine our current thinking as to who or what actually constitutes a "victim". The present day tyranny of the "poor victim of circumstance" syndrome virtually allows some people of this mind-set to even commit crimes of shocking violence under the umbrella of this excuse. In truth, such terribly wrong attitudes debilitate and spiritually degrade society. We should recognise this for the wrong attitude, the "emotional disease", that it actually is and set up re-education programmes to smartly correct such incorrect, aspiritual thinking.

That is not to say, however, that help should not be offered to those in need. On the contrary, with this correct knowledge, *exactly the right kind of help* or education can be given, thus allowing for the possibility of the complete elimination of this societal "illness". This would provide the necessary foundation for nobleness and ***individual responsibility*** to become the norm instead of the present practice of socially or culturally entrenching the totally wrong idea of "non-responsibility" into the very people who desperately need a complete change of thinking.

Consider, also, if the earth could be rid of all diseases and the causes of human suffering, any souls that needed to experience such suffering would not have the opportunity to be able to incarnate here. Consequently, we can further extrapolate that if we – all humanity – really strove to be truly noble in all our thoughts, words, aspirations and activities etc., it would become impossible for any unworthy spirits to incarnate on earth simply because *the connecting bridge of attraction* would not be there. Through this recognition and process, a more enlightened humankind could make the earth what it was originally ordained to be – ***a Paradise***. More to the point, that is what could and should have happened. Our choice, our responsibility – solely.

To this end it is important to understand that the present thrust of globally entrenching the concept of "my rights", transgresses virtually every aspect of Spiritual Law. Almost nowhere now do we hear of responsibilities, duties, or obligations. We hear only the increasingly strident and selfish cry of **"my rights"**! In the case of the relationship between parents and children, this translates into a mad tyranny where children's *rights* have become more important than their *responsibilities*. Just as parents have responsibilities to their offspring, so, too, should children be taught to fulfil this aspect of Spiritual Law also.

By first putting in place the attitude of responsibilities and duties to each other, we automatically create an environment where rights can become synonymous with duties, for under Spiritual Law fulfilment of duty and responsibility must come before any claim to rights. Therefore children can only claim rights if they loyally perform their duties.

3.5 Gravity – The Spiritual Dynamic

The Law of Spiritual Gravity

In accordance with *Newton's* "Law of Universal Gravitation", the idea of a force of gravity is readily understandable in the physical sense of the word. Quite logically, heavy objects fall to the ground whilst very light substances may rise. So the effect we see materially is the form by which this Law manifests on earth.

The everyday unconscious outworking of the effect of "The Law of Gravity" is revealed in earthly sayings which reflect this concept in society as a whole. However, whilst the effect of this particular Law clearly displays obvious physical characteristics, it is first and foremost a *spiritual* one. For instance, we often speak of "heavy thoughts" and "light thoughts", or the effect that a "heavy person" may have upon us as opposed to the much more enjoyable company of a "light person". Evil thoughts and practices are rightly recognised as being of a "heavy nature", whilst noble thoughts and deeds are similarly accepted as occupying a far higher level.

Thus the same gravitational effect that takes place in a physical setting also occurs in a non-physical environment. It is one, moreover, which impacts very decisively on the fate of man *after* his earthly demise! That is because the actual person or individual is more than just a heavy physical body. Our true self, or actual conscious personality, is that of our inner animating core – our spirit. **That is who and what we actually are.**

At earthly death, therefore, we simply discard, or step out of, the physical form that all human beings are obliged to take upon entry onto the earth plane. This shell, our "overcoat", is then subject to the natural processes of decay and disintegration in accordance with The Laws of Nature – which are the results of the *earthly outworking* of The Spiritual Laws of Creation. This completely natural process thus allows the soul body, which consists of a number of non-physical bodies enveloping the spirit, to become free of its previously heavy "garment". However, it is not then able to go wherever it wishes, for this process is determined by The Law of Spiritual Gravity acting upon all the "works" connected to each individual. For, as is stated, *"their works shall follow them."*)

Base propensities and activities whilst in the physical body on earth weigh the *coverings* of the spirit down causing it to sink, to fall away in a direction opposite to its true origin in The Spiritual Realm. Thus the entity regresses. The depth to which it sinks is strictly determined by the extent to which it indulged in wrongdoing which, in turn, gives it its corresponding "spiritual weight" or heaviness. That particular level will be peopled by those with similar base propensities or weaknesses in accordance with The Law of Attraction of Similar Species.

It is important to understand that under The Eternal Laws only here on Earth can good and evil live *side by side*. Every other plane of Creation is formed according to its comparative "weight" – lightest and purest at the top, and heaviest and darkest at the bottom. In this lies the most wonderful justice because each individual spirit automatically ends up in the plane corresponding to its personal volition, thereby automatically receiving what it strove for most.

If a recently departed spirit has lived a life of, say, lust and greed for example - a very good illustration given the deplorable state of humankind today - it will be drawn to the same level as others similar to it. In such an environment similar souls will give full vent to their propensity for lust and greed upon each other continuously. This same happening will be repeated in other places at other levels where the propensities for violence, drunkenness, nicotine and drug addiction, gluttony, laziness, and anger etc., hold sway. There, in situations as depraved and potentially as hopeless as that described, is the place we call "hell". Yes, **hell is what we have created**, but need not, and should not, ever have done so.

Yet even there The Eternal Laws, which also automatically incorporate Divine Love, are ever watchful for souls who, through inner recognition, finally become disgusted with themselves and their tormented environment and petition for their release from it. With this personal awakening to the truth of their situation and the longing to be free of it, a way is automatically opened for such souls to begin their ascent to the next higher level.

Through their awakening to personal recognition and desire for change, they would have become different in nature to their particular environment, thereby ensuring an automatic separation from it in accordance with The Spiritual Laws – notably The Law of Attraction of Similar Species and The Law of Gravity under the outworking of The Law of Movement. In this way, The Law of Attraction of Similar Species then becomes a "Law of Repulsion of Dissimilar Species". Thus any soul can ascend, even out of such grievous circumstances, if its desire to do so is sufficiently strong.

Contrast that situation with one where a soul has striven to do noble deeds all its earth life, where it had sought to find Spiritual Truth, where it had offered compassion and kindness, where its thoughts and aspirations had sought elevation. Such a life makes a spirit light and buoyant. Upon shedding its physical shell at earthly death, its spiritual lightness draws it upwards toward Planes of Light. There it will find spirits who exhibit the same kinds of noble traits as itself. Whereas the inhabitants of the lower regions are surrounded by their own base volition, those in the higher planes of Light experience the living reality of the greater contentment and happiness synonymous with striving for more noble aspirations. Thus, Perfect Justice!

For those who choose to believe that spiritual ascent lies *solely* in a belief of faith in Jesus, consider His severe words:

> "I tell you indeed, that you will not depart until **you** have **repaid the very last farthing.**"
>
> (Matthew 5:26, Fenton.)

And again in part:

> "...that until the heavens and the earth shall pass away, a single dot or hairstroke shall not disappear from the law, until **all has been completed.**"
>
> (Matthew 5:18, Fenton.)

The Law of Spiritual Gravity has logically existed since time immemorial, yet it is interesting to note that Newton's theories and discoveries in the earthly environment paved the way for a rapid increase in knowledge of astronomy and allowed for further interstellar discoveries. Moreover, the simplicity of The Laws that hold the moon in stable orbit around the earth without either crashing into it through its stronger gravitational pull, or simply heading off into space, convinced Newton that only *"a few natural laws apply to the whole universe"*.

He demonstrated that The Laws, which govern the planets of our solar system's elliptical paths around the sun, are the same Laws that also govern all moving bodies, and therefore apply everywhere in the entire universe. Notwithstanding the Hermetic adage of "as in heaven, so on earth", his radical view of the time generally put to rest a conflicting belief that there is "one set of laws for heaven and another here on earth". Because Newton believed that the same natural laws applied everywhere in the universe, this would clearly have posed a potential "crisis of faith" for any orthodox church view of God. Newton's own faith, however, was never shaken. On the contrary, he regarded the natural laws as *proof* of the *existence* of a great and Almighty God.

3.6 Balance in Life – A Vital Necessity

The Law of Balance

> "Virtue, then, is a disposition involving choice. It consists of a mean, relative to us, defined by reason and as the reasonable man would define it. It is a mean between two vices – one of excess, the other of deficiency."
>
> (Aristotle, from *Nichomachaen Ethics*, Book 2)

Had Aristotle lived today he would probably be horrified at the excesses relating to such things as extremes of wealth, and in personal body-development. In his view these kinds of activities and practices were just as unbalanced as someone who only uses his head. He considered such extremes to be an expression of a warped way of life. Aristotle also applied the "Golden Mean" to human relationships. He believed that we must be neither cowardly nor rash, but courageous (too little courage is cowardice, too much is rashness), neither miserly nor extravagant but liberal (not liberal enough is miserly, too liberal is extravagant). The same applied to eating. He thought it was dangerous to eat too little, but also dangerous to eat too much. The ethics of both Plato and Aristotle contain echoes of Greek medicine. **The Law of Balance**, in its perfect outworking, is Aristotle's 'Golden Mean'.

Aristotle believed that for some acts there is no mean at all; their very nature already implies badness, such as spite, envy, adultery, theft, and murder. These are bad in themselves and not in their excesses and deficiencies. One is always wrong in doing them.[10] Achieving a happy or "harmonious" life, therefore, can only be attained by exercising balance in temperament.

Generally regarded as probably the first philosopher/scientist, Aristotle divided everything in the natural world into two main categories. In one corner he placed what he termed the non-living things such as rocks, clumps of soil and drops of water etc., and in the other the classification of "living things". He further divided this latter group into two other categories: "plants" and the "other creatures". This last was finally divided into two sub-categories: animals and humans.

Aristotle further reasoned that the "form" of man comprised three parts; a plant-like part, an animal part and a rational part (the soul or "divine reason"). In his view, man could only live a good life and achieve happiness by using all his abilities and capabilities. In the three forms of happiness that he identified, the first was a life of pleasure and enjoyment, the second as a free and responsible citizen, and the third as a thinker and philosopher. All three needed to be present at the same time for happiness to be attained within the individual, for he rejected all forms of *imbalance*. Thus The Law of Balance was well understood in those early years.

In spiritual terms this Law, in its effect and outworking, should reflect the necessary *balance* between "giving" and "receiving". In everyday tasks, many even mundane things automatically obey this law. Like a baby taking its first faltering steps, or a young child learning to stay upright on a bicycle, waiters balancing plates of food in cafes, or even the simple act of walking. On construction sites we observe large cranes with enormous working booms counter-balanced by opposing shorter boom lengths appropriately counter-weighted to achieve safe working balances. The activities of trade and monetary transaction may require the use of scales for various purposes. In many judicial systems, justice is depicted by a set of scales held by a blind-folded woman, traditionally meaning "Justice is blind". Perhaps, however, reflecting the wish that a correct weighing and examining in the Courts might be the outcome, for if there is no balance where lies justice? *Justice should not be blind, however, but all-seeing and spiritually discerning.*

The simplest and most quietly obvious example of The Law of

---

[10]Samuel Enoch Stumpf, *Philosophy History & Problems*, p 99

Balance is in breathing. We must naturally balance exhaling with inhaling. Correct breathing is vital for optimum health, but shallow breathing into the top of the lungs only does not provide this. The solution in this case is to regard the *exhalation* as the key. Exhaling properly and emptying the lungs will automatically ensure that a full breath will next be inhaled. Many a respiratory disorder can be at least relieved with consistent and correctly-balanced breathing.

In the home and in the nation, the need to balance the budget is important in order to live within our means. The daily intake of food generally indicates a basic understanding of the need to try to achieve a "balanced diet" for optimum health, i.e. different kinds of foods in appropriate proportions. Quite obviously, too much of just one type of food is not only inappropriate and tiresome, but is also not beneficial for the normal digestive system. Balancing the necessary intake of food is the need to eliminate body wastes as a natural result of this process. Any imbalance resulting from poor digestion or constipation makes us feel unwell.

Workaholic burnout as a result of "all work and no play" is also a transgression against The Law of Balance. Conversely, a life characterised by no work is equally harmful, even after retirement. The right kind of work for each individual should be a feature of the retirement years to help maintain the health of the body until death. Where the elderly happily engage in appropriate activity, higher levels of health are achieved. And where job opportunities are not readily available for someone wishing to work, low self-esteem may be the outcome resulting in a decline in the emotional and physical health of that individual.

The Laws of Creation show us that they inherently possess Divine Love. Love is thus the greatest Power. Also inherent in this as a part of Divine Love is Perfect Justice. The two cannot be separated. The Law of Balance, under the aegis of the power of Love and Spiritual Justice, ensures that "everlasting rest" is not the reality of the after-death situation. No one "rests in peace"! That is surely one of the strangest "human inventions". We are compelled to accept the responsibility of our life's decisions and "live them out", so to speak, even after our physical demise. Then, our "personal books" are audited to determine where there is imbalance, after which we must spiritually address it, i.e., put it right!

Perhaps if more people recognised this stark reality – which cannot be circumvented in any case – there might arise a better attitude to many things, since earthly death is the "great leveller" for all. A knowledge of The Law of Balance would therefore certainly benefit the elderly, and those consciously approaching death through illness or accident. Perhaps a greater effort might then be placed on "balancing one's spiritual account" long before being *overtaken* by earthly death.

Unfortunately, however, our present way of thinking clearly shows a general propensity for two things. Firstly, to seek as much wealth in the shortest possible time, and secondly, for a life of ease ever after on earth. Great wealth can achieve wonderful goals and is not, in itself, a bad thing. However, if it is used for base, superficial or selfish ends, it loses its great potential and value and spiritually degrades the holders of it. It is a sad indictment on today's society that spiritual goals or earthly activities with a spiritual content are not regarded or valued highly as befits their true worth. The scales of society are well and truly tipped toward overindulgence, base passions and immorality, to our spiritual detriment.

Benjamin Franklin (1706-90) observed that if there were no limiting factors in Nature, one species of plant or animal could engulf the entire globe. The balance is maintained because many species hold each other in check. Man is the only "spanner in the works" here, as his activities invariably create imbalance.

In what is arguably the most difficult yet necessary part of the everyday life of the human spirit, i.e. that of personal relationships, the correct application of The Law of Balance between "giving and taking" offers the key to harmony and progress in all situations. Whether in marriage between partners, in a family situation between parents and children, between employer and employee, or between groups or nations, in each particular case the concept of giving and taking needs to be correctly understood.

Parents desiring to have children must be aware of the need to balance this with the duty to care for the child in the right way. The huge rise in child abuse and paedophilia, even in family groups, clearly attests to terribly imbalanced and sick societies. But where parents offer spiritually-correct protection and nurturing to their children, this must be balanced by the obligation of the offspring to then respect their parents. But only where parents or caregivers have *earned the right* to be respected, of course. For why should parents be *automatically honoured* by offspring if they are not deserving of honour?

The ostensibly sacrosanct Commandment, "Honour Thy Father and Mother" should be very carefully thought about as to its **correct** meaning. Societal statistics clearly reveal the fact that many parents are not worthy to be honoured in any way at all by their children. Violence, drunkenness, drug-taking, abuse etc., can never be raised as the kinds of examples and behaviour for children to be exposed to. And certainly not to aspire to. Even though individual souls are brought together in family groups under the precise and lawful outworking of Spiritual Law, it still behoves parents to live – and thus teach by example – the correct spiritual principles of life.

We should understand, therefore, that this Commandment was given **first and foremost for parents!** For parents to **honour Fatherhood and Motherhood**. So that they *would* become such parents as *could* be honoured by their children. For it was surely not the children born to their union who made the decision for their parents. In the light of Perfect Love and Perfect Justice, it is *absolutely inconceivable* that the Perfection of The Creator would *command* children to honour parents who had no right to be honoured. That is the true meaning of this Commandment; that parents live correctly according to The Law, and thereby *imbue* the status of parenthood **with honour!**

Yet, for one or two churches, the letter of the law is so strictly enforced that some family groups within live not in love and harmony, but in fear. We may therefore wonder how many children, raised by strictly religious parents who, themselves, did not obey the Commandments or live correctly, yet nevertheless still hypocritically demanded that they be honoured. I am sure that many a child or young adult has suffered greatly under this kind of arrogant and hypocritical injustice.

Once the child has reached an age where it is physically able to assist in the home, it should be required to do so in order to balance the parental care it receives. Its form of assistance would be commensurate with its age and abilities. A child brought up *without* the application of this Law in its life may not develop any kind of purposeful work ethic, nor garner the correct social skills and attitude necessary to interact in a naturally balanced way with others. An attitude of personal selfishness is often the outcome which, unfortunately, may become ingrained for life. The spiritually correct concept of "tough love" for wayward children today might not have been needed for many had The Law of Balance been applied from the outset.

It should not be assumed, however, that the overall application of The Law of Balance must necessarily require a *similar* kind of return contribution or payment to that received. Personal circumstances may decree otherwise. In such cases the recipient will fulfil the requirements of this Law if he evinces deep and genuine gratitude for the help received. Or perhaps he may be able to tender some good advice which his benefactor may well be able to put to good use for himself. So, regardless of personal situations, everyone is able to fulfil the demands of The Law of Balance in some way. The fact that many do not do so stands as a reflection of our level of spiritual immaturity where the unhelpful human traits of selfishness, thoughtlessness, or just plain bad habits have become more the norm.

Thus, in respecting this Law, we should not unnecessarily worry about what should be given in return. It behoves us to simply give the best of what we have and what we can, *relative* to what was received and what we are *able* to give. If this should mean genuine thanks only, without guile or deceit, then the demands of The Law are fulfilled. Legal contracts are not included here, that is a different matter. Everybody, rich or poor, is therefore able to *live* this most necessary Law. Even the poorest can give out of themselves, either gratitude, a heartfelt prayer, or even a kind look to the giver. So long as the heart is pure and the intention genuine, the essential considerations from the standpoint of The Spiritual Laws will have been fulfilled.

The outworking of The Law of Balance in the present time can be powerfully observed in a specific problem area now coming to acute prominence. Mankind's questing nature and technological drive guaranteed that he would journey to and explore lands far from his birthplace. And, of course, colonise and settle some of them. Major wars have also been a driving force for people to flee to nearby safer areas, and perhaps settle there. Prior to the Age of Exploration such "refugee movements" were generally confined to the continent of Europe. Because the population numbers were not high, the "resettling" impact could be absorbed much more easily than is the case today.

During the Industrial Revolution, however, the situation changed dramatically. The industrialised nations – of which many were the main maritime ones also – shipped in thousands and thousands of workers from other places around the globe. Some went voluntarily, others were enslaved. Whilst it made some nations and individuals very wealthy, the balance of the world's peoples was, from then on, more drastically altered than at any time before. The huge dislocation caused by the Second World War compounded the problem considerably.

With a global population now exceeding six billion and increasing, more people seeking a so-called "better life" in lands sometimes at an opposite end of the globe. The huge and fundamental imbalance in the ethnic mix of peoples in the different countries of the world that began in earnest just a few centuries ago has now become like a "sword of Damocles" hanging over many countries of the more wealthy West. That unfortunate legacy has produced desperate acts of violence, political instability, social unrest and urban terrorism on a new and frightening scale. It has resulted in demands for stronger measures to curb immigration in the refugee crisis of the present day.

The ostensibly compassionate practice of Western Nations accepting refugees from parts of the world where unstable, corrupt or oppressive regimes hold sway does not *ultimately* solve the problem for the people of the country concerned. *They, themselves, should strive to bring about correct change within.* Unfortunately, however, external influences often undermine well-intentioned efforts to influence such change. Dubious foreign policy objectives of some Western Governments, big business dealings, UN mandated operations and badly monitored aid programs have all contributed to abuse, corruption and incredible suffering for millions.

It is precisely this kind of aspiritual, greedy and ignoble behaviour which has driven much of the refugee problem. It is not our purpose to analyse the global situation of the why of refugees to any depth here. The world's news and refugee agencies do an admirable job in highlighting these problems, and constantly supply a surfeit of visual images.

What we must state, however, is the fact that the world, its peoples, its systems, its religions etc., are in serious and dangerous imbalance. For not one thing, not one decision, stands alone in the world. All are ultimately connected. Because they *are* all in some way connected, a decision in one part of the world produces a ripple effect in every other – even if not perceived immediately or at all. This lawful effect can thus be seen developing *more and more strongly* in the international and religious tensions now surfacing over refugees and immigration.

Desperation and riots, people smuggling, religious and ethnic tensions and hatred; these extreme outcomes simply reveal the emerging end-effect of this particular outworking under the aegis of The Law of Balance. It places increasingly stronger spiritual pressure on all of humanity to recognise and understand why there is so much conflict in a practice that "seemingly" seeks to *help* the downtrodden. That in itself is a noble and correct ideal of course, and forever will remain so. If not applied and effected spiritually-correctly, however, then disaster will be the end-result. That is the path we currently tread. There may well be a place for refugee assistance in other countries, **but the reason must be a spiritually correct one in the first instance.**

The refugee group and the Government accepting the entry of that group to their country should fully understand the import of such a decision. For The Law of Balance will *ultimately redress imbalance* wherever it occurs, irrespective of the reasons for the original decision. In the case of latter-day pressures to accept refugee quotas, The Law of Balance does not mean *equal* balance of ethnic numbers, it is more about the *balance of harmony* - for that country and that society and culture. Refugee groups that refuse to integrate in an harmonious way should perhaps consider whether they should have remained in the country of their ethnic origin after all.

The various peoples and cultures of the world **are meant to be different and diverse.** Those essential differences, however, are obviously most powerfully reflected and *harmonised for the benefit of all peoples of the world* in and through the "beauty of the peoples and cultures" *within the borders of the lands that represent and actually are of that people.* Of course we all understand that movement and settlement into other lands to seek a better life or freedom from oppression or persecution is a natural aspect of humanity. And without those sorts of motivational considerations, many millions of the world's peoples would not now be generationally-settled into countries far removed from ancestral homelands.

The increasing and strident racist vitriol from so many quarters we now hear may not be so much racist but more a sub-conscious knowing that *so much* ethnic resettlement over such a relatively *short period* has not permitted sufficient time for *normal and natural assimilation* as was the situation previously. In any case, there are no solutions or answers in the same old arguments that each "side" – the "pro" and the "anti" –s continue to push. Because the problem now virtually feeds on itself, the only alternative insight that *might* have *once* brought order out of increasing chaos is probably no longer viable. Therefore, in accordance with the mandated purpose of this work, we unequivocally state that the posturing and bluster of politicians and concerned individuals and groups worldwide for increasing refugee quotas into so-called "better" countries will fail without the correct insight.

Equally for those individuals and groups who stand in opposition, they, too, must take into account the essential knowledge of Spiritual Law if they are to correctly understand the true nature of what is currently fermenting to its final conclusion. Spiritual knowledge and concomitant application of it by both groups – the authorities on the one hand and the supplicants on the other – would have been the only solution. It is unlikely that that will be the outcome anywhere now. The Law of Balance has been transgressed very seriously for a long time now. Therefore, balance **will** be restored *equally seriously*. ***But in a much shorter time period!***

3.6.1 To Give, or to Take?

"It is more blessed to give than to receive!"

(Acts 20:35, Fenton.)

These words of Jesus, like many of them, have been so misunderstood or so grossly misinterpreted that it has become difficult to fulfil His words of The Law in the way He originally taught them, even with the very best of intentions. Yet the question of whether one should give or take is readily answered in the understanding that in The Law of Balance between giving and taking, *giving* always ranks first. Unfortunately, through the well-intentioned but misplaced "generosity" of some social groups, "taking" as a "social right" has become a way of life for some people and families who have no idea that they should also ***give*** *something* in return.

Whether intentional or not, this transgression of The Law of Balance has a detrimental effect on the one who is a constant receiver, not least to the individual's self-esteem and self-respect. Moreover, children raised in this environment may become unwitting transgressors of this Law later in their life, also to their detriment. Thus, through a lack of understanding of an Eternal Law, well-meaning people can actually perpetuate and enlarge a social problem as their good intent, in certain cases, does not always translate to giving the correct and necessary kind of "spiritual" and material help actually needed.

A thorough knowledge of The Spiritual Laws is the only way that humanity can address its increasing social problems. In determining the best way that we might offer help, we should always be cognisant of the ancient Asian saying:

"Give a man a fish, and you feed him for a day. Teach him to fish, and you feed him for life!"

At the beginning of this Chapter we stated that each Law examined would intermesh with all the other Eternal Laws to produce a perfectly balanced whole, and that the reader should be able to perceive the connections between them all. In this case, and as a simple example, one can easily deduce that *giving* in the correct way is better because it is connected to The Law of Sowing and Reaping. The act of giving is identical with the practice of sowing. For each seed will, at its appropriate time, provide multiples of the same kinds of seeds for the *giver*.

Conversely, that which one extends the hand for – the seed taken or received – is like a harvest. Once consumed, it ceases to exist. With each receiving, a cycle is closed. Whenever we give, however, we start a new cycle. Through this process, therefore, it is always better to give than to receive. Of course, any giving should not be coloured solely by the selfish desire for a large return, thus losing sight of the correct spiritual reason to want to give in the first place. When viewed in this light, the words of Jesus take on a far deeper and richer meaning than might previously have been understood.

As we noted earlier, the current social propensity to demand one's rights, whether individual, children's, youth, ethnic, cultural, social, legal, religious, or any other, in the first instance belongs to the aspect of "taking"! In the sense of The Spiritual Laws, it is a negative and selfish attitude, for rights are only obtained by the fulfilment of responsibilities or duties. Therefore, **the fulfilment of duty and responsibility must come before any claim to rights**. This vitally necessary attitude should be inculcated into every individual through education in the home, in the schools, in the collective workplaces, and perhaps more especially in the gaols.

Consider the effect on society if, instead of demanding more and more "rights", we all immediately and radically changed our way of thinking to encompass a new, more tolerant and giving attitude which saw us all become concerned with responsibilities, duties and obligations. Toward each other, between parents and children, teachers and students, employer and employee, between religions and ethnic groups, even between individuals within those ethnic groups, and between the individual and society.

In one single stroke of "attitude", our present kind of oftentimes selfish society could be instantly transformed into one that actually lived the completely beneficial aspects of Spiritual Law, particularly that of The Law of Sowing and Reaping. Virtually overnight, all manner of social problems and crime could disappear, and confrontation could also quickly become a distant memory – a memory of pointless, debilitating argument, anger and violence. Whilst this may seem an unworkable utopian ideal, nothing more than a pipe dream, it is exactly possible. In any case, without such a change the misguided "Human Rights first" ethos will continue to ensure that the current "my rights mantra" will simply further entrench selfishness in society.

Thus one should give out of a genuine desire to help, and in the manner most *spiritually* beneficial to the recipient. The Eternal Laws therefore urge everyone to give, and no one should practice or indulge in one-sided taking. As previously stated, however, it would be wrong to expect any kind of *particular* return from the person to whom one has given, as the act of giving is then denigrated to an unspoken, selfish, strings-attached, silent demand – for something in return. In the strict lawfulness of this process, what should be recognised is that what might be received in return for what one has given does not necessarily depend upon the recipient. This may initially be a difficult concept to adjust to. Yet whether or not it is believed the recipient deserves it, whether or not he is grateful or ungrateful, and even whether or not he is actually aware that he has been helped, all such considerations are ultimately irrelevant. In any case ingratitude for any kindness shown will bring its own "reward" to the "ungrateful one".

It is a very human trait to seek recognition for any kind of help offered, yet the outworking of The Law of Reciprocal Action applies here equally as much as our attitude toward the suffering. What comes to us as our exact due – our reward as it were – arrives in the manner and at the time so ordained under The Spiritual Laws. Since we do not necessarily harvest in the same season that we sow, the time of its return may not be immediate. The immediacy of financial transactions is a different matter, concerned solely with business expectations and practices, unless perhaps fraud or deceit is planned.

The same principles should apply whether the giver or receiver is an individual, a group, or a nation. Here, also, it is more blessed to give than to receive. Many developed nations give aid and technical assistance to others, and this serves to promote a large measure of peace, harmony and goodwill in the world. If every recipient nation were to give something in return, a wonderful system of dynamic exchange and interaction would emerge, thus promoting global development in the right way. Every recipient nation *can* give something in return, be it only in cultural exchanges.

At this point it is timely to reiterate that under the increased spiritual pressure now pouring onto the earth and its inhabitants, all past imbalances will be forcibly, and therefore severely, corrected. In future, deviation from The Law of Balance will not be sustained for as long as has been possible thus far. The present structural problems that can be observed in the national and global economies, in particular through failing banks and financial institutions, are a direct result of mankind's total disregard for, and lack of understanding of, The Law of Balance. The disruption inherent in the economic and social stress of major restructuring programmes worldwide is the result of the effect of this increased pressure now culminating in urgent attempts to restore balance where, previously, there was imbalance, even if it appeared *not* to be the case.

Therefore the first task of the restructuring agencies should be to ensure that the process is carried out for the right reasons and under the knowledge of this Law, with due regard for the respect and integrity of those duly affected. Restructuring purely for the sake of doing so, without clear reasons and goals, will only ensure unnecessary upheaval. So it behoves the architects of necessary change to become thoroughly conversant with The Eternal Laws, especially The Law of Balance, if they wish to succeed. Quite obviously, only those areas that actually *need* restructuring should be worked upon. Any area that is already in balance should be left alone, whether in international trade, in the financial system including setting exchange rates, in the determination of prices for goods and services and in industrial relations.

Since most company restructuring involves the down-sizing of work forces and their pay rates, with the generally greedy practice of those who institute the changes greatly increasing their own salary levels, it would be timely for such people to become cognisant of this Law, if only for their own spiritual growth. Otherwise their "greed", or their "works" will one day pursue *them*. For The Law takes no account of supposedly "sharp" business practices. In terms of the attitude of such "Boards of Directors" or "CEOs" to the workers who help produce the business profits for them, the correct application of this Law is well illustrated in the admonition attributed to Jesus: "...for the workman is entitled to his wages." (Luke 10:7, Fenton.)

In the international arena, the practice of advancing huge loans to poorer, under-developed nations, and then expecting outrageously exorbitant interest charges from them, has been rightly likened to a blood transfusion – *"from a **sick** patient to a **healthy** one"*. Where is fairness and balance in such cases? To cite global monetary vagaries as the reason why cheap loans cannot be advanced from rich nations to poor, quite clearly shows that we should quickly set about bringing it into balance. Thankfully, a new idea is fermenting among some lenders. Any system that permits the electronic transfer of large currency amounts to reap huge profits simply because of a small shift in an exchange rate somewhere in the world is clearly obscene. Such practices should serve as a warning that this completely out-of-balance, globally-interconnected monetary system cannot be sustained, simply because the spiritual pressure of The Law of Balance will one day bring about its collapse.

Interestingly, the December 1996 Edition of *Time* Magazine noted a subtle but growing shift in the attitude of *some* of the richest Americans. In the opinion of billionaire Ted Turner, the wish of the majority of those Americans to make *Forbes* magazine's listing of the 400 wealthiest, "...is destroying our country," claiming that the "ole skinflints" are so afraid of slipping down the *Forbes* list ... that they hoard, rather than share, their wealth."

Turner issued a challenge: rank the biggest "givers" instead of the biggest "getters" (takers). Picking up the glove, Microsoft's online magazine *Slate* took up that challenge launching the *Slate 60*, a list of the largest charitable donations in the country by families or individuals gathered from publicly available sources.

If this list becomes as important to the rich as the *Forbes* list has thus far been, it may well open up a veritable floodgate of financial help where it is needed most – in assisting the unemployed back to work and to self-esteem. For under Spiritual Law, the wealthy have a duty to provide, not hand-outs, but means, schemes and employment, whereby the less fortunate can contribute meaningfully toward their respective societies, and to their own personal worth.

The Gates Foundation, founded, of course, by Bill and Melinda Gates, directs many millions of dollars to health aid in Africa – just one of the Foundation's philanthropic activities.

Notwithstanding *winds of change* in the ranks of the super-wealthy, we should not leave this particular segment without offering this most wonderfully appropriate Biblical quote:

> *"For what will it profit a man if he should gain the whole world and forfeit his life?" (lose his soul?)*

(Mark 8:36, Fenton. Parenthetic addition mine.)

A quote from Stephen Lampe's "Building Future Societies: Spiritual Principles of Nation Building", Chapter 2, p 39, Millennium Press, offers a further reflective note:

> More than 150 years ago, a French economist, Pierre Boisguilbert came to the recognition of the utmost importance of balance. He wrote:
> "Only equilibrium (balance) can save everyone; and nature alone, to repeat, can achieve this. On our part, we should give and give, and nature will restore balance."

The right balance must be struck in all aspects of our lives and not just economic re-structuring. The rapid increase in one-parent families shows the urgent need to restore balance in personal relationships, in social interaction with others, and in all human activities. The breakdown of large nations to smaller ethnic states is nothing more than the restoration of balance to peoples once forced to become, for them, part of a larger and often alien system.

The British Commonwealth is one example of this ongoing process. Once an empire of disparate countries and peoples ruled by the force of arms of the "mother country", it has now developed into a *relatively* easy voluntary association of most of those former colonies, bonded by more or less common goals, aspirations and ideals. Such links, moreover, have allowed the many varied races in the Commonwealth to develop a generally greater degree of knowledge and tolerance toward each other, particularly in the areas of race and religion, than might otherwise have been the case under continued British military dominance. And that is as it should be.

In its current format, the British Commonwealth, *thus far*, stands as a reasonably good example of what can be achieved through voluntary goodwill, with the concomitant ability to play a beneficial role in international affairs. However, if the common binding force were the knowledge and application of The Spiritual Laws of Creation, the Commonwealth example and its resultant international effect would be much more powerful.

The Law of Balance between Giving and Taking will one day play a fundamental part in true international understanding when peoples and races finally stand *side by side*, helping and furthering one another in mutual respect. The ideal time for such a process to begin is always in the present of course. Notwithstanding that current non-realisation, the recognition that every people, every race, possesses earthly and spiritual values which are indispensable for humanity as a whole, will eventually arrive. And because other peoples and races may not inherently possess exactly the same attributes, a vital exchange of those values will then become the norm. But such exchanges that occur must reflect the right balance in accordance with the outworking of this Law between Giving and Taking.

Whilst the inherent characteristics of The Law of Balance can obviously be applied to most situations, the most critical should be to urgently seek the correct balance between the *material and spiritual* in our individual lives. In the intellectual sense man presently stands astride the apex of his technological pyramid. Spiritually, though, he grovels in the dust at the base, stunted and blind. If any kind of reminders were needed to induce us to begin to redress the balance of the scales toward The Spiritual, one need only look at everyday world events. In that clear revelation *humankind unequivocally reveals the level* ***it has chosen!***

3.7 Rebirth – Fact or Fiction?

The Law of Rebirth

The one absolute we all accept without question, irrespective of race, religious beliefs or political leanings etc., is the factual reality of birth, life and death. These three facets, at least in their physical happening, also represent the only belief or reality for many. The processes of all three, moreover, are absolutely identical for all individuals insofar as the *mechanics* are concerned. Only the individual life paths will be different due to the factors of race, geographical location, education, wealth and status etc., but both the *spiritual and physical* **processes** *for each remain the same.*

The term "miracle of birth" reflects our amazement and wonder at this event. The Spiritual Laws that govern the development of the growing individual and determines the final characteristics of it are constant and unchangeable. Thus the many billions of human births have followed the same lawful process. Inherent in The Laws is certainly the provision for development, but not for wrong experimentation, deviation or transgression, however. So even when using the procedure of in-vitro fertilisation, doctors are not able to operate outside the parameters dictated by this universal Law.

It is the same with the death process. Without exception, we are forced to accept the absolute inevitability of it at some point in life. Universal Laws operate here in their immovable perfection too. For the step from a living, breathing, animated physical body to a cold, lifeless shell is exactly the same everywhere in the world. The manner of dying may be vastly different, i.e., disease, war, illness, accident – in peaceful sleep even – but the process is nevertheless identical. Indeed, it could not be otherwise. Yet whilst we are able to observe the physical processes of the steps of birth and death, and can clearly see the after effects of birth, we do not necessarily accept that there may be after effects of earthly death too.

Why not, however? If the evidence of our own eyes with regard to the irrefutable processes of birth and death governed by strict, consistent laws in the *physical* happening can be readily accepted, why should it not be a simple step to know *intuitively* that the outworking of The Spiritual Laws does not simply come to a convenient halt at that point simply because we may believe or wish otherwise?

By virtue of the inviolability of The Spiritual Laws, humankind can do nothing else but submit to them, for there is no other choice. In cases of suicide or murder the physical processes still cannot change. However, even though The Laws are physical in their visible effect, they are, nevertheless, still spiritual in origin. It may be worth deep consideration that even The Son of God, Jesus, had to be born of a woman on earth. The Creator could not just simply place Him on the earth as a fully grown man – notwithstanding the strong religious conviction among many that: "God can do anything He pleases".

From this standpoint consider, again, the later words of Jesus:

> "Do not imagine that I have come to abolish the law and the prophets; I have not come to abolish, but to complete them. For I tell you indeed, that until the heavens and the earth shall pass away, a single dot or hairstroke shall not disappear from the law, until all has been completed."
>
> (Matthew 5:17-18, Fenton.)

Thus the "Natural Laws" could not be circumvented, not even by Jesus Himself, nor can they be today – or ever. Not by force of arms, wealth, political power, scientific disbelief, rationalist theories and, not least, by religious dogma. Ultimately there is no choice for humankind but to submit to the processes outlined, since it is

Spiritual Law which drives everything in Creation. By virtue of our free-will we *can* choose to *oppose* those Laws. However, the outworking of them will eventually guarantee the appropriate kind of hard and bitter reaping for such opposition.

What we cannot change at all is the *actual* and lawful outworking of the death process. Since not one thing can happen without a reason or not have some kind of starting point or origin, it should be a simple matter to deduce that any sudden, unexpected arrival of painful experiences in our lives can only be the result of a previous decision made elsewhere. *We constantly stand, therefore, in the centre of all our "returns", both good and bad, exactly in accordance with all the free-will decisions responsible for every returning reciprocal effect.*

However, because there may be no recollection of the actual originating decision or event in the present lifetime of an affected individual, or in the lives of others closely associated with that person which could have brought about such a consequence, any such end-effect clearly presupposes another possibility, i.e. the concept of more than one earth life from where such an outcome could originate. As previously stated, this is not a view readily accepted in Western thinking, though it is a basic tenet of billions of the World's peoples. So just as we can reduce the question of whether there is life after death to either there is, or there is not - for it surely cannot be both - we can also ask the same of *one life versus many*.

Current Western thought in the scientific and intellectual disciplines, as well as in religious doctrines, offers few genuine solutions to society's increasing problems within the restrictive parameters of a "one-life concept". Unfortunately, therefore, disbelief or ignorance of The Law of Rebirth cannot, in any way, alter the truth of its actual reality and outworking. This widespread "unbelief of the West" *can* be accepted if there is nothing more than a purely physical body to contend with. Conversely, if the body *is* no more than just the physical shell – the cloak housing the *real person* – then, just as the processes of The Law allow for **one** birth, why could it not allow for **others** where another, but different, "overcoat" is simply taken on in accordance with such Laws?

This particular insight provides the meaning about the promise of ".. the resurrection of the flesh", again stated by Jesus. This "resurrection" does not mean that bodies long dead will suddenly rise out of their graves at some point soon and become clothed in the flesh of the original owner. This strange and totally illogical belief seemingly derives from the Scripture which ostensibly states that: "All the dead shall awaken." However, in the light of the rapidly increasing degeneration of all aspects of global human activity, if we exercise logic and reason to strive to determine what it might truly mean then we will intuitively recognise that it is actually a *warning*. It is a warning, moreover, that fulfils the essence of The Law of Reciprocal Action, and is thus a severe warning to humankind to *spiritually awaken*.

The true meaning is, therefore: "All **that is dead** shall be awakened." Thus it is the awakening of *all, everything*, that is *spiritually dead*.

With that vital revelation, the *global increase* in our problems may be much more readily understood. All belief systems, all disciplines of human endeavour, everything that we have held sacrosanct or sacred, everything that we might thus far have stated to be inviolable, all must now be forced to show where it truly stands in relation to The Spiritual Laws of Creation. Thus the spiritual pressure that is now being exerted more powerfully with each passing day upon *all* our beliefs and activities, *forces the awakening* of those belief systems and activities. It does not matter whether they *ostensibly* hold scientific, philosophical, religious or political "truths". Without exception, *everything* will be subject to this severe and relentless cleansing and clarifying process.

All that does not stand true – thereby suffering collapse in the awakening – thus reveals that it **was** dead and *needed* to be **awakened**, i.e. *that it did not have as its foundation and guiding principle,* **the knowledge of The Spiritual Laws**. This "awakening process", this *resurrection*, applied in accordance with the inviolability of The Law of Rebirth, thus permits each one the opportunity to "put right" the past wrongs. Through this mechanism of Divine Grace, man is gifted the means whereby he may *earn* the possibility of returning to his spiritual origins, his true home. "Resurrection of the flesh" is thus a Divine Grace providing the means whereby we are given numerous opportunities to return to the earth to atone for past transgressions committed in the earthly.

Despite inherently possessing clear and ultimately irrefutable logic, reincarnation as a concept has fuelled debate for centuries. Even though a very large proportion of the world's peoples accept it as a factual part of man's *total* existence, the Judaeo-Christian religions generally do not. The basic belief of reincarnation in some form or another has been accepted by most in the Indian subcontinent for the past 2,500 years, and in other parts of the world for a long time too. It is interesting to note, however, that the so decisively important doctrine of reincarnation – of rebirth as a human being – was only expunged from Christian creeds by a very small majority decision at the Council of Constantinople in 553 AD. What was effectively lost through that decision of appalling ignorance and ego was the greater understanding of the *seeming* inequality of the world and, indeed, the Love and Justice contained in The Creative Will.

Consider, if at that fateful Council meeting only a few men had decided differently, *reincarnation would now be a matter of course for Western "religions" also.* Had that happened, there would not exist the present fortress of doubt and prejudice against it. In its place would be greater freedom of thinking rather than this terribly unfortunate constraint into which our current thought-processes have fallen, and solely because of that unfortunate decision taken by a few powerful men centuries ago! In general, it has succeeded in removing any possible larger outlook to the greater connections of our existence, and to the incredible vastness of Creation as a whole.

Because of that decision, we have created the unhealthy situation of not readily accepting death as a natural part of life, or as an ongoing transitional step in our complete existence.[11]

The great difficulty with trying to meaningfully grapple with the rapidly increasing problems in society, is that there often *appears* to be no logical cause for it all. Is it any wonder that suicides are on the increase, particularly among the more impressionable young who are often too emotionally immature to cope with the *seemingly* insurmountable? They seek answers but no one will give them the only correct one. Our so-called "educators" reject the very thing that would provide the necessary enlightenment. Yet even *they* continue to ask – "Why"? Australian Children's Advocate and "National Treasure", Professor Fiona Stanley, on the subject of increasing youth suicide there, soberly observed: "Despite all that we now know, and all the research that's been done, **nothing is getting any better**."

The concept of reincarnation will need to be accepted as fact if society wishes to find answers to its problems, for the deliberate rejection of it only blinds one to the impending day of reckoning. It must be understood, however, that reincarnation is governed by the strictness of The Spiritual Laws too. Contrary to some beliefs

---

[11]The details of that meeting are examined more specifically in specific later Chapters which outline the actual death process.

and misconceptions, therefore, one *cannot* return as a tree, an insect, or an animal.

So, in direct contrast to the cultural or ethnic beliefs of various peoples, our ancestors cannot be such things as those. Inanimate objects have no connection with human spiritual origins, and neither do psychically produced forms that some indigenous groups revere. Even living, animate creatures such as eagles, tigers and whales etc., must forever remain their own kind. Humankind's collective spiritual ancestry can *only* be that of *human spiritual origin*.

Simply and logically put, The Laws of Nature absolutely decree that we *cannot change our species*. They thus further decree that under The Law of Rebirth we can only return as human beings. Carrying with us, moreover, all that we have "***previously sown***". Some experiences we are forced to live through may well have their origin in previous earth-lives. How we live our life now will determine what will come our way in the future, perhaps even in a later earth-life.[12]

The Western medical profession's general refusal to accept this logical view of a multi-life concept and become locked, instead, into a single one unfortunately translates into the practice of often attempting to go beyond reasonable limits in order to preserve "life". At all costs is the view, rather than simply accepting the dignified inevitably and reality of a "natural transition" to earthly death. Of course life should be extended for as long as it is reasonably possible to do so, but not at the expense of unnecessarily prolonging what should be regarded as the completely normal process of exiting earth-life. Neither should death be *desperately fought against* when medical reality clearly indicates an imminent demise. The dying one is not actually helped thereby.

Reincarnation offers the only viable mechanism for mankind to make rational sense of the misery, the suffering and the tragedies that beset the world today in such a relentless manner. Whilst it also brings good fortune and happiness for some, it is the tragedies that need more urgent clarification.[13]

---

[12] Whole nations and races must collectively reap what they have sown as well. The destruction of the Axis Powers during the Second World War is a particularly good example.

[13] It is not the purpose of this book to deal with this subject to any great degree, though we will briefly return to it in a later Chapter to help clarify another contentious religious issue – the "Second Death". However, as the actuality of reincarnation is a "Living Law of God" – which no one can change – it behoves us all to learn what we can about the actual mechanism and

The sage Paramahansa Yogananda wrote much about how to live correctly. Perfectly correct living, however, is really only possible with the knowledge of all The Laws of Creation. Even though actively seeking what he intuitively perceived was that complete knowledge existing somewhere on earth during his lifetime, certain pre-conceptions he harboured effectively prevented his taking the final step to personal recognition when given the crucial opportunity which would have led him to it. Notwithstanding that missed vital moment, his inherent wisdom nevertheless offers a good blueprint for basically correct living. His knowledge of reincarnation offers a brief insight into his truthful wisdom.

From the Sub-heading: **"How We Live This Life Determines What We Are in the Next"**.

> "We have been given the power to reason out where we go and whence we have come. But we don't take enough pains to analyse ourselves and our lives. Otherwise our common sense would tell us that whatever our character is today it will continue to be after death - perhaps a little better or a little worse, depending on how much effort we are making to improve ourselves. You go along 365 days a year, year after year, and perhaps you have made some progress, but your nature will be the same after death as it was before death. You will not become an angel just because you die! Only the body changes. Death makes no difference, otherwise. Death is like a gate you will pass through. Your body will be gone but you will be in every other respect the same. If you have a violent temper, you will not leave it behind, at death, with your physical body. Your violent temper will remain with you until you conquer it. If in your present life you have observed The Laws of healthful living, in your next incarnation you will possess a healthy body. The last portion of life is more important than the first, because what you are at the end of this life is what you will be at the beginning of the next.
>
> The first part of life is usually stupidly misspent, in a sort of bewildered state. Then romance comes, and finally disease and old age; the struggle with the body starts ... The body is a trouble most of the time: ... Always trouble, trouble! *That is why it is so necessary to your happiness that you realize you are not the body...*"
>
> (*Man's Eternal Quest*, p 219, Italics mine.)

---

process which, in its concept and outworking, actually provides the greatest measure of certainty about earth-life and life thereafter.

An apt description from The Bible refers to the body as "the deadly carcass". - - -

As a final notation on this subject, reincarnation, as an inviolable Spiritual Law, must live the fullness of that fact without deviation. This Law also naturally exists within The Laws of Nature, which themselves are a reflection of The Eternal Laws. All dovetail into each other in perfect outworking. As previously stated, perhaps the refusal of many Westerners to accept reincarnation may be due in part to the promoted belief of some Eastern religions that one may be required to return to the earth – for various purposes of atonement – as an animal, a bird or an insect even.

Atonement is a most necessary requirement in the outworking of our inherent free-will decision-making ability under The Law of Reciprocal Action – a Law which unequivocally states: "...what a man sows, that he will also reap." (Galatians 6:7, Fenton.) Reincarnation therefore provides the only "earthly" *long-term mechanism* under which this spiritually ordained atonement **can** be expiated. As it is also a Law of Nature or a natural Law, we must reiterate that such Laws state that it is not possible to change one's species, *irrespective of any belief to the contrary.*

The inner animating core of man – his life-force – is **spirit**, whilst that of the animal is **soul**. Two different species of animating power from two different levels in Creation. Therefore, in this context, the human spirit must always remain a human spirit, with absolutely *no possibility* that it could somehow transmigrate across *immovable spiritual boundaries* to become a life-form **different** to that ordained for it by the unalterable Laws of Creation. So humans remain humans, they cannot become animals. And, just as surely, **animals cannot develop into humans!**

In summary, the process of reincarnation, whereby a human spirit is ordained by Law to accept rebirth on earth, is subject to, and affected by, the collective outworking of all The Spiritual Laws of Creation. The free-will decisions of his previous life, or lives, will determine who he will be in the next one, what his spiritual lessons will be, and what he can also spiritually offer that group of souls into which he will be incarnated – to those who will be his earthly family. That, in turn, will determine such factors as to whether he will be born handicapped or complete, whether his new circumstances will be one of wealth or struggle, whether of the same race, geographical location or religion as his last incarnation, or one completely different.

Irrespective of these considerations, however, the circumstances of his next incarnation will precisely offer the necessary conditions he will need for his further spiritual maturing. The key point in all of this is the fact that he is still master of his own destiny. In that sense his inherent spiritual free-will provides the mechanism whereby he can still set in place new decisions which might offer a better or worse life than that originally ordained for him by Law through the outworking of all his previous decisions. Certain *"experiences of the spirit"*, however, will be part of his necessary path and may perhaps even provide a lifetime of hard struggle.

Whether or not that is the case may well depend upon the lawful outcomes of previous personal decisions acting upon him as he lives out his present life. Even if he should live spiritually correctly, yet experience a lifetime of struggle, The Spiritual Laws will still set in train beneficial returns for a future time. For the more *powerful experiences* will be impressed upon his spirit *in any case*, be it through *great joy* or *tragedy*.

Thus The Laws of Creation intermesh to bring about precisely lawful outcomes. Yet it always remains with the individual as to what those personal outcomes will be. As stated regularly throughout this book, only the ***decision*** is **free**, the ***consequences*** are **not!** Thus, in cases where two options are presented, whilst we will always have a **50%** option or **choice**, there is always only a **100% outcome** *after* the decision has been taken. Of course there is nothing to prevent one from modifying or radically changing the original decision with a second, or even third one. Those decisional changes, of course, will ultimately be reflected in their corresponding outcomes at some future point.

3.8 Grace – A Gift of Divine Love

Even though not a Law in the strictest sense, the inclusion of the key aspect of Grace in this Chapter about The Spiritual Laws is vital because the concept and outworking of the spiritual attribute of Grace impacts decisively and beneficially on the fate of anyone who recognises the error of their ways and subsequently seeks a more enlightened path. The entry of Grace into one's life, therefore, will manifest through the outworking of Spiritual Law in reciprocity deriving from spiritually-correct decision-making – even if the particular decision required needed to be a material one.

Grace is an inherent quality of Divine Love. Also inherent in Divine Love is Justice. However, the Love that is defined here has no affinity whatever with humankind's emotionally-distorted idea of this most noble Power. Thus, under the outworking of Grace – which *originates* from The Divine – help and guidance are given to humankind with each passing moment. In order to reap the benefits, however, the guidance needs to be recognised and lived accordingly.

Since The Spiritual Laws contain both the cornerstones of Love and Justice, they return only what is *spiritually* beneficial. By heeding Spiritual Law, we give no cause for any such "unwanted returns". In its distilled essence, therefore, "Spiritual Love" is pure, even *severe* if necessary. In certain cases it *needs* to be *severe* in order to bring about the necessary *awakening* to force the question "***why***"! Yet we must ever be mindful of the fact that we ourselves will have given cause for that event or trial somewhere, sometime, in accordance with the inviolable outworking of The Spiritual Laws.

Thus the kind of Love outlined here is not the caricature spawned and given form by collective humankind, and which has become so distorted that it is now used to encompass virtually every kind of debased activity under "modern", liberal thinking. This human distortion carries no justice within it. In keeping with current, prevalent attitudes, attempts are continually made to separate that which cannot be separated - genuine Spiritual Love from true Spiritual Justice.

In the most wonderful of ironies, the twin forces of Spiritual Love and Justice will eventually teach humankind that they are, indeed, inseparable. We have produced a weak form we call love but which, in reality, is more often than not a mask and poor excuse for overly-liberal, over-emotional and vacillating *self-indulgence.* In short, we have substituted the pure Power of Love with earthly emotionalism. In its pure form genuine Love stands far above such incorrect ideas. Compassion should not be confused with what is described here either, for compassion is an attribute of unconditional Love. When one has accepted, understood and finally worked through all that must be personally expiated, The Spiritual Laws or Rules then become strong and furthering helps for one's spiritual growth, thus expressing the Power of the genuine Love. The "Gift of Grace" lives in the essence of that inviolable Truth!

The "Gift of Grace" therefore permits even the worst transgressions to be completely expiated, if one *genuinely* seeks to put right his wrongs. Despite the fact that The Spiritual Laws operate strictly, here, too, the overriding attribute contained within the outworking of The Laws in this case is that of Grace and forgiveness. If being "pursued by one's works" presupposes a "return" of even severe difficulty and hardship, it is important to understand that by simply *changing* our spiritual volition for the better, we automatically begin the process of *altering* the forms (both their intensity and severity) of "our wrong works" previously produced. For they will, at some future point, surely return to us.

Therefore, under the process of reciprocity in "awaiting our works", someone who has lived a life of dark, horrific deeds is absolutely condemned to fully reap his "personal whirlwind" either here on the earth or when passed from it, *so long as there is no effort or attempt to change his ways*. Total ignorance of this cause, or even disbelief of it, cannot alter the returning effects either. As we need to restate, this lawful path reflects Divine Justice which, at the same time, is also Divine Love.

The returning reciprocal effect to a hardened soul should thus provide the necessary experiences and potential for a spiritual awakening, a re-appraisal of one's personal situation, and some deep "soul-searching". Should that individual stubbornly fight against this process, more of the same is assured. Yet this should not be seen as some kind of retributive punishment from some arbitrary God or Power. It is simply the "personal reaping" from the *personal* "sowing", irrespective of when sown or why.

What of one with many years of living a depraved or evil lifestyle, and with total and selfish disregard for the welfare of his victims, however? What happens when such a one suddenly finds himself faced with the unnerving reality that his attitude and conduct were "all wrong"? What then? Ordinarily, we would probably say he still deserves to pay for everything he inflicted on others. According to societal Law, that would probably be the case and society would no doubt be well pleased with such an outcome. Indeed, it is appropriate that correct punishment be meted out, for society has a right to protection from such individuals. In any case, our earthly Laws should reflect the clear recognition that we cannot function without order.

Therefore, even if a "criminal" has been dealt with by the justice of the earthly courts, this does not mean that all is necessarily "paid for". The more crucial debt, **the spiritual**, may still await resolution. However, if our miscreant – through the honest recognition that his previous ways were wrong – then genuinely seeks to mend them and make atonement, he sets in place for himself the mechanism whereby the impact of the returning retroactive consequences of his previously dark volition can be greatly lessened. Of course the desire to want to change must be an absolutely genuine one, for The Spiritual Laws are not fooled by the subterfuge and deviousness that human beings often engage in. Genuine humility, moreover, must be an accompanying factor in such a change.

What, then, is that process? Because we possess the inherent attribute of "free will", and because there is only **one** *neutral power* streaming through and animating all of Creation including the material worlds, our "free will" endowment ensures that this *neutral power* is *refracted through us* to good or evil purpose, **according to how we choose to use it.** Under The Law of Attraction of Similar Species, if our volition is dark, we automatically make connections to, and attract in and surround ourselves with, similar species. If the opposite is the case, via the same process of connection and attraction, we lock ourselves into a vastly different kind of "power stream", one which brings beneficial effects.

Thus, in the voluntary spiritual change that the felon of our example has undertaken, he has changed his "nature of attraction" from one originally leaning toward dark things to those much lighter. Since this change is subject to The Law of Spiritual Gravity also, there occurs within and around him a lightening effect as a result of his decision to change his ways for the good. Now he attracts to himself beneficial "forms" corresponding to his new volition. But where does this place him with regard to the returning effects of perhaps a long life of degrading deeds? The Law of Sowing and Reaping must still hold sway. That cannot change.

Now, however, through his newly-activated, lighter connections corresponding to the new volition with which he now surrounds himself – quite automatically – a lighter and stronger force envelops him. This acts like a cocoon against which some of the retroactive effects of his past volition can be deflected. Some may still penetrate to him. In which case they will be of such a nature as he still requires for growth and ascent and, moreover, may therefore need to be fully experienced materially for complete expiation under Spiritual Law.

The experiences from it, however, will enable him to further develop spiritually. Some returning effects may only need to be redeemed symbolically, perhaps something even as innocuous as a kind word to a complete stranger. Each case will be different for every individual but it will be in strict and inflexible accordance with Spiritual Law operating in concert with the Gift of Grace, so demonstrating both Perfect Justice and Perfect Love, two important cornerstones of The Spiritual Laws of Creation.

Therefore, if we do not wish to be pursued by any former "unpleasant works", it is essential that the knowledge of The Eternal Laws be regarded as a serious spur to help nullify the reciprocal effects of them. Thus, via the perfection of The Laws, we are enjoined to strive only for what is good. Such striving will ensure the reciprocal effect of greater peace and happiness under the "Gift" of Divine Grace!

3.9 Conclusion

"Power comes out of the barrel of a gun!"

(Mao Tse Tung.)

"Physical strength will never permanently withstand the impact of spiritual force."

(Franklin D. Roosevelt.)

"The pen is mightier than the sword!"

(From the original, "Arms give way to Persuasion!" – Cicero.)

Three vastly different quotes occupying opposite ends of the "spiritual spectrum". Each, however, generating its own specific kind of "return" under the aegis of The Spiritual Laws. The first concerned solely with earthly results, but ultimately returning certain spiritually-driven corresponding ramifications of no small import, and the other two having connections to both. In the first quote are sown the seeds of its own destruction because its inferior "form" is correspondingly attached to weaker, and therefore lower and baser levels.

The latter, however, if writing *Spiritual Truth*, is equal to the second because of its powerful connection to The Source of all Life. By virtue of that fact, any such writings connected to that source produce "forms of spiritual power", as opposed to the "baser forms" produced by the gun *if* the use of it is for strictly totalitarian purposes with the aim being control and/or enslavement.

Whilst The Spiritual Laws are the infallible and unalterable *driving mechanisms* which produce the consequences or outcomes for every decision made, it is vital to understand that any spiritual transgression incurred will be made more against the "rules for correct living". They are those that all the great religions and spiritual and philosophic teachings have recognised and espoused over millennia. Thus one *can* transgress The Law of Balance. In the true sense of the word, however, one cannot actually *transgress* The Laws of "Rebirth", "Attraction..." or "Spiritual Gravity". However, transgressions against the "rules of life" such as are stated in The Ten Commandments, for example, even if done in complete ignorance of them, nevertheless unequivocally set in motion the driving *"return"* mechanism that is inherent in the *power* of Spiritual Law. In this case, more specifically in The Law of Reciprocal Action (Sowing and Reaping.)

The reader should thus understand that **The Ten Commandments**, which the Law-Giver Moses received for **all** of humankind, are the necessary accompaniment of **The Spiritual Laws of Creation**. For both issue from the hand of **The Creator** for the harmonious order of **His Creation**. However, whilst they are the Rules, so to speak, The Laws that drive and sustain everything are vitally important to know so that we may understand *why* **The Ten Commandments** must be regarded as very necessary "Rules for correct living".

It is equally important to recognise, also, that it is *spiritual power* that we actually use in all decision-making. Even our thought processes utilise the same power. It permeates every part of Creation, for that is the life force of the whole. However, it does not at all mean that our utilisation of that power necessarily produces genuinely spiritual outcomes. Unfortunately, and as global societies clearly reveal, the volition of humankind has produced mainly aspiritual ones. Clearly evidenced by the global situation, the mechanism inherent in The Spiritual Laws drives everything to its particular outcome.

Thus The Spiritual Laws have been outlined in this earlier Chapter as a most vital adjunct to the correct understanding of the overall purpose of this book. The degree to which those Laws have been explored should be sufficient for our purpose. For only with the help of the knowledge of them am I able to attempt a book that assumes so much. Throughout the rest of the work, therefore, regular reference to these Laws will be made in order to explain every other aspect of our story as it interlinks and connects all the relevant threads.

It is also vital that we recognise and understand our origins too. Whilst The Spiritual Laws are very necessary for understanding what our free will decision-making process will return to us, that knowledge cannot stand completely alone. We also require the further recognition of our Spiritual, and therefore actual, Origins – our "whither and why". For to *that home* we can return provided we have made the correct decisions throughout life to achieve that desirable outcome. Irrespective of whether made consciously or unconsciously, they are choices nevertheless driven by, or taken under, the aegis of The Spiritual Laws of Creation!

In that regard, let us now discover our very beginnings, from the **Spiritual** Origins of **all** of humankind irrespective of the colour or shape of the outward physical form that may clothe our individual spirits today. Or of the differing Creation-beliefs that man's many and varied religions and cultures have produced!

Chapter 4

The Origins of Man – "Genesis" and Science Agree.

4.1 Our Spiritual Origins

"When we consider thy heavens, the work of thy fingers,
The moon and the stars, which thou hast ordained,
What is man, that thou art mindful of him?"

(E. B. Szekely, *The Gospel of the Essenes*, p 175)

"Where does the world come from?"
"She hadn't the faintest idea. Sophie knew that the world was only a small planet in space. But where did space come from?

It was possible that space had always existed, in which case she would not also need to figure out where it came from. But could anything have always existed? Something deep down inside her protested at the idea. Surely everything that exists must have had a beginning? So space must sometime have been created out of something else.

But if space had come from something else, then that something else must have come from something. Sophie felt she was only deferring the problem. At some point, something must have come from nothing. But was that possible? Wasn't that just as impossible as the idea that the world had always existed?"

(Jostein Gaarder, *Sophie's World*, p 8, Phoenix Press.)

The questions that young Sophie finds herself faced with in Gaarder's international bestseller are the very same that men have asked since time immemorial. The fact that this particular publication was a "bestseller" illustrates the keen, ongoing interest in such ideas from far more than the scientific or philosophic community. For, quite logically, there should be a natural, inherent curiosity in each of us which brings forth these very same questions by virtue of the fact that we exist on planet earth in the first place. Let us join Sophie as she asks more questions:

> "How was the world created? Is there any will or meaning behind what happens? Is there a life after death? And most importantly, how ought we to live? People have been asking these questions throughout the ages. *We know of no culture which has not concerned itself with what man is and where the world came from...* But history presents us with many different answers to each question."

(*Sophie's World*, p 12, Italics mine.)

Thus far Sophie's second question has been addressed from the standpoint of The Spiritual Laws. This, in turn, should provide the answers to the fourth question, namely how we should live. The third question on life after death will be addressed in a later Chapter. For if we do not know where we originate from, we cannot know who we are, what we are, or what our purpose is. That leaves only the first question to be answered, "How was the world created?" That question we examine here – in this Chapter!

The philosopher Plato believed that there had to be a reality behind what he termed the "world of ideas". He thought that we could never have true knowledge of anything that is in a constant state of change. We can only have knowledge of things that we can understand with our reason. Plato also believed that man is a dual creature with a body bound to the world of the senses – which he thought were unreliable – and an immortal soul which is the realm of reason. He also believed that the soul existed before it inhabited the body.

Even though Plato wrote extensively about this dual concept, it was widely believed by many Greeks before him. Plotinus (c. 205 - 270 AD) knew of similar ideas from Asia. Plotinus also believed that the world is a span between two poles with The Divine Light at one end, and absolute darkness at the other which receives none of The Light. He believed that this darkness was simply the absence of light, without any existence. Thus The Divine Light becomes increasingly dimmer the further one travels from it. Finally, he believed, there is a point that it cannot reach. He believed, moreover, that the soul is both a spark from, and illuminated by, The Divine Light: a fascinating insight because this particular view contains much basic truth, as we will illustrate in this Chapter.

Whilst the philosophers have mulled over this question for millennia, the mainstream religions have generally not needed to do so. The acceptance of an immortal soul or spirit – whether it becomes "one with the universe" or retains its "personal self-conscious form" after earthly death – is part and parcel of most religious beliefs. Even within this field, however, there is no clear position either. Yet pre-dating the early philosophers and the main religions, we find that in some places "cave-men" buried their dead with flowers and small items that were probably personal possessions.

This indicates that the funeral ceremony was conducted with a certain ritualistic air, perhaps reflecting the first stirrings of a belief in the duality of man in the early progenitors of humankind. A degree of reverence for either the burial process or in the belief of a soul departing from the body is evident here. This offers a different perception of these early humans, once depicted as stereotypically brutish.

Democritus (c. 460-370 BC), on the other hand, believed that people and animals were constructed solely of atoms, and that neither possessed immortal "souls". According to him, souls were built up of atoms that are dispersed to the winds when people die. In contrast to that particular view The Spiritual Laws of Creation decree that there are both animate and inanimate life-forms. The inanimate we may designate as that which is anchored in place such as trees and mountains etc. Rivers, lakes and glaciers also fall into this category. The animate is naturally the opposite and comprises those life-forms that are, in essence, ***mobile!*** They include the insects, birds, fishes, animals and, of course, man.

The "mobile group" is further divided into those forms that have free will and those that do not. In fact, only man possesses free will. The *mobile life-forms* of the natural world do not. They do, however, possess instinct. The designation "mobile" means that all such creatures possess an "inner animating core" *separate* from their "physical form". We can picture that "inner core" as a "power pack", the "battery in the machine", so to speak. However, because there is a huge and fundamental *inherent* difference between the *free will* of humans and the basic *instinct* of all other mobile life-forms, there is, similarly, the same great difference in the *respective kinds of animating power* contained within the "individual species".

We explained the concept of free will in the previous Chapter. Because its nature has puzzled thinkers for centuries, however, – free will being inherently necessary for any decision-making process – the *non-understanding* of what free will actually is and how it works essentially limits our ability to comprehend and deal with the many problems that beset us. Problems appear which seem to have no causal reason at times.

Immanuel Kant, (1724-1804) a German idealist philosopher, Protestant and an ethical man, believed strongly in three things; that man has an *immortal soul*, that God *exists*, and that man has a **free will**. These aspects, he believed, were essential factors under which the necessary virtue of morality could flourish. By exercising free will in his decision-making process, man moulds and shapes his individual personality in accordance with the strict outworking of certain immutable Laws, thus determining his future. The subsequent "level of development" attained is then his alone. This simple yet absolute mechanism explains how inequalities occur – why men are not equal.[1]

In order to fully understand our true nature as human beings, it is important to also understand what exactly constitutes the three main parts of the complete entity, earthman. In simple terms, they are the material or physical body, the soul, and the spirit.[2] Unfortunately, the designations "soul" and "spirit" either cause great confusion in the differences not being understood, or are thought to be the same thing.

Essentially, we can designate "spirit" as being the **innermost animating core** of man. His "spirit" is that which inhabits and drives the material body. *It is the actual animating power or force.* **The Spirit is thus the actual person!**

The soul body and physical shell are respective ***outer cover-***

---

[1] We have explained this in The Spiritual Laws of the previous Chapter.

[2] The mind and the feelings are part of the physical aspect because their contribution largely stems from the activity of the brain.

ings that *clothe* the "spirit". We may thus regard the soul as being composed of **all** the **"other-world" coverings** that **envelop** the **spirit** but is **not that** which is the **material** body. In the Ethereal World of the "beyond", however, it is the *ethereal body* that envelops the spirit. The material body at this time has been vacated.

To reiterate; The Spiritual Laws therefore decree that human beings have both a physical body and an "other-world", non-material one collectively called the *soul*. The soul, in turn, envelops the inner essence of who and what we actually are – our **spirit**. Therefore **we are spiritual beings first and foremost.** So, whilst spirit and soul are closely linked together inside man's physical form as part of the complete entity, by virtue of their different origins they serve a slightly different purpose, even though still being animating aspects of that singular entity. What we now need to know is the how and why of our spirit, the how and why of our various "coverings" of the "soul-body", and finally how they all fit together.

Now, whilst man possesses **Spirit** as his "innermost animating power", this is not the case with animals. Their "inner life force" may be designated as being *soul only*, because their ultimate place of origin stands at a *lower level* in Creation than man's *higher level* of Spiritual Origin. Therefore animals do not possess the *spiritual responsibility* inherent with a free-will attribute as does humankind, and are thus not subject to the outworking of the "Law of Reciprocal Action" in the same sense that we are.

From those brief explanations it can be safely deduced that *inanimate objects* cannot therefore possess *either* soul or spirit. What is sometimes *perceived* or *felt* around great trees and around waterfalls, or in mountains and forests, is something entirely different, which in a sense can be called "soul" but is not of the same kind.[3]

Having determined the nature of free will, soul and spirit – the Origins of which we will discover in this Chapter – the next vital step is to address the question of the Creation-process itself. Since there has never yet been complete agreement about the "origin of the world" and all that it contains, let us add our voice to the debate and offer our explanations for mankind's beginnings to try to resolve that first question that Sophie is struggling to come to terms with. The reader should thus discover for himself that the following explanations do provide clear and logical enlightenment

---

[3] This "force" is examined in the later Chapter on "Elemental Lore".

to this *seemingly* perplexing question.

From our analysis of The Spiritual Laws of Creation, in concert with the discoveries of anthropological science, traditional, cultural and indigenous beliefs that state that ancestors were "things" or "beings" other than human, should be dismissed. To reiterate, human beings are *not* descended from rivers or mountains or half-men or demi-gods that some indigenous beliefs allude to. Nor from any other form that superstitious belief or legend has dreamed up, and neither is any other race different with respect to the truth of this. Interestingly, this is not a "European" or religious truth, or even a "scientific" one. It is the Truth simply because the human form is the **only one** ordained for any creature that possesses *spiritual free will* under the outworking of **Spiritual Law** – that Law which overrides and transcends all man-made beliefs.

Let us, therefore, begin this particular part of the book with a particularly bold statement! Those souls presently living on planet earth, who have wandered *individually* for thousands of years through perhaps *many incarnations* in many *different races* have, as their common spiritual origin and therefore their true home, **The Spiritual Realm of Creation!**

What do we mean by this, and what is the *Spiritual* Realm of Creation? Is there such a place? Can there even be such a place? If there is, are we possibly "related" to all other races on earth by virtue of our same place of origin? If so, were we once all there together as different races etc., or are these "recent developments" which provide us with a reference point for our natural, physical differences? Moreover, do we all automatically return to our place of origin at earthly death as a member of "our own particular *earthly* race" as a matter of course? Or are there other possibilities?

Where and how do we find the answer to this most necessary of questions – our Origins? For there is surely little point in journeying through life uncertain, confused, even angry at vexing questions such as race, racial mix and ethnic origins. Or whether one truly belongs to one race or country more than to any other. So, in the context of this particular Chapter, where should we begin?

We know that most races, cultures and religions have, as a common theme, a story of "Creation". The myriad views expressed in cosmology and Creation-theory etc., are as diverse and as numerous as the thought-processes that have spawned them. Yet very few of the many thousands of varying ideas completely agree with each other, and will therefore not be completely correct in their *entirety*. Certainly many aspects may be similar and have elements of the truth contained within them. It would be equally true to also say that in the natural process of evolution and development, certain races would have garnered insights which would have required previously accepted beliefs of "truth" to be discarded, in the sure knowledge that the "new" contained more "truth" than the "old".

The transition to the 'new' was not necessarily without great travail and societal and religious upheaval, for man's precious ego does not easily allow him to "let go" what he considers to be his "great well of truth". Yet in the major issues relating to our origin, to our entry and exit from the earth, we remain just as ignorant and without real knowledge as we always have.

Fortunately, however, through the great Wisdom contained within The Creative Will, certain especially chosen ones unveiled the Truth to humankind in accordance with the developing spiritual maturity of the particular people into whose midst they were incarnated. Those teachings were given to mankind in a manner that could be understood by the race or nation ready to receive them at the time. This took place over many thousands of years. Man, however, could not leave the Teachings alone. He had to alter their original clarity.

In essence, the reluctance to discard precious pet beliefs reflects the inexplicable inability of mankind to leave such teachings in their pure and uncorrupted state. Rather than simply *living* the teachings as instructed, man chose to dissect them to suit his own personal wants. This unfortunate fate has befallen all the great spiritual teachings – **without exception.** Even the setting up of the major religious institutions of so-called "higher-learning" has not advanced the cause of *Truth* a great deal.

In reality, its unfortunate "dissection" has been directly responsible for the incredible proliferation of so many *different religions*, with each generally purporting to be the only true one. After being offered the great Truths, man subsequently converted them all to mere "religions". In a kind of perverse irony, if all the Teachings had been lived in a purely unadulterated way by those peoples to whom it was given, there would now only be *one single unified Teaching throughout the world today.* And that would have been **the complete Truth.**

Even though admitting to the existence of an "unattainable truth", The German philosopher, Hegel, (1770-1831) believed that "truth is subjective" and "all knowledge is human knowledge". He thus "rejected the existence of any 'truth' above or beyond human reason". He believed, moreover, that because human ideas changed from one generation to the next, there could not be such a thing as "eternal truths" or "timeless reason". In his view history provided the only fixed point that philosophy could cling to. Since history in the philosophic sense is more or less constant reflection, Hegel believed that certain rules applied for this "chain of reflections".

Thus a thought is usually proposed on the basis of other, previously proposed thoughts. However, the proposal of one thought is invariably contradicted by another, thereby producing tension between the two opposing views. That is basically the current position with regard to the Creation versus evolution debate. Hegel postulates a method whereby such entrenched positions can be "softened", so that the tension is resolved by the proposal of a third thought which accommodates the best of both points of view. Hegel calls this a *"dialectic process"*.

Unfortunately, the belief still persists that science and religion will probably never be truly reconciled, and that perhaps they should not be. However, since our purpose is to move from a simple faith/belief position to genuine conviction as to the truth of it all, the knowledge contained within The Spiritual Laws perfectly permits a reconciling of the two viewpoints. We will, therefore, in this Chapter, utilise Hegel's "dialectic process" to identify which of the respective main points of each argument can offer mutual accommodation without losing any genuine substance from either, thus merging the two into one complete and logical whole!

Classically, the subject of Creation has provided the perfect forum for completely opposing views – that of orthodox Christianity and Creationism against that of the scientific community generally tending toward Darwinism or evolution. Galileo, Darwin and others, whose findings challenged Church dogma, were invariably branded as heretics, and the polite way to reconcile science and theology was simply to agree that each would keep to its own area. Basically, science would ask and answer the questions what, why and how empirically, and the church would do the same from the religious, faith-based standpoint.

In April 1997, what was billed as the Great Noah's Ark Trial was held in a Sydney court. Whilst not a case of an "evolutionist" versus a "Creationist" in the classic sense, Dr Peter Pockley, a freelance journalist, nevertheless reported that "...the trial had pitted the belief of many fundamentalist Christians in the literal truth of the poetry in Genesis against the conclusion of science for a 4.5 billion year old earth."

In reality, there is no conflict between the two positions, as this

Chapter will illustrate. The disagreement exists only in the minds, and therefore in the *incorrect interpretations*, of the proponents of the respective points of view. Moreover, essentially *the same battle*, which we note later in the Chapter, was fought in an American State Supreme Court years ago.

So even with the current strong corporate-earth mindset today, the age-old question of "man or monkey" still produces passionate debate. Since this Chapter offers clarification of that debate, and with what we have at our disposal, let us now employ Hegel's "dialectic process" to determine where such truth lies in discovering an origin for ourselves that makes sense. Thus where science and religion blend into one, each supporting the other without conflict, as it obviously should be. For we, the human beings of earth, are the proof of this one simple reality. **We exist! We are here!**

In the evolutionist's corner, Charles Darwin (1809-1882) – once described as the most dangerous man in England because of the direct challenge to the teachings of Christian orthodoxy that his work of evolution brought proposed that "all existing vegetable and animal forms were descended from earlier, more primitive forms" via the simple mechanism of biological evolution. And that evolution was the result of "natural selection". Until quite recently science had "pushed back" and accepted a geological "birth-date" for our Solar System and the earth as approximately 4.6 billion years. Darwin thought the age of the earth to be about 300 million years. The age of the universe itself is believed to be around 14 billion years or so.

Historical anecdotes of Darwin's ideas possibly being correct actually sent shock waves through the "establishment", with even a distinguished scientist noting that it was "an embarrassing discovery", and "the less said about it the better". One "upper-class lady" expressed the hope that it was "not true", but if it was, then the further hope that it would "not be generally known".

> *"Much of the vitriol directed at Charles Darwin a century and a half ago came not from his ideas about evolution in general but from his insulting but logical implication that humans and the African apes are descended from a common ancestor. ... Along the way they [palaeontologists] learned, among other things, that Darwin, even with next to no actual data, was close to being right in his intuition that apes and humans are descended from a single common ancestor – and, surprisingly, that the ability to walk upright emerged millions of years before the evolution of our big brains."*

(Time Magazine, Oct. 9th, 2006. "How We Became Human".)

So, standing in the opposite corner to Darwin stood the Creationists and Genesis "literalists". In Darwin's time, both the ecclesiastic and scientific views were virtually sacrosanct with regard to the doctrinal idea that all vegetable and animal *species* were created only once in each and every respective form. The views of Aristotle and Plato were not dissimilar to the Christian beliefs, since they basically thought that all animal species were patterned after "eternal ideas". This Creationist outlook, in concert with the Biblical, genealogical time-frame back to "Adam", postulated that the earth was "created" about 6,000 years ago.[4]

In determining the various arguments for the "Creation versus evolution" debate, and in the context of the subject matter in this Chapter, it is vitally important to know what evolution means - exactly. There is a view in some scientific circles that evolution means "selection by random chance", and not perhaps to a precise developmental path. British Astronomer, Sir Fred Hoyle, has stated that "...believing that the first cell originated by chance is like believing a tornado could sweep through a junkyard filled with airplane parts and form a Boeing 747". Professor N. Chandra Wickramasinghe, co-author with Sir Fred Hoyle of "Lifecloud: the origin of life in the universe.", has also dismissed the evolution idea.

Overall, however, the science of astronomy believes it *can* trace the evolution of the universe – "...on the assumption that matter is created; but just **how** it is created is another problem altogether, and no theory has given indication of how this came about."[5] Yet some scientist/theologians believe that evolution provides clues to the very nature of God.

Plato, (428-347) who was basically concerned with what was eternal and immutable on the one hand and what "flowed" on the other, found mathematics very absorbing because "...mathematical states never change". Much later in the seventeenth century Galileo observed that the book of Nature "...was written in the language of mathematics". "Measure what can be measured, and make measurable what cannot be measured" was his view.

The actuality of Immutable Laws, and therefore a Creator of those Laws which *automatically* govern "His Creation", negates the

---

[4] In fact, using so-called biblical genealogy James Ussher, a 17th century Bishop, calculated that the earth "began" at 6pm, October 23, 4004 BC.

[5] *The Atlas of the Universe: Origin - or Evolution*, p 214

idea, for example, that life on earth could ever have been the result of "random-chance" development. This image does not hold up because the creative process, under the outworking of The Spiritual Laws, translates that very mechanism into precise *mathematical formulae* in the material spheres. Thus, **"The Spiritual Law of Numbers"** is also mathematical Law which can be noted in everything, everywhere.

Even the "primordial soup", produced at the birth of our planet aeons ago, had to have the appropriate formulae out of which eventually developed all the *physical* life forms and substances for planet earth. For within each of *them* will be found their own *personal-species mathematical formula*. Change the formula and you change the substance or thing; if such change can be achieved within the bounds of scientific law which, in reality, is Spiritual Law.

Since this Law provides for development, but not for alteration outside of what is possible, science, therefore, *cannot actually create anything new at all*. It can only discover things not previously known. It can, however, produce new combinations, but only from substances which *already exist*. Even then, only within the parameters of what is scientifically and therefore spiritually possible under The Creative Will.

The Bible alludes to this mathematical precision in the exactness of The Laws of Creation by stating that everything is counted and nothing goes unnoticed. As a simple illustration of this lawful truth, scientific formulae decree that only a precise number and configuration of certain atoms can form molecules of a particular substance. Change the number and a different substance is produced, or the experiment may not work. For example, one atom of copper, one of sulphur and four of oxygen will combine to produce $CuSO_4$, which will forever be copper sulphate. Copper sulphate, quite logically therefore, cannot ever be $CuSO_6$ or $CuSO_9$. In the same way common salt, chiefly sodium chloride, will always be $NaCl$, not Na_2Cl_6 or any another formula. And sodium bicarbonate, commonly used in the kitchen in the form of baking soda, can only ever be $NaHCO_3$, not Na_5HCO_7 or anything else.

Physicists have noted signs that the cosmos is custom-made for life and consciousness. It turns out that if the constants of nature – unchanging numbers like the strength of gravity, the charge of an electron and the mass of a proton – were the tiniest bit different, then atoms would not hold together, stars would not burn and life would never have made an appearance. John Polkinghorne, a former distinguished physicist at Cambridge University and now an

Anglican priest, sagely observes: "When you realise that The Laws of nature must be incredibly finely tuned to produce the universe we see, that conspires to plant the idea that the universe did not just happen, but that there must be a purpose behind it."

Charles Townes, who shared the 1964 Nobel Prize in physics for discovering the principles of the laser, goes further: "Many have a feeling that somehow intelligence must have been involved in The Laws of the universe." And the authors of "The Mystery of Life's Origin", concluded that: a ..."**Creator beyond the cosmos**"... *is the most plausible explanation of life's origins.*

On the question of evolution, other scientists sharing similar views to Fred Hoyle and N. Chandra Wickramasinghe include Colin Patterson, senior palaeontologist at the British Museum who, after believing in evolution for more than 20 years, claimed he was "duped". Charles Darwin seemingly noted that not one change of species into another is on record, and he could not prove that a single species had been changed. In 1984, the former President of the French Biological Society, Professor Louis Bounovre, stated: "Evolutionism is a fairy tale for grown ups."

On the other hand, Arthur Peacocke, a biochemist who became a priest in the Church of England in 1971, has no quarrel with evolution for he finds in it signs of God's nature. He infers from evolution that God has chosen to limit His Omnipotence and Omniscience. In his apparent view, it is the appearance of chance mutations, and the Darwinian laws of natural selection acting on this "variation", that bring about the diversity of life on Earth. Theologian, John Haught, founder of the Georgetown Centre for the Study of Science and Religion, believes this process suggests a Divine humility, a God who acts selflessly for the good of Creation.

The sticking point in this whole debate is perhaps not actually that of Creation versus evolution in any case, but probably more that of the time frame required to produce either one, or both together! For if a time period for such a thing as "evolutionary-Creation" can be logically established, then both viewpoints can be accommodated in perfect harmony. In my view, therefore, the one **key** question in this debate that must be considered – yet rarely is – is: **"Can Creation also be evolution?"** And vice-versa? Our reply is an unequivocal: **Yes, it can. And, moreover, it is!**

The simple recognition that "evolution" *can* actually be a necessary and vital part of the "Creative process" should logically develop into the clear conviction that evolution **is** the creative process. At the same time, the Creative process **is** evolution. Fact! And simply because The Will of God must inherently be both natural and logical in **all** processes. That fact also inherently stems from the Perfection of His Creative Will. Therefore, since it is vitally important to understand what we actually mean by "evolution" – or what it is supposed to mean – from our particular standpoint we shall state it to mean, and also encompass and promote, *"natural development"!* We do not mean "random selection", or anything even remotely equating to any kind of "chaos theory" either.

Unfortunately, the respective default settings of science and religion presently seem to be so irreconcilable that there would appear to be no grounds anywhere for a meaningful merger of both realities. On the one hand science seems generally to hold to a kind of "eternal doubt" paradigm whilst the basic core of religion is faith. Since a major sticking point remains the possible time period necessary to accept both the scientific and religious or theological viewpoints, these two contentious aspects will nonetheless be drawn together to show that such a merger is not only possible, but is actually the *true* position – notwithstanding the many interpretations to the contrary from proponents of both disciplines.

To begin with, the very first thing is to revisit and clarify exactly who and what we are. If we unequivocally state that our true origin is that of The Spiritual Plane of Creation, we logically imply that we cannot be purely physical in origin, just as the early Greek philosophers surmised. Therefore it may be presumed that the earth plane of the material world is not our *true* home but a *material* one for the time that we are ordained to live on it. Yet the apparently obvious reality appears to indicate the opposite. We see, hear and feel everything around us as being solid and material. To all intents and purposes, it seems logical to believe that we are *solely* material beings. Should we expect that to be the last word if our "Spiritual Origin" is *not that* of the world of matter, however? In this lies the key!

From our examination of The Law of Spiritual Gravity we know that heavier objects will sink whilst lighter substances will rise. Whilst being obviously so, it is nevertheless important to reiterate this fact again at this point. Thus, in the structure of Creation, a *material* object will occupy a lower level or plane than a *spiritual* one, simply because the higher the Plane of Creation, the finer and lighter is the substance of which it is composed. It is the same for the particular inhabitants of those respective Planes.

Therefore, only the earth of the material plane is the home of the flesh. In this material world we marvel in awe at the vast expanse that we see in the night sky. Astronomers speak of interstellar distances so incredibly immense that the human brain can scarcely even begin to comprehend such figures. We are reminded of the magnificence of such a work through the insights of the poets and philosophers in their attempts to understand our place in the universe, vis-a-vis:

> "When we consider thy heavens etc., ... What is man, that thou art mindful of him?"

A powerful question indeed, and one that we should all ask of ourselves from time to time. For in the stupendous scale of things, it is vital to understand that the mind-numbing, incomprehensible immensity of just the physical universe alone can only be the ***smallest and lowest part*** of the ***whole of Creation***. Our galaxy, on its own, contains something in the order of 100,000 million stars. The known universe, in turn, contains literally billions of such vast galaxies. The higher Spiritual Planes, by virtue of their far greater spiritually-expansive attributes, are therefore incomprehensibly and immeasurably far more immense.

If, then, our Origin is out of The Spiritual, yet our earthly existence is obviously material, the only conclusion that we can logically draw here is that we must have both these aspects contained within us, i.e. the human being is both spiritual and physical. ***And that is so!*** Only on the earth, however, can this duality be utilised. Indeed, it is the only way that humankind can meaningfully exist here at all.

For the spirit needs the material body to fulfil its purpose whilst on the earth, and the body needs the power of the spirit to animate it here also – to give it life.

Earthly death, therefore, is little more than the separating out, the drawing apart of the two; where also at this time the "spirit" *should* strive to free itself from the material world. The material shell then returns to the earthly components from whence it came in the normal process of decay that The Laws of Nature decree must take place. Hence the words of The Law, "earth to earth, dust to dust", which we hear at funerals, and which only applies to the empty, discarded shell. The process is simply outlined in Fenton's Bible, Job 10:9-12 (Italics mine.):

> Remember You made me from clay,
> That to dust You will make me return!
> And did You not curdle the milk,

> And fixed me together like cheese,
> Then clothed me with skin, and with flesh,
> And with bones and with muscles compact?
> And gave me my life and my reason,
> Then last, *fixed my **Spirit** in me*?

Accompanying the process of establishing the physical/spiritual connection is the requirement to locate relevant reference points pertaining to the respective origins of both those parts to man in order to gain the necessary understanding. To thereby learn why, in the development of man and transition to human perfection, the spirit was fixed last – as Job states.[6]

Therefore, of all the *religious* works that *purport* to have the Truth – insofar as most Western peoples are concerned anyway – The Bible is probably the best known and accepted by virtue of the fact that it is the one where the person of Jesus Christ is the key figure. Because of His particular Origin and pivotal role for humankind as documented in The Bible, we will therefore accept this book – at least among the *religious* works – as being *more able to provide* the answers we seek.

Thus, in one single, simple sentence from The Bible, both our *physical* and *Spiritual* origins are actually clearly revealed. In its stupendously far-reaching yet stunning simplicity, it **destroys** the "great divide" that religion and science have constantly promoted and clung to. We ask why?

The King James version, Genesis 2:7 states:

> **"And the Lord God formed man *of* the dust of the ground, and breathed into his nostrils the breath of life; and man became a living soul."**

Here has lain ***one part of the answer***, for centuries unnoticed, unseen perhaps, but clearly not at all understood.

Now, if this particular Scripture is thought about in purely literal terms or from solely a fundamentalist viewpoint, a picture more or less naturally arises of The Creator, The Power of All that exists, descending to the Earth and building the shape of a man out of its substance – the mud of it. Then, what would effectively be a model of a *mud-man* would be instantly transformed into a living, breathing, walking, talking, internally-pulsating human being by the simple act of being "breathed into" in the literal sense.

---

[6]Where possible we will derive those points from certain mainstream writings.

Is that the method by which one could believe man was first formed? The crudeness of such an idea is difficult to reconcile with a creative-force responsible for the Creation of the immensity of the physical universes alone, never mind the far higher spheres spoken of in all religious works. With all that we have learned about our multi-faceted world today, is there any point in continuing to cling to such a preposterous idea?

Moreover, there is a major and insurmountable problem for literal fundamentalist thinking here in that The Bible alludes to the fact that God cannot descend to the earth for it would be completely consumed by His Power. Immediately there is a contradiction, *if* we view it in a purely literal sense. Quite unequivocally, there can be **no** contradictions anywhere in the *actual Creation process itself*.

We should be very careful, therefore, not to apply any kind of heretical or blasphemous labels to an idea that may be markedly different to any current or orthodox church one. We should, instead, objectively allow the intuitive inner reason the *spiritual freedom* to determine the true nature of what is proposed here. Perhaps a wider vista might then suddenly open up offering the spirit the potential to "soar" instead of being shackled by too rigid an interpretation that refuses to allow even the "possibility" of such a thing as "evolutionary-Creation".

The much-celebrated "Tennessee monkey trial" or "Scopes monkey case" of 1925 in Dayton, Tennessee, provided the key forum for exactly this debate. A high school biology teacher by the name of John T. Scopes who taught the theory of evolution was accused of violating the Butler Act, a Tennessee law that forbade the teaching of evolution because it contradicted the account of Creation in The Bible.[7] The trial received world-wide publicity and was conducted in a circus-like atmosphere. And because of the popular belief that evolution meant humans were descended from monkeys, the press dubbed it the "Monkey Trial".[8]

Because of its far-reaching educational implications, not least for many of the scientific disciplines, the Education Department hired the famous criminal lawyer Clarence Darrow as their defence counsel, whilst a former US Secretary of State, William Jennings Bryan, appeared for the prosecution. Clarence Darrow and his

---

[7] Trials along the same theme have taken place in the USA even in more recent times.

[8] The similarities between man and the anthropoid apes evidently caused Darwin to believe that both probably evolved from the same progenitor.

team argued for the scientific validity of evolution and against the constitutionality of the Butler Act. According to anecdotal reports, and after both views were aired, the case hinged on one crucial question which Darrow addressed to the opposition. The question concerned the existence of dinosaurs and the time-frame in which they lived.

Since their existence could not be denied, the challenge and case could not be upheld. Had fundamentalism won that day, the State Supreme Court would have had no option but to order schools to teach only "the 6 days-of-Creation belief", and any concept of evolution would have been officially suppressed. The Butler Act remained on the State Statute books until 1967. Paradoxically, that court case need never have taken place simply because, as is our premise, the *evolutionary process* is actually part of the *creative process*, and naturally so. *Indeed it could not possibly be anything other than a natural union.*

Yet, even in the year 2007 of the 21st century, the science of "biological anthropology" still persists with the totally incorrect belief that it is **solely *genetics*** that has determined the so-called "evolution" of "primate to human". Researchers from the Broad Institute of MIT and Harvard have evidently coined a new "anthropological term" – **the human-chimp split**. Their ***basic*** hypothesis and time-frame *is* correct. An ancestral ape-species ***was*** the ancestor of the human race a very long time ago, **but only as the physical-form vessel, nothing more!**

Science must recognise and learn to understand the huge and fundamental difference between that ***physical/material-form of vessel/body***, and **the animating life-force within it**; i.e., within **every human being**. Only with that essential knowledge as the primary foundation for any further research – if it is deemed necessary – might the current, strong scientific emphasis on genetics and the human genome find its ***correct connection***. Rather than constantly needing to change hypotheses, this particular branch of science might, instead, begin to build *constant* upon *constant*.

So if we revisit our previous Genesis quote from the King James Bible, in Chapter 2 Verse 7 we discover therein the amazing revelation of *"the actual human/chimp split"*.

That key Verse states:

> "And the Lord God formed man of the dust of the ground, and breathed into his nostrils the breath of life; and man became a living soul."

Therein lies the *overarching answer* to the most amazing evolutionary processes that, in the most natural and logical way, *separated out the first human beings from their physical-form progenitors*. Thus, The Bible described **the real human/chimp split** a very long time ago. And human science has not yet caught up with this fundamental Truth. The detail of this singularly-decisive event for humans more fully unfolds as we continue our journey, and clarifying explanations flesh out the primary aspects.

Despite the incredible nature of what has been revealed here, it is still only a part of the complete process, albeit a stupendous one for human beings. A far *greater* revelation, however, is written in The Book of Genesis, most relevantly of course in Chapter 1. Verse 26 therein states:

> **"And God said, Let us make man in our image, after our likeness."**

Verse 27 continues:

> **"So God created man in his own image, in the image of God created He him; male and female created He them."**

Those two primary quotes from The Book of Genesis reveals, very clearly, what science and theology have not only **not understood**, but **missed completely**; **the second part of the answer**. And that is; that there are **two separate** "Creations of man". Thus, in the above Chapter **1**, we have **both** *male* and *female* beings *created*, **but not out of the dust of the ground**.

Conversely, in Chapter **2**, (our first quote) we initially have only man being formed, **but from** the *dust of the ground*. Later, after a plea for company, the Bible narrative describes the first *woman* as being *fashioned* from a rib of the first *earth-man*. All this, however, took place **AFTER** the **First** *Creation* of "man" i.e., male and female.

Is there a contradiction here? No, there is not! We have simply not at all understood what the Creation process, as described in Genesis, really meant exactly. This great degree of non-understanding has seeded the assumption for many that all this had to have taken place in the physical-material environment of the earth. Such an assumption would be perfectly valid **if** we were only and solely physical substance. Since we are not, then other realities obviously need to be considered.

So, from the standpoint of general Christian thinking, the acceptance of a single Creation-concept for the formation of man is regarded as the norm. Yet the orthodox Bible, from which the Christian Church takes its teachings and spiritual substance, clearly states otherwise. Anyone can pick up *almost* any Bible and find the same for themselves. So what should we make of this?

What we should not fear to undertake is a keenly searching examination of a possibly contentious religious issue whereby the deepest and most wonderful revelations are missed. Moreover, it should be exactly the role of the churches *in the first instance* to **fearlessly** seek out the Truth, and to immediately discard any untruths discovered. That would be the right thing to do. With **bold courage and spiritual certainty**, that is what we will do here!

At this point in our search for answers, it is timely to examine a Bible that is not accepted as possibly being "church-standard" but is, nevertheless, one which comes closest to providing what we now know to be the *correct* interpretations to the answers we seek. The following comparative passages are taken from "**The Holy Bible in Modern English**" by Ferrar Fenton. The author of this remarkable work heads the very first Chapter in The Book of Genesis with the words:

The First Creation of the Universe by God = Elohim.

This is clearly an exceptionally significant statement, and a radical departure from orthodox thinking in that Fenton *identifies* a **First Creation**. In a comparison of the relevant Verses it is patently clear that the probability of a complete and fundamental misinterpretation of Genesis regarding the Creation of man has entrenched itself in our thinking for the last two thousand years. To the point, unfortunately, where we are now too afraid to even question this possibility, and thereby completely missing what is our rightful and ordained heritage - the actual truth of our origins. So let us take the next steps boldly and examine, from Fenton's Bible, the *two* Creations of "man" in sequence.

The *comparative* verse 26 in Chapter **1** is preceded by the heading:

Creation of Man under the Shadow of God.

The verse reads:

GOD then said, "Let Us make men under Our Shadow, as Our Representatives."

Verse 27 continues,

"So GOD *created* men under HIS own Shadow, *creating* them in the Shadow of God, and constituting them *male* and *female*."

Now, very significantly, Verse 7 in Chapter 2 is also preceded by a relevant heading:

The Formation of Man from the Dust of the Ground by the Ever-living God.

Thus we have clear and unequivocal clarification of a huge and fundamental difference – the ***first*** as an ***immediate Creation*, close to** The Creator. The *second* as simply a *forming*, **very far from** The Creator.

The actual Verse regarding the *forming* of man reads:

"The EVER-LIVING GOD ***afterwards*** *formed* Man from the *dust of the ground*, and breathed into his nostrils the life of animals; **BUT MAN BECAME A LIFE-CONTAINING SOUL**."

(Some emphases mine.)

The last phrase of the above sentence should be marked well because it provides **the actual key** to a true understanding of this whole question of our origins. Significantly, **it is printed in bold capitals in Fenton's Bible**. To state once more in reinforcement – the most significant aspect is the clear and unequivocal reference to the *first* happening; with man - both "male and female" – being directly *created*. In stark contrast to the second phase, with man being only ***formed*** – and from out of the "dust of the ground". The same relative Scriptures, moreover, appear in the same respective places in both the King James Bible and Fenton's, as it does in most.[9]

---

[9] It is probably pertinent, at this point, to mention a few facts about the author of The Bible from which the last passages were taken. In 1853, Ferrar Fenton resolved to study The Bible in its original languages and to re-translate it completely into English. Fifty years later, he had accomplished his task of translating the complete Scriptures of the Old and New Testaments from the original Hebrew, Chaldee and Greek. Whilst the general thrust of the recog-

Thus far we have basically established that man is both a spiritual being and a physical one. And, moreover, further noted that only here on the earth can these "two parts to man" co-jointly exist as a single, completely whole and integrated entity. What has not been explored yet is *how* they are co-joined. Again The Bible holds the key. Since the complete process naturally implies that there had to be a beginning for man and his earthly home, this is so stated.

Let us return once more to "Sophie's World" and join her as she struggles to make sense of a concept that we may never be capable of grasping in its "living reality". That by virtue of the vast natural gulf existing between the Creative Power of all that exists, and us – the *lower **formed** entity* that is man. Such an idea is simply beyond our ability to ever comprehend.

> "They had learned at school that God created the world. Sophie tried to console herself with the thought that this was probably the best solution to the whole problem. But then she started to think again. She could accept that God had created space, but what about God Himself? Had He created Himself out of nothing? Again there was something deep down inside her that protested. Even though God could create all kinds of things, He could hardly create Himself before He had a "Self" to create with. So there was only one possibility left: ***God had always existed***."
>
> (p 8., Emphasis mine.)

---

nised story of Genesis is obviously still present, there are seemingly small but extremely significant changes to some passages, changes which throw a whole new slant on some strongly-entrenched beliefs. Throughout his work he explains translation errors, mainly in the Greek and Latin Versions, by showing where and how they occurred. Most importantly, however, the "small changes" he identifies allow for a vast expansion of perception regarding the clarification of the problem of interpreting the *time* taken for the Creation-process, not to mention the whole concept of our relationship with The Creator.

Ferrar Fenton's intuitive insight into a more logical and correct explanation of the *seven days of Creation* resulting from his re-translation of The Bible may well signal a note of warning to purveyors of the status quo and to more recent Bible translators whose own efforts may have been clouded by religious preferences rather than a purely objective and logical analysis. For the purposes of this discussion, if his re-translation of the Creation part of Genesis is correct, it might be wise to carefully consider whether this man's ordained spiritual purpose was to help bring clarification to those Christian Churches and Bible translators who still hold to the literal view of seven days for the Creation process. Fenton's re-translation of Genesis in this case clearly offers a more stupendously correct interpretation, given its ability to accommodate both the viewpoints of scientific evolution and a Creation-process in a **logical** scenario and time-frame.

Via this simple mechanism of logical elimination Sophie has hit on the only credible answer to the question. Assuming, of course, that one accepts the belief of a Creator in the first place. Therefore, from the unequivocal acceptance of that premise – *and that is the standpoint from which this book is written* – in order to have Planes of Creation to "fill the void", including the material worlds of the observable universe, there had to be set in motion a "Creation process" to bring this about.

So, through the stupendous and humanly-incomprehensible process of Creation, driven by The Power of The Creator in The Divine Ordination and Command **"Let There Be Light!"**, the Creation-process of the forming of all the worlds in all the various planes began. As the lowest and therefore last *precipitation* of all the levels in Creation – and under the outworking of The Spiritual Laws of Creation, particularly *The Law of Spiritual Gravity* – the vastness of the *material* universes also came to be. Contained within just that lower immensity, our earthly home. Thus the **void** was filled.

Because of the sheer impossibility of ever being able to picture or understand what is for human beings an inconceivable process anyway – for what words in the many languages of the world could one possibly use to even attempt to describe it – what kind of earthly example could we employ to *try* to explain *how* the separation between the respective Planes of Creation occurred? If we are able to arrive at some small degree of comprehension of *at least the mechanics of the process*, we can at least develop an inner awareness of our *true place* in Creation. That kind of recognition should also help in the understanding of what our *Spiritual purpose and thus our actual reason for being* really is.

As a very basic and crude analogy, we can perhaps relate the main points of the Creation-process to that which occurs every hour of the day throughout the world in the numerous oil refineries of the petrochemical industry. This process is called fractional distillation. It takes place in a "distillation column" whereby heat-generated crude petroleum vapour rises inside a tall metal column. At specific heights within the column, the vapour condenses to form various liquid petroleum products.

Each **different** distillate **will form itself** from the condensing vapour **at its appropriate condensing level as it cools.** This will be determined by the **weight and consistency** of the particular distillate being condensed **from the vapour at that level.** The distilled product at **each level** will thus precisely configure itself to **its own specific type of material substance**, and at its *specific temperature*.

I have highlighted particular terms in the previous paragraph in **bold italics** to help explain certain points that we will now outline. The explanation given basically accords with all such processes under the influence of gravity. Whilst this one example is earth-orientated, i.e. operating from below upwards, the process of Creation naturally works from the Highest Heights downward to the material worlds, but obviously still subject to The Law of Spiritual Gravity. Though we will never ever be able to even remotely understand this stupendous event – for even a combined distillation of the most ennobled aspects of all the world's languages could not even begin to offer a summary of words sufficient enough for the process – I believe we should nevertheless strive to achieve at least some small insight. Even a diagrammatical picture in the mind would be of value, for that is better than having no picture at all.

In the actual Creation process, then, we might perhaps envisage something approximating an unfathomably vast, white-hot mass of "downwards-moving" substance suffused with the stupendous Power of The Divine, vast enough to eventually form the incomprehensible immensity of the material universes – ***after the far greater Creation of the Higher Spheres – The First Creation***. And all driven from the immediate proximity of The Light and Power of **The Creator** through the "Creation-Words":

"Let There Be Light!"

Because of the obviously immense power and pressure in closest proximity to The Creator, only the strongest and purest of beings could come to immediate consciousness there in the planes of their sphere of activity – i.e. *closest to GOD*. At heights we could never comprehend, and certainly never ever reach in our spiritual form, occurred:

The Creation of Man in the First Creation.

Man *created* in the **Image of GOD**, (Genesis 1:27, Fenton) – and **not** man *formed* later in the **second** Creation – from out of *the dust of the ground.* (Genesis 2:7, Fenton.)

Now, basically similar to the distillation process we examined earlier, the pressure of The Power of The Light drove the Creation-process to its completion. As each **different species within Creation** found its **appropriate level of consciousness**, as determined by its **weight and consistency** – i.e. its own **specific**

gravity so to speak – so, too, could the planes for those inhabitants **form around them** in the **cooling off process.**

This process was repeated all the way down to the material worlds. The governing factors which determined those levels of forming were the same as in our oil-refinery example, the *lighter and finer* in the **Higher Spheres**, the correspondingly *heavier and coarser* toward the **lower levels**. Thus each realm formed itself at its appropriate place, corresponding to a level or plane whereby the *distance* from the Creative-Light permitted a *cooling off* and a condensing and thus an eventual *awakening to consciousness* there of that plane's particular inhabitants.[10]

Only in the separating out and cooling off stage, roughly similar to the earthly process of *sedimentary deposition*, could worlds and landscapes form in which all the inhabitants of Creation would be able to fulfil their purpose, exactly as we must do here. For we should not suppose that only in the material sphere are there worlds of lands and rivers etc. This difference is clearly alluded to in Genesis, Chapter 1, where worlds, animals and fishes were *created*, before the **first** *Creation* of *male* and *female* in the **Image of God.**[11]

And only in Chapter 2, in an incomprehensible time-frame representing the aeons-long evolutionary process concerned with the physical world of Planet Earth, do we then find the animals, fishes and birds being "...formed from the dust of the ground". Earthman, "formed" the same way – "from out of the dust of the ground" – thus enters his new world. It is a world of incredible diversity and pristine beauty.

> "And out of the ground the LORD God *formed* every beast of the field, and every fowl of the air..."
>
> (Genesis 2:19, King James. Italics mine.)

The same Scripture in Fenton's Bible states:

---

[10] Each individual happening, each minute and incremental change in the cooling off process clearly spans immense spaces and distances which, once again, we can never even begin to understand. The distances of interstellar space in the physical universes alone are simply too incomprehensible to grasp, never mind concepts of the vastly larger realms of The Spiritual – or the even greater Divine.

[11] By The Spiritual we do not mean the near-earth places that we generally associate with departed souls and occult or psychic activity, but a far greater spiritual reality. "In my Father's house are many mansions." [John, 14:2]

"Therefore the EVER-LIVING GOD, who had *formed* out of the ground every animal of the field as well as every bird of the skies, took them to the man to see what he would name them. And whatever the man with the Living Soul called them, that was their name."

(Italics mine.)

(The exact nature of the "forming" is of crucial import, for it reveals the science in the whole Creative process.)

The major difference between the lower and coarser physical worlds and the infinitely Higher and lighter Spiritual Realms is the *consistency* of the *substance* of which the *respective levels* are *composed*. Thus the First Creation is of *spiritual* substance whilst the second, out of the dust of the ground for the earth and physical universes, is obviously material.

The key point to reinforce and understand here once again is that **each level represents a different consistency**, lightest and finest in the Highest Spheres – increasing incrementally with each subsequently formed level – until the heaviest and thus lowest in the material world. Such a far-reaching concept should not be all that difficult to understand. The statement of Jesus that: *"My Kingdom is not of this world"*; reveals the sure fact that His World [*"I came from The Father and I return to The Father"*.] could not possibly be some kind of barren or filmy, amorphous expanse for He gives the strongest hint that His World is anchored in its infinitely more powerful and Eternal reality. Many of the great religions speak of an attainable Paradise if one lives one's life **based on The Laws of God** (but not, however, according to the rules of Churches and Religions.) Every Realm above the material would therefore become progressively more paradisiacal.

Quite logically, therefore, the consistency and substance of the various Planes of Creation must necessarily be the same as that of their inhabitants. This implies that each realm must also feel, and be, very firm and real for those who reside there; exactly as with humankind on earth. Any idea to the contrary is simply unrealistic. Nowhere in all the Spheres of Creation, therefore, do any of the inhabitants float about aimlessly, as is sometimes depicted in religious interpretations or films. Every inhabitant and every thing in the various planes is thus *anchored* in the *substance* of its particular "realm" through the *consistency* of the level concerned.

We have previously and unequivocally stated that The Eternal Laws operate throughout all of Creation, and the effects of The

Law of Spiritual Gravity are felt in every sphere also. The Law of Movement, too, implies **activity** – everywhere. Thus we may note the perfect outworking of those Laws in the Creative process. Understandably, however, any sudden adjustment to this kind of conceptual perception may require a leap of quantum proportions. All we need do to achieve this, however, is to use the abilities of our inner spiritual core, the real you and me. Abilities given to us precisely for this purpose, to understand our "Spiritual Origins" which are explained in this Chapter.

What about those Spiritual origins, however, that of our higher Spiritual home? Because we are clearly only developed or *formed* beings (i.e., from *spiritual* **non-consciousness** to *personal* **self-consciousness** and not actually *created beings* as with man of "The First Creation" (as Fenton reveals), we did not therefore possess the inherent strength **to awaken to consciousness** *close to GOD*. Our level of *spiritual residence*, therefore, had to be *far lower* – in a kind of second-level Spiritual Realm. Yet even at that huge distance from **The Creative-Light Source**, we still did not possess sufficient strength to take on form and become conscious of self there either.

That state of *non-consciousness* therefore meant that we would require a home of transition – a material one – in which to *acquire* self-consciousness. Quite logically, any kind of material home could only be below that of "The Spiritual Realm". And only in that lower, material world would we be able to *develop to personal self-consciousness*.

Thus, in our non-conscious state at the very lowest levels of The Spiritual Realm – our true home – we, the future spiritual human inhabitants of the earth, awaited our time to *incarnate* in the material worlds far below. We awaited the **completion of the "evolutionary developmental process" that would bring forth the appropriate physical vessel – that of the primate** – via *"...the forming of man from out of the dust of the ground"*. And into which **the immortal Spiritual aspect of man could first be placed** i.e., *"...the breathing into 'it' of the breath of life"*.

Therein lies part of the understanding of the Creation of man. And therein, also, lies part of the reconciliation of the Creation-versus-evolution debate. That contention is, in reality, a totally unnecessary argument since there is no actual reason for this division save that which the proponents of the two opposing views have "created" themselves.

The complete process still requires further clarification, however. So apart from the earth being the place of transition for our awakening to self consciousness and spiritual awareness, was there a greater purpose for being permitted the opportunity for self-conscious life? Unequivocally yes! The material paradise of our earthly home was not only the place where we would develop to personal self-consciousness but, more importantly, **where we were to learn the truth of our Origins.** We were also tasked to protect and nurture the earth and its creatures given over to our stewardship as stated in Genesis and, having achieved spiritual purity through a voluntary adjustment to The Laws of Creation, i.e. **The Rules**, we could then return, *ascend,* to our true home – The Spiritual Realm.

That particular sphere is the promised *Kingdom of GOD* for we human spirits. Thus, we are not even beings who stand close to The Creator, but just *developed* ones far from The Light. To reinforce this Truth, an appropriate quote from John 1, Verse 18 of the King James Bible notes:

"No man hath seen God at any time."

Fenton writes:

"No one has ever yet seen God;"

For the purposes of spiritual clarity, the understanding that the level of our origin lies far below that of The Divine, the "Abode of The Creator", is imperative. This fact, therefore, forever precludes us from ever personally knowing the All-Powerful Creator we far too loosely call God. The Eternal Laws unequivocally impose the completely natural barrier that a creature can only possess "actual knowledge" *as an "inherent part of itself"*, **up to** its "source of origin". It is clearly not possible for any creature to *fully understand* levels beyond, or higher than, its own beginnings.

A simple but pertinent illustration is the difference in the level of intelligence and "awareness" between animals and humans. How much greater must the difference naturally be between humans and He Who permitted us form and conscious life? To believe that we are at, or can attain to, the same degree of knowledge and power – as some scientists occasionally imply – is simply ludicrous and foolishly arrogant. Just as ludicrous is the belief among some eastern religious groups that they will one day become "one with God".

Whilst we cannot "consciously know" more than that which our level of origin would permit, we can, however, *perceive* things from above such a level, as in the case of the Jewish people's intuitive recognition of the one invisible God when most of the rest of the world at the time were worshipping a variety of idols. We also possess the capacity to perhaps roughly *visualise* levels above our origins if we are given this information from One Whose Origin is from a higher level. The tidings and knowledge of the Higher Spheres given to us by Jesus is such an example. To believe, however, that we have, or can achieve, the ability to absolutely "know" in this way is incorrect. It is simply beyond the capabilities of even our Spirit, whose actual home is from a far higher point in Creation than this lower-level material earth.

A simple test of this "truth" is to try to picture the concept of *infinity*, just as "Sophie" is attempting to do. To accept that there is a Creator logically means that there has never been a time when God did not exist. He has always existed. He will thus exist forever. We, on the other hand, need beginnings and ends as frames of reference to help in the understanding of everything connected with our existence and with time, and thus cannot even *begin* to grasp such a concept. The mind rebels and almost shuts down against such an alien thought because it has no affinity with such a far-reaching "idea". Only One who has no beginning and no end can logically "live" this kind of "infinite reality". For us, with our very limited perceptive ability, it is simply an impossible thing to grasp.[12]

For the moment, however, the problem of needing to completely reconcile the ongoing conflict between orthodox science and fundamentalist religion as to the origin of man has not yet been fully resolved. Some major points in previous paragraphs have offered many insights, but more explanations are needed. As previously stated, the real tragedy here is that this great difference of opinion exists only in the minds of the proponents of the respective opposing views, for it **cannot actually exist in reality.**

In other words, the pointless arguments that have marred this path since the initial stirrings of scientific thought brought the first rumblings of disquiet into the previously sacrosanct church view could not, quite obviously, have had *any bearing whatsoever* on the **actual** *forming of the worlds* in its stupendous scope and

---

[12]This concept may sit uncomfortably with some, though might serve to inculcate a more realistic attitude in our self-perceived relationship to the "Creator of all the Worlds".

scale, however long ago it may have been. That reality will forever stand separate from all human opinion, as it obviously must.

Continuing to rigidly and stubbornly hold to a personal or professional viewpoint at all costs, and sometimes even against the quiet warning of the inner intuitive voice, is a sad reflection of much that is wrong with humankind. Yet for the sake of a clear, true picture of our origins and for peace of mind, resolving this totally unnecessary debate is imperative. However, this can only be achieved with a completely open, fearless and enquiring mind and, most importantly, without preconceptions.

The Bible once more offers the final resolution to this *apparent* quandary. The question here is one of interpretation or, more precisely perhaps, incorrect interpretation. The standard view of fundamentalist Christianity is that the "7 days of Creation" scenario is non-negotiable, and probably because of the view that The Bible itself *seemingly* states that this is so. So strong has been this belief that it is now an entrenched and apparently immovable cornerstone for many. Rather than being a correct and thus sacrosanct anchor point for the church, it is one which causes dissension and confusion.

Clarification of a previous key quote from Genesis should help to consign this division of opinion to its proper place in the sure relief of finally knowing the answer, thereby allowing the differences to be safely expunged. Thus, in the last phases of the great Creation our world of the lower, material sphere could take on form too. As the last level of precipitation from out of the Creative process, this vast world of matter took billions of years to coalesce into roughly the form we know.[13]

That long, slow, evolutionary process eventually allowed for all material life forms to emerge, including "...the formation of man from out of the dust of the ground..." and the breathing into his nostrils "the life of animals". This is exactly what science has discovered: that incredibly long evolutionary process saw the emergence and preparation of the *physical vessel* – the development of the primate – that would ultimately house *Spiritual* man.

The preparation of the physical vessel for man is clearly revealed in Fenton's work where that particular happening is separated from the formative process by its denotation in his key capitalised phrase. The two primary events are revealed in this key

---

[13] The vast world of matter referred to here is infinitely more than that which cosmologists believe they know. Both its true nature and its size (inasmuch as can be envisioned) are discussed later.

Scripture:

> "The EVER-LIVING GOD afterwards formed Man from the dust of the ground, and breathed into his nostrils the life of animals, BUT MAN BECAME A LIFE-CONTAINING SOUL."
>
> (Genesis 2:7)

Now, if this "sacred Scripture" is separated into two parts and simple logic applied to both, we discover a crucial point. From the King James Version, the first part reads:

"And the Lord God formed man from the dust of the ground..."

This small, seemingly innocuous, part-sentence actually holds one of the key components to resolving the Creation versus evolution debate between Christian fundamentalism and science. In it is revealed the science of Creation that quite clearly equates to that aspect of the overall **Creation-process** denoting the long evolutionary development of the physical vessel – the primate – *formed from the dust of the ground* to one day house "Spiritual man".

Now the second part states: *"...and breathed into his nostrils the breath of life; and man became a living soul."* Equally clearly, the "breath of life breathed into the nostrils" *is* **the animating aspect for that physical vessel**. So simple yet so profound in concept, and so stupendous in scope and scale.

Perhaps many a reader may now recognise the correct picture with this explanation. For, as we state once more in reinforcement, the "...forming of man from the dust of the ground..." was simply the evolutionary process by which all creatures developed after the formation and cooling of the material earth. From the first minute microscopic life-forms out of the primordial soup, to the fishes, insects, plants, birds and great lizards, and thence from mammals to the first primates. Thus did our **physical-form** ancestors slowly develop to their particular zenith – the refinement of form ordained for **Spiritual-man**. A marvellous and completely logical happening quite naturally divorced from any *fundamentalist* connotations when viewed correctly.

The associated aspect of the *time-frame* needed for evolutionary development, and how that could possibly be reconciled with a complete Creation time of just 7 days as depicted in The Bible requires clarification too. The 7 days account, though accepted by well-meaning Christians world-wide, is essentially rejected by the scientific community? Even the more recent "new and supposedly definitive translations" such as The Jerusalem Bible – compiled by committees of "learned" theologians – still persist with a literal 7 days Creation-time.

The scriptural quote: "...and a thousand years are as one day..." (2 Peter 3:8) scarcely suffices to place even the smallest dent in the time period required for *evolutionary development*, given that the dinosaurs alone reigned for some 180 million years. Why, then, do such a large slice of humanity still persist with the absurd belief that just 7 earth-days – *that equates to 7 earth-days of 24hr time* **as we experience it here on earth** – accounted for **every facet of the whole Creation-process.**

Do we really believe that just a few thousand years ago, dinosaurs marched into the Ark two by two, as some Creationists are desperately striving to promote?

The true answer in this case is one of *incorrect interpretation* and non-understanding perhaps resulting from an incorrect translation of the original writings, or perhaps from simply accepting a symbolic "spiritual" term that was never meant to be so read. And then applying to it a literal, earthly point of view. It is, in effect then, *an incorrect "spiritual interpretation".*

WHAT, THEN, IS THE CORRECT INTERPRETATION?

The correct interpretation lies in recognising the fundamental differences between Chapter 1 and Chapter 2 of The Book of Genesis! The misinterpretation from Christian orthodoxy lies in attempting to ascribe two very different processes – one, **Creation**, the other, *primarily* **Evolution** – to a singular 7 earth-day Creation time-frame in Chapter 1, and attempting to also include in that time-frame the completely separate processes that Chapter 2 explains. That inexcusable error embraces the erroneous belief that the First Creation of Man – both male and female – refers to man on earth.

The scientific misinterpretation on the other hand lies in either completely disregarding the Creation aspect *as correctly outlined in The Bible*, and/or viewing Creation as a singular, material cosmological process out of which sprang the evolutionary developmental phase of the various earth creatures – including man

– *through physical/genetic processes solely.* Fenton's Bible both delineates yet also harmonises the earth-science and Christian fundamentalism points of view so completely that both are effectively neutralised in their individual positions, yet conjoined perfectly when brought together.[14]

The "7 days of Creation" – **The First Creation** – described in Chapter 1 was therefore not immediately the Paradise of the human spirits, or the earth. It describes actual spiritual happenings at heights and distances immeasurable and thus inconceivable to earthly humanity. We should therefore not become confused with the term, earth, used in the account of Creation in Chapter 1. That word ***does not*** refer to any kind of "local" association with our planet. It must be understood as a ***concept of Creation which applies to "dry land"***.

> "And God called the dry land 'earth': and the gathering of the various waters He called 'seas'."
>
> (Genesis 1:10)

In the First Creation, therefore, there are also mountains, forests, meadows, seas, animals and men – as we have previously and strongly noted – but of inconceivable beauty and perfection as prototypes for all subsequent Spiritual Creation, all of which could only come into being ***after*** The First Creation.

Thus it is stated:

> "Let the earth (the dry land) produce seed-bearing vegetation, as well as fruit trees according to their several species, capable of reproduction upon the Earth." and that was done. The Earth (the dry land) produced the seed-bearing herbage according to every species, as well as the different species of reproductive fruit trees; and GOD saw that they were good. This was the close and dawn of the third *age.*

---

[14] Perpetuated by the Christian Church, earthly science and committees of PhD and degree-toting Bible "scholars", this "triune" of earthly power and flawed education persistently clings to and continues to intellectually debate this foolish divide. Riding on the back of so-called "expert" translations and opinions, the main Bible Publishers similarly continue to reproduce the same appalling error. Despite this dreadful suppression of the truth about Creation by the "educational elite" of the "Christian" part of global humanity we, guided in the same way that Fenton surely was, will, with his essential contribution, together reveal the processes that facilitated our [human] entry into spiritual life on earth.

(Genesis 1:11-13.)

Now, what is this new and very different word – *age* – describing the Creation-process? A quick comparison of our two main reference Bibles reveals a vastly different contrasting picture with exactly that one small word making all the difference. The King James Version of Genesis 1:1 reads:

> "In the **beginning** God created the heaven and the earth."

This Bible, as with most others, goes on to state in Chapter 1 Verse 5:

> "And God called the light Day, and the darkness he called Night. And the evening and the morning were the ***first DAY***."

And so on to Verse 31:

> "And God saw everything that He had made, and behold, it was very good. And the evening and the morning were the *sixth day*."

And thus to Chapter 2, Verses 1 and 2, which state:

> "Thus the heavens and the earth were finished, and all the host of them. And on the ***seventh DAY*** God ended his work which he had made; and he rested on the ***seventh DAY*** from all his work which he had made." (Bold emphases mine)

Surely we are able to acknowledge that this word **day** is nothing more than a symbolic term for a particular "time-period", and was never ever intended to be taken literally. The example from *Verse 4* of the *same book* quantifies this premise because it states:

> "These *are* the **generations** of the heavens and of the earth when they were **created,** in ***the* DAY** that the LORD God made the earth and the heavens."

(Bold emphases mine.)

As previously stated, the literal acceptance of the word *day* in the singular here, for the complete Creation of both the heavens and the earth, and the unequivocal and clear reference to the word ***generations*** in the same creative phase, surely calls into question any literal acceptance of 7 earthly days for this whole creative process, for there is an immediate and obvious contradiction here.

In stark contrast, Verse 1, Chapter 1 of Genesis in Ferrar Fenton's re-translated Bible reads very differently:

By **Periods**[15] GOD created that which produced the Solar Systems; then that which produced the Earth.

It is crucial to understand here that a vastly different conception of time must inherently exist in spheres that are obviously non-material. The diurnal rhythm we experience here on earth simply cannot apply to such spheres, for the passing of time can only be experienced in material spheres. In Realms that are Eternal, time, as we believe we know it, simply does not exist. Time, therefore, does not *pass* there. We on material and finite earth, however, *experience its passing* every second of our earthly existence.

So in comparison with Verse 5, Chapter 1 of the King James version, Fenton states:

> "And to the Light GOD gave the name of day, and to the Darkness He gave the name of Night. This was the close and the dawn of the **first AGE**."

And so on to Verse31:

> "And God gazed upon all that He had made, and it was very beautiful. Thus the close came, and the dawn came of the *sixth age*."

And Chapter 2, Verses 1 and 2 comparatively state:

> "Thus the whole Host of the Heavens as well as the Earth were completed. And GOD rested at the **seventh AGE** from all the works which He had made."

In similar vein, Verse 4 reads:

> "These were the productions for the Heavens and the Earth during their Creation at the **"PERIOD** of their **organization"** by the LORD GOD of both the Earth and the Heavens."

(Bold emphases mine.)

And *only after* that *direct Creation* phase did God *then* subsequently *form* earthman – via a long evolutionary process – from "...out of the dust of the ground...", along with the animals and

---

[15] Fenton's translation of the word, "Periods", equates literally to, "By Headships". He writes; "It is curious that all translators from the Septuagint have rendered this word (-as-) B'reshitii, into the singular, although it is plural in the Hebrew. So I render it accurately. F.F."

birds etc.. This scenario fits perfectly with the scientific view of a very long developmental phase for the earth after its birth before even the ancestors of the very earliest primates could emerge.

It is patently clear, therefore, that the difference between an "earth-day" and an **age** is immense indeed. Simple logic should suggest that the designation of an **age** to denote a **phase of Creation** utterly stupendous and incomprehensible to human thinking in its scope and scale makes eminently more sense than the literal acceptance of an earthly 24 hour time-period that Christian fundamentalism has perhaps interpreted as meaning a Genesis **"Creation day"**.

And neither should that correct view clash with any religious interpretation regarding the awesome greatness of the Creation-process by The Creator Himself. Religious fear and blind faith do not supply answers. They only serve to perpetuate spiritually-wrong concepts with the resultant effect of producing adherents afraid to think for themselves. Perhaps the explanations outlined here may induce the tentative religious reader to become less afraid to question worrying uncertainties.

After all, how often do we hear the common phrase or variations of: *"It wasn't like that in my day!"* Generally used to compare an earlier time-period in a particular life to that of the present, the connotations here are surely obvious to all. Such references do not refer to a single day.

Even though the previous explanations offer solutions to some contentious questions, there is still the need to provide further clarification to particular points for our complete elucidation. In one area at least, however, our discussions thus far should offer the clear recognition that we, *as the complete entity man*, are **not descended from the primates**. The physical body which we inhabit today is a refinement of form that developed from the very first primates during the long and natural evolutionary process that eventually led to upright man.

Therefore, let us re-state once more that this "body-form" is nothing more than *a physical vessel only*. It is, however, one we absolutely need in order to live in the material environment of the earth. The animating power that separates itself out from the physical shell at earthly death, that some in the scientific community refer to as "the ghost in the machine"; *that* is the real you and me – our individual Spiritual core whose home and Origin is **not of the earth**.

The above explanations may also answer the question as to what happened to the many varied species of primates that disappeared virtually overnight, and why the search for a so-called missing link is a difficult one. With the entry of the human/spiritual aspect into the most advanced species, all others *striving to develop to that same point* – but who *could not provide* the necessary *strength of attraction* for the *Spiritual part of man then reaching the earth plane* – simply died out. As a natural consequence of insufficient development and the inability to compete with this newly arrived "Spiritual force" in the shape of early Spiritual man, all other primate groups that *could have* developed to become **"that particular vessel"** were rendered superfluous.

Now, whilst we have a resolution to both parts of this religious/scientific debate, **how** the human/spiritual aspect actually entered the appropriately developed primate species or group requires further clarification. For only then could the true "human being" now multiply within its own new species and thus populate the earth and develop into the world's peoples.

We have established the fact that the human being is both spiritual and physical and possesses the attribute of *free will*. It is also clear that without the *Spirit* as the animating force within the human body, the physical vessel has no life of its own i.e., it is naturally and necessarily dead. In this particular state, it follows the decree of The Laws of Nature and decomposes. It can thus be deduced that all other *mobile* life-forms of the earth, such as birds, insects and fishes etc., must similarly have an inner animating core in order to have life. Their inner core is, however, not spirit, but **soul**, from which is derived the discernment of **instinct**.

As with man on earth, animals, too, have an original home above the material world from where they draw their life-force. However, because they do not possess the attribute of *free will* – which is synonymous with *personal spiritual responsibility* – their *place of origin* is **below** that of the human spirit. That plane of origin is designated as the Animistic, or Elemental Realm; which is that of the Nature Beings and the Elemental Forces of Nature. Whilst these other *mobile* creatures of the earth do not possess *free will*, they do have the driving power of the *instinct*. This inherent attribute allows all such creatures to develop their ordained place and purpose too.

It is crucially important to therefore recognise that **up to** the incarnation or arrival of Spiritual-man, *animal-man* (earthly primate) **possessed soul as his life-force**, and quietly developed the perfection of form that was ordained to provide the vessel via which the entry of the *human/spiritual* onto the earth plane would be effected.

To this end, over the many millions of years of evolutionary development of the earth's creatures to the perfecting of the form of *animal man*, the human spirit (us), slumbering in a state of non-consciousness in the lower levels of the *Spiritual Realm*, obeyed an *unconscious inherent urge* to develop to *personal self-consciousness*. Since this could not take place there, and as a result of that "inner petition", the non-conscious spirit-seed – in terms of its individual journey – was *driven or expelled* (from out of The Spiritual Realm – the Garden of Eden) downwards toward the material worlds. **This is the mechanism whereby we ask to be born, precisely to develop to self awareness of who, what, and why we are!**

Now, as it traverses the intermediate planes below The Spiritual Realm all the way down to the Material Plane, the human "spirit-seed" – (Note: "A sower went forth to sow.") – is compelled to accept a covering or cloak of the same *consistency* as that of the plane through which it is journeying. In the great immensity of what we refer to or understand as being "the beyond", there are "many mansions" too. Those "mansions" are the Realms or levels we must traverse to get here.

Thus, the closer the *now-stirring spirit-seed* gets to earth, the *heavier* its outer coverings become. We may refer to them as the bodies or coverings that pertain to, and are of, the particular *consistency* of the *different Realms* traversed. Through this process, we become more than just an entity comprising a Spiritual core (the real us) and a physical body. In reality we possess a number of "cloaks" or coverings, each one telescoped into the other, so to speak, with each one having a different consistency exactly *commensurate* with the *sphere* or *plane* from which it is *derived*.

This *collective* covering is the *soul-body*, distinct from the inner Spiritual core. The final cloak, of course, is that of the physical body, taken on when the *Spirit*, with its enveloping "soul-coverings", *enters, incarnates* into the growing foetus of a pregnant woman under the perfect outworking of The Law of Spiritual Attraction of Similar Species. This outer physical body becomes the earthly vessel for that "complete soul body" and its "enveloped spirit".

The processes that determine whether a male or female is born in this first incarnation will have been decided by the journeying spirit's *intuitive inclination* as it travels downwards toward the material world and the earth. From an initial *non-conscious* state, it gradually begins to slowly *awaken* the closer it gets to the world of the physical. During its transition downwards, it begins to sense the life-stream currents of the various levels through which it passes.

As it descends further, it becomes more and more firm *in its inclination towards the experiences it wishes to make its own.* With this increasing certainty comes the firm decision to choose either an *active* and, therefore, *male incarnation*; or a *passive* and, therefore, *female one.* (Passive in this context does not mean weakly submissive.) Thus, the *nature of the activity it chooses* **determines its body form.**

This explains the *mechanism* of *personal* choice that *determines* whether the entity's final form will be male or female. From that point onwards, in its successive incarnations, it *can* change its outer forms depending, of course, on whether it changes its activity. Thus it is possible for a spirit to incarnate in alternate male and female bodies, which enables it to experience and develop both the male and female abilities inherent in the Spirit. However, it can also happen that such a situation generates for that individual, spiritual and emotional uncertainty as to its true ordained place. *In this explanation lies the key to the many emotional and/or psychological problems of humankind with regard to sexual orientation.* [Everything has its answer – its origin and end – under the outworking of The Spiritual Laws.]

Now the stage is almost set for the entry of the human/spiritual into the world of matter, therein to determine his future spiritual outcome. The earth, up to this point inhabited by prolific numbers of varied creatures, did not yet know Spiritual man, nor the effect that this particular creature would exert on their natural, pristine world. Unknowingly awaiting the advent of this new stranger were the most highly developed species of primate quietly furthering their role as the chosen vessels through which this event would be fulfilled.

With the unnecessary conflict between science and religion in *one* aspect of the "Creation versus Evolution" debate incontrovertibly resolved, let us complete the process by examining the *second* part of our wondrous yet contentious Genesis Verse to determine the final happening. This is tightly bound to our old friend, Verse 7, Chapter 2 in Genesis of the King James Version of The Bible. As previously stated, two distinctly separate parts to this verse can be readily identified. Quoted in full once more, it reads:

> "And the Lord God formed man of the dust of the ground, and breathed into his nostrils the breath of life; and man became a living soul."

What we are now concerned with are the words:

> "*...and breathed into his nostrils the breath of life...*"

As previously refuted, this surely cannot be taken to mean that God Himself descended to earth to literally blow His breath into a model of a mud-man. Though brief and simple, this part of the Scripture clearly depicts something else. It depicts the **animating** of the future **physical vessels** for humankind, facilitated through **"...the forming of man from out of the dust of the ground..."** That "forming" occurred quite naturally and logically during the aeons-long evolutionary process. Through those vessels – the especially prepared species of primate – man would eventually exert his new and far-reaching *Spiritual influence* in the material worlds at the ordained time for this to occur.

Now, in order to answer, from The Bible, the question of how the entry of the human/spiritual aspect into that species of highly developed primates prepared for its reception was effected i.e., those possessing a soul as their animating life-force – *animal man*) – we need only re-visit Verse 7, Chapter 2, but *this time* using Ferrar Fenton's translation of Genesis to find the *true* connection. Fenton offers that actual revelation. It is one, moreover, which gives a far clearer understanding than we have thus far found in other "scriptural writings".

So, once again we read:

> "The EVER- LIVING GOD afterwards formed Man from the dust of the ground, and breathed into his nostrils the **life of animals; – BUT MAN BECAME A LIFE-CONTAINING SOUL.**"

The *difference* in wording here from commonly accepted Scripture represents a huge leap forward in our knowledge of the understanding of Creation and may well reflect Ferrar Fenton's *intuitive* grasp of the true happening to enable him to detail it precisely, but without *actual* confirmed knowledge.[16]

---

[16] Fortunately that new knowledge is available today, hence the unequivocal and unapologetic nature of this Essay. Fenton's clearer "spiritual insight" enabling him to clarify the terrible error/distortion about Creation – so long

The fact that the evolutionary development of the *primates* necessarily required the symbolic "*...breathing into the nostrils the life of animals...*" also simply reflects the creative and actual necessity for all mobile creatures of the earth to have **an inner animating core.** Thus that which is referred to here as "*...the life of animals...*", is the ordained life-aspect that all animals must possess in order to live. It is that of *soul.*

However, the reference to the word "soul" pertaining to man in this particular translation of the Biblical account can be taken to mean "spirit", since there is clearly a fundamental difference between the life-force inherent *"...in the man breathed into..."* and **what he then became** as a result of this *"breathed-into process"*. Moreover, there is a stated delineation with the use of the conjunction – **BUT**! This can be further extended to logically mean "...**but** *nevertheless became*...". We can conclude, therefore, that this inherently logical process that Ferrar Fenton alludes to is that which actually facilitated the entry of Spiritual man onto the earth.

It thus depicts the amazing event of the *incarnation*, the *entry* of the **human/spiritual** from out of his previously *non-conscious* state in The Spiritual Realm, into the most highly developed **species of primate** then existing on earth. Similarly, the final part of the Scripture in the King James Version i.e.; "**...and man became a living soul...**" essentially states the same thing.

Spiritual man now stands on the earth!

The reader who supports Bible Scripture literally and solely may now begin to see that there is no conflict after all between the Creation account and evolutionary development since both, in their co-joined natural perfection, could only have issued from the hand of The Creator Himself in any case. Utilising Hegel's dialectic process and Fenton's more correct Bible, we have succeeded in bringing together the appropriate connecting threads from both the scientific and religious disciplines to offer the reader definitive clarification of the Creation-process.

---

accepted without question – is revealed toward the end of the "Explanatory Note" of his remarkable work and sublime 'Calling'. It now finds voice here too. To those few of his assailants who 'sneered' that his work was 'not a translation but a mere paraphrase', he writes: "The remark shows that they do not know the difference between one and the other, or a perusal of my rendering of the Hebrew of the *two first chapters of Genesis*, and my note thereon, ...would show to them the purely philological basis of my translation." (Italics mine.)

So there stands our Spiritual Origin; that of all humankind. From that stupendous happening, Spiritual man, in his material home prepared over millions of years, began his new journey of development towards personal self-consciousness and knowledge. This journey, however, would span a certain, precisely ordained period of allotted time requiring accountability at the end of it. For with his request for conscious life came the responsibility of correct stewardship of his material home; the earth and all its creatures, as was once commanded!

The division and separating out into the races, peoples and languages of the earth still lay before him. History records that stewardship as one of mostly degradation, destruction, blood and war, with few intervals of true peace, grace and nobleness. Now, however, the time of accountability has arrived. We stand in the midst of the reciprocal effect of our bad stewardship as The Spiritual Laws set about the grim task of "balancing the books". That necessary "auditing process", which we now begin to observe with some considerable degree of alarm, is effected via the increasing outworking and activity of the unassailable power of the Elemental Forces of Nature!

The clarification herein of humankind's origin and entry into the material world of the earth as home should provide meaning and insight for many readers. With clarification should also come quiet confidence and peace of mind as to who and what one really is. Here, we outlined and explained the basic happening of the coming-into-being of Creation, and of man. We accompanied him on his journey downwards, from a non-conscious spirit seed in The Spiritual Realm to incarnation and conscious personal responsibility on the earth, and thence to the employment of his free will to determine his spiritual future under the outworking of The Eternal Laws.

Naturally, we should expect that there is a lawful process by which he leaves this earth too. Whilst considerable detail is given to this process in the Parent Work, it is appropriate to conclude here with a short paragraph to very briefly outline the reverse process of his return journey, thus completing our cycle of *spiritual* life in this segment. (The reader should note, however, that this particular outline only explains the return ascent *if* The Spiritual Laws have been heeded. The process for a human spirit who **chooses** a path *opposed* to those Laws is, unfortunately for that human spirit, a very different one.)

So, upon earthly death and *release from the physical shell,* **and** *providing he has earned the right to do so,* he begins his *return journey upwards* to his true Spiritual home. As he passes *into each correspondingly lighter sphere* – **the same that he traversed on his journey downwards** – the heavier covering of the previous lower level is automatically discarded in accordance with its corresponding weight and that particular level's corresponding density. In this manner his ascent continues until, finally, he stands at the threshold of The Spiritual Realm from whence he originated.

This time, however, not as a non-conscious, unknowing spirit-seed, but as a fully conscious, purified, spiritual being – the true Spiritual Man. Here, he sheds the last cloak and is drawn across that boundary into his Eternal home, radiant in his Spiritual Purity having **earned** "...the crown of eternal life". Thus is fulfilled the invitation of Jesus who stated:

> "In the home of my Father there are many abodes. If it were not so, I would have told you: because I am going to prepare a place for you."
>
> (John, 14:2)

In order to earn this right, however, the next scriptural quote should also be accepted:

> "I tell you indeed, that you will not depart until you have repaid the very last farthing."
>
> (Matthew 5:26)

Therefore, to this end under The Laws of Creation i.e., spiritual/foundational science, we read;

> "You, however, should be perfect, as your Father in heaven is perfect."
>
> (Matthew 5:48, Fenton all.)

Given the possibly contentious yet potentially mind-extending implications of this essay, detailing the main points of the Biblical sequence of Creation here at the conclusion may provide simplified clarification via a greatly condensed overview.

Key Points

The Utterance of the stupendous Creation-Words – "**LET THERE BE LIGHT!**" – thus resulting in: **The First Creation – (The Spiritual Realms.)**

1. The Creation of the Heavens and the Earth of **The First Creation** – "By **Periods** God created *that which produced* the Solar Systems: then that which produced the Earth."

    (Genesis 1:1, Fenton.)

2. The **Creation** of day and night (in the Heavens.)

3. The division of the waters which were **under** the expanse (firmament) from the waters which were **above** the firmament (expanse.) The firmament/expanse then named the Heavens.

4. The commanding of the waters **below** the Heavens to be collected in one place, and for dry land to appear.

5. The **Creation** of flora.

6. The Creator sets two great lights which divide day and night for earth.

7. The **Creation** of fish and bird life.

8. The **Creation** of animal life.

9. Then, the great **Creation** of man **in His Image** – both male and female – and the Blessing to rule over all flora and fauna.

10. The **completion** of the Creations at the end of the **sixth Age**. The Creator rests at the **seventh Age** and blesses and hallows the seventh **day**.

Note Scripture: Genesis 2:1 (Fenton) "Thus the whole Host of the Heavens (as well as the Earth were completed.)" This is the completion of The First Creation (i.e. Spiritual Realms.) (Parentheses mine.)

And only then:

The Creation of the Worlds of Matter, including our universes, solar systems and earth – **as planned by its Creator.**

11. After the completion of **The First Creation** (**The Spiritual Realms**) including all that was then **created** (as described in Genesis 1:1-3), **The Creation of the Worlds of Matter** through a long process of evolution leading to the forming by God of earth-man from out of **the dust of the ground** who, following a suitable time of evolution, became the first human being – **the man with the Living Soul**.

(Genesis 2:19 All emphases mine.)

12. Earth-man gives name to every creature – **formed** from out of the **dust of the ground also**.

13. Even though God had **already created** "man" in His Own Image (both male and female) in **The First Creation**, and had subsequently **formed earth-man** from out of **the dust of the ground**, there was still no earth-woman. (Biblical tradition states that she was constructed from a rib of the man.)

Now, whether this sequence is viewed literally, symbolically, pseudo-scientifically or any other way, there are clear pointers illustrating a number of very different and very distinct happenings that occurred. This is clearly contrary to the one single sequence that the main churches generally believe and accept as having ostensibly **created** man/earth-man. And, moreover, him only. Fenton unequivocally delineates these separate, stupendous events in clear sub-titles.

1. **The First Creation of the Universe by God = Elohim.**

2. **Creation of Man under the Shadow of God.**

3. **The formation of Man from the Dust of the Ground by the Ever-living God.**

Therefore, if we take careful note of points 3, 4, 9, 11 and 13, and similarly note the above sub-titles 1, 2 and 3 from Fenton's translation, a vastly different and more stupendous picture arises than the present, general belief of an aspiritual humanity somehow being in close proximity to a Power that we cannot even begin to comprehend. Points 3 and 4 *on their own* here strongly indicate two different places very far apart: one above the Heavens and one below the Heavens. The Creator of all the Worlds is clearly far further from us than we might want to believe. (In any case recognition of that fact arrives to all not too long after earthly death.)

The sequence we have outlined here (from The Bible) concurs with many of the scientific findings of anthropology and astronomy. Taken in concert, both views actually trace a path of evolutionary development that is consistent with rational logic and, moreover, encompasses and co-joins both the religious and scientific points of view. More importantly, however, this more logical sequence places man (us) in his correct place very far from a Creative Force that inherently possesses the Power to Create all that we know – and all that we do not – simply by an Act of Will. In short, by the Power of Creative thought. That is a power and an ability utterly incomprehensible to us. Such stupendous Power, moreover, will forever be beyond our extremely limited comprehension.

However, instead of that particular recognition being somehow problematical for us, we should be grateful for the fact that the incomprehensible immensity of the Creations graciously provides all that we will ever need for life here – **and life eternal**. And should thus actually offer the largest possible measure of inner peace and spiritual security possible. That is provided, of course, that we voluntarily choose to – **obey the Rules!**

Therewith are the long-contested arguments of Creation versus Evolution – Christian fundamentalism versus intellectual science – **perfectly reconciled and harmonised!**

Chapter 5

The Emergence of Language – The Legacy

The Development and Spiritual Ramifications

"Spirit and language are inherently inseparable!"

Picture *Spiritual Man* aeons ago at his very first beginnings. Into the environment of the physical world, he takes his first faltering steps. The earth thus far has only known the activity of the animal kingdom, countless millions of different species interacting in perfectly balanced cycles of life, and each with its own particular call. Some loud, raucous and dangerous, others mellow and sweet. All contributing to the symphony of the earth's natural sounds for that time, however. The voice and languages of man would be a new sound, an intrusion perhaps? Yet one that held the potential for noble enhancement, or vulgar coarseness.

The rich diversity of man's languages was still far in the future. Before that could happen, this new addition to the world's creatures would need to develop into a fully-fledged human being. For it was not *fully developed* human spirits that incarnated into the most highly developed anthropoids that were prepared for this event, but *spirit-seeds* from The Spiritual Realm, the actual "home" of Spiritual man.[1]

They had first, therefore, to develop into individual personalities in the World of Matter. As formerly stated, the physical body

---

[1] Consider the parable: "A sower went forth to sow..." Matthew 13:3

of man is, indeed, derived from the animal, but the inner animating core is from the higher Spiritual Realm. Thus the "receptacle-body" for those *spirit-seeds* necessarily underwent a fundamental and far-reaching change with the arrival of the human-spiritual aspect into it. In place of the previously existing animistic *souls* which were the "driving energy" inside those "ordained forms", the new inner animating "life-force" of the human *spirits* now became established in their place through incarnation into the prepared vessels – the most highly developed anthropoid forms. So, in accordance with that requirement, male *spirit-seeds* or spirit-sparks incarnated in animal bodies of the male sex, and female *spirit-seeds* in those of the female sex.

Leading on from these very first incarnations, continuing incarnations of human spirits could now take place through the natural procreative process under The Law of Attraction of Similar Species. This process resulted in the demise and extinction of those groups of anthropoid apes which did not develop to a level sufficient to *attract* the human-spiritual aspect then preparing for its entry into the material world. Anthropologists have discovered that in the early history of man, a number of branches of the "anthropoid family tree" terminated for no *apparent* reason. Thus preventing any further "transmigration".

For that species which was successful, however, the ensuing entry of human spirits naturally permitted the next stage of development for it. This great evolutionary change from animal-man to spiritual-man thereby allowed for the development of that originally-prepared, select anthropoid form, to our more refined, present-day physical form.

With the arrival of The Spiritual into the animal bodies, a critical event occurred for this new race called man. **This was the concomitant development of human language.** It was a singularly evolutionary event of huge proportions with obviously far-reaching implications. The inherent urge of the human spirit to seek communication with others gave vocal expression to his thinking, volition and intuitive perceiving, and allowed the formation of the organs necessary for this. To this end an important and closely-linked change took place in his physical form, clearly demonstrating the difference between man and animal, a difference only discovered relatively recently.

That vitally important distinction was *the gradual sinking downwards of the larynx*. In the world of the animal, but more especially that of the apes, there was no change in the position of the larynx. Only through this *sinking of the larynx*, this re-positioning of that organ of communication could the *simultaneous forming of the human shape of mouth and nose* occur. That crucial event made possible the complete voice and vowel reproduction that is probably the defining and characteristic feature of humankind.

The development of the organs of speech permitted communication between members of the budding human race. The projection of only the most basic sounds in the beginning, to eloquent oratory and abstract intellectual theorising in the later millennia of his grand march forward, was not an instant happening, however. This process of development necessarily required a long period of time as humankind formulated new words to "frame" ever new discoveries and new and evolving concepts to add to his continually developing vocabulary.

For it should not be supposed that spiritual man arrived on the earth with the innate and automatic ability to instantly converse with great skill and eloquence from an inherent vocabulary of already known words and some form of pre-programmed meanings. If we accept the literal interpretation of the forming of man from out of the "dust of the ground", then we *may possibly* accept that scenario. However, that is not the reality. In our part of Creation, evolution and development are the norm rather than the exception – in both the great and the small.

Therefore, the development of sufficient skill and ability to enhance the medium of speech as an effective means of communication from simple interchange, to more complex discussion, to the area of conflict resolution even, could not possibly be attained in just a few short years. The process was necessarily long and exacting, and probably in concert with the parallel development of larger and larger social groupings.

Interestingly, however, this process of speech development and vocabulary acquisition which, for man, took hundreds of thousands of years, can be seen *in one single lifetime* anywhere in the world in the natural growth of children from babyhood to the teen years. Therefore, today, when a new-born begins its earth-life with a cry, and through the process of imitation learns to speak within the first few years, it undergoes all the stages of development which humankind necessarily underwent over that long period of time. This is achieved by the sinking of the larynx and is repeated with each new birth. Research since about 1905 has allowed embryologists to establish that this "descent of the larynx" begins at the end of the first year of life and lasts up to the eighth or ninth year.

Lieberman and Crelin, in their essay, "On the Speech of Neanderthal Man", state this same process in rather more technical terms:

> "Of all the living primates only man has an extensive supralaryngeal pharyngeal region that allows all of the intrinsic and extrinsic pharyngeal musculature to function at a maximum for speech production by changing the shape of the supralaryngeal vocal tract."

(Negus 1949, p 216)

Lieberman's study of the anthropoid apes and of the other apes, including macaques, has shown that "...they are denied the true, correct vocalisation: simply because they do not experience the descent of the larynx."

Consequently this "...descent of the larynx to its lower position in adult man.", would thus confer "...advantages in communication." Interestingly, Lieberman and Crelin also state:

> "The adult human laryngeal position is not advantageous for either swallowing or respiration. The shift of the larynx from its position in New-born and Neanderthal is advantageous for acquiring *articulate speech* but has the disadvantage of greatly increasing the chances of choking to death when a swallowed object gets lodged in the pharynx... The **only function** for which the **adult vocal human tract** is better suited is **speech**."

(p 218, Emphases mine.)

Thus, via this "shift-mechanism", a space is formed at the back of the throat, one which the anthropoid apes (and all other apes) do not have. It is a space necessary for the utilisation of our freely moveable tongue to make the very fine movements required for vowel vocalisation. In essence, it is a true vowel space. It can therefore be clearly seen that the formation of our own human language, especially of the different vowels, is only possible with this "vowel space".

In the opinion of these two researchers, Neanderthals possessed an essentially non-human vocal tract, but probably made maximum use of his large brain to establish vocal communication. That utilisation, in their view, would perhaps "provide the basis for mutations that lowered the larynx and expanded the range of vocal communication in modern Man's ancestral forms." (p 218) With regard to the time-frame required to perfect vocalisation skills, Lieberman and Crelin observe that with this stage of man's evolutionary development, particularly his speech:

> "...limited phonetic ability was probably utilised and that some form of language existed. Neanderthal man thus represents an intermediate stage in the evolution of language. This indicates that *the evolution of language was gradual*, that *it was not an abrupt phenomenon.*"

(p 221, Italics mine.)

They state: "The reason that human linguistic ability appears to be so distinct and unique is that the intermediate stages in its evolution are represented by extinct species." (p 221) They further state: "Fully developed 'articulate' human speech and language appear to have been comparatively recent developments in Man's evolution."

From our particular perspective we note their view that: "They may be the primary factors in the accelerated pace of cultural change." Their research into Neanderthal's linguistic ability coupled with this observation is, in their opinion, "...consistent with the inferences that have been drawn from the rapid development of culture in the last 30,000 years in contrast to the slow rate of change before that period."

(Dart 1959, p 220)

The conclusion can be reached that man's ancestral form, which has quite clearly evolved from some basic shape close to that of the apes, was similar in configuration to the vast majority of mammals, in that the epiglottis reached right up to the palate. Thus why the **Spirit** was necessary for man to begin the process of language development, which parents can observe in the first few years of their own offspring's development. The simple yet unequivocal logic contained in this process should offer greater certainty as to the how and why of our early development, and serve to further strengthen our assertions on humankind's origins in the previous Chapter.

Despite the clear conclusions reached by these two researchers, science still persists in trying to establish a language-potential in primates. Dr Tecumseh Fitch, recently writing for the journal, *Science*, noted that the key principle common to all human languages is beyond monkeys. They could not encompass complex rules called "phrase structure grammar" that underpin every human language, he said. These findings clearly show a sharp limit to the ability of animals to engage in open-ended communication. Because studies had shown monkeys to have a rudimentary grasp of grammar, scientists had hoped they could master more complex language. Research by Dr Fitch and Professor Marc Hauser from Harvard University suggests this was wishful thinking. Working with cotton-top tamarins, a New World monkey species, the scientists found that the tamarins were able to perceive the breaking of simple grammar rules, but were oblivious to more complex violations.

Clearly Tamarins cannot master language. It is simply impossible for primates, both apes and monkeys, to reach any evolutionary point whereby speech could naturally develop. And despite the fact – reported in the "Independent" – that Dr. Nancy Minugh-Purvis, an anthropological scientist from the University of Pennsylvania, has discovered a gene responsible for the heavy jaw muscles in primates to have been "switched off" 2.4 million years ago – thus permitting a lighter jaw and concomitant enlargement of the brain case in the probable branch of our human ancestors – such "scientific" findings in no way change the absolute parameters required for speech. That specific requirement is inviolable. The ability to speak requires the animating power of the "spirit", an attribute which only human beings can, and do, inherently possess.

Therefore, for science once more, it is impossible for animals, even monkeys and apes, to possess the innate ability to "speak". It is only through **the power of the spirit**, the inner, animating core of man, **that permits him the ability to do so**. Animals, who possess **the inferior animating core of soul**, *cannot ever*. **Those are the Rules from out of The Laws of Creation!** Lieberman and Crelin have already scotched any such possibility.

Does science really believe that "new scientific discoveries" can somehow circumvent or change Inviolable Law?

So, back to our journey: In those far-off days of man's humble beginnings, how did the forming of the language proceed? Spiritual man was like a baby needing to formulate new sounds to be new words with distinct and clear meanings. In their evolutionary physical development, the posture of early man gradually changed from a bent ape-like one as they walked, to the upright stance we have today. As the larynx descended and the human mouth developed to its present shape, the initially hoarse and probably guttural sounds would have gradually become much more clear vocally. In the beginning, humankind probably communicated with familiar gestures and sounds gleaned from the natural world around them. Individual sounds would then become groups of sounds which became words. These words subsequently became sentences. The ability to produce whole sentences allowed for the extension of the language, with the eventual capacity for far greater expression.

As we explained previously, each *word* became the actual *form* of that particular *sound*, evoking a clear and concise *picture* as to its *meaning* in the minds of all who heard it. This was man's great responsibility in being given the gift of speech – to use the formative power of the spoken and written word to *upbuild*. Unfortunately it has too often been employed for the opposite. Today, with many thousands of languages and dialects scattered throughout the world and its peoples, the spiritual power inherent in the formed word is no different now from what it was when man took his first, hesitant vocal steps into what was his spiritual future.

What is important to realise is that language was intended only for the good. Yet our historical record clearly reveals thousands of years of wrongful application by humankind. Therefore, because every language has the same relative or comparative degree of power for the race that is using it, all languages should be treated as a spiritual gift offering the most wonderful of means to express, in a precise and specific way, all that a race, culture, or nation is capable of attaining. Thus the medium of the "spiritual power" inherent in all speech and language decrees that we not only produce all our *works*, but we actually also ***"form"*** our particular cultures.

A fine example of the power of correct use of language from a much earlier time can be noted in the great philosophic debates of the Greek and, to a lesser extent perhaps, the Romans. This power they understood well.

> "Then there is the marvellous and godlike gift of speech. Do not you Academics call it 'the mistress of the world'? Through speech we are able to learn things of which we would otherwise be ignorant and to impart what we have learnt to others. Through speech we can encourage, persuade, console the sorrowful, dispel the fears of the terrified, restrain the headstrong, cool anger or lust. It is the power of speech which has bound us together in the bonds of justice, law and citizenship. It has raised us from a life of brutal savagery.
>
> It is almost incredible to those who have not studied the

subject what pains nature has taken to confer on us this gift of speech."
(The Nature Of The Gods, Cicero, Book 11, p 183)

It is shameful that we in the 21st century have allowed language to be divested of its inherent power for spiritual elevation through uncaring attitudes towards it. The slovenly practice of "txting" in this electronic age is a prime example.

Whilst it is clearly an aid and time-saving device, what is not at all understood is the Spiritually-Lawful and inviolable relationship between individual letters – one to another – and the subsequent building of those letters into words, and thus the **forms** produced. Shortening words for convenience **changes** their form, and their subsequent effect on the world. The whole insidious process is, in the final analysis, one more serious transgression against immutable Law. In this case, that of **The Law of Numbers**. Txting, too, will add its unfortunate share to the final cleansing event!

Nonetheless, the momentous potential in the transitional effect of animal-man becoming spiritual-man would be that which the power of the spoken and, in turn, the written word would spiritually exert on his world. Not just on the earth, but in his part of Creation also. However, man would tread many diverse paths, produce much offspring and people many lands before the full and generally unfortunate impact of this "speaking ability" could be gauged and measured. Separating out and populating the different parts of the earth guaranteed the formation of new languages with new words to give name to newly-discovered flora and fauna, along with sights and sounds not seen or heard before.

Via this vital and stupendous evolutionary happening, the way was now cleared for spiritual man to begin to record his exciting yet sometimes painful journey through "history". The establishment of "ground rules" whereby these small bands of "new humans" could consolidate and begin to prosper, would be an obvious advantage. In a very quick journey of compressed time, we can visualise the emerging family groups banding together to form larger, clannish organisations. This would serve the purpose of increasing their chances of success in hunting and for gathering food, provide protection for the group and allow for greater social development. Continually expanding groups would also prevent the possibility of inbreeding, which would be a consequence of maintaining a small group for any great length of time.

The slow, gradual process of building groups of families into tribes, and tribes into confederations of tribes and so on, until whole nations and races became fully established across the ancient "known world", would occupy a span of many, many thousands of years. The primary medium of communication, the language, would provide the pivotal role in this process. Language offered the means to formulate practical, working rules to maintain cohesion and harmony in the growing organisations, vital preparation for the very much later and more difficult task of governing empires stretching across many lands. That was a long way into a very distant future, however.

Incidental to this procedure, therefore, was the requirement for expanding groups to seek new lands and territories – sometimes far from their origins – thus giving rise to the establishment, over time, of a different language from that of the old homeland. One perhaps similar, but perhaps not. Even with this diversification, however, certain elements in the languages of particular ethnic groups were retained as the basic root-foundation, thus indicating a common origin which we can trace today – particularly within the Indo-European group of people. Most Indian and Iranian languages belong to this Indo-European family of languages. Some Asian, South American, and Pacific Island languages share similarities also.

Humankind's territorial expansion did not result in an equal and uniform level of language development among the increasing numbers of different races and nations, however. For example, races that were more concerned with merely the basics of life and with a limited view of the world naturally developed a simple language that reflected limited knowledge about fewer things. That was not the case with people who were developing more technological societies. Thus the different, emerging peoples began to develop their own particular culture and characteristics in concert with their language. Some qualities would already have been inherent in the respective core group, but certain other traits would have developed as a consequence of various factors affecting their development, such as environmental ones for example. For each group, however, every phase added to their respective store of knowledge and word-usage over-all.

Environmental aspects such as a warm or temperate climate with favourable food-producing conditions might allow an emerging race the luxury of food surpluses for trade and, therefore, the accumulation of wealth. A colder or harsher environment enforces the need for a more or less constant survival attitude with perhaps less scope for large-scale trade activity. It is not surprising therefore that, generally speaking, the earlier, more advanced civilisations first emerged in the warmer, more fertile regions of the earth, notably around the Mediterranean, North Africa and the Middle East, and in parts of China, India and South America. Of course, favourable climatic conditions were not the sole reasons for such an emergence. An inherent questing and technological bent were also required, since some societies in other warm climes remained basically simple and tribal.

The acquisition of food was always the primary need of man, with shelter being a close companion. Climatic factors would naturally be a strong determinant here too.[2] If, then, the question of food and shelter in a "friendly climate" is resolved to the point where it does not present a problem and allows time away from the activities of food gathering – hunting, fishing or agriculture – this "spare" or "leisure" time from such activities can then be channelled to other pursuits.

Dwellings, for example, which may have begun as rudimentary shelters could then be expanded to become much more comfortable and elaborate homes. From humble beginnings later gradually arose the great civilisations featuring large, planned, paved cities with public buildings, places of worship, and even piped water etc. In terms of language and vocabulary extension, this "expansion of the people" allowed the intellectual aspect of the race to evolve toward greater expression of abstract thought and philosophy.

Maslow's "hierarchy of needs", defines this process in latter-day "psycho-babble". Abraham Harold Maslow (1908-1970) developed a theory of "motivation" which describes the process by which an individual progresses from basic needs such as food and sex to the highest needs of what he called "self-actualisation". In his opinion, "humanistic psychotherapy", usually in the form of group therapy, was the best way to help the individual through these stages.

We would opine that the better, simpler and more sure way to achieve that desirable state is to embrace The Spiritual Laws and live by them. Self-realisation (or "self-actualisation") derived from *genuine* spiritual knowledge and awareness would produce a more beneficial and natural outcome from such a decision.

The overall drive, energy and population levels of the various emerging races might well determine who would become the greater nations and empire-builders – as opposed to those who would be administered or absorbed by others. The establishment of larger

---

[2] It is certainly a truism, that it is easy to be a conservationist until one is cold or hungry!

groupings of peoples into complete nations by the most energetic or magnanimous races might mean a correspondingly faster level of development of their administrative and building skills than perhaps those who were simply conquered or enslaved. History records the fact that some groups simply became slaves or servants of the strong.

Generally speaking, the languages of the "empire-builders" flourished as a result of continually evolving capabilities. This expansive attribute now developing in those particular groups allowed for the subsequent emergence of a different way of thinking and speaking. Literature, religion, poetry, music composition and art gave impetus to a large degree of elevation in the language. Abstract or intuitive ideas and views became the science of philosophy which required the development of a whole new vocabulary to clarify such thinking. This process quite naturally took some considerable time. Did the language development of humankind, however, proceed in accordance with the design of The Creator Who, under the aegis of The Eternal Laws, granted us human spirits the gift of conscious life? Since this work is concerned with that "reality", it is important to examine this question further.

Early man still retained contact with the non-physical world from whence he came, thus holding an innate understanding of his connections there. His "spirit", guided by that still-clear connection to those other realms and to higher Spiritual Teachers led his thinking and intuition. Consequently, the forming of words proceeded in accordance with the power inherent in The Laws of Creation. With clear guidance and strong, intuitive perception, man was able to give the *correct spiritual form* to all that he gave name – remembering that The Spiritual is actually the *foundation* for all that exists in the material. The non-material or abstract concepts also received their particular *word-coverings*. They, too, *resonated* with their *correct spiritual meanings*. So as long as men "built" their language *spiritually* in the early epoch of development, they received the "reciprocal returns" of peace, happiness and advancement, since all forms of ennoblement are founded on The Eternal principles and application of The Spiritual Laws.

Unfortunately, in the course of man's development, the purity of his previously strong intuition and volition began to falter. This was brought about by strengthening the use of his intellect to a point where the necessary balance between the spiritual and intellectual aspects within him tipped more decisively toward the intellectual side. Consequently, that original, clear guidance suffered because a natural barrier was erected which blocked the formerly strong connections. The language *subsequently formed* began to degenerate under the power of the greater and denser *materialistic thinking*. Through this event man *severed* his connections with the lighter Spiritual Realms of his origin and became enmeshed in darker thinking which was alien to his spirit. Increasingly *cut off* from the knowledge of its origins and walled-in by the *all-dominating intellect*, his **spirit** could no longer exert sufficient influence to alter his newly-chosen, aspiritual course.

This was the "great fall of man." Referred to in many legends and religious writings, the actual fall *was the placing of his* **intellect** *in the* **leading position** with the subsequent relegation of his **spirit** to an *increasingly* **reduced** *role*. Thus, a **turning away** from The Creator and His Eternal Laws. This definitive happening in the evolutionary history of humankind is depicted in The Bible as the story of the building of the tower of Babel which resulted in the great "confusion of tongues". (Genesis 11:1-9)

The story of the Tower of Babel denoting the *scattering of the languages* should be viewed, in the first instance, as a *spiritual event* describing a process that, in this case, was **not** primarily a *literal* building of a tower to heaven. It is vitally important to understand the true spiritual meaning of this happening. The edifice of Babel was a tower of *arrogance and presumption* fuelled by man's personal ego through his greater and greater disregard for The Eternal Laws. More especially in relation to language in this case. What should have been retained and developed further was *spiritually appropriate employment* of correct word usage. By choosing an opposite path, a confusion of the language gradually spread to all of the world's peoples.

This should not be interpreted to mean the development of many *different* languages, for *this would have been the natural situation in any case*. That was not the problem, and not the process. Neither does it mean that communication between the various peoples with their different languages would necessarily have been difficult either. The "scattering" represented far more than just simple, physical differences in word-sounds, structure and meaning. In reality, it was an event of decisive *spiritual* proportions!

Men no longer *understood* each other because the spiritual qualities of honesty, nobleness and purity that were the hallmark of the early development of the *form* of the language, underwent drastic change. Disregard for The Laws of God brought about a fundamental and far-reaching shift in the "kinds of forms" *created* by collective humankind. These new, *mutated forms* of pride, ego, selfishness, personal advantage and disregard for their fellow-men, became the normal produce of mankind. In that process is revealed the meaning of the *"scattering of the languages"!*

With that event, a wrong volition and attitude entered the earthly languages. Words appeared which had not until then existed, and which were alien to the pure volition of the first human spirits. Words that were dark and evil, words formed from out of the evil deeds and thoughts of men. Like an insidious virus it spread throughout the languages of the peoples. Through this process, all the evil that can possibly occur in this world was inflicted by humankind upon one another over the thousands of years since. In accordance with The Spiritual Laws of Creation mankind had no choice but to give name to each evil, because the various *forms* produced *arose within us human beings* - exactly *corresponding* to our *free will* choices. [3]

Thus today we can readily see the culmination of all those past errors. The spiritual transgressions against the language which humankind thoughtlessly engage in clearly reveals how it is misused more and more through meaningless rubbish, empty talk and evil thinking. Ever more carelessly the meaning of words is distorted, particularly under the now socially accepted standard of "political" or "cultural correctness" and crass political power aspirations. This insidious process is just one of its soiled shields, and even debate in the various political chambers of many countries – the very place where one would expect such standards to be, at the very least, upheld - sometimes degenerates to foul-mouthed mud-slinging.

The high concepts of justice, love, purity, truth, humanity, freedom, peace and faith, whilst still bandied about, no longer hold the elevated position within society that even a few short years ago they would have. In accordance with man's present nature, he imputed to those ideals insidious meanings corresponding more to his increasingly selfish, material goals. Aims far removed from the pure application that these inherently noble concepts actually mean and represent.

It should thus be perfectly clear to any keen observer that the degradation of the language and its latter-day use conclusively reveals the depths to which we have *voluntarily* fallen. Once the "darker deeds" and the associated "growing evil" had given birth to the **living form** *of the* **words** *connected with the* **deed** and en-

---

[3] "Tower of Babel" insights sourced from "A Gate Opens" by Herbert Vollmann.

tered the *language* of the race, both these aspects became *alive within that particular race*. The whole then became a "dark well" into which all could dip and drink, with the "forms" even becoming "culturalised" and perhaps deemed to be "politically correct". And the true magnitude of this "terrible disaster" is not at all understood – or even recognised.

Thus, today, the language has, to a large degree, become befouled, evil and ugly with even the youngest children contaminated. But who really cares? Very few. For all of humanity have fallen away from the pure connection to the higher spheres that were once enjoyed in former, more spiritually-enlightened times. A time sometimes referred to as the "golden age of man". Thus words used to describe dark and evil deeds within any language are clear proof that such things are an inherent part of that particular race, since those members, alone, have spawned the deed and its associated "living word forms".

Consequently, the objective examination of any language will quickly reveal the true "inner condition" of the "collective soul or spirit" of that particular race. Whilst all languages inherently encompass concepts and "forms" of enlightenment, the balance scales of all races are also clearly weighted toward baseness too. Some more so than others.

Therefore, when speaking of the "fall" of man we should intuitively understand this to be his "spiritual" fall, which we should clearly recognise as the loss of the once sacred, strong and necessary connection to The Source of Life. By supplanting the *spiritual* part within us – the *leader* – with the *intellectual* part – the *assistant* – we could do little else *but* fall away. The difficulty in redressing that balance today is exacerbated by our *inability to recognise* that this adulation of the intellect **actually constituted the fall of man *to begin with***. That inability, in the strangest of ironies, is caused by our too-strong a reliance on *that very intellect*, in the belief that it, and it alone, can provide all answers and solutions. Unfortunately, that is what is directly responsible for the worsening problems of humankind. As a further irony, the propensity of "modern man" to want to "intellectualise" everything – even *spiritual* matters – would *not have been possible without the means of the language* to express such incorrect and inherently unworkable concepts in the first place, the forms of which are now very self-evident.

A sharp differentiation should be made here between the more natural, intuitive beliefs associated with genuine knowledge and

Truth, and the need for earth-sciences to utilise that intellectual talent and ability to actually construct workable concepts for the benefit of humankind. Despite the obvious need for intellectual input into earthly existence, the fact that the intellect is *unable* to recognise spiritual truths because of its ordained purpose in fulfilling the earthly or material task, modern intellectual man *has lost the very means* by which he can *actually* and readily recognise Spiritual Truth in the first place, i.e. via his spirit. A spirit now paradoxically very much suppressed by the all-powerful and much-lauded intellect.

As probably the best example of the power of language to initiate sweeping change down through the centuries, we need look no further than to the influence of Jesus Who was sent to this earth to guide mankind back to knowledge of the Truth. As previously stated, in accordance with the "Law of Attraction of Similar Species", He could only incarnate into a race that had developed sufficient spiritual insight to intuitively accept the "reality" of the One Invisible Creator. So it was that Jesus was born, by Law, into the Jewish race, a people with the necessary level of spiritual development for this connection to be made. A people, moreover, whose law and language, through the admonitions of their many prophets, clearly reflected that understanding.

As we have already noted a birth into any other race could not have been possible – aside from being totally pointless. Only a people with some degree of even symbolic affinity or understanding could prepare the way for a Being Who stands far *above* The Spiritual even. The language and spiritual form of the "Torah" basically provided the bridge. The entry and purpose of Jesus in the world gave man a far different perspective of the power of language through His use of it in the purest, spiritual way. His whole ministry was remarkable for the fact that He taught the Truth via the medium of the *spoken word* and not that of the written. Thus the "living power of language" is best illustrated in the manner in which Jesus "spoke the Truth", and its resultant and undeniably powerful effect upon the world.

However, even this stupendous event and help from Above still did not change man's basic intransigence toward the pure truth given at that time. The distortions and errors caused by the "playing with the language of the Truth" have caused great confusion, particularly among the numerous Christian Churches.

Another distortion, ultimately no less important than that of the words of Truth handed down to humankind, was that associated with the "gods of legend". Through the unfortunate development of greater intellectual sophistry in the new peoples collectively, the original strong and natural connection to, and knowledge of, his spiritual origins became more and more clouded as the intellect grew disproportionately more influential. The inevitable result saw spiritual man's once secure ties to his higher origins virtually severed. And with it a particular and vital connection that was meant to be an ongoing and special help in his earthly activities for all the time of his earthly stay.

In the beginning, he lived his life completely aware and accepting of the other-world (ethereal) currents around him, and of his connections to what we term the "beyond". More importantly, he worked in concert with other beings who have their origin in another plane of Creation and who are active not only on the earth but in every other Realm of Creation also. Indeed, without their essential activity, man would never have had an earth to call "home" in the first place. Today, only a very few people scattered throughout the various races have the ability to still see these "helpers", even though we all see and feel the effects of their necessary activity every minute of the day. These are the "Nature Beings" and Elementals whose names are found, *virtually without exception*, in the languages of all races on earth.

This cutting away and rejection of the "Elemental Forces of Nature" through the elevation of the intellect guaranteed that a huge gap of knowledge would develop in the history of the peoples. Some would consciously retain this knowledge longer than others. In virtually every case, however, what was once sure and certain truth, securely and knowingly embedded in the languages of the various peoples, eventually became relegated to the realm of uncertain myth and legend. Rather than being retained as clear knowledge, it was transposed into just the "culture" of the race.

Some of the more intellectual races, notably those from Western cultures, have virtually severed this connection totally, not even bothering to retain them as fables in the culture. The so-called more primitive or not-so-advanced races have at least retained a strong belief in the validity of their legends as possible truth. Unfortunately for Western Nations generally, their god of science has determined that such "notions" cannot possibly be entertained as belonging to a "rational, logical and intelligent" society. Interestingly, however, the main book of their religion, The Bible, speaks of them quite clearly. Thus the relegation of what was once accepted as factual knowledge to the realm of myth and legend by "intellectual reasoning", is to our detriment. Notwithstanding this particular path, the many languages of the world's various peoples still bear testimony to a time when man accepted the evidence of his factual experiences, and thus gave name to all that he knew existed in the Elemental World of Nature.

As previously noted, the rightful place of the intellect was to facilitate and assist man in the fulfilment of his *earthly* duties, which is why it is vital for scientific endeavour and why it has produced such technological marvels and great feats of construction. In those particular endeavours the language naturally provided the exact parameters by which this aspect of man also developed. As ordained from the very beginning, however, the spirit was to lead and the intellect to assist. Sadly, spiritual man, with the potential for achieving true greatness in the material world and in Creation, became merely intellectual man more concerned with earthly analysis and theory. Paradoxically, greater spiritual activity would have produced correspondingly greater intellectual works.

Ironically for modern-day man, the purpose of science was always to explain - via the language of course – the workings of all the "Spiritual Laws" and their effects in the physical world. By this process, man could re-discover his true place in Creation. Instead, he denies for himself the very knowledge and connection that can bring about that re-discovery – his spirit. Now, instead of a powerful, uplifting, spiritual language at our command we have, in its place, only a weak shadow of what it should be, thus **contaminating** virtually all the "works" that we currently "produce".

We should therefore not forget the lessons that history can teach us. For in that grand sweep can be seen how the power of language has stirred men and nations to great deeds. The welling up of nationalistic fervour by the generation of powerful and emotional oratory has galvanised whole peoples to destroy even numerically superior forces bent on their conquest or destruction. The greatest conflict the world has ever experienced produced especially stirring words of power from Winston Churchill which greatly helped the British people withstand the onslaught of Hitler's Air Force. The noted American radio journalist, Edward R Murrow, opined that Winston Churchill "...*mobilised the English language and sent it into battle to fight for democracy*".

Jostein Gaarder, author of Sophie's World, in his analysis of the German philosopher Hegel, writes of Hegel's philosophy with regard to language: "Reason manifests itself above all in language. And a language is something we are born into." He argues that a language can manage quite well without the personal involvement or input of an individual of that particular race, but the individual *cannot* manage without that language. "*It is thus not the individual who forms the language, it is the language which forms the individual.*" (p 307, Italics mine.)

A quite logical extrapolation from that truism thus accepts the premise that *whole races, also, are "formed" by their individual languages*. We recognise, or perhaps inherently associate, various characteristics of different races with their language. The fact that specific languages generally "belong" to particular races is usually sufficient to conjure up images that "fit" the people of those races. Conversely, our natural acceptance that other races will invariably be different from us automatically inculcates the belief that they will probably speak a language different from ours also.

The power of language to move people patriotically can be clearly and powerfully seen at events where National Anthems are played. The words are sung with great feeling and emotion and are an obvious pointer to the power inherent in all languages when used correctly. It is the "living form" *embodied in the words* which actually produces that effect, thus which holds and strengthens the corresponding connection for each race to their particular homeland.

The same effect can be felt when the hymns or *spiritual* songs of a given people are sung at times of great distress or during reverent worship. There the inner spirit perhaps senses its lost connection to a Higher, intangible force far removed from the problems of everyday living. A strong upwelling of emotion is invariably felt then. The particular *forms* of distress, loss, or inner joy felt at that moment strive to find solace Above by seeking to establish or re-establish a connection with an intuitively-perceived Higher, more powerful, protective presence. Here the words *clothe* the form and power of the spiritual meaning and are thus felt emotionally. Of course, this is also true with opposite kinds of living word forms, but these bring forth ugliness and conflict. The potential for self-imposed distress, therefore, provides the very reason to use language only in an ennobling way.

What of the less developed races, the smaller groups and tribes around the globe, however? And what comparative level of language development did they achieve? In general their more restricted view of the world, governed by narrower perceptions reflecting less knowledge and of fewer things, and perhaps strongly laced with superstitious views, resulted in comparatively simpler languages. Thus, through the many diverse languages, we *see* the different, historical life-paths and subsequent fortunes of the world's various peoples quite clearly written on the pages of time. Recorded history has generally been written by dominant races with perhaps stronger, more assertive languages.

Certainly, the history of humankind clearly records many instances of suppression of the language, history and culture of minority groups within the sphere of influence of totalitarian regimes. Yet, whilst such activities in other societies past and present are rightly condemned, the same kind of "official" language suppression and distortion "at home today" virtually enshrines the dangerously insidious practice of "political" or "cultural correctness" too. The madness of it all is too clearly evident when it becomes a criminal or cultural offence to speak on certain issues - even with correct language usage - in case it offends someone, somewhere. By hijacking a word for a particular labelling purpose, even words once simply understood have become so distorted that previously unacceptable practices have become "main-stream acceptable". Racial issues involving change or distortion in language meaning also occupy this wrongly elevated place. Unfortunately, a spade cannot always be called a spade today.

Notwithstanding all that is wrong with our use of it, certain languages have developed to a point of convenience and value where they are now regarded as the world standard for particular activities. Thus, for example, we have Latin for scientific classification of flora and fauna, the German language generally synonymous with precision and engineering excellence and English as the preferred language of international business and aviation. Nevertheless, for all its obvious necessity, the language in its general application, formed by the power inherent in the human spirit, is now a sad, polluted and degraded shadow of what it could and should be. Whilst it will continue to evolve, it should do so only under the umbrella of The Eternal Laws – if it is to be of maximum benefit for humankind.

This should not mean the relaxation of even basic rules of grammar and spelling under "modern and enlightened" educational curricula simply because it fits with some misguided notion that it somehow provides a more "level playing field" for all students. No longer do we appear to strive for individual excellence as would befit the outworking of Spiritual Law. Far easier to adopt a "herd-mentality" and simply produce average "automatons" who won't be "emotionally disadvantaged" by not having the same "level of achievement" as the rest of the herd! That kind of neutering process offers nothing more than a lowering of standards within the particular society because it rejects the vital necessity of sound, healthy discipline which is ultimately voiced through language. To use a "modern" term – "dumbing down".

Despite the fact that languages are important to retain within individual cultures in any given land, a particular language may not necessarily be the best one for general, everyday use, however. Therefore, where there may be indigenous bi-culturalism associated with a more globally-accepted dominant language within the land, such as English for example, that will probably always be the main medium of language communication. Simply because, in terms of sheer logic, it is a commonsense position. Certainly, the less-dominant language should be retained, for all languages are a gift *through which the peoples' culture* **can** *be more nobly expressed.*

Its retention, however, must ultimately be the responsibility of the people concerned, for it is *their* language after all. It is not anyone else's. If, however, there is insufficient interest in retaining it *for themselves*, then that would simply show the lawful process of how and why the demise of part of the cultural heritage of a race occurs. It would thus reveal that particular race's *own unwillingness* to hold on to it. Latter-day renaissance interest for languages almost lost is clearly a correct and admirable thing. For the language of any people perhaps offers the greatest medium for the complete cultural expression of that group, and therefore should not be allowed to die out.

In summary, language, with its inherent "forming power" under the aegis of Spiritual Law, can either uplift a people or drag them down. Upliftment or degradation will depend upon whether that medium is used to spiritualise the talents and abilities within the group, or is used to pervert or coarsen those gifts. For from the thoughts are produced the words, and from the mouth via the respective language, the issue of those words. The words then frame or clothe the *form* of the corresponding activity or deed.

The Book of Matthew offers a strong pointer to this spiritually-lawful and precise relationship between the use of words for good, or for the opposite. He recounts how Jesus rebuked the Pharisees intent on entrapping Him. In Chapter 12, verses 34-36, (Fenton) Matthew notes this reference to the power inherent in language.

> "...how can you preach purity, when you are yourselves depraved? The beneficent man draws from his treasury of purity, goodness; and the depraved man can only produce

depravity, from his stores of depravity! I tell you, however, that every vile *idea* that men give expression to, they shall render a reason for it in the Day of Judgement."

And the King James version (Matthew 12, 37) completes it thus:

"For by thy *words* thou shalt be justified, and by thy *words* thou shalt be condemned."

(Italics mine.)

A further powerful statement is made in Chapter 15, verse 11, where Jesus proclaims to a large crowd:

"Listen and understand! What goes into the mouth does not corrupt the man; but what comes out of his mouth does corrupt him."

And in reply to His disciples obviously puzzled by His explanations, He said to them:

"Are you ignorant even yet? Do you not know that everything going into the mouth proceeds to the stomach, and is from there evacuated? But what come out from the mouth proceed from the heart, and corrupt the man. For there come from the heart wicked thoughts, murders, adulteries, fornications, thefts, perjuries, blasphemies. These are what corrupt the man..."

(Verses 16-20, Fenton.)

Thus all languages possess words which run the complete gamut of human volition. From soaring forms of spiritual upliftment, to ugly and befouled ones. The particular "word forms" chosen for general discourse or debate which issue from the mouth of speakers of any given language will produce the corresponding "living forms" of either upliftment or debasement, exactly as Jesus explained. Therefore liberal beliefs that Biblical pronouncements of the kind we have quoted have little relevance for modern man and equate to nothing more than "fire and brimstone" preaching, are themselves rendered irrelevant by the reality of rapidly degrading societies world-wide. For global societies are ultimately the *end excrescence* of all the "forms" produced by **the many aspiritual deeds in the medium of all the diverse languages of collective humanity**.

Therefore, *we should never forget that inherent in the human word are vestiges of The Living Word of God*, out of which Creation – and thus our life and being – arose. Whilst not possessing any *creative* power as such, it nevertheless still exerts a powerful *formative* influence on the environment. This sets in motion unseen forces which, if wrongly applied over a long period of time, produce devastating consequences. So it is vitally important to use earthly language in the right sense. We can achieve this by using a manner of speaking that is controlled by the spirit. Only in this way can man work constructively through the language, and thereby develop its inherent life and potential to the fullest and highest expression of human-spiritual ennoblement.

Chapter 6

The First Death!

The Process? The Same for all of Humankind!

"And do not shrink in fear from those who kill the body, for they are not able to kill the soul."

(Matthew 10:28, Fenton.)

"Do not dread those killing the body, and who after that have nothing worse to do."

(Luke 12:4, Fenton.)

"The more spiritually one lives, the less fear there is of death."

(*The Soul – Whence and Whither*, p 186 Hazrat Inayat Khan.
)

The essence of the above *Biblical* quotes clearly indicates that physical death is not that which humankind should be morbidly fearful about. Of course, we should not be flippant or superficial about any death, or whether it affects us personally or not. That is not the intended meaning behind the quotes anyway. By them we are meant to understand that death is not the end, and that earthly death is only a transitional phase or process. One of many in the complete time-frame of our total existence.

Moreover, if analysed from the standpoint of The Spiritual Laws, those particular Scriptures should be readily accepted as a viable and logical outcome of being born onto the earth in the first place. For there appears to be little point in living for one generally indeterminate length of time only to have it all end in a complete expunging of the conscious personality in "blackness" in a hole in the ground. The terrible circumstances and life-path that millions are born into must logically presuppose clear and precise reasons for such outcomes. To simply subscribe to a belief that fatalistically accepts that such dire situations are out of our control is to also accept that we are no different from animals which are governed by instinct alone.

Since humankind possesses the attribute of free will as an inherent part of his spiritual heritage, to accept "any station in life" in dumb resignation in the belief that it cannot be changed, or believe that we cannot institute change within the society or group we may find ourselves in, is to allow the perpetuation of that wrong belief to flourish. And via this attitude or belief, bequeath to future offspring the same straitened circumstances and the same spiritual apathy. By exercising our free will in the conscious recognition that the outworking of The Spiritual Laws *do* offer inherent Justice, we automatically tap into the life-stream of that Universal Power and the outworking of the Justice contained within it.

We arrive, thereby, at the sure knowledge that physical death is nothing more than a transitory phase – a rebirth into the next world for our further experiencing. Of course, strict **rules** govern the process, as it does everything in Creation. By adjusting ourselves to The Laws or Rules, however – with the subsequent gaining of the spiritual knowledge that is a natural accompaniment of them – we can fully understand, and thus *consciously experience* one inevitable day, this ostensibly "fearful" thing called **Death!**

The great unknown that has surrounded the inevitability of earthly death has taxed the minds of the greatest thinkers, philosophers, scientists and theologians since man's beginnings. However, even though much thought has been devoted to unravelling this "mystery", no clear and unified position has ever issued from their ranks. Since the death process is exactly that – a process, and the same for all – it is thus eminently clear that the individual standpoints of the respective disciplines on this issue differ greatly in interpretation or belief as to what exactly does take place. In other words, **they do not know**.

Over the centuries, various mediums, visionaries, clairvoyants and mystics have all sought to divine the actual happening too. Many have claimed to have made contact with people in the "beyond". Some have published their claims. Except for the few who keep at least a reasonably open mind on the subject, most of these kinds of stories are dismissed and ridiculed. Still, the fact remains that we *do* leave the earth at death. The dead body we leave behind in our likeness is testament to that. We, as a living entity, are no longer in it. So, where have we gone?

The one constant that can be absolutely relied upon in life is the certainty of dying, sooner or later. Chapter 7, verse 6, from the "Wisdom Of Solomon" (The Apocrypha) states it wonderfully succinctly:

> "...there is for **all mankind** one entrance into life, and a **common departure**."

(Emphasis mine.)

Therefore since death comes to us all without fail, it would be logical to believe that we would occupy ourselves far more with the how and why of it than we actually do. Most, however, push it away. It is too fearful to even contemplate.

Still, it should at least be thought about from time to time, but in a constructive and objective way. For if after earthly death *life* does continue on, is it not reasonable to assume that upon that discovery many people who *have* passed on would then want to contact those whom they had recently departed from – those whose lives would have been so intimately intertwined with theirs whilst on earth? Cold logic would aver that that would probably be the case. However, because a major separation from the physical/material environment of the earth has occurred, any kind of subsequent contact could only therefore be via a non-physical method.

Now, consider, what if a few mediumistic people were able to be the portal by which people in the "beyond" could pass on their experiences? Should we automatically reject all such stories? Or should we perhaps see in at least some such claims the possibility of a clear Grace from Above whereby we *can* be helped to a clearer understanding of the transition through the death process to "further life" in the next "realm"? Since this book unequivocally accepts that premise, let us note one such person's desire to offer us this very help.

In 1895 a Mr A. Farnese transcribed the experiences of a "Spirit Author" who gave his name as Franchezzo. The work, *"A Wanderer In The Spirit Lands"*, describes his journey after earthly death. From the perspective of the major thrust of this book – namely the explanation of The Spiritual Laws of Creation – the dedication by him in his work is very interesting since it perfectly concurs with what we state is imperative for humankind to recognise! Key aspects are noted here.

> "To those who toil still in the mists and darkness of uncertainty which veil the future of their earthly lives, I dedicate this record of the Wanderings of one who has passed from earth life into the hidden mysteries of the Life Beyond, in the hope that through my experiences now given to the world, some may be induced to pause in their downward career and think ere they pass from the mortal life, as I did, with all their unrepentant sins thick upon them.
>
> It is to those of my brethren who are treading fast upon the downward path, that I would fain hope to speak, with the power which Truth ever has over those who do not blindly seek to shut it out; for if the after consequences of a life spent in dissipation and selfishness are often terrible even during the earth-life, they are doubly so in the Spirit World, where all disguise is stripped from the soul, and it stands forth in all the naked hideousness of its sins, with the scars of the spiritual disease contracted in its earthly life stamped upon its spirit form - never to be effaced but by the healing powers of sincere repentance and the cleansing waters of its own sorrowful tears.
>
> I now ask these dwellers on earth to believe that if these weary travellers of the other life can return to warn their brothers yet on earth, they are eager to do so. I would have them to understand that spirits who materialize have a higher mission to perform than even the solacing of those who mourn in deep affliction for the beloved they have lost. I would have them to look and see that even at the eleventh hour of man's pride and sin, these spirit wanderers *are* permitted by the Great Supreme to go back and tell them of the fate of all who outrage the laws of God and man. - - - -
>
> As a warrior who has fought and conquered I look back upon the scenes of those battles and the toils through which I have passed and I feel that all has been cheaply won - all has been gained for which I hoped and strove, and I seek now but to point out the Better Way to others who are

yet in the storm and stress of battle, that they may use the invaluable time given to them upon earth to enter upon and follow with unfaltering step the Shining Path which shall lead them home..."

(From the Dedication of FRANCHEZZO, *A Wanderer In The Spirit Lands*.)

The "Better Way" that Franchezzo alludes to in his warning plea to humankind clearly means a "better way" than that which the world presently practices and which, as he so correctly terms it, is *"the downward path"* which *"outrages The Laws of God and man"*. His clear recognition reveals that *only* by heeding The Spiritual Laws and living the "Better Way" might we thus then be able to step upon the "Shining Path" to return "home".

That first step on the true path "home" – after living the "Better Way" however – is transiting through the process of earthly death. What we all know to be true is that death is invariably accompanied by huge emotional struggle and anguish for those left behind. Yet this simply reveals the large degree of non-understanding of the actual process. If the *mechanism* of the death process were understood, that must surely help to ease the pain of those grieving. For there would not then be the non-comprehension that is the usual demeanour of those who gather at funerals. The emotional hurt at the loss of a loved one can generally be coped with, but the reasons why to other questions that may surround this process are often a far different proposition.

6.1 "Death, the Great Leveller"

For the one shortly to travel that path, the first reaction is usually disbelief, then perhaps denial. Denial brought about by the fear of it. Or the thought of how unfair it may seem to be, and possibly not wanting to leave family and friends. However, for those who have the knowledge of the process of death, and thus of The Laws which govern it, that person is better able to accept the earthly inevitability of it. With calm confidence he can approach his time knowing that it is a necessary transitional step with the opportunity for greater enlightenment, **"if The Laws have been lived correctly"**! Franchezzo's harder experiences suffered after departing the earth offer the very reason to heed those Laws.

The wide reluctance to accept death as a completely natural process, coupled with most people's fear of it driving an associated desire to "stay on the earth forever", has given rise to the offering of substantial rewards from wealthy individuals for a formula to stop, or considerably slow down, the ageing process. This line of thinking has thus resulted in the insanity of not only freezing corpses for exorbitant fees, but also just heads for a lesser fee. To ostensibly await a "re-awakening" and cure from the expectations of future, "advanced medical knowledge".

However, as we have firmly stated in previous Chapters, it is the ***spirit*** that is the animating "power" within the physical shell. Once that severs itself from the material body the natural laws decree that the shell will decompose. Therefore regardless of how far medical science may develop to, it will never be able to effect this particular miracle. All that has been achieved here is the provision of a very expensive, refrigerated grave. And, of course, the inevitable decomposition of the corpse once thawing occurs, with absolutely no chance of a re-awakening.

Relatively recent Frankenstein-like scenarios which call for "head transplants" have emerged. The cloning of humans and the growing of foetuses for replacement body parts has been widely discussed, and probably already experimented with. There was also, until quite recently, the belief that there would be an inexhaustible source of animal body parts – mainly from pigs - for xeno-transplantation into humans. All this from people who are, supposedly, "highly educated and intelligent". Medical science had since recognised that such operations could trigger a global pandemic of a deadly new disease. Experiments by the Natural Environment Research Council of Britain have revealed that pig hearts and kidneys carried potentially deadly animal retroviruses, "...dashing hopes that animals could one day supply spare parts for human surgery."

Notwithstanding that clear "scientific" message, xeno-transplantation has once more reared its totally unnatural and ugly head whereby a new group of "medical experts" are revisiting the "pig concept". One wonders what form those who promote and support such aberrant ideas might take once free of their physical shell, thereby faced with their new, non-earthly body under the aegis of Reciprocal Law.

Researchers have noted that cancer viruses *will* jump species, "...in the real world, not just in artificial laboratory settings." Virologist Robin Weiss, who first demonstrated that pig viruses could infect human cells, said: "Xeno-transplants do not *seem* to pose a big risk. But then BSE and HIV were not *thought* to pose big risks when they were first discovered." (Italics mine.)

This particular recognition will *not* come as any great surprise to the spiritually aware, for any kind of cross-species tampering is a serious transgression against The Spiritual Laws producing equally grave reciprocal returns. In the case of "head transplants", there still appears to be "approval by association" from at least one Christian church so far.

Dr Robert White, Professor of Neurosurgery at the Case University in Cleveland, Ohio, has proposed exactly this idea – where a person who has a complete and healthy body but is brain-dead, could be "married" to one who is quadriplegic or similar, but who possesses a "good head". This "marriage" would ostensibly produce one good and whole "productive unit". The key question is - who would that person actually be? Which one of the two "part-units" inhabits and *animates* the "completed new body"? For only one can. That means the other one must die to facilitate the union – if the operation is successful to begin with. For both "spirits" cannot co-exist as dual "animators" in the "new unit".

Once again, the problem with all medical researchers who subscribe to this kind of "medical advancement regime" is that they seem not to even *begin* to understand that The Laws of Life decree that we are *very much more* than just a material body. We only have life during the time that the inner animating core – the spirit with its outer soul-coverings – is **present** in its individual "physical form". Earthly death is the *separating out* of the physical "overcoat" from the "soul-body" and "spirit-core". **It is that simple, that logical and that perfect!**

Dr White, who claims to have already successfully transplanted the head of a monkey onto another more than twenty years ago, states himself to be a committed Catholic, is a frequent visitor to the Vatican, is a member of the Pontifical Academy of Sciences, and helped to set up the John Paul II committee on medical ethics. Why, I wonder, do we not hear of these kinds of medical "experts" proposing to set up committees on "spiritual reality"? In fact, it is precisely because they lack any true knowledge of the connections between the material body and the inner animating *spiritual* core, that they do not. For they, too, must also possess the exact same "configuration", otherwise they could not live to wax expert on such matters. **This "life connection" is the very knowledge that should be taught as the key foundation for all healing and medicine in all Medical schools.**

Yet there is another insidious and evil practice that has arisen through this non-acceptance, or lack of knowledge, about death and life-after. That is the reported growing trade in body organs. Given the sometimes dark nature of man, there is probably no doubt that some unfortunate people are murdered for selected parts. Anecdotal evidence from investigative television journalists probing into such allegations strongly suggest that in parts of India – which is one source – children have already been sold for this trade. Chinese prison guards have been convicted and jailed for selling body parts of prisoners.

Unfortunately for all involved in this dark, repulsive "replacement body-parts business", it is not only the murderer who will reap the consequences of the deed in this case, but also the recipient, the surgeons who perform the operations, and finally all those who harbour similar thoughts of organ acquisition. All share *spiritual responsibility* for such a crime under the outworking of The Spiritual Laws, even if they believe otherwise. In any case, all participants soon discover the huge error of their wrong belief when they, in turn, die. It is then that they must fully experience the consequences of their chosen belief and deed.

Let us keenly examine this "death thing" then. Knowledge empowers whilst ignorance clouds! The problem with attempting to understand the death process is that, for the most part, it is an unseen and unknown happening. What exactly does happen when we observe the last exhalation of breath from a body? At this particular point, what was a living, breathing, talking entity has suddenly become a still and silent, rapidly-cooling shell. What has happened to the "force", the energy, the power that a few short moments before gave this now lifeless shell the ability to live, laugh and love during its tenure on earth? Can such a thing as its "life" simply dissipate into nothingness?

It would seem to be inconceivable to believe that an energy source such as that which can enable human beings on the one hand to produce great architectural works, wonderful symphonies and technological marvels, and on the other to stand incredible tests of privation and extreme cruelty of so many perverse kinds over long periods of time – and still survive – can simply dissolve into nothingness at earthly death. Yet that is the belief of many.

The other possibility is that this "animating power" does not disappear into oblivion but is actually a different kind of living form from that of the physical body. There are those who believe that. For those who subscribe to such a view, the general acceptance is that the physical body is really the outer shell from which the person who previously occupied it has now vacated. There is a large third group who do not know what to believe about this apparently uncertain process. For the purposes of this introductory phase to this Chapter, let us initially assume that we do not have any answers.

The question of whether there actually is such an inner animating force has already been resolved. Yet those within the Medical profession, who work intimately with the living entity, invariably evince uncertainty about the true nature of it all. Moreover, these are the people who utilise their considerable talents to slice, cut, remove and sew. The beating heart in the chest could well induce one to arrive at the belief that we are, after all, just a physical body animated by a very efficient pump for blood flow whilst also possessing an electrically-driven brain-computer programmed to control all other functions and life's decisions. If this is so, then the demise of the body at what we term death is simply a process of the pump stopping, a cessation of electrical activity in the computer of the brain – or vice versa – with a subsequent stilling of all bodily functions. This belief necessarily rejects the possibility of a separate animating entity which leaves the body at this time. A black hole of nothingness *is* the only logical end here.

The obvious fact governing these differing ideas is that we have only two choices for arriving at a correct conclusion, and we have an equal **50%** chance of getting it right or wrong - in terms of **the choice**. Either there *is* an inner animating force, or there *is not!* There cannot be two positions here. However, that even-chance choice must necessarily translate to a **100% outcome**. To be wrong is to be *completely wrong* with either choice – and not just be **50%** in error.

For those who ostensibly claim no interest or concern, such an outcome might be considered to be a personal non-event. However the *actual* reality of the death process will quickly shake the foundations of that particular belief. For those who wish answers, however, it surely behoves one to choose correctly, for initial peace of mind at least. Malcolm Muggeridge, the famous British social commentator, was once asked if he believed in "life after death". He thought that the more intelligent thing to do was to "hedge one's bets", even if one found it difficult to conceive of such a possibility. In his words – "just in case"![1]

The question of personal responsibility for how one has lived

---

[1] In ultimate spiritual terms, the term death-process to denote *earthly death* is actually a misnomer, for it is really a "transitional-life process". Nevertheless, we will continue to use the term to simplify matters.

one's life is a further factor which may have a bearing on one's attitude toward possible concern about death. If the "notion" of "life after death" is dismissed out of hand, we might perhaps assume that proponents of such thinking, even if conceding that *possibility*, might not necessarily equate the process with a concept of ultimate personal responsibility for the individual life lived – if a "less than noble lifestyle" has been the case.

Yet what of believers who unequivocally accept that the physical body is the material shell of the animating life-force – that of either a soul or spirit? The question which needs to be addressed here is whether or not there is complete dissipation of this "power source" at earthly death, or a retention of it in some form. In this particular situation we can once more reduce the outcome to only one of the two possibilities. Again, *it can only be one or the other.* One more **50% choice**, and one more **100% outcome**.

For any firm conviction of absolute dissipation or dissolution of any such "innate energy-source" is, quite logically, completely incompatible with a concept of "personal responsibility" for how one has lived one's life. Quite logically, also, full acceptance of "personal responsibility" can only *naturally* apply where there **is** the retention and continuation of a "life-force" in the form of a *complete and conscious being*, otherwise there is no point or purpose to such a concept. For ultimate ***personal responsibility*** logically requires some ***form*** to ***act on and through – for itself and its outward expression***. For our part, little more need be said for the completely wrong belief in a deep black hole of "nothingness".

Within the context of this work, therefore, let us examine the other possibility open to us. Here we have a concept of the acceptance of the physical body containing an animating "energy source" which, upon earthly death, retains its form and accepts personal responsibility for its "life lived". Religious leanings of many persuasions teach this very concept. At this point the issue becomes somewhat clouded with many varying ideas as to the final outcome. Now whilst some are decidedly similar in content, any difference in belief as to the *actual end result* nevertheless logically represents a point of conflict regarding the true and unequivocal nature of the happening. Quite simply, there cannot possibly be any differences since the *actual death process itself*, apart from the naturally differing events leading up to it, ***must be exactly the same for all***. And, moreover, totally in accordance with The Spiritual Laws of Life itself.

That is our absolute premise and contention! Irrespective of one's race, colour, religion, belief, geographical location or any other factor, the process is the same for all. Indeed, the idea that there may be differences because of the aspects mentioned is completely untenable, and really quite foolish. Unfortunately, not being able to physically see every individual step has produced an impossible maze of opinions and theories to cloud and confuse the issue. If, however, the premise that the "death process" is subject to absolute Law without deviation is correct, all that is required is to *recognise* the outworking of those Laws and apply them to this contentious subject for our complete edification.

At present there are many books on the subject of "near-death" or "out of the body" experiences and a number of researchers have compiled reports from the experiences of the dying. Dr Raymond Moody is perhaps the best known. Dr Moody's research noted that at times of severe illness or injury resulting in such a "close encounter with death", all subjects recorded very similar experiences, with the *consistency* of the experiences being the common constant. The many differences in race and nationality, social and economic status and religious preference produced no differences in the experiences. Even suffering different diseases or illnesses and receiving different medical treatment, the basic event was remarkably similar. Yet, should this be a surprise? If it is a lawful process without deviation as we contend, we should expect to discover exactly this fact.

Therefore, if there can be such a thing as an out-of-body experience, then there must necessarily be another body perfectly capable of existing consciously outside of the physical one. This we have already outlined in Chapter 4 in the explanations of our spiritual origins. There, we identified our inner life-force as having its origin, and therefore home, in The Spiritual Realm far above the material plane of the earth. That "energy source" which is the animating force for our physical body, we know as the spirit. It is the true, and very real, you and me.

Plato, who accepted the belief that the soul leaves the physical body at earthly death, interpreted its particular realm as the "world of ideas". He also noted the fact that most people have a superficial attitude toward these ideas, being content with a life "among shadows". As a consequence of this they "paid no heed to the immortality of their own soul".

Plato perhaps also intuitively understood the idea of a proffered "attribute of grace" in the connection of the soul to its origin. In his philosophical comment he states, "...when perfect and fully winged she [the soul] soars upward." (*Philosophy History & Problems*, p 63) Thus the soul yearns to fly home to the world of ideas. It longs to be freed from the chains of the body. Yet even *after* Plato's enlightened teachings for the time, Epicurus, (341-270 BC) a Greek philosopher who accepted the teachings of Democritus and his "dispersal theory" of "soul atoms", believed that death should not concern us because as long as we exist death is not here. And when it does come, we no longer exist.

Unfortunately for Epicurus, his incorrect views would have been swiftly demolished at his death. It is important to therefore define and understand the nature of spirit, which we possess as our actual inner being and by which we are drawn upward to our origins in The Spiritual Realm after the completion of our "schooling" in the material world. Provided, of course, we have not placed a barrier between the two thus preventing our return. In any case, the many designations that people ascribe to this word, spirit, should be clarified so as to more clearly understand its meaning.

People who are highly educated, witty, intelligent and widely-read, and able to converse well about all they have learned are often regarded as being "rich in spirit". Or perhaps they may be gifted with a talent for producing original ideas. But the designation "rich in spirit" is not strictly correct in either case. Neither can we call a person who is steeped in knowledge about their particular traditions and culture "rich in spirit". Unless there is a conscious and knowledgeable connection to the higher spheres, such knowledge is really only concerned with culture or tradition.

Therefore spirit is something completely different. As previously explained, the true Spiritual Worlds lie far higher than the earth plane, and form the upper and lightest part of Creation. Therefore "spirit" is more an "independent consistency" composed of that substance which comprises the Spiritual nature of those Higher Spheres. Spirit can perhaps be best described as having, or expressing the quality of, "deep inner feeling", but is not the same as being "highly intellectual".

Neither does spirit refer solely to the emotions. They are given to enable us to fully *live* an experience – irrespective of whether it be joyful or painful – to the greatest depth possible. Being emotional is not the same as having "deep inner feelings" of a spiritual kind either. The spirit, being the producer of the language, is therefore able to express itself in writings and in activities of sublime beauty such as art and music. The spirit, which possesses the inherent ability to "intuitively know" the emotions of love, hate, joy and sorrow, also naturally possesses inherent longing for its original spiritual home, as Plato correctly perceived.[2]

As formerly explained in the Chapter on our Spiritual Origins, the journey of a human spirit from the plane of The Spiritual to the Material necessitates the need to traverse all the intervening Realms. Each one is a different consistency, lightest toward the higher planes and heaviest towards the lower, exactly according to The Law of Spiritual Gravity. As we journey downwards, we are required to take on or wear a cloak or body of the consistency and material of the particular plane being traversed, with each plane becoming more dense the nearer we come to the gross material plane of the earth. Thus, by the time we reach the earth, we will have enveloped our spirit, our inner core, the actual us, in a number of coverings, each one exactly corresponding to the consistency and the material of the particular plane descended through.

Now, we might well wonder where all these *coverings* are? Since each, in turn, envelops the previous coverings on the journey downwards, they are logically all inside us. By virtue of the different consistencies, however, they are prevented from *blending* with each other. We may view this as a kind of uniting, similar to the way a collapsible telescope is held together. The huge difference between that basic material example and the human process is the mechanism or force which holds us together as a complete and self-conscious entity. That power is "radiation". It is that which holds together everything in Creation – from the greatest thing to the smallest.

The science of physics has long recognised that everything radiates, and that the "apparent" solidity of all material substance is due to just this radiation. It is a specific radiation which, in a sense, "magnetically" connects the elementary particles.[3]

---

[2]The cause of the seething restlessness, frustration, discontent and anger that seemingly pervade the peoples of the world like a terminal disease today, may possibly lie in the anguish of a collective humanity which has lost its true place in Creation and is no longer able to find its way.

[3]It is interesting to note that this radiation, which emanates from virtually everything, can be captured by Kirlian photography, either still-life or on video. The truly amazing aspect of the process, however, concerns the constant movement of the various colours being radiated. These appear to correspond to the different properties of the subject being photographed, particularly the relative strengths of the various parts of the energy-field. Whilst there is a school of opinion which deems this energy-field to be the actual aura of things, science states the radiation to be electro-magnetic. Still, radiation all the same. Perhaps the word aura is too unscientific, too new-age! Nevertheless, that is what it seems to be.

The physical body is obviously the immediate first part of "us", the complete entity. It is that aspect which allows us to interact with our physical environment. With it we are able to utilise the senses of sight, smell, hearing and touch etc., to enable us to carry out earthly tasks and fulfil particular desires. In itemising the *three key components*, and working from the material body inwards, we find that the outer mortal physical cloak – that which can be seen in the mirror – has a closely connected "astral" body, the prototype of the physical, whose consistency is roughly similar to the physical as it is still composed of material matter. It is not as dense, however.

These two, in turn, envelop other body-coverings that correspond to their respective spheres of origin beyond the earth. In the Ethereal World – that which we loosely call the beyond – the *ethereal body* covers the soul. Inside all these coverings resides our "spirit" – the real you and me! To reiterate once more – the "spirit" and its immediate coverings enveloped by the ethereal body, but *excluding* the physical and the "astral" can **basically** be *collectively designated* as the "soul body". It is important that we clearly identify and understand the three main parts of the total entity, for we will need to remember them in order to follow the complete process of earthly death, since we will repeat those various designations.

The phenomenon of "phantom-pain" that many amputees experience derives from the fact that we possess these different "bodies" of varying consistency within each of us. When an amputee loses a limb, the corresponding "limb" of his "astral" body remains complete within him because, obviously, it cannot be physically severed. However, the various non-material bodies that reside within his, now, less than whole "physical form", nevertheless still exert a subtle influence upon him and his physical environment. He may, therefore, from time to time, "sense" or still "feel" the "lost limb". Anecdotal evidence would strongly suggest that those in the medical or psychiatric profession are highly sceptical or dismissive of such beliefs. However, as we will state often within these pages, either a thing is so, or it is not. Since we are dealing here with the fact of inviolable Spiritual Law, this so-called "phenomenon" unequivocally resides in the *"is indeed so"* category!

Thus, within the material substance of our physical body resides our spirit, the actual animating power – the life-force – for the now multi-layered body. However, in order to *connect* the individual coverings so that the volition of the spirit can act on the complete entity, we require a "connecting" or "linking" mechanism whereby this can be achieved. That necessary connection from the spirit to the soul, ethereal, astral and physical bodies is provided by something called the "Silver Cord", mentioned in various spiritual works and The Bible. It is this connection that enables the animating power of the spirit to produce its earthly works as it *impresses its volition* on the "coverings" that envelop it. It also provides the very animation and life-warmth for the physical body, without which it could not live. These last points provide the *major* keys to a full understanding of the complete death process!

Whilst it is the power of the spirit which animates the body, it is the intermediary function of the brain which supplies the electrical impulses that permit the end physical motivation – but nevertheless still under overall *command* of the spirit.

In a broad sense, we can liken the "Silver Cord" to the umbilical cord that connects the growing foetus to the womb of the mother. As a very *basic* analogy, that cord provides life and warmth to the young life too, as well as nutrients to nurture the body. However, what it does not do after a specific point in pregnancy, is provide the *spiritual* life-force. The entry of an individual spirit into the foetus at the appropriate time assumes that role.

Because the concept and knowledge of the "Silver Cord" is crucial to understanding the "death process", some views about it from two of the main schools of religious thought offer interesting comparisons. Cruden's Complete Concordance to the Old and New Testament and the Apocrypha is still highly regarded in the Christian world as an accurate and reputable publication even though the first edition appeared in as far back as 1737. The explanation of the "Silver Cord" in Cruden's work may perhaps still represent the fundamentalist Christian understanding of it today.

> "By this, commentators generally understand the pith, or marrow of the back-bone, which comes from the brain, and thence goeth down to the very lowest end of the back-bone, together with the nerves and sinews which, as anatomists observe, are nothing else but the production and continuation of the marrow. And this is aptly compared to a cord, both for its figure, which is very long and round, and for its use, which is to draw and move the parts of the body; and it is compared to silver, both for its excellency and colour, which is white and bright, even in a dead, and much more in a living body."

(Crudens, p 445)

The above interpretation is obviously only a physical one concerned solely with the materiality of the body, for the wording of the text clearly refutes the idea of the Silver Cord being a connection between the physical body and the spirit. Compilers of more recent Concordances do not offer an interpretation of this "cord" aspect as Crudens did. The actual connection, of course, must first be recognised and understood correctly in order to be able to explain it thus.

Eastern philosophical beliefs on the other hand have long held that the "Silver Cord" *is* the link connecting the soul to the body as a kind of "ethereal umbilical cord". The "Silver Cord" is also believed to link the various energy centres or "chakras" which are situated along the axis of the spine. While not physically visible, the "chakras" correspond to various nerve centres and organs of the body. It is the conduit or channel through which energy and the "life-force" pass to these centres during the course of our life on earth. After death the cord is severed, thus allowing the soul to be released from the material body which, in turn, then decomposes into its original elements.

Having established the main points of reference for our elucidation of this fascinating event, let us now begin our actual journey into death by first examining the similarly reported phases of out-of-body experiences, as recorded and distilled by Dr Raymond Moody in his second book on this subject, *"Reflections On Life After Life."* (Bantam. p 5/6):

> "A man is dying and, as he reaches the point of greatest physical distress, he hears himself pronounced dead by his doctor. He begins to hear an uncomfortable noise, a loud ringing or buzzing, and at the same time feels himself moving very rapidly through a long tunnel. After this, he suddenly finds himself outside of his own physical body, but still in the immediate physical environment, and he sees his own body from a distance, as though he is a spectator. He watches the resuscitation attempt from this unusual vantage point and is in a state of emotional upheaval.
>
> After a while, he collects himself and becomes more accustomed to his odd condition. He notices that he still has a "body", but one of a very different nature and with very different powers from the physical body he has left behind. Soon other things begin to happen. Others come to meet and to help him. He glimpses the spirits of relatives and friends who have already died, and a loving, warm spirit of a kind he has never encountered before - a being of light - appears before him. This being asks him a question, non verbally, to make him evaluate his life and helps him along

by showing him a panoramic, instantaneous playback of the major events of his life. At some point he finds himself approaching some sort of barrier or border, apparently representing the limit between earthly life and the next life. Yet, he finds that he must go back to the earth, that the time for his death has not yet come. At this point he resists, for by now he is taken up with his experiences in the afterlife and does not want to return. He is overwhelmed by intense feelings of joy, love, and peace. Despite his attitude, though, he somehow reunites with his physical body and lives.

Later he tries to tell others, but he has trouble doing so. In the first place, he can find no human words adequate to describe these unearthly episodes. He also finds that others scoff, so he stops telling other people. Still, the experience affects his life profoundly, especially his views about death and its relationship to life."

Contained within the above report are some of the points thus far outlined. Note that the being of light communicated "non-verbally". We can assume from this that one's earthly language is of no importance at this point, and that communication is perhaps more via the spiritual intuition – a kind of "other-world telepathy". The obvious separation of the physical body from the non-physical is an especially clear point. In accordance with the knowledge we now have, we are able to recognise the reference to "moving rapidly through a long tunnel" as relating to the drawing out of the non-physical body from the physical.[4]

More importantly from the above report, however, was the requirement to evaluate the key phases of one's life, this aspect under the direction of a powerful spiritual being. Here can be observed the necessity for accepting the fact of "personal spiritual responsibility" for all ones thoughts, words and deeds, exactly as The Spiritual Laws demand, and which we continually reiterate in this book. In this regard, again consider the warnings of Jesus, "...that until the heavens and the earth shall pass away, a single dot or hairstroke shall not disappear from the law, until all has been completed." (Matthew 5:18) Consider, also, what we might regard as a further "spiritual" qualification of the above once more:

---

[4]This "long tunnel", in terms of its perceived length, does not refer to the length of the physical body as the soul-body exits the physical shell. It refers to an altered aspect of time, which has a vastly different reference value in that non-earthly sphere.

"I tell you indeed, that you will not depart until **YOU** have *repaid the very last farthing*."

(Matthew 5:26, Fenton, Emphases mine.)

To be faced with the need to confront one's past life in the very early stages after one's earthly death may well presuppose the unsettling probability that the next stages of the process call for atonement and expiation in some way. That really is the inescapable reality, exactly as the above Biblical quotes clearly state. For the description from Dr. Moody's work ***does not*** explain the process of *actually dying*, it merely describes *only the very first steps in just being* ***"out of the body"***. In short, the person concerned has not died. Many researchers in this field have concluded that the feelings of love and well-being that are experienced at this time represent the *totality* of the after-death situation, but that is not the complete picture by any means. Through insufficient knowledge, they are not able to take into account the absolute and full outworking of this process - a process which can be only be understood with the knowledge contained within The Spiritual Laws of Creation.

Having determined that we must accept "personal spiritual responsibility" for our deeds, we need to draw the veil aside a little more in order to reveal the next step into earthly death. The actual happening is quite simple. Because the connection between the physical and the non-physical parts of man is that of a radiation process, all that is required to effect a complete separation is for one or the other to become so debilitated as to not have sufficient *radiating strength* to hold itself *locked to the other*. We see this in severe illnesses, or during a long fast where the body can be considerably weakened.[5]

On the other hand, the "soul body" can also lose its "radiation-connection" to its physical counterpart such as in the case of giving up the will to live. So even where there may be no obvious physical reason for separation to occur, nevertheless, according to Spiritual Law, this must eventually take place if there is no re-strengthening of the necessary "connecting radiation" in such cases. Thus, as the radiation-attraction between the soul body and the physical body becomes progressively weaker, the point of separation is finally reached.

To clarify the process once more, where a body has been forcibly destroyed, ruined by disease, or weakened by old age, and can no

---

[5]The same Law operates here as in the process of amalgamation.

longer offer ***sufficient strength of radiation*** so as to maintain ***a strong attraction between soul and body***, the soul must sever itself from its earthly body or covering. That, quite simply, is earthly death. In terms of natural Law, which at the same time is Spiritual Law, it is just the lawful process of *two species of matter*, once united on the earth through a *mutually-attracting radiation*, but which must separate out again when one of the two *different species* can no longer fulfil its *attracting* role.

Now the soul, at the moment of severance, draws the astral body[6] with it away from the physical body. The soul needs to draw the astral body out of the physical shell because, unlike the physical body *at this particular moment* the astral becomes, but only for a very short while, the next "material" cloak for the spirit. This phase of the death process is the actual exiting and departure from the physical shell where the soul ***draws*** the ***astral body with it*** out of ***the physical body***. Since there was never a *fusion* as such, but only a *sliding into one another* – as with the example of a collapsible telescope – the soul simply ***pulls the astral from the physical*** as it strives to free itself from its former "material partner".

In doing so, the soul does not draw this astral body very far, because it is still connected not only with the soul but also with the physical body. Moreover, the soul, which initiates the actual movement, needs to detach itself from the astral body too, and strives to get away from it. The astral body always remains near the physical body after the earthly departure of the soul. The further the soul moves away, the weaker the astral body becomes. The continuing detaching process of the soul eventually brings in its train the decay and disintegration of the astral body, which, in turn, immediately brings about the decay of the physical body too. This is the normal process under the lawful outworking of The Spiritual Laws.

Whilst this explanation should be relatively easy to follow, particularly when viewed pictorially, as a further aid we can perhaps also consider the visible birth process to offer *some* understanding. At this time a separation also occurs between mother and baby, where the new-born similarly seeks to initially strive out of, and away from, the mother's body. For it, too, is connected to its mother and to the placenta via its "life-cord", the umbilical, and must also "disconnect" from both. Whilst this may be regarded

---

[6] In previous explanations we learned that the astral body is like the "prototype" of the physical.

as a very crude analogy, the reader may find greater clarity to understanding the death process through this example, even though a kind of reverse view. However, the reader should not regard one process as perhaps being an exact mirror image of the other, though there are certain aspects which can possibly provide some enlightenment.

In Dr. Moody's description of just the "out-of-body" experience, the outworking of The Law of Spiritual Gravity is immediately evident, where the lighter, more mobile part – the soul body – floats away from the heavier material body. It is important that this particular point be carefully noted. For whilst we have now described the death process, that is only with respect to a "normal happening", which is that for a soul who is quickly able to sever its connection or tie to its material body. Obviously the soul is still subject to The Spiritual Laws and must now follow its particular path into its new environment, into its new world. However, it can only embark upon its next journey when the "Silver Cord", that had once served as the necessary link between the "power source" of the spirit and its material counterpart, is completely severed. In the same way, a baby cannot be completely free of its physical tie to its mother's body until its life-support cord is similarly cut.

We now enter the little understood, and perhaps less believed, area of "personal spiritual responsibility". As the death process is subject to strict and firmly established Spiritual Laws, including that of The Law of Justice, what criteria governs the situation where a soul is not able to easily sever itself? And what does this mean for that soul body – that individual?

Whether or not a soul detaches itself quickly from the physical body will absolutely depend on *how that person has lived his life on earth*! **That is the short, blunt truth of the matter!** The spiritual nature of the individual human being is the decisive factor in this. We need to understand that it is not the teachings of any particular religion or belief that is decisive here, it is **how we are in our being, how we stand spiritually, individually**. The Law of Spiritual Gravity is a key aspect in our explanations now, for this Law operates in every sphere of Creation, and not just in an obvious way on earth where its physical effects can be readily observed.

We previously explained this Law and its effects, and stated that everything we do, every thought we think and every action we take corresponds to a precise spiritual weight. Thoughts and actions of good are *spiritually lighter* than those that are not.

Throughout our lives, therefore, we are naturally subject to all the different experiences that our personal choices will generate. The changing circumstances of them – but perhaps more particularly how we cope with them from an attitudinal standpoint, sometimes well, sometimes not – will all contribute to the final *"specific spiritual weight"* of our soul-body at earthly death.

A life of superficiality without concern for spiritual matters, or of seeking only the acquisition of material things to the exclusion of any elevating influence – even without necessarily evil intent – will ensure that the "Silver Cord" becomes darker and thicker precisely corresponding to the degree of superficiality or materialism lived. It thus naturally follows that a life of violence, crime and debasement, regardless of the circumstances that might have brought it about, will actually produce a spiritually far "heavier" individual. This perceived effect has entered our language where we describe such persons as being or feeling "heavy".

Unfortunately for such people this "heaviness", with its associated and perhaps personally-desired intimidatory effect, whilst perhaps generating a tough, "untouchable status" on earth, will likely set in place a very painful death experience, *if* no genuine change of spiritual direction is embarked upon before that time arrives. The effect of this "heaviness" on the "Silver Cord" is to darken and thicken it considerably, with serious consequences for that soul at earthly death.

Now, when the time comes for severance to occur, the spiritually darker and heavier person with the correspondingly thicker cord will discover that this cannot be effected so easily. It may be very many days, perhaps weeks, before the Cord eventually begins to wither and disintegrate, thus finally setting the hapless soul free of its now decomposing shell. This particular example in the process clearly reveals the outworking of the Justice of The Laws in the exercising of our free will for evil or debased purposes. Choosing an opposite lifestyle, however, especially one where *spiritual considerations* are a regular and normal part of one's life, will ensure that the "Cord" remains lighter.

It is important to reiterate that only **our decisions are free. The consequences are not.** These must be fully lived out under The Law of Sowing and Reaping. Thus the consequences for a soul who has lived a life without thought or care for any of the higher spiritual aspirations will mean an unnecessarily longer time tied to his physical body than need have been. Through the still strong attachment via his thicker and heavier "Cord" he will therefore feel all that the physical body undergoes in that time, including any autopsy, and perhaps cremation. In longer-tied periods, even the decomposition process itself. The actual moment of his release will have been precisely determined by The Spiritual Laws, in exact accordance with his "attitude and chosen lifestyle" during his life on earth.

The exact same death *process*, however, offers a *vastly different experience* for a person who has lived a more noble life. His severance will be effected much faster and he will be quickly free of the shell. That is one reason **why all** the great spiritual teachers over the ages have constantly admonished mankind to always strive for the good. Those warnings were not the incoherent ramblings of foolish old men, or the strident fire and brimstone preaching of doomsday prophets. They should therefore not be ridiculed, mocked or ignored, for such serious warnings simply, yet powerfully, state the Truth of The Eternal Laws.

The effect of thousands of years of man's stubborn refusal to accept the truth of it all has now brought us to the most serious point that mankind and this earth have ever reached, and we are well into the process of reaping the results of all our personal and collective choices, alive or dead. What will be experienced by humankind more graphically, however, is the exponential factor of much more in much less time. **Hence the impending Apocalypse and World Judgement!** - - -

With this new knowledge of the death process, and aside from the practice of autopsies, at what point can a person be safely pronounced dead? Some years ago, Dr. Lyall Watson wrote a book called "The Romeo Error". The subject matter was precisely about the difficulty in determining the exact moment of death. He recounted many instances where persons had been certified dead, even to the point where the early stages of decomposition had set in, and yet still returned to life. More harrowing were the experiences of the relatives of deceased where death certificates had been issued for the one apparently very dead, where funeral preparations and burial service were undertaken, and where the casket was duly consigned to the earth and the grave filled in. These particular cases recorded relatives requesting the exhumation of the deceased because of strong feelings and even dreams that indicated their loved ones were not actually dead at the time of burial.

Because of the need to convince the appropriate authorities of the urgency of the matter – with official scepticism being an unfortunate time-barrier in such cases – subsequent exhumations did reveal persons "buried alive". Their short time awake was evident by the efforts they undertook to try to free themselves from their tomb. The most notable factors being the dishevelled arrangement of the clothing, fingernails ripped from gouging the casket lid and, probably the most harrowing for the friends and relatives, the look of frozen horror on the faces of the "now deceased". Dr. Watson also outlines the curious state of "Catatonia" in many of these cases where, in his opinion, the body appeared to be completely dead with no detectable or discernible life within it, yet still alive.

Indeed, today, with the supposedly huge advances in diagnostic medical science, bodies still "come to life" even in the morgues of the most advanced hospitals, much to the very great surprise and consternation of medical staff. The explanations for these tragic errors lies in that which we currently explain in this Chapter, where the vital knowledge and purpose of the "Silver Cord" is not accepted or believed, and which the Medical Profession should take urgent steps to learn about.

The frightening situation of how one could possibly be accidentally buried alive surely begs the question how, and why? From the standpoint of The Spiritual Laws, and irrespective of what we believe or may *wish* to believe, whatever takes place on earth is not solely the result of pure chance. It may be comforting to continually insist that such is the case, particularly when we might be personally affected detrimentally, but every event, every incident, even the most minute, will have been brought about by a *decision made by human beings somewhere, sometime.*

Indeed, it cannot possibly be otherwise for it is *we* who *cause* things to happen through our inherent spiritual ability to make decisions in the first place. But, as we need to continually emphasise, only our *decisions* are free, the *consequences* await to eventually be faced. So, if we are ever to make any sense of the *why* of the problems that beset us, a huge and fundamental leap into a *different* way of thinking must be made. A way of thinking that actually and finally accepts the absolute validity and inflexibility of every single one of The Spiritual Laws of Creation, which return to us **every** consequence of **all** our decisions.

If, now, the question of "accidental" burial or any other *apparently* inexplicable human misfortune is considered, we should quietly reflect on the outworking of The Law of Sowing and Reaping. Whether in such cases that *that* is the mechanism which had *"returned"* the reciprocal effect of an unfortunate decision made in the past – even if long distant – to the individual affected, a decision that perhaps once affected **another soul very detrimentally**. One, therefore, which might require a similar kind of experience in order to expiate any such past deed.

To return to the existence of the "Silver Cord" and its purpose: its vital function in the life and death of humankind brings into question the medical "wisdom" of organ transplants. In such undertakings it is vitally necessary to ensure that the organs are taken from a body very recently "presumed" dead, or conveniently pronounced "brain-dead", to ensure the "freshness" of the product. This means that the "donor" will almost certainly still be *attached* to the physical body and, depending on the density of the "Cord", may well feel considerable pain at the removal of organs. Viewed from the higher knowledge of Spiritual Law, organ transplants add little to the overall "life" of a person, as earthly death is merely a transitional phase in the total existence of an individual in any case. This is aside from the horrendous financial considerations of such "operations" of course.

The emotional turmoil associated with the thought of "losing loved ones forever" coupled with the medical profession's general disbelief in these matters has resulted in the propensity to want to extend physical life way past what sometimes appears to be a natural and desirable point at which to exit from earthly life. Consequently this has changed the nature of how we relate to every other human being. Today we are all potential spare parts units. Of course, it is correct and proper to seek to extend life where possible, but surely not to the point where the lawful process of dying a completely natural death is actually hindered. Yet do we ever read of anyone dying of old age anymore? Hardly ever. Where death occurs in the very aged, medical protocol must always find the exact medical words to attempt to describe this completely natural process of ageing, even where it may logically be something as simple as plain organ deterioration. But where indeed, in all of this, is *true* Knowledge? - - -

6.2 Jesus – "The Calling of the Dead to Life"

The astute reader should have little difficulty in recognising that the Silver Cord is the key to understanding how one can "return to life". As long as the cord is still attached to the body, the *possibility* exists for a *return*. In such a case, it is merely a question of the re-strengthening of the radiation-connection between the physical shell and the soul body which offers the potential for reconnection. The condition of the shell or corpse does not necessarily prevent such a reunion either, though a severely ravaged one will probably not allow for a reunion of any great length of time. As already noted, Dr. Watson records that even in cases where decomposition of the body had begun, people still returned to life. In all cases, however, the possible return of the "dead", or the inability to return, will always be subject to strict Spiritual Law without any kind of arbitrary intervention.

The strict outworking of The Spiritual Laws in such cases permits a fascinating insight into *how* Jesus was able to call the "dead" back to life. What we should not lose sight of here is that Spiritual Law is also Natural Law. Indeed, The Spiritual Laws could not possibly be anything other than "completely natural". Thus the "miracles" that Jesus wrought never over-stepped the naturalness of the highest Spiritual Laws. He came, "...not to overthrow the laws, but to fulfil them", as He Himself firmly stated (Matthew 5:17).

We, too, strongly state once more: It is unfortunate that the followers of all the great Teachers have invariably distorted the clear Truth of their original Teachings, probably more so with those of Jesus, Who came from out of The Living Law Itself. In His unequivocal reference to "fulfilling" The Laws, He firmly indicated that even He, as The Son of God, could not circumvent or overthrow The Spiritual Laws of Creation, but had also to submit to them. Thus even the "miracles" He performed were similarly subject to the strict consistency and inviolability of The Eternal Laws. The *miraculous aspect* of His work, however, was in the *acceleration* of the *healing effect* of the cures He wrought simply by virtue of the fact that He possessed the **power** to bring that about.

This does not lessen the greatness of those miracles, however. Indeed, the very fact that He absolutely had to operate within The Laws shows the sure certainty and naturalness of them whereby we human beings can also live in the supreme confidence and perfection of the same Laws. If, now, a reader may wish to use the argument that God, and therefore Jesus, could do anything without constraint from the very Laws which The Creator placed into Creation by virtue of being part of The Godhead, the very vital and critical point of **"The Perfection of God"** is called into question!

As we have stated previously, if we accept the premise that

God is, and must be, Perfect by virtue of His **incontrovertibly-natural Perfection**, then His Laws of Creation must similarly also be Perfect. The possible contention that a Perfect God would produce imperfect Laws is completely untenable, though it clearly reveals our human propensity to attempt to ascribe emotive human values to the **Creator of All the Worlds!** For, without such Perfection in The Godhead and The Eternal Laws that have issued from It, the whole idea of Laws that actually are Eternal, inviolable in their "Perfection", and therefore unchangeable, becomes an absolute and illogical *impossibility*.

Therefore, the common belief that God can change His Laws at will in order to bring about a particular event, can only mean that The Law needing to be changed to effect such a thing was not perfect to begin with. Intimately connected with that assertion is the obvious further assertion of an imperfect God unable to put into place Perfect Laws from the very beginning. When we gaze at the night sky in awe and veneration and marvel at its incredible vastness, the idea of such imperfection and changeability cannot logically be considered – not even as the tiniest thread of some kind of remote but nevertheless *humanly-assumed* possibility.

Having clarified the validity of the impossibility of altering The Spiritual Laws – which we examine more fully in a later Chapter – let us assess the "miracles" of Jesus with regard to the "dead". We can now easily understand that the soul-bodies of those He called back, **travelled back to the physical shell along the Silver Cord which had not yet been completely severed.** Whilst this is a lawful process, the key point here is that Jesus **possessed the power to do so**. Issuing as He did from The Godhead – without which nothing could come into existence – He naturally and lawfully possessed the **Power** to **command** the souls to return.

Thus He clearly demonstrated the fact that death is only a transitory phase and that we should not fear it. However, a vital aspect of those particular "miracles" is not the fact that He *could* order the souls to return, but the *different manner* in which He *commanded* them to do so. With the young maid who was very recently dead, He simply says:

> "My girl arise." 'Her breath thereupon returned, and she at once got up. And He gave orders for her to have something to eat'."

(Luke 8:54-55)

In the case of the young man from Nain, who has been dead longer and is about to be buried, His command is stronger, more urgent, where He calls:

> "Young man, *I say to you,* Arise!" '...the dead man sat up and began to speak. And He handed him to his mother'."
>
> (Luke 7:14-15)

Finally, in the case of Lazarus who had already been in his tomb for four days, we read that Jesus, after ordering the cave-stone to be removed, first ***prays for help***, before ***commanding*** Lazarus to rise. The Scripture states that:

> '...He called ***with a loud voice***': "Lazarus, come out!" He who was dead accordingly came out, swathed hand and foot with bandages, and his head wrapped in a napkin. Jesus told them, "...loosen and let him walk".
>
> (John 11:42-44 Fenton all. Emphases mine.)

It is interesting to note that John the Disciple records Martha, sister of Lazarus, as objecting to the expressed intention of raising him from the dead when she stated to Jesus: "Master, by this time the smell must be offensive: for this is the fourth day." (John 11:39, Fenton) The Disciples, who were also aghast at the thought of Jesus bringing back to earth-life a man dead four days, protested to him to not be so foolish. His reply was one imbued with Divine Wrath at their presumption. He accordingly told them that with Lazarus, the Power of God through Him would be revealed for the world to see, and that they should not dare to oppose Him.[7]

Thus we see that in these three cases, the longer the person had been dead, the ***stronger the command required*** by Jesus to effect a return, a clear indication of the relative "distances" the respective souls were from their bodies. So long as the cord is still attached the "dead" have the possibility of returning, which is the sole and lawful reason ***why*** Jesus ***was able*** to bring this about, aside from *possessing* the power to do so. Once the cord is severed, however, it is not possible for any return. Even though possessing the power of The Divine, Jesus would *not* have been able to alter The Eternal Laws to achieve that, as He clearly pointed out!

---

[7] It is also interesting to note that in each of the three respective cases, Jesus gave different instructions to the families of them. In the case of the young girl, however, we may deduce that the order to give her food was to immediately re-strengthen the "radiation-connection" between her soul body and material body which she had recently vacated.

His miraculous healings did not require a "Law change" either, as everything can only take place under the umbrella of The Spiritual Laws. It was simply a case of His Divine Power, which stands far higher again than The Spiritual, *accelerating* the normal process of healing by a very large degree so as to make it seem instantaneous, and thus miraculous. He intimated that humankind, too, would one day be able to achieve similar results once we had reached the appropriate level of Spiritual purity. The Bible narrative records that the Disciples also effected healing "miracles" *after* the Ascension.

According to the historical record, shortly after his resurrection, Lazarus left Palestine and the persecution of the Christians, and journeyed to Cyprus where he was ordained as Bishop by St Barnabas. Lazarus apparently lived there for a further 30 years and it is reported that he rarely smiled having seen the plight of the souls in the beyond. We should remember that he journeyed well past just the "out-of-body experience" of initial release from pain etc., into the actual state of earthly death where it is recorded that he spent four days in that "beyond" before being commanded to return to physical life.

The co-authors of "The Holy Blood and The Holy Grail" paint a rather more esoteric version of the fate of Lazarus. They state:

> If the "beloved disciple" did not go to Ephesus, what became of him? If he and Lazarus were one and the same that question can be answered, for tradition is quite explicit about what became of Lazarus. According to tradition, as well as early Church writers, Lazarus, the Magdalene, Martha, Joseph of Arimathea and a few others, were transported by ship to Marseilles. Tradition maintains that - - - Lazarus [died] at Marseilles after founding the first bishopric there.
>
> (p 361, 362)

We have reached the stage where the soul-body is about to become free of its former "partner in earthly life". Firstly, however, we should briefly return to the long, dark tunnel phase of the first stages of the death process to offer a more complete explanation of it. The subjects claimed that they felt "as if they were gliding through something dark and narrow, a valley, a dark shaft, a tunnel", and they used words like being "pulled out" in attempting to describe the sensation.

What is described here is the striving away of the ethereal soul *from* the astral body, the soul's pulling-out from the latter. At this moment of transition - during the striving away movement – the spirit can no longer see through the eyes of the earthly or astral body. Nor can it see through those of the ethereal soul body, which is not yet completely free. Therefore the spirit temporarily has the impression of darkness. We can liken this phase to that of being in a lift moving between two floors. Before we can look out again we must wait until the next floor is reached.

The next stage is the emergence from out of this dark tunnel into the bright light of the next world. As previously stated, we can note some similarities in the birth process, in the striving away, the dark tunnel, and the emergence into a bright new world. For, in reality, *earthly death* is simply *birth* into the ethereal world. This new, bright world for the soul is, however, still close to the earth, but with a vastly altered time-perspective. Here, in this new, lighter world away from the constraints of the heavier physical body and the gross material earth, everything is more mobile, more "speeded-up".

For the departed one, this phase might be marked by much confusion. More so if he had paid no attention to this matter of death during his life. Now, in death, he discovers he has the ability to see and hear all that is taking place around him, but finds he is not able to make himself heard or felt. He sees the emotional anguish of those he left behind, and strives to reassure them that he is not actually dead, that he lives. But he cannot! If those of his family members have the same attitude to death that he previously had, he will be forced to endure the emotional upheaval and non-comprehension of his kin that his death has produced. Because of this he may seek to make himself understood but, as he cannot with his "new soul-body", the only course open to him is to try through the earthly organs of speech of the physical one he has left behind.

His attempts to do so bring about a renewed strengthening of the cord with perhaps a corresponding increase in feelings of pain, which he would recently have become free of. This effort on his part unnecessarily prolongs the death struggle which can last for days, and which his loved ones will anguish over. Thus his well-meaning attempts to offer solace to those around him actually only add more confusion for them. And sometimes fear. The feelings of anguish and loneliness for a soul who finds himself in such circumstances must surely be considerable. Far better if we all occupied ourselves with this vital question instead of pushing it away, as if that act might keep earthly death away forever. Since knowledge empowers, it is far better to know than to not know!

The severing of the Silver Cord is not always easy. The Spirit-Author, Franchezzo, whose Dedication we included earlier in this Chapter, offers a sobering insight into this difficulty. After his physical death he sees, standing by his grave, the girl he loved. When she leaves he tries to follow her but is unable to.

> I strove with all my might to follow her. In vain, I could go but a few yards from the grave and my earthly body, and then I saw why. A chain as of dark silk thread – it seemed no thicker than a spider's web – held me to my body; no power of mine could break it; as I moved it stretched like elastic, but always drew me back again. Worst of all I began now to be conscious of feeling the corruption of that dead body affecting my spirit, as a limb that has become poisoned affects with suffering the whole body on earth, and a fresh horror filled my soul.
>
> Then a voice as of some majestic being spoke to me in the darkness, and said: *"You loved that body more than your soul. Watch it now as it turns to dust and know what it was that you so worshipped, and ministered and clung to. Know how perishable it was, how vile it has become, and look upon your spirit body and see how you have starved and cramped and neglected it for the sake of the enjoyments of the earthly body."*
>
> (*A Wanderer in the Spirit Lands.* p 11, Emphasis mine.)

The Silver Cord, which in this case has thickened and become dark, binds the departed one very firmly to his physical body. Only much later, after he has recognised the wrong of his earthly life, can he sever himself from his mortal shell. When the disintegration of the Silver Cord does finally occur, the departed one experiences the effects of The Law of Spiritual Gravity in its full manifestation. In accordance with previous explanations the soul is forced, through the consequential effects of its recently lived lifestyle, to then begin to "reap what it sowed". This is achieved under the outworking of The Spiritual Laws where the soul is "propelled" to the particular plane which corresponds with its ethereal or "spiritual" weight. In accordance with The Law of Spiritual Gravity, only on the earth can good and evil live side by side. On no other plane of Creation is this possible.

Thus upon earthly death a separation takes place between all the departed. In accordance with that separation, they must then occupy the particular plane that their ethereal weight has decreed for them and those of similar mind and propensity. Therefore souls will always find themselves surrounded by others of the same weight and essentially of the same nature. In this lies the Perfect Justice of The Eternal Laws, in particular the outworking of The Law of Attraction of Similar Species.

> And Man seeks his Long Home,
> And the Mourners will walk round the streets -
> *Ere the Silver Cord's loosed...*
> And Man goes to the earth that he was,
> And his Soul will return to the GOD Who gave it!
>
> (Ecclesiastes 12:6-7, Fenton. Italics mine.)

6.3 The Nature of Hell

Much uncertainty surrounds this question of the nature of the place called "hell", or even if such a place exists, or could exist. Some earlier philosophers postulated a duality of forces, i.e. a good and a bad one, and a light and a dark one. Such a view clearly presupposes that two forces must exist, and that there are two separate powers we can choose between or connect ourselves to. This belief is still strong for many people today probably because, on the surface at least, it appears to be a reasonable assumption. The dark force, moreover, is invariably deemed to be the "creator" or "owner" of hell. The assumption or proposition that such a separate "dark force" exists has certainly been used often enough as a reason or excuse where horrific crimes have been committed. "I was told to do it" they say. "Voices from somewhere made me do it." and so on. The voices would be real enough, but their origin is the key consideration here.

St Augustine, a theologian who lived from 354 to 430 AD, was preoccupied for much of his life with what might be termed the "problem of evil". In essence where evil came from. For a time he was influenced by the Stoic school of thought which held that there was no sharp division between good and evil. A major contributing influence was that of Neoplatonism which espoused the view that all existence is divine in nature. A philosopher to begin with, Augustine had nevertheless long felt that there was a limit as to how far philosophy could go. It was not until he became a Christian that he found the peace he sought, a peace anchored in faith. "Our heart is not quiet until it rests in Thee," he wrote.

Schelling, (1775-1854) the leading Romantic philosopher, sought to unite mind and matter. He believed that all of nature in both the human soul and the physical reality was the expression of one Absolute or world spirit. He saw this "world spirit" in nature but he also saw it in the human mind. He also accepted the idea of a development from earth to rock to "mind" governed by his "world spirit" beliefs. Schelling stated explicitly that "the world is in God". He believed that God was aware of some of it, but there were other aspects of nature which represented the unknown in God. This was the "dark side of God" in his view.

In reality, however, there is only **one** power streaming through all of Creation. It issues from out of the "Creative Will of God" and is completely **neutral**. Being, in essence, the "Living Power", it creates and sustains all life. However, in the case of we humans who are inherently endowed with the attribute of free will and who also stand in this power stream, we occupy a singularly consequential position, for we are like lenses. This "power" is ***"automatically refracted through us"*** precisely according to how we choose to use it and where we choose to direct it – either for good, or for evil! This unstoppable free-will mechanism ultimately determines how we finally live our lives, and thereby also determines our end-fate.

So, whilst we absorb a *neutral power*, our free-will volition then *converts it* to whatever we choose – good or evil. Or, to word it differently, to either the correct principle or the incorrect principle. By this process we automatically "form" our environment thereby bringing in its train our personal reaping, the reaping of our society, our nation and global family of nations. Now, since all written history quite clearly attests to wars, blood and violence on the grandest possible scale, consider the forms we have created over thousands of years, and continue to do so. So because we have created them, only through a fundamental change in attitude and way of being can we destroy them and become free.

Yet, is there any move towards seeking to change the mostly dark forms of our free will volition? Generally speaking, no! How many on earth are truly prepared to accept the reality of The Law of Reciprocal Action? Very few. Instead, we not only add to those forms but greatly nourish them in our selfish desire to "do what pleases us". In concert with "The Law of Attraction..." we are forced to reap more and more from that growing monster under the "iron law of karma". Unfortunately, however, with additional burdens lawfully imposed via the aegis of the *whirlwind constant*.

The knowledge and outworking of Spiritual Law permits the

concept of hell to be simply explained. It is, therefore, **not an institution ordained and created by God**. It is composed of those levels in the world of the afterlife that we (humankind) have created through giving full and unbridled rein to our evil dispositions over countless millennia. The rejection of genuine spiritual ideals and the gravitating toward material pleasures and vices, with the natural accompaniment of evil activities, have caused the formation of the "planes of hell". From there, its forms go forth to influence the decisions of humankind under the outworking of The Law of Attraction of Similar Species. Down there, also, the darker like-minded are forced by Law to reside until such time as a genuine spiritual longing to be free of it permits ascent for that individual under The Laws. Therefore, *humankind is the landlord and owner of the place we loosely call hell!* Under the interrelated workings of all The Spiritual Laws, perfect spiritual justice may be clearly discerned via this lawful mechanism.

In striking contrast, the same process has also formed planes of light and joy, where like-minded souls enjoy the peace and beauty of the afterlife they have earned. Suffering and tragedy, therefore, are **not** willed by God. We bring that on ourselves via the same process, paradoxically, whereby we could enjoy continual peace and happiness, i.e., by the simple application of directing our free will toward the good.

The often bemoaned cry of "Where lies justice?" is quite clearly explained in the above discussion. If we consider the following Scripture, moreover, we can readily see that "Justice", down to its last ramification, is absolutely served. Perhaps not immediately on the earth under human law, but most assuredly later under the Perfection of Spiritual Law! Through its outworking, we can more readily understand the following scriptural quotes, key ones of which we have previously mentioned:

> "And as they have sown only Wind, the Whirlwind alone shall they reap!"
>
> (Hosea 8:7, Fenton.)

> "Yet we know who says PUNISHMENT IS MINE, I WILL REPAY."
>
> (Hebrews 10:30, Fenton.)

> "I place Life and Death before you, – the Blessing and the Curse! Therefore choose for yourselves the Life, – that you and your posterity may live!"

(Deuteronomy 30:19, Fenton.)

In each of the above Scriptures, the clear admonition to *choose* correctly is evident, and only with a free-will ability can we do so. Therefore all choices are ultimately ours and ours alone, and the automatic outworking of The Spiritual Laws subsequently delivers to us the ensuing consequences.

There is one final question that remains to be addressed with regard to the *end-fate* of human spirits in terms of the *complete death-process*. That is the subject of our next Chapter. For the moment we have arrived at the end of a basic explanation of this inevitable yet vital earthly happening. It is, however, a basic overview only. For greater understanding, the reader may wish to avail himself of *certain* other publications which offer more insight into the subject. The reader should note, however, that whilst there are *very many* books which *purport* to give correct explanations of the death process, in fact only a very few *actually* can. **And only *one* completely so!**

6.4 The Ramifications of Loud Wailing

Whilst grieving is a natural facet of virtually all peoples at funerals, some races appear to inherently display a level of emotion that can sometimes border on unhealthy over-emotionalism. Whilst there will always be a normal and naturally healthy level of grief, for departed loved ones in particular, without the knowledge of the death process to guide us we could not ever have been sure of the *effect* that displays of very deep emotional grief and loud lamentations might have **on the very ones for whom we grieve**. Now that we do have clear and unequivocal understanding it behoves us, regardless of race, culture or tradition, to take cognisance of this knowledge, and begin to more fully understand the effects that our behaviour might have on the very recently departed.

We should therefore ask ourselves the key question: *"What should we do to help those who are struggling to become free from the earthly body and associated ties?"* Given the huge amounts of emotion and stress invariably present at funerals, perhaps the more relevant question is: *"**What** should we **not do** when grieving for the dead?"* Equally importantly, **why** should we not do it? Even though a brief explanation is already previously offered in this Chapter, it is probably appropriate to re-define the relevant aspects again.

People who are present at a death bed should strive ***not*** to break out into loud expressions of grief! When the grief at parting is too strongly expressed, the person in the process of detaching himself from his physical body, or who may already be standing beside it in ethereal form, may hear or feel it and be emotionally disturbed by it. If he should then feel pity for those left behind, the wish may awaken within him the strong desire to say a few words of consolation. In his attempts to make himself ***understood*** to the grief-stricken mourners, his "struggle" binds him more strongly to his physical body.

Now, because of his renewed efforts to establish a closer connection with his physical body – *which is the only medium by which he is able to communicate* – the ethereal body, which was still in the natural process of detaching itself, not only re-unites itself more closely with the physical body, but will be drawn back into it again. Consequently the pains from which he had already been delivered will be felt once more. When he next seeks to detach himself from his physical shell – and which he must inevitably do – it will be made more difficult and may last for several days. As previously stated this produces the prolonged, so-called "death struggle" which loved ones and relatives anguish over and which not only causes them more grief as they observe this process, but is also painful and difficult for the soul wanting to depart.

The blame for this unfortunate situation, as difficult as it may be to accept, lies solely with those who are unable to curb their emotions, and who express it in loud wailing and lamentations of grief. Because of this *the natural course of development for that soul is held back as* **he** *struggles to cope with it.* From an earthly standpoint such behaviour is understandable. From that of the purely Spiritual, however, it is actually one of selfishness because the grieving ones are more concerned with *their loss* than for the lawful transition of their loved one into his next life, or for *his* emotional struggle as *he* observes *their* grief.

This quite unnecessary interruption of the normal process, even if only a weak attempt at concentrating on making himself understood, ensures that a new and forced connection occurs. Dissolving this unnatural connection again may not be so easy. Unfortunately, because it desired this reconnection itself, no assistance can be given. Moreover, so long as the physical body is still not yet completely cold and the "Silver Cord" – which may not necessarily tear for many weeks – is still intact, such "reconnections" can still be effected. *We should thus always consider the suffering of the dying one* **first**, *and not the thought of our own loss.* The ideal situation for this serious event, therefore, should be one of absolute quiet, therewith offering the departing one the necessary dignity as should befit the importance of the hour.

These vital considerations should induce each of us to seriously reflect upon our own particular attitude at such times to ensure we are not remiss in this area. Would we want the experience of a painful death struggle? Clearly not! Unfortunately it is what we invariably visit upon those we *most care for* during **their** *death process*. At such times, therefore, we should resolve to place our personal sense of loss in a secondary role and consider more the plight of our friend or loved one as he struggles to stand free of the shackles of the earthly body. More particularly if there has been a prolonged illness or a restrictive and painfully-debilitating accident. A quick merciful release from that should be our *primary* concern, and not our own personal wish to *hold him to us*.

To this end, it is important to clearly differentiate between the **differences** that actually exist between a natural, **emotional experiencing** at such an event, and a situation where this aspect is perhaps **unconsciously subjugated** to a state of **overwrought emotionalism** brought on by the collective, emotional upwelling of the occasion. Even though the emotions are given to us to **deepen** every experience – irrespective of whether it be joyful or painful – there is a vast difference between the two positions in this case even if, on the surface and to the onlooker, the grief may *appear* to be the same.

One is naturally healthy having a spiritual foundation as its wellspring of understanding, whilst the other is basically earthly emotionalism. For **The Spiritual** knows only high, pure, cool objectivity with Spiritual Love as its foundation, and not that of earthly emotionalism. Therefore displays of *unnecessary emotionalism* have little affinity with true spirituality but, in its earthly manner, invariably focuses more on the person/s displaying it.

Only by accepting that **death is a far more serious and important occasion for the departing one** than it is for us, might we learn to leave behind the loud wailing and lamenting that has invariably accompanied death and funerals for so long. If we need to grieve, we should replace loud lamentations with quiet, controlled, natural and dignified grief, thus offering the help of a quick release and peace and dignity to the one being farewelled. As we would no doubt want that also, we should remind ourselves once more of the following, appropriate words of Jesus, given from out of The Living Law:

"And as you wish men to do to you, do the same to them."

(Luke 6:31, Fenton.)

6.5 Death of a Soldier

For those who accept that life continues after physical death, a loved one's sacrifice in battle may be easier to deal with emotionally. But what of the actual sacrifice itself, the extinguishing of a life in battle for a particular cause? Where can we place that in spiritual terms, and are we able to? The simple answer is "yes"! There are spiritual effects for every soldier in the ultimate sacrifice.[8] So if death is the outcome in a just and righteous cause nobly and bravely carried out, the "after-effects" will be vastly different from those which "brutal adventurers" in an ignoble war will experience. A brief examination of relatively recent history can probably conclude that there will have been very many acts of noble sacrifice, by virtue of the need to stop the madness of megalomanic despots.

What then spiritually happens for the soldier who bravely pays the ultimate sacrificial price? In order to answer *this* question, we must refer back to our explanation of the origin and nature of man. We know that the human spirit is an amalgam of a number of bodies telescoped, as it were, into each other, with each "body" corresponding to the nature and consistency of the particular plane to which it belongs. From our origins in The Spiritual Realm we are required to accept and occupy each appropriate body corresponding to, and consistent with, the nature of each plane we must traverse on our journey downwards to personal self-consciousness on the earth in the material world. At earthly death, the reverse process takes place whereby we discard each body at the height of its appropriate realm or level, as we ascend on the journey home, assuming, of course, that we have earned the right to do so.

Connected with Spiritual Law and the higher realms are all the virtues, one of which is *heroism*. By virtue of its particular nature, its place of origin can only be in the higher planes. The gift of free will that is inherent in every human being means that in our chosen life-path, whether as an individual or even as part of a nation,

---

[8]The term "soldier" is used to describe the activity of all servicemen. Therefore the equally valuable role of the sailor and the airman in war on the earth is the same as that of the soldier.

we can choose either the uplifting benefits of the virtues or the debasing, destructive energies of the vices. This means that certain activities will inherently have either uplifting or debasing qualities. Now, whilst war may generally be regarded as destructive, particular elements within it or, more particularly, certain kinds of actions that war inevitably produces, *can* be connected to the higher virtues.[9] So, in the case of a soldier who recognises that his participation in a just war is necessary to preserve freedom, who carries out his duties with quiet efficiency, with objectivity for the cause and without hate for the opposing side, and who is killed during an act of heroism in the course of his serving, this soldier – in spiritual terms – has released the virtue of heroism within him. It is thus connected to him.

This act of heroism in its *spiritual form*, through its release via an heroic act, is attracted upwards under "The Law of Attraction of Similar Species", to its ordained place close to The Spiritual Realm of our Origin. This particular plane of Creation is commonly alluded to as the "home of the gods" of many of the ancient cultures. It is that level which the Greeks, particularly, sought inspiration from to nobly emulate that loftier vision and apply it to every aspect of their society, including the military training of their young men. Their spiritual insight allowed them to "see" the activity and nature of the inhabitants there, such as the Elemental Lord Zeus, whom they erroneously believed to be a god. They named their "home" Mt. Olympus.[10] Thus every heroic act is connected to the essence of the natural power and nobleness of those "Elemental forces".[11]

It is from the noble volition of the spirit – the real us – that heroic acts are generated. The "living form" of each heroic act is thus connected to its origin in the Higher Realms. That *form* is "released" from the soul body of our noble soldier at his death in battle. It is drawn upwards to the topmost level of its ordained place where it is cared for until the day the "owner" of the heroic act – our soldier – might reach that point of spiritual ascent. If he does so it is automatically returned to him, since it was his alone. This he carries with him to the next level of The Spiritual Realm,

---

[9] The Bhagavad-Gita offers a precise explanation in this regard, since its narrative is based on the duty and responsibility of a true hero and soldier, Arjuna, to his people, as instructed by Krishna.

[10] The "formerly noble ideal" of the Olympic games has its origin here too.

[11] Even in the animal kingdom the inhabitants there will defend territory or young, to the point of dying for that cause.

his origin and home. There it adorns him as a spiritually visible sign of his selfless sacrifice.

The ancient Nordic peoples also perceived the truth of this process and named that particular kingdom or level "Valhalla". This high "fastness" housed the "resting place" of their heroes killed in battle too. However, whilst they and the Greeks, among others, divined the existence of this sphere and the activity of the beings therein, they had not reached a sufficient level of knowledge to fully understand the outworking of The Eternal Laws and the associated process that determines this complete happening. Today we can fill those gaps with the relevant knowledge from particular spiritual works now available to us.

That, then, is the spiritual meaning of selfless and noble sacrifice of a soldier in a just cause! Thus, whilst wars are a curse and a blight on mankind, they do provide opportunities whereby returning potentially severe fate, under the "Law of Sowing and Reaping", can be expiated by an individual during such deeds of ultimate bravery. Therefore the common saying, "... better to be a live coward than a dead hero" does not actually occupy any truly spiritual place. Cowardice, historically, has been reviled by most of the world's peoples, and the aftermath of various wars have seen known cowards executed anyway.

Finally, the words of Jesus best explain the true meaning and greatness of what is termed, the "ultimate sacrifice", when He said:

> "Stronger love has no one than this, that one should lay down his own life for his friends."
>
> (John 15:13, Fenton.)

In such noble deeds the greatest power in Creation is invoked, that of the power of Love. This, however, is the pure love contained in true *spiritual* activity and is not the unfortunate distortion of base emotionalism produced by humankind's earthly interpretations and activities relating to this word.

Chapter 7

The Second Death

"The conqueror shall never be injured by the second death!"

(Revelation 2:11, Fenton.)

"Do not smile about it for it is true; Your thoughts, words and works are recorded in the "Book of Life" *by none other than yourself*."

(*Heavenly Thoughts*, Karl May. Emphasis mine.)

The title of this Chapter may seem incredulous to many. Perhaps more particularly for people who are uncertain or unbelieving regarding the nature and process of just the physical deaths we will all see in the course of life. To state that there is such an event as a "second death" will surely cause considerable disbelief in the minds of many. Yet, just as we outlined the process of *earthly death* in the last Chapter, so can an explanation for a seemingly radical idea of a *"second death"* also be offered.

As with death in the earthly sense, the reality of the "second one" is equally as subject to immovable Spiritual Law. Indeed, only from that standpoint can it be so possible and be explained, by virtue of the simple fact that all things, from the smallest to the greatest, exist under these Laws. Neither does a "second death" conflict with the Biblical statement wherein it states that, "...it is appointed to men to die once." (Hebrews 9:27, Fenton.)

Quite obviously if there were such a conflict we could not logically have any allusions to such a thing as a "second death". Yet we find in Revelations two more clear and unequivocal statements about it.

"...over these the *second death* has no authority."

(Revelation, 20:6)

"...that is the *second death* – the lake of fire."

(Revelation 20:14, Fenton both. Italics mine.)

Allusions to "second deaths" and "lakes of fire" may sound religiously crass to many living in our increasingly technological and computerised society strongly directed to the ethos of the "god-corporate". However, perhaps such ostensibly "archaic religious ideas" should be viewed as simply being "symbolic explanations" of **particular and very precise lawful processes and outcomes!** In any case, from the point of view of the Judaeo-Christian school of thought – upon which Western society is largely moulded – we have at least established that the "second death" idea is very much "alive and well" in The Bible.

Moreover, the *spiritual meaning* of the *conqueror* in the Biblical quote under the title heading of this particular Chapter should be understood to mean one who has succeeded in **conquering himself!** He has conquered **his own base weaknesses** and is thus far more spiritually mature and knowledgeable than "before the fact". His increasing spiritual awareness may also allow him to be more accepting of such an idea as "the second death". Establishing the Biblical fact of a "second death" therefore permits us the use of this foundation to assess the ramifications of how we might be affected by this "event". First, however, let us read the interpretation of it that Cruden's Concordance offers:

[2] "A separation of soul and body from God's favour in this life, which is the state of all unregenerated and unrenewed persons who are without the light of knowledge, and the quickening power of grace, Luke 1.79. This is *spiritual death*."

[3] "The perpetual separation of the whole man from God's heavenly presence and glory, to be tormented forever with the devil and his angels, Rev. 2. 11. This is the *second death*."

(*Cruden's Concordance*, p 96)

If we accept that there is such a thing as a "second death", as The Bible clearly states, then we should expect that however it is brought about it can only be so under the strict outworking of The Spiritual Laws. Since The Laws of Nature and scientific law both have their validity solely under the umbrella of the higher Spiritual Laws, let us approach this particular subject matter, not from a purely "religious" perspective, but from the combined intermeshing of all the above Principles, as we did with the "first death".

In the current Biblical interpretation from Cruden's Concordance, *three* different kinds of deaths are noted. Yet The Bible does not appear to indicate anywhere that there are three in all. Cruden's mentions physical death, with which we are all familiar, and states that there is a "second death', and also a "spiritual death". Utilising The Spiritual Laws as the foundation for our assessments, we will endeavour to show that, aside from physical death which all must experience, there is the **"actual reality"** of the "second death" to contend with. There are not two *different kinds* of *further deaths*, however, but a ***single secondary one only*** – the **"second death"**! *This second death is thus* **spiritual death.** Therefore we can safely conclude that any opinion to the contrary will be solely due to an incorrect Biblical interpretation on this particular subject.

But what exactly is a "second death" – if we have already "died" in the earthly sense? In order to find a starting point of explanation, we must first consider the differences between that which is Eternal and that which is not. The earlier Greeks, Indians, Persians and Teutons – the ancient "Indo-Europeans" – shared a common view that history is cyclical, with no beginning and no end. But in an "eternal interplay between birth and death", different civilisations rise and fall. This view, however, is not quite the "eternality" that we mean.

Let us compare that idea with the notion of Rene Descartes, (1596-1650) a French philosopher and mathematician who rejected all previously held beliefs and built his own philosophy on the one premise he held to be indisputable, the existence of himself as a "thinking subject". This is reflected in his *personalised statement* – **"I think, therefore I am."** As a "dualist" philosopher, Descartes believed that whilst there are two different forms of reality or substances – *thought* or mind, and *extension* or matter – he nevertheless maintained that *both substances* originate from God, because "...only God Himself exists independently of anything else". He thus came to the conclusion that man is a dual creature – of the mind, and of the body. Yet even though philosophically equating the mind with spirit, he apparently did not extend that thought to encompass a separately-existing "Spiritual Realm" as the originating place of the spirit.

Sartre, (1905-80) from out of his existentialist beliefs, thought that man had no eternal nature to fall back on, and it was therefore pointless to search for the meaning of life. Existentialism, in the philosophic sense, appears to represent the 20th Century's answer to all other philosophical beliefs of the past. It is therefore interesting to note the path that philosophy has taken. An early and strong acceptance of a separable soul or spirit before the birth of Christ became interspersed with diverging philosophic/religious views at varying intervals up to the present.[1]

But in the century preceding Sartre's, another European philosopher had already rejected the values of Christianity. Friedrich Nietzsche, (1844-1900) regarded the Christian ideal as "slave morality". In his opinion, both Christianity and traditional philosophy had turned away from what he termed "the real world", and instead directed their thinking toward 'heaven" or the "world of ideas". He urged people to be "true to the world" and not to be seduced by any offers of "supernatural expectations".

In terms of an actual truth or a distortion of that truth, his reference to Christianity as being a "slave morality" could quite clearly be viewed as a "truth in itself" if, in the course of centuries, the original teachings had become so badly distorted that only rigid fundamentalism or a religion of fear was left. Without the vitality and vibrancy that only a "pure truth" can offer, apathy, superficiality and non-understanding – with the obvious potential to lead into cynicism and hypocrisy – may well then become the "way of that religion". Of course, this applies to all beliefs and teachings, and not necessarily religious ones.

As explained before, we know that Creation consists of two main basic parts, The Eternal and the non-eternal or Material. For human spirits, The Eternal part is that region of Creation from which we issued as *unconscious spirit-seeds* on our journey down to the earth in the non-eternal Material. For its part, the Material is that region to which the earth and the physical universes belong and in which it was ordained we were to develop to a fully conscious state, thereby hopefully recognising both our origin and our life's

---

[1] Perhaps we might now see existentialism and its general denial of the spirituality of man as the almost final excrescence of our lauding of intellectual prowess above all else.

purpose. And, therefore, with the concomitant potential to return to The Spiritual Realm in The Eternal part of Creation as a fully purified spiritual being. In fact, that is the *only* state in which we *can* return home!

In order to understand why there is a "second death" reality, there needs to be the further recognition that there is necessarily a "time-frame constraint" for all the Material Worlds of Creation. The Spiritual Laws decree that everything in the material worlds must inherently have a finite lifespan. The Eternal Realms, quite logically, do not. In the material world of the earth and physical universe, it is a simple matter to observe the vast number of diverse creatures and inanimate life-forms with varying life spans. From fractions of a second for sub-atomic particles, to hours for the most minute creatures, to days for some insects and on to years for those of the animal world. Man, as the only creature on earth with an inner animating spiritual core and free will, has a life span of 70 odd years approximately. The great trees, though, can live for thousands of years.

But out in the vast tracts of the universe, suns and planets are born, live out their allotted life-span over billions of years and then disintegrate to be reborn as other celestial bodies aeons later. The far larger galaxies have a life span running into millions of light years.[2] Notwithstanding such incomprehensible measurements of distance and time, everything in the Material World nonetheless has its time of birth, life and disintegration.

The Material Part of Creation is therefore finite with a strictly ordained time of existence, after which it must also disintegrate back to its primordial components to be reformed into a new Material Creation. Obviously such a time span is difficult to comprehend but it behoves each one of us to concern ourselves with this concept, for the disintegration of a whole part of the Material World cannot take place without huge and unimaginable dislocations and upheavals. Whole galaxies and universes would be absolutely convulsed in this process under the immensely powerful outworking of The Laws of Nature. Quite logically, therefore, we, the inhabitants of the very small planet earth, can expect similar kinds of convulsions also, with a correspondingly large degree of dislocation and destruction *when our time arrives!*

Now, being of the spirit in his inner animating core, and being

---

[2]One light year is the distance a ray of light travels in one earth year – approximately 6 million, million miles. Or more precisely – 9.4605 million, million kilometres.

of the material in his body of flesh, man, in reality, **stands in both parts at the same time**. With his origins from out of The Eternal Spiritual he has the potential to return there, and to reside eternally. With his other foot in the Material, however, he has an equal chance of remaining there tied, as it were, to it. The choice is solely his, and his alone. And therein lies the key to the understanding of the "second death".

In the granting of conscious life to humankind, and the accompanying formation of the Material Worlds for the many journeys man must make in order to spiritually develop and mature, The Spiritual Laws that govern this process also determine the total time of existence for this part of that World - in strict accordance with The Creative Will. Thus this earth, and therefore man on it, naturally has the exact same amount of allotted time – *in terms of its total existence in this part of the Material World*. At the close of that time period, it will undergo its disintegration phase too, exactly in accordance with the established Spiritual Laws which then transform the component pieces into a new part of the material world in a vast, humanly incomprehensible cycle of birth, life and disintegration over a similarly stupendous time-frame.[3]

Of course, it should be realised that whilst such concepts of time are mind-boggling for humankind, in terms of eternity under The Creative Will it is not even a "snap of the fingers". Our general inability to come to terms with such a concept owes itself to the fact that the human spirit, even though possessing the *potential* to live *eternally* as a self-conscious personality, was never inherently so. So it is important to remind ourselves that we will never be able to form a *knowing concept* of eternity. It will forever be beyond our grasp for we are merely "developed" beings only, and not "created" ones, as we have already noted.

Having thus established a basic framework of time through which the ramifications of the current subject can be further explored, let us continue our explanations. As previously stated, the precisely determined and ordained time of life for humankind on earth is necessarily exactly the same as the far larger and clearly defined part of the Material World **to which the earth belongs**. This fact decrees that that ordained time-span is naturally also the total amount of time given for our **spiritual maturation**. This period we can designate as *part* of the time of our **complete spiritual existence**.

---

[3]Later we will correlate the findings of astronomical science and Spiritual Law to more precisely detail the disintegrative processes.

As previously explained, also, the basic earthly concept of a *single lifetime* of birth, life and death is totally in error. One lifetime hardly suffices to gain even the faintest recognitions of Spiritual Truth. Since it is barely possible to become spiritually mature in the course of one lifetime, we are therefore able to designate a single-life time-period as being just a very small part of our complete existence.

7.1 One Life – or Many Lives?

We now return to the contentious question of a single-life concept versus a multi-life one. As with other similar choices, what we determine for ourselves in terms of a "belief of conviction" about this particular concept has a corresponding and natural flow-on effect into every other aspect of how we live our individual lives and how we relate to everything and everyone around us. The question of choice here is once again a **50%** one, but with the same **100% outcome**. Therefore, just as a personal choice over the question of "life after death" might logically presuppose a certain attitude and lifestyle in its *100% acceptance*, so might the question of "one life versus many" also produce a particular conviction as to one's perceived purpose and final outcome in life.

Yet the problem remains that if the *wrong 50 percent choice* is made – for whatever reason – that choice necessarily translates to being *100 percent wrong*, with all its attendant incorrect opinions and views. On the subject of reincarnation, therefore, a huge, consequential reciprocal effect under the outworking of Spiritual Law. Since we contend that it is not possible for the human spirit to acquire all the spiritual knowledge that it needs in one lifetime, we must therefore state our unshakeable conviction that the concept of multi-lives, or reincarnation, under The Spiritual Law of Rebirth, is the only correct possibility. **Thus have we chosen our 100 percent outcome!**

> "Man is a spirit and his body is the dress, the clothes it wears while it is on the earth. Just as an earthman changes his clothes but remains the same person, so the human spirit changes his physical body in the process called death. But the spirit, the owner of the body, lives on after discarding the body.
>
> Belief in reincarnation is simply the acceptance of the knowledge that a human spirit, in one continuous existence,

is given the opportunity to come to the earth more than once. On each occasion, the human spirit takes on a different human body.

This simple concept is the key to the unravelling of many so-called mysteries, the explanations of the inequalities, apparent injustices and inequities that worry so many well-meaning people, and the understanding of some exceedingly important but difficult passages in The Bible. Reincarnation leads us to a conviction of *"the relative* **insignificance** *of tribe, race, and nationality"*, a conviction that is absolutely essential in moving mankind from its present-day chaos into a just and joyful social, political and economic order."

> (*The Christian and Reincarnation*, Stephen Lampe, Millennium Press, p 1, Italics and emphases mine.)

The New Testament of The Bible offers an interesting insight into the thought processes of the people of the day regarding this belief, including the disciples of Jesus. In the story of the healing of the blind man, the question the disciples put to Jesus regarding the reason why the beggar was born blind must clearly presuppose a belief and basic understanding that certain afflictions can only be the result of a spiritual transgression *from a previous life*. Conversely, an exceptional talent or genius in a particular field, such as that which child prodigies display, can stem from the same process too.

Thus we read:

> His disciples accordingly asked Him: "Teacher, **who sinned**; **this man**, or **his parents**, in consequence of which **he** was **born blind**?"

> (John 9:2, Fenton, Emphases mine.)

It is clear that the disciples would not have asked this question if they did not believe that a man *could* be *born blind* as a *consequence* of a previous sin committed somewhere else in time. A sin, therefore, that could only have been committed in a previous life, in order *to be born blind*. Equally clearly, Jesus did not admonish them as fools for believing in such ostensibly "stupid beliefs". On the contrary, *in this particular case* He informed them that *"neither* the man *nor* his parents had sinned", but that **this man** was born blind "...in order that the workings of God may be displayed through him." (John 9:3, Fenton. Emphasis mine.)

The obvious connotation from this discourse between Jesus and His disciples is that reincarnation was a fact of life for them and, moreover, offered exact reasons for hard afflictions such as being born blind. Thus the puzzlement of the disciples over this man's blindness was not about *whether* reincarnation was factual or not, but *which* of the *two possibilities* (the blind man or the parents sinning) in this particular case might have *caused* his blindness.

The Old Testament offers a number of relevant passages about reincarnation also, a few of which we can include here. In narrating his call to prophethood, Jeremiah stated:

> Now the word of the Lord came to me saying, "Before I formed you in the womb, I knew you; and before you were born I consecrated you, and I appointed you a prophet to the nations."
>
> (Jeremiah 1:4-5)

The case of the prophet Elijah is also worth analysing:

> "Behold, I will send you Elijah the Prophet before the great and terrible day of the Lord comes."
>
> (Malachi 4:5)

Whilst there might be uncertainty as to what the "great and terrible day of the Lord" refers to – the coming of Jesus or to the Last Judgement in which we now stand – there should be no uncertainty in the clear message that Elijah the great prophet *would* be sent back to the earth again. During the period of Christ's ministry, some Jewish people interpreted that particular prophecy in the sense of a reincarnation in that he would be born as a baby. Some therefore thought that Jesus was a rebirth of Elijah:

> And they said, "Some say John the Baptist; some Elijah, and others, Jeremiah, or one of the prophets."
>
> (Matthew 16:14)

In the context of multi-earth lives, if we follow this basic thread about Elijah further then the reply by Jesus to His disciples with regard to the identity of John the Baptist is especially revealing.

> "And *if you are willing to accept it*, he is Elijah who is to come. He that has ears to hear, let him hear."
>
> (Matthew 11:14-15, Italics mine.)

The contentious question of reincarnation, at least for the many who subscribe to the generally accepted ideas of current Western philosophical and materialistic thought, has rarely been given the chance to be intelligently debated. Invariably it has been dismissed as Eastern religious nonsense or, in the worst extreme view expounded by some Western churches, as something evil stemming from, or having connotations to, Satanism. To be totally dismissive of an idea in such a highly emotive way might stem more from fear and ignorance rather than from rational, reasoned objectivity. Historically, the record of mankind reveals many instances of clinging to views that were clearly incorrect. Such an unfortunate stance does not necessarily advance the cause of real knowledge for mankind.

Consider the flat earth theory held sacred for centuries, regardless of the beliefs of more intelligent and logical men. Socrates was killed because he "disturbed" his fellow citizens" more conventional ideas when he tried to light the way to "true insight". Consider the trials of Dr. Joseph Lister, 1827-1912, (later Lord Lister) of England, who for years attempted to enlighten his fellow doctors and surgeons to the fact that poor hygiene was actually causing the deaths of patients in operating theatres in British Hospitals. At that time, surgeons did not necessarily wash their hands before surgery, and neither was there a high priority placed on any kind of cleanliness of the operating tables or instruments. Gangrene and other infections were thought to be caused by bad air. Yet despite Lister's efforts to keep his new surgical rooms and instruments clean at the Glasgow Royal Infirmary, the mortality rate remained close to 50 percent.

From initiating a practice of spraying the air with carbolic acid without any real reduction in rates of post-operative infection, he fortunately came across the germ theory of Pasteur in 1865. Utilising this knowledge and applying carbolic acid to instruments and directly to wounds and dressings, Lister reduced surgical mortality to 15 percent by 1869. His work in antisepsis met initial resistance, and even after demonstrating increasing levels of patient recovery through his simple procedure, it was not until the 1880's that his methods were finally accepted by the "medical establishment".

Gaarder, a latter-day philosopher and author of "Sophie's World', in analysing the philosophy of Seren Kierkegaard, a Danish philosopher (1813-55), noted Kierkegaard's belief that truth did not lie with the masses. His views suggested that "the truth is always in the minority". And that "the crowd is the untruth".

Such "lone voices in the wilderness" outside the "organism of the crowd" can sometimes launch huge changes in the consciousness of their fellow-men for the betterment of all. Of course, obvious physical changes cannot be so easily disputed in the same way that a physically intangible "idea" can. Like "unseen germs", reincarnation might be deemed to fall into that category. Nevertheless, many hundreds of millions of human beings over millennia have accepted reincarnation as a fact in their lives. This could hardly be likened to a "lone voice" situation. The seeming problem in reincarnation for most Westerners appears to relate to the many differing views that are offered as explanations or as fact about it. Some, of course, are clearly so bizarre as to be completely untenable.

As with all aspects of life and death, however, even the smallest ramifications of reincarnation are subject to the strict and inviolable outworking of Spiritual Law. The major difference between the respective religions of the Eastern and Western worlds is probably that of the *concept* of reincarnation. Present Eastern religions generally state that the purpose of one's existence is to strive for release from the cycle of rebirth and thereby finally merge with the "cosmic consciousness" and "become one with God". This is achieved, for the most part, by self-communion and meditation.

On the other hand, the three great Western religions of Christianity, Islam and Judaism all share the same fundamental idea that there is only one God, and that there is a distance between God and His Creation. With this view, man's purpose is to seek redemption from sin and blame. This is assisted by prayer and the study of the respective Scriptures, and perhaps certain austerities. The Christian Church has the added aspect of "faith and belief in the resurrection of Jesus".

Of course, not all beliefs of reincarnation share exactly the same views about it either. Arguably, perhaps the most difficult aspect for the Western intellect to accept is a particular belief which promotes the view that we can return to earth in a form *other* than human. Either for lessons of experiencing in a personal wish situation, or being forced to in atonement under The Law of Karma - The Law of Reciprocal Action.

The reader will be familiar with our premise that only man possesses spirit as his "inner life-force". In a previous Chapter we outlined the reasons for this. In another, explanations as to why The Laws cannot be circumvented – including what we may regard as The Laws of Nature – were given. Therefore the inviolability of The Spiritual Laws absolutely decrees that any kind of cross-species transmigration of the human spirit into another and different kind of life-form is not only inherently incorrect, but impossible. The general thrust of life itself offers each species the natural ability to procreate or otherwise produce its own, irrespective of however diverse that ability might be for any given species. For only with that "procreative reality" can any species exist. Any attempt to procreate across clearly-defined, natural barriers will ultimately fail.

One can quite easily observe this "naturally lawful fact" in just one group of creatures, in that of the animals. Even in those most closely related, such as the big cats for example, the inability to produce offspring between the different kinds should be regarded as clear proof of the inviolability of *any* transgression of Natural Law, regardless of any particular faith/belief-mode outlook. Thus in the case of a "liger" – a hybrid produced by the mating of a female tiger and a male lion – or a "tigon" – the offspring of a male tiger and a female lion – we note that all offspring from either union are sterile. It is the same for the mule, a sterile hybrid of a male ass and a female horse. "Mother Nature" will simply not permit cross-species tampering, for that is as it should be.

If that were not the case, and different species were able to cross-breed with any other kind, we would not have a clear, consistent classification of fauna as we now have. It short, it would be disastrous. However, this does not remove the opportunity for natural change or mutation within each species, because that is simply the process of continual natural development, an entirely different situation altogether. Therefore, according to the "Spiritual Rules" of the creative process for all things, **humans can only be re-born into human form**!

Rebirth, however, is not the same as that which Jesus alluded to in His enlightening statement when He stated to Nicodemus,

> "Most assuredly I tell you, that unless anyone is born from above, he cannot see the Kingdom of God."
>
> (John 3:3, Fenton.)

That particular "birth" is a *spiritual* or *inner awakening* or *realisation* and does not, in any way, conflict with multi-earth lives which are obviously physical births.[4]

---

[4]For the reader who wishes to examine these same questions that have puzzled great thinkers and church leaders for centuries, and wish to be finally offered the explanations that eluded those erstwhile individuals, he should read

Now, since the idea of a "second death" necessarily travels into the area of multi-lives, it behoves the need to give sufficient explanation to this subject.

As a prime example let us examine just one particularly vital aspect of this subject from Stephen Lampe's work at this point. It will supply the reader with an explanation of how the early Church determined its final position on this matter of reincarnation. We should also recognise that there have always been, and there currently still are, a number of very eminent Christian church leaders who have publicly stated their support for reincarnation, with the further far-reaching view that the concept ***does not*** contradict the teachings of The Bible.

In addition, many eminent people from all walks of life believe it also, and recognise within it the inherent sense of true Justice which reincarnation offers. Therefore, if we are to fully understand how there can be so many apparent social injustices and inequities amongst the world's peoples when we speak of absolute Justice contained within The Spiritual Laws, and how there can be a "second death" separate and distinct from being re-born "spiritually", then we must openly and objectively examine this matter of reincarnation.

Since the generally accepted orthodox Christian view is to basically deny or refute the validity of such an idea, even with some of its leading clergy *accepting* of it, a need to define a starting point by which we might gain some insight into how the official Church position arose is vital. Stephen Lampe offers clarification about it in his book, "The Christian and Reincarnation". We would state the following excerpt to be a crucial "knowledge-imperative" for all Christians.

"The Second Council of Constantinople (553 AD)"

> "The history of the official Church position on reincarnation is a very complex one. Many assume that the Second Council of Constantinople (552 AD) also called the Fifth Ecumenical Council of the church, condemned the teaching of reincarnation, but this assumption has been called into question by some competent church historians.

---

the book, "The Christian and Reincarnation" by Stephen Lampe, (Millennium Press.) This well researched work, with much of the material culled from The Bible, will clarify many uncertainties for the serious seeker as to the validity and purpose of reincarnation, and will provide a disturbing challenge to those who might wish to scornfully dismiss the concept out of hand.

The Second Council of Constantinople was called by Emperor Justinian and convened on May 5th, 553 AD under the presidency of the Patriarch of Constantinople. However it was the Emperor, who had engaged in bitter conflict with Pope Vigilius, who controlled the proceedings. Even though the primary objective was to reconcile the churches of the East and West, the arrangements heavily favoured the East. It is reported that of the 165 bishops who signed the acts of the final meeting on June 2, not more than six could have been from the West. The request of Pope Vigilius for equal representation of bishops from East and West was refused. In protest, the Pope boycotted the meeting, even though he was in Constantinople, the venue of the meeting. However Pope Vigilius eventually accepted the decisions of the Council, an action that was not popular in the West, and which caused some dioceses, including that of Milan, to break off communion with Rome. Milan remained out of communion with Rome till the end of the sixth century.

Because of the protestations of Pope Vigilius, the Second Council of Constantinople did not open on schedule. While the assembled bishops were waiting Emperor Justinian ordered them to consider a subject (Origenism) that was not an item in the previously announced agenda. During this extra-conciliary session, fifteen condemnations (anathemas) proposed by the Emperor against the teachings of Origen (who had died three hundred years earlier in 254 AD) were approved. Apparently, one of the condemned teachings was the idea of pre-existence of the soul, and by implication, reincarnation. There is no evidence that Pope Vigilius, who was at the time protesting against the arrangements of the Council approved this action taken by Eastern bishops outside the formal sessions and before the opening of the Council. Thus, it is understandable that some Catholic scholars disassociate the Roman Church from the condemnations of the teachings of Origen, and therefore argue that the Roman Catholic Church has never really condemned the teaching of reincarnation.

Many otherwise knowledgeable Christians are unaware of the confusion surrounding the Second Council of Constantinople and the inconclusiveness and uncertainty of its decisions. For this reason, some imagine that they are obliged to uphold this ancient condemnation of reincarnation.

In any case Christians should appreciate that they should not necessarily consider themselves bound by decisions taken by some bishops more than 1,400 years ago. Did not the Church condemn Galileo's scientific support of the Copernican theory that the sun, and not the earth is the centre of the solar system? And the ordinary Christians of that day of course dutifully joined Church officials in denouncing the Copernican theory. Christians at that time probably imagined that the idea which contradicts the Scriptures must have been put in the mind of Copernicus by Satan! Today some Christians, unfortunately, have a similar view of reincarnation."

(Chapter 1, 8-9)

One of the main points of interest regarding this important meeting was the fact that such an incredibly far-reaching and definitive decision could have been taken in a side issue separate from the main agenda. The either-or aspect of a one-life concept versus a multi-life one decided that day actually calls into question the very essence of much of Bible teaching, the cornerstone on which supposedly rest many of our beliefs and ideals.

For a few men, therefore, to cast the disturbing shadow of such a definitive decree down through the centuries surely smacks of religious machinations, particularly the edict issued against the Christian theologian, Origen, who believed in reincarnation. Among other things the edict stated that anyone who said or thought that the souls of men had had an earlier life (pre-existence) and were now incarnated in bodies ... would be anathematised!

One might question the true motives of the Roman Emperor Justinian in *ordering* the bishops to consider condemning, among the other fifteen "anathemas", the concept of reincarnation. Perhaps the idea of being forced in future lives to "reap what one sowed" – with the probability of some of those incarnations being lived out in less than favourable circumstances – was, in itself, considered blasphemous to one very much accustomed to living a role of absolute power and wealth. The possibility of "inheriting" anything less than that must have been "anathema" to Justinian, since the line of Roman Emperors considered themselves to be divine and descended from the gods themselves.

So the very thought of reincarnation and atonement for an Emperor's possibly debased excesses needed to expunged from the day consciousness of the Empire in general. From the spiritual point of view, of course, no amount of legislation, debate or decree could have possibly altered the fact of The Law of Rebirth. And even a mighty Roman Emperor must obey this Law too.

Notwithstanding this decree, Stephen Lampe observes that, "Finally, Church historians point out that no papal encyclical against reincarnation has ever been issued – a point that should be of particular interest to Roman Catholics." (p 11)

Thus Christianity embraced reincarnation for three hundred years before the Emperor Justinian declared it "anathema".

The knowledge of reincarnation was thus withheld from many people who, with this knowledge, could have gained a deeper meaning and greater significance to their lives on earth and in the beyond. We should therefore *expand yet again* our horizons to encompass the recognition that only repeated earth-lives offer the human spirit the means whereby it is *able* to accumulate sufficient experiences "of the spirit" to gain true spiritual insight as to its origin and purpose, enabling it to develop genuine spiritual maturity.

The intervals between incarnations should be regarded as a very necessary time of learning also, as the life experienced in the "beyond" will be a direct result of the *kind of life* lived whilst on earth under the outworking of The Laws of "Sowing and Reaping", "Attraction..." and "Spiritual Gravity". Each further earth-life, also strictly governed by The Eternal Laws, will bring the soul to the correct circumstances of family and race that it will need for its further maturing. Either in terms of its own learning, or to provide the same for others in its new environment, or to expiate past misdeeds there.

Whatever the reason for an incarnation, it can only be in accordance with the strictness of The Spiritual Laws, so he will be justly placed in terms of circumstances and the requirement to experience that *which he once sowed*. A purification of the whole person is a necessary part of the overall learning process, provided, of course, that the path taken for this purpose truly aspires to "genuine spirituality". Even if this were not voluntarily the case, however, the same Laws would work on regardless, still bringing to that particular individual the consequences of previous decisions at the appropriate time.

Now, because our inherent free-will endowment determines what will return to us under The Spiritual Laws, this "constant-return" process takes effect whether we are on the earth or in the "planes of the beyond". **Thus we continually stand in the "reciprocal-effect mechanism" of all our past decisions.** Not necessarily the return effect of all at once but, nevertheless, in whatever is lawfully ordained for that particular point in time. In this lawful and completely inviolable process, there is no escape!

As we generally vacillate between making good and bad decisions, we can naturally expect a life of changing fortunes. Therefore, some will always be better off than others at any given moment, and some will be worse off, simply by virtue of the reciprocal effect of The Spiritual Laws. That is the reality for all. Since changing fortunes are a fact of life for most people, the concept of repeated earth-lives not only provides clear solutions to the worrying problems and trends current on the earth, but allows an insight into the Wisdom and Grace of The Creative Will in granting humankind the opportunity to "make good" all past mistakes. We must do so in any case, if we are not to suffer potentially hard fate continually.

With regard to the changing fortunes of the numerous philosophical ideas throughout history, Kierkegaard, in fine contrast to what we affirm, believed that we are "all unique individuals who only live once". He also attacked the reliance on ritual and dogma in Christianity, and what he thought was essentially the empty faithlessness of the adherents. He believed they had to do more than just believe "Christianity" is true. In his view, having a Christian faith meant following "a Christian way of life". Kierkegaard, who rejected the basic thrust of "Hegelianism", also thought that the individual is "responsible for his own life".

It is therefore imperative to "recognise the need" to make good one's transgressions. Once we have left the *relative protection of the physical body* at earthly death, it is too late to then lament the fact that we were too disbelieving, too superficial, too blind and stubborn to accept any view different to that which we personally wanted to believe. Because, there, in the far more *mobile* environment of the non-material world, all movement – even the effect of ones thoughts – are "speeded up" considerably. So, too, are the waiting reciprocal effects for the individual. Life in the physical body in the more ponderous world of the earth at least allowed a "stay of proceedings", so to speak.

It is precisely the time spent on earth that is crucial for correct decision-making, particularly at this point in the evolutionary development of this material part of Creation to which we and the earth physically belong. Unless one were completely insane – in which case one could not be held spiritually accountable for one's actions[5] – one would logically wish to be treated with respect and kindness by one's fellow men.

From our explanations of the death process we know that lighter spiritual thoughts and deeds produce a corresponding lightness of

---

[5] Naturally other karmaic events lead to this condition, which we will not delve into at this stage

the soul. Darker, heavier thoughts and actions produce the opposite under The Law of Spiritual Gravity. We therefore know that through personal choices, "heavier" souls will sink to the level corresponding to their particular "spiritual weight", there to live out their propensities with like-minded souls.

It is especially important to now understand that such levels *still remain in the* **Material Sphere,** *even though not actually on the earth*. All souls inhabiting those particular levels are therefore necessarily subject to whatever *finite* fate may befall them there. That is not the case with souls who gravitate to higher, lighter planes, however. There, the more spiritually enlightened thus more fortunate souls are not oppressed like those in the darker regions who have surrendered their free-will choices to baser propensities. Unlike those unfortunates, the souls who have earned the right to ascend to the higher levels are more easily able to *continually further ascend* to that region of Light which is **above the pull of the Material World and its finite time**. Becoming sufficiently enlightened whilst on earth so as to live correspondingly similar thoughts and deeds, guarantees an ascent into lighter planes after earthly death.

The horizons of the inhabitants there are vastly more expansive than those who languish in the much more restrictive environment of the lower, darker planes. Partaking of the great joy and happiness that exists in the lighter planes further imparts the natural wish to want more of the same, thus allowing still further ascent. The souls who have chosen the experience of the lower levels, set in place by their personal wish for the exact same things whilst on earth, enjoy no such peace. Theirs is literally the torment of being inflicted upon by others in the same way that they once did. Yet, as formerly stated, The Gift of Grace gives even those sad ones the choice to leave their surroundings behind.

As a precursor to providing definitive explanations about the "second death", it is timely to examine more closely the "awakening" in the beyond of a previously *disbelieving soul* just released from his physical body. With such a soul, however, let us first revisit the process and consider, once more, some of the things he may experience in the moments before burial when "friends" and relatives arrive to pay their "respects".

This usually difficult time invariably produces the whole range of emotional reactions in the psyche of the bystanders to the event. Human emotions at such times run the full gamut from deep and genuine grief, to curiosity, to superficiality, sometimes to anger and sometimes to gladness at the death. However, what is generally not accepted is that the "departed" one *can still see and hear all that takes place around his "discarded shell"*. So one can easily imagine his reaction to eulogies and speeches in his memory or honour and so on, particularly when those whom he believed he knew well whilst on earth now perhaps reveal a different side to their character.

In some cases, he could well re-evaluate the relationship of those kinds of people. Sadly, it would be difficult to express gratitude to those who might now reveal genuine respect and friendship towards him, those whom he did not realise held him in high regard when he was alive. To all intents and purposes, however, his visitors – both the genuine and the superficial – believe him to be dead, and he has no way of proving to them that he is still "living".[6]

Because of the lawful outworking of The Spiritual Laws in this common situation, it should not be difficult to picture the anguish of the departed one as he follows the whole procedure of his own funeral even. Yet he is unable to offer clarification about his situation to those most affected. Thus we can relate to him as he attends the burial of his earthly shell, and empathise with him at the moment of greatest grief, when the casket is lowered! One can picture him in a state of great despondency and desolation at this time. After a while, tiredness would overtake him and he might find some solace in sleep. The reader may find this curious, but just as the physical body tires through exertion, so will the soul-body.

When this soul finally severs itself from its tie to its former physical body, (via the disintegration of the "Silver Cord") it will invariably find itself in a plane closely corresponding to its previous state of "attitudinal-volition" during earthly life. If this had been one of disbelief or disinterest in "life after death" then, when he awakens, he will be surrounded by darkness. He will discover, however, that he is no longer connected to his physical shell. He is free, but in a strange and silent, oppressive darkness where he cannot even hear the sound of his own voice. And no matter what he may wish to believe about his situation, still the darkness presses

---

[6]The reader will recall the "Silver Cord" being a mediating connection to the earthly organs of sight and speech through still being attached to the physical shell. It is the special nature of the "cord" that makes it possible for the departed one to see and hear all that takes place around him. Despite this connection still permitting him sight and sound access to his recent world, he is nevertheless unable to make himself heard or felt by those still alive *because he no longer stands in a body of the same consistency as the material world* and therefore cannot "touch" anything of the earth, including his loved ones.

in on him.

In its new and unfortunate surroundings, the soul *lives* as it did on earth. For this is the *real* person except, now, freed from his physical body. He experiences all the travails and joys in his soul-body in the same way that he experienced life in his physical one. He weeps, laughs, tires and sleeps. For his new world is just as real as the physical one recently left behind, purely because his new body is of the **exact same consistency as his surroundings**. Whilst his new body is not a physical one, it is not his spirit-body either for he is still very, very far from the genuine Spiritual Realm from where he originated. His spirit – **the real man** – **is still the inner animating core of his new body**. This "new body", however, is subject to the much faster vibration of the non-physical world of the "beyond" – his world at this time.

His "faster environment" may induce a stronger urge to find out *why* than might have been the case on earth, and he may seek answers *more desperately*. We can readily understand that the restless need to seek is borne of a desperation to find an explanation for his rather sad circumstances. But how to know exactly *what* to seek? He only knows that he **needs** answers to his plight. Yet to find an answer may take such a soul years, even decades, for time has a vastly different meaning outside the physical realm. Until such time as genuine yearning to be free wells up in the soul of one in this position, however, all he can look forward to is the continuing condition of dark uncertainty. So we can be sure that much inner searching would take place as he struggles to understand what had brought about his sorry plight. Hopefully his seeking will bring about the realisation that this, after all, must be the "other world" he refused to believe in!

Such an inner awakening for this soul must surely presuppose, at the very least, the *dawning* of the recognition of obviously still being alive, yet clearly physically dead. Even that realisation, however, may not be *sufficiently strong* to bring about a *change* in his surroundings. The simple wish for change must further develop into a deep *longing* from which springs a genuine petition for help, even if only a timid prayer at first. For such a longing is suffused with "the purer intuition born of desperate need".

Finally, with the entry of humility and submission into his soul through deep and genuine prayers for help, the outworking of Grace upon him and his surroundings takes effect because, now, a connection with the higher and lighter Spiritual Spheres of Love and Grace is established. Consequently for this soul, the darkness would then give way to a kind of twilight. He would feel a corresponding lightness in his "body", and experience a sense of soothing comfort. Now he can take stock of his surroundings and is better able to determine his next move.

The "lightening" of his surroundings also at last allows him a glimpse of a light in the far distance. That far-away light becomes a beacon of hope and a means of understanding his new world. It is the only point of welcoming focus. The light comes no nearer to him but he intuitively knows that he must journey towards it, for he recognises that it will lead him out of his "twilight zone". Thus, gratitude and humility would begin to suffuse this soul as it senses more strongly the gift of Grace granted to it.

Humility, as an attribute and quality of the greatest power – Love – is a most necessary trait to develop if one seeks spiritual ascent. To practise opposite traits such as arrogance and cynicism with regard to Spiritual Truth will ensure similar kinds of experiences for such believers as those outlined here. Whilst our example is basically that of the initial experiences of one soul in the Ethereal World of the "beyond", they could not be said to be those of a "bad" person. Just one who had given no thought to his fate after earthly death; one who did not want to be "bothered with it".

In summary, anyone who in his earth life refuses to acknowledge that there is "life after death", or that there is a concomitant requirement to one day render account for all that he has done and all that he has left undone, is blind and deaf when he finally passes over into the Ethereal World of the "beyond". Only for the time that he remains connected with his discarded physical body can he still partially observe events around him.

Once he is freed from his disintegrating physical body, this possibility is lost to him and he no longer sees or hears anything. Yet that should not be viewed as punishment. On the contrary, it should be recognised *as a perfectly natural consequence of his own attitude toward "life after death" whilst he lived*. Because he refused to "believe" – which is tantamount to "blindness" and "deafness" – he thus **forms for himself** his future ethereal environment which he must fully experience if, in the meantime, there is no change from his "disbelieving position" before his death arrives. After that transition, only a voluntary change in his soul will allow him to see and hear again.

The necessary condition for such a change after earthly death is the *desire of the individual himself to* **want** *to change his circumstances*. The time frame for this also solely depends upon him. It may take years or decades, perhaps far longer, but is the concern of the individual alone. The exercise of his personal free will brought him there in the first place, and can also release him from it – *if* he so desires. It cannot be forced upon him. The light that the soul was finally permitted to see as a result of his inner change was *always there*. It was his *spiritual condition* that **prevented** him from seeing it. The **condition** of the soul thus determines *how* he sees it – whether strong or weak, or not at all!

The example we have outlined shows a soul experiencing the outworking of The Law of Sowing and Reaping in stark relief. It received what it had wished. Thus what it brought to itself in accordance with that wish, simply because it had refused to believe in the reality of "life after death". What should be clearly and fully understood is that **the soul cannot, by any means, abolish the continuation of life for itself**. The reason is beautifully simple and final – *because it has absolutely no jurisdiction over it whatsoever*. Disbelief of this fact cannot alter that lawful outcome by one single dot!

This knowledge should be regarded as the key consideration as to how one should resolve to live one's life. Not from fear, but from true knowledge, in the realisation that we simply cannot alter The Spiritual Laws to suit our personal wishes. A human soul, purely via his inherent free-will ability, can bring himself to either a dark or light region in the Ethereal World. Even if finding himself in the former, all that is required for him to ascend out of such a place is to generate a spiritually pure volition of genuine humility in the recognition that he and he alone was responsible for the circumstances of his condition. With this first and most necessary step, he can begin the process of ascending out of the lower, material spheres of the beyond to the higher, lighter planes far from the inexorable and ordained path of the earth and its interstellar environs as *it tracks towards its time of disintegration*.

If this is the position in which a relatively "decent" individual in the earthly sense would find himself after earthly death, how much more dire would the situation be for those whose earthly lives are given over totally to baseness? We would have to conclude that in their regions of darkness, there would surely not be any light to speak of! Now we may begin to understand why Jesus was so severe in His admonishing of those who were not prepared to change their ways, for He certainly understood all of The Law in its strict and inviolable Justice.

The explanations offered allow us to easily picture the fate of some past races, and perhaps even some present ones too. Members of races who live according to cultural traditions and beliefs which do not encompass any elements of Spiritual Law *as it actually is* may well descend to lower regions of darkness after earthly death. There to live out the reciprocal effects of their self-willed and self-chosen path.

If even a relatively half-decent life brings about a sad and less than joyful outcome, it should remind each individual to carefully consider his attitude toward this inevitable event called death. Just as importantly for parents and society in general, the necessary schooling and explanations about it should be provided for the young, to thereby help to beneficially change the very nature of society itself. Via this recognition and educative method, we may perhaps even lessen the unacceptably high rate of youth suicide – *suicide being a serious spiritual transgression*.

Unfortunately, such souls as described in our example probably make up many, many millions on the earth today. They have no wish to learn about God, spiritual things, or eternity, yet may be good and decent people. However, *since **The Laws have the final say in all matters human***, the end-fate of those who are simply evil-minded speaks for itself. Despite the obvious fact that we must all die, many people are reluctant to even acknowledge that it just might be in their best interests to think about their own time of exit from the earth.

So, what might be the experience of a person who *does* believe in life *after* death and thus recognises the need to live correctly *whilst* on earth? What might he experience upon awakening in the "beyond"? At the beginning of this Chapter we noted the plea of Franchezzo for humankind to awaken to the truth of life after death. And we further described the basic experiences of a soul who did not believe. In strong contrast, here is an opposite account.

H. Dennis Bradley, an English poet who died in 1934, had promised to communicate after his death, if this were at all possible. Shortly afterwards he apparently did succeed. Through a medium he gave a good description of his experiences. What is interesting is the great difference between the kind of environment he experienced, and that of our example, of one who did not believe. Bradley's narration follows:

> "The landscape in which we live is a great deal different from that of the earth. It is of a blessed purity and clearness. There is a tremendous amount of light, and nothing is grey or even dark.

There is soil here too, as well as an ocean, trees and flowers, but everything is more beautiful and more wonderful than on earth.

Even the plumage of the birds is more radiant and more colourful. But strangest of all are the flowers. They not only exude fragrance, but also emit delightful sounds which the physical ear cannot hear, and which are different for each kind of flower.

There is no weariness here and no need for rest, instead one feels oneself overflowing with a wonderful strength. Time is of no importance. One is always busy; for there is a million times as much to learned as on earth.

There are millions and millions of departed souls to be found here. The spirits can communicate with one another, even though they spoke different languages during their earthly lives.

The ability to move from one place to another is also wonderful. It is not the same as on earth, for there are no physical bodies here. Even though I do have a form that could be compared with a body, it does not bind me.

Here it is enough simply to wish to be somewhere, and immediately you are there.

In the future it will probably again be possible for human beings still on earth and souls in the beyond to communicate. But for this it is necessary for the human being in simple trust to open the gates of knowledge which he has closed to himself by his lack of belief. "

A few key points about Spiritual Law and Bible Scripture can be clarified from Bradley's description of his experiences in the particular level of the beyond he had *earned the right* to be in.

1. Note Bradley's description of the landscape in which he found himself, with the same physical features and flora and fauna as on earth. Just as we explained in a previous chapter. Naturally more perfect, however.

2. The soul of *our* example, in being heavily burdened with non-understanding of the why of his plight, needed to rest. Bradley and those of like spirit, animated by the purer surroundings of their higher, lighter realm, were filled with energising strength.

3. Note, also, the reference to "so much more to be learned there than on earth". In this statement lies the meaning of

the Scripture: "And a thousand years are as one day." In other words, what would take a person a thousand years *to learn* in the heavy, ponderous physical realm of the earth, would only need one day of ***spiritual experiencing*** in the higher Realms of Light.

4. Even though not possessing a physical body, the soul, with the spirit as its core, retains the bodily form as an envelope for the spirit. This "body form" is only shed if and when the entity ascends to the point of his origin – The Spiritual Realm.

5. Finally, Bradley's recognition of man's paucity of spirit in closing himself to the knowledge he needs for the greater overview of the why of his very existence, the vital knowledge of the *beyond* and how he is *lawfully* connected to it.

As a reflective assessment of this "paucity of spirit", perhaps we should collectively consider what has developed in the state education systems of some Western societies particularly. Over many years, that has taken the form of insidiously stripping away from schools the once regular practice of Biblical or religious instruction and prayer. Once there was at least a *basic* societal recognition of a Creator and inviolable Laws accepted by far more people than might accept such a view today. In the present, such ideas are more likely to be deemed superfluous and unimportant – a trampling on "human rights".

Such a foolish and quite stupid term. As if any human being could produce the perfection that we are permitted to live in. In the 21st century, we still produce only war, terrorism, ethnic cleansing, environmental degradation ... – should one go on? Too many forces within our present societal infrastructure deem "religion" unnecessary for society's continuing function in these more "enlightened times" of "economic roulette" on "corporate earth".

The blatant and dangerous hypocrisy of this "modern educational practice" is glaringly revealed as a false sham when these same societies are hit with disaster and tragedy. ***Then we see the desperate prayers to GOD!*** Even those who impose the new educational thinking upon society – the politicians and their servants – even they must bow to a clear truth experienced by soldiers placed in harm's way: **"When the chips are down, everyone calls out for THE MAN!"**

Ferrar Fenton, from whose Bible we mainly quote, states, in his introductory notes, that one Professor Karl Behr of Munich, insightfully argued for the retention of religion within the state or society if it was to survive.

Fenton notes that on the Philosophy of History, Professor Behr observed:

> *"That the best-established doctrine of Historical Philosophy was, that all the power, prosperity, and mental energy of a Race or Nation sprang from and lived by its Religion; that when its Religion ceased to be its Faith – that is, its energising principle – the intellect, power, vigour, and prosperity of that Race or Nation died away in proportion, and ultimately perished, both mentally and physically."*

And Fenton further observes:

> *"...how he illustrated his doctrine by a wide survey and a series of illustrations from the history of all nations, Asiatic, African, and European, both Ancient and Modern, dwelling especially upon the fact that this Law of National Life did not depend upon any particular Religion, but was manifested by them all, Pagan, Jewish, Mohammedan, and Christian?"*
>
> (*The Holy Bible in Modern English*, Explanatory Note, p xi, Ferrar Fenton.)

Fenton goes on to say that Professor Behr's doctrine "...did not urge a regard to that Law of History for any ecclesiastical purpose..." for he was not a professed member of any particular Christian Church. Professor Behr therefore emphasised it by a review of the Arabian Civilisation under the Kaliphat.

What Professor Behr refers to as a "Law of National Life" is, of course, Spiritual Law. His revealing insight offers clear reason for an acceptance and adjustment to The Laws for the betterment and, indeed, survival of our societies and nations! **Teach religion as a step of faith to begin with, but teach The Law for true knowledge and conviction!**

7.2 Earthbound Souls

One issue that requires examination before finally exploring the actual meaning of the "second death" is that of how and why souls can become "earthbound". The term "earthbound" is one with which many are possibly familiar but are perhaps not completely sure of the processes that determine the "binding". Even though much has been written about such situations there is little real knowledge as to why! The many recorded cases of hauntings, of poltergeist activity etc., even though true enough, do not give the full picture at all.

Poltergeist "energy", whilst often producing "noisy" and perhaps frightening phenomena, actually concerns only a very small number of souls. The vast majority of the "earthbound" continue their particular activities without humankind being aware they are about. At various times the close presence of one may be "sensed", and people with clairvoyant or psychic ability can see them on occasions. With all processes and activities in Creation, however, the reason for the close presence of one will be subject to strict Spiritual Law, and will invariably be associated with land, a place or dwelling, or to a person or persons in that particular place. Or with an *activity* there to which the "earthbound" one is drawn. There may be other ties but those outlined will invariably hold the reason why.

In the first place, there should not be cause for fear if a poor "earthbound" soul is recognised as being about, because the binding of one to the earth is also a perfectly natural process. Many presently alive now may well find themselves tied to the earth after their time of death too. Whilst we know that this should *not* be the normal process, nevertheless it is brought about once more by man's refusal to live correctly, i.e. according to Spiritual Law. The knowledge of that Law would help him to leave behind all pointless and unnecessary ties to the earth. A few brief examples as to how this sorry state can come about should offer some clarification of the process.

Let us examine the case, unfortunately quite common, where a questioning child is continually told by his parents that there is no such thing as "life after death". In the beginning the child may intuitively sense that there *is* life after death, or may have heard about it from school or in church. Uncertain, he seeks confirmation of it from his parents, let us say his father. The father, through his own fear or lack of interest in the matter, dismisses the whole idea of it and forcefully imparts this view to the child. With continual reinforcement of this belief, the child begins to doubt, until finally accepting the opinion of adults that there is no life after death.

However, the time comes when the father dies and, much to **his** horror and dismay, finds that death is not the end after all.

The deep wish now arises within the father to impart the truth of this to his child, and this strong desire binds him to it. The child, unfortunately, can neither hear him nor sense his presence, for it now has the firm conviction that its father *has ceased to exist*. This conviction acts as *a completely natural and impenetrable wall between the child and the father's efforts*. Now the father must live the painful reality that, through misleading his child, there is the very real danger that he may take a path leading him further and further from the truth. Moreover, as the child grows into adulthood and gathers future generations around him, the same misleading error is passed on through them with the added danger of his child, *through **its** increasingly narrowing perceptions*, falling further.

Perhaps this is one meaning of the "sins of the father" visiting themselves upon successive generations. In any case, this forms the father's so-called "punishment" for misleading his child. In such circumstances, it would be extremely difficult for him to communicate to his offspring the knowledge that life continues on. Consequently, he will be forced to witness how his previous wrong idea is carried on down through the generations, and all as a result of his own disbelief. Unfortunately for him, however, he cannot be released until one of his descendants finally recognises the error and adjusts his life to the right way, hopefully also influencing the others. Only then will the father be gradually released. And only then can he consider his own need for ascent.

A very typical and more insidious way in how one can be earthbound is through the connection to cigarette smoking. It is a situation which impacts hugely and detrimentally on human health in two ways. Physically in the first instance, and spiritually in the second.

An habitual smoker who dies takes over with him the strong craving to smoke. In its strength, it is actually a *propensity* which thus has a *connection to the "spiritual intuition"*, albeit only at its outermost edge. His propensity produces the need for gratification and he therefore seeks out smokers. There he is able to satisfy his craving because the changed nature of his "body" after earthly death enables him to enjoy **the inner sensations of smokers** to whom he is held.

If there is no stronger reciprocal effect waiting to bind him to any other place, the sensations he feels are, for him, generally pleasant ones. So such souls may not be aware that being tied to others on the earth through their propensity is actually a self-imposed punishment. This is also the case with drinking, so-called harmless recreational drug use and aberrant sexual desires. Given the heavy emphasis today on one's "right" to sexual gratification by any and all means, many might not consider this last a punishment at all. Yet any binding to the earth prevents such souls from recognising that their "primary craving" – which overshadows all else – is actually a punishment stemming solely from their own aspiritual personal decisions and subsequent lifestyle whilst alive on earth. Consequently, the longing for something better, more noble and higher, cannot easily develop to become the main focus which would then free them from such base desires and uplift them.

Yet even if this main desire should reach a point where it begins to die away, other lesser desires, which a soul may still carry within, may then rise to take the place of the original, strongest propensity and subsequently transport him to a place where those lesser desires can be lived through. Eventually, with sufficient good will for his own ascent, he will finally succeed in clearing all the dross that had previously prevented any chance of release from his bind to the earth. For only when the earthly sensations are gradually outlived or let go, associated with a longing for what is higher, purer and therefore more spiritual, can he steadily ascend. The variations here will be many but these few examples illustrate the *kinds* of circumstances that *can* allow a soul to become "earthbound".

The act of suicide can also produce very strong ties to the earth for a soul that decides to exit earth life by this means. With suicide, certain aspects in that individual's life will hold powerful sway prior to the deed. A stronger than usual emotional component, invariably seen as insurmountable, will help drive the thought toward suicide, so is often a powerful precursor to the final act. In concert with any problem that *appears* to have no solution, the inner strength of the one so assailed will ebb to a degree commensurate with the perceived degree of hopelessness of the particular situation faced.

However, notwithstanding the reason for such a desperate "solution", the very act of ending one's own life prematurely means that that soul has *rejected* the gift of life. A life, moreover, that it had petitioned for. Exiting before the fulfilment or completion of its life's purpose ensures that the soul is held to the particular level of "maturity" or experiencing attained up to that point in time. It therefore "passes over" in an immature state. Because of the very strong psychic/emotional "feelings" generated within and around a suicide, the site of the incident may become the strongest point of focus for it after death, and may thus bind the soul to that place for some time.

However, since The Laws demand spiritual fulfilment in all things right down to the smallest ramification, this soul must then again incarnate on earth to "catch up" with and then complete all that it did not attain to or fulfil previously. Because it personally chose to commit suicide as perhaps an apparent "easy way out", it will carry with it into its next life *the same unresolved aspect*. Only through recognising The Laws of Life and adjusting its thinking and activity to them, might it then expiate the previous unlawful deed to begin again its path of natural ascent – if it should so choose.

In the "strange but true" category, *sudden* and quite *unexpected* deaths, such as might occur in a random shooting, in war, terrorist bombings, an aircraft explosion etc., can happen so quickly that those killed *do not realise they are actually dead*. In a "normal" death situation, the connection to its former cloak should provide a reference point for at least some level of understanding for the one recently departed. But the complete disintegration or vaporisation of the physical body in an instant, not altogether uncommon in certain extreme situations in recent times, may preclude that possibility. In such cases, the person affected is literally forcibly wrenched or ejected from the physical shell – the mortal cloak – in a split second, and thus stands alone and stripped of its now virtually non-existent body.

After the Second World War, it was revealed that during the Battle of Britain where many *young* Allied pilots were killed in air combat against the German Luftwaffe, a very senior RAF Commander from time to time worked with a medium to try to contact his dead pilots to help them leave the earth. Anecdotal reports at the time strongly indicated that some were not aware they had actually died, for a number were "haunting" the Air Bases from which they had operated. More especially in exploding fighters – but also in bombers – death came very suddenly and very quickly to very young men of incredible courage and daring, to "boys" who readily understood that their *life expectancy* in total air combat might only be a matter of minutes.

So for very young pilots now a world away from childhood, teenage years and families, the Air Base became their new "home". It was a Base from which the battle was fought, but a place of rest and relative safety between missions as well. It was also where strong physical and emotional attachments of deep camaraderie and mutual respect would inevitably develop between skilled pilots and brave men. Men who understood they were engaged in a life and death struggle with an enemy bent on the destruction or enslavement of their homeland. Deriving from sheer psychological necessity to mask the seriousness of the struggle, the dire situation of the time drove pilots to adopt a devil-may-care, almost cavalier approach to their task. For given the very high attrition rate, it was imperative to yet believe that one might nevertheless survive to the end.

Powerful spiritual forces bond servicemen in this kind of desperate yet noble struggle and sacrifice to the utmost degree. Even though rarely voiced by the people involved, that bond is actually **Love**! The Air Base and all that it contained thus represented the entirety of their life at the time, in the machinery of war and in the intangible essence of enduring comradeship forged through necessary sacrifice for a just cause. Very significantly in this particular situation, however, it was the ***last earthly anchor point*** they would know before death overtook some of them. Therefore, to ***their*** "Base", ***their*** home and ***their*** fellow pilots, did some ***return*** after their personal sacrifice.

It may sound incongruous to believe that one cannot know that one has died, yet that is the reality that some will inevitably experience.[7] Relatives or friends who possess some measure of *understanding* about the truth of "life after" should therefore consider helping their very recently departed to at least a similar measure of "knowing". To help them more easily transit the passage from the near-earth environs to their next ordained level of existence after the Silver Cord is severed. As formerly stated, the time to so explain is in the days immediately after death.

7.3 Hypnotism – a Spiritual Crime

The effect of hypnotism derives from the foregoing explanations on "Earthbound Souls" and is thus also important to visit at this point. Whilst its practitioners *can* be tied to souls on earth, the more insidious effect of it is to become tied to lower levels of the "beyond" after earthly death. It is a practice that certain branches of medicine – psychological, psychiatric and general etc.. – employ on a reasonably regular basis. Its use is ostensibly touted as being of great benefit for patients in certain categories of medicine. It is also regarded as an important crime-fighting tool by some law

---

[7] In this regard, some films like "The Sixth Sense" *can* depict a certain measure of the truth.

enforcement agencies in certain types of investigations.

A seemingly innocuous practice that *appears* to be of benefit to mankind in certain situations is, in truth, **an extremely serious spiritual transgression** – *for the hypnotist particularly,* **but for the one hypnotised too**. The spiritually astute reader should recognise why this would be so. The *effects of the application* of hypnotism are so far-reaching that, *if fully recognised*, practitioners *in every current field of practice* would, in horror, **immediately and voluntarily cease all such activities**. In blunt terms, hypnotism *binds* the personal and free will of the subject to the *control* of the hypnotist, and therein lies the seriousness of the transgression. It lies in the *binding* of the *spirit* of another human being. In other words, the one hypnotised is open to receiving whatever spiritually adverse currents or forces may wish to attach itself thereto at that moment, because the individual is not able to resist, or protect itself against, such influences.

Even if used to relieve chronic pain, to help stop smoking or heal a bodily disease, any apparent subsequent improvement *resulting from* the "treatment" should be regarded as temporary alleviation. Since it has been the spirit that has been bound, and irrespective of the "condition" for which hypnotism might have been sought, what will be achieved will be more a "suppressive effect", but not *real control* of the problem or condition. Intervention by hypnotism is not any kind of ultimately beneficial panacea, for only with a *free and uninfluenced volition* can a human being take full control over its life-problems and destiny. A destiny or fate resulting from its own decisions in any case.

Whilst the effects of being hypnotised are not at all helpful for the one hypnotised, the end result for the hypnotist is *far more dangerous*. Because he is the one who has *bound* the *spirit* of the other – and irrespective of the reason why – he is, from that point on, psychically tied or bound to that other person. Forcibly binding the spirit of another through hypnotism simultaneously binds the hypnotist to his subject. And because *he* retarded the free development of that person, *he* cannot be released until *he* has helped him to advance as far as he would have done were it not for his intervention in the binding of that spirit.

The ultimate horror for all hypnotists after earthly death must surely be the realisation that they are tied to *all* whom they once bound through hypnosis. For even after both have left the earth the hypnotist must, by Law, go where the spirit he once bound goes. Even to the lowest realms of darkness if need be, for each connecting tie to all whom he hypnotised must be redeemed, *one link after the other*. The hypnotist cannot ascend until the very last of his subjects has begun their ascent. Should any yet remain in the lower realms **he, too, will stay**!

In the light of this knowledge, consider how hypnotism is used in a comedic way in vaudeville and stage shows. Ostensibly all very hilarious, but ultimately foolish and dangerous in the extreme. As we state quite often, any transgression of The Spiritual Laws will always return the reciprocal effect. Not in accordance with human opinions, but according to the full strength and perfect justice of The Law!

For what humanity sows, humanity must reap!

7.4 The Danger of Leading Astray

A similar fate awaits those who, in seeking followers through religious or "spiritual" activities, distort the Truth to such a degree that the followers are completely led astray – away from the direction leading to the possibility of spiritual ascent. Good intentions hold no mandate here. Neither does it matter if the "leader" is trained in a Theological College, or holds an official position in a mainstream Church, promotes New-Age philosophy, or sets up a personalised, charismatic-type "church".

Writers, especially, need to be absolutely aware of the inviolable outworking of The Law in this regard. For their writings can live on and continue to influence long *after* they have left the earth. It was not without high purpose that one of the great Religions specifically warned *against* the written word being used for wrong purposes, for those very words would stand *with* the authors at the time of their Judgement. The incredible proliferation of so many books literally "churned out" in the millions stands as clear testimony to the use of the gift of language for oftentimes spurious purposes.

Of course it remains the personal, free-will choice of any individual whether or not to accept a particular teaching, or follow a particular "leader". Notwithstanding that inherent truth, the historical record contains very many instances of so-called "religious leaders" who *actively* seek adherents – not to fulfil some kind of altruistic or spiritually-ennobled purpose, but to gain personal power, and political or financial advantage. Self-promoting egotism seems to be a common trait here. Therefore, even if, in the meantime, such "leaders" had come to the shattering recognition that they were wrong, those so influenced by them must also be helped to reach the same recognition.

In summary, those who promote, teach and otherwise foment incorrect ideas about the how and why of Creation and human existence and thus lead people astray – away from Spiritual Truth – will discover to their horror upon their own death, that they were completely wrong. And that all *those* so led astray by them must first recognise how wrong were the "teachings of the "leader" *they* once followed before they, the particular "leaders or teachers", can begin their ascent.

There, on the "other side" away from the safer environment of the earth, the once "sure leaders" must wait until the very last they had led astray comes to recognition of that wrong decision and path, just like the hypnotists. Only then can they, the "leaders", begin their own ascent upwards. In just the Christian Church alone – and deriving from the legacy of the murder of that so-called "trouble-maker", Jesus – how many well-meaning "church-servants" over centuries have preached sermons that badly distorted His Pure Teachings and thereby leading people astray? How many still do so today! For **everyone** on earth, the warning out of The living Law to be very sure of one's chosen path is simple, yet stark.

To return now to the Scriptural warning of the "second death", in order to fully understand it we must again revisit the concept of reincarnation. It is a concept which needs to be recognised as, or likened to, a "school of learning". Thus, each earth-life lived represents a class or stage in which our spiritual development can be furthered – *if we so choose*. However, we should not be so naive as to believe that each successive incarnation *automatically* places us on the next highest step. Whilst that may be a desirable idea, and one which has its adherents in some religious beliefs, the reality is vastly different. With each earth-life, we are given **the opportunity to re-awaken** and once more advance – **nothing more**. In **every** case, in **every** incarnation, we must **recognise the purpose** for which we were born, and *live accordingly*. Therefore, to this earthly school, we must return a number of times.

The "extra classes" allow us more time to learn and to fulfil our spiritual purpose thus helping our ascent. It is equally true, however, that one may *never* recognise the purpose for which one was incarnated, irrespective of how many "classes" one might "attend". Consequently, thereby, one may continually gravitate toward material or even evil pursuits. That kind of path helps to re-strengthen quite unnecessary binds to the material, from which one will need to strive harder to break away **if one wishes to ascend out of the final chaos of the earth during the apocalyptic times**.

Finally, after many "classes", examination day for *everyone* arrives. The result will determine whether one graduates from the "school" and achieves spiritual freedom, or whether one fails to pass the "examination" and must be expelled. With regard to we human beings currently in material Creation, the examination is now due, with fewer opportunities for a "recount". This "reality" is reflected in the increasing problems within society, and in the enormous and rapidly increasing amount of *reaping in suffering* that we witness daily on a global scale. As previously stated, the length of time under which our "school" was ordained to run for is exactly that of the equally ordained time of life for this part of material Creation to which the earth, our "classroom", belongs.

Once more in reinforcement, whilst the Grace of being able to "right past wrongs" is a constant promise, the time available for any such expiation is precisely that under which the material part of the world is ordained to exist as our physical home. At the end of the allotted time, everything that is part of that materiality or connected to it will go through a disintegration process. Unless we have reached a degree of spiritual maturity and inner purity sufficient to take us above the pull of the earth, any human spirits who have not managed, or not bothered, to spiritually mature adequately enough will be caught up in the destruction too. Yet it should always be remembered that this whole process is a completely natural and ordained one, even if difficult to comprehend in terms of reason or scale.

Now we have reached the stage where a definitive conclusion to the meaning of the "second death" can be offered. What is vital to understand is that whilst the *earth* is the obvious home of mankind in the *material* sense, and the *Ethereal World* is the transitional experiencing plane for souls in the beyond, *both "planes" or "spheres"* belong **solely** to the **"non-eternal" Material Part** of Creation. The true Spiritual Realm, as we now clearly know, stands far higher in The Eternal.

Thus from its earliest beginnings the Material Creation was inexorably bound to the unalterable Spiritual Laws, which also bring about evolution and dissolution. As already noted, what are referred to as The Laws of Nature are, in reality, the ***expression of* The Will of God *on earth***! In its expressionistic activity, therefore, it is continually forming and dissolving worlds, exactly as astronomers observe. Moreover, The Creative Will – out of which the Ethereal World of the beyond and the Material World of the earth plane issued as one inter-connected whole – is present throughout all of Creation.

In a time scale that we can never ever comprehend it is necessary to at least *strive* to understand that **only the cycle of Creation is eternal**. And not necessarily the life of individual component parts of the material world as a whole. Only in a "continuous" coming-into-being, disintegration and re-formation is the "cycle" **eternal** and **without end**, thus **infinite**.

It is therefore within this great and stupendous happening that all the many revelations and prophecies are fulfilled. Within this framework, also, there one day comes the last, i.e. the *final* "sorting out" for *each* material celestial globe. However, whilst this does not take place simultaneously in the whole of Creation, it is a process connected with that part of Creation which reaches the point in its cycle where its disintegration must occur, so that it can once more begin the process of renewal in the fulfilment of the Eternal Cycle.

It should be further understood that in strict accordance with the consistency of the Natural Laws, the exact point at which disintegration of each celestial globe must begin is precisely determined. Most importantly for humankind, therefore, *and **irrespective of the condition of the celestial globe concerned or of its inhabitants***, the process of ***disintegration*** must develop at a very definite point in time. In accordance with The Spiritual Laws, the Eternal Cycle drives every celestial globe irresistibly towards this point, enabling its particular hour of disintegration to be fulfilled. However, as with everything in Creation, this actually represents simply a transformation – albeit a mighty one – which thereby provides the opportunity for further development.

Once this collective point of its ordained evolutionary development is reached, however, this Material part of Creation, along with the earth and all its inhabitants, will be "ripe" for the "final sorting". That is the moment of our "either-or" – our final **50% Choice** and **100% Outcome!** Either we are raised upwards to The Light if we have followed a spiritual path or, if we have become convinced that material or aspiritual considerations are more important or more valuable, we are held fast to the World of Matter. Thus, through our own personal desire to seek things other than those which hold true spiritual values, we must then be drawn, with the World of Matter, into *disintegration*! That, then, is **"spiritual death!**

Thus have we finally explained the meaning of the *second death*. **It *is* "spiritual death"!**

Long development over millennia from an unconscious spirit seed in The Spiritual Realm to its first incarnation onto the earth plane permitted the newly arrived human beings to reach the necessary state of personal self-consciousness, and then journey through the first stages of speech development. Continuing on through the era that we designate as early man, through the transitional stages of tribalism and thence into nationhood and the world stage via many different incarnations, that long often tortuous path now finally nears its zenith.

This lengthy development to "personal self-consciousness" will unfortunately be terminated for those who, through their rejection of Spiritual Truth, are irrevocably drawn into the disintegrating process. They will therewith experience the piece-by-piece shredding of the *"ego of personal self-consciousness"* during the dissolution process of this part of the Material World. Piece by piece, until the once "conscious" personality is reduced to an "unconscious" spirit-seed as it was at its beginnings. Thus reduced to the state of *spiritual death* – **the "second death!"**

For those who do ascend out of the chaos of disintegration and dissolution, the specific meaning of one particular Scripture in Revelation can be readily understood:

"...over these the second death has no authority!"

(Revelation 20:6, Fenton.)

In the closing part of this Chapter it is important to clarify a key aspect of the human spirit's development to *spiritual self-consciousness* and the reverse process of its possible loss in the disintegration of the "Material World" in which it had developed to that self-conscious level. We have identified that the "spirit" originates from The Eternal Part of The Spiritual Realm and arrives in its first incarnation without yet having developed to the state of "personal self-consciousness". This can only be effected by that "spirit" in the "Material World", for it is its *personal experiencing in this **earthly** medium* that offers the mechanism for its necessary development to self-consciousness. Therefore, even though the *unconscious spiritual part* of each human entity is originally of The Spiritual Realm, it can only *acquire **personal** "self-consciousness"* in its wanderings through the Material Realms, particularly whilst on the *earth!*

Therefore, the stripping away of its *spiritual* self-consciousness to the unfortunate condition of *spiritual death* can equally only occur during the *disintegration* of the *material* part of Creation in which it developed to its *self-conscious state*, and to which the necessary "experiences" to obtain this desired level belong. This "stripping away" does not occur in the actual Spiritual Realm of Creation as the words may seem to suggest, for that is **not** the area where the human spirit is ordained to *develop* to personal self-consciousness. This particular "schooling" takes place in the various levels of the Material Realm, and naturally includes some time on earth.

Thus it is The Spiritual Realm that the human spirit ascends to when it has gained sufficient spiritual purity and maturity to earn its place there. There in The Eternal Spiritual, secure in its eternal reality within the bounds of its original home, it is able to fulfil its complete spiritual potential – **eternally!**

The reality of the "second death" should not be equated with the beliefs of those who interpret this process as being similar to the attainment of "nirvana", the "desired" state of spiritual bliss expounded by some Eastern religions. Spiritual Law decrees that the human spirit is ordained to develop to **personal** *self-consciousness* only, which means it retains its ***individuality*** and therefore must render ***personal responsibility*** for all its activity. It was never ordained to merge with a collective "cosmic consciousness". This is a seemingly pleasant idea but does not accord with Spiritual Truth. The "either-or" **choice** here means **either** *individual spiritual life*, **or** ***individual*** *spiritual death*, in strict accordance with inviolable Spiritual Law. The choice once more, of course, is solely that of each person alone.

There is one further important aspect of the "second death reality" to address at this crucial time in the earth's and humankind's development. The words, "eternal damnation", are usually synonymous with fanatical "fire and brimstone" religion. Yet, in reality, it well describes the quite natural and lawful processes for any human spirit drawn into disintegration, for he ***ceases to be personal***. From any standpoint, this must surely be the worst fate that could possibly befall any individual. For it is exactly synonymous with effacement from The Book of Life itself!

Moreover, this separation of *spirit* from *matter* is, itself, a completely natural process. Under the aegis of The Creative Will, and in accordance with The Spiritual Laws, *it is already now taking place*. **It is the so-called "Last Judgement".** This final "sorting out", *not yet "full-blown"*, however, is necessarily connected with great upheavals and transformations but will be on a scale not previously known. The Book of Matthew offers a strong insight into this time. It was given when the Disciples of Jesus asked Him what signs will portend "the completion of this age." (Matthew 24:3, Fenton.)

Verses 19 to 22 are particularly chilling in their portent.

> "But alas for those with child and those who nurse in those days! Pray, however, that your flight may not come during the winter, nor upon a Rest-day; for there shall then be wide-spread affliction, such as has not been known since the beginning of the world until now, no, nor will ever be known again. And if those times were not cut short, not a man would be saved; but for the sake of the chosen ones, those times will be cut short."

These particular passages, as with most in The Bible, become far more clarified when assessed from the knowledge of The Spiritual Laws of Creation. It would be a tragic mistake, therefore, to regard these explanations as just religious "fire and brimstone fanaticism" without any relevance to societal beliefs or norms today. The very fact that virtually everything is collapsing globally should be evidence enough that there is some exceptionally powerful *reaping* taking place already. We can be sure, therefore, that even what we observe daily is not yet the culmination – the final – *collective reaping* so to speak!

Consequently, it should be a simple matter to recognise that the earth and "its inhabitants" must surely be approaching a major and climactic point, simply because more is happening faster. The separation among men reveals itself more and more sharply every day as smaller and smaller splinter factions in religion, politics, or ethnic groupings, break away from parent organisations. Thus what had previously only manifested itself in "opinions and convictions" now reveals itself more and more as intransigent positions, often marked by violence or the intimidatory threat thereof.

Therefore the present state of the world should be viewed with alarm and concern, with the urgent need to seriously recognise where we *actually* stand spiritually. In order to stand "right", however, we must exert the greatest strength to leave behind all base thoughts and activities, seek out Spiritual Truth and begin to live accordingly. If we do not, we are in danger of being chained to the World of Matter and being drawn with it towards complete disintegration.

Cultural and ethnic traditions will also be placed under this immense pressure, and no amount of believing in one's "ethnic spirituality", or one's indigenous right to it, will alter the actual and lawful outcome of this **unstoppable**, "separating force". All races must be absolutely sure that what they regard as "high spiritual beliefs" *are truly so* according to The Spiritual Laws. It will not be enough to simply *imagine that they are*. For The Eternal Spiritual Laws are not the least bit interested in the beliefs of any people and their imagined "spirituality". The Law will sift without favour and in complete objectivity – as it must in any case.

Yet, in the final analysis, that process will simply be the separating out of the opposing principles of Light and Darkness along with their respective adherents, irrespective of what ethnic or religious group they may belong to. For the end result is one of *individual and personal standing*, and **not** that of any *collective grouping*.

For those who strive for The Light, however, the *uplifting* attraction of this spiritual force will apply here equally as powerfully as with the *destruction* of all that opposes it. Thus those souls who hold more noble aspirations and goals will gradually become freed from the World of Matter, with the correspondingly greater opportunity to ascend more quickly to planes of Light, to the home of all that is spiritual. With that separation from the baser elements of humanity, the judgement is fulfilled for them!

The correct knowledge now at our disposal, enables us to shed light and clarity on much that was previously veiled in mystery and uncertainty. We shall conclude this Chapter with a particularly relevant Scriptural quote. It, too, once more offers us the final **50 percent choice** and **100 percent outcome!**

> "Bear witness to me, now, Heavens and Earth! I place Life and Death before you, – the Blessing and the Curse! Therefore choose for yourselves the Life, – that you and your posterity may live!"
>
> (Deuteronomy 30:19, Fenton, Italics mine.)

Chapter 8

Elemental Lore of Nature

"Understanding the **true nature** of "The Forces of Nature" provides the clearest *foundation* for a more *correct* understanding of the World!"

(Author.)

"Blow, blow, thou winter wind. Thou art not so unkind, as Man's ingratitude [to Man!]"

(Shakespeare, "As You Like It", Act II)

"I happen to believe that if you treat the land with love and respect (in particular for the idea that it has an almost living soul, bound up in the mysterious, cycles of nature) then it will repay you in kind."

(H.R.H. Prince Charles – The Prince of Wales. National Geographic, May 2006 Vol. 209 - No 5)

The above few quotes spanning an historical time period encompassing many thousands of years perfectly accords with the main thrust of this particular Chapter. It explains the inviolable interconnectedness between our inherent free-will attribute to make decisions in the first place, but more decisively sheets home the stark fact that consequences must then ensue from every decision made. Since the material world of planet earth is one where the Forces of Nature quite obviously impact on every nuance of every facet of both the natural world and thus upon the humans who inhabit it, the crises now facing global societies should never have arisen.

That, however, is the present reality. The Forces of Nature are therefore the final arbiters of how events will finally "play out". The explanations of The Laws of Creation outlined in an earlier Chapter automatically give to those inexorable and lawful "Natural Forces" the mandate to so return to humankind the consequences of quite stupid and ultimately inexcusable actions. Humankind should therefore understand that the key to our future relationship with "Nature" cannot possibly find mutual accommodation with the purely intellectual parameters which drive general and scientific education today, for it would never accept such a "childish notion" in this present age of "intellectualism at all costs". That non-acceptance will, however, be completely shattered by the very Forces that human science has relegated to the realm of nonsense.

8.1 The Circle of Life

"Man has a poor understanding of Life. He mistakes knowledge for wisdom.

He tries to unveil the Holy secrets of our Father, the Great Spirit.

He attempts to impose his Laws and ways on Mother Earth.

Even though he, himself, is part of Nature, he chooses to disregard and ignore it for the sake of his own immediate gain.

But the Laws of Nature are far stronger than those of Mankind.

Man must awaken at last, and learn to understand how little time remains before he will become the cause of his own downfall.

And he has so much to learn. To learn to see with the heart.

He must learn to respect Mother Earth – She who has given life to everything;

to our Brothers and Sisters, the Animals and the Plants;
to the Rivers, the Lakes, the Oceans and the Winds.

He must realise that the Planet does not belong to him,
but that he has to care for and maintain the delicate balance of Nature

for the sake of the wellbeing of our children and of all future generations.

It is the duty of man to preserve the Earth and the Creation of the Great Spirit.

Mankind being but a grain of sand in the Holy Circle which encloses All Life."

> (Attributed to White Cloud, a principal chief of the Iowa tribe. More probably stated by "Wa-cha-mon-ya" – regarded as the tribe's greatest orator.)

The clear wisdom of the Native Americans is beautifully and powerfully encompassed in the above statement. The advent of satellites and manned space stations has, for the first time in humankind's history, shown us all how incredibly beautiful, fragile and "lonely" the earth – our "blue planet" – actually is. The deep wisdom inherent in those words from a technologically-illiterate Native American people from the 19th century reveals the spiritual emptiness of much of Western "culture". Paradoxically, however, it is really only since those first space photographs appeared some years ago now, that the realisation has gradually dawned that we are not separate groups, races or nations with our own closed ecosystems divorced from every other.

Such pictures have reinforced the unequivocal fact that every action on earth will ultimately impact globally somewhere, somehow, some way. Just like ripples radiating outward from the impact of a stone thrown into a pond. At least that is the realisation among those who are sufficiently awakened to understand the truth of this. Unfortunately, however, too many of earth's inhabitants still regard their own personal space and aspirations as being the most important thing. Nevertheless, those who are too obtuse or too ignorant to care, will one day experience the Iowa tribe's sage, intuitive observation that "Man must awaken ... and learn to understand how little time ... remains before he will become the cause of his own downfall." This Chapter will offer explanations as to why – and how – "White Cloud's prophecy" **will be fulfilled!**

Interestingly, in our time, the world of science which we look to for answers has also offered a sobering prediction. One, moreover, that reinforces White Cloud's *vision* for the earth. The 1992 Earth Summit in Rio, attended by one of the largest gatherings of Heads of State in history, was heralded as a singularly-definitive eco-event. One designed to produce a lasting international accord for protecting the world environment. Yet, on 18 November, 1992, just five months after that ostensible environmental milestone, more than sixteen hundred senior scientists from seventy one countries, including over half of all Nobel Prize winners, released a signed document titled, "World Scientists Warning to Humanity". The document began:

> "Human beings and the natural world are on a collision course. Human activities inflict harsh and often irreversible damage on the environment and on critical resources. If not checked, many of our current practices put at serious risk the future that we wish for human society and the plant and animal kingdoms, and may so alter the living world that it will be unable to sustain life in the manner that we know. Fundamental changes are urgent if we are to avoid the collision our present course will bring about."

The warning went on to list the crises in the atmosphere, water resources, the oceans, the soil, the forests, bio-diversity and human over-population. Here the words become more stark:

> *"No more than one or a few decades remain before the chance to avert the threats we now confront will be lost and the prospects for humanity immeasurably diminished. We, the undersigned, senior members of the world's scientific community, hereby warn all humanity of what lies ahead. A great change in our stewardship of the Earth and life on it is required, if vast human misery is to be avoided and our global home on this planet is not to be irretrievably mutilated."*

Surely an apocalyptic view in any sense of the word.

> "Nevertheless, when the "World Scientists" Warning to Humanity" was released to the press, Canada's national newspaper and television network ignored it, while in the United States, the *Washington Post* and the *New York Times* rejected it as "not newsworthy".

(The Sacred Balance, David Suzuki, p 4-5)

Whilst this eminent group of clearly learned men have rightly identified the gravest crisis humanity has yet faced, the scientific field in which they operate is, however, still not able to offer exact and definitive answers and solutions to most of their concerns. Dr

David Suzuki's recent work notes this paradox inherent in all science. That is precisely because earth-sciences are constrained by the very parameters it imposes upon itself, i.e. its narrow world of empiricism. We once more restate a key point of this work: that this unfortunate "scientific" viewpoint fails to take into account or even acknowledge – let alone understand – that all scientific endeavour must embrace Spiritual Law first if it is ever to offer complete and meaningful answers to the never-ending questions it continually finds itself faced with.

Thus David Suzuki points out:

> "Scientism, the aura of authority carried by scientists, has made us believe that knowledge obtained by scientists is the ultimate authority, that as we accumulate information, our capacity to understand, control and manage our surroundings will grow correspondingly. But the basic principle of scientific exploration contradicts this faith: knowledge comes from empirical observations, which are "made sense of" by hypotheses, which in turn can be experimentally tested. All information is open to being disproved. As Jonathan Marks has pointed out":
>
> "...the vast majority of ideas that most scientists have ever had have been wrong. They have been refuted; they have been disposed of. Further, at any point in time, most ideas proposed by most scientists will ultimately be refuted and disposed of... Science, in other words, undermines scientism."

(The Sacred Balance, p 19)

The more recent "Johannesburg Summit on Sustainable Development" revealed that few of the recommendations from the Rio Summit were fully implemented. The Johannesburg conference, whilst notable for all the right ecological speech-making, will probably suffer the same fate as the previous Summit – namely all talk and little action. Concerned scientists will once again continue to try to influence the political leaders and the industrial power-brokers of the world to change direction "before it is too late". Unfortunately, we have already reached the "too late".

Notwithstanding White Cloud's appropriate introduction for this Chapter and the inherent truth of it harmonising with those eminent scientists, the subject matter contained in this segment may appear, at first glance, to have no connection to the Chapters preceding this particular one. Yet it is essential that this vitally important aspect of the sum total of knowledge that is our rightful inheritance be well understood. If we are to have a more greatly clarified and harmonious existence in our material world, then the knowledge of the "true nature" of the "Elemental Forces of Nature", perhaps more than any other, precisely offers that mechanism whereby scientific ideas need not be "refuted and disposed of" in the future.

Prince Charles, in the past ridiculed quite savagely for his ideas on the environment, modern architecture – but perhaps more for what were once considered fringe ideas on sustainable growing and farming practices – has, in the new brutal reality of a poisoned and polluted planet, been completely vindicated.

In any case it was quite clear to anyone with even the smallest amount of common sense that the comments made by Prince Charles even many years ago did ring true. The sustainable farming and gardening methods he has introduced and developed at his Highgrove estate has now captured the attention of farmers and agriculturalists.

Poundbury, a new village architecturally designed with environmentally sustainable principles for people first and cars a very distant second set on 400 acres of the Prince's Duchy of Cornwall, has also attracted serious attention. The British Government has embraced the Poundbury principles, and city planners and high officials from numerous countries as far afield as the United States and even Saudi Arabia have visited the village. Others are planned. Will there be an ongoing and expanding legacy from Prince Charles' vision?

The National Geographic article notes:

Two decades ago when he began this crusade, many British farmers felt his experiments were a rebuke to their efficient modern methods. "He was publicly ridiculed. It was withering," recalled Patrick Holden, director of the Soil Association, the main organic growers body. But since then, the area in Britain farmed organically has increased more than a hundredfold. How much of that can be put down to Prince Charles and Highgrove?

> "I don't think it can be overestimated," Holden said. "He has emerged as the clear global leader of the sustainable agriculture movement, and rightly so."

(Emphasis ours.)

Another high-profile global leader of environmental note is Al Gore. A similar crusader over decades, and similarly ridiculed in the beginning, he has emerged as the "voice of clear reason" highlighting global warming.

His very important documentary, "An Inconvenient Truth", in one sense also concurs with White Cloud's visionary statement and prophecy. But in another, Al Gore's seminal work hugely extends that ancient wisdom via the aid of exceptionally good science. The documentary should perhaps now be understood as almost the final evolvement of the work that a few insightful scientists began in earnest just a few decades ago and who had the courage to speak out about their concerns, and the ongoing work by more and more concerned scientists since. The disturbing trend of human activity and its impact on the planet and its resources is incontrovertibly clear in the documentary.

Al Gore's almost "tongue-in-cheek" comment at one point in his documentary actually reconciles the science/religion divide, at least on this crucial issue, for global humanity. Scenes of devastation of human "works" and desolation of natural landscapes in the documentary brought forth the wry yet fundamentally truthful comment: **"It's like taking a major hike through The Revelation."**

Whilst the scientific discoveries and concomitant analyses of his documentary are, in a word, brilliant, the ultimate knowledge that inherently underpins all earth-sciences must be taken into account too. That way, the ancient wisdom of White Cloud, and the modern knowledge of science, harmonise perfectly. So if we are to have a more greatly clarified and harmonious existence in our material world, then the knowledge of the "true nature" of the "Elemental Forces of Nature", perhaps more than any other, precisely offers that mechanism whereby scientific ideas need not be "refuted and disposed of" in the future.

Instead, via the knowledge of The Spiritual Laws, science can finally become "genuinely knowing" through recognising and understanding the connection with those forces which govern the immediacy of our earthly environment. Forces, moreover, that also operate in direct correlation with our attitude and behaviour, thus our collective decision-making process. Unfortunately, it is a human behavioural attitude which, for the most part, is based on ignorance of the Natural Laws which, however, then impact detrimentally on both the natural world and the societies we create.

Therefore, as we observe the increasingly unpredictable and sometimes disturbing "weather-havoc" globally, the explanations of the "Elemental Forces" will hopefully offer greater understanding. Whilst the foundation for the process we outline is still that of The Spiritual Laws of Creation, in the context of the subject matter of this Chapter, the outworking of the reciprocal return of our free-will decisions is placed in the hands of those "elementals" whose activities we loosely refer to *as* "The Forces of Nature." Thus the "**Lore** of Nature" that we refer to in the Chapter heading is also the "**Law** of Nature!"

Under the mantle of that duality it is important to understand what The Laws of Nature refer to and actually mean. Let us state quite unequivocally that whilst these Laws are Spiritual in origin, their *main* effects can be clearly observed and felt as *"weather"* – in all its myriad forms. Alternately soft and gentle at times and raging and destructive at others, the destiny of mankind is irrevocably intertwined with the "elemental" activity contained within the weather patterns. What exactly are we implying here? This is clearly a concept vastly different to what meteorology teaches us.

It will probably therefore require a leap of quantum proportions for most to even *deign* to consider such an idea. Yet the strange and unpredictable weather patterns and the uncanny rapid rise in natural catastrophes world-wide must surely be cause for concern and, no doubt, some speculation as to the actual cause. Even the more spectacular weather effects which trigger catastrophic natural disasters are not divorced from humankind's collective earthly activity. Since all things are interconnected and intermeshed in some way, humankind, even though a very small component part of the whole, nonetheless exert a *disproportionately large measure* of decisive influence *in our part of Creation* through the constant exercising of its collective free-will endowment. The consequences which flow from that decision-making process under The Law of Reciprocal Action ensure that we do, indeed, *"reap what we sow"*.

A large and increasing measure of that "reaping" *is returned to us by way of natural disasters.* We need to be constantly reminded that only our *decisions* are free, the *consequences* are not! In that single reality lies humankind's immense responsibility through being granted the gift of free will. Understanding the *true nature* of **The Forces of Nature** therewith offers meaningful answers to many of our collectively-induced problems, **and to the reason for all natural disasters.** Let us therefore once more reinforce a key aspect of The Law, from which this particular Chapter derives its mandate. The fundamental truth that: *"***The Laws of Nature are the earthly expression of The Will of God on earth!***"*

We began this Chapter with a rather grand but possibly enigmatic statement regarding the necessity to understand the *actual nature* of The Forces of Nature, thus perhaps presupposing a very radical view of the natural forces around us. Perhaps radical in the sense that it may not accord with current scientific thought, but certainly not radical in its spiritual reality. What do we mean by this?

Most assuredly, humankind stands aside in stunned awe when the Elemental Forces of Nature spectacularly destroy his works, whether by earth, wind, fire or water. As we are all aware, the forces that can produce gentle lapping waves and soft summer breezes can also spawn winds and waves of immense power capable of unbelievable destruction. So, too, the healing warmth of fire in winter can be quickly transformed to raging conflagrations in forest and city.

Interestingly, the narrator of the 1998 four-part series on global weather from the "Our World" programme (BBC) quite regularly used the term *"species of weather"* to describe some of the different kinds of more severe weather events that we are subjected to.

It is an interesting and unusual description to emerge from out of a purely scientific documentary. If not exactly "species of weather", our clear contention is that we *are* talking about actual **Forces** of Nature – forces that can bring either gentleness or raging destruction. The history of early man provides testimony to his belief of the "supernatural" nature of these forces. He feared the lightning and thunder, and could no more control the elements in his time than can modern man today, despite his technological sophistication. Herein lies the paradox! Ancient man accepted the elements as living entities which gave him the forest for building materials and food, the sea for other foods, and good weather for the ripening and harvesting of his crops.

Those same "beings" could also visit great desolation upon him and his works with destructive weather formations. His naturally close connection to the "Elemental Forces" enabled him to give name to each being associated with a particular elemental activity. Through his developing knowledge, he identified male and female beings with clearly demarcated tasks, with each occupying a precisely defined place in their hierarchy.

Because early man had no control over "elemental" activity and believed he was at the mercy of these powerful beings, appeasement and worship of them became a living reality for that particular stage of his development. It is significant to note that, virtually without exception, *every developing race* has recorded the presence and existence of these "nature beings" – from the tiniest to the gigantic – depending on their particular role and activity. In his observations of the "gods", as he came to regard them, he ascribed human traits to them. The vagaries of the weather at times, as though he were being played with, gave rise to a mischievous entity – a joker. Kings and queens ruled over this huge and powerful elemental domain and over all the lesser "gods" who inhabited it. Every race acknowledged their existence and gave them appropriate names out of their language and incorporated this "knowledge" into their respective cultures.

Conversely, traditional science has determined that weather is *caused* by a combination of precisely configured and measurable scientific formulae involving all aspects of meteorology. Insofar as the visual and material effect of weather is concerned, that is obviously the case. We observe approaching storm fronts and feel their immediate effects, and we also enjoy clear skies and bask in the warmth of high pressure systems. From the cosiness of the lounge in winter, we can be entertained by well-groomed, witty and knowledgeable weather presenters who offer a dazzling presentation of the next few days' weather assisted by a world-wide network of sophisticated satellite detection and measuring equipment, all assessed by banks of powerful computers.

Yet, even with this vast array of modern wizardry, there are still reasonably regular, embarrassing glitches in weather forecasting, with sometimes even glaringly opposite outcomes to particular forecasts. As we move from there into the arena of volcanic and earthquake activity projections, it becomes much more difficult to be absolutely precise in predicting either the various levels of projected activity relating to them, or the time of the disturbance. Or whether such activity might be waxing or waning if it is not clearly obvious. So even though undeniable advances have been made in the better detection of impending geological incidents utilising modern sensing instruments and analytical techniques, we are still a long way from any scientifically-acknowledged breakthrough-mechanism to accurately predict such potentially devastating events.

In very recent times, however, we have a precisely recorded event where the population of a major Chinese city (Haicheng) was evacuated before being struck by a powerful earthquake. That precaution resulted in literally tens of thousands of lives being saved. Moreover, this was achieved not so much by technological means but by careful observations of the behaviour of animals and birds, and via the monitoring of ground-water levels.[1] Thus we have two vastly differing mechanisms for the prediction of this kind of *elemental-force* activity.

This Chapter will offer explanations as to which method will produce the greatest benefit and protection for modern man, provided that he does not cling to his solely intellectual pursuit of technological sophistry to the exclusion of all other possibilities. A key requirement is that he is open enough to allow his spirit to lead him to a greater understanding of the true nature of these awesome forces. Then, rather than believing he might one day be able to "control" this power – which he cannot in any case – he will be able to work "consciously" with it, for his obvious benefit.

If the development of man's spiritual or religious leanings from his earliest beginnings is examined, the various stages that he had to travel through can be readily observed. Since he did not possess the sophistication for total discernment that we today are able to have – by virtue of having travelled along this developmental path for a far longer period – the brave new world of early man mostly offered a bewildering array of powerful forces that had to be fought, appeased, or worshipped. In the beginning, therefore, animism as a belief and religion held powerful sway over his everyday world for a long period of time.

Thus he observed and learned the ways of not only the animal and plant worlds, but also those of the elemental forms that inhabited every part of his "natural" world too. He gave name to them and to a large degree regulated his life around the activity of what he "knew" to be fellow inhabitants of planet earth. Different from him both in form and activity, but nevertheless as much a part of the world as was he, and who could offer the greatest help to him. So from them he learned the properties of healing herbs, how to grow his food and what to harvest from the wild. He also learned the ways of the weather and heeded their warnings of impending natural catastrophes. This knowledge is the vitally necessary connection we have long since lost.

During this phase of animistic worship, he sometimes incorrectly ascribed elemental entities to the natural fixed forms such as trees, rocks and mountains. He was not able to discern that these particular aspects of the natural world did not possess their own life force such as animals or humans have – as is still believed by

---

[1] China currently has an earthquake monitoring force of 10,000 scientists and observers.

some of the world's peoples today – but have a different kind of life-energy. The fixed forms of the natural world nevertheless provide *habitations* for the elemental *beings*, which early man observed in and around them.[2]

As his developing world expanded so, also, did man's understanding of the "elemental world" around him. From observing the simple activity of the Nature Beings close to his immediate environment, his inner sight began to reveal the higher levels of their Realm where far larger beings of greater power exerted the greatest influence on everything in the material world. Thus certain races whose development proceeded according to the ordained path that man was to take, recognised the Higher Realm of the Elemental Beings, the gods of the legends. They attempted to emulate their activity, and borrowed from them ideas that they could incorporate into their everyday life.

Arguably the peak of this particular path of development probably culminated in the classical Greek period known as Hellenism which had its flowering from near the end of the fourth century BC to approximately 50 BC This particular race of people refined quite advanced mathematical principles and constructed magnificent buildings of great beauty in symmetry of form. In the classical perfection of their architecture and their flawless sculptures, we can readily note the purity of form reflecting the application of **The Spiritual Law of Balance**, and the concomitant usage of pure mathematics in **The Law of Numbers**.

Great strides were made in medicine, too, not least aided by the great philosophical debates and treatises of men like Plato and Aristotle who sought to define and understand the nature and place of man in the known Universe. And, moreover, the relationship and possible reality of a dualistic concept of man in being both a material form and a spiritual or "soul" entity as well. This highly accentuated preoccupation with the form and inner aspect of man may well have resulted in the perfection of form evidenced by Greek sculptures of the human body.

---

[2]In terms of the justice of Spiritual Law that permeates *every* part of Creation, it would be totally against every idea of perfect justice whereby *immobile* life forms such as trees, plants and rocks would have an inner animating core such as that which animals and humans possess. Only in beings or life forms who are *able to take flight*, or otherwise *offer resistance when danger threatens*, is that kind of inner life force present. Were this not the case, the harvesting of trees for housing and warmth, or the taking of rock for road construction etc., would take on vastly different "spiritual" overtones than purely one of general beneficence for man.

Paradoxically, the *philosophical ideas* of Plato and others, essentially being only a step toward the *sureness* of *spiritual knowledge*, might not have been necessary had man's original spiritual connections been retained. Rather than philosophy and theory by Plato, we might have had more "Spiritual Truth" by him and others. Of course, elements of the truth may certainly be contained within those essays, but they cannot be stated to be definitive works of *absolute* truth.

The Greeks nonetheless achieved a profound level of knowledge through their greater recognition of the Elemental Beings even though, similar to most other peoples, they also wrongly regarded them as gods in their polytheistic beliefs. Nevertheless, they were the first to *more completely* understand the relationship between themselves and the Animistic Realm which their particular level of development permitted them to "see". Thus, because they were able to "perceive" the activity above and around them, all the benefits of that Realm were available to them. That insight allowed them to "borrow" themes and ideas from the higher levels they were permitted to *see*, and the Greeks built much of their society accordingly. Thus their history, culture, medicine (the Hippocratic oath) architecture and language, expressed their correct recognition of the place of these *forces* probably more vitally than most other races did.

The attitude and thinking of the Greek philosophers toward the ruling deities in their pantheon of gods (the Animistic Beings) is well illustrated in Cicero's "The Nature of the Gods" in which representatives of the Greek schools of philosophy speak about them in the form of a dialogue. A condensed, brief thread of thought provides that easily understood insight.

> "My belief is that the universe and everything in it has been created by the providence of the gods and is governed by that providence through all eternity. - - If you grant their existence, you must admit that the world is governed by their providence. - - So you must either deny that the gods exist at all,... or else, if you admit their existence, you must also admit that they are active in the higher sense. What could be better then that their activity should be the government of the world? Therefore the world is governed by the wisdom of the gods.
>
> *If it were otherwise, it would follow that there must be some power better and stronger than that of the gods*, whatever this might be, inanimate matter or the great blind forces of necessity, which have created all these wonderful

works that we see around us. In that event the nature of the gods would not be supreme in excellence. It would be subject to that other nature or necessity which ruled the earth and sky and sea. *But nothing is more excellent than the divine and to divinity must belong the government of the world.* God is not subject to obey the laws of nature. It is nature that is subject to the laws of God.

If we admit that there exist beings of divine wisdom, then we cannot exclude the working of their providence in the great design of the universe. Or are they unaware of what is of importance and of how such matters should be ordered? Or too weak perhaps to undertake and sustain such great responsibilities? But such ignorance would be contrary to the nature of the gods and it is not in accordance with their majesty and power that they should be too weak to sustain without effort the burden of their office. From which it follows, as we seek to prove, that the world is governed by the wisdom and foresight of the gods.

If gods exist (and they do exist) then to be gods they must be living beings. But not only living beings. They must also be rational beings, joined one with another in a sort of peaceful and harmonious commonwealth, ruling the world as though it were a single state or city. There must be found among them the virtues which men recognize in truth and reason. The same law too which seeks to foster justice and expel evil. From this we can see that it is from the gods that wisdom and good sense are given to men. In recognition of this it was the custom of our ancestors to pay divine honours to Reason, Faith, Virtue and Concord. - - If Reason, Faith, Virtue and Concord are to be found among men, whence can they have come down to earth but from the gods? Since we have some measure of sense, rationality and wisdom, the gods must have them in far greater measure. They must not only have them but use them too in the greatest and most admirable works. Now there is nothing greater or more wonderful than the universe as a whole. Therefore it must be governed by the wisdom and the foresight of the gods."

(Book 11, p 155-157)

Whilst that particular discourse is an indication of the Greek perspective of philosophic thought with regard to perhaps a more elevated concept of the role of their gods as rulers of the universe, there was also the recognition and acceptance of the other helps that assisted mankind. Cicero noted that whilst there were other philosophers who held it true that the entire world is kept in order and ruled by divine insight and reason, at the same time they believed the gods also looked after the life of men in a counselling and helping way.

> *"In their opinion fruits and other products of the soil, changes in the weather, the seasons and the planet generally, by which everything the earth produces is made to grow and ripen, are gifts of the same gods – for mankind.* And since this belief in gods was not the result of education, old custom or law, and since universal agreement among the philosophic community was well established, there was therefore the firm conviction that the gods existed. Such a conviction could only stem from an inherent, implanted or, as he avers, *"an inborn conception of them.*
>
> As this point is almost invariably given unlimited recognition, not only by all philosophers but also by the uneducated, we must certainly admit that there is in us the pre-comprehension of the gods, as I have called it before; or should I call it pre-knowledge."

Therefore, Cicero believed, the existence of the gods must be admitted.[3]

The Greeks' correct spiritual development to that particular point permitted them the insight to "know" that much more existed in Creation than just the material world, by virtue of their recognition of the Elemental Beings (their gods). Unfortunately they basically concluded that the "Gods on Mount Olympus" – as they perceived them to be – were the absolute height of Creation. Yet the Apostle Paul, in his first address to the men of Athens, noted that the Greeks had divined the probable existence of the One invisible God when he stated to them:

> "Men of Athens, I perceive beyond everything how deeply religious you are, for, going about and studying your objects of worship, I even found an altar upon which had been inscribed:
>
> TO AN UNKNOWN GOD
>
> What therefore you unknowingly worship, I proclaim to you. The God. Who made the Universe and all in it."

---

[3]The mechanism by which we inherently possess such pre-knowledge has already been explained, but will also be briefly re-visited later in this Chapter.

(Acts 17:22-24, Fenton.)

Without sure conviction of a "Divine Realm" or a "Higher Creation", any further spiritual development for the Greeks was stunted by that uncertainty. The one race that did conclusively divine the Highest Spheres – in fact all the way to the seat of The Godhead – was the Jewish race. Their recognition of The Source of All Life paved the way for an eventual connection which would allow Jesus, The Son of God, to incarnate among them. Their prior recognition of the elemental "Forces of Nature" can be clearly noted by the help accorded to the Israelites by these "Nature Beings" – sometimes spectacularly so – on many different occasions during their exodus from out of Egyptian bondage under the leadership of Moses.[4]

From the Greek homeland, the same knowledge was used to create a new Empire – that of the Roman. Because the transportation of this belief and culture was effected by a relatively small number of Greeks, the native Roman people who had not developed to the same "level of seeing" *as a complete race*, did not have the natural recognition of this higher realm that the Greeks possessed. So whilst the Roman Empire flourished and grew very powerful, the connections to, and worship of, their "gods" were far more tenuous than those which the Greek Empire enjoyed.

Certainly history records that the Romans feared their differently named deities and proffered many gifts and sacrifices to them over millennia, but this was probably based more on dogma and doctrine than actual conviction. The end result was that the Roman Emperors eventually became convinced of their own direct lineage from these "stone gods". This corruption of their belief brought about the demise of their empire and allowed for the subsequent new emerging force of Christianity to supersede both Greek and Roman thought.

Christianity has been the main religion of the Western world since its dissemination thereto via the Roman Empire. From out of The Bible it has striven to supplant the "stone and wooden gods" of those races to whom they introduced their new, more enlightened teaching. Yet even though we live in an increasingly sophisticated world, a surprising number within *certain* races today

---

[4]We may note the same interaction between man and the "elementals" in other places within The Bible, examples of which will be used later in this Chapter to illustrate the spiritual and physical validity of this "elemental-force premise".

still retain ties to, and revere, some of their gods of old. *Such intransigence surely reveals why humankind is burdened with so much distress. For it shows that we do not really advance spiritually, but in many ways remain stagnant and locked into flawed and unworkable concepts.*

By way of example, the Old Testament Prophet, Jeremiah, wrote a letter to those taken captive to Babylon by King Nebuchadnezzar. Jeremiah, the weeping Prophet, was left alone to remain in the land. His advice to those taken away illustrates that even amongst the Jewish people of the time – with all their long history of worship directed *away* from "stone idols" – fear of the Babylonian "gods" was nevertheless present among some. Jeremiah explained why they should not fear the Babylonian gods. For exactly the same reasons, carved effigies today should not be acknowledged, revered or, worse, worshipped. Jeremiah's almost "tongue-in-cheek" advice amazes one by its stunningly-clarifying analysis of the stupidity of such fear-ridden worship.

> "Now in Babylon you will see gods made of gold and silver and wood, which are carried on men's shoulders and inspire fear in the heathen. So take care not to become at all like the foreigners or to let fear for these gods possess you. Their tongues are smoothed by the craftsmen — but — cannot speak. When — dressed in purple robes, their faces are wiped because of the dust from the temple, which is thick upon them. ...the god holds a scepter, though unable to destroy anyone who offends it. It has a dagger in its right hand, and has an axe, but it cannot save itself from war and robbers. Therefore they evidently are not gods, so do not fear them."

Jeremiah continues with the observation that when they [the gods] are set up in the temple, the attendant priests and the believers do not seem to notice the fact that they are actually lifeless, yet still attend them and ostensibly worship them.

> "Their eyes are full of the dust raised by the feet of those who enter. They do not notice when their faces have been blackened by the smoke of the temple. Bats, swallows and birds light on their bodies and heads; and so do cats. From this — they are not gods, so do not fear them."

A key point of Jeremiah's letter about the foolishness of such practices is wonderfully stated in the next few passages.

"Having no feet, they are carried on men's shoulders, revealing to mankind *their worthlessness*. And those who serve them are [a]shamed because through them these gods are made to stand, lest they fall to the ground. If any one sets one of them upright, it cannot move of itself; and if it is tipped over, it cannot straighten itself; yet gifts are placed before them *just as before the dead*."

"These things that are made of wood and overlaid with gold and silver are like stones from the mountain, *and those who serve them will be put to shame*. Why then must anyone think they are gods, or call them gods?"

(*The Apocrypha*, "The Letter Of Jeremiah", Extracts from p 178 and 179, Emphases mine.)

Today there are probably more gods than ever before, for we have technological ones, scientific ones and monetary ones now. These, too, are worshipped, revered or feared by those who serve them in their different associations and ways. So it is extremely vital that the explanation of the "gods of legend" are offered, because the timely recognition of their true nature as Elemental Beings will offer to those who do so recognise, vital protection when the time of humanity's trials burst in full strength upon us. **Then all false gods, whether stone, technological, scientific, monetary or whatever, will have had their time too!**

Like the Greeks and Romans, other races such as the Nordic and Germanic peoples also reached the level necessary to recognise the Nature Beings and thus also the knowledge of the Elemental "gods", with the Norse naming their high fastness, Valhalla. During their depredations in other lands, the Norsemen came into contact with Christianity and they, too, eventually embraced the new religion. This acceptance of a completely new idea ensured that the original, once-sure beliefs would eventually die away. Notwithstanding that unfortunate demise, certain aspects of the old beliefs were still retained in the fables, myths and legends of those groups.

The active retention of this kind of knowledge was held more strongly in the less-developed tribal groups in the different parts of the world still untouched by this new thought of Christianity. Unfortunately, the generally superstitious minds of most of these tribal groups allowed major distortions to enter into their view of the Animistic world, and they did not reach the degree of actual knowledge necessary to recognise the higher levels of that realm. Moreover, their particular views generally produced fear and wrong worship which effectively kept the door to greater knowledge firmly closed. So whilst a natural and necessary connection to "otherworld realities" was retained, to all intents and purposes the vitally necessary working knowledge of, and connection to, the realm of the Elementals and Nature Beings above us was effectively lost here also.

And whereas some of the "indigenous peoples" have at least retained a strong belief in the validity of their legends as possible truth, other more "intellectual races" – including those of European origin in the new worlds of America, Canada, Australia and New Zealand – have virtually severed this *connection* completely, not even bothering to retain them as fables. With the embarkation of millions from old Europe to the new lands in a relatively short space of time, the severing of strong family and cultural traditions developed over centuries was considered more or less necessary in order to face the challenges of a new way of life freed from the constraints of a dogmatic and blinkered Europe. This dogmatism was epitomised either by the superstitions of the rural peasantry, the bigotry of the controlling political and religious authorities, or the arrogance of the ruling aristocracy.

"Freedom from restraint" from old Europe paradoxically seeded a strange "new idea", especially in America. Historically we are able to note the curious emergence of the concept of "Manifest Destiny", itself just as bigoted, and probably more arrogant, as that which was ostensibly left behind. In essence it decreed that the new lands were more fit for the new people than for the indigenous inhabitants. In place of a benign, caring and conservation-minded approach, with a mutual merging of cultures offering benefits for both peoples, the goal was to exploit and *tame nature* in the frontier land, and subjugate and civilise the "primitive natives" in the process. The "new Americans" and the actual land of America itself would have been far spiritually richer today had the concept of "Manifest Destiny" espoused humility and the biblical admonition to "...do unto others..."

This "new way" of the new world peoples clearly and unequivocally illustrates our assertion that the necessary connection to the "Elemental forces" was no longer a part of their life. This loss, in the same way and for the same reasons that the Greeks eventually lost it – rapidly developing and generally crass intellectualism almost completely supplanting the intuitive-spiritual insight – guaranteed the seeds for the material degradation of planet earth. For without genuine veneration and gratitude for the earthly home, we sow the seeds for our eventual demise, drowned in our own poison. It may be that we will one day look back and recognise the technical revolution itself as a perilous path opposing all that was natural and spiritually lawful in the world.

Unfortunately for "Western Nations" generally, their god of science has determined that such notions as "Elemental Beings" cannot possibly be entertained as belonging to a "rational, logical and intelligent" society, even though the "face-book" of their religions, The Bible, speaks of them clearly enough. Moreover, missionaries who ventured forth out of Europe into the new "heathen lands" generally condemned this natural and necessary connection ordained by The Creative Will, and applied various labels such as superstition, blasphemy and even demonism to it. Thus the relegation of what was once accepted as factual knowledge, even if not fully understood, to the realm of myth and legend by man's new "intellectual sophistication", is to our grave detriment. For the more correct place of the intellect was to assist man in the fulfilment of his earthly duties, which is why it is vital for scientific and other earthly endeavours. In this, its proper and ordained place, it rightly produces technological marvels and great feats of construction.

Sadly, spiritual man, with the potential for achieving true greatness in the material world and in Creation, became merely intellectual man more concerned with earthly analysis and theory, rather than spiritual activity producing corresponding deeds. This can be largely attributed to his rejection of the twin-realities of the knowledge and outworking of Spiritual Law and the existence of the "Elemental Forces".

Two key events in the history of man had a major bearing on the acceptance, or otherwise, of "Elemental aspects". One was the religious madness of the Dark Ages, and the other was the later, perhaps more enlightened, Age of Reason. During the course of the Dark Ages and the later Inquisition, the Christian religious authorities, who were at the height of absolute temporal power, decreed that anything remotely connected with "Nature Beings" be branded as heresy and "demonism". Consequently, even the simple and innocent act of picking herbs or fungus in the forest for food or medicine resulted in the torture and death of perhaps thousands of harvesters, mostly women, who were invariably accused of being witches and in league with the devil.

During the exploration and colonisation period when the "white cultures" of Europe exported religion and criminals to the lands of indigenous tribal peoples beginning about the 1700s, the church once more came up against strong conviction about the existence of "Nature Beings". However, if it was totally unacceptable in their own societies where innocents were killed in the name of their God for this "heresy", it would certainly not be tolerated in the new lands. Consequently, it was quickly opposed and suppressed in the new lands as well. Thankfully, the madness of "torture by religious numbers" finally relinquished its hold on the psyche of the European Church with the beginnings of the more scientific "Age of Enlightenment" in the 18th century.

Yet what did our erstwhile, budding scientists make of the previously unseen world around them then? With the greater surge of intellectualism to scientifically rationalise the natural world, the catchwords, "prove it", became the rationale of empiricism that everything had to bow to. What could not be physically seen, touched or heard was relegated to the realm of nonsense until such time as the new religious god of science decreed otherwise. Of course, as more powerful instruments were developed, what was very recently dismissed as impossible was revealed as living reality. It is curious that the scientific community, even in our present age of so-called great enlightenment, still tenaciously clings to that same view of "not possible" until proven *scientifically*.

Yet the reality for all time will be that, regardless of the adulation they may heap upon themselves with each new "discovery", scientists seem not to understand – or at least publicly acknowledge – that what might be lauded as a major discovery has, quite naturally, *always existed*. Even with the production of a new element which science might suddenly produce, it was never a question of an actual *creation* of a new substance, because the necessary building blocks for that fusion were *always available*.

Therefore, if we apply the same criteria to both science and religion – each generally vehemently opposed to any such notion of "Nature Beings" – to that exact same subject, we have the factual reality that **either** Elemental Beings exist, or they do not! Only one reality is possible, it cannot be both. If, in fact, they really were a figment of emerging man's fertile and fearfully superstitious imagination, then the problem resolves itself and we need no longer bother with it. However, if the *opposite* is true and they actually *do* exist and they *are* a living part of the total activity in Creation and thus also here on earth – even if outside of our physical senses – then that clearly poses a huge problem for both science and religion. For an accommodation would have to be made somewhere in both disciplines, and one that actually fits.

Since nothing can exist in the world of science or religion except under the umbrella of The Spiritual Laws, it naturally follows that any actual existence of "Nature Beings" will have been ordained by The Creative Will. The same Will, moreover, under which both those erstwhile disciplines are permitted to exist. Quite logically, then, if "Nature Beings" do exist and ancient man did understand their place and *actually observed them,* then the obvious reality for latter-day man is that *we have lost the ability to see them.* What, then, might that imply?

Since modern science has relegated "Nature Beings" to the realm of superstitious myth and legend, and because their existence probably cannot ever be proved by scientific means, it follows that the scientific community will probably never accept even the possibility of such beings. Notwithstanding this attitude from that particular direction, Dr Lyall Watson, an eminent Biologist, (perhaps one of the very few "knowing voices in the scientific community") has produced a remarkable series of books exploring the intellectually-perceived "no-go zone" between empirical science and the "other-world reality". In that series he has documented some stunningly remarkable and totally unexpected insights

In particular, his books, *Supernature* and *Gifts of Unknown Things* reveal amazing incidents inexplicable according to man's accepted scientific criteria but naturally factual under the higher knowledge of Elemental and Spiritual Law. As a scientist, he was able to bridge the *humanly-created* "impossible zone" between the discipline of science and the less clearly defined area of religiosity, and logically marry many aspects of the two-world beliefs. His research has greatly helped to dispel the myth that such a "no-go area" *actually exists in the first place.* In reality it cannot, for all things between the *tangible* and the equally real *intangible* are, in various ways, precisely and lawfully connected anyway.

And what of the Church? Is there anything in their doctrines of faith that even faintly allude to the existence of such beings? For they are certainly accepted in many races, religions and teachings other than the orthodox Christian one. We have already mentioned the assistance afforded Moses. Two instances of particular note were the parting of the Red Sea, and the "pillar of fire" which guided his vast caravan. The others being "manna" from heaven for bread, low flying flocks of birds for meat, and water produced by Moses who knew exactly where it was flowing under the surface of the rocks.

The Bible contains examples of even supposedly savage animals not offering harm to particular individuals where, in the situations described, they perhaps normally would. Daniel in the lion's den stands as a prime example. But perhaps a very brief examination of one especially celebrated event from The Bible may offer the greatest relevant insight into this question of "Elemental Beings" and their ordained activity alongside humankind.

Most people with even a rudimentary grasp of The Bible, even from "Sunday School" level, are probably aware of the story of the "miracle" of Jesus calming the wind and waves during a storm on the Sea of Galilee. In this particular instance the disciples, alarmed at the increasing strength of the storm were fearful for their lives.

From The Book of Mark we read:

> "And a very heavy gale began to blow and the waves rushed into the boat, so that it was rapidly filling. And He Himself was at the stern asleep on a cushion. They accordingly aroused Him, exclaiming, "Teacher! Do you not care if we perish?" Upon awakening, He restrained the wind, and said to the sea, "Silence! be still!" The wind then lulled and there was perfect calm."
>
> "Why", He asked them, "do you doubt in this way? How is it that you cannot yet have faith?"
>
> But they became terrified; and said to one another, "What can He be? for even the wind and the sea obey Him?"
>
> (Mark 4:37-41, Fenton.)

That particular event is accepted by Christians as one that actually occurred but are probably inclined to label it a miracle. However, what may not be generally comprehended was *what actually took place* in this most interesting happening. To understand it fully, we must apply the knowledge of The Spiritual Laws of Creation to it, since not one thing can take place in any part of Creation except under the aegis of them. Because Jesus Himself declared that He had "...not come to abolish the Laws but to complete them", the calming of the wind and the waves could only be possible under those Eternal Laws. Now, by virtue of His origin from out of The Divine, He would clearly have known of the "Elemental Beings of Nature".

Moreover, not only would He have been aware of them but, because of His High Origins and associated power over all else below that level, all "Nature Beings" and their activities **would have naturally been subordinate to His Command**. For it would be foolish to believe that He was rebuking the *actual substance* of water and wind. No, the clear illustration here is that He was admonishing some force or energy that has its field of activity in what we loosely call the natural world and weather. A "force" which gave rise to the increased agitation of the wind and water that instilled fear in the disciples, thus the forces, or "Beings", of Nature!

Acceptance of this event as being one of unequivocal truth presupposes the clear inference that the only viable mechanism under which the "calming of the wind and waves" could have occurred in the manner illustrated – in particular being **commanded to cease their activities** – is via the activity of "Nature Beings". Therewith do they fulfil their ordained purpose under the umbrella of inviolable Spiritual Law, of which Jesus would have perfectly understood every single ramification.

Through this clearly recorded incident, we are able to offer one more illustration that it is the "work" of the "Elemental Forces of Nature" that *produce the effects* of the varying levels of interrelated weather outcomes in storms, natural disasters and catastrophes which so effectively destroy man and his works. This occurs through the direct correlation between spiritually-wrong *personal and collective decisions* produced by *our spiritual volition,* and their subsequent outcomes returned to humankind under The Law of Sowing and Reaping.

Such a radical view will no doubt produce smiles of incredulity, perhaps more so on the part of weather scientists and forecasters. Yet, as stated previously, it does not take all that much imagination to wonder at the increasing frequency and intensity of storms world-wide. Or of extreme weather patterns producing intense and prolonged droughts virtually alongside areas of devastating flooding. What we are also observing is the more frequent use of superlatives needed to *attempt* to describe the continuing catalogue of Mother Nature's "handiwork".

Words such as the heaviest, longest, driest, severest, worst in living memory, and worst ever recorded, etc., clearly reveal an emerging pattern that is not solely the product of journalistic jingoism. Something very different is now taking place on earth the like of which we have not experienced before. Something that is producing a feeling of uncertainty and unease in the minds of more and more people. And something that cannot be completely explained by the felling of the rain forests, the enlargement of the hole in the ozone layer, nuclear proliferation, global warming, or a burgeoning global population. Even the feared "El Nino" phenomenon, which is clearly capable of producing great devastation, is simply only the activity of these Elemental forces.

It is interesting to note that the U. S. Geological Survey, the body responsible for monitoring earth-movements in the United States and elsewhere, has observed a large increase in world-wide earthquake activity over 7 on the Richter scale in the decades *from* the 1930,s and 40's. Up until the point when records were first kept, numbers of earthquakes of that magnitude were relatively infrequent. The most interesting aspect of these findings is that various people who have studied this data do not know *why* such a huge increase has occurred. However, since nothing can occur without a reason, and as everything must take place under the umbrella of The Eternal Laws, the answers can be found within *those parameters*, even if "scientifically unacceptable" *at this point in time.*

For the purposes of clarification, let us suspend any disbelief in such a seemingly preposterous notion, greatly extend *our personal parameters of possibilities*, and allow vastly different perceptions to hold sway for the moment. Let us assume the correctness of the assertion that "Elemental" activity is the mechanism by which weather patterns and related geological activity are generated. And, moreover, that the increasing extremes of natural phenomena via this mechanism have a definite cause and purpose. What, then, might be the trigger? To understand the cause, we need to revisit the structure of Creation so that we may understand the "whence, whither and why" of the "Elemental Beings" also.

We have already offered explanations as to how and why Creation came into being. The reader may wish to return to Chapter 4 to familiarise himself with the complete process. At this point we will quickly skim over the main happenings in a brief memory refresher. In answer to the petition of many varied creatures who could not come to conscious life in the immediate vicinity of the immense power of The Creator, lower planes of habitable worlds at necessarily vast distances from His "Proximity" were permitted to come into being under the Creation-Words: "Let There Be Light!"

As each Realm coalesced out at its ordained level of Creation, the inhabitants for each of those planes were able to take on form and begin their conscious existence. The final outcome of this "fractional distillation process" was the forming of the material worlds encompassing the earth and the vast physical Universes. But because the denser, physical realm of mankind must naturally occupy that lower part of Creation which is *not eternal*, it was unable to generate its own "warmth" to produce the requisite parameters for conscious life there.

By "warmth" we do not mean the interstellar mechanisms of thermonuclear energy etc., that gave rise to the formation of the billions of suns and star systems in the physical Universes. We refer to the "warmth" of the *life-force* of Creation Itself which is separate from the immense heat generated during the formative processes of all celestial globes, but which nevertheless allows those formations to come into being also. This particular "life-warmth" is naturally present in both The Eternal Realm of The Spiritual and also in the Elemental Realm.

The material worlds, which did not inherently possess this necessary "warmth" or "animating life-power", received it from what we might term the "Elemental Realm." All the "Beings" of the Elemental forces – the powerful and the small – have their origin there, but carry out their activities throughout all the planes of Creation. Thus, it was the "energy" of The Spiritual, utilised by the "Nature Beings" involved with the formation of the vast Universes, that gave life-warmth to our material home. Perhaps as a clearer description, we may liken the "nature beings" to the "maintenance workers" in the hive holding everything together. There we have the "whither, whence, and why" of the "Elemental forces" too. Not "scientifically rational" of course, but nevertheless spiritually correct in its basic overview.

The reason for man to know of the existence of "Elemental Beings is quite simple. As explained in Chapter 4, the human spirit, as he journeyed downward from the realm of The Spiritual to seek incarnation in the material planes in order to develop "personal self-consciousness", necessarily traversed other realms including that of the Animistic. As he traversed the lower planes, each of which was of a naturally heavier consistency than the previous higher one, he was logically compelled to accept a covering, or "body", of the same substance and consistency of the particular plane journeyed through. Consequently, one of our "cloaks" corresponds precisely to that of the Animistic Realm. It is this particular covering or "body" that allows us to connect to, and understand, the "Elemental Beings" of the "Forces of Nature" and their activity.

This necessary connection offers us the means whereby we "can" work consciously with them as once the early races did. Such a working on earth could produce a wonderful reflection of the beauty and harmony of the higher Spiritual Spheres, for our material benefit also. But because we voluntarily cut off this vital connection, we have produced a mainly intellectual world devoid of any real Spiritual-Truth aspirations. Thus we struggle to make sense of an increasingly poisoned and degraded planet, for which we seem unable to provide meaningful, long-term answers. If we do not now strive to re-establish that vitally important connection and begin to seek out the necessary knowledge and understanding of them, there will be nothing to look forward to except more problems wrought by more people crowding into reducing areas of increasing degradation! A truly apocalyptic end.

That will be the ultimate end result anyway, simply because of our stubborn refusal to accept this reality. Paradoxically, because we of humankind desperately need this vital connection for our very survival, it is critically important to offer the very knowledge that may turn the tide for those who still hold the desire to learn about them. Those who genuinely embrace this desire would gain a greater level of insight into the inner and outer workings of the natural world. Whilst intimately involved in the formative processes of, and activity in, all the spheres of Creation, the Elemental forces, by way of a precise and lawfully ordained process, are also concerned with all human activities.

To explain the further *why* of this connection, we need to **fully** understand that, of all creatures in Creation, only the human spirit inherently possesses the gift of free-will. Every other inhabitant within Creation carries out their life and activity in strict accordance with The Creative Will, including the Elemental Beings. From free-will, however, derives the ultimate spiritual responsibility of **accountability**. Accountability for all our thoughts, words and actions.

Now, at this time in the spiritual and evolutionary development of mankind, our collective "karma" over millennia – which for the most part consists of dark, debased and degraded activities – is being returned to us with increasing strength and frequency under the lawful outworking of the interlinked and inviolable Spiritual Laws. This lawful process marks the closing of all cycles – again activated by our free-will – for *this Material Part of Creation*. It is the unenviable task of the "Elemental Beings", through the generation of increasingly severe effects of the world's weather patterns and catastrophic natural disasters, that "returns" a large part of this "payment" to us. It is thus in exact accordance with both the *individual* and *collective* spiritual volition of all humankind under the outworking of The Law of Reciprocal Action in the first instance.

In the previous Chapter we explained the meaning of the "Second Death" for man and outlined how such an event could occur. The same process is also employed for the "collective reaping" of mankind, since *individual outcomes* are *simultaneously* being resolved within the parameters of the *collective happening*.

That is because the Material part of Creation was firmly bound to the unalterable Laws of evolution and dissolution from the very beginning, in strict accordance with The Creative Will. This "Creative Will", of which The Laws of Nature are part, is the power or force which, in its activity, continually forms and dissolves worlds. Exactly as can be observed in interstellar activity. Again, the key point in the previous paragraph is the reinforcement of our assertion that the "Laws of Nature" are the "Will of God". In other words, the "Elemental Forces of Nature", in their ordained purpose and activity, carry out The Eternal Will. Under the inviolable Law of Sowing and Reaping, the "Elemental Beings", both the large and the small, produce the reciprocal effect of mankind's decisions.

So, what is the actual mechanism that will ultimately bring about our "collective fate", and how will the "Forces of Nature" achieve this? To understand that point we need to briefly revisit the process previously outlined in our analysis of the meaning of the "second death", and thereby show how the Elemental activity of the Forces of Nature is so strongly connected to the fate of humankind! Whilst a "second-death" concept necessarily represents a finite one – as must the life-span of each material globe – it is the *continuous coming into being* of the star systems contained within the "*cycle* **of Creation**" that is "eternal and without end", thus *infinite*! Individual suns and planets *within* such systems simply undergo their time of birth, life and disintegration in this overall, infinite continuity.

Moreover, it is a process necessary for any particular part of the material world which finally reaches the defining point of its life-cycle whereby its disintegration permits a further renewal for its continuing evolution. Each globe has its ordained time for this process. The key aspect contained within such lawful outcomes is the fact that the outworking of the Natural Laws precisely determines the point at which this disintegration process for each celestial globe must begin. Hence the reason why our own planet earth cannot be exempt from this ordained event either. What colours our situation most markedly is the fact that this "inevitable happening" will proceed at its precisely determined moment, *irrespective* of the *condition* of the *earth*, or *its inhabitants* i.e., *we humans!*

We should be perfectly clear from the above explanations, therefore, that the "Forces of Nature" *will* bring about the "renewal" of the earth under the outworking of the Natural Laws which are, at the same time, The Spiritual Laws. We should thus carefully note the key point – that these events will occur at the precisely ordained time, "**irrespective**" of the "**condition**" of the "**inhabitants**". The term condition in this case means the *spiritual condition*, or level of *spiritual maturity* of the inhabitants. Therefore, as we continually reinforce, since most of man's decisions for all his time on earth have leaned more toward war, strife and degradation of his material home, we can expect that the collective reciprocal return of that volition will be severe and destructive, returning tenfold our original "choices", albeit in perfect justice. Unfortunately for humankind, however, under the aegis of the "whirlwind constant".

Moreover, if we *actually are near the point where disintegration is due to set in*, we should then be able to detect the *beginnings* of that process via *increased Elemental-force activity*. This effect should thus clearly reveal itself in more and more disruptive and destructive weather patterns. Quite obviously, there *is* such increased activity, the like of which even weather scientists now view with alarm. This new "weather development" therefore clearly heralds this impending disintegration process.

As our fate is tightly bound to the spiritually-lawful activity of the "elementals" who are ordained to return to us the reciprocal effects of all our deeds, in the same way that we must reap "our bad", it is equally true – and certainly more desirable – that we will also reap any "good" that may be ours at this time. Therefore, if we wish to survive this disintegration activity that is now "waiting in the wings", we need to do what this work has constantly enjoined thus far, and will constantly stress throughout. We need to become voluntarily accepting of, and conversant with, The Spiritual Laws of Creation. By changing our attitude and volition to one of conscious recognition and acceptance instead of perversely maintaining one of cynical, disbelieving rejection we would reap, instead, the benefits that ensue from working with and alongside the "Elemental Forces of Nature" under the inviolable outworking of those Perfect Laws!

The first step is to re-establish connections to the "Elemental Beings" by first recognising that they are a very real and necessary part of life in the material worlds. By this change we fulfil our ordained purpose in consciously working with them. With their guidance and help we *could* have created a reflection of paradise on earth, and thereby have been true "stewards of the earth" as was once commanded for humankind. Now, however, under the *serious need of their protection*, we *may perhaps* survive the disintegration of our poisoned home when its ordained time arrives. The sure guarantee of not accepting this "life belt of hope" is that of destruction in any case, exactly in accordance with our collective volition.

Such a "doomsday scenario" will invariably produce different responses from within the various sections of any society of course, and there have been *imminent* doomsday predictions for centuries. Yet whilst there are many believers in an approaching "end-time" today, there will surely be disbelievers too, both from within and without the various religious groups. Intellectual science, also, by virtue of its basically aspiritual nature, will be generally unreceptive to such ideas. Nevertheless, the outcomes alluded to will conform to "scientific laws" – as explained in Chapter 14 – because they, in turn, can only derive from the higher Spiritual Laws, as we continually reiterate. What we have not previously had before are the necessary **spiritual** explanations whereby *greater* sense can be made of the increasingly severe weather patterns and geological activity globally.

The views of disbelievers are ultimately **completely irrelevant** anyway. Irrespective of what they may espouse, and from whatever discipline or source they may derive their beliefs, what is outlined and explained here **are** the connective-processes that will bring those events which humankind must soon experience, set in motion by the very Laws of Life. It is the same "mechanism of Law" that gave rise and life to all disbelievers and to all science in the first instance. Therefore all we need do is *quietly watch and wait* as the verification of what has been stated, and why, becomes the living reality for all. Since we contend that that is the inescapable reality, let us continue on with our analysis of "Elemental Lore" and offer other insights into this "brave new world" for those who may yet still awaken spiritually. We will, however, still offer respect for all other beliefs, in accordance with humankind's ordained free-will right to choose individual paths.

Western societies – and perhaps more particularly America, with its greater technological bent and promotion of the corporate, capitalist ethos – will generally have scant regard for "Elemental" beliefs. It is interesting to note, however, that Japan, that dynamo of corporate wealth and global trend-setting, actually retains extremely strong links to "Elemental beliefs" behind the corporate facade the country presents to the rest of the world. Not only are there many shrines and temples to "Elemental Beings" in the strong animistic religion of Shintoism, the language itself actually incorporates the sounds and sound effects of "Elemental" activity. Yet, in a perversely selfish paradox, this same culture has no qualms about stripping much of the world of all that it materially needs to feed its own personal wants in apparent direct contravention of a strong religion that ostensibly venerates all that the natural world offers.

The Fairy Tales from old Europe that many fondly remember from childhood directly trace their origins to Elemental activity. The early Teutons and other similar European groups unequivocally accepted "Nature Beings" as factual reality. And in many rural areas of Europe today, such acceptance is still strong.

Paradoxically, had we retained an unbroken connection to the Animistic Realm, the world could have been much more than classical Greece once was. For such clear insight would have guaranteed greater help and advancement from precisely those Elemental Beings placed in Creation to assist us in what would have been our natural, step-by-step, spiritual development. The proliferation of chemical poisons and the development of some of the world's current energy systems which offer only nightmarish end-scenarios, would not have arisen. In their place would have been **given** natural, sustainable energy and natural sowing and harvesting methods.

Instead, much of what we have produced on the planet without that vitally necessary connection are areas of poisoned, denuded and degraded "chemical deserts". The mega or super-cities of the so-called "first world" harbour areas that are little more than ugly, decaying hell-holes holding thousands of diseased, drug-ridden or malnourished human flotsam housed in filthy slum areas – or not housed at all. The third world's starving equivalent are camped out in refugee hovels in unproductive desert lands. Because of the bounty of the earth overall, we should *never* have reached this point.

Yet that point has finally been reached for millions simply because we severed the connection to our greatest help in the foolish belief that man could do it better. In the most "bitter-of-pills" scenario, it will probably only be the *continuing reality* of such nightmarish situations that may finally induce humankind to awaken to the only true knowledge with which to alleviate the suffering of millions of our fellow travellers.

The reader may recall the explanations regarding the "life-power" that maintains and sustains literally everything in Creation; that power which is neither good nor bad, but **"neutral"**. Precisely because of our spiritual origins and inherent free-will attribute, we humans act like refracting lenses and are thus able to direct this "power" to whatever purpose we choose. Moreover, we cannot stand divorced from or even **stop** the process as it is completely automatic. Therein lies the "accountability" that we must accept for the stewardship of planet earth – our material home. The consequences derived from this free-will "refractive-mechanism", whereby the "Elemental Forces" return to us the reciprocal effects of all our deeds, must logically correspond precisely to the kind of stewardship *chosen*.

Therefore, if we compare the reality of man's history against the command to live according to The Spiritual Laws, it is not difficult to understand that an incredible amount of reciprocal effect is heaping against us like a huge tsunami about to break. We are in the vanguard of it at this present time as we observe how more and more strange and virulent diseases appear and mutate, the increasingly changeable and unpredictable weather patterns, the natural catastrophes of greater and greater frequency and intensity, and the insurmountable problems of all kinds. However, all that "angst" is still nothing more than just the "beginnings" of the "complete reaping" yet to occur.

8.2 Native American "Spirituality" – A European Philosopher's View

Let us digress from our present thread for a moment and very briefly examine the attitude of the North American Indians to their environment, particularly the beliefs of those of the Great Plains and the forest-fringe dwellers.

Jostein Gaarder, author of Sophie's World, notes that in this present time of great concern for our poisoned "home", a new thought of "ecophilosophy" has emerged. Arne Naess, a Norwegian philosopher and one of the founders of this "idea", coined the word, "ecosophy". He and others – mainly in the West – believe that "western civilisation as a whole is on a fundamentally wrong track, racing toward a head-on collision with the limits of what our planet can take." Moreover, the idea that man is "... master of nature ... could prove to be fatal for the whole living planet."

Consequently, these particular philosophers "...have looked to the thinking and ideas of other cultures... and have also studied the thoughts and customs of so-called primitive peoples – or 'native peoples' such as the **Native Americans** – *in order to discover what we have lost*." (*Sophie's World*, p 384-5, Emphases mine.)

The life of the Native Americans of the Northern United States revolved very much around the sharply delineated seasonal changes that characterise the Continental United States. The mountain range of the Rockies running in a north/south direction rather than across the land means that sudden unseasonable Arctic blasts can occur unpredictably, reaching as far south as Florida at times. By striving to understand their "feeling" for the environment, we may deduce whether or not there existed genuine knowledge of the Elemental Forces of Nature. And not simply a fear-ridden, superstitious attitude of resigned acceptance to the natural forces surrounding them, either in the movement of life-sustaining animals, or in the vagaries of the weather.

The Plains Indian, utilising mainly the bison to provide virtually all of his shelter and clothing needs, was *acutely attuned* to the most minute changes in the natural environment surrounding him, and therefore to the weather too. Whereas certain Indigenous peoples fearfully saw dark and dangerous entities at every turn – forms that had to be *appeased* or countered in some way – the Plains Indian, in stark contrast, generally saw only *the greatness of the "Elemental forces" serving, nurturing, and protecting his world.*

In his veneration of those "forces", he not only gave thanks for all that he was given but sought to emulate their goodness in the way he related to those animals and birds whose lives he took for food, clothing and shelter. The ethos of the Native American Indians before the arrival of the European inherently encompassed that elevated outlook, where gratitude to the "Great Spirit" was invariably the first consideration. It was not fear of their environment but rather respect for life and veneration of its "Giver"! That recognition is well exemplified in one short sentence taken from a lengthy address by "One of the most important figures among Native American leaders of the eighteenth century..." (*North American Indian Chiefs*, Karl Nagelfell, p 18)

This "most important figure" was a Seneca leader popularly known as "Red Jacket" because of a British Officer's jacket that he wore. His actual name was Sogoyewapha.

From "Red Jacket's commentary on the spiritual beliefs of the Native Americans (1805)", we read:

"For all these favours we thank the Great Spirit, and Him only."

(p 18, Emphasis mine.)

One can note powerful, intuitive insights here that closely approximate the essence of The First Commandment. In the case of the Native Americans, however, it is a clearly a voluntary reverence stemming from a quite natural recognition of the beneficence of the natural world which, in turn, draws its offerings from the Great Spirit – their term for The Creator! Contrast that stance with the fear element promoted by some churches toward the same Commandment from the time of the Dark Ages even to the present.

Red Jacket addressed the European colonists attitude to land and religion too. In the following observations, he sagely notes:

"You have got our country, but are not satisfied... You want to force your religion upon us... We understand that your religion is written in a Book... Brother, you say there is but one way to worship the Great Spirit. If there is but one religion, why do you white people differ so much about it? ... Why not all agreed, as you can all read the Book? ... We are told that your religion was given to your forefathers... We also have a religion which was given to our forefathers and has been handed down to us... It teaches us to be thankful for all the favors we receive, to love each other, and to be united. **We never quarrel about religion.**"

(p 19, Italics mine.)

In this exceptionally noble outlook lived the strongest connections to the Elemental Forces, and equally powerful veneration of the "Giver of Life". Even though sometimes needing to take the lives of his own at times, it was not generally in complete disregard for that life; again in stark contrast to that which other peoples savagely displayed. Whilst the Indian "brave" was most certainly a fearless warrior, it is unlikely that this aspect of him ever degenerated to the more and regular blood-thirsty practices of some races. Generally it remained as noble as it was possible to be in the circumstances of his existence, in both the pre - and post-European phases of his life.

For even under extreme provocation and duress at the encroachment of European settlement, and the more brutal behaviour of the "frontier Army" at times, the demeanour of this people generally remained far more noble than should have been expected of any race. His veneration for the natural world that was inherently carried within, instilled in him the strength he closely identified with in the power of the elements, and in the power and natural nobleness of the bison and the eagle.[5]

Thus, what we have lost is exactly that for which we offer explanations here, and is exactly that which the Plains Indians had to an ennobled degree. Even though these latter-day philosophers are endeavouring to find that lost knowledge, which they obviously believe exists, will they be able to accept the notion of non-material "Elemental Beings"? Invisible to most of us, yet capable of exerting huge, weather-induced, physical effects on the environment. Effects that, in a clearly material way, have the power to devastate man and his works.

With regard to the Plains cultures once more, and our assertion that it was most likely the vast openness of the land that produced or strongly influenced such an ennobled outlook in the inhabitants, Colin F. Taylor, in his book "Native American Myths and Legends", notes the powerful effect the Great Plains exerted. The following notation reinforces our premise about it.

> "There seems to be something within the unique environment of the Great Plains which causes a people to live with such vivid intensity and an awareness and understanding of the things around them. The Plains Indian was so much in daily association with his environment and so dependent upon it, that not only animals but plant life and even some inanimate objects were believed to have a spiritual existence. There was an awareness of a great power – the energy or moving force of the great universe – which, in the sacred language of the Lakota shamans, was called Skan or To and the blue of the sky symbolised its presence."

(p 41)

And in the same publication, a senior Cavalry Officer whose Military Service encompassed this part of America, had this to say about the initial effect the Plains could have on people.

---

[5] In my view, if one even cursorily examines the attitudes of most races to the "natural world", it is patently clear that this lost knowledge-connection sought by Arne Naess, could only be found – in its deepest reverential and natural expression – in some of the Native American peoples. Perhaps more particularly before the influence of, and corruption by, the "new Americans". Their way of being and interaction with their environment, even around that genocidal time-period, provide that particular essence of reverence and veneration for the natural world that the philosophic-seeking would more readily understand.

"The first experience of the Plains, like the first sail with a cap full of wind, is apt to be sickening. This once overcome, the nerves stiffen, the senses expand and man begins to realize the magnificence of being."

(Col. Richard Dodge, 1877, p 41)

If a European could experience and realize "the magnificence of being" without possessing an inherent veneration for the environment of the Great Plains, consider how deep that respect had become for its inhabitants – a respect nurtured for obviously far longer than Europeans. A more striking example of the deep, innate understanding that the "Red Man" had for his environment, however, is now preserved for posterity in what is probably *inadequately described* as "...the most beautiful and profound statement on the environment ever made."

Like "White Cloud's statement" of great wisdom at the beginning of this Chapter, there does not appear to be anything else in existence to even remotely approach the pure nobleness of the address given by the Great Chief Seattle, Chief of the Duwamish, upon "surrendering" his land to Governor Isaac Stevens in 1854. After the "Great White Chief" in Washington made an "offer" for a large area of Indian Land and promised a "reservation" for the Indian people, Chief Seattle "offered" *his* wisdom! Surely, the most noble address on the environment ever, and from which *we* will *offer* a few quotes. Such a wonderfully powerful document should grace every home!

8.3 Excerpts from Chief Seattle's Address

"The Great Chief Washington sends word that he wishes to buy our land.

For we know that if we do not sell, the White Man may come with guns and take our land. The idea is strange to us. If we do not own the freshness of the air and the sparkle of the water, how can we buy them?

We know that the White Man does not understand our ways. One portion of land is the same to him as the next, for he is a stranger who comes in the night and takes from the land what he needs. The earth is not his brother, but his enemy and when he has conquered it, he moves on.

His appetite will devour the earth and leave behind only a desert. The sight of your cities pains the eyes of the Red Man.

There is no quiet place in the White Man's cities. No place to hear the unfurling of leaves in spring or the rustle of an insect's wings. The clatter only seems to insult the ears.

The air is precious to the Red Man for all things share the same breath – the beast, the tree, the man, they all share the same breath.

The White Man does not seem to notice the air he breathes. Like a dying man for many days he is numb to the stench.

I have seen a thousand rotting buffaloes on the prairie, left by the White Man who shot them from a passing train.

I am savage and do not understand how the smoking iron horse can be more important than the buffalo that we kill only to stay alive. For whatever happens to the beasts soon happens to man. All things are connected.

Whatever befalls the earth, befalls the sons of the earth. If men spit upon the ground they spit upon themselves. This we know, the earth does not belong to man, man belongs to earth. Man did not weave the web of life he is merely a strand in it. Whatever he does to the web, he does to himself.

Our warriors have felt shame and after defeat they turn their days in idleness and contaminate their bodies with sweet food and strong drink. It matters little where we spend the rest of our days. There are not many.

But why should I mourn the passing of my people? Tribes are made of men, nothing more. Men come and go like the waves of the sea. Even the White Man, whose God walks and talks with him as friend to friend, cannot be exempt from common destiny. One thing we know, which the White Man may one day discover – our God is the same God. You may think now that you own Him as you wish to own our land, but you cannot. The earth is precious to Him and to harm the earth is to heap contempt on it's Creator. The whites too shall pass; perhaps sooner than all other tribes. Continue to contaminate your bed and one night you will suffocate in your own waste.

But in your perishing you will shine brightly, fired by the strength of the God who brought you to this land for some special purpose... That destiny is a mystery to us for we do not understand when the Buffalo are all slaughtered, the wild horses tamed, the secret corners of the forest heavy with the scent of many men and the view of the ripe hills blotted by talking wires. Where is the thicket? Gone. The end of living and the beginning of survival.

So if we sell you our land, love it as we have loved it, care for it as we have cared for it... And with all your strength, with all your mind, with all your heart, preserve it for your children and **love it** – as God loves us all.

One thing we know. Our God is the same God. The earth is precious to Him. Even the white man cannot be exempt from the common destiny. We may be brothers after all."

(Chief Seattle, 1854, with very kind permission of "Friends of the Earth.")

We have woven a particular thread from out of Chief Seattle's complete and extremely powerful, painful address. Contained within his address is much of The Living essence of The Spiritual Laws of Creation which we can easily recognise. If used as a guide, the exquisitely noble words of great wisdom by an equally great and noble Native American Chief can help all peoples to understand the difference between that which they may believe to be spiritual, and that which the substance of Chief Seattle's wisdom points to in its actual reality.

It is thus vitally important to accurately discern between psychic, elemental, and genuine spiritual activity. Only man's wrong volition is responsible for the production of aspiritual *psychic forms* and *their* associated activity. It is **never** produced by *Elemental* or truly *Spiritual* forces, for both serve only The Creative Will! By this measure, we may understand *how* to differentiate between genuine *Elemental messages* of warning that might be given for our safety, and unreliable *personal feelings*, perhaps generated by the emotions or by fear. Most importantly, though, we need to learn to recognise clear Spiritual Guidance. For such guidance will ***always*** be beneficial. That will be the measure of its validity.

The history of man certainly does record numerous incidents where warnings received from strictly Elemental activity or "signs" resulted in the prevention of accident or death in some way. That is not to say, of course, that every single natural event involving all the elements of nature, and every animal, insect and bird that we see, or that might otherwise catch our attention, means that something is "absolutely going to happen". To believe that is to nurture foolish superstition and generate uncertainty and perhaps fear at every turn. More often than not such things will be the normal and natural activity of all the other natural life-forms around us.

Warnings, nevertheless, are sometimes given for our protection and, if recognised as such, should be acted on immediately. Discernment is the key in knowing what to listen for, and what to ignore. It naturally follows, therefore, that superstition cannot provide that appropriate level of discernment. The only sure way to absolutely know is to be thoroughly conversant with the workings of "Elemental Lore". For it is the "Elemental Forces" that will sound any such warnings, since our continued existence is interlinked with their ordained activity. To achieve that level of discernment, however, the sufficient understanding of the higher Spiritual Laws is the first imperative. It is unfortunate that we have become so obtuse that the warnings *constantly* being given to us now are rarely heard. To our serious detriment, we have virtually lost the ability to correctly perceive "**protective discernment**"!

8.4 The Elemental Connection to the Animal Kingdom

To illustrate how we can learn and benefit from animals, some examples of their natural ability to sense impending changes in the activity of the earth offer a serious guide. Because earthquake lore invariably records the fact that many animals become agitated before any major earth-movement, we should briefly examine this phenomenon. Earthquakes can trigger other crustal changes or movements such as in volcanic activity, which can also set in motion hugely destructive tsunami. Since many of the world's great cities are clustered around natural harbours for purposes of maritime trade, and the frequency of larger earthquakes is increasing, perhaps more attention should be paid to the activity of animals in these areas, particularly.

For many years the scientific-intellectual mind-set of seismologists tended to dismiss stories of precursory animal behaviour as scientifically useless or as something akin to greatly exaggerated folk-tales. However, recent large quakes in China produced thousands of reports of strange animal behaviour which were so compelling that earthquake scientists from other countries are now reconsidering such phenomena. We restate our previous contention that this has always been the natural pattern because earth movements are an *Elemental activity* to which all animals are closely attuned. And "Elemental Lore" takes no account whatsoever of what earth-sciences may so decree. It is therefore extremely heartening to note that on 19 July 2002, Discovery Channel screened a programme from its "Natural Mystery" series precisely about the precursory behaviour of animals, birds and fishes. On this programme, Jim Weir, a retired American geologist, stated, ***"Mother Nature is far more reliable [than science]."***

Modern seismic instruments are capable of detecting even the most minute changes in the earth's electrical and magnetic fields, even patterns of sub-audible sound. Yet whilst these changes may be subsequently shown to precede seismic activity, they do not always. However, in the long history of recorded phenomena of this nature, animals, birds and fishes, far more sensitive to such tiny stimuli, react immediately in the sureness of *knowing* that an earth movement is imminent. Therefore, we can surely state that we have a "constant" in this behaviour pattern, even if a non-scientific one. Yet clearly far more reliable than much of our "modern" detection equipment.

So what might we deduce from this? Marine scientists marvel at the sonar abilities that mammals of the order Cetacea (whales and dolphins etc.) possess, but are unable to definitively explain it apart from using scientific terms that perhaps closely approximate their theories. Similarly, animal reactions of the kind we have outlined cannot simply be slotted into a solely scientific pigeon-hole either. Whilst the physical event can certainly be recorded as electrical activity or something similar, nevertheless, it is an *elemental happening in the first instance*. And one driven by *a higher* power. This is the mysterious factor that science cannot measure with its instruments, and to which the animal world, itself strongly connected to the Elemental world to the strongest possible degree, reacts.

A few examples recorded in "The Handbook of Unusual Natural Phenomena" (Eyewitness Accounts of Nature's Greatest Mysteries) by William R Corliss, Arlington House Crown Publishers, New York, may offer clearer illustration.

In the sub-Chapter, "The Curious Supersensitivity of Animals to Impending Quakes", Corliss records how the consternation of dogs, horses, cattle and other domestic animals are referred to in the records of most great earthquakes. Fish are also frequently affected. In the London earthquake of 1749 roach and other fish in a canal showed evident signs of confusion and fright. Moreover, he records that, sometimes after an earthquake, fish rise to the surface dead and dying. During the Tokyo earthquake of 1880 cats inside a house ran about trying to escape, foxes barked, and horses tried to kick down the boards confining them to their stables.

Whilst we may not be overly surprised with such frightened behaviour of animals *during* a tremor, it is an entirely different matter when animals clearly sense something *about* to happen when contraindications appear to suggest otherwise. As if aware of an earthquake's imminent arrival, Corliss recorded that:

> "...ponies have been known to prance about their stalls, pheasants to scream, and frogs to cease croaking a little time before a shock..."

(p 291)

Interestingly, geese, pigs and dogs appear more sensitive in this respect than other animals. Calabrian folklore, after the great earthquake there "...recorded that the neighing of a horse, the braying of a donkey, or the cackle of a goose was sufficient to cause the inhabitants to flee their houses in expectation of a shock." (p 291)

At the time of this quake, sand-eels, which are usually buried in the sand, came to the surface. Many birds are believed to show their uneasiness before an earthquake by hiding their heads under their wings and behaving in an unusual manner.

Some South American peoples believe that certain quadrupeds such as dogs, cats and jerboa rats give warning of coming danger by their restlessness. And sometimes immense flocks of seabirds fly inland before an earthquake, as if alarmed by the commencement of some sub-oceanic disturbance. In Chile, before the shock of 1835, all the dogs are said to have escaped from the city of Talcahuano. One scientific explanation for such behaviour has been advanced by Professor Milne who believes that some animals are sensitive to the small tremors that precede almost all earthquakes. He suggests, moreover, that animal intelligence, as the result of their own experiences which will have taught them that small earth tremors may be precursors to a large shake, would then register alarm at any future indications of major earth movements.

Interestingly, Corliss states that signs of alarm days before an earthquake are probably accidental. This statement is clearly contradictory in my view for, quite obviously, any signs of alarm even days before an earthquake *actually occurring* must logically be cognitive prescience on the part of the animals concerned, purely by virtue of the *arrival* of the quake, so can hardly be deemed accidental.

But what do other publications report about this interesting phenomena. Corliss records the "American Review of Reviews" as itemising the following:

> "In connection with the fearful catastrophes of recent date in Italy, California, and elsewhere, which, like so many others of like nature will long retain a hold on human memory, attention has ***again*** been called to the fact that many animals give intimations of such great disturbances in advance by certain particular and often unusual conduct. It is particularly such animals as have their abode underground that often indicate, days before the event, that something unusual in nature is about to occur, by coming out of their hiding places underground into the open.
>
> Aelian mentions that, in the year 373 before Christ, five days before the destruction of Helike, all the mice, weasels, snakes and other like creatures, were observed going in great masses along the roads leading from that place. Something similar was noticed also, later, though not to so marked an extent as in the case mentioned by Aelian. This leaving of their subterranean abodes by underground creatures on such occasions might possibly be explained by the emission of various malodorous and noxious gases during these disturbances of the earth."
>
> (Emphasis mine.)

However, not only do animals living under ground furnish indications that something out of the ordinary is about to happen. The larger animals on the surface, such as cows, horses, asses, sheep, and many birds, even, seem to get premonitions of particular natural phenomena and events.

Corliss records that in 1805, during an earthquake:

> "...the cattle at Naples and its neighbourhood set up a continuous bellowing some time *before* the event, at the same time trying to support themselves more firmly by planting the forefeet widely apart; the sheep kept up a continuous bleating, and hens and other fowl expressed their restlessness by making a terrible racket. Even the dogs gave many indications of uneasiness at the time. The actions of animals observed during the great earthquake of 1783 seem to have been most remarkable. Thus the howling of the dogs at Messina became so unendurable that men were sent out with cudgels to kill them."

Corliss further notes that their noise was most marked during the progress of the earthquake, while it was difficult to pacify the animals in the vicinity for some time, even after the cessation of the shocks. Dogs and horses ran about meanwhile with hanging heads, or stood with outstretched legs "...as if aware of the need of planting themselves firmly." Horses that were ridden at the time stopped and stood still without orders "...trembling so at the same time that no rider could remain in the saddle."

Corliss mentions Scophus as telling the story of a cat during an earthquake at Locris "...which set up a most dismal caterwauling at the approach of each new shock, meanwhile constantly jumping from one point to another. The roosters kept up a continual crowing, both before and during the earthquake." In the fields Scophus also observed hares: "...so under the influence of the terrestrial disturbance that they made no attempt to escape and seemed in no way disturbed by his presence. A flock of sheep could not be kept on the right road, notwithstanding the efforts of shepherd and dogs, but fled in affrightened haste to the mountains."

Birds, also, seem to have premonitions of the coming of such catastrophes. During the earthquake of Quintero, in Chile, in November 1822 "...the gulls uttered all sorts of unusual cries during the whole of the preceding night and were in constant restless motion during the quake." And on February 20, 1835, the day before the earthquake at Concepcion, also in Chile, at ten in the morning "...great flocks of seabirds, mostly gulls, were seen to pass over the city landward, a phenomenon not to be explained by any stormy condition of the weather. It was fully an hour and a half after their passage, at 11:40 of the forenoon, before the earthquake came, one so disastrous that nearly the entire city was reduced to ruins." Even the fish in the sea seem to be disturbed at the approach of an earthquake. Alexander von Humboldt, the famous traveller and naturalist, tells of having observed "...the crocodiles of the Orinoco leaving the water and fleeing to the forest during an earthquake."

During the 1930's some scientists wondered whether the growing mountain of anecdotal evidence on pre-quake animal behaviour might be sufficient to help predict impending earthquakes. Corliss cites the publication, Nature, as reporting that the Japanese undertook the first experiments – perhaps not surprising given the huge amount of tremors Japan experiences.

Corliss notes that "...two Japanese seismologists, Dr. Shinkishi Hatai and Dr. Noboru Abe, observed that catfish (Siluroidea) in natural conditions showed signs of restlessness about six hours before earthquake disturbances were registered on their recording apparatus." Since catfish are ordinarily placid, unresponsive creatures, experiments were made to test that seeming precursive responsiveness. Catfish placed in an aquarium were tested three times a day by tapping on the supporting table. When no earthquake was impending, "...the fish moved lazily or not at all." But about six hours before a shock "..the fish jumped when the table was tapped and sometimes swam about agitatedly for a time before settling down upon the bottom again." Several months of testing showed that in a period when 178 earthquakes of all degrees of severity had been recorded: "...the fish had correctly predicted 80 per cent of the shocks." They showed no discrimination in their movements between slight local shocks and more serious distant shocks. The experimenters think that the catfish "...are made sensitive through electrical changes in the earth, since it was only when the aquarium was electrically earthed, through the drainpipe, that they responded to a coming earthquake." (*Nature*, 132: 817, 1933)[6]

The Chinese have always believed that the earth provided all the messages required to predict earthquakes. Sometimes the messages are so clear that precise predictions can be made and lives saved. Such was the case in the Haicheng earthquake of 1975 where dozens of abnormalities pointed to an impending quake. Apart from solely animal behaviour, sudden changes and unusual fluctuations in groundwater levels were also catalogued. Two days before the quake struck, 90,000 residents were evacuated. At 1030hrs on the precise day predicted, the final warning was given and the rest of the city emptied. Nine hours later the quake struck. Measuring 7.3 on the Richter scale, it destroyed or damaged ninety per cent of the city's buildings but few deaths resulted from it. (Source: Encarta, BBC and "Our World" programme – "The Savage Earth")

The world's greatest recorded natural disaster occurred in China in 1556 in Shensi province where a single earthquake killed 800,000 people. Such devastating earth movements have prompted Chinese officials to collate testimony concerning premonitory signs from the rural populace, particularly farmers. China currently possesses the world's largest computer network for collating earthquake data. With hundreds of millions of people tied closely to the earth, and

---

[6]In terms of "Elemental Lore", it is quite logical that the catfish should respond when the conditions of what would be their more natural environment were re-created, whereas any form of shielding *might not necessarily* provide that same response.

who are perhaps more attuned to subtle changes in their environment than people resident in cities, the authorities have achieved some success in earthquake prediction.

Unlike Haicheng, however, the "messages" from the Tangshan quake, whilst very numerous, were not as clear. After the Tangshan earthquake the following report was filed by Shen Ling-huang, a Chinese writer:

> "A stock-breeder in Northern China got up to feed his animals before dawn on July 28, 1976. He is a member of the Kaokechuang People's Commune which lies only 40 kilometres away from the city of Tangshan. When he went into the stable, he found that instead of eating, his two horses and two mules were jumping and kicking until they finally broke loose and dashed outside. At that moment, a dazzling white flash illuminated the sky and huge rumbling noises were heard. The Tangshan earthquake (magnitude 7.8) had struck.
>
> This occurrence was reported to Chinese scientists during a survey of the earthquake-affected areas around Tangshan. Their mission was to find out about the feasibility of an earthquake prediction programme that made use of observations of animal behaviour. This survey, covering Tangshan and 400 communes in 48 counties around it, was conducted by Chinese biophysicists, biologists, geophysicists, chemists, and meteorologists shortly after the earthquake.
>
> Through interviews and discussions with local people, the scientists collected information on 2,093 cases of unusual animal behaviour in the time shortly before the earthquake. Nearly all of the anecdotes were passed on to the scientists by survivors of the earthquake themselves; the majority of the reports involved domestic animals. Some examples included goats that refused to go into pens, cats and dogs that picked up their offspring and carried them outdoors, pigs that squealed strangely, startled chickens that dashed out of coops in the middle of the night, rats that left their nests, and fish that dashed about aimlessly."
>
> (*Earthquake Information Bulletin*, 10: 231-33, 1978, Corliss, 291-94)

In the case of the Haicheng earthquake, the authorities, armed with similar kinds of information – and completely accepting of its validity – took the precaution of being "wise before the event" and ordered the evacuation of the city before the quake struck.

Compare this example with the people of Messina who went out to kill the howling dogs. Humans cannot match the sensitivity of animals to earthquake precursors, so the subtle signs that set dogs to howling often pass by humans undetected. This unfortunate state of affairs is solely the result of humankind closing a necessary connection to the same forces and signs that animals immediately react to, and which is a potential lifesaver. For we also possess a similar ability. All we need do is recognise such forces and then utilise that ability to heed any warnings received for our protection too.

The observation of animal behaviour predating the occurrence of earthquakes goes back centuries. In fact, even in 100 AD, Pliny, a Roman writer, advocated then that such behaviour be used for predicting earthquakes.

Volume II of "Earthquakes and the Urban Environment", G. Lennis Berlin, CRC Press, records interesting observations of animal behaviour.

> "Zoo animals refuse to go into their shelters at night; snakes, lizards, and small mammals evacuate their underground burrows; hyperactive insects congregate in huge swarms near seashores; cattle seek high ground; wild fowl leave their usual habitats; domestic animals become agitated."

In the United States, the earliest published accounts of unusual animal behaviour were for the 1906 San Francisco earthquake where a Miss Finette Locke kept detailed notes of this phenomenon from cases reported to her. In a summary of her notes published in the 1908 report of the State Earthquake Investigation Commission, several of her observations were:

> "Horses whinnied before the shock... Several instances were reported where cows stampeded before the shock was felt by the observer. In other cases cows about to be milked are said to have been restless before the shock... Lowing of cattle at the time of the shock was very commonly reported, and in some cases this is said to have occurred a little before the shock. The most common report regarding the behaviour of dogs was their howling during the night preceding the earthquake."

The lowing of cattle at the time of the shock should surely be a natural expectation. So it appears surprising that such behaviour should be considered unusual, in contrast to that preceding a tremor. Vol. II of "Earthquakes and the Urban Environment" offers an interesting insight into the changes in attitude that are obviously occurring within some of the disciplines. The following quote reflects this new awareness.

> "Until quite recently, accounts like these were usually met with skepticism (scepticism). However, this view is changing, largely due to the apparent successes the Chinese have had in using erratic animal behaviour as an earthquake precursor.... farmers are instructed to watch for unusual activity in their animals, and observers are even stationed in the Peking Zoo to watch for any unusual animal activity. Erratic behaviour is reported to a local seismological brigade."

A booklet issued by the Seismological Office of Tientsin offers observers hints on how to use unusual animal behaviour for predicting earthquakes. A translated summary states:

> "It is easy and simple to use animals to predict earthquakes. Certain organs of animals may acutely detect various underground changes before earthquakes. Both historical and recent surveys of large earthquakes prove that animals have precursory reactions."

And an earthquake prediction verse from the same translated publication notes that:

> "Animals are aware of precursors before earthquakes: Let us summarise their anomalous behaviour for prediction. Cattle, sheep, mules and horses do not enter corrals. Rats move their homes and flee. Hibernating snakes leave their burrows early. Frightened pigeons continuously fly and do not return to nests. Rabbits raise their ears, jump aimlessly and bump things. Fish are frightened, jump above water surface."

Upon being rescued from her damaged apartment building after the Taiwan earthquake of 1999, a Mrs Chu reported that the fish in her tanks became agitated the night before. She noted that they kept swimming into the sides of their tanks so forcefully as to cause bleeding. (Discovery Channel documentary.) And in the recent, devastating earthquake and tsunami aftermath affecting the countries bordering the Indian Ocean, CNN reported many deaths in the destruction of a Tourist Hotel located in a National Park. Officials feared the worst for the wild animals resident in the protected area – which was why the Hotel was located there. Expecting to discover large numbers of dead animals, they found, to their amazement, that they had left the area and moved further inland, above the farthest reach of the waves that *subsequently* washed inland. Using senses that we have no comprehension of, they simply moved out of harm's way – before the event.

The high geological activity of the San Andreas fault in California offers ideal monitoring conditions for American geologists. This very visible fault is generated by the Pacific Plate moving past the North American Plate. However, even though both plates are moving in the same northwestwards direction, the Pacific is moving faster than the North American. That "speed differential" effectively means that the "relative movement" of the two Plates is in opposite directions. It is generally accepted that the San Andreas fault will one day produce one of the largest earthquakes ever experienced by man.

Increasing "Western" scientific interest in the possibility of utilising animal behaviour for earthquake predictions is illustrated by a perhaps belated admittance from U.S. scientists at a 2 day conference sponsored by the USGS (US Geological Survey) in October 1976 in noting that: "...there may be some truth in the belief that animals can sense some environmental change that precedes an earthquake."

The Conference heard that:

> "...the activity of captive pocket mice and kangaroo rats is being monitored at sites near the Palmdale bulge, and the motor activity of cockroaches is being monitored at sites near Hollister, Twin Lakes, and Anza - sites close to active faults. Preliminary results from the second study indicate that before the occurrence of small earthquakes, there is a marked increase in their motor activity."

(Conference Notes, p 38-9)

Having examined a few examples of connected elemental and animal activity for our purposes, and apart from our previous reference to Jesus and the storm on the Sea of Galilee and the help given to Moses, are we able to cull a little more from The Bible to illustrate our assertions that other "ordained beings" such as "nature elementals" are a reality. One of the Psalms of David offers a curiously worded Scripture. But not so curious when the knowledge of Elemental Beings is taken into account.

> "Thou Who maketh Thine angels into winds and Thy servants into flames of fire."
>
> (Psalms of David.)

An interesting passage in The Book of Isaiah also sheds further light on this "reality" in terms of a definitive, relative place within Creation for such "entities" – at least as indicated in The Bible. The prophet, Isaiah, sometimes referred to as The Great Prophet, is generally held in high regard in possessing greater clarity of spiritual perceptive depth than perhaps some of the others. In Isaiah 18, Verse 3, he states:

> "All ye **inhabitants *of the world*, AND dwellers *on the earth***, see ye, when He lifteth up an ensign on the mountains; and when He bloweth a trumpet, hear ye."
>
> (Bold emphases mine.)

In this Scripture we can readily note a clear delineation of **two** distinctly separate groups having their sphere of activity in **two** different places **not closely connected**. It seems perfectly clear that the "**inhabitants *of the world***" are **not** the same "beings" as the "**dwellers *on the earth***". This separation is further accentuated by the wording of "inhabitants *of*" and "dwellers *on*". And in the use of the conjunction *and* in the sentence. From our explanations of the various Planes of Creation, we could well conclude that Isaiah might actually have possessed the spiritual insight to *see* some of the other inhabitants of Creation aside from just the "dwellers on the earth". Whether this was so or not does not alter the obvious fact of his seemingly sure statement here.

Throughout history, what humankind term the instinct of animals has provided us with wonderful tales of near misses and lives saved from disaster when unusual behaviour of domestic pets such as cats and dogs, have alerted their owners to imminent danger. Anecdotal evidence also reveals that domesticated animals such as horses have refused to continue along a path for no apparent reason, even with the strongest urging. Then, onto the very area that the animal refused to enter, the rider escapes a slip that comes crashing down.

In such cases it is *not* any inherent instinct of the animal that causes it to shy away from certain areas at those precise moments, even if it had taken the same path regularly for many years. It simply heeds a warning given to it that danger is imminent, because it is able to see where the warning comes from. Today only a few people possess that similar faculty. This inherent ability in animals can be explained by the fact that their animating core (the inner life-force) originates in the Animistic Sphere. That is also the plane of origin of those Beings that have their field of activity in what we usually call Nature, i.e. air, fire, earth and water, about which, among others, Isaiah seeks to enlighten us. Therefore the similarity of their origins naturally provides the clear possibility for each to recognise the other.

Despite the fact that our origin lies in the higher Spiritual Sphere and we are "Spiritual beings" in essence, we nevertheless also possess an Animistic "body" as well as other "coverings", as explained in Chapter 4. We are therefore perfectly equipped to recognise the "Elemental Beings", by virtue of that inherent Animistic "attribute". Yet, humanity as a whole generally derides such "childish" or fanciful notions. Unlike the animals whose origins stand closer to them, and who thus live consciously in this "creative reality" we, supposedly, more "aware" human beings have allowed the same and necessary connection to virtually die within us. Paradoxically, because it is precisely the "elementals" who are tasked with the preparation and bringing about of those happenings we call natural disasters and catastrophes, **we will yet re-learn and fully experience the foolishness of our attitude toward this vital God-Willed activity. For it is they who know exactly when and where sudden changes in Nature are about to take place.**

Therefore all events in this category, such as landslides, sudden water eruptions, the bursting of a dam, tidal waves and floods, volcanic eruptions, rocks dislodged from mountains, trees falling, the caving-in of land undermined by water, and virtually everything connected with **natural events**, are all the ordained activity of the "Nature Beings". If, then, such an event is imminent, the possibility exists for an animal or person approaching the spot to be warned by these "elementals". Their presence and warnings, even though generally unseen by human beings, may produce feelings of distinct apprehension or unease such as a "cold feeling" or "hair standing on end", and may be sufficient to induce an individual not to want to proceed further. The behaviour of the animal may be markedly different, however. It is invariably startled, its hair bristles, and it may simply *refuse* to go any further.

Without this knowledge, such an experience of distinct unease or apprehension would probably imbue one with fear, particularly if one's cultural frame of reference encompassed the belief of forest or mountain entities, or psychic or phantom forms, or even the fear of earth-bound souls. We may wonder how many such warnings from out of the compassion of The Light have been given to humankind over millennia, and how much of it was treated with fearful apprehension, or totally ignored, or obtusely not perceived at all? Given the increasing frequency and intensity of storms world-wide, we should be careful that any such "help" given is not pushed away out of fear or derision. We should, instead, learn to gratefully accept such beneficial help!

Now, if we recall the earlier explanations in this Chapter regarding the connections between our free-will ability and the return of all our "sowings" via the activity of the "nature beings", we may begin to discern the reasons why man very often finds himself in dangerous situations with the potential for death or serious injury. For this reason we should emulate and refine the Chinese example and pay more attention to animals and thus learn from them.

Therefore, if we coolly and *objectively* observe the increasing "Elemental activity" world-wide in natural disasters and catastrophes of greater and greater intensity and frequency, it is very clear that man does, indeed, **stand blind to the true nature of the happening!** These explanations may offer the reader the possible connecting reasons why some intensely hot Eastern Australian, or Californian bushfire-storms, which can completely destroy a brick dwelling and melt cars, will sometimes leave a next-door *wooden* dwelling virtually untouched. Ordinarily, such intense heat would generally "explode" the wooden structure even before the flames will have reached it.

And perhaps why, during the Ash Wednesday firestorms around Melbourne in the early 80's, some of the houses that were left relatively intact, even though directly in the fire-path in some cases, were then reported destroyed or severely damaged by major flooding a few months later. For under the outworking of The Spiritual Laws, much that we are **forced to experience**, and the **timing** of that experience – even in natural disasters and catastrophes – is **not** necessarily an arbitrary happening. As we have clearly stated, what we term catastrophes and disasters are often just simply "changes" in the natural world around us. The fact that many may die during such upheavals is due to the obvious reality that wherever such increasingly-more-frequent changes occur, there will invariably be people in the way. Sometimes relatively sparsely populated, at other times in areas where millions reside. That is humankind's blunt reality!

What should again be recognised here is that the "Elementals" are active in every Sphere of Creation, and not solely on the earth. Just as we have small "Nature Beings" whose area of activity is concerned with the smaller plants of the world, and larger ones concerned with seas and mountains etc, so are there also beings of immense size and power whose field of activity reaches out into the forming of galaxies, suns and planets. All active under the aegis of The Creative Will![7]

A *conscious knowledge* of the *workings* of the "Elemental Forces of Nature" should offer the clear realisation that no race or people can lay claim to "ownership" of land, rivers or the air. We are enjoined to be stewards and nurturers of the land over which we must pass. And further enjoined to leave it in at least a good a state as, or preferably better than, that which we might have inherited. Therewith to produce beauty and harmony for the time we are permitted to be on it.

Such powerful statements of truth regarding "ownership of land" should be marked well because, at any moment, the incalculable power of the "Elemental Forces of Nature" can quickly devastate any tract of land, or destroy any works on it. *It is a process, moreover, that occurs somewhere on earth every hour of the day* – **and it is increasing**. This fact alone should sound a cautionary warning to develop more humility toward the inherent "Elemental power" within the land, and therefore caution also in foolish demands to "own" or "control" it.

Therefore, in terms of establishing the strongest possible connection to the "Elemental Forces" in our overall relationship with them and their ordained activity, we should learn *never to curse the weather*, regardless of the reasons we may wish to do so. For in doing so we curse the actual *ordained activity* of those "Elemental Beings" of the "Forces of Nature". And, by extension, that perfection which is The Creative Will! Far too often we use human-emotional terms in describing the weather as bad, ugly, lousy, rotten or shocking, etc. Since weather cannot intrinsically be such as that, to hear this more or less constant litany of many expletives, even, unequivocally reveals how far we are from any real

---

[7] Perhaps we may now understand that it was the activity of the "Elemental Beings" whose "ordained work" brought into being our own planet earth and raised the various lands out of the sea. Thus we may view the "Creation-legends" of different Indigenous peoples as "Elemental events" brought about by the larger and more powerful "Nature Beings" of the earth.

understanding of the "true nature" of the "Forces of Nature".

Weather is just weather!

Elemental activity may *produce* very stormy conditions which, in turn, may also *generate* violent winds and destructive waves. Or the same kind of activity may *produce* searing heat or bone-chilling cold which may even result in deaths. Such *productions* are **not arbitrary**, however. That is the "imperative of weather" which humankind needs to learn quickly if they are to understand the reasons for the unusual weather patterns which will **yet bring far greater destruction than at present**!

Quite clearly, then, all of humankind is subject to every nuance of weather change and activity, and not solely in terms of food production. At the Meteorological Society's Weatherwatch conference held in Auckland in November 1996, (New Zealand Herald report) the CEO of the Insurance Council of New Zealand, Mr David Sargeant, stated that extreme weather is a growing threat to New Zealand's economy. He also noted that: "...catastrophic weather events, such as damage from the severe winds and flooding brought by hurricanes, represented the greatest threat to the survival of the world's insurance industry. **And that the rise in natural catastrophes should not be ignored.**"

(Emphases mine.)

Our assertions that "elemental activity" will yet bring far more destruction through natural disasters more quickly, thus seriously affecting every aspect of the economy, appears to be well illustrated in the graph which accompanied the N.Z. Herald article. In the years from 1960 to 1984, costs to the Insurance industry world-wide from such events remained more or less manageable, fluctuating between a few hundred million U.S. dollars to a high point of about 24 billion, equal to an average annual cost of approximately 5 to 7 billion. Yet, the decade from 1985-1995 shows an almost year by year increase depicted by a steeply-rising exponential curve, culminating in a 110 billion dollar cost in 1995.

Mr. Sargeant attributed the increase in weather damage of recent years to a combination of factors that generally all scientific agencies subscribe to. Factors noted were: "Population density, increased living standards, industrialisation in high-risk areas and vulnerability of technologies, along with changing climate conditions." However, whilst these factors are constantly put forward as the reasons for severe weather increases, the same conference was told that even with global warming still on the rise:

> "...*scientists still could not attribute the observed effects to a specific cause.*"
>
> (Emphasis mine.)

Professor K.U. Sirinanda of the University of Brunei said, "People are not attuned to climate change. We need to have environmental education on a democratic scale or whatever you call it ... to convince policy makers of the importance of these issues." Such clearly correct views are, paradoxically, probably just a pipe dream, and that conference just another in a long line of them which will bring no real change at all – simply because most of all preceding similar ones have not. A very appropriate Biblical quote for this present time has resonance for most conferences now.

> **Take counsel together, and it will come to nought.**
>
> (Isaiah 8:10)

So whilst the "Weatherwatch" conference produced the standard reasons for the increasing concerns about the severity of global weather patterns and noted the end results of these changes, it was unable to "*attribute the observed effects to a specific cause*". In other words, the conference delegates did not *understand* or *know* the **actual causal reason** for them. As we have explained in this work, the reason lies in the spiritual connection *between* our inherent free-will decision-making ability and the *returns* we must experience through *wrongly using* that "spiritual gift" *to continually break the rules.*

As we must reinforce often, the "reaping from our sowing" is returned to us via the ordained activity of the Elemental Forces of Nature acting under The Creative Will. That is the precise reason why such conferences achieve no real change, and will not do so in the future either. That is simply because most of society, including those of influence or power who could institute the greatest change, generally regard such ideas as religious or "fringe-garbage".

However, since an exponential factor can be readily observed in all events now, all we need do is sit quietly back - and watch and wait. In the meantime, perhaps we should be crassly religious here and, again, state the answer of Jesus to His disciples when asked what the end-time would be like:

> "...for there shall then be wide-spread affliction, such as has not been known since the beginning of the world until now, no, nor will ever be known again. And if those times were not cut short, **not a man would be saved**."

(Emphasis mine.)

To this end, we should once more carefully note Chief Seattle's beautiful words of powerful truth and understanding. "If men spit upon the ground they spit upon themselves ... to harm the earth is to heap contempt on its Creator."

In probably the saddest of prophetic and paradoxical ironies, and simply because he voluntarily allowed the knowledge of the "Elemental Forces" to die within him, man will surely *curse* the power of the weather *as brought by them*, when it *finally destroys him and all his **wrong** works*. Thus at the very time when he would **need their protection to the greatest possible degree**. In what will obviously be a stupendously-powerful happening on a truly apocalyptic scale will be revealed the inviolable truth alluded to in Chief Seattle's address. For mankind on earth, that humanly-wrought destructive phase – which we unequivocally state must and will occur – shall be experienced as **the ultimate justice and outworking of Spiritual Law in the collective reaping of our collective whirlwind!**

As this is the prophesied happening for humankind that will shortly visit itself upon us, it behoves every person with even the faintest hint of "intuitive unease" today, to begin the process of setting within himself the knowledge that will offer understanding and protection at that time. All peoples, therefore, irrespective of whatever their particular societies or belief systems might deem correct or valid, must first begin with a thorough grounding of "Elemental Knowledge" and all its interrelated connections to the activity of man. After which should be taught all other Truths.

However, this clear need may require far more inner-seeking, value-change and discipline from certain races who currently demonstrate that they are incapable of *collectively* generating this particular requirement at present. This reluctance, or plain outright disbelief, runs the gamut of all peoples within the cultural spectrum globally. Thus, from the fearfully superstitious to the sophisticated scientific and technologically superior, most peoples will aver that they already know it all and will thus invariably be derisively dismissive of the kind of vitally essential knowledge as is offered here.

In very broad terms, therefore, the basic cultural parameters of Indigenous and Western Races overall may well determine where each group stands in relation to any recognition of the Elemental Beings of the Forces of Nature. Indigenous peoples *should generally* be more easily able to develop the greater recognition and a more correct attitude toward "Elementals" than perhaps the Europeans can - *as a complete group*. In reality, of course, there should be no difference whatsoever between the two groups, for The Law states quite unequivocally:

All can see – if they really wish to!

Further to that, however, must be the realisation that **it is the individual, alone,** who must ultimately accept full and personal responsibility for all his beliefs and decisions under the outworking of Spiritual Law – even ones concerning Elemental Beings.

Becoming more accepting of the other-world reality of Nature Beings thus offers all of humankind the means whereby – if he so chooses – he can establish the correct and necessary foundation for his physical and spiritual protection against the greatly accelerating "elemental activity" that we already observe in the almost daily news items world-wide. This powerful, unstoppable activity, that even scientists are now beginning to refer to as "weather disasters" and "weather havoc", will soon completely engulf our rapidly deteriorating and degraded planet earth. For we have **not** been true stewards of our earthly home, and it is now time to pay! Recognition of Spiritual Truth *as it actually is* automatically provides the strongest, natural connection to the "Elemental Forces".

Therein lies the Divine promise that, *"The Meek Shall Inherit the Earth!"* But the meek in this case are not the weak, the earthly subservient, or the servile. They are the *humble* who by their *humility and modesty* have become *spiritually strong* through genuine and grateful acceptance of **Spiritual Truth** – thus **Divine Truth!**

In the ultimate choice of whether to believe or disbelieve – irrespective of whether we label that Truth Elemental, Spiritual, or even Divine – in the final analysis it is still a 50% pick. That individual choice, however, unequivocally equates to a personal and final **100% outcome.** We should all mark this well, *for there is no other way. Not for Indigenous Peoples, nor for the more technological Western Races!*

> **"And there will be signs in the sun, and moon, and stars; and upon the earth nations in despair, as when in terror of the roaring and raging sea; men expiring from fear, and apprehension of what is coming upon the world..."**
>
> (Luke 21:25-26)

Chapter 9

Where to Now?

9.1 Where to Now?

We ask, "Where to now?" The answer is simple. Despite the fact that the greater part of "Elemental knowledge" was lost by virtually all races, the imperative is still to stand correctly on that step. That is a necessary foundation for any further evolvement toward the genuinely spiritual. That should be **"The First Step"**. By teaching the *correct understanding* of **Elemental Lore** through the knowledge of the **Spiritual Laws**, the appropriate level of discernment can be attained whereby the recognition of what constitutes genuine "Elemental activity" can be *consciously* strengthened. Through a *voluntary* and *sufficiently strong*, conscious strengthening, human beings *can* benefit from the protective umbrella that the Elemental Forces of Nature offer.

Notwithstanding the fact that the main thrust of this book is about what must shortly come to pass for global humanity as a whole, this particular Chapter nevertheless still offers advice on how we should yet still proceed. For we cannot ultimately know who will stand or who will fall. What we certainly *can* observe is a clear separating-out process taking place more and more rapidly amongst the world's peoples. Such things include the separation of religion from state, ethnic group from ethnic group, GM science from GM opposition, the increasingly wealthy from the increasingly poor, first-world societies from third-world societies etc.

Interestingly, the process is not strictly confined to one particular country or major religion, as one might ordinarily presume. It is a much broader, all-encompassing separating process which automatically impacts on *every* area of human life. That is clearly as it should be for there is **not one aspect** of human endeavour that will **not** be subject to this relentless sifting and purifying process during the apocalyptic destruction that must take place. Moreover, it is the inherent perfection contained within The Spiritual Laws that drives to fruition this inviolable outworking of sifting and separating.

That is the accompanying Judgement! A Judgement, moreover, brought solely upon ourselves through our blind refusal to heed and live the inviolable Laws of Life. It was thus always our choice. As a global humanity, we very foolishly chose not to.

Our arrival to this most unfortunate point should have been a journey of a natural, spiritual progression of all races and peoples from the time of our first hesitant steps on the earth. A long and arduous journey from *small family groupings* to *tribes* and thence to *single, unified nations* to begin with. Those very early beginnings would have been embarked upon with conscious knowledge of the Elemental Forces of Nature. All that deep experiencing should have prepared the ground for the next step to evolving into *a people of planet earth*, and thence to the final and necessary spiritual understanding that we are all ordained to be "**Spiritual Citizens of Creation**".

Thus *complementing* each other as peoples and nations, mutually respecting ethnicity and geographical origins. For just as the different classes within any given race or society were meant to live and work *"side by side"* and not one above the other, so the same was ordained for the world's many and varied peoples. That acceptance, however, was always going to require far more inner greatness than we have currently demonstrated thus far. Nevertheless, that was the demand in terms of the spiritual responsibility that had been placed on each of us in the first instance, and no individual or race of people was exempt from that "directive"!

Since each step on our journey so far has outlined the how and why each individual connects to every other, the ladder thus produced offers the steps away from the "redundant old" into the knowledge of the "Spiritual new". This new ladder, like Jacob's, reaches up to The Source of **All LIFE**. With such a foundation, a wonderful spiritual potential for *some* can perhaps still yet be realised. However, The Spiritual Laws demand work to achieve it, *spiritual work* in the first instance. That means working on oneself so that the necessary change may be wrought whereby the transformation of each individual produces the possibility for that "potential". And therefore the best possible spiritual outcome.

To this end, however, there must develop the desire to embrace the only knowledge that can offer this realisation. Any other alternative will simply not produce that result. Perversely, **man on earth still clings to a deluded, collective idea that his many and varied religious and cultural traditions and beliefs somehow hold the key to spiritual harmony on earth.** *Why, we must ask, does he continue to persist with such a delusion?* For none have produced that ideal thus far, even though being given many, many opportunities to do so! That is simply because the truth of "Spiritual Law" is not at all understood. It is hardly even recognised. For those who now choose to, embracing the truth of Spiritual Law automatically means accepting the reality of Elemental Lore also – if the very many problems facing us are ever to be transformed into solutions.

Because the myriad problems of humankind detrimentally impact on a large part of the world's population, it is clear that a huge *"upwelling of longing"* for a better world now permeates the planet. However, any "longing", *other than* the "longing for the Truth", actually leads *downwards*. The first *connection*, therefore, must be to the Higher Realms, upward to The Source of All Life, that we may recognise our Origins and thus our actual **home** – thereby fulfilling the admonition to "Seek ye first..." That can only be achieved through the recognition and application of The Eternal Laws in one's life.

To *tie oneself* to earthly goals or pursuits – even if they be ennobled or altruistic – in the belief that that is the spiritually correct thing to do *first,* logically means that one places the most vitally important and naturally far higher Spiritual connection on a *lower level.* Whether this is believed or not is irrelevant, for that is the actual form created by the one who places the "lesser longing" first.

In turn, because that unhelpful *form* belongs to the one who possesses the "longing" for it, and which therefore surrounds that individual, any potential connection to the Higher Spheres is weakened because the wish for other things remains the strongest desire in the individual. Of course, we need earthly pursuits and activities for the natural and necessary purpose of everyday life and basic fulfilment. That is not the issue here, however. It is a question of what should ***first*** be spiritually considered, ***and why***!

As an indication of how we should undertake to live our lives and effect that necessary change, we should always strive to live the **First Commandment**. There is not one good thing in the whole of Creation that does not have, as its beginning, substance and end, any part that does not exist in the "Living Form" of this First and Greatest Commandment. Since **"The Word"** is **"The Living Law"** and **"The Law"**, in turn, is the **"The Living Word"**, The First Commandment logically encompasses all the good in Creation. Therefore, *if correctly understood*, The First Commandment holds the key to all higher knowledge and to the way upward, simply because all Power and higher knowledge naturally and inherently reside in it.

This fact needs to be recognised and understood by the purveyors of all religions and belief-systems today for it has *nothing to do with religion in any shape or form*. ***It is simply and precisely why we have our life and being in the first place.*** Irrespective of whomever brought the various Teachings to the different parts of the world and the peoples therein at the time, **The First and Greatest Commandment stands above all else for all time.** All of the great religions have their source contained within it, and the blessed "Bringers of those Truths" understood this living reality.

So regardless of what their followers today may decide for themselves about the particular religion they might choose to embrace, or whichever Prophet they may deem to be the greatest, every nuance of every thought-idea cannot divorce itself from the fact that: **The First Commandment Stands Supreme!** Therefore any deep and genuine spiritual volition in the veneration of this greatest of Commandments will, by virtue of the outworking of all the interconnected Spiritual Laws, naturally impact on any such believer to the greatest beneficial degree in all areas of that individual's life.

So must it be with a complete group of people too! In the first instance, however, the reciprocal help connected to any spiritually-correct attitude will *first be felt in the necessary process of the shedding of all errors*. This may mean a time of quite painful struggle as the individual fights to free himself from the binds of those past errors and any entrenched wrong attitudes still holding him tightly to spiritually-wrong concepts. The one struggling, however, must absolutely **know** that the fight to become free is a battle – *with, and within, himself*. It will invariably be his own incorrect ideas that he must conquer. Genuine recognition of the truth of The First Commandment – to absorb and live its meaning – can be the greatest help in achieving this vital goal.

Whilst there is the need to recognise one's *individual* spiritual purpose, the different races are here to spiritually fulfil their particular role too. Both, however, within the ordained purpose of the whole of humanity, automatically driven by humankind's petition for conscious life aeons ago under the aegis of The Creative Will. Humankind, however, seem not to collectively understand this particular reality. Fortunately, in some races there are individuals or groups who are aware and awake, and who do attempt to spiritually re-awaken the connections to this once-known Truth. Unfortunately, however, as must be restated in this work, this was generally lost through turning away from true Spiritual knowledge and replacing it with beliefs that, for the most part, are actually opposed to it.

Sadly, the few who do feel the calling to assist the re-awakening process of humankind are like "voices in the wilderness", with their entreaties mostly blown away in the wind of disbelief. Now, however, even with general intransigence towards such ideas so pervasive among crassly materialistic human beings, because of the increasingly compressed time-frame of opportunity left to humankind to re-awaken, the time for procrastinating is virtually over.

That notwithstanding, from time to time a spectacular event of stupendous spiritual significance may occur which offers an *immediate opportunity for complete races to embrace a very large measure of Spiritual Truth at the one time*, thus providing the strongest foundation for their Spiritual fulfilment in the intertwined threads of all humanity. And even if there are other races present who are aware of such an event but choose to remain unmoved, the fact remains that the race that so recognises has greatly advanced its Spiritual purpose. Such opportunities of immense grace were given to humanity through those Called Prophets and spiritually enlightened men who founded the great religions. By association, the peoples thus blessed at the time were called to embrace and live those Teachings too.

All races will develop certain strong and beneficial talents that will enable them to more effectively manage their particular societal and cultural way of life. The great Teachings given to the various peoples *at the particular times ordained for them* were so given because they had developed sufficient knowledge and maturity to be able to absorb and understand them. Any benefits accrued from that higher knowledge which might subsequently result in an ennobled elevation of their everyday life and culture might then be an example for other races not similarly blessed to aspire to.

For by applying The Spiritual Laws of *the given Spiritual teach-*

ing ordained for a particular people at a particular time to any societal problems that may be present then, optimum levels of social, material and spiritual benefits *within that particular society for that particular time* can develop thereto. Administering Spiritual Laws correctly provide both the example and mechanism whereby the same formula can be offered to *other peoples* who may need the same recognitions to evolve further. However, one can better help others when one has first undergone the associated recognition and learning experience first.

9.2 Recognition or Rejection?

Because the subject matter in this book describes the now and near future of humankind, the above heading relates, in the very first place, to the reality of The Spiritual Laws of Creation. If we objectively assess the present state of humankind, make simple comparisons to what we once accepted and believed in even just a few short years ago, it is eminently clear that the world and its crowded mass of humanity has not at all followed the *true way*. That fact therefore actually answers the question in the above heading. As a global humanity, we have not *genuinely* recognised the great truths in the *correct way* at all. We have, instead, **effectively rejected The Living essence of Spiritual Truth** given to us by the Prophets and messengers of The Almighty!

Is there, then, still time to change our ways before the full force and power of The Law of Reciprocal Action, particularly, destroys all that refuses to bend or bow? For those who might believe there *is* still time left to change, we offer a few pointers for consideration. Before any *collective* spiritual potential can be embarked upon to fulfilment, *individuals* within the collective must not only recognise the goal or potential, but also the need to accept the means or "rules" whereby the potential can be fulfilled *collectively*. For if there is not sufficient insight or recognition of the necessary mechanism required for the task, then the end result will clearly not be the realisation of that spiritual potential. What will emerge, instead, will invariably be divisiveness and mistrust, invariably driven by narrow, personal-wish parameters, ultimately set in place through ignorance. Is that not a good description of global societies today?

Therefore a beneficial, spiritual direction or task in the collective sense should only be embarked upon if the individuals within the "collective" fully recognise the validity of The Spiritual Laws in the first instance. Only from a foundation consistent with such Laws can any group then collectively and beneficially engage in a concerted task and bring it to harmonious fruition.

Apart from that key recognition, there would need to be the strongest discipline to fully understand that such a spiritually-expansive role could not afford to have any overtones of egotistical grand-standing attached to it in any shape or form. That, unfortunately, is a very ignoble yet also very human trait. Spiritual-cum-humanitarian goals need to be carried out with the utmost natural humility. For that is where true nobleness and wisdom reside. Elevated ideals provide the potential for any people to break free of previously wrong and unworkable concepts to thus fulfil the highest spiritual abilities and aspirations possible for them.

The story of Saul in the New Testament provides a perfect example of how a singular, particularly powerful trait, if wrongly directed, could so easily produce the opposite of what the owner might actually desire. This man, who later became the first Apostle, Paul, possessed an exceptionally keen intellect. Whilst believing he zealously protected and defended the letter of The Law of Moses, he failed to apply compassion to it in the "Spirit of The Law". As a member of the Jewish Religious Authority, his relentless persecution of the first believers in Jesus eventually led to the stoning to death of Stephen, who became the first Christian martyr.

Saul's implacable conviction about the correctness of his beliefs and the methods he employed to enforce them were shattered and transformed when he was struck blind during a journey to Damascus. The event we know as the "Conversion of Saul" resulted in a far more spiritually powerful ministry by this man of intensely strong convictions. The powerful trait was still there but now utilised for a vastly different purpose and towards a very different outcome than he could have ever foreseen under the domination of his previous volition. A volition driven by the soulless intellect and not that of his living spirit.[1]

Nonetheless, the "Conversion of Saul" perfectly illustrates how any individual – or even whole peoples – *can transform* certain

---

[1] Notwithstanding Paul's elevated position today in certain Christian Churches and among some theologians, we should nevertheless note quite marked differences between Paul's teachings and those of what was known as the true Church of Jerusalem under "James the Just", the earthly brother of Jesus, and also other religious figures. Those differing opinions have produced strong debate among Bible scholars and theologians for a long time, e.g. the "Faith Vs Works debate".

particularly strong but unhelpful traits and utilise that *transformed energy for a higher, more powerful cause in true Spiritual serving.* Therefore, in the context of this particular Chapter, "Where To Now", a similar "conversion" of all individuals and of all peoples is urgently required. For the very state of our earthly home clearly attests to that need.

Even though offering pointers on how to perhaps personally mitigate the effects of the approaching Apocalypse, have we, as a **collective**, global group of human beings, already reached the time of the "too late"? Our unequivocal answer is an immediate and resounding **"yes"**!

Just as Paul's world was shattered when he was struck blind – because he was actually spiritually blind to the Truth prior to his "conversion" anyway – so will global humanity shortly suffer similarly. Simply because we, too, stand blind to what The Spiritual Laws and the Elemental Forces are trying to show us.

Therefore we, also, will be shattered – either for our renewal, or for our demise.

Chapter 10

Humankind's Lost Potential

If, then, real conversion and transformation is urgently called for, that change will need to be global for it to work and bear permanent good – at least for those who may survive. A study of the religious history of humankind will reveal that certain teachings stand out more powerfully than others in the major global racial or ethnic groupings. These will also be connected with particular geographical areas of the earth in terms of the "origin of the teaching". As men spread further afield from their "home areas", their teachings went with them. Essentially, however, we identify certain groups of people with a particular religion, with each religion having a "founder" from that particular racial or ethnic group in a clearly defined part of the globe. Over time, those beliefs provided the religious and social framework for the life and activity of the people in the main region to which such teachings originally belonged.

The spread of those main religions to neighbouring regions might offer a challenge to the ruling authorities there, and such a challenge might produce severe opposition and reaction against that particular group or religion. More particularly, perhaps, if such a religion was ideologically opposed to The Laws or beliefs of the governing body of that particular region. Generally speaking, though, as long as the teachings remained simply religions and were contained within their boundaries of geographical origin, they could pose no perceived threat to any other group of people.

However, given the natural human trait to seek new lands, the possibility of religious differences clashing increased proportionately with the amount of movement away from originally clearly defined and stable, singular areas of religion. As exploration and trade increased, many diverse religions were transported to different countries, and eventually all over the globe. Either to be the mainstream belief wherever they touched, or to become isolated pockets. Some, of course, did not take root at all.

Those that did make a considerable impact in countries other than that of their origin include Hinduism, Buddhism, Judaism, Islam and Christianity, as well as some lesser known. Unfortunately, the end result of the different beliefs has been a "competition-mentality" between their proponents. Its particular excrescence is too often translated into the visual images of brutal reality that are shown almost nightly on television screens. That of bombs, bullets, suicide-terror and their associated destruction, and curiously, in complete opposition to the tenets of the original founders of those teachings. Yet nevertheless set in motion by narrow and rigid fundamentalism where interpretations are so far removed from the original, clear texts that it is difficult to comprehend the inner workings of the minds of such interpreters.

That reality, however, offers a key clue as to the reason for such intractable views of intolerance toward others. Whilst such intolerance may clearly reflect the religious bent of the particular groups involved in their sometimes desperate struggles, it also invariably reveals their personal and political agendas. Such incorrect interpretations surely cannot be solely religious. And they most certainly **do not** derive from anything **genuinely** Spiritual.

With virtually all of the primary religions emerging prior to the "Age of Reason", there was no such thing as hard science to really challenge the religious ideas of the main teachings before that time. Before the so-called "Age of Enlightenment", the churches or main religions were the dominant force ruling all thinking and providing all answers. Paradoxically, whilst the age of science and reason was an obvious and beneficial step forward and did provide enlightenment to all manner of questions, the pendulum effect actually swung too far with the result that the scientific community became almost too afraid to revisit the Spiritual question. Or totally dismissed it as a meaningless aspect of life altogether. Yet it should be realised that integration of The Spiritual and the material, as was originally ordained, is not, nor should it be, a denial of one or the other!

The unfortunate consequence of this one-sided aspect of science and "reason" is that too many people are afraid, even against their own "gut-feelings" and personal experiences, to admit that there is anything other than the material world. It might almost be described as a new dark age. A retrograde step backward to before the much-vaunted "Age of Enlightenment". The Dark Ages was not a time of any genuine understanding of The Spiritual Laws. It was more a dark phase of religious and superstitious fear which provided the perfect breeding ground for all manner of base activities carried out in the name of the God they purported to serve!

The key question here, if we are to make any sense of the religious conflicts that have plagued mankind for centuries and which are becoming increasingly bitter in more and more countries is: "Did the founders of the original teachings advocate the present outcome?" Given the strident proclamations of some of their followers, we may be excused for believing so. Certainly, particular events in history may appear to offer irrefutable evidence that this was the case and, moreover, with the "apparent" sanction of the founder.

Yet all the major teachings clearly promote the tenets of compassion, tolerance, kindness and all the other virtues associated with true spirituality. Therefore we can reduce that question to "either-or"! Either the founders of the main religions advocated violence and senseless killing as part of the religion, or they did not! The essential content of the teachings allows us to safely conclude that the founders taught and gave only what was spiritually beneficial for their people, with Spiritual Law incorporated into the necessary, everyday material affairs of the society concerned for that particular time. We should note that Laws of justice were an inherent part of the teachings too.

If, therefore, violent opposition to other religions was not part of any of the original teachings, and given that we must accept that the founders obviously knew what they were outlining and why – for they were the "bringers" of the "Teachings" after all – the only sure and logical conclusion for the increasing strife today is that the *followers* of those teachings have disastrously distorted the original meaning. A clear fact we have previously determined, but an imperative to restate in this particular Chapter. Such dangerously narrow interpretations are the actual cause of so much destructive chaos of greater frequency and intensity, which we incredulously observe in the present time.

The ultimate reason for the huge levels of violence committed by evil people upon their fellow men today is not necessarily because of political considerations, or ethnic or racial conflict, or wealth versus poverty or any other excuse. Those are simply the societal or religious parameters that offer the framework under which they carry out their evil works. The *true* answer will be found in Chapter 3, where we discussed The Spiritual Laws. The problem today – which has nevertheless been with us for a long time now – is precisely about the *kinds of human souls permitted entry onto the earth from darker regions in the beyond* to whom fellow humans on the earth should never have stretched a hand.

Quite simply, through the justly lawful process of procreation and incarnation under the aegis and outworking of "The Law of Attraction of Similar Species", particularly, *doors have long been opened to the lower regions of the beyond.* The huge numbers of the more evil-minded human souls forced to be there under The Law of Spiritual Gravity are offered a bridge by which they can return to the earth. The bridge of attraction, in the first instance, *are the mothers of the various global communities into which they incarnate.* We speak of responsibility as being one of the key factors for creating a better society, *but ignorantly refuse to accept, or even believe in, the very kind of ultimate responsibility that would prevent such dark humans from arriving on earth to wreak murderous havoc in their later years.*

The main contributing factor here are the terrible distortions of the original religious teachings. Such twisting of the clear original sets the parameters whereby whole societies today now live their respective delusions about the absolute rightness of their particular religion, solely. Within those societies the children, especially, are exposed from birth to every nuance of societal interpretation of the particular religion. Thus one more powerful reason why there must, and will, be an Apocalyptic end for global societies with associated destruction on an unimaginable scale.

Such a final end will bring to a juddering halt any further opportunity for the evil-minded to incarnate on earth. For, quite obviously, *many* of the parents of the world, and especially women, inculcated from birth with the particular "mind-set" of the various races, cultures and religions **into which they <u>chosen</u> to incarnate**, and who therefore **primarily** provide that "bridge of attraction", will not be here either.

The reader should seriously dwell awhile here and strive to understand **why Jesus, The Son of GOD** should so strongly warn His Disciples in the *way* that He did, when *they* asked Him to tell *them* what would come upon the earth and humankind at the closing of the age – these times now!

A specific warning goes out to the women who will be mothers at the time.

> "But **alas for those with child and those who nurse in those days**! Pray, however, that your flight may not come during the winter, nor upon a Rest-day; for there shall then be wide-spread affliction, such as has **not been known since the beginning of the world until now**, no, nor will ever be known again. And if those times **were not cut short, not a man would be saved**; but for the sake of the chosen ones, those times will be cut short."
>
> (Emphasis mine.)

The warning also clearly and strongly hints that the destructive period will come upon the world suddenly and unexpectedly, but last only for a relatively short time. Hence his further warning that the period of destruction would therefore need to be on a scale **"...not seen before, nor will be seen again"**, in order to *"complete the job"*. Thus the need to cut the times short ***or no one would be left***. Do we believe, or do we mock?

Whilst the measure for interpreting Bible Scripture – particularly the words of Jesus as recorded in the Gospels – is often a very broad one with many offering their personal ideas on meaning, far too few interpretations exist for just *this* one verse. Since we have stated what will surely produce outcries of horror from women's groups, and civil and human rights advocates as well, let us now analyse what that specific warning to the world's women – **from One in Whom inherently resided The Living Law** – might *actually mean* from the knowledge of that Higher Law.

The whole thrust of this work has sought to enlighten and point the way to that All-Truth from which we derive the knowledge so written herein – that knowledge so stated at the end of this work![1] Therefore, in terms of a soul incarnating via a mother anywhere in the world, to any culture, race or religion, the ***primary aspect*** of the event is that the ***new-born*** is *not* the ***personal property*** of either the mother, the associated family, or the particular group into which it is born. In the very first instance, it is its *own individual person*. It is a singularly *individual spirit* which has journeyed

---

[1] For a more comprehensive understanding of what we state here, the reader should revisit Chapter 3, in particular the subsection, "Families and Children".

through this part of Creation primarily for *its spiritual purpose*. The various families *into which it had previously and successively incarnated* under The Law of Rebirth unequivocally reveals that it is **not** the property of anyone else.

New-born babies are invariably welcomed, nurtured and protected by most mothers of the world, and strong bonding is a natural and desirable feature of the mother-baby relationship. That we certainly agree is absolutely the right thing. However, since we are assessing the *actual meaning of Christ's warning to mothers* at this end-time, then other, more powerful considerations must come into play here if there is to be any kind of logical meaning according to the outworking of "The Spiritual Laws of Life". Obviously, the deaths of babies and children strike us hardest. That is because we adult human beings invariably see only the physical happening, the death of a small, vulnerable and often helpless little person. What we do not see is that from that small body is released the *actual person* – that *spirit* who would have grown to adulthood – now *free* of the body, but at a tender age. Sometimes the loss is so great for the nurturing mother who *carried* and *delivered* the *soul* into the world that her emotional grief may be inconsolable. Therein, however, lies the *substantive meaning* of the *warning to women*.

Thus the gift of a child is exactly that – a gift. As the inviolable Spiritual Law unequivocally states: children may arrive *when least expected or planned for* and, as is painfully obvious to all, **can be taken at any time without the parents permission being sought**. Therefore, the loss of *any* child should be spiritually understood to have been *a gift* **for whatever time** *was ordained for it*. For the mother, particularly, but also for the wider family. Unfortunately, at the moment of greatest grief, sometimes – perhaps too often even – someone must be blamed for the loss. Regrettably, if that blame should be directed towards the One Who gave life to all anyway, including the grieving mother, then the outworking of The Law of Reciprocal Action must, and will, run its eventual course.

So, in the case of an Apocalyptic destruction of global societies and their human populations, and because the demographics of the earth's population show a large proportion now quite young, any destructive effects may impact on this group perhaps disproportionately. One can readily understand the prophecy where at that time, the "great wailing and gnashing of teeth", will occur. The Indian Ocean tsunami tragedy is a case in point. So much outpouring of aid globally, but so many children dead, and so much inconsolable grief and anguish.

The one element in what we are stating that *could* serve to *help* mothers, particularly, over the loss of children, is the lawful fact that babies and young children, *because they have not reached the age of spiritual responsibility,* are **not** so subject to the outworking of The Law of Reciprocal Action – **the iron Law of Karma**. Therefore, unlike adults who *are* so subject to that full outworking, and who thus are lawfully propelled to that plane which they had prepared for themselves, babies and children, precisely in accordance with the Perfect Justice of The Spiritual Laws, will find themselves in one of the more luminous planes, there to be cared for and undergo growth and development alongside other human beings residing there also.

The clear connotation here, in concert with the warning of Jesus to mothers, is **to seek out and strive to understand the knowledge of The Eternal Laws**. So that, should the situation arise where a mother must *let go* one she has brought into the world, she will do so *with* ***understanding gratitude*** to He Who granted her the ability *to **bear** the child in the first place,* and gratitude ***for the time*** *she was permitted to be with that soul*. As previously stated, for those who would curse in hate or anger, The Law must, and will, bring the reciprocal effect! Such inviolable outworking simply cannot be altered!

That is precisely why it is stated that, for the few who are left, the millennial phase will be one of peace. In the first instance, it will be forced upon those who survive through the discipline of *adjusting* to The Law as it actually is, as we should have done long ago. Secondly, those who *would have* refused to bend or bow will simply *not be here*. Only then, when the evil-minded *through their* **personal** *choices* have self-destructed, will there then be peace and harmony for the remnant left on earth. That is why the earth will be cleansed so comprehensively. Quite clearly, it simply cannot, and will not be permitted to, continue on its present course for much longer.

What, then, was the point of the different religions that sprang up at various times in history from diverse areas of the world out of different peoples, if only to degenerate much later into mad savagery? Or were they ***actually different*** religions insofar as the **Spiritual Principles** that ***anchored the original beliefs*** were concerned? If we believe so, given the parlous state of religious intolerance today, then we must further believe that the founders of the main teachings had exactly that in mind, intolerance and bigotry. However, since the main tenets of the "great religions" clearly reveal only spiritual virtues as their foundation, the sad conclusion that we must draw is that we, the various groups of human followers, are clearly too blind, intolerant and immature to even begin to emulate the high level of spirituality shown by all the great "Spiritual Teachers of Mankind". In short, we are a "spiritually-destitute" humankind.

In place of their sacred and ordained mission to bring the substance of spiritual enlightenment to all of humanity, we have, instead, generally defiled those very truths with base and opposite outcomes to that envisioned by those highly advanced men. As formerly noted, the proof of this particular pudding can be readily observed depressingly frequently on the television screens and in the newspapers each day.

We have designated the "founders" as "Teachers of Mankind"! Was there, then, a higher plan ordained for humankind under the leadership of those men through careful guidance from Above? If we carefully examine the times of their emergence and balance that against the particular level of spiritual maturity of the people concerned we can, indeed, readily observe a precise pattern whereby nations and peoples could be taken, step by careful step, to the final recognition of all Spiritual Truth. That is: **The "All-Truth" reserved for this present time!**

That this carefully guided process did not happen can be placed squarely upon our shoulders. The responsibility for that failure is ours alone. We, the followers, through our arrogant and foolish belief that we could *know it better than the ones who were carefully prepared and ordained to bring the respective teachings to humankind,* are the cause of all religious strife throughout history and today.

Because Truth is Eternal and unchangeable, it must forever remain the same. It is therefore recognisable to us in The Spiritual Laws of Creation, including The Laws of Nature which are equally unchangeable. By extension, the recognition of these inviolable Laws leads without deviation to God because His Will is revealed to us in The Spiritual Laws. Through them we learn what He Wills.

The "Teachers of Mankind", to whom all this was known, were "Forerunners for the Truth". We can identify some of them as Zoroaster in Iran, Lao-Tse in China, Buddha in India, Moses and the Prophets, and Mohammed in Arabia – as well as Krishna and others. Their appointed task was to mediate the knowledge of the truth *exactly adapted to their peoples and countries, and formed according to their spiritual maturity at the time*. These "Teachers for Mankind" thus brought that unchangeable Truth in a *form* understandable to their particular people. Mankind was therefore meant to be carefully guided step-by-step over thousands of years to the recognition of Truth. And thus eventually into *one single acknowledgement of Divine Truth* – the **"All-Truth"** that The Son of God Himself warned to watch for at the end of the Times. Today, in its Pristine and Inviolable Perfection, now here on earth is the very same **"All Truth"** about which Jesus stated would ultimately be recognised, *but only by the few.*

The symbols of some of the different teachings, which are still in use today, possess precise spiritual meanings. The lotus flower of Buddhism symbolises the necessary requirement to strive for purity. In its place in flowing water it exemplifies the need for a strong connection with the stream of life. The Star of David is the sacred symbol of Judaism where the two triangles symbolise the inseparable connection between the visible material and the invisible non-material worlds. The crescent moon of Islam is linked with the sacred obligation to honour women at all times. Naturally, however, *if women wish to be honoured they should ensure that in their everyday manner and activity they live and behave honourably.*

Thus, in the beginning, all the teachings were pure in their origin. Moreover, had mankind kept them pure and not distorted them over thousands of years for their own base ideas and selfish ends, those individual teachings would have long since converged and today be recognised as only *transit and concomitant teachings to The One Truth!* Unfortunately, the paths which the individual teachings illuminated came to an end in the temple or church of the particular religion. Through the non-understanding of the followers of those various religions, the teachings did not, and could not, then lead on to *the final Temple of Truth*.

In summary, what was ordained and set in place was a careful, step-by-step process whereby there would have been only one single, unified Truth permeating the very consciousness of all the world's peoples right across the whole earth today. *It was meant to be that simple*. Unfortunately, however, there has not been the necessary understanding or openness to permit any kind of meaningful examination of individual beliefs to ascertain whether or not they might accord with The Eternal Laws. There has, instead, been very much entrenched and rigid dogma; hence the reason why there is so much ongoing and tragic "reaping" now.

As we have previously stated, the Truth, which is anchored in The Spiritual Laws of Creation, should not just simply be acknowledged, but clearly understood also. That vital need, however, presupposes the requirement for a level of discipline serious enough to critically examine *oneself* with regard to those Laws in an objective assessment of *one's own attitude toward them*. Then finding the courage to change whatever needs to be "personally changed" in order to live them correctly. From correct "personal changes" should flow similarly correct collective, global changes.

Yet the relatively recent emergence of one aspect of totally wrong thinking – even if on the surface it might appear to be a spiritually-enlightened policy of great fairness for all – clearly shows that even within the world leadership, there is little understanding of what is desperately required to effect spiritually-correct global policies to bring about positive and beneficial change. It is a policy, moreover, that is not only promoted by the U.N. and the E.U., but actually now legislated for by these ostensibly august bodies. And also by most Governments of Western Nations.

In this particular instance, we are referring, once more, to what are euphemistically termed "rights". Thus we now have "rights" of every shade and hue. Individual rights, ethnic rights, children's rights, the rights of the aged, of students etc. *ad nauseam!* Whilst on the surface this may seem an admirable and enlightened, humanitarian advancement, **the vital point of Spiritual Law is completely missed**, both in meaning and ultimate outworking. The Law of Reciprocal Action, particularly, must be applied to this policy. All "human rights" policies should therefore be seriously re-addressed, but only by correct-thinking leaders who are able to recognise the inherent truth of what is stated here, i.e. *the huge and fundamental difference between* **rights** *and* **responsibilities**.

Let us, once again, reiterate the vast difference between **rights** and **responsibilities**, put right this socially devastating and dangerously insidious error, and set in *form* the "Spiritual Truth" of it. Firstly, we, the human beings of this material world, do not actually possess any "absolute rights" of any kind. Neither, therefore, do we have the "right" to make any "absolute demands". The fact is that by being *permitted* the gift of conscious life – "solely at our request" – we naturally abrogate any right to "any rights". Instead, *by that very petition for conscious life*, we are charged with *total spiritual responsibility* for all that we think and do.

Thus, in perhaps uncomfortable reality for most, we ultimately have only *duties and obligations*. Firstly to that Source which gave to us life, and then to our fellow human beings, and to the earth that provides our home and sustenance. "*Any so-called rights will only eventuate as a direct consequence of first fulfilling our duties, obligations, and responsibilities*." Therein lay the means whereby a better and more tolerant society *should* have developed. If the differences between rights and responsibilities are carefully considered, only with the latter is it possible for a more equitable global society to develop, for this ideal lives The Law that:

"It is more blessed to **give** than to receive."

(Acts 20:35, Fenton, Emphasis mine.)

Through ostensibly well-meaning but insidiously dangerous and misguided concepts of political and cultural correctness, our present societies are now too strongly imbued with the attitude of "non-responsibility". The permeation of this spiritually-weak and perverse mindset of "my rights" throughout global societies is virtually complete. That has set in place clearly wrong beliefs that have no understanding of the higher Spiritual Law – let alone any meaningful connection to it or any understanding of the Justice of it. For the whole unfortunate business is based more on *emotionally-generated selfishness* which promotes the "taking first" in the arrogant acceptance now that "rights" are absolute, rather than on clear objectivity which would promote the "giving" – the according of obligations and responsibilities – to each other first.

Moreover, this totally incorrect attitude and direction has produced an inordinate amount of polarisation between various groups within many societies. This, in turn, has unfortunately bred great mistrust and fear, and very much violence. Most certainly fear of doing the wrong thing, of breaking this new law if one stands up for rapidly fading values. Fear produced by the very tyranny that such selfish demands, initiated by certain kinds of unscrupulous individuals and groups. This new societal reality has also become a goldmine for lawyers who willingly defend "those who demand". They are the weak who will not accept responsibility for their own, in very many instances, perversely-foolish decisions and subsequent actions. And everyone must bow to this new, insidious evil. Few there are that possess the spiritual insight to recognise the clear truth that **responsibility *must* precede rights**.

However, in a refreshing change, the 2002 Conference on environmental issues and sustainable development held in Johannesburg produced one speech on exactly this issue from Kofi Annan, then Secretary General of the United Nations. In his address towards the end of the conference the key concept of his speech *was* responsibility. He called on world leaders to be responsible, to accept responsibility for their decisions and therefore for the state and fate of the planet.

However, not withstanding the obvious weight that the Secretary General might offer towards a new mind-set, it will inevitably be argued that it is all the same in the final analysis, that rights and responsibilities are both sides of the same coin. Yet the rapidly changing patterns of behaviour and increasing violence, even among children, have been recognised and acknowledged by many social commentators, politicians, social scientists and Police Forces. So something has changed radically and dramatically – and relatively recently – to produce such rapid change in societal behaviour.

The legal promoting of "rights first" in place of "responsibilities first" has had the effect of allowing both personal and social discipline to be subverted. For that is exactly the end-excrescence of such a policy. It is the final outcome of a distorted application of what was once a more noble reality, deriving from a formerly innate acceptance amongst people of a higher ideal: to be responsible to, and for, others.

Therefore, given the gift of such a beautiful planet for our earthly home, it is saddening to recognise that we did not possess sufficient inner grace and courage to put in place an ideal such as "responsibility" first, thereby nurturing complete spiritual harmony across the globe. As altruistic as it clearly is, it is not enough to give *only* when disasters occur, for the true form of correct giving is ultimately a spiritual one, which means that it should have developed to become a "spiritual constant" within the very psyche of humanity.

The irony of it all is that the knowledge required to bring about this clearly desirable state has been available to us for a long time. If the courage had been there also, then all that was required was to find the necessary amount of genuine humility from all political, religious and cultural leanings on earth to fulfil the "collective potential". And, by that, actually achieve true harmony in genuine tolerance towards everything pertaining to this planet and its many different peoples; something probably not achieved in any previous human era.

Can this be seen as just an unrealistic, unworkable and foolish "pipe-dream"? Yes, it virtually is *now*. Yet, under the outworking of the "Law of Attraction of Similar Species", it could equally have been realised long before now through the power of opposite thought processes and deeds – in simply believing it was possible. Therefore in my view, and precisely because of the particular parameters we have outlined, human intransigence and non-understanding of Spiritual Law will no doubt continue to hold in place the perverse policy of "my rights first".

Therefore, in accordance with the Truths the "Teachers of Mankind" brought to the earth's peoples, it naturally follows that all races and religions should have lived both their spiritual duty and responsibility. To thus ensure that their beliefs encompassed the true essence of what are actually The Spiritual Laws of Creation. For that was the foundation upon which all the great Teachings were unequivocally anchored in the first place.

Through such correct spiritual choices we *would have* gifted to ourselves a *present experiencing* of a true flowering of spiritual harmony under the outworking of those Eternal Laws. In its place, however, is an opposite and potentially terrifying kind of world which we can all plainly see. Despite that obvious reality, the sole foundation for any kind of better future **must yet still follow** –even if only symbolically now – the Teachings of the Forerunners of the Truth, those of Krishna, Zoroaster, Lao-Tse, Buddha, Moses and the Prophets, Mohammed and others, in their original, **undistorted form**. Then to the more complete knowledge brought by Jesus, The Son of God. And, finally, on to the ultimate and **All-Truth** now on earth at this time. To recognise the gift of that Divinely guided path for humankind and to strive to embrace it completely was our *primary purpose in life*.

The choice, as it must always be, however, is an individual, free-will one in the first instance, and obviously lies in the hands of all the diverse peoples of the earth! What will we ultimately choose, we may wonder? Or, perhaps more relevant given the huge problems facing humankind today and brought about solely by foolish choices we have made thus far, **what have we already chosen?** Thus how "hard" and "destructive" must the "final reaping" **now be** in **our collective, 100% outcome?**

Chapter 11

Jesus – His Birth, Death and Resurrection

> "Do not imagine that I have come to abolish the law and the prophets; *I have not come to abolish, but to complete them.*"
>
> (Matthew 5:17, Fenton, Emphases mine.)

Chapter 10 explained the path humankind should have taken if it was to bring about a spiritual and harmonious "paradise on earth". That path was to have been through the great Truths given to humankind through those Called for the purpose. Clearly, that did not happen. Even the powerful and sublime intervention of The Son of God Himself still did not induce humankind to genuinely recognise the actual nature of the Perfect Truth that He brought.

In its place, and founded upon it, we have, instead, just religions. Thousands of them. Within all, distortions of that Truth to varying degrees. Yet all claiming to have the correct interpretation. Therefore, within the very broad parameters that Bible *interpretation* currently encompasses, i.e. the broad, easy path, and since we state that we unequivocally accept the Perfection of The Laws of God for all things, we must, by virtue of such a sure conviction, also include a critical assessment of the two "seemingly" contentious issues in the life of Jesus that *this* particular Chapter addresses. Laws Perfect in their inception, conception and fulfilment. Perfect? Unequivocally yes. And perfect in accordance with the very Laws which Jesus came to fulfil. Any "imperfection" or contention, therefore, will only be "formed" and given life and credence by human opinions and beliefs.

In order to ensure that we do, indeed, possess a clear mandate for what we now state here, let us formulate for ourselves a series of questions to show exactly that. In any case, irrespective of whatever one may choose to believe about the birth, life and death of Jesus, the particular questions posed here must be faced honestly. If not faced thus, then he who still doubts *automatically denies* the inviolable Perfection of The Creator.

1. Question: Can the **"Perfection of God"** be called into question?

   Answer: No!

2. Question: Can a Perfect God produce imperfect Laws?

   Answer: No!

3. Question: If we accept the premise that The Almighty is, and must be, Perfect – by virtue of His Nature – must His Laws of Creation similarly also be Perfect?

   Answer: Yes!

4. Question: If His Laws are Eternal, Inviolable in their "Perfection", and therefore Unchangeable, can any event then take place *outside* the parameters of that stated *Inviolable* Perfection?

   Answer: No!

5. Question: Would such an absolute and illogical impossibility reveal believers of any such event to thus be gravely in error?

   Answer: Yes!

6. Question: Would any such beliefs therefore pit themselves *against* the very Laws that The Almighty Himself has ordained for all of Creation?

   Answer: Yes!

7. Question: If the answers to all our previous questions unequivocally deny any *imperfection* in The Almighty and His Laws, can we still continue to believe that He can change His Perfect Laws at will in order to bring about a particular event?

Answer: No!

8. Question: If we, nevertheless, still persist in incorrectly believing that He can somehow transgress His Own Perfect Laws to "do as He pleases", would that suggest earthly religious doctrine as being the *fostering agent* for such views in order to thereby suit a said dogma?

Answer: Yes!

9. Question: By virtue of such an inherently flawed concept, can we thus therewith illogically and very incorrectly impute to The Creator, Who must forever innately be "The Perfect God", the *earthly human failing* of imperfection?

Answer: Clearly and unequivocally – No!

Thus, only with such Perfection in The Godhead and The Eternal Laws that have issued from It, could there be a Creation for Jesus to enter in the first place. And, by extension, a Creation for human debate today exactly about the issues of a virgin birth, crucifixion, resurrection and ascension.

By virtue of the only correct answers that could possibly be given to our series of questions, we have gifted ourselves a clear and honest mandate to continue.

11.1 The "Virgin" Birth – The Immaculate Conception

Just as the *physical* death of Jesus at the end of His life marked His exit from earthly life, so did His birth as a baby herald His *physical* arrival onto the earth and into earthly existence. For in accordance with the inviolability of The Divine Laws He came to fulfil, The Son of God could not circumvent The Law that to be born of woman on earth, the seed must first be placed within the womb by a natural procreative event. Subsequent to that seeding, a lawful gestation period of nine months in that exalted womb. Here, however, a singularly contentious question arises with the inescapable truth that in the twin realities of *physical* birth and *physical* death, one must obviously always follow the other. Since the purpose of this book is to boldly question certain strongly entrenched sacrosanct beliefs in Christian theology, the key one now is the truth or otherwise of the so-called "virgin" birth of Christ.

Since we cannot deny the fact of Mary's earthly pregnancy or the earthly birth of Jesus as a baby, should we dare to believe that those *earthly* processes might just have been *preceded* by an *earthly* conception too? Or is that going too far? Or is it simply a matter of religious fear masquerading as the "ostensible" guardian of "religious righteousness" standing ready to condemn any attempt to delve logically into what was a completely natural event, i.e. Jesus issued, and was delivered, from Mary's womb. Though natural, it was, without doubt, a birth of stupendous import. One ordained and sanctified by Divinity Itself.

Now, because every human spirit incarnating on earth requires a physical vessel in which to dwell and through which to work, Jesus, too, needed a physical body to carry out His Work. However, all physical bodies entering the earth plane in baby form can only do so with an earthly conception to begin with. Does the idea of an earthly conception, then, denigrate the greatness or purity of the person of Jesus or His inherent Divinity? Of course not. Then what about the purity of Mary herself, or her exalted calling? Would we regard her as being somehow soiled or impure if a conception was necessary before Jesus could be born onto the earth? Once again, of course not.

If we did it would be very difficult, indeed, to reconcile the birth of The Son of God from out of a woman of the earth whose necessary purity for that purpose was somehow compromised through a natural act of copulation. So, would a possible father for the purposes of a necessary conception debase the body of Mary who would carry to full term the earthly vessel which Jesus, in His Divine reality, would inhabit and work through? Moreover, for such a high and purely ordained purpose, might not such a man be similarly chosen from Above? And would such a union for that highest possible purpose not therefore constitute an **"immaculate conception"** in the truest sense? If not, then why not? And if not, would it be because The Bible "appears" to state otherwise?

The birth of Jesus out of Mary must be very correctly regarded as being of the most sublime purity. That correct recognition, however, should not automatically condemn every other mother before or since as being unclean or impure simply because a normal conception was obviously naturally required before a subsequent birth could be realised. If the resultant viewpoint from *some* religious quarters is of that mind-set for all other births, then it is one that is clearly dangerously distorted. For any such misconstrued stance would foolishly denigrate the very ordination of The Almighty in the outworking of His *Perfect Laws* which state that if a man and woman wish to produce offspring in the ordained *natural manner*, they must firstly become "one flesh". Surely no argument there. Even animals have to do that.

In any case the state of marriage should not necessarily be regarded as the only institution under which a child should be conceived. If we fully understand that the inherent key attribute of The Almighty must be *Love in its Divine Purity*, then the very notion of a *completely pure yet natural process* of conception to birth, as in the case of Jesus, offers the same *potential* for purity for every other human mother too.

A clue to the reason for the wide Christian acceptance of "the" virgin birth as truth may lie in the interpretation by Matthew of the title, the "Holy Spirit". For he reports:

> "...the origin of Jesus the Messiah was thus: Mary, His mother, was promised in marriage to Joseph; but before their union, she was found to have conceived ***from*** the Holy Spirit. Her husband Joseph, however, was a righteous man; and not wishing to degrade her, felt inclined to divorce her privately. But while reflecting about it, he saw a messenger from the Lord appear to him during a vision, saying":
>
> "Joseph, son of David, you need not be afraid to accept your wife Mary; for what is conceived in her was ***produced by*** the Holy Spirit:..."

(Matthew 1:18-20, Fenton. Bold emphases mine.)

Because it was so stated by one of the Disciples, it is now forever regarded by two billion odd Christians as sacrosanct in its *"apparent"* meaning. That is, that the egg inside the womb of Mary, from which the **physical foetus** would grow to become the **physical vessel or body of Jesus,** was somehow literally impregnated by The Holy Spirit simply to produce **just the mortal or physical cloak**.

What needs to be fully understood here once more is that the *mortal cloak* of Jesus **was not Him solely and completely**. It was simply **the body** which **housed** His **Divine core**. As explained in Chapter 4, we should understand that the ordained path of *every* physical cloak is to return to the earth out of which it is ultimately constituted.

> "And man goes to the *earth that he was*,
> And his Soul will return to the GOD Who gave it!"

(Ecclesiastes 12:6-7, Fenton. Italics mine.)

It was **His Divine core** – which at the same time **was He personally** – which **returned to become One With the Father**. The forming of His physical body **did not require** the Power of The Holy Spirit to produce it. Physical bodies by the score are produced every day of the week on earth.

*However, the entry of Jesus The Divine into the depths of the material world from **out of The Divine Realm**, to subsequently incarnate **into a human body on earth**, clearly did need **The Holy Spirit to effect it.*** So, one of the keys to a final understanding of this whole question must take into account the true meaning of the Title, **Holy Spirit**, in strict concert with the way that Matthew refers to it for the conception of Jesus, but this will be examined a little later.

For the moment, however, two points must be considered if the question of the "virgin birth" of Jesus is to be finally answered satisfactorily-correctly. One is the inviolability and absolute Perfection of The Living Laws of The Almighty, of which we have already made a clear determination. The other is the *true* meaning of the word conceive, and of the word, virgin. The Christian Church's imposition of a narrow, intellectual constraint upon the meanings and usage of the words in this particular case fail to understand that *word meanings relating to activities and ordinations from The Living Light* **must inherently be fundamentally more comprehensive and far-reaching in scope than any earth-orientated faith-belief dogma or doctrine.**

In human thinking the word, conceive, is invariably and immediately associated with pregnancy:

1. "To become pregnant with".

2. "To begin or induce the conception of".

However, let us apply other "possible" meanings to the word:

1. "To form in the mind, to become possessed by".

2. "to *formulate; devise: conceive a plan*".

Now a far more comprehensive aspect suddenly emerges! If we revisit Matthew's narration about this matter, we have the phrase, "***conceived from*** the Holy Spirit"; and a second, "***produced by*** the Holy Spirit". Yes, it could be seen to be "playing with words".

But what actually **was** *conceived from* and *produced by* The Holy Spirit here? Our other two Bibles of reference use slightly different phrasing, but all must *ultimately* mean the same thing, simply because Jesus was *physically* born to Mary – under the aegis of the Grace of The Almighty and His Inviolable Laws!

Matthew's narration in The Jerusalem Bible states, "...she was found to be with child through the Holy Spirit." The angel of the Lord then says, "...because she has conceived what is in her by the Holy Spirit." From the King James Bible the same passages respectively read, "...she was found with child of the Holy Ghost." And from the angel, "...for that which is conceived in her is of the Holy Ghost."

With such "apparent" clarity, it is eminently clear why so many well-meaning Christians will not even begin to question the so-called "virgin-birth". Unquestioning loyalty to a high ideal carries a certain measure of greatness. Where it is a matter of the truth or otherwise of a particular event, "set in motion" by The Living Laws of God, however, then any *assumed* absolute sureness of the given belief must inherently conform to, and comply with, those very Laws. A position that does not do so – irrespective of how strong or self-sanctified the belief may be from a human or religious viewpoint – must therefore *set itself against* the **very sanctity** and **Inviolability** of the Perfection of The Laws of God. **And therefore against The Almighty Himself!**

If, however, we accept the idea of a *physical* resurrection and ascension for Jesus, then the current, accepted belief of a *virgin-birth according to Christian theology* **might** make sense. However such an idea would need to somehow accommodate the possibility of a Divine Being from the Realm of The Almighty Himself in some way becoming physical in a kind of **Divine totality** on **earth** through some kind of *physical conception from* that High Source. Using the more logical, more rational meaning of the word conceive here inherently encompasses a far greater reality that transcends and transforms narrow earthly parameters.

Thus to *form in the mind*, to *formulate*, to *devise*, to *conceive* – a **plan**, whereby Jesus, The Son of God would incarnate on earth in a human body. That was what was **conceived from**, and **produced by**, The Holy Spirit. An **Immaculate Conception**, **conceived** in **Plan and Ordination**, and thus **"produced by" The Holy Spirit**! We should recognise that the term, *Holy Spirit*, is a *Divine Title* relating to a **specific Being** of Divine Origin. It is not some kind of amorphous, super-endowed force or power which can perform any act arbitrarily, against the very Laws which are in Him and which He fulfils without flaw or deviation. For that is the meaning of Perfection – without flaw!

It does not refer to the simple, earthly matter of the impregnation of a human woman, of which there are millions at any given time.

Therefore, whilst the earthly foetus was formed according to natural processes, the entry of The Divine Core of Jesus into that earthly vessel was, indeed, carried out **in accordance with The Divine Will through Divine Activity!** In other words, **The Living, Divine Essence of Jesus, as a Part of God, was brought down to the earth from out of the Highest Heights to then enter the vessel prepared for Him.** Upon His death, He had then to return to His Origins and become "One with the Father", as He Himself stated. Simple to understand, but truly stupendous as a living happening!

In its earthly aspect, the historical record from that time shows that the "chosen earthly father" for the pregnancy which would house The Divine Core of Jesus was known to many, hence the inclusion into the historical narrative. That reality simply serves to show the complete naturalness of the whole event in the first place, as it must clearly be if it is to accord with the Perfection of The Living Law in all matters.

If we now analyse the meaning of the word, virgin, the reader may perhaps intuitively recognise a far greater reality of interpretation here too. Even though we believe our previous analyses have offered a clear enough picture of the forces and processes that brought Jesus onto the earth, we should still nevertheless go through this last little exercise in word meaning. Thus the accepted meaning in current doctrine regarding Mary interprets virginity or the virgin birth as stating that she had not ever had sexual relations with a man. We must therefore conclude that Mary became pregnant through a method that somehow precluded all the natural processes that The Living Laws of God unequivocally state to be inviolable. Such a notion, of course, would have to go against the very Laws that Jesus Himself stated He had come to fulfil.

If we therefore apply broader parameters to the *concept* of virginity in the context of the *complete organic process of childbirth*, then we may begin to discern a far deeper and more natural meaning for the word than is currently applied in the case of Mary. Moreover, if we extend the very essence of the word "virgin" and apply it to a *process* that had *not ever come into activity before*, then we can correctly state that *prior to* the particular activity the key aspects associated with it must have been *virginal*. Within Mary, therefore, the organs of procreation and reproduction were ***virginal*** for the birth of Christ. They had not come into activity in this manner prior to that exalted birth. So a ***virgin birth for Jesus*** was the reality. Thus did Jesus fulfil every last nuance of The Law by which, and for which, He came down to the earth!

One final word on this subject: if we are able to grasp the fact that The Holy Spirit, both in Term and Title, is exactly synonymous *with* The Holy Will, then we will see that the *true* Title here is **The Will of God!** Therefore the whole, almost incomprehensible nature of the entry of Jesus onto the earth was ***conceived from***, and ***produced by***, **He** Who was then, and Who is today, and Who forever will be – **The Will of God!** Exactly as will be clarified in the next Chapter, "The Two Sons Of God!"

Were this the reality that God is imperfect because He could change His Laws at will, we should ask ourselves why He did not place Jesus on earth as a fully grown man? Thereby obviating the need for His babyhood and childhood phase. For The Laws governing earthly procreation just as naturally also reflect the inviolability of their unchangeable Perfection. This fact offers the absolute premise once again that, even here, *in the conception of the earthly vessel for Jesus*, The Laws *could "not be overthrown"*, as He Himself clearly stated. An earthly procreation can only occur when the natural Laws governing this process are fulfilled, and this was so with Jesus. By that natural act of procreation to produce His earthly vessel, every other act carries a similar potential for a pure conception too. Unfortunately, however, many conceptions today occur as a result of drunkenness, drug use, or general social debasement, and cannot be considered even remotely pure.

Nonetheless, let us take this argument of the perfection vs. non-perfection of The Laws to the next obvious step and "allow" God to make us all sinless and perfect, but of course *without* free-will and *personal spiritual responsibility*. There would then have been *no need* for Jesus to come to the earth at all. He would have thus been spared His life of struggle against an intransigent people who, even though awaiting **His** Coming, nevertheless ***still murdered Him***. Thus the words of Jesus in declaring that He had come to "... fulfil the Law", must surely mean exactly that. Without exception, we are all born under The Law, we produce "our works" under The Law, and we die under The Law. Throughout our complete existence, for however long that may be, we receive the "returns of our works", good or bad, under The Law.

Let us once more in reinforcement reiterate the fact that since the physical body is *not* the animating "power" of the individual, the "inner animating power" that actually *was* Jesus, was therefore *not* that of His physical body of the earth. His "inner being" – which revealed Itself *through* the *powerful radiations emanating from* the physical shell He was obliged to take upon entering the material world – in strict accordance with The Eternal Laws He came to fulfil – was of Divine Origin. These facts naturally call into question the believed *physical* resurrection of Christ. Notwithstanding what we think are sufficient pointers in the above explanations for the spiritually-perceptive reader to deduce the Truth of what actually occurred there as well, we will offer further pointers to a greater clarification of not only the Resurrection, but the Ascension also, later on in the Chapter.

11.2 Mission of the "Three Wise Men"

An interesting theme emerges with the whole issue surrounding the birth of Jesus, His subsequent and difficult Mission, and His death as a supposed necessary propitiatory sacrifice to cleanse the world and humanity from sin. It is actually quite a strange and illogical view when looked at brutally objectively. Nevertheless, if that were the case, what role did the three Kings or "three wise men" play in the overall picture, in terms of what *they* achieved? More to the point, perhaps, what might have been their *actual* role and mission?

We have their names and, according to recent research, we have a clearer picture of who they were and where they came from – probably Parthians from the Persian Empire. We also know they travelled for a long time to finally arrive at His birth-place. Was this just guesswork? Highly improbable. For how could they know where to go by simply guessing? History informs us that they were wise in the art of astrology – the forerunner of astronomy – and thereby divined the event that was the birth of Jesus. After so much preparation and "guidance" – never mind the long camel or horse journey itself – why then just bring expensive gifts to the Child ... and simply ride away?

If, however, we are prepared to consider another and more spiritually-meaningful reason – in terms of so much preparation to locate one Child, albeit a very special One – then we should reflect on their status to begin with. In the first place they were kings in their own right and so possessed great wealth – the gifts were very expensive. Secondly, they were evidently highly regarded as wise men and rulers. And thirdly, *all three* were carefully and *collectively* guided to find Him.

A logical extrapolation of those three points would suggest they were especially "Called" for that task. By virtue of the fact that the Mission of Jesus was constantly opposed by the religious authorities of the day who saw in him a danger to *their* authority and who subsequently succeeded in their plot to kill Him, might it not be possible that the *primary purpose* of those three powerful men was to take Him into their care and protection? So that He might carry out His Work relatively unhindered?

Consider how different His mission would have been had they accomplished theirs'. In the first place, it would not have been so tragically cut short. Under their protection His sublime Commission would have unfolded to its utmost point, which was **not death by crucifixion**. Given that the Three Kings recognised Him as The One sent from Above, we would further expect that royal scribes would probably have been appointed to record His every Word, all His Teachings. How different the "Christian world", particularly, would be today. However, because the Three Monarchs failed to recognise their true calling and task, what we subsequently have as a result of that unfortunate error is a more fractured, divided and divisive "Christian religion" than *would otherwise have been the case* had Jesus received that protection. Such a powerful potential is, of course, a moot point now.

It may not ultimately have prevented a violent death at some point in His life, but a strong blanket of royal protection from the "Three Kings" *might* have induced certain religious authorities to tread more carefully with regard to His Person. At the very least, however, we might have had historical access to a far longer Ministry by Him with perhaps His Teachings eventually recorded by Him personally. Of course this is all supposition. Interestingly, though, the strange view that many of the religiously inclined subscribe to which states that if a particular thing takes place it does so because it must automatically be The Will of God, does not want to accept the reality that *human beings have free will in all matters*. Therefore the path of a prophet, or even of a Son of God, can either be helped or hindered by those who might cross that path.

The Three Kings, by not placing Jesus under their care and

protection – *even though clearly guided to find and acknowledge him as The Awaited One* – nonetheless ultimately hindered His Mission. Not purposely or from dark intent, but rather through not fully recognising their primary purpose. The fact that Herod – fearing the prophecy about the "King" that would be born in his time – in ordering the slaying of all male children up to the age of two years, surely reveals that the true purpose of the "Three Kings" in their ordained journey was to find and protect the Child. Their error unfortunately bequeathed to the future Christians and the world the ongoing contention about His life and Mission. And thus even the very issues we address here. The *apparent* final resting place of those men – or at least their skulls (revered and crowned in gold and precious stones) – is the Cathedral of Cologne. It was especially constructed to house those very relics.

11.3 Resurrection and Ascension

The resurrection and ascension of Jesus must surely rank as one of the most religiously contentious issues ever. In bygone days, any opposition to the once all-powerful church position that Jesus was resurrected physically, would certainly have bought an immediate death sentence and execution. Yet the very Scripture we use as the introduction to this particular Chapter clearly state that precise rules hold unequivocal sway for all, including The Son of God Himself Whose words we accept they are.

Physical resurrection and ascension! What should reasoned and objective logic tell us about it? For we are surely enjoined by The Living Law Itself to employ what all humans are gifted with, the attribute to think and weigh with intelligence, logic and reason. If forcibly locked into either an earthly empirical or a fundamentalist-religious framework, the issue under discussion here might appear to be satisfactorily validated for some. Or perhaps even for many.

In the final analysis, however, an event such as a *physical* resurrection and ascension, which radically departs from "natural" processes, cannot be held up as being logical in any way whatsoever. Correct clarification, therefore, must inherently rely on the truth and outworking of the very Laws which Jesus Himself stated could not be overthrown. And which He, according to the lawful parameters thus contained within them, also had to submit to at His death.

Because our mandate derives from the Perfection of The Spiritual Laws, we can also now seriously question and challenge the second crucial part of this particular Chapter, i.e. the strong, entrenched belief within some Christian circles that a physical resurrection and ascension is somehow valid. To this end a key question needs to be asked with regard to the "resurrection" of Jesus. Can a man, any man, in a flesh and blood *physical body*, weighing somewhere around 70 to 80 kg, perhaps, and very surely pronounced dead, realistically rise from that dead state to then live some kind of *physical* reality, **eternally?** Whilst we certainly accept that Jesus was able to call the dead to life, it was done so under the strictest aegis of The Living Law – as we explained before – of Which He Himself Was and Is a Living Part.

If we therefore employ the knowledge of Spiritual Law to apply the processes of death to the fate of Jesus, we are left with His irrefutable statement – that we must often reiterate – that He had *not* come "to overthrow the Law, but to fulfil it". Not just to fulfil it to a somehow convenient earthly-belief level, according to mere religious dictates, but to fulfil it completely. That being the case He, also, was absolutely subject *to the natural and therefore lawful processes of the normal exit of His personal inner animating core from the mortal cloak He was obliged to take upon being born of a woman on earth*.

If we now track to the end of Jesus' life, the extremely tenuous rationale offered to ostensibly support a "physical resurrection" has always been that He *had* to have risen in a physical body *simply because His own was not in the tomb* in which He was placed. *Such a one-dimensional view is almost superstitious in its supposed "reasoning".* Quite clearly, Jesus *had no choice but to vacate* His broken, bleeding and dying body on that cross of death when His time of exit thereupon arrived. Jesus died a physical death, as all who are born onto the earth must. Since the Perfection of The Laws of God simply do not allow for anything other than complete naturalness in all things, those Perfect Laws thus represent the *ultimate* level of pure naturalness. Therefore, whereas the inner core of human beings is that of spirit, corresponding to our point or Realm of origin, the inner core of Power *that actually was Jesus then* was, and is, Divine. Precisely corresponding to His Origins from out of The Godhead.

The explanations on the inviolability and Perfection of The Laws of Creation in a previous Chapter about the "calling of the dead to life" by Jesus should offer sufficient elucidation for a clearer understanding of the issue under discussion here too. The reader can therefore use those same explanations as the foundation for understanding the standpoint upon which we base the what and why of this particular statement. For that Chapter provides sufficient information to similarly understand the portent of this particular segment too.

We know that after His death Jesus was taken down from the cross and buried in a tomb owned by Joseph of Arimathea. What do we read post-crucifixion, however? That even those closest to Him *did not recognise Him when He appeared before them.* Mary *did not recognise Him to begin with.* Mary Magdalene, too, *did not recognise Him immediately.* Even two of His disciples on their way to Emmaus *did not recognise Him for hours* even though *He walked and spoke with them.* How could it be possible that after a short interval of *just days*, those closest to Him *did not recognise Him immediately*? What does this clearly infer? **It unequivocally infers that had He been in His original physical body, recognition would have been immediate.** Therefore, and in concert with the lawful outworking of the earthly death process, it is obvious that it must have been **another and different body they saw**.[1]

Spiritual Law informs us that a less dense envelope is able to penetrate denser objects. His sudden appearances inside locked rooms in which the disciples regularly gathered thus testifies to the fact that He could *not* have been in a *physical body*. It is not lawfully possible to "rarefy" a physical body. Physical bodies cannot penetrate material doors or walls. Not His physical body, therefore, but one which we all possess too. A non-physical Ethereal body of the consistency of that Realm through which we journeyed down to incarnate on earth, and through which we must journey back up to return home – unless, through our own aspiritual deeds, we remain trapped "in the world". It is thus a body that can exist on the earth – hence the millions of earth-bound.

This "other-body" thus answers the question of *how* Thomas could *feel* the wounds of Jesus. It is simply a matter of the same kind of "body" within Thomas, i.e. of the same consistency, bearing witness to the world of this lawful event. Thomas was *invited* to

---

[1] The "substitution-premise" that some writers and theologians hold dear seemingly answers this particular question for them. For them, the answer to most of the issues surrounding the Crucifixion and resurrection seem only to make sense if there was a substitute for Jesus on the cross. Some researchers point to Simon of Cyrenaica as that substitute. Jesus was even supposed to have watched His own "death walk" hidden from sight. Or that He survived the actual crucifixion, then later on left the Holy Land with His "wife" (or, according to other accounts, with His mother) to live elsewhere on the planet.

"touch" and "feel" purely because he was "Thomas the doubter".[2]

An obvious question begs an answer here. What really did happen to the physical body of Jesus? We know that guards were posted outside the tomb to prevent the theft of it. Therefore, the story goes, it could not possibly have been stolen. For thieves would have been seen. So the only possibility left is that we all meekly submit to the belief that Jesus did rise from the dead in His physical body. And that apparently seems to satisfy the majority of Christians in their various churches.

Of course, the other logical possibility must not ever be entertained **lest the whole carefully nurtured structure totters and comes crashing down**. For the reality is that soldiers on sentry duty *do fall asleep*. Or they can be bribed to turn a blind eye. Or perhaps the sentries, in strict concert with The Law under The Will of The Almighty, were rendered unconscious for a time. To thereby graciously permit a few especially chosen ones to quietly remove the body so that it might be placed where it would **never ever fall into unbelieving hands**.

For if that particular scenario is regarded as an impossibility, as blasphemy or heresy even, then we have a **major and insurmountable problem** with the fact that Jesus had to subsequently **return** to The Father. To thus levitate and ascend in that same supposedly **physical body** to a realm that is obviously **non-physical**. And, moreover, to a level far beyond the incomprehensible reaches of the farthest universes even. Such an idea simply beggars description, for it is implausible in the extreme. In fact, **"it is patently impossible!"**

As He stated to his disciples, He would one day leave the earth and become, again, One with The Father. In the light of His sure statement, the question that must be put to the issue of the ascension is: "What is the natural reality of God?" Of course, that cannot ever be answered by human beings. We cannot possibly know anything *above* our particular origins. By asking that question, however, *we are not seeking an actual answer to it*. We are simply yet graphically illustrating the fact that a huge and fundamental problem exists with any belief that Jesus ascended to become One with The Father **in His physical body**.

Do we therefore also believe that The Almighty sits down to a meal? Or that He needs to relieve both bowel and bladder, as we

---

[2]Interestingly, Thomas's fulfilment of his amazing mission to India after that must surely be seen to be one of *transformed conviction* from a previously doubting nature.

must in the physical world? Of course not. It is an utterly ludicrous thought, and one certainly leading towards the blasphemous. **However, that kind of physical reality must be accepted as inescapable for anyone who persists in the patently absurd notion that Jesus ascended in His physical body.** He said often enough, "My Kingdom is *not* of this world" and "I come into the world and I leave the world." What is so difficult to understand here? His Kingdom was not of the physical world that we presently occupy. It was of a non-material reality – above the heavens even!

If such a simple reality cannot yet be grasped and one still persists in the belief of a physical-body ascent, then the next question is: "At what point or level in the ascent did the necessary transition from a physical form to a non-physical one take place, *in order for The Son of God to become One with God The Father?"* And: "did Jesus take any food with Him for the return journey?" Staunch Christians may regard such questions as a mockery or a defilement of an ostensibly sacred or holy belief. If so, then it is clearly a closed-spirit viewpoint. For the questions posed are extremely valid and must be honestly answered if any actively-promoted, conceptual belief of a physical-body resurrection **and** ascension is to hold any credibility whatsoever. For one must follow the other in terms of any credible physical-mode answer.

This particular distortion may possibly derive, wholly or in part, from an incorrect interpretation about the fate of the dead at the end-time. This, **once again,** ostensibly states, that then: "All the dead shall be awakened." This sentence as it stands conjures up horror-filled images of all the dead emerging from their graves and being somehow fleshed out to physical specifications conforming to their original bodily appearance. And presumably to the same level of knowledge and belief they possessed when they died. How they could ever possibly understand the why of the very different world they will supposedly enter after emerging from their earthly graves, no one seems to have answered. And how can they? Because that is not the meaning of the prophecy in the first place anyway. **It is not even the correct wording.**

It is not that "all the [earthly] dead" shall be awakened but that:

"All that is dead shall be awakened!"

The difference in wording here is huge and fundamental and immediately conjures up a more *correct* picture. ***All that is*** spiritually dead *shall be forced to awaken*. This does not at all refer to, or mean, those who have long since died. It means literally *everything* that has not adjusted itself to the correctness of The Spiritual Laws. Everything that has not voluntarily adjusted itself to The Law will be *forcibly awakened* to thereby reveal its true nature. Social structures, concepts, attitudes, religions, families, nations etc., will be affected according to the level of compliance or non-compliance of The Law previously undertaken prior to this crucial point. At this present time we can observe this "awakening and revelatory process" in such diverse activities as are practised within the corporate world and in the churches. And, by extension, in the previously hidden activities of leaders and senior persons within them.

Nothing will escape this now necessary and unfortunately long-ordained "spiritual-cleansing" process. Not one thing, organisation or activity, is, or will be, exempt. The perceptive reader should readily now understand the great gulf between a belief that incorrectly says "all *the* dead", and that which correctly states, "all *that is* dead"!

Since we have presented a logical explanation of events pertaining to the birth and death of Jesus, it is interesting to note the many attempts to deny His Divinity; that He was just an ordinary man. Should we once more tiresomely reiterate the absolute fact that all born onto the earth must use the form ordained for that purpose, the physical form of either man or woman? There, we did! **That is the sole purpose the body serves.** It is simply the vessel, the cloak, the overcoat that the life-force that is each and every one of us needs as an habitation for physical life – down here.

So simple a concept, and so perfect. Yet it provides such fertile ground for scenarios that are so ridiculously impossible that one wonders how the authors could have possibly thought them up. The truly amazing thing about "other-body" realities is that the time eventually arrives for each one of us to be forcibly thrust into exactly that separating-out process we call earthly death. So was it for Jesus too.

Then, yes then, through the experience dawns the realisation for most that they had wasted their lives on things that really did not matter, but would now cause them major problems in their non-earthly body. In any case, the academic world's seeming preoccupation with Jesus and his earthly physicality *completely misses the point* of the whole quite stupendous event – His entry onto the earth as a very necessary act of "Truth-bringing". "Heed The Word, not the Bringer" should be the primary consideration. In the very first instance it is *what* He brought, His Teaching, the Truth inherent in His Divine Core, that should always have been *the first* and *principal thing* to be understood. For it was, and is still, *decisive* for all on earth.

What we have today, however, is a virtual cult based on the "personality of Jesus". Evangelical Christians promote the rather strange idea of the necessity for a "personal relationship" with a Power that human beings could not even approach. After His earthly death He warned Mary Magdalene not to touch Him. Having exited His physical body the Power that was always inherent in Him from birth **was no longer constrained by the heavier physical body.** His Power therefore radiated much more strongly from Him. Even as a "man among men", the Power was still sufficient to effect healing from solely the radiations emanating from just His physical "covering".

Unfortunately for the Christian Church mainly, but for all of humanity ultimately, the true meaning and purpose of His coming from the Highest point in the **non-material**, Eternal part of Creation all the way down to the lowest point of the **non-eternal**, material earth has not ever been understood correctly. And to teach that a **physical body** can somehow rise to the **Highest part of the non-material, Eternal Divine Realm** is surely the ultimate blasphemy. Blasphemy: it is the word that Christians are often wont to use against those whom they believe denigrate their ostensibly sacrosanct interpretations of Bible Scripture.

I am sure we all accept that The Laws of God are sacrosanct. We would probably further accept that their outworking must be so too. Therefore, in concert with Jesus' serious admonition that He had come to "fulfil The Law" – the reciprocal outworking of which is clearly explained in this Work – what fate must await the Christian Church and its followers for continuing to promote a belief that is not only completely illogical, but absolutely wrong? The Law *will bring without fail* the commensurate reciprocal consequences to all who would dare to denigrate the **Perfection of The Law!**

So here, in concert with that Perfect Law, we both ask and answer, the key question: "What really did happen to the body of Jesus?" Well, should humankind ever be **permitted to find** the **actual location** of His earthly cloak, the many who have written about Jesus and The Holy Grail and have propounded final resting places in locations as diverse as India, Pakistan and even the South of France, and certainly all Christians who believe He ascended to His ***non-material*** *Eternal Home* in some kind of transfigured ***earthly body***, will then know that they were ***all very, very wrong!*** The approaching and inevitable appearance in the sky of the **Sign** of The Son of Man will produce the same recognition; and very much more besides.

So what, exactly, will be revealed to the world should humankind ever be *permitted* the discovery of the exalted earthly body of Jesus, and how will we know that it truly is He? What we herewith present in this Chapter are the keys that will provide the clearest revelation that, ***prior to any such discovery***, it ***will be "proof positive"*** that ***it is the earthly cloak of Jesus.***

His body rests in a sealed cavern under Jerusalem. At the entrance to the cave three crosses are engraved over the right hand arch. The body inside will show evidence of crucifixion, ***but the bones in the legs*** **are** <u>**not**</u> **broken.** In the row of upper teeth in the skull, ***an eye-tooth is missing.*** And on the gravestone which covers His body is engraved a specific sign or mark – **His Sign!**

The missing eye-tooth is obviously singularly significant. But why have we emphasised the fact that the legs on this special body are not broken?

The particular agony associated with crucifixion centres around the fact that being suspended from nailed palms or wrists means; that to prevent compression of the lungs and subsequent asphyxiation, the naturally-sagging body must be held erect. However, as one can readily note when gymnasts perform the "crucifix position" on "the Rings", only the strongest and fittest men in very good health and in their prime can hold such a position for any length of time.

Therefore, the very position of the arms affixed in that "crucifix position" in an ***actual crucifixion*** means that it is virtually impossible for crucified and probably tortured men to do so. What they could and did use, however, is the leverage point that the *nailed feet* offer. It is the only means whereby the crucified one can relieve the crushing effect of a sagging body – in effect, to push up, to stand, on that driven-through spike.

The burial Laws at the time required that bodies of Jews crucified on the Sabbath be taken down and buried before sunset, so the breaking of the legs ensured a quicker end on that **"Cross of Torture"**.

The Book of John, Chapter 19, Verses 31-37, provides a clear account of that part of the process.

> "The Judeans, therefore, since it was preparation-day – for that day was the Great Day of the Week of Rest – so that the bodies might not remain on the cross on the Sabbath, requested Pilate that they might be removed after their legs were broken. The soldiers, therefore, came and broke the legs of the first, as well as of the other one crucified with him; but when they came to Jesus, and seeing that He was already dead, **they did not break His legs.** One of the soldiers, however, with a spear pierced His side; when blood and water issued from it.
>
> "And the eye-witness gives this evidence, and his evidence is truthful; and he himself knows that he speaks true, so that you may believe. For these events happened, in order that the Scripture might be verified: A BONE OF HIM SHALL NOT BE BROKEN."
>
> (Emphases mine.)

But what of that group of human beings who first hailed him as the Messiah with Hosannas? And then later shouted: "Crucify him!" They, the Jewish people, called to receive The Son of God in their midst. Where do they fit in the outworking of Spiritual Law which ordains that all transgressions against The Divine Will must be expiated to their final point of resolution? The historical record clearly shows that the Jewish authorities continually sought the death of Jesus to the degree of fabricating lies about Him. The legal term today is "entrapment". The failure of the Three Kings to recognise that their mission was to protect Him set in motion the train of events that would finally bring about His murder.

As previously noted, Herod ascertained from the Magi the exact time the star made its appearance and instructed them to learn all they could about the child and report back to him. However, having been instructed by a dream not to return to Herod, they returned to their own lands by another road. Furious at being tricked and fearing the prophecy that a King had been born there, Herod ordered the killing of all new-born male children at the time of Jesus' birth up to the age of two years.

Upon the instructions of a "messenger of the Lord", Joseph and Mary fled to Egypt to escape the reach of Herod. Upon Herod's death years later, Joseph was further instructed "...to go into the land of Israel." His long absence in Egypt was surely instrumental in helping to expunge the memory of that exalted night of the Divine birth to the world from the consciousness of those who were meant to bear witness. As previously explained, the Three Kings, *called* to be the primary witnesses for all time, would have changed the course of history then and forever had they fulfilled their primary task of protecting the child.

The non-recognition of Jesus as the prophesied Messiah by the Jews – *who waited for Him then and are still waiting for a Messiah today* – hinged on the fact that the prophecy about Him correctly named Bethlehem as the town in which the Messiah was to be born. However, Jesus became known as "the Nazarene", for that is where Joseph lived – in Nazareth. Could the Jewish people state such an error to be a simple and legitimate mistake, and therefore not expect any repercussions from His murder? Ordinarily, that might possibly possess some saving grace – just a mistake.

The Book of John, however, in recording the arrest of Jesus, reveals what was surely the murderous attitude of many within the Sanhedrin toward "the troublemaker".

> "The troops, then, headed by their colonel, and the Judean officers, arrested Jesus, and having bound Him, they conducted Him in the first instance to Annas; because he was the father-in-law of Caiaphas, who was high priest for that one year. Now it was Caiaphas who advised the Judeans that *"It is profitable for one man to die on behalf of the people."*
>
> (John 18:13-14 Fenton. Emphasis ours.)

In this case, therefore, the stakes are crucially higher. What might be now dismissed as a "simple mistake" was a hypocritical calculation to get rid of Jesus. That action resulted *in the torture and murder of an innocent man* in the first instance. That in itself is wrong. Secondly and crucially, that particular *murder* was against The One Who, gifted in Love and Grace from The Creator, *came to help humankind out of the mess it had mired itself in.* But Who then, however, was *rejected* by the very people who were called from the time of Moses to prepare for His Coming. Is that not incredibly arrogant and foolish?

If there was, or is yet still to be, severe reciprocity from that repulsive act of blind hatred against The Light Itself, what form might it take? *Or might it just perhaps have already occurred?* We should note here the discourse of Pilate to the baying crowd, and their replies to him.

> "What then," asked Pilate, "shall I do with Jesus, Whom they call the Messiah?" "Let Him be crucified!" was their unanimous reply.
>
> "Why?" he asked; "what crime has He committed?" In reply, they yelled out more savagely than before, "Let Him be crucified!"
>
> Pilate ...took water and washed his hands in the presence of the mob, saying, "See, I am innocent of the blood of this just Man; look to it yourselves!"
>
> Then in reply to him, the whole mass shouted out, **"Let His blood be upon us and upon our children!"**
>
> (Matthew 27: 22-25. Fenton. Emphases ours.)

And so Pilate handed Jesus over to be crucified.

In that last terrible and hate-filled imprecation, the inviolable outworking of the very Laws given to that race by Moses began their silent and long-reaching work. It was that race that was tasked to lead the way back to the correct living of The Spiritual Laws – through their elucidation of them by Jesus – and thus under His initial guidance. They failed in their task, for they did not want it. Because of that murder the ancient prophecy that foresaw His death was fulfilled. Not, however, because it was the Will of God that it be fulfilled, but because it could be seen that ***the Jewish people would go against the very laws and prophecies they were meant to obey.*** Thus the failure was prophesied long before Jesus came onto the earth.

"The Spiritual Laws of Creation" in Chapter 3 offer clear explanations of all The Laws and their outworking. A previous Chapter: The Spiritual Laws of Creation – *The Crucial Knowledge for Humankind*, provide the keys for greater understanding of reciprocity for the murder of Jesus which we examine at this point in our story. Especially note "The Law of Reciprocal Action".

What can we therefore deduce from the events of 2.000 years ago for those who shouted, "Crucify Him!"

The Book of Luke records the Admonition of Jesus to "The Daughters of Jerusalem" as he was led to Golgotha.

> And a large crowd of the people followed Him, including women, who were beating their breasts, and lamenting Him. Jesus, However, turning towards them, said, "Daughters of Jerusalem, weep not for me; but weep for yourselves and for your children. For now the days are coming, during which they shall say ,'Happy are the barren, happy the childless, and happy those who have never nursed.'[3] Then they will begin to SAY TO THE MOUNTAINS, 'FALL UPON US'; AND TO THE HILLS, 'BURY US'; because if they do this with the green tree, what must happen to the rotten one?"
>
> (Luke 23: 26-31. Fenton.)

The Spiritual Laws of Creation unequivocally offer clear explanations of all The Laws and their outworking. Chapter 3: "The Spiritual Laws of Creation – *The Necessary Knowledge*" will provide greater understanding of our analysis about reciprocity for the murder of Jesus. See, especially: **The Law of Reciprocal Action**.

Bible prophecy and Scripture speak of the fact that "...generations will not pass until all has been fulfilled." And we further know that our works or deeds follow us into the beyond after earthly death and, under the aegis of The Law of Rebirth, may wait many centuries before exactly the right time and circumstances for expiation converge. Therefore, the notion that "crimes of enormity" committed against certain races throughout history are always committed against innocent people does not at all correspond with the perfect and inviolable outworking of The Laws of Creation.

The concept or claim of innocence for dark deeds committed can be used for at least two reasons:

1. Ignorance and/or disbelief of any inviolable and thus constraining Laws to begin with.

---

[3] His warning to the women of the time, even though they lamented Him, could be interpreted as a warning about their impending wholesale slaughter under Titus. However, what we should read here is a larger warning from The Son of God that The Law of Reciprocal Action would reach down through the centuries to all the women and mothers of the world who would reject The Living Word that we must all, in the final and absolute analysis, embrace in gratitude and therefore live by. For we can clearly see, if we wish to, the ramifications of His severe warning to women at the end-time. "Woe to the woman who is with child and who give suck [at the breast...]" See full explanation in sub-heading, "Why there is so much Violence and Evil on Earth", Chapter 3 – **The Spiritual Laws** *The Necessary Knowledge.*

2. The recognition that inviolable Laws may or do exist and that the consequences of dark actions are inevitable, but that any potential for a "possible guilt aspect" may hold at bay, even subconsciously, any acknowledgement and thus acceptance of the long-committed deed.

The obvious ramifications that such *inviolable* Laws presuppose for the individual or group in the necessary expiation of particularly heinous deeds such as the murder of One from out of The Godhead means that The Law will, without fail, one day "visit the appropriate reaping" on such a group.

"Ignorance is bliss!" In terms of expiating past transgressions, ignorance of The Laws does not stop their sure outworking. Ignorance or disbelief, therefore, **cannot stay** the reciprocal return. The same applies to the second point. Knowledge of, but refusal to accept, the lawful reciprocity of dark deeds may add **more suffering** to the **inevitable reaping** for the **deed perpetrated** than otherwise might have been the case. The darker and more savage the act, the stronger will be the "lawful return". In the case of serious transgressions by whole peoples, it naturally follows that the group as a whole may, at a future time, *"yet reap together"*.

However, due to the lawful outworking The Laws of Rebirth..., Attraction... and Reciprocal Action..., it does not necessarily follow that the group present at a particular event in history that must require expiation – such as the murder of Jesus – will all incarnate together at a given future point for that expiation to occur. Yet they may. In any case, unless the individuals present at the event who did contribute in even the smallest way to the deed *had not come to recognition of their part in it since that time*, then the long reach of the Justice of The Law would require them to be back on the earth around the time it was ordained that *all karmaic cycles must close.*

In the case of the murder of Jesus, it is not only those who shouted: "Crucify Him", who will "reap the appropriate return", but all human beings who have rejected Him and The Living Truth He brought to humankind. In the case of those directly and indirectly involved in the actual, incomprehensible event – those who took part in his murder and those who were willing servants of the plotters and planners – all would need to be on earth when **The Son of Man** proclaimed His presence. And therewith to recognise Him through the All-Truth He would bring which would clarify the Truth surrounding the life and true Mission of Jesus – **The Son of**

God. Recognition of that crucial Truth by the perpetrators and supporters could bring expiation for them.

The Christian reader, particularly, should very carefully read and strive to spiritually absorb the contents of the next Chapter: "The Two Sons of God." In truth, however, the crucial knowledge about "The Two Sons of God" is for every human being on earth and in the beyond. In short, for all!

Since all karmaic cycles have been closing rapidly for some time now but more exponentially in the present – hence the "increasing reaping" everywhere on earth today – we should yet note how history records countless events where various races perpetrated horrific acts against others. In those kinds of unfortunate episodes in human history, we may thereby better understand the inviolable aspects of The Law.

World War II saw perhaps the greatest concentration of dark deeds perpetrated against many races in many parts of the globe. The world also witnessed the curious phenomenon of mass non-responsibility from the citizens of the main perpetrating groups. They gave as their excuse or reason; they were just "following orders", or had no choice – particularly where they were led by a megalomanic/charismatic leader. In any Nation or race, however, the inviolable outworking of The Law does not absolve any person – who simply "follows a leader into mad savagery" – of personal responsibility.

The "one-life-only" school of thought, which does not take into account the lawful outworking of precise and inviolable Laws, will naturally describe those on the receiving end of "crimes of enormity" as innocent victims. The reality is, however, that under those very Laws, what has taken place is simple reciprocity under the aegis of The Laws of Rebirth, Attraction... and Reciprocal Action – "What we sow, that shall we reap" – in the first instance. So races and peoples who continually lament that they are the victims need to recognise, understand and accept that The Laws do not deliver injustice. That is impossible. At this rapidly-closing time of humankind's odyssey, people and races receive or "reap", **simply because they once "sowed the seed"!**

That does not at all mean, however, that the "perpetrators of the deed" possess the "right" to so deliver retribution. That belongs to the Justice of The Light. "Vengeance is mine, I will repay", states The Law. Therefore, the only sure way to not suffer severe and traumatic "reaping" is to recognise, understand, and live the Truth of The Law. That process offers the sure mechanism whereby "hard reaping" can be nullified or lessened, and ultimately expiated completely.

Readers, observe the increasing suffering of the earth's peoples; of those around you, and *understand* the processes that have brought it about! The "reaping from the sowing" will surely and inexorably increase exponentially anyway. So learn The Rules and at least lessen some aspects of "future reaping"!

11.4 The Revelation and The Holy Grail

As we are presently discussing the life and earthly death of Jesus and how His death, particularly, has created a virtual industry around it, we should examine a singular feature that many writers have connected Him to. It is a connection which, for millennia, has imbued many individuals and diverse groups with the unquenchable longing to embark on, ostensibly, the greatest spiritual quest of all – the search for The Holy Grail. The numerous stories that history holds about this worthy task are steeped in the highest and noblest aspirations that human beings could possibly bring to bear on any endeavour. The key element in the search for The Holy Grail is the seemingly inherent "knowing" that it is an object so holy and sublime that its very existence seems supra-earthly in nature. To seek so assiduously for something so apparently unattainable over such a long period of time carries with it a certain kind of nobleness-of-spirit almost worthy of the object itself.

For all that, however, no one researcher has actually produced what can be definitively stated to be The Holy Grail. It is believed by some to be the cup which Jesus used at the Last Supper, by others the cup which was used to catch His blood. A number of claimants around the world hold different kinds of cups or vessels, but the very fact that there *are* numerous claimants obviously calls into question the authenticity of any to lay claim to being *the* icon – *in terms of what the object is believed to be and the power it is felt to hold*. This "search", like so many "other-world" research efforts, suffers from the common human condition of only seeing the subject matter from the earthly point of view. Solely from the physical-material.

It is therefore puzzling that the many authors who have written about The Holy Grail – even though professing a strong belief that it is something so high and sublime that only the purest of human spirits are permitted to behold it – can still publish reams of paper trying to *conclusively prove* that it somehow exists *in material form on earth*. Even the many documentary and filmmakers who have looked at it seem not to be able to leave the material-earth paradigm.

So an object ostensibly worthy of the highest veneration, and which only the purest can serve, in the human mind ultimately comes down to something so mundane as an ordinary, everyday clay or wooden cup – notwithstanding the iconic status of those vessels. Certain authors and claimants, however, have tried to link The Holy Grail to an earth-based, Jesus-connection by hypothesising a substitute at the Crucifixion and a marriage to Mary Magdalene. Thus producing some kind of genus different to the rest of humanity by virtue of a postulated Divine, thus royal, bloodline. Thereby bequeathing to humanity an earthly genealogy ostensibly carried by certain, mainly European, families living today. That hypothesised "sacred bloodline", at least for them, apparently seems to be, or hold, the secret of The Holy Grail - as postulated in the book, "The Holy Blood and the Holy Grail".

How insidiously influential such damagingly-incorrect ideas can become is evident from unprecedented interest in runaway book sales of one publication, Dan Brown's "The Da Vinci Code", on exactly this subject. As was expected, it was made into a motion picture and became a blockbuster, thus further influencing many millions more globally and taking them all away from the *actual* Truth of it. It is a specific Truth crucially vital for all human beings to know. So, now, for increasing numbers it would seem, The Holy Grail was, or perhaps still is, a woman. Clearly, a woman's body *is* a vessel in living form. It receives, and it delivers. Unfortunately for such believers, however, it is not, or ever was, or ever could be, the pure Vessel, the Pure Chalice that is **The True Holy Grail!**

In any case, who dares ask the obvious question, where are the pure human spirits "down here" who would be worthy enough to hold or guard it? None. Why? Quite simply, **because the true Holy Grail is not of the earth**. How could it possibly be? That is why it is so Holy! We, therefore, cannot ever actually see it in its "living reality" – let alone get anywhere near it.

The **form** that is associated with The Holy Grail – that of a Chalice – is known simply by virtue of the fact that especially blessed ones long ago received a "radiated picture" of it. From them it entered the consciousness of a particular group of humanity whose "spirit" was thereby awakened to a longing to seek it out. Even in recent times, however, others have received "pictures" about it. *Music Forms*, a book by Geoffrey Hodson, offers a tantalising glimpse into what Wagner may have seen – or at the very least perceived – when writing his great work, Parsifal. Dr Gordon Kingsley, Music Director of Beverley Hills Church in Hollywood, California, worked with Geoffrey Hodson on this project. Hodson was renowned for his amazing "second-sight" abilities, and employed it to analyse the forms of some of the noted classics from the great composers. Wagner's "Parsifal" was one chosen.

In "The Overture From Parsifal", Dr Kingsley offers his comments on what he believes the music represents and symbolises. A few short extracts indicate the sense of majesty he perceived in it.

The Eucharistic Motif

In his music drama "Parsifal" Richard Wagner reached a height of sublimity which even he had not previously attained ... there is added another element – sacredness.

We are on holy ground. The first sounds of the prelude convey a sanctity not of this world, a peace, indeed, which passeth all understanding. It is the motive of the Eucharist. - - - "it is the old, old story of man's ascent to God." It is only natural that the composer should represent this conception in a musical motive which in itself seeks to carry the listener to higher realms.

The Grail Motif

The Grail is the chalice which contained the "life-blood" whose ruby radiance streaming forth in blessing, enveloped everything within the sphere of its mighty influence. The very structure of the music suggests this all-embracing benediction...

(Dr. Kingsley's Comments. (bars 45-47) p 32-33)

Geoffrey Hodson described what he observed in each of the two Motif compositions. More importantly in this case, he also produced colour-prints of what he saw: a Chalice clearly not of the earth. As with the other great compositions chosen for the project, the pictures really are "worth a thousand words". Wagner must surely have perceived that it was supra-earthly in nature to bring forth both words and pictures indicating that. So why did so many Grail researchers attempt to tie it in with Jesus on earth? For once the tidings of it reached all the way down to earth through the few gifted to perceive its existence, the answer was always available to any earnest seeker dedicated to unearthing the mystery of it.

We had previously stated that we would quote from The Revelation the Scripture identifying the actual Holy Grail. Since many researchers have connected it with Jesus and His earthly Mission, this is the appropriate Chapter to show exactly *what* it is. A clue lies in the words He spoke to Pilate on the day of their fateful meeting: *"My kingdom is not of this world"*. The very note of His words clearly indicates something very different to the ongoing notion of any kind of *earthly* association here. The words reveal that in the final analysis *direct* connections to Jesus not only do *not* lie in the earthly, but ultimately *cannot*.

By virtue of its supra-earthly nature The Holy Grail can truly be stated to be a "Sacred and Holy Vessel". Over centuries and even to this day men have racked their brains to try to solve what is ultimately a Divine Mystery. A mystery in the sense that we can never behold it or know anything of it in its living reality. Not, however, a mystery about what it is or, indeed, that it *really does exist*.

From The Bible, the "Revelation of John" tells us exactly what The Holy Grail actually is. Dr Kingsley's comments about the "life-blood" streaming forth in blessing are surprisingly insightful.

> Then He said to me, "**It has come! I, the Alpha and the Omega, the beginning and the end. I will freely give to the thirsty from** *the fountain of the water of life*."
>
> (Revelation 19:6, Fenton. Emphases mine.)

Through just those few stupendous words we can more readily understand parts of the legend of The Holy Grail where, if the power, "the water of life" that streams forth from The Chalice, is withdrawn, *everything* decays and dies including, of course, unbelieving humanity. The *actual* Holy Grail, therefore, is what we are all meant to recognise and know as literally the *"fountain of the water of life"* dispensing Divine Power for all of Creation. And thus for all here on earth too. **From God, through Imanuel – The Holy Spirit – The Alpha and the Omega – His Will! Thus, The Holy Grail is the Highest Creation of God!**

Grail researchers need only adjust their thinking to this inviolable Truth and very much that was hitherto regarded as once unknowable would quickly fall into place. Determined, but ultimately fruitless efforts to prove some kind of Jesus-Holy Grail-earth connection deny Him His very Origin from out of The Divine. The Lawful and humanly unbridgeable gulf naturally existing between such Divine sublimity and our far lower level of earthly humanity automatically precludes, as a matter of course, any such connection.

Jesus came to Earth to lead humanity back to **THE LIGHT** through the knowledge of **THE ONE LAW**. He therefore gifted all on Earth the opportunity to return from whence we originally came – our *true home* in a Higher Realm. [We all surely know His words of Divine Love which reveal that fact: 'In my Father's House are many mansions. I go to prepare a place for you.'] However, any possible 'return home' is absolutely predicated on living that **ONE LAW** – **CREATION-LAW** – *inherent* in **HIS Divine Essence**.

He did not come to found a Divine bloodline; by any standard a *nonsense-notion* focusing *solely* on human ego. Yet the extreme foolishness of such an idea nevertheless continues to be promoted. Men had became so entangled in wrong ideas and teachings that *the way home was effectively lost*. Had The Love of The Almighty not inclined towards an erring and spiritually-sinking humankind to send a Part of Himself to Earth in Jesus, mankind would have sunk irretrievably. He was not sent to die, therefore, *but to rescue mankind.*

Despite all the trials and indignities He suffered, He did not shun physical death when it drew near but remained resolute, deliberately facing it for the sake of **The Truth** He brought into **The World of Matter**. By shedding **His blood** on that terrible "**Cross of Crucifixion**", He placed **His** very "Seal of Conviction" on *all* that **He** had *said* and *lived*. With His death, the way to **The Light** was now open. He had won the victory for **The Love of The Father**, for the **Love of Truth** and the *Love of Man*. For He had subjugated the powers and forces that had striven to destroy **His Message** and **His Work**! And therewith, as the incontrovertible historical record unequivocally reveals, man's *faith* in **The Truth** of **His Word** was *strengthened* by **His Victory**. *So Jesus died* for – *thus* **because of** – *the sins of men*.

If He had given up His Work in fear of His many enemies, doubt would have assailed the faithful. The seeds of Truth He sowed in the spirits and consciousness of men then would not have taken root to subsequently spread to all corners of the Earth.

Had it not been for *the sin* of *turning away* from **The Creator and His Perfect Laws** and thus *introducing* dark and evil forms onto the Earth in the first place, ***Jesus would have been spared His Coming, His suffering and His death on the Cross.***

It is correct, therefore, to say that for the sake of 'the sin' which led to mankind's 'fall', Jesus came, suffered and was crucified, but that irrefutable fact is not a blessing for Christians or mankind in any shape or form. Those who had the chance to save Him from a terrible end – the once-chosen and blessed Jewish race – agitated for Barabbas over The Son of God. To Pilate, they shouted: 'Crucify Him'. Standing as an *indictment* against all of mankind from that singularly-dark moment of far-reaching portent, it was and still is an especially damning indictment against the Jewish race. For even today, they still refuse to recognise that **The One** sent to them *at their petition*, really was their **Awaited One** at that time.

His Crucifixion was not, and could never ever be, an act of "necessary sacrifice" to take away the sins of a weak and spiritually-lazy, earthly humanity. The millions upon millions of Crucifixes that have *inundated* the Earth for millennia should thus be looked upon *far differently* to what has been the case thus far.

Yes, the Crucifix *should* be approached with awe and reverence, **but see it for what it really is, and therefore what it truly means!**

11.5 Crucifixion of The Son Of God: Medical Forensics Speak

Up to this point we have examined a number of issues of contentious moment centred on the life, death and its aftermath for Jesus, The Son of God. Irrespective of the many differing viewpoints about these events, however, a clear and absolutely unequivocal Truth is nonetheless sacrosanct here. And that is:

That the actual happenings in the Life and death of Jesus could only have occurred according to firmly established, inviolable Laws. As we have already explained, it is impossible for anything to take place except under precise and lawful processes, irrespective of what human/Christian opinion – either from lay persons or academics – might wish to state or believe.

Since that *is* an inviolable Truth in itself, let us put aside all selfish notions of how wonderful it all was that The Son of God Himself was sent down to this Earth in an act of Noble Love on the part of The Almighty to save *us* from *our* sins. Instead, and from a scientific/medical perspective, let us *really and closely* examine the whole process of the Crucifixion of Jesus in a probing, 'blow-by-blow', assessment of His 'journey of terrible suffering'.

While doing so, we should very seriously understand that the incredible pain He suffered throughout *never let up*. It was *constant*. It was not at any time relieved by 'first-aid' or convenient pain-killers such as we would immediately grasp for at the onset of even very mild, 'inconvenient', pain.

From childhood, Christians are conditioned with a mind-set which *superficially* and ***incomprehensibly*** says that Jesus suffered and died on The Cross to save *them* from **their** sins. Nothing, however, about what that suffering *really meant* **for Him**. Not, however, for the 'believing Christian' who will *never ever* experience such a thing, but who nonetheless preens himself with sickening false piety in the truly strange belief that he is 'absolved' from all **his** sins and 'thereby saved'.

That being the perverse and pervading belief in Christendom, let us all journey with Jesus to His agonising death. Whilst on that grievous walk to His place of execution, we should put aside every shred of 'religious' thought, and – **objectively** and ***logically*** – try to fathom *how* and *why* around two billion otherwise well-meaning humans on Earth can *accept* and even *strongly promote* a belief whereby the excruciatingly-painful torture that **The Son Of God** was cruelly subjected to can *somehow* be the *'right thing'*. Even in an earthly Court of Law, such an idea would be 'thrown out' as unjust. Yet so many believe that **'The Power of All Creation'** would nonetheless *sanctify* such an *appalling injustice*.

[Perhaps we should **all** have long-understood that just as **The Creator** is **Perfect Love**: **He** is *also* **Perfect Justice!**]

Firstly, then, we should watch the terrible 'scourging' by Roman soldiers. Secondly; the mocking and the placing of a 'crown of thorns' upon His head. Next; accompany Him every step of His cruelly-agonising 'death-walk' laden under the crushing weight of a heavy wooden beam. And thence finally arrive with Him at Golgotha: His place of execution.

Are there any hand-clapping, 'praise the Lord' Hallelujahs there? No! Of course not. It is too cruel, too painful, *too unbelievable*. Yet every Easter on so-called 'Good Friday', hundreds of millions of Christians in their thousands of Churches across the world perversely 'celebrate' this *worst* of *all* murders.

"BLACK FRIDAY!" That is the reality for all time.

Note: The medical and forensic analyses of the Crucifixion of Jesus we now outline is sourced from the History Channel Documentary called **"Crucifixion"**; screened on **'Black Friday'**, 2009. It is a harrowing Documentary that *all* Christians should view, for it is to date the most graphic depiction of Jesus's painful suffering. [In this writer's view, far more so than Mel Gibson's, "The Passion of The Christ"; itself regarded as a very graphic depiction of The Crucifixion.]

The primary contributors for the *Biblical/historical narrative* of the medical forensics associated with the **Crucifixion of Jesus** are:

- **Dr. David Ball, M.D.** ER Chief, Ret., Tri-Lakes Medical Center.

- **Dr. Robert M. Norris, M.D.** ER Chief, Stanford Medical Center.

- **Jonathan Reed, Ph.D.** Professor, University of La Verne.

- **Richard J. Hoffman, Ph.D.** Professor, San Francisco State University.

- **Sarah Stroud, Ph.D.** Professor, University of Washington.

- **Dr. Mark Benecke.** Forensic Biologist.

- **Daniel Smith-Christopher, Ph.D.** Professor, Loyola Marymount University.

This particular segment of our overall journey of *logical* enlightenment is offered as a help primarily to those Christians who are 'content with their faith'. However, the 'blind-faith' attitude that many Christians seemingly display is really no faith at all, for it simply demands that *the faithful* 'accept without question' all they are told. Specifically and especially on the question of whether or not Jesus came to Earth 'to take on the sins of men' and 'die on The Cross to save them'; without keen examination of this subject from either the 'Christian teacher' or the 'Christian follower' to ensure an absolutely correct answer – i.e., according to **The Will Of God Whom** all Christians will state they want to serve – the warning of a very well known key Bible Scripture should be the primary driver to "get it right"!

"When the blind lead the blind, all will fall into the ditch." [abyss]

Since there are a number of quite different interpretations and beliefs around this question, it is patently obvious that many Christian 'congregations' have thus 'not got it right' at all. Yet every one of them will *swear* that *they* are *saved* by *their* belief, and/or their *group interpretation*. Unfortunately, as we all surely and logically understand, the *correct answers* that must *inherently reside* in the events and meaning surrounding Jesus's death *cannot possibly* allow for an *infinite number* of 'saviour-scenarios' here.

The knowledgable analyses of the above contributors will help the average or 'seeking' Christian make more sense of a momentous and portentous event that ultimately affects **all** of humankind.

Crucifixion: A slow death of maximum suffering, used as a method of Capital Punishment for over 3,000 years. It was practised in various forms long before Roman Legions occupied the land of Judea at the time of Jesus. From the more simple but excruciatingly-painful practice of 'staking' a body to hang suspended from an upright stake, true crucifixion – the body affixed in the 'crucifix position' on a wooden 'cross' – was perhaps a 'torturous refinement' of 'staking'.

Death by crucifixion was essentially designed to discipline the many peoples conquered by Rome. Her vast Empire required policing methods designed to ensure that the "Pax Romana" – 'The Peace of Rome' – was kept. Crucifying criminals, dissidents and revolutionaries alike who threatened that 'peace' set a severe example to others contemplating the same. Instilling fear of a terrible and agonisingly-painful death in Roman subjects probably did help hold the 'Pax Romana'; for crucified victims were often left to decompose on the cross for all to see. A further unsettling dimension for both the crucified and the travelling public was the fact that crows often sat on the heads of victims to peck at the eyes. Perhaps the most notable crucifixion *event* was the execution of 6,000 gladiators taken from the slave Army of Spartacus after his defeat. They stretched 125 miles along the Appian Way from Capua to Rome.

By the time Jesus walked the Earth, the Romans had well-perfected the 'art' of crucifixion as we know it today. Two forms of 'the cross of crucifixion' were used by the Legions. The **Tau** – in the shape of a **Capital T**; and the **Latin** – in the shape of a **lower-case t**. Both consisted of two parts: The **Stipe**, the *upright beam*; and the **Patibulum**, the *cross-member*.

Since the Roman Army crucified countless thousands, their no-nonsense approach to all they undertook would have ensured a practical, efficient method for the purpose. The **Tau**, being simpler, was therefore probably more commonly used because the top of the **Stipe** is in the reach of soldiers.

A new look at the whole question of Roman-style crucifixion offers greater insights into the death of Jesus. Notwithstanding the obvious fact that Roman soldiers were well practised in the *mechanics* of crucifixion, considerable effort in time and manpower would nonetheless have been required to nail and/or affix the many tens of thousands crucified over the term of the Roman Empire; if the Latin Cross was the preferred option.

The simpler and thus more likely method was to first set the upright beam – the **Stipe** – in the ground. The wooden cross-member – the *mortised* **Patibulum** weighing about 100 pounds to which the victim was affixed – was then lifted up by soldiers and fitted onto a matching tenon on the **Stipe**.

11.5.1 The Roman 'Flagrum': The 'Scourging' of "The Son Of God"

scourge *n.* **1.** A whip used to inflict punishment.

2. Any means of inflicting severe suffering, vengeance, or punishment

scourging *tr.v.* **1.** to flog.

'Scourging' commonly preceded crucifixion. It was carried out by soldiers wielding the Flagrum, a Roman whip designed to flay skin, tissue and muscle, and thus produce excruciating pain and terrible wounds. It consisted of several strips of leather into which were tied pieces of metal, nails, glass, bone and lead weights; basically anything that would cut into flesh.

> "To be crucified was to say that you were no better than a slave. You are worthy of death. And part of the crucifixion process – you might say the drama of crucifixion – was to scourge you."
>
> (Richard J. Hoffman, Ph.D.)

The victim was stripped of all clothing save perhaps for loin coverings, and tied by the hands to a wooden post. Two Roman soldiers would stand either side of the victim and alternate whip strokes. The severity of the flogging was largely determined by the viciousness of the soldiers. Long-practised in war and killing, soldiers of the super-efficient, well-disciplined and ruthless Roman Army were very far removed from the more squeamish nature of modern Western peoples who often require counselling as a way of coping with what are often just the simple realities of life on Earth. Since crucifixion as a punishment was common, soldiers would often experiment on the hapless victims. Dr. David Ball explains:

> "What you would expect from a Roman Flagrum would be complete tearing away of the skin down to the ribs. And this results in bruising to the inter-costal muscles, which impairs respiration ... and actually causes bruising to the lungs... And that leads to a very serious medical problem called 'pulmonary contusion'. That will lead to 'pulmonary oedema' and impaired respiration. It is a very serious injury."

In this medical-trauma analysis of 'scourging' and crucifixion, we reiterate that it is an analysis of *the suffering of Jesus*, primarily as recorded in The Bible.

Dr Ball notes that scourging a human being with the Roman Flagrum produced wounds that [are] "...so severe that it has been compared to a shotgun blast at close range."

Robert M. Norris, M.D. explains:

> "The muscles would have been torn, hanging; basically ribbons of flesh that were bleeding profusely ... deep tissues

of larger vessels that can't clamp down so easily. Profuse bleeding decreases blood supply leading to hypo-bulimic shock ... not enough blood circulating around heart to profuse vital tissues; the muscles and the organs."

A prime purpose of 'scourging' was to:

"Create a mutilated body up on the cross ... [for] ... a mutilated, visceral experience on the part of the viewers who were attending the crucifixion. ... We don't really know how Jesus was scourged. The Gospels don't give us much detail. But it's quite possible that it was fairly severe because Jesus dies within a day. And He dies before nightfall."

(Jonathan Reed, Ph.D.)

"He was beaten nearly to death. He was macerated. He was bruised. He had massive damage to the backside, and massive damage to the inter-costal muscles, and massive damage to the lungs and the kidneys themselves through the bruising process."

(David Ball, M.D.)

Narration: 'When the scourging is finished, Jesus's back is an unrecognisable mass of torn and bleeding tissue. This brutal beating will dramatically affect the final hours of Jesus's life.'

11.5.2 The 'Burden' of the Cross

The present, widely accepted, notion in Christendom is that Jesus was made to carry or drag a complete **Latin Cross** weighing several hundred pounds roughly a mile to Golgotha, then nailed onto it whilst it was on the ground, both raised up together, and the Cross then positioned in a pre-prepared hole. If that *were* the true scenario, it would have taken a superhuman effort to carry or drag such a weight that distance with a body severely-weakened and already near death as a result of the torture and mutilation at the hands of the Roman soldiers ordered to 'scourge' Him.

The Bible narrative reports that 'Simon of Cyrene' was seconded to carry Jesus's Cross after His strength finally gave out.

"I do not think it is either practical – from a Roman perspective – to have individuals carry entire crosses. Nor do I think it is likely possible as a physical feat."

(Sarah Stroud, Ph.D.)

Experts generally agree it is more likely that Jesus would have carried only the Patibulum, which nonetheless weighed around 100 pounds – a huge weight for a badly tortured man to carry any distance.

> "For this point the victim would already be in some degree of shock due to blood loss from the scourging. So now we've put a 100 pound beam on the person's back; strapped their hands to it. And now the heart is tasked to pump even harder and harder to supply the leg muscles to get him to the execution site."

(Robert M. Norris, M.D.)

Whipped up by Caiaphas and key members of The Sanhedrin, the emotional turmoil connected with the trial and sentence of Jesus would surely have wrought tumultuous agitation among those who watched Him walk His last pain-wracked mile – to Golgotha. The Bible tells us that Jesus fell under the weight of the Patibulum. Dr. Norris explains the 'medical' ramifications of such a fall.

> "The full force of His body and that 100 pound weight on the backs of His shoulders would have been centred on His chest. That slammed the heart against His breastbone, the sternum, inside. That could bruise the heart."

> "A bruised heart is a very serious injury. The muscle has been damaged, and so it tends to stretch. And as the heart is pumping, that stretch increases and you have a balloon we call an 'aneurysm'. That 'balloon' becomes thin-walled and can rupture."

(David Ball, M.D.)

This type of injury is similar to chest trauma sustained in a car accident when an unrestrained driver impacts onto the steering wheel. Now bearing the added pain and trauma of a bruised heart from His fall, Jesus is forced to continue His grievous walk to his place of execution.

11.6 The 'Murder' at Golgotha

11.6.1 The 'Nailing'

> "The bio-mechanics of a crucifixion is quite interesting. It all depends very much on the angle in which you secure the

> limbs and all the body parts because this will determine how much physical stress will either be on the bones or connective tissue. ... The maximum stress that you can have on the tissue, on the bones, is between 40 and 60 pounds. This may cause the tissue to rip or the bones to break so that the whole system of crucifixion won't work..."
>
> (Dr. Mark Benecke.)

It was found that in tests with arms set at an angle in a crucifixion:

> "...*each* hand bears the whole weight of the body, and not *half* the body-weight for each as we might ['logically'] expect. Therefore, an average weight man will tear away from the cross if nailed through the hands."
>
> (Dr. Mark Benecke.)

Dr. Norris explains that if the nails were placed instead into the wrist, i.e., into the small bones of the wrist where there are [dense] fibrous sheaths around these bones:

> "...they would have held. The pain, however, would be excruciating because the large median nerve which provides sensation to the forearm and hand passes right through this area of the wrist."

Commenting on the 'pain factor' when the wrists are 'nailed, Dr. Ball states that:

> "The median nerve, whether it's lacerated, or whether it's impinged upon as the nail pushes against it ... it's going to be like *burning, severe pain.*"

The Gospels imply that Jesus is nailed through the hand. In the ancient Greek language, in which The Bible was originally written, the word for hand describes both the hand and the wrist. So the bony area described is where most experts believe the Romans drove the nail into Jesus's hand. They would probably not have relied on the nails alone, so also tied the arms to support the weight of the body. Dr. Norris notes:

> "The ultimate outcome in terms of how long the person survived probably was dependent in some particular way in how the feet were attached."

The feet were most likely attached in the 'stacked' position – one foot on top of the other as commonly depicted. This position, whilst encouraging a quicker death, produced excruciating pain.

> "If you place the soles of the feet flat against the upright, the individual cannot lock their knees. They have to support their weight with the thigh muscles. Or hang completely from the [hand] nails."
>
> (David Ball, M.D.)

This fiendishly torturous position made it far more challenging for the victim to breathe. Scholars of crucifixions generally do not believe that artistic portrayals in paintings and Hollywood movies depicting a wooden block under the feet of Jesus are correct. For why, after such prolonged torture, would the Romans then offer *any* victim even the smallest measure of 'comfort'?

> "There are a series of nerves that pass through the feet in that area that would cause tremendous stimulation of those sensory nerves and just [exquisite] pain from that. And every time the victim would try to rise to exhale, that would stimulate those nerves."
>
> (Robert M. Norris, M.D.)

Dr. Ball says:

> "A person nailed to the cross is going to be searching for a comfortable position. He may relieve the pain on the medial nerve and lift himself up, but he creates muscle pain. When he drops himself down he relieves the muscles but he finds the pain has recurred in the medial nerve and the shoulders."

In excruciating agony Jesus tries to find relief from the intense pain wracking every part of His body. He strives to breathe freely by pushing up on the spike driven through His feet. In doing so the exposed nerves on His cruelly-mutilated back rub on the rough-hewn post. Robert M. Norris, M.D. concurs:

> "Every time He would lift Himself up on the Cross, that would drag these torn shredded tissues of the back across the rough wood of the Cross, reopening the wounds, re-stimulating the nerves in the back causing further bleeding and, again, causing tremendous pain."

Dr. Ball notes that:

> "There is no comfortable position on the Cross. There is no position where He is even relatively pain-free."

Narration: 'Jesus hangs in agony. The end is near. He's beaten, dehydrated, exhausted. He's suffering from external trauma and internal injuries; all life-threatening conditions. But what ultimately kills Jesus? Today, science may have the technology to decode the ancient evidence and discover the exact cause of Jesus's death on the Cross. ... Since His arrest nine hours earlier He's been beaten and abused. His crucified body is wracked with pain as He struggles to breathe. The cruelty is clearly taking its toll. But what is the ultimate cause of Jesus's death?'

> "There were so many things that were going on at the same time. Any one of them at a certain point could cause someone's death; the dehydration, the blood loss, just the severe trauma to the muscles."
>
> (Robert M. Norris, M.D.)

Medical experts believe that Jesus's physical deterioration begins with exhaustion, for He has not slept for over twenty four hours. Moreover, since His arrest He has had nothing to eat or drink.

11.6.2 His Final Moments

> "The death-process is definitely underway. ... the scourging started the process with the contused lungs, bruising to the muscles, damaged kidneys."
>
> "I don't think that it's fair to say there is one cause of death on the cross. I think it is multi-factorial, and all of these things are taking place in a typical crucifixion."
>
> (David Ball, M.D.)

Narration: 'His blood-loss is made worse by the constant tearing of the wounds on His back as He moves up and down on the Cross in order to breathe deeply. The loss of bodily fluids means He's probably suffering from hypo-bulimic shock; a condition in which the heart is unable to pump adequate blood to the organs, muscles and vital tissues. On top of that, decreased respiratory volume means carbon dioxide is building up in the lungs and reducing oxygen in the blood; a condition known as hypoxia. Ultimately, this could lead to suffocation.'

> "He's probably becoming somewhat hypoxic at this point, Again, from the increased work of breathing, and inadequate blood volume circulating around. He is near death."
>
> (Robert M. Norris, M.D.)

Deriving from His fall with the weight of a 100 pound Patibulum on His back, it is very probable that Jesus is suffering from 'blunt chest trauma'. 'The ensuing internal damage could easily include a bruised heart.'

> "When an individual has sustained a bruise to his heart, this bruise creates a soft spot in the muscle. Every time the heart pumps, there's pressure on that soft spot that has the tendency to cause a ballooning out. Or, as we call it, an aneurysm."
>
> (David Ball, M.D.)

Narration: 'Jesus's cardiovascular system is under enormous stress. His heart is pumping upwards of 170 beats per minute. An aneurysm puts Him at even greater risk. If left untreated it can rupture. And there's another factor that can contribute to the death of any victim on the cross.'

> "The pain of crucifixion is unimaginable. ... the pain over time is so excruciating that the bodily functions give out. You die simply of pain."
>
> (Jonathan Reed, Ph.D.)

Narration: 'Any one of these [conditions] can be fatal. But Jesus has not yet given up. According to The Bible He is able to speak despite His weakened condition.'

> "He was carrying on conversations that were lucid and clear. So we know that His brain was being adequately supplied at this point with enough [oxygenated] blood."
>
> (David Ball, M.D.)

Narration: 'After several hours, Jesus seems to know that the end has come. The Bible says that he called out His final words – and then dies.'

His final words: **"Father. Into your hands I commit my spirit."**

Dr. Ball states factually that:

> "If He had died of hypo-bulimic shock – as some people say – He would have fainted. He would not have been able to holler out with a loud voice and then suddenly die."

Whilst some see asphyxiation as the cause of death, Dr Ball explains why that is very unlikely. He sagely observes that if a crucified man has: "...enough air in [his] lungs to holler out, [he] will not be in any danger of dying of asphyxiation. That cannot happen."

> "That He had enough strength and enough mental clarity to cry out very effectively means to me that something catastrophic was happening. And He knew that it was happening."
>
> (Robert M. Norris, M.D.)

Given the searching medical analysis of the final moments of Jesus's life, experts believe that the most likely cause of death is from His bruised and damaged heart. Dr. Norris explains the process: "Gradually His heart is failing. The fluids would begin to back up in the lungs, around the lungs, and actually around the outside of the heart; inside the heart sac – the pericardium."

The pericardium is a sac of fibrous tissue filled with a water-like solution that surrounds and protects the heart. Dr. Ball explains:

> "With His pulse rate going to 180 or even more, He is under an enormous cardiovascular stress load."

Dr. Ball opines that under such extreme stress, the bruised heart of Jesus ultimately ruptures. It would feel like a heart attack, and Jesus would know His death is imminent. The ruptured heart continues to beat. With each pulse, however, it pushes blood into the pericardial sac until the heart finally stops.

That is the one, single, blessing for The Son Of God in His whole unbelievable journey of horrific, agonising torture to His execution on the 'death cross' at Golgotha:

For His terrible ordeal at the hands of men is finally over.

> "You've got a heart that is ruptured. It's not functioning any more, it's not pumping. But you've got a pericardial sac that is under pressure. Taut."

(David Ball, M.D.)

The spear of a Roman soldier reveals the proof of Dr. Ball's medical analysis of the actual death of Jesus.

> "According to the Gospel of John, a Roman soldier takes a spear and sticks it inside Jesus to make sure that He's dead."

(Jonathan Reed, Ph.D.)

The Gospel narrative states that blood and water 'come out' from the wound. Dr. Ball explains what has taken place:

> "What you have to understand is they've gone through this pericardial sac to get to the heart. The pericardial sac is under pressure. The blood has settled. So immediately you've got this flow of blood followed by clear fluid, which is described as water in The Bible."

Narration: 'After about six hours on the Cross, Jesus Christ is dead. It's a relatively short time for crucifixion [by Roman standards], which can last for several excruciating days.
Arrested on the Thursday night of the Passover holiday; by Friday morning soldiers are preparing to nail Him to the Cross. By that afternoon He will be dead.'

The final act played out both on Golgotha and for those in the Sanhedrin who actively plotted to bring about His death, was wrought by a powerful earthquake. Sufficiently strong to shatter the floor of the Temple of Jerusalem, the convulsive transfer of energy from the Earth to the great building tore asunder the heavy curtain that protected **The Holy of Holies.**

The odds of **that** particular earth-tremor occurring with such precise convergence to, *ostensibly,* **'*coincide*'** with the exact moment Jesus died, would surely be in the order of millions to one. That natural event should be *proof enough* of how terribly wrong His execution was, for even the **Forces of Nature** vented their anger and fury at the *murder* of **The Son Of God: He Who** once Commanded *the same* to cease their 'storm-work' activity on the Sea of Galilee with the admonition: **"Peace. Be still!"**

For the Jewish race, what was once the Holiest Treasure on Earth – the *sanctuary* of which even **Moses the Law-Giver** *could* *not enter* on the decades-long journey to the 'promised land' – *was no longer so*. The curtain that formerly 'spiritually-symbolically' protected it, rent in two by the power of the tremor at the murder of **The Son Of God**, signified the *separation* of man from **The Almighty** – *not the opposite*. It was not a *reconciliation*, as many from 'Christian academia' will argue. The Jewish Priesthood, once Called to serve and protect that Holy Treasure; by *their* dark deed were made *redundant*. For, shortly after, the Jewish race lost possession of The Holy of Holies and it *disappeared from history*; a *further* indication of the ***singular enormity*** of that particular crime.

The historical aftermath of the execution of Jesus saw develop among Christians and their Church a radical but nonetheless strange change in perception concerning the 'Latin Cross of Crucifixion'. Initially His death only reinforces the perception of the cross as an horrific tool of oppression. Yet, over time, the symbolism of crucifixion underwent an ironic transformation. Very interestingly, the documentary, **Crucifixion**, asks the most pertinent question of all in this regard.

> *"How does this implement of torture and execution become an iconic symbol of hope and salvation despite the fact that it continues on into the 20th and 21st centuries?"*

The answer is brutally logical.

A Teaching, a Church or a Movement that has **Truth** *at its core and as its* **practice** *would not, indeed* **could not**, *possibly accord such an instrument of torture the perversely altered state of reverence and even worship that the Latin Cross/Crucifix now holds for around one third of global humanity. Only a* **religion** *could bring such a thing about, for religions hold very little of* **The Pure Truth**. *Hence the unbelievable state of hate and violence between religions in the present.*

The path to that detrimental point of 'altered perceptions' probably began when the Roman Emperor Constantine became Christian after 'seeing' a vision in the sky prior to a battle. It is said that an accompanying voice told him: "In this sign you will be victorious." Believed by Christians to be the 'Latin Cross', Constantine's victory on the battlefield thenceforth set 'that' cross as 'the form of salvation' for the Church and its followers.

"It's under Constantine's rule that the cross becomes a positive symbol for the first time. And it's a symbol of Christianity. And because of that, you can no longer use it as a tool for shameful death."

(Jonathan Reed, Ph.D.)

So in the strangest of 'turnarounds', the cross, once identified with the most fearful kind of death, and an object to inspire terror in the hearts of men, is now a symbol of piety and faith which Christians now use in the shape of their churches, for their rituals, and in their art.

Christianity becomes the dominant world religion. Despite the long history of cruel torture inherent in the practice, crucifixion is almost exclusively associated with Jesus. Even though documented crucifixions are rare after the Romans, this brutal punishment nonetheless persists throughout the centuries. The crucial event of The Second World War saw Hitler's Nazi regime use this method of torture. Sarah Stroud Ph.D, notes:

"It was a display of power. It's always a spectacle, and it's always sadistic. ...it was often used against individuals who actually posed some sort of threat or had committed a wrong against the State. [However] The use of it against individuals who were already victims or already captives and completely powerless seems especially perverse."

Even today in the Sudan/Darfur region where genocide is rampant, crucifixion is sanctioned as a method of execution. In 2002 Amnesty reported that 88 people, including two children, were sentenced to death by crucifixion. Perversely, then, it would seem; the image of Jesus's agonising death on the Cross remains one of our most powerful icons. Jonathan Reed emphasises the fact that:

"When Christianity adopts the Cross as its key symbol, it also defines itself as a *religion* that focusses itself on suffering, and a *religion* that focusses on atonement. And so the Cross itself, maybe more so than any book written, has had a profound impact on how Christians think about their religion, and their religious experience."

Narration: 'Yet the cross and the roots of crucifixion reach back long before Jesus. He was just one of the many [countless] victims of this brutal death sentence. From ancient civilisations to modern regimes, crucifixion carries the same meaning. It's not just about killing. Crucifixion is about torture, fear and control.'

> "Crucifixion should be a *warning*. Crucifixion should make us *ask questions* about *unjust* and *horrific treatment* of other people. The cross should be a symbol that says: **Never treat someone like this!**"
>
> (Daniel Smith-Christopher, Ph.D. All emphases mine.)

The murder of The Son Of God stands as the most heinous crime in the history of the world, for He came to lift humanity out of the depths to which it had *voluntarily* sunk. Human ego and religious power had subverted Spiritual Truth and Law. Proclaimed by the Old Testament Prophets, the subversion of It resulted in a rigid dogma that wrought suffering for many, and meant that Jesus had to come to Earth to Light the Way back to **The Truth**.

The later Messengers of His Truth encountered the same blind perversity. The explanations of The Truth which they were called to Teach to the peoples among whom they were incarnated, became – in short order after their deaths – just religions.

Historically, have we human beings ever really revered **Envoys** from **The Light** or, indeed, **Its** Prophets? Almost all suffered from human perversity and mockery, *when* they proclaimed *on Earth*. If stripped down to 'bare bones', it is the **adulation of human beings by human beings** that has long-reigned supreme in the world. Today, the rock stars, sports stars, movie stars and the fashion models etc., are the *things* of adulation, even reverence.

That being the case; apart from the regular 'Easter Shopping Guide', what do we invariably see advertised as a *primary enticement* for the 'Easter holiday period' the Christian West celebrates? Yes, there are the Church services. And there are re-enactments of His Crucifixion which, *in no way whatsoever for the 'participants'*, could possibly give *any* degree of understanding of the terrible pain and suffering that The Son Of God had to endure at the hands of blind, religious fools. In truth, it is a *perverse mockery* to re-enact His torturous suffering.[4]

So: On every anniversary of His hideous execution, the one thing that probably most Western Christian children look forward to are chocolate eggs, laid – in the strangest, impossible concept –

---

[4] It is something akin to the 'annual fast' that overfed Western children in communal 'rah-rah, jolly-jolly' groups take part in for *just* 40 hours to *somehow* gain *understanding* of the plight of children so starved that, for many, **death** is **their** outcome. Unlike the 'empathists' who receive a hearty meal and congratulations at the end of their 40 hour 'famine ordeal'.

by a rabbit; the wealth-producing 'Easter Bunny'. Is that surely not the most perverse distortion of a crucial date that all Christians should *fully understand* in its *true* meaning? For in its **yet-to-be** rapidly-closing spiritual reciprocity, the long-reaching outworking is one of menacing and *growing* portent for global Christendom.

Of course, it's all just fun for the children, isn't it? That is what Western society has determined as being suitable for Easter. Well, the end-cleansing – **already upon us and increasing in scope and scale** – will sweep that and every other kind of appalling distortion aside and away for all time; along with all those who cling to aberrant ideas which distort **The Truth**.

A dangerous aberration stemming from the Crucifixion of Jesus centres on the so-called 'Christian Cross of Salvation'. The *shape* of the Latin Cross produces the *form* of a "sword". As a 'belief-token' or symbol *ostensibly* declaring that by His death on the Cross **The Son of God** took away their sins and that of the world; this terrible and appalling *Christian distortion* of the execution of Christ means that the wrongly-revered Crucifix 'spiritually forms' a **"Sword of Judgement"** for all who wear, revere or display it!

If Christians, particularly, do not believe thus, yet still say they follow the Teachings of Jesus; then how do the two thousand million that make up global Christendom reconcile His warning to the world? In the truly strangest of ironies, He – **A Part of The Godhead** – was perversely accused of *blasphemy* by Caiaphas and others of the ruling Sanhedrin for *being* What He *actually* Was and Is: **The Son Of God**. Yet He was nonetheless executed.

Since an exponential factor can be readily observed in all events now, let us **restate** the answer of Jesus to His Disciples when asked what the end-time would be like. His reply is chilling. From Matthew 24:21-22:

> "...for there shall then be **wide-spread affliction**, such as has **not been known** since the beginning of the world **until now**, no, nor will **ever** be known again. And if those times were **not** cut short, **not a man would be saved**".

Centuries before Jesus came to Earth to admonish humankind to obey **The Law** if they wished to *live and return home*; Isaiah, 24:5-6, 'the great Prophet and Servant', had long warned so.

> "The 'Earth' also is defiled under the inhabitants thereof; because they have

> *transgressed* the Laws,
> *changed* the decrees,
> *broken* the everlasting covenant.
> Therefore has the curse devoured the 'Earth', and those that dwell therein *are desolate*:
> therefore the inhabitants of the 'Earth' are ***burned***[5] and ***few men left***."
>
> (Fenton both. All emphases mine.)

Now you, Christian believer, and perhaps even you, "Bible scholar"; but certainly all who live tremulously in piety in the belief that The Son of God, sent down to Earth by The Creator of all that is good to bring The Living Word to a base and evil humanity: Now that you *better-understand* the ***true*** horror and suffering of He Whom *you* profess to follow; where in His admonition or that of the great Prophet, Isaiah, do you find the sure salvation of two billion Christians? It is ***arrant nonsense***. It is, in truth, *a dangerous death-delusion.*

Do you honestly believe that The Son of God went willingly to an horrific death to save ***you*** from ***your*** personal sins? Do you really believe that the Perfect Justice of God is displayed there; that an innocent man should be put to death for ***the wrongdoing and evil of others***?

Such an injustice is not even accepted in earthly courts of law. If it were, imagine the outcry – from all of you especially. So why and how can human beings who proudly call themselves Christians accept a notion that such a thing would be acceptable to The Creator Himself: **He Who is Perfect Love, but also Perfect Justice?**

If you truly believe that such an aberrant tenet would be acceptable to The Almighty, then you must also logically accept the notion that the group of Roman soldiers who actually carried out His Crucifixion *were blessed for all time*, and would follow Jesus into Paradise. If His death was a necessary sacrifice blessed by God, then that is the only logical conclusion for you to draw. If you do

---

[5] The term, 'burned' – describing a recurring theme of End-time destruction that numerous Bible 'scholars' have puzzled over for many centuries – *in this case* does not refer to fire in the ordinary sense. The Scripture pointedly states that only the 'inhabitants' of the Earth are 'burned', *not* the Earth itself. A full and detailed explanation can be read in Chapter 12: **The Two Sons Of God**: Sub; **Destruction by "Fire"**.

not believe that they were so blessed in that way, then your whole absurd Christian ethos centred round "His necessary sacrifice" fails utterly.

Notwithstanding the pure truth of that statement, if you yet *still seriously believe such a thing*, then do not hide behind 2,000 years of earth-time to shield you from that most insidiously-evil event. Instead, have the inner courage to put yourselves in the place of the small group of executioners at His Crucifixion and actively take part in the murder of The One whom you profess to believe in; be part of that Roman squad on that terrible day – **Black Friday.**

Help to lay the flayed and bleeding body of The Son of God on that rough and splintered Cross of Death. Feel His blood splashing on your skin – for there are no niceties such as rubber gloves to protect your delicate hands. Next, take up the hammer and spikes and drive them through His flesh. Ensure, however, that you do it correctly so that the weight of His body will not tear ***His once-healing hands*** away from the spike when that dark, death-cross is raised.

But as you drive home those spikes, look into His eyes and say to Him:

> *"I nail you to this cross because in this deed I prove my great Christian love for you since you came to die for me and my sins. Even though you have already suffered so much already, I offer you yet more pain and torture. I know you will understand and will one day welcome me into your Kingdom because I have now proved my faith to you by helping you to die on this cross."*

How foolish a belief. How utterly absurd.

Such a belief is tantamount to idolatry of the worst kind, but self-idolatry – of human beings – and not of reverence and worship of **The Most High** or of He Who was and is a Part out of **Him**.

JESUS: The SON OF GOD; designated as both **The Word Of God** and **The Love Of God**; that is who you symbolically murder each time you tremulously "...thank 'Him' for dying for *your* sins".

Even the words of **The Bible** – that *especial* Work which you hold up to the world as **The Living Word Of God** – condemns that terrible act in no uncertain terms. Peter, the Apostle designated by Jesus as "the rock" upon which His Teachings could be built, "tells it like it is". After receiving "Power from On High" at Pentecost and speaking in the various dialects of the region, the crowd that had gathered accused the Apostles of being drunk. Peter countered with the following:

> "Men of Israel! Listen to these statements: Jesus the Nazarene, a Man pointed out as from God by powers, and wonders, and signs, which God did through Him amongst you, as you yourselves know; *having betrayed*, you *murdered Him by crucifixion* through *lawless hands*..."
>
> (Acts 2:22-23, Fenton.
All emphases mine.)

What happened next? The words are certainly clear enough; *betrayed*, *murdered*, through *lawless* hands! Was there great cheering that they were *saved* by His "death on the Cross"? That is certainly the *seemingly* unbreakable belief amongst latter-day Christians. Yet, what do we later read as "The Effect of the Discourse" of Peter in Acts 2:37? The exchange between him and the gathered crowd shows that at least some there had recognised the wrong in *that* Crucifixion.

> Now on hearing it, they were *stung to the heart*, and said to Peter and the rest of the apostles, "Men, brothers, *what shall we do?*"
> But Peter said to them: "*Change your minds...*"

Quite clearly, if they *had* been pleased and *at peace* with 'the Crucifixion', they would not have replied in that way. The recognition for at least *some* there had finally hit home, for they were "...stung to the heart...", did not know what to do, and were now *afraid*.

When the horrific realisation finally sinks in that such beliefs were so illogical and wrong that they border on a kind of *religious insanity*, it will be among you Christians, primarily, that a very large measure of the "great wailing and gnashing of teeth" will occur. What will you say then?

In conclusion, let us quietly reflect upon a singularly poignant "poem" about the life of *this* Son, **Jesus**; perhaps the greatest radical to have ever set physical foot on the earth. As we unequivocally state, however, will not do so again, for **He is The One** who *returned* to **The Father**. Yet Whose very Words – from out of **Divinity** Itself – many were "called" to disseminate amongst the world's people. Illustrated in the following poem is an unknown author's salute and great love for Jesus and His Highest and most Noble form of **Radicalism – Perfect Love!**

Radically noble in the sense that He was ***prepared to accept death on that Cross* if that was the only way by which He could anchor the Truth of His Teaching in the consciousness of humankind for all time.** He, as **The Word and Love of God** and surely the most innocent of all – even though suffering the grossest indignities until finally succumbing to the brutal act of murder perpetrated against Him – *yet still offered up the greatest prayer of intercession ever for the senseless blind who committed that atrocity.*

His noble prayer thus stands as an indictment against those who murdered Him then, *and against those today* who still very wrongly believe that His painful and brutal death on His "Cross of Crucifixion" could somehow be sanctified and Divinely Blessed by An Almighty God as some kind of loving act of propitiatory sacrifice to cleanse the evil and sin of an undeserving humanity.

The very words of the prayer itself stand in rightful accusation against such an evil distortion of the great and incomprehensible Love of The Creator.

"Father forgive them, for they <u>know</u> <u>*not*</u> <u>what</u> they do!"

Thus, ***they did the <u>wrong</u> thing***.

Through an anonymous yet spiritually-insightful poet, the pure and ennobled form of the Christ's Mission rings down through the centuries and is baptised in its own unequivocal message of **sublime radiance and great Spiritual Power!**

One Solitary Life

Here is a man
who was born of Jewish parents
the child of a peasant woman...
He never wrote a book.
He never held an office.
He never owned a home.
He never had a family.
He never went to college.
He never put foot
inside a big city.
He never travelled two hundred
miles from the place
where He was born.

He never did one of the things
that usually accompany greatness.
He had no credentials but Himself...
While still a young man
the tide of popular opinion
turned against Him.
His friends ran away.
One of them denied Him...
He was nailed to a cross
between two thieves.

His executioners gambled for
the only piece of property
he had on earth... His coat.
When He was dead
He was taken down;
and laid in a borrowed grave
through the pity of a friend.

Nineteen wide centuries
have come and gone
and He is the centrepiece
of the human race and the leader of
the column of progress.
I am far within the mark
when I say that all the armies

that ever marched,
and all the navies
that were ever built...
have not affected the life of man
upon earth
as powerfully as has that

One Solitary Life!

Chapter 12

The Two Sons of God!

An unusual Chapter heading. Perhaps even blasphemous. Should we designate it a question, or a statement? Standard Christian beliefs generally accept an approaching end-time of great tribulation and destruction and the concomitant need for there to be the return of Jesus to earth to, *ostensibly,* fulfil the revelatory prophecies from Biblical Scripture. Even Time magazine, Issue 1 July, 2002, devoted their lead story to this growing belief. Yet the contention that there *is* Another *other than* Jesus will, in all probability, be dismissed as ludicrous and impossible by many. However, let us keep an open mind and follow this key thread to its particular conclusion too.

In a previous Chapter, we traced the line of Religious Prophets and Truth-Bringers via the teachings they brought to the earth at their particular time. We further intimated that Jesus, The Son of God, brought a *more complete* knowledge of the Truth than had yet been given to mankind up to that point. In fact He brought the whole of the Truth **living within Him**, but humankind were too spiritually closed to fully recognise His Sacred Mission to be able to accept and absorb all that He brought. In the last Chapter we examined the strong beliefs still pertaining to Him that He was born of a woman on earth but without an earthly father, and the notion that He rose from His death in His physical body and ascended to His Origin in it.

The time-line of the great Prophets and Truth-Bringers shows an almost evolutionary spiritual-knowledge path of Truth up to the present. And that is correct in its basic outline. The premise that this particular Chapter postulates absolutely unequivocally, however, is that Jesus stands at the apex of Truth, since He Himself is a Part of It. **And He, as the Part thereof designated as "The Love of God", therefore forever stands as One of The Two Sons of God.** If we did not state that reality as a living conviction in these pages, this book would, of itself, be blasphemous, and would thus serve *to corrupt and distort the truth of The Living Word Itself*. That we will not do since the purpose of this work is to offer signposts to the *whole* of the Truth.

The danger of denying that which is of The Living Truth Itself lies in the outworking of The Laws of Creation on those who so deny. That outworking rests completely and lawfully in The Law: "What a man sows, that shall he reap." Since we aver that there are actually Two Sons of God, a denial of this fact will ultimately visit its particular "reaping" too. Therefore, as we have designated Jesus as a Son of God and this Chapter Heading reads "The Two Sons of God", Who, then, is the Other?

As background to our bold claim, in a very compressed journey in time, we need to once more look at the path, and impact on both the civilised and the new worlds, of Judaeo-Christian beliefs after the time of Christ. The rise and fall of the many civilisations of the "Ancient World", particularly those written about in the Old Testament, ultimately prepared the stage for the Teaching of Jesus to begin its journey out into the world. Initially across, and out to the borders of, the Roman Empire, but thence to its future dissemination to the wider world through the later European Empires. The general religious foundation of the latter is basically derived from the Judaeo-Christian ethos as outlined in The Bible. However, its entry into the European psyche to the present time saw it undergo many upheavals resulting in huge differences of meaning from the original simple and pure teaching of Its Bringer – Jesus.

The religious authorities were not content to simply accept the clear truth He brought but chose, instead, to erect huge monasteries and "schools of learning", behind which doors they could dissect the original teachings. As a result of this long process of analysis and debate, the original clear meanings underwent change, some subtle, some far more radical. What has finally emerged today from that fermenting crucible of *intellectual religiosity* differs vastly from the *spiritual original* given by Jesus. Not only that, but for a time was also removed from the ordinary people. Thus, what little the masses were permitted to have, even that was used to enforce and maintain religious power over them by the few.

As we have reinforced often in this work, the simple and sorry fact is that the Light constantly strove to give the great Truths to men. Men, however, unfortunately subverted them all to just religions, and/or splintered offshoots of. Religions, for the most part, of earthly power, wealth and *religious* subjugation.

This dark volition can be readily traced through the mad, religious fervour of the Dark Ages and the equally insane Inquisition. The wealth and excesses of the Papacy seeded the wonderfully enlightened protestations of the great spiritual scholar Martin Luther who, in 1520, launched the Protestant Reformation. His opposition to the, then, entrenched religious view found a kindred soul in King Henry VIII. By the Act of Supremacy in 1536, Henry effectively formed a new English Church and broke with Rome.

Later, via exploration and colonisation, the gradual expansion and consolidation of the European Maritime Nations to the New Worlds was effected. Thus along with the export of European ideas (and some of their criminals) went the zealous missionaries and their Christian religion in its more or less final, distilled form.

Whilst that was obviously an expansion of the European Empires, it was not at the same time an expansion of Spiritual Truth. As already noted, what was exported to the new lands was far less spiritual than the original pure Teaching. The religious madness of the Dark Ages and the Inquisition had ensured that certain ideas of religious rigidity, formulated as dogma during those years of bigotry and cruel torture, were henceforth retained as inviolable tenets of the new religious thinking. That is what arrived in the New World to challenge and then, for the most part, subjugate the peoples to whom it was usually forcibly introduced.

However, even though the "religion" had lost much of the essence of actual Spiritual Truth it was at least, in many ways, far more enlightened than anything some of the Indigenous peoples of the New World possessed. Thus, in accordance with their "Divine Mandate" as they believed it to be – and paradoxically probably should have been - European explorers and Missionaries carried *their* version of The Word, once delivered spiritually pristine from out of the mouth of Its Bringer, to many parts of the earth.

What arrived to those far-off lands was therefore not truly a correct interpretation of the Teachings of The Bible and of Jesus. Religious scholars in great Universities and Theological Colleges today still argue and debate many points of religious disputation. Uncertain theoretical or theological argument should have no place in the dissemination of The Living Word given to humankind from One Whose Origin hailed from the very Source of that Word Itself!

For any such wrong interpretations must logically be accepted as a dangerous transgression against The Living Laws of God Himself.

A radical statement concerning two Sons of God, then, would surely be described as too blasphemous to even consider, given that no past or present-day clergy or religious authority has publicly mooted this "possibility". Yet, such radical assertions cannot be made without some relevant form of Biblical or Scriptural foundation to begin with. For that is the standard measure by which to flesh out such a premise, at least in the world of Christian religion. In *this* book, however, *other avenues – of exceptional knowledge and clear spiritual insight – immeasurably assist us in our premise.*

Despite the clearly contentious nature of what we are saying, we nevertheless urge well-meaning Christians and Biblical scholars to be sufficiently open-minded to at least *objectively* examine this matter. We categorically state, however, that we do not, in any shape or form, seek approbation or approval from any said religious or Christian authority or church anywhere to state what we assert in this Chapter – or indeed anywhere else in this book. For, in reality, the debates that still rage among the "religious-learned" are simply the final end-excrescence of that process that began so many centuries ago, even pre-dating the church-theology of Medieval Europe.

The relative times differ vastly of course in that today we possess far greater scientific knowledge about much more of the world. Unlike the Dark Ages when the church held absolute power, a non-partisan Police Force and Judiciary today protect citizens who might wish to challenge the religious status-quo. To have asserted then what we assert here now would surely have resulted in charges of heresy and blasphemy, and thus a death sentence. One invariably preceded by cruel torture to try to force a recant, no doubt.

As with most questions, however, the obvious reality is that *either a thing is so, or it is not!* Particular historical times and events can never alter *that* particular truth. So is it with our radical assertion. Either there are two Sons of God as we unequivocally state, or there is only one – Jesus. If, as we assert, there are two, then that clearly poses huge and fundamental questions for all Christians – and not least for the time that is referred to as the "Final Tribulation". Therefore let us now consult The Bible and the Scriptures and reveal the relevant passages. And from those let us intuitively strive to recognise and understand the far-reaching ramifications of such a claim.

The starting point of The Bible is, of course, The Book of Genesis, and it would probably be fair to say that the general Christian belief about it would aver that Genesis states, "seemingly", that *prior* to the Creation event there was only ONE GOD. A God Who has existed from eternity, the darkness of a formless void, and nothing else. No life save that of The Creator.

Yet John, the beloved of Jesus, makes a fundamentally more profound statement in the very first verse of his Book. We know from New Testament Scripture that John and the other Disciples – who all lived literally cheek-by-jowl with Jesus – were given the greatest amount of Knowledge that men had yet received about Creation, life and The Law. Since their Teacher **was The Son of God Himself**, we should surely expect that certain passages written by at least some of the Disciples *might just carry within them* far-reaching insights of tremendous spiritual import for *all* of humankind.

For the world of Christianity in this case, however, spiritual import of a potentially explosive nature. Thus we read in John, the beloved of Jesus, Chapter 1 verses 1-3:

> "The **WORD** existed **in the beginning**, and the **WORD** was *with* God and the **WORD** *was* God.
> *He* was present *with* God at the beginning.
> **All** came into existence by means of *Him*; and nothing came into existence apart from *Him*."

(Fenton, Emphases mine.)

If we analyse those passages with an open, objective and questing spirit and mind, we immediately see that there was not just God and the empty void, as Genesis might "appear" to indicate. There was Another – *with* God! The key question must surely then be: Who was *"He Who was present with God...?"* Was **He** Jesus, as might be currently accepted? Or was **He** the Other, to **Whom** we refer?

A vital point we need to grasp is that Whomever it was that John referred to was not simply *present With* God, but *present With God* at the beginning. Moreover, the use of the personal pronoun **He** is a clear pointer as to *Who this particular One actually is*. As a second vital pointer to the answer, the Scripture also clearly states that **the Word that was with God was the "He Who was present at the beginning". And that all came into existence by means of Him!**

To reiterate the key point of that particular Scripture once more: *He* Who was *with* God was *also* the *Word of* God too, and that *all* came into existence by means of *Him!* Surely simple enough to understand. Or are we trying to find something there that does not exist? A mystery perhaps? No! Not any kind of mystery at all because The Bible identifies **Who** that **"Other"** actually **Is**. Moreover the identity of **Him** offers clear answers to other points of religious disputation.

To further flesh out our premise that He "Who was with God at the beginning" was the same He Who created "all things", all we need do is very briefly go to Verse 2 of Chapter 1 in Genesis. We will quote from our three Bibles of reference:

> "And the earth was without form, and void; and darkness was upon the face of the deep. And the *spirit* of God moved upon the face of the waters."
>
> (King James.)
>
> "Now the earth was a formless void. There was darkness over the deep, and God's *spirit* hovered over the water."
>
> (The Jerusalem Bible.)
>
> "But the Earth was unorganised and empty; and darkness covered its convulsed surface; while the **breath** of GOD rocked the surface of its waters."
>
> (Fenton.)

The unequivocal reference to a **"Creative Spirit"** in all three differently-sourced Scriptures clearly show that it was not God Himself Who Created the "heavens and the earth", but **He Who was with Him!** The very fact that it is so written shows that the ancient writers of the original texts understood this. Of course, we should readily understand that Creation itself nevertheless proceeded only *according* to **God's Design**. Under **God's Power and Authority**, but **through He** Who was *with Him* as a **Part of Him**!

A note of caution should be sounded here. We should not attempt to interpret the *complete Creation-process* as involving just the *earth* and its immediate, *material* interstellar environs. A clearly stupendous happening of colossal and *humanly-incomprehensible magnitude* would thereby be brought down to a superficial level of human-earthly non-understanding. Fenton's sub-heading, discussed earlier, provides the vital spiritual insight, vis-a vis: "The **First Creation** of the Universe by God..." For the word "earth" does not refer solely to our earthly home but is symbolic of a *far larger Spiritual Reality.*

Now, just as the same basic reference to the **Other With God** can be read in the King James version so, too, can the solution also be found in both our main Bibles of reference and, indeed, in virtually all the different Bibles. The King James version notates the same Scripture thus:

> "In the beginning was the **Word**, and the **Word** was *with* God, and the **Word was God.**
> The *same* was in the beginning *with* God.
> All things were made by *him*; and without *him* was not anything made that was made."

(John 1:1-3, Italics mine.)

The Jerusalem Bible (1985 edition) states it similarly:

> "In the beginning was the **Word**
> the **Word** was *with* **God**
> and the **Word was God**
> *He* was *with* **God** in the beginning.
> Through *Him* all things came into being
> and not one thing came into being except through *Him*."

(Emphasis mine.)

In order to more completely clarify this issue we should very carefully note that whilst **He** of the **Word** was **with God**, both **He** *and* the **Word** were *also* **God**. Yet whilst **He** is the **Word**, and the **Word** is **God**, there is nevertheless a clear *separation* between **He** Who brought all things into being *through* the **Word** - and **God** out of Whom came the **Word!** Surely simple enough to understand...!

If we now track to certain other Bible passages where **Jesus** is similarly referred to as the **Word**, then apparent discrepancies do "appear" to develop. However, the general belief that the **Other with God** was **Jesus** as the **only Son** fails to take into account the meaning of the following references and inferences:

> "And the Word was made flesh and dwelt among us, (and we beheld his glory, the glory as of the *only **begotten*** of the Father) full of grace and truth."

(John 1:14, King James, Emphases mine.)

The word *begotten* in this particular Scripture provides the vital clue. For one who is regarded as *begotten* cannot logically be The One who was *present **from the beginning*** – as existing from *eternity*. The Scripture therefore stands spiritually correct. Jesus was the *only begotten* Son. Not just the only *"begotten"* Son, however, but also The Word too. ***That Part of The Word of God*** that *had* to incarnate 2,000 years ago, if humankind was not to fall utterly and irretrievably.

Now, what of this other "Son of God"? We know that the Christian Churches – who should surely know their Bible after all – have always spoken of only One Son of God, Jesus! And that He, as The Living Word also, therefore brought the complete and final Truth to mankind. He, as a Part of The Living Truth Itself, certainly *brought "the whole"* **within Himself**. Due to humankind's spiritual immaturity at the time, however, that consequential inability to receive the Truth fully from Him meant that the writings of those who were closest to Him – His Disciples – are incomplete with regard to the whole that He brought ***living*** within Himself. The obvious ramification that such an assertion must presume is that The Bible, therefore, *does not contain the whole*.

The Apostle Paul provides the relevant insight in his letter to the Corinthians. We should carefully note that the words of Paul were written *after* the Crucifixion, and *after* the Outpouring which, according to some religious "scholars", *was* the watershed event that would "lead" them [the Disciples] into all-Truth". Thus the time when Jesus would send The Holy Spirit. Notwithstanding the obvious spiritual power that must have been experienced by those present, Paul states very clearly:

> "For we know *in part*, and we prophesy *in part*. But when that *which is perfect is come*, then that which is *in part* shall be *done away*."

> (1 Corinthians 13:9-10, King James.)

Fenton translates the same passages thus:

> "For we know *imperfectly*, and we teach with *imperfection*; but when the *perfect* arrives, the *imperfect* will *become useless*."

And The Jerusalem Bible says:

"For our *knowledge* is *imperfect,* and our prophesying is *imperfect*; but once *perfection* comes, all *imperfect* things will *disappear*."

(All emphases mine)

Simple logic must lead us to the obvious conclusion that Paul could not have been referring to Jesus Himself as "the ***part***" or the ***imperfect,*** for He, being Who He was, was ***complete*** in **Knowledge** and **Perfection**. In all of Paul's ministry, nothing to the contrary was ever so stated by him. In any case, it would be ludicrous to try to argue that Jesus, as The Son of God, or His teachings, could be ***done away*** with, ***become useless***, or ***disappear***. Paul certainly knew that, as did the Disciples. For Jesus Himself stated in admonishing warning that:

"The heaven and the earth may fade away; [*disappear*], but My Declarations [the Truth] will never pass away."

(Matthew 24:35 Fenton.)

Theologians and Bible scholars could be forgiven for believing that the Outpouring was, after all, the event where The Holy Spirit gave the *"**complete and perfect**"*, the All-Truth, to the Disciples. For the strength of the happening was such that they all spoke in tongues and became seeing. Yet, a simple analysis of it all points to a very different conclusion. A conclusion that Paul understood quite clearly. Therefore, if Jesus was not "the ***part***," – and He surely was not the ***imperfect*** – then Who or what was Paul referring to? Who would bring the Perfect, and when?

12.1 The Disciples' Confusion

The answer lies in the following Scriptures given by ***Jesus*** in reply to questions from His Disciples regarding the end-time. The singular, strong aspect here is the clear statement that **The One to come** would instruct **in all the Truth**, meaning that Jesus had not done so. In other words, what He was *able to give for that particular time* in human spiritual evolution and have it at least basically understood, was just a ***part*** of the whole, ***not*** the ***complete*** thing.

This is so stated in John 16:12, *"I have still much more to tell you; but you are not able to bear it."* In other words it would have been too much for them to understand or assimilate, even though they were instructed to a far greater level of knowledge than probably any other human beings to that time.

Therefore another, **The Other**, would have to come and bring all the truth.

> "...because if **I** do not depart, the Helper will certainly not come to you; but when **I** depart, **I** will send *Him* to you. *He*, on *His* coming, will bring conviction to the world..."

And also,

> "When, however, the Spirit of Truth *Himself* comes, *He* will instruct you *in all the truth*... *He Himself* will honour Me..."

> (John 16:7-8,13-14, Fenton. Emphases mine.)

The clear inference in all of these Scriptures is that the use of the personal pronoun, **He**, denotes an *actual* person in the same way that **Jesus** was an *actual person!* And, moreover, would be **The One** Whom *Jesus would send*, but only *after His* (Jesus's) *Own departure*.

The "Second Coming of Jesus" has been "accepted" as a non-negotiable event for centuries now by virtually all Christian groups. The ostensible sureness of that happening as espoused by them, however, is clearly thrown into question if a brutally objective assessment of particular Scriptural statements is embarked upon. For *if* **The Other** *is* to come, and that event becomes the ultimate reality and Christianity, or humankind in general, ignore it and embrace instead a totally different, and therefore wrong, concept, the end result will surely not then be as Christians might hope or imagine.

Whilst we may accept that Jesus said He would "return", He did not say where or how, or *precisely* why. In other words, in what "form" would such a "return" occur and for what purpose, given that **The Other** – the actual **Bringer of the All-Truth – would be here on earth with that All-Truth?** Another mystery perhaps? Not with the complete knowledge contained within that All-Truth. What we may deduce, therefore, is that contained within the **All-Truth** which Jesus Himself stated would be brought to the earth by **The Other**, would be revealed not only the *how* of Jesus's "return", but also the *why!* If true, it would seem that we have some kind of dual working here, and for the obvious spiritual benefit of mankind.[1]

If we now look to The Revelation, in Chapter 1, Verses 4 and 5, we should singularly note, in cool objectivity, a further strong statement of differentiation between the Two.

> "Blessing and peace to you from **the One** Who Is, Who Was **and Who comes**; and from the seven Spirits which are before **His throne; and** from Jesus Christ."
>
> (Fenton.)
>
> "Grace to you and peace, from **Him** who is and who was and **who is to come**; and from the seven Spirits who are before **His throne; and** from Jesus Christ,..."
>
> (New American Standard Bible. Emphases mine.)

It is patently clear from the above Scriptures that there is more than just one **"One"**! Moreover, the strongly denoted conjunction *"and"* draws a clear line of demarcation between Jesus *and* the **Other** – "Who Is, Who Was **and Who comes**"! We should further note that the one "Who is, Who Was and **Who Comes**", is also the **Alpha and the Omega**, the **Word of God Who exists** – the **All-ruler**! The **One Who comes** is also **enthroned**, and so He is *not* GOD The Creator Himself, even though He is a Part out of Him![2]

His entry onto the earth with the complete and perfect whole of the All-Truth would thus ultimately fulfil the prophecies of Jesus and statements of Paul in that it would render any accumulated knowledge and belief, past and present, individual and collective, religious and scientific – *that did not perfectly accord with it* – superfluous and therefore useless. That is exactly the *"in part"* that shall be *"done away"*; and the *"imperfect"* that

---

[1] The reader might be surprised to learn that a dual working *is precisely stated* in The Revelation. That particular Scripture, along with others of revelatory insight, is quoted further on in this Chapter.

[2] **Note**: Jesus in the presence of the **One enthroned** *could* be interpreted as Jesus in the immediate presence of God – Who would naturally be Enthroned. Clearly, however, the One Who is enthroned here, Who is *also the One Who Comes*, cannot possibly be God, the One Whom **"no man hath seen at any time"**. The fact that the blessed recipient of this vision *could behold* The One upon the Throne Who is to Come *automatically tells us* that He is not The Creator but the Part out of Him, Who is enthroned above all Creation as His Living Creative Spirit!

will *"become useless"*. It is when "all *imperfect things* will *disappear"*.

Thus it is actually for *this present era of humanity* with its concomitant spiritual and technological development that the *whole*, the *complete*, the *perfect,* was intended for. And **The One Who Comes** is **The One Who** would bring it. The same **Who**, as **The Spirit of Truth**, Jesus was to send. Moreover, the All-Truth that He would bring would speak of Jesus, as we have previously stated. Thus: **"He Himself will honour Me!"**

The two thousand years since the time of Christ have permitted us the luxury of greater understanding and awareness of the world around us than the people in His time could ever have had. Because of the greater level of overall knowledge now taught as a matter of course through scientific disciplines, institutions of "higher" learning and in the general education systems today, the presupposition should therefore be that we are now also sufficiently *spiritually* equipped to recognise this complete whole when it arrives. And thus similarly recognise **The Bringer** of it. **The Spirit of Truth, The Holy Spirit, The One Who Comes, The Eternal Mediator – The Son of Man!**

Since it is *our present time* that is spoken of, the spiritual faculty within each one of us *should*, therefore, at least *intuitively* perceive that such an event is imminent – **or has possibly already occurred**. Yet, almost the whole of the Prophetic utterings of Jesus and the Prophets within the pages of The Bible clearly show that the majority of mankind **will miss the moment**, will **not be awake at the time**.

If we do *not recognise* in time, if we miss that moment, if we simply refuse to accept – *even if it should pass before us* – what happens then? If we stubbornly cling to what we presently believe out of fear of letting go, what will that mean for the one who has missed it, or for the one who is asleep? In turn, what will it mean for global humanity, **if the majority of the world's people are blind to the happening?**

Then, as we intimate, **if** there has not been sufficient recognition and spiritual growth and change in humankind:

"...all the tribes of the earth shall mourn..."

(Matthew 24:30, Fenton.)

"...then too all the peoples of the earth will beat their breasts..."

(Matthew 24:30, New Jerusalem Bible.)

Matthew, Chapter 24, offers key pointers to this question of whether Jesus was or is to return. For example, from verses 3, 4 and 5:

> Afterwards, when He was resting upon the Mount of Olives, His disciples approached Him privately, asking, "Tell us when this will be; and what is the signal of Your presence, and the completion of this age."
>
> "Take care," said Jesus, in reply to them, "that none may deceive you. For many will come in My Name, asserting "I am the Messiah", and will lead many astray."

Verses 23 to 25 offer more indications.

> "Then if any should say to you, "Look! the Messiah is here," or "there" do not believe it. For false prophets will make their appearance; and will give out great and terrible omens, so as to mislead, if possible, even the chosen. However, *I have forewarned you*."

Here Jesus surely indicates that many would pretend to be Him and that the disciples would need to exercise the greatest possible degree of alertness and spiritual discernment when the time for the entry of The Son of Man onto the earth arrived. That logically means that The Son of Man, The Eternal Mediator, *would be here at the time when many false prophets would claim to be Jesus*. Historically, messianic claims are nothing new. It would be fair to say, however, that the 20th century probably saw the public emergence of perhaps more false messiahs than ever previously recorded. And, of course, many are alive and well in the 21st century too. So **where is He**?

Matthew gives the key sign which will herald **The One** Who comes. The following Scriptures not only add more Biblical weight to our premise, but they further illustrate the fact that Jesus does not refer to Himself in the first person but clearly infers that there really *is* Another.

> "...and then will appear the signal of the Son of Man in the sky. And **He** will send out **His** messengers - - - and they will collect all **His** chosen..."
>
> (Matthew 24:30-31, Fenton.)

Matthew offers another powerful statement from Jesus in support of the **Other One**. Again, He *does not* say **"I"** will do this or that, but that the **Other One – He, The Son of Man** – will fulfil it!

> "But when the Son of Man appears in **His** Majesty, and all **His** angels with **Him**, then **He** will take **His** seat upon the throne of **His** Majesty; and collect all nations before **Himself**."
>
> (Matthew 25:31, Fenton.)

In that particular Scripture, as in many others, we would at least expect Jesus to say, "**I** will collect all nations before **Me**" – if **He Himself** was to fulfil that role in the end-time. Yet that is not what **He** says, even though instructing and enlightening His Disciples as to what to expect then!

Further Scriptural quotes flesh out our premise. John 14:26:

> "...but the helper, the Holy Spirit, Whom the Father will send... **He** will teach you everything." Luke 18:8, "When the Son of Man comes, however, will **He** find this faith upon the earth?"

A further example is John 16:10:

> "...proved by my going to the Father and your seeing Me no more."
>
> (The Jerusalem Bible.)

And John 16:28:

> "I came from the Father and have come into the world, and now I leave the world to go to the Father."

Despite the fact that we *can* find passages where Jesus *apparently indicates* He will return, it is The Son of Man Who is to Come as The Eternal Mediator – as Jesus clearly states. For too many other statements by Him show clear reference to the **Other** Whom **He** is to send. If it was unequivocally and absolutely certain that Jesus was **The One Who Comes**, then we would surely expect that *all* statements, references, Scriptures, inferences etc., would carry the **"I"** and not the **"He"**, so clearly evident in so many places. If it was so absolute, as Christian thinking today states so emphatically, then surely the men who were closest to Him, even though not fully understanding all that He gave them, would have written so in every case. But that is not what we read, for that is not what they wrote. **For that is not what He told them in this case!**

The validity or otherwise of the Four Gospels has been the subject of much scrutiny and debate by scholars and theologians for centuries now. It is clear that the original writings or, perhaps more specifically, the original words given to the Disciples from Jesus underwent much change and editing through many translations, but also through the personal or religious bias of various scribes and translators. So we know that The Bible today is a heavily re-worked publication set in a more-or-less final form that powerful, tyrannical Church leaders, operating under the guise of spiritually-enlightened and infallible scholars, determined it should take. More recent researchers have seized upon this fact to call into question the actual validity of the Four Gospels of the Evangelists.

The co-authors of "The Holy Blood And The Holy Grail" make much of this to lend credence to their particular premise. It is surely impractical and illogical, however, to believe that the Disciples of Jesus would report everything that transpired during their association with Him in *exactly* the same way. They were chosen *not* because of their *sameness* but because of their *differences*. They would therefore likely report events in the short yet hugely eventful Ministry of Jesus in historically volatile times differently from each other. Certain events would no doubt obviously impact more decisively on some than on others. So the very fact that they apparently *did* report things slightly differently, with one or two clearly important events omitted from some Gospels, should not detract from the main and critical message ultimately contained in the Four Gospels. Rather it should be seen as a convincing insight into a much broader sweep of their overall connection and association with Jesus. Thus what they were tasked to pass on to the world.

Therefore, despite the obvious fact that the Evangelists were very different individuals from diverse educational backgrounds, The Books of the Four are *remarkably consistent* with regard **to what we are postulating here**. They no doubt made mistakes and perhaps did not report exactly all that transpired, and they clearly did not understand all that He told them, according to His own statements. However, one could assume that if there were *huge and irreconcilable* differences and not simply minor ones in terms of what they were told by Jesus – or believed they were told, or grossly misinterpreted what they were told or heard – then we would surely see evidence of that in their individual writings. That is clearly not the case, however. In fact the *consistency* with which references to **The Other**, obviously from Jesus Himself – ***for where else could they have possibly gotten it from*** – faithfully reproduced in the four Gospels by the four Evangelists clearly indicates a singularly important aspect of what Jesus was trying to impart. And the four, in essence, recorded exactly that.

So, a strong example of what we are explaining here can be found in Mark, Chapter 8, Verse 38.

> "If anyone, however, is ashamed of **Me** and of **My** teachings in this adulterous and wicked race, then will the Son of Man be ashamed of him, when ***He*** comes with the holy angels in the majesty of ***His*** Father."

(Fenton.)

In this example, Jesus does not say; "...when **I** come... in the majesty of **My** Father." as He surely would have if He was to fulfil that role in the future. Such statements reveal that Jesus knew He would *not* return to the earth as "The Eternal Mediator", and that He knew Who *would*. He therefore prepared the Disciples, and thus mankind through their writings, to expect such an event.

A singularly important aspect of His Coming would require it to be strongly linked to the appointed time and thus to any indicative signs that *might* precede this event. As previously stated, the key requirement must surely be the **CRUCIAL RECOGNITION** that such an event was imminent. *Or perhaps had already taken place*, and thereby been *completely missed by most*. The fact that such a scenario *might* ultimately turn out to be the reality for the greater majority of humankind is very clearly spelt out in the Scriptural warnings from Jesus – He Who would send **The Other Who Is to Come**.

The entry of The Eternal Mediator onto the earth surely poses huge and fundamental problems for all Christian groupings that accept the validity of the return of "someone". In the first place, who will He come to? Since only cool, clear objectivity offers the key to a logical interpretation of prophetic Scripture and not emotive, Christian religiosity, then we should understand that the All-ruler, the Alpha and the Omega, The Eternal Mediator, will not, and indeed cannot, ally Himself to any one group or denomination. That would be just plain silly!

From the Disciples of Jesus, from those who recorded His Words, we offer a few more of His admonitions. Warnings to be fully awake and alert, to not get so bogged down in everyday matters or pleasures that the spirit inside falls asleep and misses the moment forever. Should this event not be recognised, that non-recognition will not stop the tribulatory effects that will be associated with it. **For**

His arrival heralds the judgement for the earth, for all its peoples and their religions and beliefs!

> "Keep guard, therefore, for you know not what hour your Lord may come."
>
> (Matthew 24:42, Fenton.)

> "On account of this, be ready! because it may be that the Son of Man will appear at a time you do not expect."
>
> (Matthew 24:44, Fenton.)

> "Be you also ready; for it may be that the Son of Man will come at an unexpected moment."
>
> (Luke 12:40, Fenton.)

> "You too must stand ready, because the Son of Man is coming at an hour you do not expect."
>
> (The same Scripture from The Jerusalem Bible.)

And in the parable of the ten thoughtless bridesmaids who were shut out of the wedding, Jesus admonishes and warns humankind to be alert and awake to this return.

> "Therefore keep awake; because you know neither the day nor the hour when the Son of Man will come."
>
> (Matthew 25:13)

Paul's contribution to this reality is well stated in 1st Thessalonians 5:1-2.

> "But about the times and the seasons, brethren, there is no need for writing to you: for yourselves know well enough that the day of the Lord comes like a thief at night."
>
> (Fenton.)

Luke, 21:34-36 [emphasis mine], gives a particularly strong warning about the crucial need to not miss the time or the moment:

> "But take care of yourselves, for fear your hearts should be loaded with debauchery, and drunkenness, **and business cares**, and that day come swiftly upon you like a snare; for thus it will come upon all dwelling upon the face of the earth. Watch, therefore, at every season, offering prayer; so that you may be prepared to escape all the coming calamities, and take your stand in the presence of the Son of Man."

The Jerusalem Bible notates the same passages thus:

> "Watch yourselves, or your hearts will be coarsened with debauchery and drunkenness and the cares of life, and that day will be sprung on you suddenly, like a trap. For it will come down on every living man on the face of the earth. Stay awake, praying at all times for the strength to survive all that is going to happen, and to stand with confidence before the Son of Man."

It is vitally important to understand why Jesus so strongly warned His Disciples to yet prepare for the entry of The Son of Man at the end of the times. Since He did not mean in His lifetime or even shortly thereafter (because we have had 2000 years of history since) how, then, could the Disciples watch and wait for such an event if they all followed the natural path of life into earthly death as they obviously all did around that time?

The answer lies in the knowledge of The Spiritual Laws of Creation explained earlier – namely The Law of Rebirth in this case. Thus the outworking of Immutable Law in concert with the spiritually lawful and inviolable processes that must occur with the First Death, and the subsequent paths that must be taken thereafter – to either life eternal, or to the Second Death.

The warning to them to watch and wait meant they should be alert and awake to the signs which would herald that arrival. His clear admonition to the Disciples of: "However, **I have forewarned you**", was to prepare them for a future end-time of great confusion. **For they would be on earth again around that time.** However, it was not just His Disciples to whom He addressed the warning. It was to all of humanity then and now – for this time – today! For this is the era of The Judgement for all! A primary statement given by Jesus to the Disciples on explanations about the end-times indicate this. From Luke 21:32:

> "Verily I say unto you, This generation *shall not pass away* till all be fulfilled."

> (King James.)

From Matthew 24:34-35:

> "I tell you indeed, that this generation *shall not pass away* until all these arrive. The heaven and the earth may fade away; but My declarations will never pass away."

> (Fenton.)

Thus the generation of that time, those responsible for His murder, would all have to be back on the earth to stand before the ***Living Truth*** of The Son of Man. Either to *pass into life* – ***if*** there had been sufficient "good works" for expiation of the deed since, or to *pass from life* – to pass away in the second death – if there had not. All generations before and since would similarly be required to face their own individual wrongs, whilst in the same period also experiencing the destruction of all the wrong that humankind had collectively produced – to also either *pass from life* or *ascend into life*.

And one more warning! From Matthew 24:37-39:

> "And as in the days of Noah, so will also be the appearance of the Son of Man. For as they were, in the days before the flood, eating and drinking, marrying and giving in marriage, until the day arrived for Noah to enter the ark, and ***they would not understand until the flood came and carried all away***."

(Fenton.)

This is that period. It *is* the time of that **fulfilment**.

> "And there will be signs in the sun, and moon, and stars; and upon the earth nations in despair, as when in terror of the roaring and raging sea; men expiring from fear, and apprehension of what is coming upon the world:..."

(Luke 21:25-26, Fenton.)

Continuing on from that very necessary explanation, let us learn more about this singularly momentous issue. For if the full import of it is truly recognised and really understood, that recognition and understanding could then open a door that would greatly assist us to *ascend into life*.

To that end it is essential to stress the fact that The Bible regularly notes *two* different *references* to *two* particular **"Names"** and *two* respective **"Titles"** in various places within its pages. The general assumption has been that both contrasting titles referred to the same **One** – Jesus! Yet, firstly, we have the two different "Titles" – **The Son of God *and* The Son of Man!** Secondly, we have the two different "Names" – **Jesus *and* Imanuel!** The Christian Churches, however, generally teach They are one and the same.

The Gospel of Luke offers a prime example of what we are saying. The message of the archangel Gabriel to Mary is very clear.

> "And listen: you shall conceive and give birth to a Son; and you shall give Him the name of **Jesus**."
>
> (Luke 1:31-32)

And verse 35 states:

> "...and therefore the holy result shall be called **"Son of God"**.

Conversely, Matthew's unfortunate mistake has bequeathed a legacy which has misled many successive generations to the present day. In Chapter 1 he writes that prior to the birth of Jesus, Joseph, knowing that he was not the father, was nevertheless directed by a messenger of the Lord to accept Mary as his wife. The Scripture states:

> "And she will give birth to a Son **and you shall name Him Jesus...**"
>
> (Fenton.)

Then, Matthew, perhaps out of his own beliefs and/or lack of sufficiently clear spiritual understanding immediately afterwards writes:

> "Now all this took place so that the statement of the Lord, as recorded by His prophet, might be fulfilled:
> BEHOLD, THE VIRGIN SHALL CONCEIVE,
> AND GIVE BIRTH TO A SON;
> AND THEY SHALL CALL HIS NAME **EMMANUEL**,
> which, when translated, means
> THE GOD AMONG US."

Joseph, however, *did not name the child Imanuel* but, *in accordance with the instructions of the "messenger of the Lord"*, named Him **Jesus**.

Therefore, what should be understood here is the fact that whereas *the messenger of the Lord* clearly prophesied **Jesus**, *Isaiah* prophesied **The Coming of Imanuel.** (Isaiah 7:14) Matthew has incorrectly attempted to make two into one, for the references relating to this in Chapter 1 of his Gospel are simply illogical.

Had he received a personal visit from a messenger from Above, he would surely have written so. In quoting Isaiah he clearly does not recognise his own mistake and neither have many since. He has, unfortunately, bequeathed a huge error to posterity because his use of the Scriptures here make no sense. They serve only to confuse and cloud a very vital issue.

12.2 "He" Who Is "Enthroned"!

If we now return to The Revelation in The Bible – that Book of which no word is to be altered - -and very carefully note the following references, we can readily, clearly and unequivocally see that there are, indeed, **Two!**

Chapters 4, 5, 6 and 7 notate this reality. In Revelation 4:2, John "...observed a throne in the heaven, and upon the throne an Occupant." We have already established that **The One Who Comes** is **Enthroned!**

Those in attendance "...give praise, honour and thanks, to the Occupant of the Throne, Who lives for ever and ever..."

(Revelation 4:9)

In Revelation 4:11, the very same state Who The Occupant is:

> "You, our Lord and our God, are worthy to receive the majesty, and the honour, and the might; for You have created all things; and for Your purpose they were and are created."

He is therefore **The One *with* God** in the beginning, ***through Whom*** all things *came into existence.*

John then saw a book "upon the right hand of the Occupant of the throne". It was written "inside and outside" and "sealed down with seven seals". Then a "strong angel" proclaimed "with a loud voice, 'Who is worthy to open the book, and to break its seals?' And no one in the heaven, or upon the earth, or under the earth, was able to open the book, nor yet to gaze upon it".

(Revelation 5:2-5)

John "wept much", because "no one was found worthy to open the book, or even to gaze at it". Then he reports, But one of the elders said to me, "Do not weep, see! the Lion out of the tribe of Judah, of the root of David, has succeeded in opening the book with its seven seals." John then saw, *"between the throne and the four Beings*, and in the *centre* of the elders, *a Lamb* placed, as having been sacrificed..."

(Revelation 5:6).

In this momentous revelation, we clearly have an *Occupant on a Throne* in the heaven *Who has lived for ever and ever, Who was with God and through Whom all things* were made. In close attendance are what we might perhaps term "the whole host of the heavens", Angels, Elders, and Beings. Now, however, *we also have the Lamb* Who is able to open this book. **Who, then, is the Lamb?** He is clearly *not* the Occupant of the Throne, for the Lamb is *between* the Throne and the four Beings. And the Occupant of the Throne is The One Who both lives for ever and ever and yet Who has created all things – "for His purpose!". **But He is not The Almighty GOD Himself! "For no man hath seen God at any time."** (Emphases mine)

Once again, the answer to Who He is that occupies the throne lies in the very first *Scripture* in this Chapter about the Two, vis-a vis:

"The **WORD** existed in the beginning, and the **WORD** was *with* God and the **WORD** was God.
He was present *with* God at the beginning.
All came into existence by means of *Him*; and nothing came into existence apart from *Him*."

The Occupant of the Throne is thus the *He Who was present with God from the beginning*. It is He, also, by *Whom everything* came into existence and, moreover, *is the One Who Comes*.

Because the issue of **The Two Sons** is so vital to a correct understanding of revelatory prophecy – and thus to the final fate of every individual on earth soon – let us formulate, very simply but precisely, the key question: *Who is the Lamb?*

Whilst the designation, Lamb, would be regarded, grammatically, as a "which" and not a "who", the sureness of the personal pronoun, He, in this case reveals that that description clearly refers to a person. Surely, then, the only logical conclusion to draw is that **the Lamb is He, Jesus.** For if we do *not* acknowledge that as the truth here, then we have a major problem with the following passages from The Revelation.

> "And He [the Lamb] came, and **took it** [the book] **from** the right hand of the Occupant of the throne..."
>
> (Revelation 5:7-8)

The very designation, *"from"*, is unequivocal in its brutally clear meaning!

Yet even with such clarity, there will yet be many who will refuse to "see", who will refuse to acknowledge the obvious truth of our assertions. Paradoxically, they may well use the very Book that we quote from to say it cannot be so. They *must* use this same Book, The Bible, for upon it are based all the many variations of Christian Church beliefs and interpretations. And ultimately, therefore, also their own "mandates" which have to individually say to the faithful of all the different, individual flocks: "only our interpretation can be correct". Of course, all will rise or fall on exactly the interpretation clung to. So, let us quote a few more Scriptural gems to further clarify the truth of what we are saying.

Now, just as the host praised the Occupant on the Throne as being worthy to receive the majesty, honour and might, so do they now offer the same to the Lamb.

> "Worthy is the sacrificed Lamb to receive the power, and wealth, and wisdom, and might, and honour, and majesty, and celebrity!"
>
> (Revelation 5:12)

Both have now been *honoured equally* – as *separate Individuals!* For the next verse very clearly illustrates this delineation between the Occupant of the Throne *and* the Lamb. The very words, themselves, so state it in the separative-conjunction – **"and"**!

> "To the Occupant of the throne *and* to the Lamb belong the fame, the honour, the majesty, and the might for ever and ever."
>
> (Revelation 5:13-14)

A far stronger message of warning about the truth that this Chapter contains can be read in Revelation 6:16-17. Here the same delineation, but a very firm reference to a *dual working at the end-time*, as we previously stated.

> "Fall upon us, and hide us from the Occupant of the throne, and from the displeasure of the Lamb; for the great day of *their anger* is come – and who is able to stand?"

What do we understand the word, *"their"*, to mean? Even to the youngest English language reader it would obviously mean what it says. It means more than one. This simple and short, everyday English word must surely be the single most important pointer to finally showing that there are, indeed, **Two Sons of God!** What else could possibly be needed?

If this crystal-clear Scripture is *not* proof enough for the doubters, then all that is left to finally force an awakening within their ranks will be the very *sign* of the Son of Man Himself. Just as we clearly understand the meaning of the word, *their*, I am sure we also understand the meaning of the word, *"anger"*. Associated with the previous key word, *their*, this powerful Scripture *should*, therefore, **be the one that finally awakens mankind**! For who are **They** angry at? There can only be one group of creatures who would deserve such **Divine Wrath**. That is mankind on earth! Who, indeed, can stand against <u>**their anger**</u>!

The spiritually-perceptive reader may now more readily discern the various connecting threads that link the subject matter within each individual Chapter to the overall premise as a whole, i.e. that there **will be** an Apocalyptic tribulation during which the Judgement of all that refuses to bow or believe is completed. We can thus connect directly to the assertions in the Chapter "The Seven Churches in Asia", and the warnings there to live correctly again, or have our "lampstand" removed. But there is more.

> "The Salvation is from our God,
>   Who sits upon the throne,
>   **And from** the Lamb."
>
> (Revelation 7:10)

As a final entry to this key issue, Revelation 7:14-17, offers the same truth. Here, John is addressed by one of the elders who asks him if he knows who the multitude are in "white robes". John did not know so asks who they are.

> "These are they", he proceeded, "who came out of great affliction, and ***they*** washed ***their*** robes, and made them white in the blood of the Lamb. Because of ***this*** they are before the throne of God, and day and night they serve

> Him in His sanctuary; and the **Occupant of the throne protects them**... because the Lamb having *ascended the midst of the throne* shall **shepherd them**..."

(Fenton, All emphases mine.)

This final reference to The Two in this Chapter from The Revelation is interesting for more than the irrefutable truth that there really are Two Sons of God. For in this particular example, we have a further clarification of very great import. Firstly, the ***Occupant of the throne*** – Who therefore sits on it – **protects** the multitude who have cleansed *their* robes (*their* spirit) and made them white (pure) *themselves*. Jesus has not done it through his *acceptance* of death on the cross. No! **They** have done it. They have achieved that state of grace by *living* His pure teachings. And have therefore *earned the right* to, *metaphorically*, "stand before the Throne" and be forever protected by its Occupant, Who is not God.

Jesus, on the other hand, Who *does **not*** occupy the Throne – because He has ***ascended the midst of the Throne*** and therefore stands on the same level as He on the Throne – nevertheless **shepherds** the throng. Again, a clear *dual* working, and one of equal majesty, power and governance.

Note In strong emphasis once more: Jesus in the presence of

the **One enthroned** *could* be interpreted as Jesus in the immediate presence of God – Who would naturally be Enthroned. Clearly, however, the One Who is enthroned here, Who is also **the One Who Comes**, cannot possibly be God, the One Whom "**no man hath seen at any time**". The fact that the blessed recipient of this vision *could behold* The One upon the Throne Who is to Come *automatically tells us* that He is not The Creator but the Part out of Him Who is enthroned above all Creation as His Living Creative Spirit!

Notwithstanding such a clear statement about ***their dual working***, the distinct demarcation between the **Two Sons of God** can be further defined by the fact that they possess **Two different Names** – **Jesus** and **Imanuel**. And They have **Two different Titles** – **Son of God** and **Son of Man**. Surely it is a simple matter to see They therefore have **Two different Tasks** also – for **Two different Purposes**. **The Son of God**, Jesus, designated as **The Love of God**, Who therefore works in Love, emphasised that He had not come to judge! (John 12:47)

The Son of Man as **The Will of God**, does, however. The Will, moreover, is the complete Will. **The Son of Man** is thus The Spirit of Truth, The Holy Spirit and the Justice of God Who brings the Judgement – a Judgement of Divine Wrath inherently imbued with the inseparable qualities of Perfect Justice and Perfect Love. *And therein lies **Their Dual Working** in the Judgement!*

Yet even though there is the individual working contained within those designated tasks, **Both** are nevertheless **in God the Father!** And **God the Father** is **in Both!** Quite simply and clearly, therefore, the **"TWO"**, and the **LORD of ALL**, comprise:

THE TRINITY – The **TRIUNE GOD!**

Taken all together, the explanations in this particular Chapter clearly point to a major error of interpretation from the Christian Churches and theologians historically. The analyses herein therefore clarify the truth and status of this "apparent" mystery and, moreover, offer clear meaning about the actual nature of The Trinity for the spiritually-perceptive seeker. Therefore the supposed mystery of The Trinity is actually not a mystery at all. Neither is it meant to be since we are enjoined by Law and Divine Directive to *seek* – and thus *find*!

12.3 Destruction by "Fire"

In this Chapter we have endeavoured to use mainly **The Bible** as the key source for our revelations. We have also ventured into other areas to cull relevant and complementary knowledge to enhance our stated premise. In the closing stages of the Work it is timely to look at one especially vital aspect of **The Law**. For this *revelation* we will marry, from **The Bible**, part of **2 Peter** with part of **"The Book of Esdras"** from The Apocrypha.

The Books of **The Apocrypha** are not *officially* regarded as having the same degree of importance as the Books of **The Bible**. Whilst still an 'addition' or 'Addendum' to the Catholic Bible, the 'Apocryphal' Books were removed from Protestant Bibles by the British and Foreign Bible Society [primarily the Anglican Church] in the 19th century. Despite the unfortunate relegation of **The Apocrypha** to almost anonymity for probably the greater mass of global Christendom by the Church hierarchy, that body of work should nonetheless be *recognised* as being *absolutely essential* for a far greater degree of elucidation around certain key questions **in The Bible** that, at present, have no logical answers from Christendom; **as in the case of the question we address now**.

The Apocrypha, in concert *with* **The Bible**, provides the answer to it, thus giving a comprehensive picture of the whole by filling a knowledge-gap not so far addressed adequately by Christian theology. However, precisely because The Apocrypha is *officially designated* as a *lesser* work by Christendom overall, quotes from Esdras may be deemed to not carry the same authority as those from The Bible. Yet the two Books of Esdras not only provide the very answer to Peter's perhaps cryptic prophecy, but in it is *the most* **powerful** and **relevant** *spiritual insight and* **revelation** *for this very time* – for the Earth and *all* its peoples.

The question of "Destruction by Fire", long mulled over theologically, has now also been assessed from the scientific standpoint. From the earth-science perspective – and perhaps to a large degree from the theological side with regard to an Apocalyptic scenario – *destruction by fire* for global humanity tends towards such things as intense and widespread volcanic activity, a meteor impact, extreme drought, and perhaps prolonged solar activity.

Yet the *real answer*, whilst simple and straightforward, is ultimately *far more profound* for we human beings of Planet Earth than any notion which might suggest catastrophic events as being the *primary* driver for *destruction by fire*, and humanity *thereby* being *physically* burned. Though, of course, with certain natural phenomena, that is not just possible but very likely for some. Moreover, even for *very many* when such phenomena finally gives vent to its *full power* at *its* time of ordination. Now, whilst that will one day be a problematic reality for humankind, the distilled meaning of *'destruction by fire'* here means something **very, very different**.

The Book of Daniel is often used to mathematically calculate significant dates in a time-line of major events which many Christians believe reveals 'the time of the end'. Ezra, in our view clearly an important "apocalyptic prophet" in the mould of Daniel, offers a *singularly vital key* to the most crucial aspect of that approaching time; what exactly it is that will constitute the actual "force" of destruction and cleansing, and Who will bring it. Or, perhaps, **Who It was that might already have brought it!** Since we have earlier clarified the identities of both Jesus and Imanuel, the exercise we undertake now is to add considerably more weight to the outworking of **Creation-Law** for a rapidly approaching time of great upheaval.

The Prophecies of Daniel *might* have some relevance – in terms of a viable time-frame – *if* an ***arrival*** is still to be ***expected***. However, if that has ***already taken place***, in exact accordance with the many quotes already offered in this Chapter such as: "You know not the hour your Lord may come" etc., then the mathematical analyses from Daniel are logically ***rendered irrelevant***. If, then, such a "return" *has occurred*, what we explain from 2 Peter and 2 Esdras equally logically fits that *possible* scenario.

Peter, towards the end of his life, offers advice to the growing numbers of Christians about what to expect at the end of the times. Fenton sub-titles Peter's discourse:

"The Irrevocable Word of God"

> "You should first recognise this, that during the latter times deceivers will come with deception, gratifying their own passions, and asking, "Where is the promise of His appearing? for since the forefathers went to sleep, everything continues the same from the beginning of the creation." For they willingly suffer to hide from them this reason, that by the intention of God the skies existed from of old, and the earth with water above and water below, arranged for the purpose of God, by means of which the then existing world perished, by the water having rushed down.
> But the *present earth and skies* are treasured up by His intention, '**reserved for fire**' at *a period of judgment and destruction of wicked men.*"

(2 Peter:3-7, Emphases mine.)

Peter's explanation of how and why the deluge at the time of Noah was possible on the scale intimated – of which there seems to be some scientific evidence – may offer some insight into understanding the "mechanics" of it. Obviously, a lot of water had to fall to achieve an inundation sufficiently large to destroy what was on *at least part of the Earth*. Equally obviously, the water had then to drain *somewhere* for the hills to reappear. It is not our intention to delve further here, but the reader may wish to contemplate on certain passages in Genesis that "seem" to complement Peter's explanation for the "deluge". As we have previously noted, the Disciples of Jesus received far more knowledge about more aspects of the world than any other men up to that time. The key point here now is Peter's statement:

> "...that the present earth and skies..." are "...**reserved for fire** *at a period of judgment and destruction of wicked men*".

The singular word **"fire"** provides the key to understanding what is not only to come, but what is *already occurring.*

What might we believe *fire* would mean in this case, however? Given that it will be a time of unimaginable desolation, we could perhaps envision a huge and fiery celestial object colliding with Earth. The Revelation does state that as an actual impending event in our probable 'near-future'. Or it could perhaps be an extremely large "coronal mass ejection" (CME) from the sun which reaches out and envelopes the Earth destroying [frying] all electrical and electronic components in everything on it; from power stations to aircraft to all computerised control systems affecting every single facet of our 'modern' world. [In 2011 NASA warned that increasing solar activity would peak sharply in 2012, with the possibility of exactly that kind of damage to global electronics that did not have the necessary shielding to protect the systems from the effects of the electro-magnetic blast/s from the sun. Modern electronics are not built to withstand such power-blasts, so will "fry" should NASA's prediction be correct.]

A massive CME that blasts the *whole Earth* would therefore effectively reduce all 'first-world' countries to 'third-world' status virtually *in an instant*, for it would cause *immediate* and *irreparable* damage to the computerised control systems that regulate every facet of our lives; even food production. The fact that all power stations would be 'knocked out' means that cities would simply cease to function – for many years. The inevitable result of such a scenario would be fear and panic, and thus anarchy.

So even though the word fire usually means flames, burning and heat, does it actually mean that here? From The Apocrypha, The Book of Esdras, Chapter 13, Verse 2, the prophet Ezra recounts a dream which is afterwards interpreted for him by the "Messenger of Light". The key to understanding the meaning of the "fire" that Peter alludes to – *and would no doubt have understood* – lies in the following relevant excerpts. Initially featuring the sea wherefrom a wind arose and stirred up the waves, Ezra's dream then showed the wind make something like the figure of a man emerge from the heart of the sea. That man then:

> "...flew with the clouds of heaven...", and wherever he turned his face to look, "...everything under his gaze trembled, and whenever his voice issued from his mouth...", all who heard it "...melted as wax melts when it feels the fire...".

After this Ezra beheld an "...innumerable multitude of men gathered together from the four winds of heaven..." to make war against the man who came up out of the sea. Ezra saw the "man" carve out for himself a great mountain and fly up onto it. But he was unable to see or recognise the region or place where it was. After that he saw that all who had gathered to fight him were "...much afraid, yet dared to fight". When the multitude rushed at him, "...he neither lifted his hand nor held a spear or weapon of war". But Ezra observed how he:

> "...sent forth from his mouth as it were *a stream of fire*, and from his lips *a flaming breath*, and from his tongue he shot forth *a storm of sparks*".

Ezra saw that all three were mingled together – "the stream of fire", "the flaming breath" and "the great storm". These fell on the attacking multitude and *burned them all up*. Nothing was left but the dust of ashes and the smell of smoke. After this Ezra saw the same "man" come down from the mountain and call to another multitude which was peaceable. In great fear Ezra awoke and besought an interpretation from the Most High. His petition was answered, and the key elements of the vision follow. The Messenger then spoke:

> "This is the interpretation of the vision. As for your seeing a man come up from out of the heart of the sea, *this is he whom the Most High has been keeping for many ages, who will himself deliver* **his creation**, and he will **direct those who are left**. And as for your seeing wind and fire and a storm coming out of his mouth, and as for his not holding a spear or weapon of war, yet destroying the onrushing multitude which came to destroy him, this is the interpretation."

The "interpreter" then tells Ezra that the time would come when:

> "...bewilderment of mind..." would come over those "...who dwell on the earth". And they would make war against

one another, "...city against city, place against place, people against people, and kingdom against kingdom". "And when these things come to pass *and the signs **occur** which I showed you before*, **then my Son will be revealed**, whom you saw as a man coming up from out of the sea."

The next segment from The Book of Esdras provides the link with 2 Peter. The aspects of ***primary significance*** in this particular analysis are emphasised either in italics, in bold, underlined, capitalised, or varying combinations of all.

"And when all the nations hear his voice, every man shall leave his own land and the warfare that they have against one another, and an innumerable multitude shall be gathered together, as you saw, desiring to come and conquer him
- - -
And he, my Son, ***will reprove*** the assembled nations for their ***ungodliness*** [symbolised by *the storm*], and will **reproach them to their face** with their ***evil thoughts*** and the ***torments*** with which they are to be ***tortured*** [symbolised by *the flames*], and will **destroy them without effort** by ***THE LAW***." [Symbolised <u>**by the fire.**</u>]

(Parenthetic additions and emphases mine.)

Here we have a clear pointer *linking* the warnings of **Peter** – thus from **The Bible** – through the clarified vision of **Ezra** – from **The Apocrypha** – to the outworking of **Creation-Law** on the affairs of mankind. Only *with* the essential contribution of the prophet, Ezra, can the *true spiritual meaning* of "**Destruction by Fire**" be answered logically. And *only* with the requisite *spiritual guidance* to *link* **The Bible** <u>*with*</u> **The Apocrypha** could we reveal that answer: An answer automatically mandated by the fact of the Perfection of **The Laws of Creation**, the explanations of which we are directed – thus graciously permitted – to offer in this and other Works of **Crystal Publishing**.

The crucial knowledge of **Creation-Law**,[3] deriving from and inherent within **Divinity Itself**, gives *back* to **The Bible** its proper place and status. The *terrible* and *inexcusable distortions* of the clear Truths in that especial Work – perversely clung to by blind millions – count strongly towards the impending *total collapse* of *all* facets of wrong *human* behaviour *and* endeavour. The

---

[3]See Chapter 3: The Spiritual Laws of Creation: *The Necessary Knowledge*; for detailed clarification.

associated destruction should be recognised as being produced by the *spiritually-lawful* **effect** *of the "fire"*; which is:

> "Whenever his voice issued from his mouth...", all who heard it "...*melted as wax melts when it feels the fire*..."

That is the key to understanding the effect of The Living Words of **The Law**! Whether written or spoken by **'The One'** – **The Son of Man** – Who brings 'the Complete': The **'Formed Word'** Proclaimed by **Him** is thus transformed into commensurate *real-time outworking* over the period of its ordained fulfilment in **The World of Matter**. And therewith is produced – under the aegis of **Inviolable Law** in Creation – the outworking of Peter's proclamatory ***"destruction by fire"*** upon our completely *aspiritual* global societies, cultures and religions. Quite obviously, therefore, very many of we – the *agglomerated* human race– will fully experience Peter's prophecy.[4]

Therefore, human works that comply *with* **The Law** will quite naturally prosper. Works that do not will suffer destruction. By this infallible measure we may recognise what is *true* to **The Law** and what is not. The **'fire'** of **The Law** thus unerringly produces the concomitant cleansing effect; [also **The Law**]. The powerful impact of *the storm, the flames* and *the fire* – which are all *already* strongly affecting mankind so detrimentally now – is solely the result of our intransigence, arrogance and stupidity in refusing to believe or accept **the one single and ultimate reality in the whole of Creation**. And that is:

That only THE LAW — <u>CREATION-LAW</u> — reigns Supreme!

There is nothing else! Everything in all of the Creations was formed from out of **The Living Law Itself: From out of The Will of GOD – IMANUEL!** It is **He** Who thus brings **The Living Law**, which is the **'*cleansing fire*'** spoken of in The Book of Esdras.

Therefore *what we even now experience* is nevertheless still just the beginnings of the storm, the flames and the fire – **The Law**. Is His arrival imminent? Or is He already here? Difficult questions

---

[4] An 'agglomeration'. 2; a confused or jumbled mass. [Kierkegaard; "It is not the truth that lies with the masses, but the **untruth**. The **crowd** is the **untruth**."]

for most, but crucial for all! The appearance of the Sign of The Son of Man "in the sky" is the key to the fulfilment of the last events for an intransigent humanity. Since His Sign "appears in the sky", we can expect that it will be a powerful one. One, therefore, that cannot be missed, even by the obtuse.

Though what will it *actually* herald? That He is about to "descend on clouds", that He is about to be born, or perhaps to be revealed? Or perhaps it will state that He really *did* "...come like a thief in the night...", that only **the few** were awake, and that the world had therefore **missed The Event**.

Because His Sign is connected with Him, it will be visible to all human spirits in this part of "the world" and not just to those living on Earth at the time. Therefore, both the living and the physically dead will know that the Sign, **clearly visible to all then**, is here!

12.4 The 'Rapture'? A Distortion of Bible Truth!

The expected return of Jesus by one very large, mainly American, group of Christians involves, for them, the interesting notion that they, and they alone as a group from all humankind, will be "saved" by being "raptured". The concept of "The Rapture" as applied in this case takes the form of an event or process more fully formulated from earlier ideas mooted by an evangelical preacher, John Nelson Darby, who arrived in the U.S. in 1862. His minister, Cyrus Scofield, expanded the evangelist's ideas in the prominent Scofield Reference Bible.

Drawn from the Apostle Paul's seeming assertion that believers could or would be "lifted up to Christ in heaven", the idea of being "raptured to heaven" must presuppose that it is in the physical body since it all happens in an instant. That at least seems to be the general conviction of believers. However, we have already correctly concluded that according to The Almighty's Perfect and thus Unchangeable Laws – which accord with Perfect, natural, Laws derived from the higher Spiritual paradigm – *human physical bodies cannot be suddenly transformed and/or whisked away to sit on clouds or something similar.*

Even The Son of God Himself could not circumvent The Perfect Laws that He came to fulfil: "I come not to overthrow the Laws..."

As you, the reader, now know, The Chapter, *Jesus! His Birth, Death and Resurrection*, details the crucial "pre-discovery information" about where His body actually lies. It is secured in *a special tomb under Jerusalem*. It is a crucified body, **but without the legs broken.**

We will once more note the prophecy about that key pointer:

> "The soldiers, therefore, came and broke the legs of the first, as well as of the other one crucified with Him; but when they came to Jesus, and seeing that He was already dead, *they did not break His legs*. And the eye-witness gives this evidence, and his evidence is truthful; and he himself knows that he speaks true, so that you may believe. For these events happened in order that the Scripture might be verified: *A BONE OF HIM SHALL NOT BE BROKEN.*"
>
> (John 19:32-37, Fenton's Capitalisation. Emphases mine.)

Do Christians really believe that the **non-material** and therefore **Eternal 'Realm'** of what is so loosely designated as 'heaven' is some kind of jaunt *'just up there'*? Jesus told Pilate that His Kingdom was *not* of *this* world. And to His Disciples that He would *return to* The Father and they would see Him *'no more'*. How can it be that many millions will accept an idea that is an absolute impossibility according to the Perfect Laws of He Whose teachings of Perfect Truth those same millions *profess* to believe in and follow?

Phenomenal sales of the "Left Behind" series which promote the "rapture" concept and which have apparently sold somewhere around 50 million copies, clearly point to at least that many believers. Yet the sage observation of key Scriptures of warning should be made by all who wish to be "raptured":

> "I tell you indeed that you shall not depart until all has been fulfilled," – "Not one farthing shall be remitted you until *you* have paid fully."

And for the authors who have made millions of dollars but in the process of growing rich *already led millions astray now*:

> **"What does it profit a man if he gains the whole world and loses his soul?"**

Should we designate the so-called "rapture" to be some kind of "Bible mystery"? After all, men prefer a mystery to Truth! No, it is not any kind of "Bible mystery" simply because the concept of "rapture", *as taught and believed by people in the Christian Church*, **is completely wrong**.

It is more an emotive concept ultimately derived from indulging human religious weaknesses. It does not exist and will not happen because the whole idea actually *opposes* all notions of necessarily **Perfect Laws** deriving from **The Almighty**. Disbelieving or dismissive Christians at this time of rapidly approaching "closures" will one day soon reel in shock and horror as the cold truth of these statements becomes brutally clear.

The rapid approach of the *end* of human foolishness, driven by increasing pressure from **The Light** Above, therefore means that all human concepts are exposed to the **Power** of that relentless *pressure*. In the case of the notion of 'The Rapture', its time of exposure and belief is perhaps at, or nearing, its peak. It has therefore gone through the necessary phase of revealing itself in its true nature; it has offered itself as a concept to those who have chosen it as truth; those choices have thus largely been made; and all that is left now is *its collapse at the appointed time*, **and therewith its demise.** There is therefore no further need to comment on what will almost certainly be:

The greatest non-event in human history!

12.5 THE PROCLAMATION!

The terribly wrong teaching of 'The Rapture' by the Christian Church pales into *insignificance* when compared with the *greatest distortion* of all; that there has only ever been *one* Son of GOD. The powerful outworking of **The Law** from ordained scriptural prophecy is perfectly proclaimed here in the Divine Warning:

"**Vengeance [THE LAW] is mine, I will repay.**"

The Law will thus visit its terrifying reciprocity on *all* who subscribe to this *appalling distortion* of **The Living Truth**!

Everyone wants from their God a soft, enervating, vacillating, personalised, emotionally-satisfying, earthly brand of constant and all-forgiving love. Few there are who *really understand* that **Justice** is an *absolute* accompaniment of **The Love** of **The Divine**! Distorting the Truth from Above sets all who so distort it *against* that very Truth, and thus *against* its **Source**:

THE ALMIGHTY!

The knowledge about **The Two Sons of GOD** is, therefore, *the most important of all* – for *all* humankind. This key Truth is not about being some kind of 'Christian truth', nor is it a point to be debated by so-called 'experts'. The religious scholars and leaders of *all* ethnic groups and cultures and *all* religions, no matter how derived, must face this Truth here, *now*, at this critical juncture in human history and evolution.

That evolution was never about the "human/chimp" split that occurred millions of years ago; that scientists have placed so much importance on. We have clearly refuted the totally incorrect *scientific obsession* surrounding that foolish belief in the Chapter: "The Origins of Man: Genesis and Science Agree!" So much wasted time and energy and research funding that would have been better spent examining subjects that could *really* benefit man.

The crucial recognition that we are not just a physical body solely is thus the key to understanding that the Earth is a place of "physical transition" only, and that our *actual* evolution was always meant to have been that of our *spiritual selves*, the *true* human being. However, just as primatologists, anthropologists and many other "...ologists" etc., have wasted valuable "spiritual-life" time pursuing something that was totally irrelevant for *real* human knowledge so, too, have the many "Christian scholars" also wasted the same kind of valuable "life-resource" in promoting completely wrong interpretations about what is the ultimate "Truth" given to mankind in The Bible:

The "Living Truth" of The Two Sons of GOD.

Religious scholars and ethnic and cultural leaders of belief-systems that ignore, disbelieve or outright oppose or condemn this Ultimate Truth will – **along with Christian Church leaders who also disbelieve or deny and thus lead astray** – live the full experience of the outworking of one of the very Laws that **One** of The Two Sons of GOD stated unequivocally He had "...not come to *overthrow*, but to fulfil."

Earth-science and all the great religions state that key Law in basically similar terms; *'The Law of Sowing and Reaping', 'The Iron Law of Karmä'* – **'The Law of Reciprocal Action'**. We can quite rightly therefore say that *no* reasons or excuses exist anywhere in the total human science/religious paradigm whereby the outworking of that great Law – with regard to the Truth *about* **The Two Sons of GOD** – could *not* be recognised. Do we not see the effect of the increasing power of this Inviolable Law every day now?

The recognition of **The Two Sons** [i.e., **Parts or Extensions of GOD**] therefore represents the critical, spiritual evolutionary-step on the path to what is meant to be humankind's final goal – *our return home*. The recognition of this sublime Truth is thus also meant to be the same kind of evolutionary step that all leaders and teachers of all religious beliefs world-wide must make, **so that The Pure Truth of He Who gave us Life could be gifted to all**. The explanations in this Work will help lead the *serious* reader to that complete knowledge.

Throughout this Chapter we have alluded to the "possibility" that **The One Who Comes** *has already been*. Since He is to be expected at a time of great travail for the human race, we have striven to pique the curiosity and spiritual intuition of you, the reader, to seriously consider what we have stated here.

Because a statement about such an event would necessarily have to be proclamatory in nature, an absolute proclamation centred around **His Return** would therefore not be at all subject to intellectual analyses – *for such analyses would automatically be rendered irrelevant* by **The Event Itself!**

At the conclusion of this key Chapter, therefore, we unequivocally proclaim what is perhaps – for the Christian Church particularly, but mankind collectively – the greatest "truthful irony" of all:

> *Bible prophecy has been fulfilled, and "the world" has missed The Event!*

Thus for all: – Bible Scholars, Popes, Archbishops, Presidents and Kings; politicians of *every* persuasion, scientists and writers, leaders of *all* Religions and Churches and of *all* ethnic and cultural Groups:

The *"Dual Working"* has therefore been fulfilled, and thus the key confirmatory-proclamation by **Jesus** that:

"He, Himself, will Honour Me!"

* * * * *

JESUS — The SON OF GOD —

– is thus **Honoured** in the **All-TRUTH** brought to Earth by:

IMANUEL — The SON OF MAN
— The ETERNAL MEDIATOR —

['GOD with us']

* * * * *

Like the foolish virgins in The Bible, a blind, intransigent and totally aspiritual humanity *did not keep the light of their spirits awake* when The SON Of MAN – IMANUEL – came!
In the profound Grace of this knowledge, and in accordance with the Mandate to so proclaim, we herewith present our Proclamation:

The SON OF MAN has indeed come like a thief in the night and He has given to mankind HIS "All-Truth"!

Chapter 13

The "Seven Churches in Asia" – The Revelation

> "Happy are the reader and hearers of this prophecy who observe its records; for the time is at hand."
>
> (Revelation 1:3, Fenton.)

> "If I have seen further than other men, it is because I have stood on the shoulders of giants."
>
> (Sir Isaac Newton.)

Thus far in this work we have examined the Laws of Life, our origins, the processes of death, the vital working of The Forces of Nature and the lives of the great Truth-Bringers, the Teachings of whom we were meant to heed. Since much of what we have looked at was meant to be examined and learned in the earthly environment, this Chapter appropriately offers ultimate insight into the wider *material* environment to which the earth obviously belongs. It reveals the *limits* of the material parameters in which we live, and allows us to know our respective place within those far-reaching boundaries. It therefore also places the singular aspect of earthly humanity's impending Apocalyptic Judgement in its correct context.

The Book of Revelation, by virtue of its seemingly enigmatic content, provides fertile ground for many interpretations, from the literal to the bizarre. That particular book is perceived to cover many prophetic aspects, though often *apparently* unrelated, and ostensibly without clear linkages. The Revelation, being part of that book which is the foundation of Christianity, is nevertheless considered by many to be virtually impossible to understand logically. Yet, if The Revelation *was* given to assist *all* of humankind *for the understanding of their purpose for being at precisely this present time in their tenure in the material world* what, then, must derive from either a wrong interpretation, or from ignoring it completely?

During his time with the Anglican Church the great mathematician, Isaac Newton, directed his monumental talent of genius to analysing The Bible, trying to discover the secret knowledge he believed lay hidden there. He further believed that some of the ancients – in particular the Greek mathematicians – had known this secret. If he could find it, he would know it too, the "plan of the world". Two major points lay at the heart of Newton's unshakeable belief:

1. A rational God made a rational universe; and

2. All wisdom lay in the knowledge of numbers.[1]

Of special interest to Newton were The Book of Daniel with its mathematical time-line, and The Book of Revelation (from which we clarify the issue of the "7 churches"). The journey we need to take for this purpose has powerful echoes to Newton and his genius for he provides the foundational mathematics of astronomy which we will need to arrive at our conclusion. Why astronomy for that conclusion? For the moment we should let that reason be a "revelation" in itself. Since we have Newton as a man of the church and a towering genius of science, he is surely the ideal companion for this august journey. Let us, then, not just take this man of spiritual and intellectual genius with us, but let us stand on *his* shoulders and discover the treasured goal that he could not find in his lifetime – the **"plan of the world"**.

Because Newton believed that only ***"a few natural laws apply to the whole universe"***, he regarded those natural laws ***"as proof of the existence of a great and Almighty God"***. Since

---

[1]The reader will recall the term used in this book as not so much being the "knowledge of numbers" as **"The Law of Numbers"**.

he was both a theologian and scientist vitally interested in apparently all things, including The Revelation, we would sincerely hope that modern-day scientists and theologians would want to journey with us too.

Any notion that states The Revelation as being an enigma and therefore indecipherable, must presuppose that some of the greatest answers to life which lie in there might be too difficult to even attempt to understand. In my view that is an illogical and untenable position. The previous Chapter revealing the unequivocal Truth about The Two Sons of God and Their dual working is clear testimony to what we affirm. After all, it *is* The Revelation, and something of paramount importance is being "revealed"! Such statements to the contrary simply reveal the actual level of *our* non-understanding.

As has been pointed out elsewhere in this book, the very fact that we are here on planet earth must logically infer that we are **meant** to discover **all** the answers to our purpose for being. Otherwise it all becomes a rather pointless exercise: of either scientific contention deriving mainly from a theoretical-supposition basis, or religious contention deriving from differing interpretations of the many and varied beliefs awash across the globe. Unfortunately, ideas, theories, guesswork etc., do not provide *definitive* answers, a good reason why the admonition, "Seek and you shall find", is so vital. That fundamentally necessary *finding* of the final and ultimate answers to the questions to life cannot be achieved with the use of our intellect alone, however.

So for the complete understanding of this particular Chapter we must *strongly reiterate* that the purpose of the intellect is to facilitate, to the highest possible level, the material and technological undertakings that humans require for their sojourn and ongoing development in the *earthly environment*. The intellect possesses no understanding of the many and far higher non-physical realms of the incomprehensible total we sometimes loosely call Creation. That is because only the physical-body part of man is derived from the material world.

So also, therefore, is its closely associated aspects of intellectual-brain activity. Thus the "seeking" of final and complete knowledge must be driven by the *"spirit"* – because it is connected to the source of Life. Such seeking, however, needs a *"clarified"* intellect as its companion. In any case no amount of intellectual or theological sophistry can change *what actually is*. So any religious or scientific pre-conceptions brought to bear here to attempt to discredit the true meaning of the "7 churches" question is, in the singular nature of things pertaining to Spiritual Truth, *immediately rendered irrelevant.*

Anyhow, it is well past the time that the true meaning *was* recognised. That essential recognition, as a vital part of the complete knowledge for humankind, permits critical threads to many of the key questions of life to be woven together to reveal a far larger picture than could ever be the case without this information. Moreover, it also provides the right structure, from the earthly viewpoint in this case, for the very necessary understanding of the previous Chapters – **"Jesus – His Birth, Death and Resurrection"**, and **"The Two Sons of God!"**.

For Bible readers generally, but more particularly perhaps for Bible scholars, theologians and the religiously learned of the Universities and Colleges of the world, the question of the "seven churches" or "assemblies or communities" in "Asia" or "Asia Minor" represents a curious and fascinating puzzle. The names of the seven "assemblies" – to each of which a messenger of God delivers an address – are given as follows: Ephesus, Smyrna, Pergamos, Thyatira, Sardis, Philapelphia and Laodicea. And, just as The Revelation *seemingly* notes, they *were* communities which *did* exist in Asia Minor.

Ephesus: Ancient Greek city of Asia Minor, in what is now western Turkey, lying near the mouth of the river Ku-cuk Menderes. It was the site of the great Temple of Diana, one of the seven wonders of the world. It was destroyed by the Goths in AD 262.

(*Great Illustrated Dictionary*, Readers Digest, First Edition, 1984, USA)

Smyrna: Now called **Izmir**. City and port in western Turkey. At the head of the Gulf of Izmir, on the Aegean Sea, it is the commercial centre of the Levant.

(*Great Illustrated Dictionary*, Readers Digest, First Edition, 1984, USA)

Pergamos: Now called **Bergama** in western Turkey. Once noted for its fabulous carpets; they were the most highly valued and probably woven with gold and silver thread. Nothing survives of these rich textiles because they were all burned long ago to extract the metal.

(Brittanica CD '97)

Thyatira: Now called **Akhisar**, a town in western Turkey, "...in a fertile plain on the great Zab River (the ancient Lycus). The ancient town, originally called Pelopia, was probably founded by the Lydians. It was made a Macedonian colony about 290 BC and renamed **Thyatira**. It became part of the kingdom of Pergamum in 190 BC and was an important station on the ancient Roman road from Pergamum (Bergama) to Laodicea (near Denizli). Its early Christian church appears as *one of the seven churches in the Revelation to John.*"

(Brittanica CD '97, Italics mine.)

Sardis: Capital city of ancient Lydia, now a small village in western Turkey. When Lydia was absorbed into the Persian Empire following the defeat of Croseus (c. 550 BC), Sardis remained the provincial capital of Asia Minor. It later became an early centre of Christianity – *one of the seven churches of Asia (Minor)*. Extensive excavations of the site have yielded the earliest known coins, dating from c. 700 BC.

(*Great Illustrated Dictionary*, Readers Digest, First Edition, 1984, USA, Italics mine.)

Philadelphia: Now called **Alasehir**, also a town in western Turkey.

Laodicea: Name given to several cities built in Asia and Asia Minor by the Greek Seleucid Dynasty in the third century BC The chief one, Laodicea ad Lycum, near present day Denizli in western Turkey, was a prosperous market town on the Roman trading route from the Orient and an early centre of Christianity.

(*Great Illustrated Dictionary*, Readers Digest, First Edition, 1984, USA)

Already now we have a strong *academic* view about what the "seven churches" *might* mean. Significantly, they were in a geographically very small area of present-day Turkey. In fact, the triangulated area encompassing the locations of those ancient "7 churches", including the nearby island of Patmos and the area of sea between it and the mainland, amounts to something like 25,000 sq. km. The total area of modern Turkey is around 780,580 sq. km. The representative area of the "7 churches triangle" is therefore only about 1/30th of that.

If we carefully read the introduction *prior* to the "messages" being given to the seven "assemblies" in Asia by the individual "messengers" of God, and then the *actual* messages, and then finally the *explanation* about The One who has authorised the messages, then a major problem immediately emerges if we hold to such a *small area of one country on earth*. The island of Patmos, where it is believed John the Disciple "received" The Revelation, is close by. So how do, or how might, the actual messages fit with such a scenario?

Each of the seven communities is addressed by its particular messenger (a Guardian Angel) who calls the inhabitants to task for various transgressions against The Laws of Creation – The Laws of God – and warns what will happen if they do not change their ways. Let us take just one message to one of the communities, and carefully note the **key** to understanding the **meaning** of that and the other messages.

The Vision in Patmos

> I, John, ... was in the island known as Patmos. I became inspired on the Lord's day; and I heard a loud voice behind me resembling a trumpet blast saying: "What you see write in a book, and dispatch to the seven assemblies – to **Ephesus**, and to **Smyrna**"... etc.. I accordingly turned to see the voice which spoke to me. And having turned, I observed **seven golden lampstands**; and **in the centre of the lampstands**, one like to the Son of Man ... and **holding in His right hand seven stars**; and a sharp double-edged sword drawn from its sheath... "Write therefore what you have seen, what is, and what will come after these. The mystery of the **seven stars** which you saw upon my right hand, and the **seven golden lampstands**, *the seven stars are messengers of seven assemblies; and the seven lampstands are the seven assemblies.*"
>
> (Revelation 1:9-19, Fenton, Italics mine.)

I have italicised the key to understanding this *apparent* mystery, for it was reserved for this point of time in humanity's journey for it to be fully understood. Verse 3 offers a further connection:

> "Happy are the reader and hearers of this prophecy who observe its records; for the time is at hand."

The next key part is the text of the address to the first assembly – **Ephesus**.

To the Assembly in Ephesus

> To the messenger to the assembly in Ephesus write:
> "Thus says the Controller of the seven stars by His right hand; *who walks in the centre of the seven golden lampstands*; I know your position, your industry, and your patience; and that you cannot endure those who are wicked; that you have put to the test those who have called themselves Apostles, and are not, and have found them false; and you have had patience and have suffered because of My Name, and have not failed. I have, however, a charge against you – that you have *forsaken your first love*! Remember, therefore, from where you have fallen, and repent, and practise your former works; failing which, and unless you alter your mind, *I will come and remove your lampstand from its place*."
>
> (Revelation, 2:1-6, Fenton. Italics mine.[2])

"From whence thou art fallen" refers to the over-cultivated intellect, which has pushed aside the spirit and caused it to fall, so that it can no longer, as before the Fall of Man, do "the first works", namely, keep awake the spiritual intuitive perception, and thus maintain the connection with God.

(*A Gate Opens*, Herbert Vollmann)

The address to Ephesus continues on for a few more sentences, then there are the further, basically similar, addresses to the *other "assemblies" or churches*. Now, if we accept such a scenario literally with regard to the "seven churches" in what is now western Turkey, then we might appear to have three possibilities. That in a past event (because those names of the particular communities no longer exist) the messengers *did* appear to the people, and *did* deliver the appropriate messages. Subsequently the cities or communities *did* disappear so one *could* believe that they did *not* "change their ways" and thus suffered destruction. However, there is no known record of such visitations or warnings to those "churches" having taken place.

We note that the name Laodicea, alone, was given to *several* cities. That is surely problematic for a "messenger" of God who is required to deliver a message of obviously great import to that particular "community". For messages at the behest of The Almighty cannot be superficial or insignificant.

---

[2]The italicised sentences are vital for the reader to remember.

That being the case, the question of *which* John received The Revelation is clearly critically important. There is a school of thought that accepts three Johns. John the Baptist, John the Evangelist – the beloved Disciple of Jesus associated with the Fourth Gospel – and a John the divine, believed to be the author of The Revelation. We, however, will embrace only two. If we accept the view that John the Disciple received The Revelation on the island of Patmos in the Aegean sea direct from The Son of Man in the Highest Heights of Creation, we must logically accept that he was sufficiently "well-connected" enough for that. Notwithstanding the fact that he was the "beloved of Jesus", such tidings of vital import must surely presuppose that only a very special individual, perhaps prepared over a long period of time, would be suitable for such a high task. Or was there a second John on Patmos?

Again from out of the work, "A Gate Opens", by Herbert Vollmann, we read:

> Only one was found worthy to receive the great Revelation of past and future happenings: John the Baptist, of whom Jesus said, "Verily I say unto you, Among them that are born of women there hath not risen a greater than John the Baptist."
>
> (Matthew 11:11)
>
> Moreover, John received The Revelation not on the island of Patmos in the Aegean Sea during his earth-life, but after his earthly death – on the Isle of Patmos that lies **in The Spiritual Realm**, even above the Paradise of the human spirits. He passed it on to a human being on earth *who was spiritually open for it,* and who translated it into earthly words. Thus the Book with seven seals, The Revelation of John, was handed down to us.

(Chapter: The Revelation of John, p 161, Emphases mine.)

Here we note that the "mansion" of John the Baptist (the "none greater") lies far above our origins. Hence the reason why only *he* could baptise Jesus, The Son of God.

Now, if John the Disciple *was* the person on earth who *received* The Revelation on Patmos, *why did he not simply travel to each of the communities to deliver the messages*? He was certainly close enough, would have been well respected in the communities, and therefore probably believed. We note that the Apostle Paul also travelled to all those "churches" to preach. So we do know they were all in existence at that time. Those *appointed* servants of God could surely have done that if The Revelation was known to them then – and *if it really was about the "7 churches" in existence there at that time*. Then there would not be the need for high messengers to descend into the physical part of Creation to utter proclamations.

So the question remains, did those small cities warrant such an exalted visit, or is it still yet to happen? But where are the names now? They no longer exist in that form. Notwithstanding the fact that it was part of the region where great religions were born and from where much recorded proclamation and prophecy is derived, such a view nonetheless still focuses on a very small geographical area on the surface of the planet, containing just a very small number of people.

The next question we might ask if we follow this improbable thread through, is what does it mean if it *was* fulfilled in some way, even though no record exists of powerful messengers from on high visiting and proclaiming to whole communities? Surely the word would have gotten out and been recorded by someone, even if not by those in the actual communities who, however, would have experienced what would surely have been a stupendous event. After all, only a relatively few people saw the Star of Bethlehem and the "miracles" of Jesus. Fewer still saw Him in His **other-world body** prior to ascending to **The Father** to become **One** again with **Him!** Yet all this is accepted by many hundreds of millions today. Can we not also accept that *if* such a major spiritual event *had* taken place *"seven times"* in such a small area, the whole of the known world would have been "buzzing". But – silence![3]

Similar uncertainty surrounds the question of the "seven churches in Asia-Minor". Again we ask the key question, *if* we accept the popular Christian view that John the Disciple received The Revelation on the island of Patmos why did he not simply *deliver* the

---

[3] Historically we know that the revolt of the Jews in 66 AD and the subsequent destruction of Jerusalem by Titus and his legions in 70 AD may have been initiated in part by the belief at the time that Jesus would return *shortly after His crucifixion* as the King/Messiah to inaugurate the millennium of peace and defeat the Romans. That this did not happen clearly shows that interpretation by the religious leaders of the day was completely wrong. Indeed, they paid very dearly for that presumption with the wholesale slaughter of almost the entire population of Jerusalem. The legacy of that kind of great error continues on in theological circles today in the ongoing uncertainty about what The Bible actually states and means about Jesus ostensibly returning and bringing with Him an Apocalyptic Judgement and great destruction around this present time.

messages to the "7 churches" immediately upon receipt of them? We know that the Disciples were instructed by Jesus to a far greater level of knowledge than most human beings to *this* point in time. So having been instructed in the far greater expanse of Creation itself vis-a vis; *"In My Father's House there are many Mansions"*, the Disciples were well aware of future events because they had all been told in no uncertain terms, **by The Son of God Himself**, what would come upon humanity at the "completion of the times" – *our* **times** – and why! We can also know this if we wish to, simply because it was recorded by them, and we can read that forewarning discourse today in any Bible.

Even though the messages in The Revelation were recorded "for all time", it was reserved *for a later time* – a future time – ***our present time***, for its wider clarification, when the true knowledge of Creation would be given to humanity as promised. Once recognised, that new knowledge could be more readily understood by present-day man through the twin disciplines of **science and theology**. Thus, via the *relative* human dimensions of man in *his duality*, i.e. **intellect and spirit**.[4]

So, if the messages were not actually for those ancient communities, what might it all mean? In order to understand this great question, a related one stands out as also being particularly important. It is the necessary understanding of where we, as human beings on planet earth in the material world, *actually stand* in re-

---

[4] The astute and spiritually-aware reader will have well recognised by this point that under the perfect outworking of The Laws of Creation – in particular The Laws of "Rebirth" and "Reciprocal Action" – a point in time is set where all cycles previously unresolved, between individuals and even whole peoples, would need to be closed off. In order for such closures to be ***fully understood*** by all those "peoples" at that ordained time, however, the evolutionary path of humankind ***should*** have reached its zenith for all by then. That *"then"*, that zenith, is this present time. As explained in the previous Chapter, the paths of religion, philosophy, science, and even the social order of all nations and peoples, ***should*** have travelled a road of unfolding enlightenment founded on the great spiritual truths – given in a carefully-guided, step-by-step process through the line of Prophets and Truth-Bringers Called from Above – to culminate in this present time where all was ordained to be revealed.

Hence the need for science and religion, particularly, to have subjugated their egoistic individual positions as the primary discipline of truth, and recognise that each had a vital part to play to lead humankind to complete and final knowledge. The window of opportunity for any kind of real accommodation in an harmonious and fully-knowledgeable working together to enlighten humanity has probably now closed. Because it is the *untruth* that mainly lies with the masses, *that task has now fallen to a few radicals, a few "voices in the wilderness", to reveal the errors and thereby proclaim for, and lead to, the All-Truth!*

lation to **The Creator**. For **He** surely cannot stand in the same part of **His Creation** as we do, i.e. as a Presence or Power *actually residing* in the *physical universes*. **And neither does He!**

Yet it should be part of one's inherent wish *to want to know* where we do *actually* stand! Do we, upon earthly death, (as so many apparently believe) simply transit from earth and be immediately in "paradise" and thus in the presence of God? If that could be so, then that would place God quite close to human beings on earth. The two other main monotheistic religions have generally similar beliefs. Yet our critical examination of Genesis and the *two Creations* clearly *negates* such a view of a close and convenient, personalised God.

A connection between the "seven assemblies" and where we stand in relation to The Almighty might not be immediately apparent, or even seem logical, **but the true understanding of what the "seven churches" actually means offers precisely that correct knowledge and relationship. A correct interpretation tells us what they (the seven churches or assemblies) actually are in their individual entities, and what it (an assembly) is in its singular, overall form.**

Now, we have determined that this is not solely a religious question only, and that *certain* disciplines within the scientific "communities" as well need to think long and hard about what it all might actually mean. Since we contend that purely intellectual seeking alone – from either of the disciplines of science or theology – will not permit any unveiling of the *true* meaning of the "7 churches in Asia", we need to take the boldest possible step in order to "find". By *merging* the two disciplines and using the clarified intellect guided by the spirit – as we have previously done with other key questions in this book – we will achieve exactly that goal. We will, thereby, indeed discover a truly marvellous revelation, **the very revelation that Newton himself sought!** It is a revelation which is literally *mind-blowing* in its ramifications for science and for *all* religions, permitting the mind, intellect, soul and spirit, *to soar in exultant recognition.*

Therefore, if *recognised and understood correctly*, the senses will reel before the true meaning of the "7 churches in Asia-Minor", for it will completely "shatter" all currently accepted ideas of the "universe" and cosmology. It also reveals therewith the huge importance of The Revelation itself. The almost incomprehensible import of such a vastly overpowering, yet spiritually *empowering*, extra-world view of where we human beings *actually stand* in Creation is virtually life-changing in that singular moment of *genuine recognition.*

As previously stated, since we have addressed the other key questions from a fundamentally different and far-reaching paradigm this particular one, too, can only be logically understood by using the same method. Because The Revelation is primarily a spiritual book indicating, in the first instance, insights into vast spiritual vistas and events that must necessarily transcend intellectual interpretations so, similarly, and by a considerable margin, must we also vastly expand our frames of reference to answer and understand the meaning of the "7 churches".

We contend, absolutely, that the premise we postulate is correct, that it is **not at all about earthly communities or churches**. The fact that those churches did once exist has clearly confused the issue. Where, then, might these places be? No satisfactory answer has publicly emerged from the Jewish faith, the Christian religions or the institutions of theology. In any case it is not about guesswork or theories, but about the knowledge of the outworking of The Laws of Creation and the concomitant knowledge of the structure of that Creation. Of course there is a correct answer, there is *always* a correct answer! So what does that imply?

Since we have concluded that the answer is not connected with the names of the "churches" in the stated general location of Asia-Minor on earth in ancient times, the so-named "assemblies" must therefore represent something *entirely different.* That logically places both the communities and the delivery of each specific address by a "messenger of the Lord" (the Guardian Angel of each assembly) *somewhere other than the earth,* in a time *different to the times* when those "communities" once existed.

Thus far we have sparred with possibilities and ideas about the meaning of the "7 churches or assemblies in Asia-Minor". If the "assemblies" are not on earth but nevertheless exist as we unequivocally state, they would nevertheless still logically **have to be** in the **material world**. For this is where The Revelation came down to, where we live in our obvious physicality, and where *the Judgement takes place!*

However, a seamless transition from current uncertain views to sure certainty in an actual answer is not a simple "fix", for it requires a huge and fundamental leap of truly gigantic proportions into a completely new paradigm. It is a paradigm, moreover, that is not simply religious in nature and import but also involves *astron-*

omy, astrophysics and cosmology on the most stupendous scale. A major problem preventing any kind of wider outlook in the present lies with the so-called academic elite from the world of astronomy and cosmology. It is their general inability to recognise that there is much, much more to Creation than just the physical universe we see in the night sky, incomprehensibly vast as it is, that stifles any other vista. For they are the "experts" in their field, and only they are supposed to know.

Despite the ability to now peer further into that great expanse with radio telescopes and the Hubble space telescope – which offers its truly marvellous dimension of stunning imagery and ever new discoveries of the cosmos – all of that *does not even begin to get close* to the actual nature and size of the material part of Creation. *Astronomers and cosmologists*, as a global group, *do not yet know this to be the case.*

In an earlier Chapter, we stated that Creation and evolution are necessarily one and the same. There is no separation in reality. The old rivalries between science and religion are just that – rivalries. And rivalries based on the narrow parameters that each side promotes for its own edification. With this current question, too, there is no separation in reality. Spiritual truth and earthly science were ordained to be *mutually inclusive under the parameters of The Laws of Creation.*

So, to arrive at the point of sure and conscious knowing about the meaning of the "7 churches", we need to now extrapolate upward and outward our present view of the physical universe. Firstly from the immediate environs of our solar system, and thenceforth undertake a mathematical journey into distances so vast as to be totally incomprehensible. Even the word itself does not nearly suffice to describe the immensity of just our "home galaxy", let alone the stupendous nature of what science believes to be the *observable* universe. We have already explained the process of the formation of the various levels of Creation in broad outline. Now we need to do the same here, but solely with the physical universes of the material part of Creation, by using the mathematical unit of the "light-year" as our measuring staff.

One light-year represents the distance that light covers travelling in a vacuum for a period of one year – approximately 9.4607×10^{12} kilometres (5.878×10^{12} miles, at a speed of 186.000 miles per second).

Our journey naturally starts from Earth, the third planet revolving around a relatively small sun in a solar system residing at the outer edges of a galaxy designated the Milky Way Galaxy. It contains 100,000 million odd stars to which the sun of our Solar system belongs. Even travelling at light-speed, sunlight takes 8 minutes to travel the 150,000,000 km before touching our face. The same light travels 5 more hours before reaching the planet Pluto at the farthest edge of our Solar System. And 4.3 light-years later, or 40 trillion kilometres away, it reaches our nearest stellar neighbour, Alpha Centauri.

Our galaxy, a disc-shaped collection of stars with the Earth about a third of the way out from the centre, was once thought to be the entire universe until discoveries in the 1920s revealed a far greater expanse beyond it. Today we know it is only one of billions of galaxies. An observer looking at the Milky Way from earth is actually looking edge-on into the Galaxy. In a broad-brush time-sweep, the Galaxy started to form some 10,000 to 14,000 million years ago, and its oldest stars are estimated to be perhaps up to 15 billion years old. Travelling at 220 km/s our sun circles the galaxy centre once every 230 million years. Our galaxy is about ***100,000 light-years in diameter***.

Beyond the "Milky Way" can be located galaxies in every direction. We are part of a loosely bound cluster of some 20 galaxies called "the local group". From the centre to its outer boundaries is roughly 2,000,000 light-years – ***4 million light-years across***.

The next larger formation we belong to is known as a "local supercluster". Clusters of galaxies – like fleets of ships – congregate in superclusters. The closest cluster to our local group is some 50 million light-years away, near the centre of our local supercluster. From the centre to its outer boundaries is roughly 75,000,000 light-years – ***150 million light-years across***.

The only step left to take now with the present level of earthly knowledge derived from astronomy and cosmology, is into what is termed "the known universe". It is that of the farthest reaches of the universe which can be observed by the use of optical or radio telescopes. Our universe is stated to be isotropic in nature and form which means it looks the same in every direction. Quasars are the most distant objects observed. Each of the brightest quasars emits the energy of hundreds of galaxies from a volume far smaller than our Milky Way Galaxy. The furthest quasars are stated to be rushing away from us at 90% the speed of light. The "known universe" was, until quite recently, believed to be about ***40,000,000,000 light-years across***. The most recent estimates to the *edge* of the universe, at least the visible part of it, places it at ***100 billion*** *trillion kilometres away*. Further recent estimates now puts the *size* of our universe at roughly **100 billion light-years across**.

Does anyone really understand such distances? If we take just the difference between a million and a billion (American = one thousand million) converted to seconds, one million seconds is about 12 days worth, yet a billion seconds is almost 37 years. It all "seems" rather meaningless when many, many zeros are slotted behind a given digit and then perhaps to the power of another number for good measure, notwithstanding the fact that present-day computer power can number-crunch very accurately. However, such determined efforts to "fix" the size of the universe have vital relevance to our understanding of the "7 churches" question. A few quotes from various people and publications over past decades nevertheless reveals the struggle to even try to begin to genuinely understand it. A simple mathematical fact sheets home the sheer impossibility of really coming to grips with such numbers.

> "My suspicion is that the universe is not only queerer than we suppose, but queerer than we *can* suppose."
>
> (J.B.S. Haldane)

> "But what came before the big bang, and how will it all end? Billions of years hence, will gravity overcome the expansion and pull matter back into its primordial state – in a big crunch? And if the universe is closed, might another big bang follow, with another expansion? Or, as many astronomers now believe, will an ever-expanding, or open, universe end in a whimper, its galaxies scattered irretrievably, their star fires spent and cold? For now, the questions are the domain of the *philosopher* as well as the astronomer."
>
> (*National Geographic Star Chart*, 1983, Italics mine.)

> "It may be that our universe is merely part of many larger universes, some in different dimensions, and that big bangs are going on all the time all over the place. Or it may be that space and time had some other forms altogether before the Big Bang – forms too alien for us to imagine – and that the Big Bang represents some sort of transition phase, where the universe went from a form we can't understand to one we almost can." ***"These are very close to religious questions."*** Dr Andrei Linde, a cosmologist at Stanford University, told The New York Times in 2001.
>
> (*How to Make a Universe* Readers Digest. August, 2004. Italics mine.)

With the huge strides made in the "science" of astronomy and cosmology, wrought by the building and use of more and more powerful instruments to observe the great expanse *"out there"*, a fascinating paradox has seemingly emerged. It would appear that because the expanse of the known universe today is simply too incomprehensible to grasp, a point or limit in our brain-capacity to truly understand would inevitably be reached. So that any greater understanding would perhaps derive initially from the conjoined and expanding paths of philosophy and religion, but only reaching a complete and final picture with, and from, the knowledge of the actual "structure of Creation" of which the material universes are, to emphasise once again, **the lowest and smallest part!**

To now move a little closer to understanding the meaning of the "7 churches" question, we should consider what might happen if we were able to travel to the edge of the universe and look beyond it. But to what, we may wonder?

> "According to Einstein's Theory of Relativity, man could never reach that point because "the universe bends in a way that can't adequately be imagined". Therefore we would, even after travelling in a straight line to the edge, eventually arrive back at our starting point because space curves in a way that allows it to be boundless – **but finite!**[5]
>
> In short, there's more space than you can imagine already without going to the trouble of trying to envision some additional beyond."
>
> (*How to Make a Universe* Readers Digest. August, 2004. Italics mine.)

That is exactly the purpose of this Chapter, however, – **to recognise that additional beyond!** So, since the science of astronomy-cosmology has seemingly not concerned itself with the great and key truths contained in certain religious writings, let us use the spiritual intuitive faculty available to the human entity to now finally explain and clarify – **for science and theology** – the true meaning of the "7 churches in Asia-Minor".

To do that we need to return to The Revelation once more, in particular to "The Vision in Patmos":

> I, John, ... was in the island known as Patmos. I became inspired on the Lord's day; and I heard a loud voice behind me resembling a trumpet blast saying: "What you see

---

[5] Here is a key understanding to the answer of the "7 churches" question. The physical universe we see and believe we know is **finite!**

> write in a book, and dispatch to the seven assemblies – to **Ephesus**, and to **Smyrna'**... etc.. I accordingly turned to see the voice which spoke to me. And having turned, I observed **seven golden lampstands**; and **in the centre of the lampstands**, one like to the Son of Man ... and **holding in His right hand seven stars**; and a sharp double-edged sword drawn from its sheath... "Write therefore what you have seen, what is, and what will come after these. The mystery of the **seven stars** which you saw upon my right hand, and the **seven golden lampstands**, *the seven stars are messengers of seven assemblies; and the seven lampstands* **are** *the seven assemblies*."
>
> (Revelation 1:9-19, Fenton. Italics mine.)

Again, the key to understanding this *apparent* mystery lies mainly in the *italicised* words. The next key part is the text of the address to the first assembly – **Ephesus**, *which we shall quote again*:

> To the messenger to the assembly in Ephesus write:
> Thus says the Controller of the seven stars by His right hand; ***who walks in the centre of the seven golden lampstands***; "I know your position, your industry, and your patience; and that you cannot endure those who are wicked; that you have put to the test those who have called themselves Apostles, and are not, and have found them false; and you have had patience and have suffered because of My Name, and have not failed. I have, however, a charge against you – that you have forsaken your first love! Remember, therefore, from where you have fallen, and repent, and practise your former works; failing which, and unless you alter your mind, *I will come and remove your lampstand from its place*."
>
> (Revelation 2:1-6, Fenton. Italics mine.)

Here, too, the italicised sentences represent a *golden key* to the final and complete understanding of the meaning of the "7 churches in Asia" and thus where we actually stand in relation to The Almighty – The Creator – during the earthly phases of our total existence. We note that the address to Ephesus continues on for a few more sentences, then basically similar addresses are given to the *other "assemblies" or churches*.

Humankind's cosmic reality is that we live in a physical environment on a small and beautiful planet in an expanse so vast as to be totally incomprehensible. Because it is so vast, the obvious assumption that could be drawn is that the visible universe may be the be-all and end-all to our total existence. If we track back to Chapter 4, however, we note that the physical worlds are purely for the purpose of developing to personal self-consciousness and maturation, both intellectually and spiritually. Whilst a good balance between the two aspects is essential for an harmonious working toward achieving necessary earthly goals, the greater responsibility of man is to develop the spiritual part within to the highest possible level attainable. And thereby *lead* the intellectual part.

A larger emphasis placed on developing the spiritual part would have thus ensured that the connection to, and recognition of, our actual spiritual origins would not have been lost, and we would not need to struggle to understand the key questions to life such as we are addressing here. Therefore the material worlds designated for man to mature in should not be assumed to be just that which we believe we know and perhaps even roughly understand, for that would, indeed, be arrogance. From an extremely narrow, earth-oriented viewpoint, earth-science prides itself in believing it has the ability to solve the ultimate riddles to life and to be able to find the answers to the ultimate questions. Ultimately, that stance represents a "delusion of denial", where the very sciences themselves become a kind of all-knowing god for their adherents. For such a belief must logically state that there cannot be any other avenue open to mankind for those very answers which science believes only it can answer.

> "Scientism, the aura of authority carried by scientists, has made us believe that knowledge obtained by scientists is the ultimate authority, that as we accumulate information, our capacity to understand, control and manage our surroundings will grow correspondingly. But the basic principle of scientific exploration contradicts this faith: knowledge comes from empirical observations, which are "made sense of" by hypotheses, which in turn can be experimentally tested. All information is open to being disproved. As Jonathan Marks has pointed out:"
>
> "...the vast majority of ideas that most scientists have ever had have been wrong. They have been refuted; they have been disposed of. Further, at any point in time, most ideas proposed by most scientists will ultimately be refuted and disposed of... Science, in other words, undermines scientism."

(Dr David Suzuki, *The Sacred Balance*, p 19)

If, then, we are able to accept even just the *possibility* of Realms or regions that are non-material and which therefore lie above the physical universes – the "many mansions" – then we gift to ourselves the *further possibility* of accepting that the physical-world part of Creation may be far larger than we could ever have supposed. By that we do not mean just what we now know exists in our universe, but that a far greater reality may exist and that the key to this stupendous knowledge may have been with us for a very long time. Since the *whole of the material world* is the physical home of man, why should we assume that the entity, man, resides *solely here on planet earth in this particular universe*, and therefore nowhere else in the *material world*. Such a view assumes that we know and understand more than the Creative Power which permitted us conscious life, and is thus a belief whereby we limit ourselves to very narrow parameters of *so-called* great knowledge.

If, then, the messengers of God did not address seven earthly communities in the ancient world, yet nevertheless did, or will, address *"communities or assemblies of men"* upon the directive of **"The One like unto The Son of Man"**, that surely reveals the stupendous scale of the actual happening. A happening that could not possibly be confined to a very small part of one very small region of one very small planet in the material world.

Since that is the actual reality of things here, we shall now simply take the boldest step and proclaim, here and now, that very truth which John, the receiver of The Revelation in the Higher Spheres, understood and passed on down to humankind for this present time. The very truth that he received came from **The One by Whom** we came into being – **IMANUEL** – **The One Enthroned – The Will of God!**

For He It was Who brought into being *the seven homes of humanity* – the *"7 churches"*. *It is He Who therefore (figuratively) stands in the centre of the seven golden lampstands.*

Thus we note: "**seven golden lampstands; and in the centre of the lampstands**, one like unto the Son of Man ... and **holding in His right hand seven stars**."

So we are not only given *indications* of what the **seven golden lampstands** actually are, but also the *key* to the *meaning* of the **seven stars**.

Thus: "The mystery of the **seven stars** which you saw upon my right hand, and the **seven golden lampstands**, *the seven stars are messengers of seven assemblies; and the seven lampstands are the seven assemblies*."

There lies the answer. The *seven assemblies, which are the seven churches – in each of which resides a "community of men" – are the seven golden lampstands* of The Revelation.

They are actually *seven universes of roughly the same consistency as the universe in which we reside*. And in each a race of men; of humanity. We of the planet earth reside in the *"assembly" or universe called Ephesus!*

The reader must understand that these "lampstands" are not simply seven universes *within* the huge expanse of the cosmos visible to us via our radio and optical telescopes. No! Each universe or "church" is an incomprehensibly vast rotating "island", *each a separate entity unto itself*. And each one similar to our own in mind-numbing size. The seven universes together *rotate* in a huge *wreath-like formation* at the *lowest part of Creation*. The distance *between* the individual universes is naturally *greater than* the *diameter* of *each individual one*. We will therefore never be able to see the other universes, and thus never be able to travel to them. The Revelation, however, permits us to know about them. The designation, Asia-Minor, used to describe the area of the "7 churches" is simply a Spiritual one, as are the names of the seven universes. Thus **the riddle of the "7 churches" is not a riddle at all.**

That is why such a fundamental leap into a far greater level of knowledge was reserved for this particular time in our evolutionary development. For it is only within the last decades that we have had the ability to see our blue planet in its wholeness from a point outside of it; a picture free of all the superstition and ignorance of the past. Just as that sublime vision has produced awe in many, so were we, via such aids as the Hubble space telescope, meant to take cosmology to new heights, in the recognition of the awesome greatness of just the vastness of the physical universe alone. The sheer and unfolding scale of it should thus have produced the certain recognition that what was being revealed in the *physical sense*, could yet only represent the heaviest and therefore *lowest and smallest part* of Creation. And that there was very much more beyond that immensity.

That should have been the watershed recognition for humankind, recognising, in humility, that we are only "developed beings" far from our Creator. Yet even though we stand a very, very long way from The Source of Life, the ever-present Grace permits us the *possibility* to eventually leave behind the confines of the material parts of Creation to return to our point of origin in higher spheres.

We have now reached the final point of this particular exercise. It is a point given explanation elsewhere in this book, but essentially needs to be restated here. Since the purpose of this book is to offer **seriously awake people** explanations and answers to some of the major questions of life – thus some understanding of the why of the rapidly deteriorating state of humanity today – in complete accord with the Title, then such a thing as an Apocalyptic Judgement must inherently have around it certain clear phases.

As we previously stated, humankind was given a long period of time in which to learn and experience all that was necessary for the recognition of Spiritual Truth. In order for there to be a Judgement with destructive and apocalyptic accompaniment, therefore, there must logically be a cut-off point preceding the final Judgement phase itself. The "cut-off point" obviously represents the moment where there is no further time left to redeem or put right all previous transgressions. That opens the way for the next phase, the cleansing or "sorting-out". After the "sorting-out" process comes the next phase – a time of harmonious peace no longer marred or harmed by what went before; that which needed to be excised and removed.

What happens, then, if the collective transgressions of a given race of humanity are so serious that there are no redeeming points whatever? What, then? If we look at the message given for us here in Ephesus, it is quite chilling in its clear import: "Remember, therefore, from where you have fallen, and repent, and practise your former works; failing which, and unless you alter your mind, **I will come and remove your lampstand from its place**."

Remember that **each lampstand** is actually **one of the 7 great Universes** in which a race of humanity resides. Now, since the whole of the material world encompassing the 7 Universes is the lowest and smallest part of Creation, a removal of one **lampstand** or universe – as vast as we recognise it is – must nevertheless be understood to be a completely lawful process for that Power which produced it and very, very much more besides. For the race of men in it, however, destruction on an unimaginable and truly apocalyptic scale which, however, is not imminent for Ephesus at this particular time on that gigantic scale. What we refer to as our earth and earthly humanity's Judgement is explained in the following Chapter. What is stated here is the stupendous, constantly-recurring "renewal-cycle" of birth, life and disintegration that *all* the 7 great universes or assemblies must undergo in a time-frame of cosmic proportions that could not ever be even imagined. Thus *finite* universes rotating through an *infinite* cycle of birth, life and disintegration.

For we, the community of the universe Ephesus who reside on the tiny speck of the earth, do we even begin to recognise from whence we have fallen? Unfortunately we do not. More unfortunately, true spiritual aspirations are often derided and dismissed as irrelevant and of no consequence or importance for 21st century man. They were not considered all that relevant last century either. What was our first love with which we no longer bother? The love for the Creator, as stated in The First Commandment, and the love for one's neighbour, as stated by Christ? Not much evidence of either in today's world. There is, however, much love and adulation for our much-vaunted, totally aspiritual intellect, precisely by which we fail to practise our former works – the far earlier spiritual ones.

Clearly, then, our former works were better than that which we produce now – **before our spiritual fall and decline** – and which we are directed to once more practise. Failing which, and unless we change our ways, our **lampstand**, the universe containing our earthly home, may well be removed. In other words total disintegration of the **whole universe of Ephesus** at some designated future point. What is this, just religious ranting? Or is it the clearest warning yet that we could possibly receive to change our ways and begin living correctly according to The Laws of Life – The Spiritual Laws of Creation?

The degraded and poisoned state of planet earth today, along with the dysfunctional social order of most societies globally, clearly testify to totally wrong thinking and wrong practices by this humanity of Ephesus. In terms of Perfect Justice, therefore, it would probably be the correct thing for most of humanity to be "taken out"! The inherent Perfection of Perfect Laws would automatically achieve that in any case. Since we are now in the end-times, and therefore **already in the Judgement phase anyway**, it is only a relatively brief matter of time before the real apocalyptic destruction of **earthly humanity on earth** begins. We are presently rolling toward that absolute and final cut-off point, and at a rapidly accelerating pace.

> "...for there shall then be wide-spread affliction, *such as has not been known since the beginning of the world*

until now, no, nor will ever be known again. And if those times were not cut short, ***not a man would be saved.***"

"And there will be signs in the sun, and moon, and stars; and upon the earth *from fear, and apprehension of what is coming upon the world...*"

(Luke 21)

In order to more fully understand what has been revealed in this Chapter, I would recommend the reader find a reasonably comprehensive star-chart of the universe showing the journey of discovery from the Solar System to the galaxies, to groupings of galaxies and so on, to the known limits of the universe. National Geographic have produced excellent charts over the years. Then, using any mainstream Bible, apply the texts used herein to a visual examination of the star-chart; the immensity of just our universe of Ephesus to begin with.

Then travel beyond that in mind and spirit into the area of material Creation occupied by the other 6 churches or universes and try to grasp the immensity of just the physical part, alone, of it all "down here". Then strive to soar upward into the non-material Realms of the Eternal part of Creation, to one of the "many mansions in His Father's house", that of our true home in the Spiritual Realm. From "there" look downwards and really strive to picture the "7 churches" or universes rotating like a huge wreath very, very far below. It really is a mind-numbing experience – **if the spirit is awake.**

The final word on this subject must go to a woman who lectured in astronomy at Auckland City Observatory, and who was at the same time also a devout Christian. Upon enquiring why I wanted to buy the 1983 edition of the National Geographic Star Chart, I asked if she knew of the "7 churches" in The Revelation? She did. When made aware of the true nature of it, she asked – literally through a mask of what I can only describe as something akin to jaw-dropping, incredulous disbelief: "Is it possible? Can it be possible?" I stated that it was the only explanation that made sense, and was therefore the actual reality in my conviction.

As both a lecturer in Astronomy and a Christian with some knowledge of The Bible, she immediately understood the full import of such a theme. A short while later when I left with the Star Chart, she said – quite clearly after some very serious reflection, however:

"Thank you for that. I've always believed we've tried to make GOD too small!"

Chapter 14

Science supports the Judgement process!

At first glance, earth science and a "fire and brimstone" Judgement might indicate an impossible or, at the very least, highly improbable proposition for any kind of successful reconciliation of two seemingly diametrically opposite views. Nevertheless, just as we used Hegel's dialectic process to analyse the science-religion "stand-off" for the Creation versus Evolution debate, so can we use the same method here to show that the findings of cosmological science do, indeed, actually support the Judgement Process.

What was stated in the previous Chapter as a stupendous, constantly-recurring "renewal-cycle" of "life and death" that *all* the 7 great universes or "assemblies" must undergo, is thus that of *finite* universes rotating through an *infinite* cycle of birth, life and disintegration. The same process also separates out and disintegrates *individual* celestial globes "within each universe" when the age of the singular globe concerned decrees that its time of useful life is complete.

What we wish to now reveal in this Chapter are the cosmological events that show how and why the "Judgement Process" can be explained from the science of astrophysics. Despite the fact that the main text quoted in this Chapter – written some years ago now by the late Dr Richard Steinpach – does not have the benefit of more recent discoveries in cosmology, the primary foundation from which he derives his "points of connection" has not changed. The ongoing discoveries in cosmology actually reinforce the basic premise of Dr Steinpach's spiritually insightful and crucial essay and perhaps, "through a new awareness, to hopefully lead many readers on to search for The Spiritual Laws that govern the entire Creation and thus our very existence."

Because the subject matter is about collapsing or imploding stars at their disintegration, we should first briefly examine some basic mathematics of the "Big-Bang" theory as an introduction to the main text. Currently thought to have brought the universe into existence, the rather impossible-to-grasp sums of the "Big-Bang" explaining how it all began and developed, at the very least, make fascinating reading.

The question of how the universe came into existence only gained real traction from the early 20th century. Notwithstanding Newton's crucial contribution to the science of astronomy, still relevant today – NASA acknowledges Newtonian physics as the foundation for its space programme – it was not until the larger telescopes and more powerful computers were developed that astronomers began to get a sense of how it might have begun and how it all might work. At this present time the Big-Bang theory holds sway. Other ideas have been mooted and subsequently discarded. Various possibilities have encompassed an "ever-expanding universe", the "steady state" theory and an open universe. On the question of the merits or otherwise of the Big-Bang, the reader must obviously decide for himself. Current thought on the how and why of the universe, even though able to now answer many previously unanswerable questions, is nevertheless still derived solely from an empirical paradigm.

As we have stated often, because the present level of "scientific knowledge" is not based on a ***Spiritual*** foundation to begin with, it does not recognise, let alone even begin to take in, the far greater expanse of the non-material worlds. Science is therefore *unable* to derive the final answers about the physical universes from out of that far greater and higher paradigm which encompasses all of the non-material worlds, upward to our Spiritual Origins to begin with.

So, the basic mathematics of the Big-Bang theory, according to more recent analyses, proposes something called "The theory of inflation" to explain its origin. It states that, "...the entire visible universe grew from a speck far smaller than a proton, to a nugget the size of a grapefruit, almost instantaneously, when the whole thing was 0.00000000000000000000000000000001 second old." (Time, June 2001. Feature article – "How the Universe Will End")

According to the "inflation model" the incomprehensible immensity of the universe came from virtually nowhere in an instant.

So small that you would have needed a microscope to find it. The inflation theory was proposed in 1979 by Alan Guth, then a junior particle physicist at Stanford University. It holds that within "...a fraction of a moment after the dawn of creation[1] the universe underwent a sudden dramatic expansion. It inflated."

The whole episode probably lasted no more than one million million million million millionths of a second – but it transformed the universe from something that could be held to something at least 10,000,000,000,000,000,000,000,000 times larger. According to Guth's theory, gravity came into being at one-ten millionth of a trillionth of a trillionth of a trillionth of a second. In a single moment, we were endowed with a universe that was at least 100 billion light years across. Feasible? Sounds impossible. For how can one individual second be logically and understandably carved up into such infinitesimal part-seconds? Anyway, who on this earth can finally say!

It is also interesting to note the opinions of astronomers such as Martin Rees:

> Martin Rees, Britain's Astronomer Royal, believes that there are many universes, possibly an infinite number, each with different attributes, in different combinations, and that we simply live in one that combines things in a way that allows us to exist... Rees maintains that six numbers in particular govern our universe, and that if any of these values were changed, even very slightly, things could not be as they are. For example, for the universe to exist as it does requires that hydrogen be converted to helium in a precise but comparatively stately manner – specifically in a way that converts seven one-thousandths of its mass to energy.
>
> Lower that value very slightly – from 0.007 per cent to 0.006 per cent, say, – and no transformation could take place: the universe would consist of hydrogen and nothing else. Raise the value very slightly – to 0.008 per cent – and bonding would be so wildly prolific that the hydrogen would long since have been exhausted. In either case, with the slightest tweaking of the numbers the universe as we know and need it would not be here.
>
> (How to Make a Universe. Readers Digest. August, 2004)

What we clearly note here is a *perfected state* for life to be able to exist at all, and a stupendously huge "home", in the physical

---
[1] Again this only refers to *just the material worlds*.

sense, for it to exist in. The Perfection of Creation overall surely precludes any notion that it all emerged by "accident".

In the previous Chapter the question of what might happen if we were able to travel to the edge of the universe and look beyond it was considered. Einstein's Theory of Relativity holds that the universe bends in a way that cannot adequately be imagined so we would, even after travelling in a straight line to the edge, eventually arrive back at our starting point. His theory suggests that space curves in a way that allows it to be boundless – *but finite*. So the physical universe we see and believe we know **is finite!**

> 'Physicist and Nobel laureate Steven Weinberg explains that space cannot even properly be said to be expanding, because "solar systems and galaxies are not expanding." Rather, the galaxies are rushing apart. It is all something of a *challenge to intuition*. For us the universe goes only as far as light has travelled in the billions of years since the universe has formed. This visible universe – the universe we know and can talk about – is a million million million million (that's 1000,000,000,000,000,000,000,000) kilometres across. According to most theories, however, the universe at large – the meta-universe, as it is sometimes called – is vastly roomier still. According to Rees, the number of light years to the edge of this larger, unseen universe would be written not "...with ten zeroes, not even with a hundred, but with millions". In short, there's more space than you can imagine already without going to the trouble of trying to envision some additional beyond."

(How to Make a Universe, Readers Digest. Italics mine.)

To achieve the incredible expansion proposed by the "theory of inflation" – from an invisible speck to a structure billions of miles across in a fraction of an instant – the speed of light is very obviously totally inadequate. Einstein's Theory of Relativity, however, seemingly permits the mathematics to fit a "faster-than-light" possibility.

> "An equally unsettling implication is that the universe is pervaded with a strange sort of "antigravity", a concept originally proposed, and later abandoned, by Einstein as the greatest blunder of his life."[2]

---

[2] Adam Riess, a Space Telescope Science Institute astronomer, has seemingly helped prove that Einstein may have been right in the first place; a mysterious antigravity force that acts like Einstein's cosmological constant is evidently quite real.

This force, which has lately been dubbed "dark energy", isn't just keeping the expansion from slowing down, it's making the universe fly apart faster and faster all the time, like a rocket ship with the throttle wide open. It gets stranger still. Not only does "dark energy" swamp ordinary gravity but an invisible substance known to scientists as "dark matter" also seems to outweigh the ordinary stuff of stars, planets and people by a factor of 10 to 1. "Not only are we not at the centre of the Universe," University of California, Santa Cruz, astrophysical theorist Joel Primack has commented, "...we aren't even made of the same stuff the universe is."

These discoveries raise more questions than they answer. For example, just because scientists know dark matter is there doesn't mean they understand what it really is. Same goes for dark energy. "If you thought the universe was hard to comprehend before," says University of Chicago astrophysicist Michael Turner, "...then you'd better take some smart pills, because it's only going to get worse."

(Time, June 2001. Feature article – "How the Universe Will End.")

From two fairly recent publications, we have noted and quoted the opinions and theories of key academics in the field of cosmology and astronomy etc.. So it seems the "Big Bang" is the theory that is current, and ongoing research appears to support and strengthen it. Thus, from an infinitesimal speck, the huge and completely incomprehensible size and mass of the universe was, by cosmologists' reckoning, "suddenly there".

The key question that obviously arises is how could this incredible mass emerge from virtually nothing? Even if we use a standard analogy of growth – say that of a human being where, at conception, the potential is simply that of a very tiny, fertilised egg but where the full potential unfolds to adulthood – it is on a scale that is easy to understand. What about a very tiny seedling which might grow to become an immense tree. That, too, is easy to comprehend. Not the Big Bang scenario, however.

The physical form of the human being eventually dies, decays and reverts to its component parts vis-a-vis, earth to earth, dust to dust – as will the giant tree. And the mass of the earth, even with billions of creatures living and dying over aeons, remains the same. What about the total mass of *billions* of galaxies, each with their *billions* of suns, however? Can we really believe that

that absolutely incomprehensible expanse could somehow explode out of something far smaller than a single dot on this page in the micro-millisecond time-frame proposed? Then very much later, in an equally incomprehensible future point in time, contract or implode, and squeeze itself back into something invisible, except through a microscope? It all seems too impossible, too strange to be possible.

A "white dwarf" is surely a good example: a very small, extremely dense star where the atoms in it have been broken up and the various parts packed tightly together with almost no waste space so that the density rises to millions of times that of water. According to scientific calculations a spoonful of white dwarf material would weigh many tons. Neutron stars, made up principally or completely of neutrons, have even greater density. Clearly, individual stars can be compressed to an incredibly small size. And in a black hole where not even light can escape, even more so. Multiply the total mass of literally *billions of* **galaxies** *worth*, and how do they fit back into that point of almost nothing?

Irrespective of what may seem to be theoretically correct from the point of view of earth-science, every event that occurs can only take place within strict and absolutely lawful parameters. Therefore, is the Big Bang theory correct? Deriving from theoretical analyses, empirical observations and mathematical calculations, is science right with regard to how it all came to be? Or has something more been missed or not understood?

In the final analysis does it really matter? Our purpose on earth was always to recognise and strive to understand The Laws by which we are enjoined to live, and to recognise our Spiritual Origins – that place in Creation from whence we came, our true home – and to where we are meant to return. So the incredible amount of energy expended on trying to understand the physical universe, never mind the huge cost of it, may be ultimately wasted – *if* these particular scientists concentrate *solely* on just one single aspect, i.e. the physical.

Unfortunately such efforts are often lauded as some kind of *ultimate* knowledge. That is a great tragedy, for under current educational parameters – at least in the Western world anyway – generations of students, obviously numbering in the hundreds of millions, simply follow academic lines of thought which are *ultimately detrimental* to any kind of **deeper-seeing** paradigm.

That is not to say we should not study the stars and the universe, for such investigation truly is the preserve of science. The ultimate purpose of such study and discovery, however, should be to reveal and explain the most powerful and profound correlation between that which is here in our material home-world, and that which exists far above the physical universes – **"the many mansions"**. As it stands today, science often appears to edify itself.

The truly intuitive scientist within that discipline will understand that the gift of intelligence, which most scientists obviously possess, is exactly that; a gift. It is one, however, which should be employed for the purpose of studying and explaining the connections between the transitory material and The Eternal nonmaterial. Science, and therefore scientists – out of themselves and *through their work* – should edify The Creator and His Work of The Creations. The very nature of scientific endeavour and discovery should bring about this recognition naturally in any case, particularly where the study of the cosmos is concerned.

For:

"When we consider thy heavens, the work of thy fingers,
   The moon and the stars, which thou hast ordained,
   What is man, that thou art mindful of him?"

(*The Gospel of the Essenes* E. B. Szekely, p 175)

Such clear wisdom from the ancient world leads perfectly into the 21st century world of the Hubble Space Telescope, powerful radio telescopes and super-computers to examine the make-up and behaviour of the *stars*. The series of questions we asked regarding the impossible-to-understand numbers, which cosmological science evidently claims is mathematically valid, might just offer the reader powerful food for thought for "digesting" the next and rather mind-blowing part of this Chapter. Notwithstanding such mathematical gymnastics, the clarified insight of Dr Richard Steinpach herewith *actually does* connect "science" with the "Judgement Process".

As previously noted, although the following essay was written some years ago, the earlier discoveries in cosmology which he uses to explain those very processes are more than adequate for our purpose. Since many of the concepts he clarifies have been covered in other Chapters, the perceptive reader should have, by this point, absorbed a sufficient level of background knowledge to follow and understand his explanations. Because the next crucial part describes the 'mechanics' of the "Judgement Process", a precise connection is therefore established with both the concept and reality of the 'Second Death'.

From Dr Steinpach's complete article we will cull certain key points to tie in this spiritually and scientifically-expansive concept with the overall thrust of the book, but otherwise generally follow the thread as he reveals it and thereby offer the significant revelations regarding the final fate of human beings. The primary 'knowledge-source' from which he derives the actual connective facts to explain it all is the Work – *In The Light Of Truth, The Grail Message*. It is the very same from which this book derives *its* explanations, especially that of The Spiritual Laws of Creation.

However, whilst Dr Steinpach's references are sourced from what is referred to as the *Three Volume Edition*, the aim of this book is to provide a bridge – and thus point the way – to the **original Work**. The complete Title may be found in **Epilogue**. So whilst the knowledge of Creation and Spiritual Law in the *Three Volume Edition* is still that of the Original text, it nevertheless represents a *change in format* from **The Original**, hence the desire and aim of "Crystal Publishing" to lead the spiritually-perceptive reader/seeker to the **Prime Source**!

We will therefore use the designations, "The Message", "The Spiritual Laws" or "The Laws of Creation" to reference some of his explanations from that indispensable Source, or as an insertion into explanatory texts where certain of Steinpach's direct reference to the Three Volume Edition would otherwise be found. In other cases, his direct quotes from the Three Volume Edition will remain.

14.1 "The Inconceivable ... Here It Happens."

(Dr Richard Steinpach.)

Steinpach, writing from the ultimately irrefutable knowledge of The Work, "In The Light Of Truth", states: "...it is only the cycle of Creation, in its continuous coming into being, disintegration, and re-formation, that is eternal and without end, thus infinite." All the revelations and prophecies are therefore "...fulfilled within this happening. And finally, "...the 'Last Judgement' for the earth will also be fulfilled in it!"

14.2 The "Last Judgement."

Steinpach continues: The concept of a 'Last' – that is, a final

– Judgement is to be found in many religious teachings in one form or another. In the Christian creed the notion of the sound of trumpets and the rising of the dead from their graves is associated with this concept. But, again, man has developed a wrong picture from revelations which were given to him for the understanding of his path through Creation. For the first time The Work, *In the Light of Truth*, has replaced this partly naive and partly fantastic attempt at an interpretation – which expects a miraculous arbitrary act of Will on the part of The Creator – by a clear description of the happening. Accordingly, the "Last Judgement" is also described as a completely natural process based on The Laws of Creation.

The World of Matter which surrounds us is not eternal; it has a beginning and an end. Just as the individual form is fashioned and then decomposes, so it also comes to pass with matter itself – but in a much larger cycle. Matter also requires renewal through transformation, which purifies and refreshes it for a new beginning.

The human being, coming from The Spiritual Realm as a spirit-seed, is "planted" in this material world for the purpose of maturing through the furthering influence of the material environment. But because the material world is subject to the continual process of "formation, evolution and disintegration", the spirit-seed of man must have developed itself to such a level that it can extricate itself from it before the world reaches that stage of disintegration. Otherwise, as Dr Steinpach notes, it will be drawn along into the process which brings about the "disintegration of matter".

The concept of disintegration is beyond human imagination or experience, for we could never understand the full magnitude of such a happening. This is because, as stated by Dr Steinpach, "...we are only able to lead a conscious life *between* the beginning and the end of matter". He emphasises that disintegration is *not* the same as decomposition, which latter only concerns the small cycle of material form. Disintegration has a much greater impact, for it "puts an end to the vastness of matter", leading it back into a primeval formless state, beyond the material condition. In this connection, Dr Steinpach offers the following interesting insights:

> "We now know that matter can be transformed into radiation from which it arose. Indeed, it is through this becoming *lighter* that sublimation occurs. Disintegration, on the other

hand — is a consequence of the excessive density of matter. Therefore its cause is opposite to that which brings about dissolution.

About a decade ago, radio telescopes began to probe the skies (which up 'til then had only been observed with optical instruments) and were able to pick up waves even beyond those of visible light. Through these observations, revolutionary discoveries were made: that in the remote expanses of the universe into which our eyes cannot penetrate, there exist stars whose condition and behaviour are without precedent.

Today, we no longer think only of "white dwarves", "red giants" and "super novae", but also of quasars, pulsars and neutron-stars. However, the subject of the life history of the stars, which seems to become clearer through these discoveries, will not be dwelt upon here, especially since science has hardly progressed beyond making assumptions regarding the various stages of development. We are only interested here in the last stage of this happening. For what takes place in galactic expanses appears like a magic trick: "a star disappears from the world". However, the circumstances under which this takes place show a remarkable agreement with the descriptions in The Message of the "disintegration of matter" and the "Last Judgement".

Thus we have to come to a correct understanding of the concept of a "material disintegration". In the following section Dr Steinpach, for the most part, lets the specialists speak. He limits himself to presenting their statements along with a few words of his own to connect them and to explain their relationship to The Message. We believe the comparisons, which the reader can verify for himself from that Source, will speak clearly enough for themselves.

14.3 The "degeneration" of Matter

"The scientific designation of these objects as "quasi-stellar radio sources", from which the shortened form, "quasar", is derived, already indicates there is only a vague similarity with stars, in the sense in which these have been known up 'til now. Gustav Andreas Tamaan, a staff member at the laboratories on Mount Wilson and Mount Palomar, in "Bild der Wissenschaft", No 3/1965 (Deutsche Verlags Anstallt) described quasars as:

> "...the most puzzling and revolutionary objects, which have most deeply shaken the physical concept of the world in recent years."
>
> Further, in volume 11/1970 of the same journal, Felix Jurewitsch Zigel, cosmobiologist of the Space Training Institute of Moscow explains:
>
> "We are still far from even partly comprehending the phenomenon of the quasar."

The riddle of these celestial bodies lies, above all, in their density. Their matter is so compactly compressed, that ... according to scientific writer Hoimar V. Ditfurth in *Children of the Universe* (published by Hoffmann and Campe, Hamburg):

> "...a piece the size of a matchbox, if deposited on the surface of the earth, would immediately break through the earth's crust and from there plunge almost unhindered into its depths, not coming to rest until it had reached the centre of the earth."

It is because of these incomprehensible magnitudes that the scientists speak in this connection of "overdense" as well as of "degenerated matter".

The designations "overdense degenerate matter" and "the over-ripeness of matter" originate, therefore, from two different sources. Nonetheless, a striking conceptual similarity exists between them. Both depict a situation that lies beyond the threshold of normality. Thus, in the considerations to follow, science and The Message are fundamentally in agreement with regard to the nature of matter.

In the mid-1920s to mid-1930s, the unique Work of The Grail Message had already clearly explained the existence of the various planes in Creation. The Grail Message states that in the World of Gross Matter there are many levels much denser and heavier than the earth. This key Work also explains that it is the "over-ripeness" of Matter which subsequently leads it to its disintegration in preparation for its renewal.

Thus, while the human spirit matures in the World of Matter, it has no choice but to join in The Eternal cycle of formation, evolution and disintegration. One day, therefore, that part of the material world in which it dwells will also reach its point of disintegration.

14.4 The Human Spirit and Matter

Steinpach notes from The Message that as long as the human spirit remains in the World of Matter it joins in part of a "...great and eternal rotating movement without realising it." One day thus comes where at last it arrives "...at the boundary line where that part of Creation inhabited by human spirits slowly drifts towards disintegration!"

Thus the fate of the human spirit during part of its wandering is connected with that of matter. Indeed the entire material world encompasses, according to the words of The Message, not only the visible gross material world, but also the completely differently constituted world of ethereal matter. Our physical bodies originate from the former while from the latter derive our soul bodies which remain as the cloak of the spirit after it has laid aside the earthly shell. Science is only able to observe the World of Gross Matter, but The Message describes the Worlds of Gross and Ethereal Matter and, above all, their influence on the human spirit that is still enveloped by matter. Its assertions go much further. In order to understand what follows, it is necessary to take note of this difference.

The subject under consideration, however, is so profound that the joyous path leading upwards toward The Light – which The Message reveals through the recognition of The Laws of Creation and which should have been the natural path of all human spirits – unfortunately barely reaches even a reasonable threshold here for most humans. It is emphasised, therefore: The Message does not threaten "eternal damnation" in the explanations which unequivocally clarify a concept which has repulsed an exceptionally large number of people.

Notwithstanding the general human aversion to "judgement" of this kind, The Laws of God – which bear **His Will** and which manifest in this part of the world in the form of Natural Laws – must be fulfilled absolutely by virtue of their perfection. The human spirit, whose free will is an inseparable part of his nature, brings about justly lawful consequences through his decisions, be they for good or evil.

Therefore, whoever is terrified at the horror that these Laws must prepare for all those who were steadily against them and thus proved themselves unworthy to be permitted to live a conscious life in this Creation, should remember that this is *not the intention of The Creator.* Only by its self-willed and continuous turning away from The Light was it possible for the human spirit to reach the stage where it could never maintain itself on its ordained path. And only in that way could it come to pass that it must suffer disintegration through having become useless. So, what is the key requirement here?

As we have previously explained, human beings bear many cloaks, not just the physical one. Within each of us, therefore, is the ethereal body, in addition to the gross material (physical) body. The ethereal body is also known as the "soul body", which remains as the "cloak of the spirit" after earthly death.

Quite simply, depending on man's spiritual state in the Gross Material World as well as in the Ethereal World, the spiritual man, the real "ego", must either move upwards, or remain chained to the World of Matter. Only the serious longing for Truth and Light will, by virtue of the change it works in him, make each person spiritually purer and thus more luminous. This most necessary condition must naturally therefore detach him more and more from dense matter and thereby drive him upwards – *in just proportion to his purity and lightness.*

He, however, who believes only in matter therewith keeps himself bound to it by his conviction. He thus remains chained to it and so cannot be driven upwards. A completely lawful and thus natural separation therefore takes place between those striving towards the Light and those connected with the Darkness. The process is brought about solely through a decision personally desired by each individual – in accordance, however, with the existing natural laws of Spiritual Gravitation.

To re-emphasise this key point once more: From our discussion on The Spiritual Laws we know that those who refuse to strive after spiritual development and instead focus only on material pleasures are weighed down according to The Law of Spiritual Gravity. This results in an enchainment, a tying down to the lower, denser gross material worlds. It is solely because of this *voluntary enchainment process* that those particular human beings – of which there are clearly millions upon millions – have to suffer disintegration. **Such a human being, therefore, has effectively rendered himself useless before The Creator and His Creation!**

For this reason, it is imperative for we human beings to strive to achieve at least some degree of spiritual recognition at just **this very point in time** in order to extricate ourselves from The World of Matter before it enters the final stages of disintegration. Beyond that point nothing of our personalities will remain if, because of our desire for only material things, we are still locked into this world.

Dr Steinpach explains this withdrawal from the world of matter in the following interesting excerpt from his essay which leads us again to the "Quasi-stellar radio source".

> "...we now turn again to the "Quasi-stellar radio source". They are – according to Gustav A. Tamaan – "...the brightest objects in the Universe and in spite of their small size radiate a hundred times more light than a bright milky way system."
>
> In considering what is to come, this seems as if the light in time wants to withdraw from the overdense "degenerated" stars. Withdrawal of light is the removal of energy which has become bound to matter. Energy, however, as the Author of The Message has shown, ...is of a spiritual nature although from a much weaker gradation than the human spirit... Thus *something spiritual is leaving the dying celestial bodies in quantity.*"
>
> (Emphasis mine.)

Regarding this, Steinpach notes the following in The Grail Message:

> "Then, however, it is high time for all human spirits which are still within the World of Matter to make haste and improve themselves to such an extent that they can ascend to the safe and luminous haven of the Eternal Kingdom, which means to find the right way and above all the shortest way of escape from the impending dangers of the World of Matter before being overtaken by them!"

(From: "I am the Resurrection and the Life...", Vol. II)

What is the nature of the final dangers threatening in the World of Matter? In all things The Law of Equilibrium maintains complete balance, and it is only through this perfection that entire star-systems and galaxies can "...pursue their respective courses and maintain themselves". Obviously, science has come to that very recognition, as stated by Felix J. Zigel, whom Dr Steinpach quotes:

> "In the final analysis, every star must be regarded as a kind of system of equilibrium, which can only continue to exist for as long as the gravity and pressure of the inner atomic

reactions retain balance: if gravity seeks to compress the star, the tremendous gas tension from within will strive to tear it apart."

Thus The Law of Balance operates in all things, both big and small! Even man is not exempt from the adamantine operation of this Law. If he is continually confronted with and oppressed by difficulties, he could eventually break down. On the other hand, if the "inner pressure" becomes too strong, he could burst with joy, enthusiasm or even anger. We can clearly see many such parallels in *every* happening in Nature. Hence, if matter becomes far too dense, its gravity correspondingly increases "...until the atomic movement can no longer withstand it". Any disturbance in the state of equilibrium will not be tolerated beyond a very definite limit.

Dr Steinpach now offers us a few more insightful quotes from both Zigel and Ditfurth (authors' of "Children of the Universe."):

14.5 The Collapse

Dr Steinpach notes: Even the specialists shy away from describing the processes that follow. Thus, before proceeding with his explanations, Felix Jurewitsch Zigel (op cit.) first states:

> "When we now attempt to explain the quasar, we are afraid that it could be mistaken for a science fiction story."

Only after this introduction does he continue:

> "Scientists came to the recognition that with extremely large masses the force of gravity is so great that it can no longer be burst apart by any radiational pressure. Gravity alone then determines the fate of such a heavenly body. Under its influence, the star experiences a gravitational collapse, which causes it to fall together like a house of cards and increases its density to about 10^{30} grams per cubic centimetre, a truly incredible solidification, which one can only grasp when one realises that the whole earth only weighs 5.87×10^{27} grams."

(Felix Jurewitsch Zigel)

> "The processes which take place as soon as the mass of the star exceeds this ominous ... limit, appears frankly fantastic,

but they are today no longer pure theory. The calculations show that the mass of such a star is so great that its own inner power of attraction is enough to destroy the atomic structure of matter..." "This is the moment of the so-called gravitational collapse: within a period of about one second the whole star which was still planet-sized collapses into a volume of between ten to twenty kilometres in diameter."

(Hoimar v. Ditfurth, *Children of the Universe*)

According to Dr Steinpach, science has already established that the critical limit (beyond which breakdown takes place) is around 1.44 times the mass of our sun. And while he admits that the sun is certainly not the measure for all cosmic processes, there is nevertheless a certain symbolism about just this particular number:

"Scientists have calculated that the critical limit at which this breakdown occurs is at about 1.44 times the mass of the sun. Now our sun is certainly not the measure for all cosmic processes. Nevertheless, it seems as if there is a lawfulness here which is worthy of attention. 1.44 is 1.2 × 1.2, thus, a hundredth of 12 × 12. We encounter the number twelve where complete order is involved. There are twelve signs in the zodiac and our divisions of time are based on the number twelve. Jesus selected twelve disciples; in the Revelation of John, the number of Sealed Ones is named as twelve times twelve thousand (Chap. 7, 4-8): in the description of the "heavenly Jerusalem" (Chap. 21, 10-21) the number twelve occurs again and again and "its walls measured one hundred, forty four cubits". In The Grail Message it is said that with all the gradations, there are twelve temperaments in all (see Temperament, Vol. III): twelve meridians traverse the human body (acupuncture is based on this).

This indicates that the number twelve, but more correctly its square, is actually a limit – "an insurmountable measure of completeness". Perhaps it is this knowledge that led to the fear of the number thirteen in ancient times. Therefore, if catastrophe develops when "the number 12 × 12 – in the present connection as an astrophysically and scientifically established limit – is exceeded", perhaps we should consider whether it is more than a mere superstition or purely a symbolic meaning, but rather an actual cosmic happening for it offers a view of lawfulness in all of creation. We must remember that it is an actual implosion taking place here, whereby "over-dense matter" collapses within itself all within a single second, as science propounds.

Whether the human being who is in the world of gross or ethereal matter is also affected by it may be understood in the descriptive words of The Message: Thus, what It has stated with more far-reaching significance, *then takes place in matter*:

> "What is false ... must collapse of itself..."
>
> (From: Earthman before his God. Vol. I)

> "...disintegrate and turn to dust."
>
> (From Submission. Vol. I)

For what happens during a gravitational collapse actually appears to be a final separation. To further illustrate the process, Dr Steinpach once again cites Ditfurth:

> "In a tremendous atomic explosion, about a tenth of the whole mass of the collapsing star is thereby hurled into the universe at a speed of up to ten thousand kilometres per second (6,200 miles per second). This is the process which causes a fixed star to collapse and then apparently leads to the appearance of an entirely new star, a supernova, which for several weeks can shine as brightly as two hundred million suns. What is left over of a supernova explosion is a star whose mass is still about as great as that of our sun, but which is now compressed into the volume of a sphere with a diameter of only ten to twenty kilometres.
>
> The power of attraction of a star mass compressed into such a comparatively small space is so great that it is no longer possible even for photons of light to leave the gravitational field of such a celestial body."

14.6 The Separation from the Light

Steinpach is careful to impress upon his reader the fact that the *seemingly impossible* is nevertheless *scientifically valid*. He states:

> "What follows sounds so fantastic that I wish to quote a number of scientists in this connection. Just at this so very important point, the impression should not arise that these are the assumptions of an imaginative layman."

Hoimar v. Ditfurth continues (op. cit.)

> "The power of attraction of a star mass compressed into such a comparatively small space is so great that it is no longer possible even for photons of light to leave the gravitational field of such a celestial body."

J. Brian Dance of the University of Birmingham writes in "Bild der Wissenschaft" No. II/ 1970:

> "If ... a star collapses under the influence of its own gravitational field, the tremendous gravity on its surface can even hold back the light which it had up 'til then emitted. Thus the quanta's of light are no longer able to move counter to the field of gravity. Thereby, the star becomes invisible, it becomes a 'black hole'. Because neither matter nor light can move out of the confines of "black holes", their existence can be proven only by their gravitational influences."

Felix Jurewitsch Zigel (op. cit.) writes:

> "The star then sinks immediately into a gravitational hole of invisibility. Only its mass, which manifests through gravity, still shows any signs of life."

And Volker Weidemann (op. cit.) writes:

> "A black hole occurs within which the dying star will always remain enclosed... The star in the black hole has such a great surface gravity that no kind of electromagnetic radiation can escape from it any longer. The connection of the collapsing object with the outside world is thus made impossible..."

And thus we have the phenomenon of a "black hole", which is able to hold back even its own light, which it had emitted up until that point. The star becomes invisible, and because both matter and light cannot move out of the range of a black hole, its existence is "proven only by its gravitational influences." Or, as Volker Weidemann (quoted by Dr Steinpach) wrote:

> "The connection of the collapsing object with the outside world is thus made impossible..."

Let us return once more to the beginning of this hardly conceivable happening and let us summarise with simple words: While the compressed star, which has exceeded the limiting value, is in a state of collapse, it hurls a small part of its mass away. In a last gigantic flash, scientifically designated as a supernova eruption, such light as is possible escapes from the star, before the remaining part is confined in darkness forever.

This is then, purely astrophysically speaking, a final separation of light and darkness. And that is exactly what The Grail Message says about the Last Judgement!

> "Then the division between Light and Darkness will be finally accomplished and the Judgement fulfilled."

This gross material event means, however, for the human spirit still in matter:

> "...a final decision! Men in both worlds (Note: the Gross and the Ethereal) will either be so far ennobled that they can be uplifted to the regions of Light, or they will remain bound in their base nature through their own volition and thereby be finally hurled down into eternal damnation! This means that together with matter from which they cannot detach themselves, they will be drawn towards disintegration."

(From: The World. Vol. I)

Here, again, we must remember the inexorable effect of The Law of Spiritual Gravity. If men become so far ennobled that they are uplifted to the Luminous Spiritual Realms, *they need not fear this final separation in the material worlds*. But if they are strongly bound to matter through their base nature and thus wrong volition, they will experience **disintegration of the conscious personality** – akin to eternal damnation i.e., spiritual death! Precisely, therefore, because they did not free themselves before the material disintegration at the end of the gross material world cycle![3]

Let us again quote from Dr Steinpach's brilliant essay on the subject:

> "Astrophysics now stands at the threshold of what has hitherto been inconceivable. Light appears to be chained to matter through its excessive density."

---

[3] Note that the incarnation of man on earth is meant to be only a temporary binding of the spirit to gross matter for "the sole ordained purpose of attaining maturity". But if the spirit develops a wrong volition, then it remains tied to the disintegrating matter, which is what takes place here.

Accordingly, therefore, the same thing would happen to the Light in relation to the human spirit: while one part escapes as a form of radiation, the other remains bound within matter.

Steinpach notes that it is characteristic that "...the escaping light originates from the outer layers which are still relatively less firmly bound, while the 'black hole' within the core of the collapsing star continues to expand."

But in the end, "...it is not only the *escape* of the light from the 'black hole' that is no longer possible; the immense suction of its gravity also *swallows* any light which comes too near. Jakov Seldowitsch, Astrophysicist of the Academy of Sciences of the USSR, writes the following about it in "Bild der Wissenschaft" No. 3/1974:

> "The name itself ... 'black hole' ... means that a ray of light or a minute particle, thus everything which approaches the surface of the black hole, would irresistibly be attracted by gravity and disappear in the hole."

The inner light of man, his spirit, is also threatened in a similar way:

> "If a human spirit permits itself to be deviated toward darkness, it runs the risk of being drawn beyond the outermost circle of its normal course towards a depth from which it can then no longer find its way back in order to ascend ... and so it is continually drawn along in the mighty cycle of material creation until it is finally drawn into disintegration..."
>
> (From: "The Mystery of Lucifer", Vol. II)

The Grail Message also speaks of the "gravity of the darkness" (see the Lecture "Rigidity", Vol. I). Actually these processes in the collapsed stars show that extreme gravity causes darkness. Indeed, the close homogeneity of these two concepts proves itself in the cosmic expanses even to the last minute detail. The English astronomer, Sir Fred Hoyle, says that:

On the strange characteristics of a "black hole":

> "...such a celestial body shuts itself off to some extent from the universe through its own tremendous gravity."
>
> (quoted from Hoimar v. Ditfurth in *Children of the Universe*.)

Furthermore, we read from John Taylor in the book, *The Black Suns* (Scherz Verlag), which, in spite of its rather unfortunate title, deals with black holes:

> "If man were to fall into the core of this terrible structure, there would no longer be any possibility for him to ever leave it again, regardless of how hard he exerts himself."

Does this not explain why The Author of "In the Light Of Truth" called out to those who refuse to learn:

> "Sink into that death-dealing horror which you have prepared for yourselves with the most stubborn efforts!" ...
> "There you shall be bound in an inescapable grip."

(From: "A Necessary Word", Vol I.)

This was no horrifying threat, but a warning to rouse them from the inescapable end to which they are heading if they continue on their path.

14.7 The Absence of Differentiation

What happens to the matter approaching its end, after the final separation from the Light? The Message says:

> "...where disintegration begins, all matter loses its form..."

(From: "The Regions of Darkness and Damnation", Vol. II)

Of human spirits who have remained bound to matter, it states further that:

Not only the gross material bodies are dissolved but that the ethereal bodies also become subject to the torments of disintegration covering thousands of years. This is the meaning of the *complete effacement* of a human spirit from "The Book of Life". It is the loss by disintegration of its personal self-consciousness built up over millennia through successive incarnations. The so-called "image of God", the basic form that humankind had acquired in the course of becoming conscious, finally disintegrates! Essentially, this personality dissolves back into the primeval constituents, the spiritual seed. This is what we have previously already referred to as the "Second Death"!

It is therefore important to read Dr Steinpach's quotes and insights on the nature of this happening:

Computer calculations have deduced what goes on within the stellar mass which is sunk in darkness. Scientists report: "Thereby a point is finally reached, where not only the electron casing of atoms collapses (this had already occurred in the course of overdensification), but also the elementary parts forming the structure of the atomic nucleus itself."

(Hoimar v. Ditfurth op. cit.)

"Through a tremendous shrinking of the volume of the star, the electrons and protons of its matter are forced to be transformed into neutrons. All chemical Multiplicity thus ceases."

(J. Brian Dance. "Bild der Wissenschaft", No 11/1972)

"Thereby, through the extreme pressure, one uniform material, the 'neutronium' is formed from the various elements and all the chemical multiplicity of our own world is compressed into the uniformity of this material!"

(Willard Frank Libby, Nobel Prize Winner in Chemistry, "Bild der Wissenschaft, No. 10/1971)

"Let us now consider the above descriptions: In The Message it is said that "...everything material loses its form". This is exactly what happens through the total destruction of the atomic structure.

With regard to man it is further said in The Message that the decomposition first affects the "ethereal body", thus the cloak which remains after laying aside of the earthly body, and only subsequently is the spirit, the core, affected. Also in matter, the cloak which is made up of electron orbits is first crushed and only later is the atomic nucleus affected.

Lastly, The Message speaks of the "dissolution of the personal ego". In matter, as has now been determined, it is fundamentally the same thing that happens. In its own way, matter also experiences a total "depersonalisation". In the end there are no longer different elements, no longer positively or negatively charged particles, but only a formless mass without any differentiation. Thus matter is also stripped of all properties and returned to a primeval state.

This stage of the happening would appear to me to be the most significant. For the variety of elements is due to the differing number of sub-particles that make up the atomic structure and thus determine the atomic number and weight. At the same time, a separation into positive and negative electrical charges exists throughout the building blocks of the universe. This can be pictured as vertical (differentiation of elements through atomic number and weight) and horizontal (separation into opposite charges) alignments which appear as a cross that embraces all material abundance, indeed from which it first came to be. Thus the death of matter assumes a shattering magnitude: For with the loss of its structure, the cross that is inscribed in it is also obliterated. The Cross is thus revealed in its true significance, as the expression of the moving, form-giving power! With its collapse, its disappearance, our well-known material world also ends."

14.8 "Torn apart and crushed..."

Dr Steinpach notes: Let us consider more closely the manner and method in which the dissolution of the personal "ego" which has developed wrongly from the spirit germ, proceed. In the previously quoted passage from The Grail Message, the ego is described as "torn apart". Yet in another place ("The World", Vol. I) as "crushed". Therefore it cannot be only the pressure of gravity which brings about the dissolution, a movement from without also plays a part. While the inner motion of the atom in the overdense matter gradually becomes less and finally ceases through the breakdown of its structure, the outer rotation increases to a raging whirlwind. This, in accordance with the Laws of Creation, is the consequence of the violation of the Law of Equilibrium through one-sided activity, the loss of balance.

That the celestial bodies which, according to The Grail Message, are caught in disintegration, will also be rotating rapidly, is easily deduced from the fact that the "sucking power of the vortex of disintegration" is mentioned. Science has now confirmed this:

> "Moreover, the black hole can suck up and tear away matter and light from the universe,"

> (Volker Weidemann op. cit.)

Dr Steinpach thus proceeds to describe the actual manner in which the dissolution of the personal "ego", the true self, takes place. He explains that it is not solely the pressure of gravity that brings about the dissolution, but also that of an *external movement*. He states that the inner motion of the atom decreases while the "outer rotation increases to a whirlwind", which is caused by imbalance, thus an upset in the equilibrium. Since the black hole can suck up and tear away both matter and light within the universe, the operation resembles a great vortex, just like the suction of whirling water. Since The Grail Message, which Dr Steinpach uses as the main source of his knowledge, also describes the process as a "vortex", it is clear that there is more than a mere symbolic resemblance. Dr Steinpach illustrates:

> "The fast rotation of the stellar mass is similar in nature to the movement of grist, as we can observe in a small way in the vortex of an old coffee mill [where] the coffee is drawn into the mill and, through its rotation, torn apart and crushed."

For [the] one being so "torn apart and crushed", however, he does himself witness the process from within his innermost being. Dr Steinpach's quotes from Zigel and other astronomers, and also from The Grail Message, yet again shows how science wonderfully confirms the immense spiritual Knowledge mediated within the pages of that crucial Work for humankind:

> "It is interesting, too, that before the inner observer becomes invisible to his outer environment, he sees the whole future(!) of his outermost counterpart passing rapidly before him within a few moments."
>
> (Felix Jurewitsch Zigel)

14.9 The experience of time

Steinpach notes that science has also viewed this occurrence (i.e., the disintegration) from the standpoint of the theory of relativity. Considering the event as an "observer", from within and without the process, Felix Jurewitsch Zigel (op. cit.) concludes:

> "It is interesting, too, that before the inner observer becomes invisible to his outer environment, he sees the whole future (!) of his outermost counterpart passing rapidly before him within a few moments."

Steinpach believes that it is "...not appropriate here to pursue further the scientific deviation offered by this seemingly astonishing fact". But he does take note of the following:

> "The 'inner observer' would, according to the above, still be able, at the moment of his fall into darkness, to experience the nature of the fate of those who can be spared his own. His own fate must then seem the more horrible to him, because he is able to recognise what he *gambled away.*"

(Emphasis mine.)

He writes that scientific observation is also in agreement with the words of The Message, which states the following about the affected one:

> "He is only stirred up so as to come to the dreadful recognition of his fall into the bottomless pit of final disintegration, of being cast out."

("The Guardian of the Flame", Volume III)

That which has been **gambled away**, then, is not some mere gift or talent, but the Grace of Everlasting Life! In a thousand torments, this personal ego completely disappears...!

It should be noted that, according to The Message the process is a "slow disintegration", although there are also references to torments "lasting a thousand years". Dr Steinpach explains this by citing both Schklowski and Zigel:

> "Because the laws of the general theory of relativity play the leading role in a shrinking process of this nature, it can also be said that for an observer from outside, everything that transpires upon such a body takes an infinitely long time."

(Josif Schklowski, Professor at the Soviet Institute for Space Research, in *Bild der Wissenschaft* No. 10/1972)

> "But an observer in the collapsing celestial body will be able to see by his watch that the entire process only lasts about ten minutes."

(Felix Jurewitsch Zigel)

The contradiction in the "observed time" is only seemingly so, however. For The Message Itself alludes to a longer period of disintegration for the human spirits trapped in matter. The contradiction arises because the scientific calculations are based on the theory of relativity, i.e. on the relationship between the motion of celestial bodies, which is nevertheless only confined within the *gross material sphere*. Thus the scientific explanations only concern the *physical body* of man, whilst ignoring his innermost core or true self, *his spirit*!

Without taking the spirit into account in all these calculations, only errors can emerge. Dr Steinpach explains the discrepancy thus:

> "This observer's watch, however, measures the course of motion of its immediate surroundings, but not the conscious *experiencing* of the spirit involved. However, a spirit which is still bound to matter which is undergoing dissolution has already become almost rigid, so that a comparison of its own motion with that of a rapid outer movement is hardly possible. Therefore, relatively, the whirling rotation around his body must seem of relatively infinite magnitude to him."

14.10 The End shall become the Beginning

Now, as everything proceeds in cycles in Creation, so too must the end be joined back to the beginning. For, as Dr Steinpach quotes from The Message, nothing can be destroyed, but merely returns to a primeval state. Therefore, although science believes that even a neutron star "...contracts into a mathematical point, to a total abstraction", thus mathematically disappearing from the universe – which is akin to the "vortex of disintegration" described in The Message – it is merely the conclusion of a cycle, beyond which there is a new beginning. Dr Steinpach again quotes Weidemann in this regard, and then proceeds to cite more evidence concerning the possible existence of the "inverse of a black hole", i.e., a "white hole".

> "According to computers, even the neutron star stage is not yet the conclusion of the star's biography. At any rate, after a short interruption, the contracting movement of this already inconceivably dense sphere begins again and then

there is no longer any halt; the neutron star contracts into a mathematical point, to a total abstraction...
How this latter information is to be understood remains to be seen. In any case, there is no longer any power left to counteract the self-contraction, to the outermost boundary of what can be mathematically calculated. In some inconceivable manner it then actually disappears from the universe."

Does this self-stricture until the point of disappearance not correspond to the suction into the "vortex of disintegration" of which The Grail Message speaks?

"It should be noted that disintegration is not the same as destruction. Nothing can be destroyed. It only relapses into a primeval state..."

(From: "I am the Resurrection and the Life...", Volume II)

This cycle of material evolution, which closes by the joining of beginning and end, is now also beginning to become clearer to science as the following suggests:

"It is extremely interesting that the primeval detonation, which set into motion the birth of the Universe is, in the mathematical sense of the general theory of relatively, almost a reverse of gravitational collapse."

(Volker Weidemann op. cit.)

The discovery of black holes automatically gave rise to the question of what then happens to the sunken matter, and as to where it disappears. The Grail Message had spoken of a "gigantic funnel" ... "...where disintegration takes place, in order to be thrust out again at the other end as primordial seed for a new cycle." (From: "The World", Volume I)
John Taylor (op. cit.) also gives the picture of such a double funnel. In contrast to the "black hole" which sucks in, he designates its opposite, which gives and creates, as a "white hole". In his opinion:
"The development of such a 'white hole' can be conceived as being the opposite of a body undergoing collapse; it would appear pictorially as if the film taken of the collapse of a rotating star were played backwards. But we have already noted that this collapsing body must have come from another universe..."

How sublimely simple the vast field of this whole happening had already been summarised in The Message:
"Because it is over-ripe the World of Matter is now entering a period of disintegration and simultaneously drifting towards a new birth."

(From: "I am the Resurrection and the Life...", Volume II)

The fate of the human spirit will obviously follow a similar pattern. For, after the complete disintegration of matter (which returns to primeval substance), the spirit is set free and *does* return to its origin, The Spiritual Realm. *Not*, however, as a consciously developed spirit, but as a mere unconscious seed, since it failed to develop its personality to a level sufficiently spiritually mature enough to fulfil its God-given task!

Obviously, we do not know the exact time of this happening for human beings. According to The Message, this Last or Final Judgement "...comes one day for each material celestial globe, but it does not take place simultaneously in the whole of Creation." Therefore, in all the millions of years comprising the development of a celestial globe, there comes one year that is absolutely decisive for it, for the "separation of the light from the darkness", which we discussed earlier. Dr Steinpach notes that this makes it possible "...for us to observe the different stages of the happening". Little surprise, then, that science admits that:

"the stars, which we see in the heavens, are not only at different distances from us and at different ages, but they belong to different successive generations."

(Ditfurth.)

Dr Steinpach summarises the whole process by quoting from John Taylor's words:

"Billions of years will pass, but in the end the black holes will engulf us."

14.11 Conclusion

"It is only the cycle of Creation, in its continuous coming into being, disintegration and reformation, that is eternal and without end, thus infinite."

(From: "The World", Vol. I)

So what was already stated in The Message decades ago, science has now come this far. It has recognised the eternal cycle of matter. Regarding this, Steinpach quotes John Taylor:

> "In this case, the whole of development would start again from the beginning – expansion, slowing down, maximum point of expansion, contraction and finally the destruction of all connected structures around us. Such a cycle would be eternal – it has always been so, it will always be so."

It therefore behoves us all to develop to the point whereby we can extricate ourselves from matter. For escaping this material disintegration automatically implies "eternal life"!

In conclusion, we can summarise the main points of what we have hitherto discussed in this Chapter with the help of Dr Steinpach's insights:

1. The cycle of the worlds of matter is eternal in its formation, evolution, disintegration and reformation. The forms change, and even matter itself must dissolve into primeval seed, which then prepares for reformation.

2. The degeneration process, which results in disintegration, is brought about by a certain degree of over-ripeness.

3. The collapse, or disintegration, takes place when a particular threshold value is crossed.

4. The complete separation between the light and the darkness occurs resulting in the utter disintegration of the inner structure and "the loss of differentiation".

5. The world finally implodes in the "vortex of disintegration", akin to being sucked into "a funnel".

Although science is primarily concerned with "measuring vibrations", scientists nevertheless have to use earthly instruments, thus mere gross material aids, to effect those measurements. Such tools can only penetrate, at most, to "fine gross matter". These aids therefore cannot measure anything beyond the gross material limits because "The Law of Attraction of Similar Species" prevents such a connection. Only gross material can perceive gross material, ethereal perceive ethereal, and spiritual perceive spiritual!

Nevertheless, using the power of the intuitive perception, and "extrapolating upwards" using the results of scientific measurement, we can certainly perceive and apply the knowledge of the same cycle of development of matter to all species in this Creation. For everything follows the inviolable outworking of ***The Law!***

In this regard, the concluding part of Dr Steinpach's essay should stimulate us to greater thinking and critical, intuitive reflection:

> Already the recognition is dawning: "The black hole not
>
> only places the sciences in confusion, it also puts in question all the opinions which man has made about the world and the place he occupies in it. For him, the consequences of the existence of black holes are equally as important, if not of greater importance, as for science. In man's attempt to understand the unknown and to answer the last of all questions, the question of life and death, of living and dead matter, the holes play an important role." writes John Taylor in his book, "The Black Suns". In weighing how this stellar
>
> process will touch the human spirit, he finally comes, from a physical point of view, very close to The Grail Message: "Therefore the spirit must continue to exist, completely sep-
>
> arated from matter, during this fateful leap [into 'another' universe] ... Otherwise, we must suppose that during this leap the spirit dies with matter."
>
> (Taylor, "The Black Suns.")

For the purpose of comparison, let us once more open The Book; ***In The Light of Truth*** [The Grail Message]. There it was said:

"What until then could not detach itself from gross and ethereal matter to cross over the highest, finest and lightest boundary and later the Sphere of Spiritual Substantiality, thereby leaving all matter behind, will inevitably be drawn into the disintegration, whereby its form and whatever else is personal about it will be destroyed!"

(From: "The Regions of Darkness and Damnation", Volume II)

These points of agreement, even to the minute details, should cause one to pay attention. For certain things were already described in detail in The Grail Message about forty years ago [from about the mid 1920's – mid 1930's], whose discovery has been made in the last decade through radio astronomy and computer technology. The question thus arises as to how the author could do this and who he was. Even today, scientists are overwhelmed by this phenomenon which they can hardly grasp. It sounds almost like an excuse when Volker Weidemann (op. cit.) writes: "In many fields of re-

search, processes have been encountered for which neither words nor concepts can be found." But what is still causing

difficulty for the specialists, [the Author of that crucial Message for humanity] had already mastered long ago. He has even – far beyond the gross material – given a description of the course of this happening and warned us *of the final crisis towards which we are moving*.

Parenthetic insertion and emphases mine.

Now the signs in the sky testify of Him and of the Truth of His Word!

(Dr Richard Steinpach.)

With Dr Steinpach's knowledgeable and spiritually-enlightened essay, our journey into spiritual life-knowledge is almost complete. Since the bulk of the references throughout the book are taken from the general format of The Bible, a short assessment on "which" Bible might offer greater insight and more logical interpretations into the great questions about life perfectly fits as the final Chapter.

As for The Grail Message itself – *"In The Light of Truth"* – by virtue of its place of absolute Primacy, It stands completely alone!

Chapter 15

Right Bible/Wrong Bible

The one constant in the world of human religious beliefs is the incredible proliferation of so many. From the reasonably logical, the lyrically beautiful, the oppressively unhealthy, the illogical, the ludicrous, the tyrannical, the superstitious and the evil. So many, and all generally self-serving. Under the outworking of The Law of Attraction, beautiful words *should* attract people of altruistic or ennobled mind. They can also imprint very strongly on the impressionable and the superficial, however. To attract even millions of followers or adherents, therefore, the simplest thing to do is write beautiful words. Pretty words, unfortunately, can often only be just that, words without real substance. So, unless such "beautiful" teachings actually translate to a logical statement showing *how and why* it all came into being and how it thus holds together – complete with perfect law and "no gaps", – then following such a teaching will not lead a *genuine* seeker to something complete and perfect.

Nowhere is there to be seen or heard what should be stated as the obvious conclusion. That we, the people of the earth, groan under our own self-imposed, massive burden of religious machinations, lies and deceit, and fraudulent hypocrisy. The Old Testament, if read either as a religious work or as an historical document, reveals this clearly.

The New Testament on the other hand, whilst certainly strongly restating the Justice of The Laws of God, is, however, also imbued with the message of the Love of God – Jesus – as its necessary accompaniment. Because we have derived much of the content herein from The Bible – and not simply from "beautiful words" found somewhere – the question will no doubt arise as to the validity of the one chosen as our benchmark: that of Ferrar Fenton. Put simply in answer to any such question, in our view it reveals a far greater level of "spiritual insight" than other Bibles and thus provides a more correct interpretation overall. Whilst we unequivocally accept Fenton's Bible for this work, it does not mean we condemn outright every other. Free-will is the benchmark here too. In any case near-future events will highlight all false writings and interpretations and the beliefs spawned by them, and similarly reveal the followers of those beliefs.

Despite favouring Fenton's Bible as our major benchmark among English-language Bibles, the linguistic work of Martin Luther in his translation should be recognised as a particular watershed in Bible translation and interpretation too. His challenge to the, then, Pope and his one-world view was a singular act of very great courage. It was one, moreover, that brought him the threat of death from the very seat of "all-power" in the Western world at the time. His stand paved the way for others to similarly question the status quo, and subsequently seeded the Protestant Reformation.

15.1 The Number 666 of The Revelation

The enigmatic number 666 of The Revelation has greatly puzzled Bible-readers, Bible students and Theologians alike. Like The Holy Grail it, too, has a bearing on outcomes which are decisive for humanity. The correct interpretation of the number is therefore a vital aid adding to the sum total in our understanding of the **why** of the Judgement. Luther's translation of that particular Scripture offers a more correct interpretation of the "mystery" than does Fenton. The relevant passage from Revelation 13:18 (Fenton) reads: "Here is wisdom. Let whoever has intelligence adjudge the number of the beast; the number is a human one; and *his* number is six hundred and sixty six." (Italics mine)

While being correct with regard to the single italicised word – for that is what the number 666 refers to – it is not *exactly* correct overall. However, by emphasising that the number *identifies the one particular man to whom it refers* Fenton may have perceived more about the deeper meaning of that number than he indicates in his full-text interpretation. The use of the lower-case *"his"* seems to show he understood it to be the number of a man on earth.

Whilst noting that probability in Fenton's Work, we can state that Luther *did* correctly translate the relevant Scripture as being the *"number of a* **man**", not a *"human"* number as Fenton did. The King James Version also translates it correctly. However, by virtue of his powerfully-guided work in shaping the German Language, what Luther gave to the "666 mystery" was the *key* to solving it. The number 666 is thus connected with the "beast with two horns":

> "I also saw another beast come up out of the earth; who possessed two horns like a lamb, but spoke like a dragon."

> (Fenton 13:11)

Various interpretations have thought the beast to be individuals, or religious or earthly powers of different centuries. However, through the *special* knowledge and insight of one man who derived his wisdom from the same source from which this book also derives its knowledge and mandate – and from which Dr Richard Steinpach could connect cosmological findings to the "Judgement Process" – we herewith include the answer to the "666 mystery". The knowledge of **The Law of Numbers** provides the solution.

> For the beast with two horns (= 2 words) stands for the *world-embracing* concept *The Sin!* But the name of the man who has the same number as the beast called *The Sin* is *John the Baptist!* The number 666 is explicitly given as the key to it.
> Like any other number, the number 666 also bears within it the sharpest contrasts. Thus with the number 666 there is on the one hand the sin in the service of the darkness, the cause of all evil, the adversary of God; it is the sin which rules the world, entices to evil, and ever again persuades to the worship of the first beast (13, 1) which embodies the absolute dominion of the earthbound intellect.
> On the other side stands John the Baptist, the high and pure spirit, the faithful and humble servant of the Light, the blessed mediator of Divine Revelation; as a powerful warrior against the sin, his name swings in the same number.

> (*A Gate Opens*, Herbert Vollmann, p 349)

Notwithstanding Luther's seminal work, the bulk of key Biblical references herein nevertheless still derives mainly from Ferrar Fenton's re-translation of The Bible. Because Fenton's work is unfortunately not all that well known, it is therefore not "mainstream". Despite that, however, I firmly believe that what it contains is so vital to a better and more logical understanding of Creation, Scripture and related theological issues, that I further believe it important for the reader to know that key people in a number of Christian Denominations and in the linguistic and theological fields supported not only the progress of his singularly amazing effort, but endorsed the finished product too. (See end of Chapter.)

For such a line-up of distinguished luminaries to support and approve a single individual's translation of The Bible – at a time when the King James version was regarded as probably the definitive holy work – must surely mean that Fenton's "translation" struck a powerful chord within the spirit of those eminent men. In my view one lone individual, genuinely and intuitively guided by The Living Light through The Spirit, will achieve a far greater degree of "spiritual accuracy" in translation than will a committee or working group engaged in the same activity. One is more strongly guided by The Spirit, whereas the many will be shackled too strongly by the collective, *debating* intellect!

A perfect example of this can be found in The Jerusalem Bible, Reader's Edition. A short introductory note from the Publishers, Darton, Longman & Todd Ltd., flesh out our assertion.

> "The English text, though translated from the ancient texts, owes a large debt to the **many scholars** who collaborated to produce *La Bible de Jerusalem*, which the publishers of this English Bible gratefully acknowledge."

(Bold emphasis mine.)

In the critical example we have chosen to show the difference in translation between one who is guided from Above and a committee appointed by earthly peers – namely Chapters 1 and 2 of Genesis – two vastly and fundamentally different interpretations of the "Creation account" can be read. On the surface such a distinction might be seen to be "splitting hairs". The opposite view, however, is inherently far more spiritually correct. That only in a true and logically correct interpretation of our origins, and therewith the recognition of our ultimate purpose, can humanity ever hope to move forward in global knowledge and harmony. For it is exactly religious disharmony and intolerance that has been one of the root causes, and still is today, of so many of our problems.[1]

In our example, *two* different Bible interpretations from just *one* religion, Christianity, are used. It is a key one, however, with very many offshoots. Yet despite the fact that the face-book for all Christians is the same – namely The Bible – almost all these many and varied groups accept a Bible interpretation virtually individualised for those self-same, diverse assemblies. If we extrapolate that small fact to encompass all the religious writings in the world, what do we then have? An impossible situation where the truth simply does not emerge clearly anywhere. It is virtually all "lost truth", just religion, which is essentially "Humankind's Lost Potential". The fact that The Bible is apparently the "best-seller" of all time readily provides a "global business" of ever new Bible translations.

Thus, in re-translating Genesis, Fenton intuitively understood that there are actually **two different Creations** of man – **one closest to God** in the Higher Spiritual Realms and **the other of "man of earth"** much further down in the *material* worlds. Whilst this whole book states that fact unequivocally, the previous Chapter clearly shows that there simply has to be such a demarcation in order for all processes, both scientific-physical and eternal-spiritual, to be fulfilled to the last ramification of Perfect Laws throughout all of Creation.

The translators of the much more recent "Jerusalem Bible" fail to recognise this key point. Their interpretation of Genesis gives **two separate accounts** of what they *believe to be* the **same Creation**.

The Jerusalem Bible reads thus:

GENESIS

1. **THE ORIGIN OF THE WORLD AND OF MANKIND**
2. **THE CREATION AND THE FALL**

"**The first account of the creation**" – which is Chapter 1. "**The second account of the creation. Paradise**" – which is Chapter 2.

(Emphasis mine)

---

[1] According to an estimate in 1950, in 3,875 years of earth history there have only been 323 years of peace, but 8,250 peace treaties. In the 55 odd years since, there has not only *not* been one single year of peace, but humanity has engaged in more conflicts in more places with many more peace treaties.

Whereas Fenton's Bible delineates the two Creations:

GENESIS

1. **THE FIRST CREATION OF THE UNIVERSE BY GOD = ELOHIM**
2. **THE CREATION OF MAN UNDER THE SHADOW OF GOD**
3. **THE FORMATION OF MAN FROM THE DUST OF THE GROUND BY THE EVER-LIVING GOD.**

(Emphasis mine.)

Such a vital and fundamentally far-reaching difference between the two Bibles can be better understood if we recognise that Fenton's monumental task was essentially guided by his inner spirit – from Above. Thus deeper insights were available to him to more correctly explain the stupendous nature of the Creation process. Conversely, the translators of The Jerusalem Bible are not similarly blessed. For their similar translation in both Chapters 1 and 2 quite clearly reveals that by not recognising a necessary demarcation line between The Spiritual Worlds and the Material universes, they thereby automatically place **The Creator of all the Worlds** on a much lower, more human, level. In other words they have produced a totally jumbled, illogical and unworkable Creation-structure, and thus transgressed against The Creative Will Itself!

A simple comparison between the *"many scholars"* interpretation of the Creation phase of Genesis in The Jerusalem Bible and that of the lone interpretation of Fenton therefore reveals a singular and vastly different outcome. As formerly stated, it is an extremely disturbing difference. For one, the Jerusalem Bible, clearly shows that it is much more an intellectual exercise of interpretation, for it views the Creation-process *from the earth upwards*. Fenton's, on the other hand most certainly guided from Above, lifts the receptive reader off the earth into a spiritually-correct awareness of an incomprehensible Creation-process that must inherently originate from out of The Divine Realm, and which then *proceeds downwards* toward the material worlds.

Interestingly, with the large amount of "Old-Testament-era discoveries" derived from modern science and archaeology, such a recent analysis of Genesis in The Jerusalem Bible, seemingly offering a more earth-orientated interpretation of the Creation process, paradoxically appears very similar to the Middle Ages church position whereby everything revolved around the earth. That "apparent" viewpoint, moreover, does nothing to reconcile the longstanding debate between science and religion on this subject. Yet, as we have strongly stated, Fenton's correct interpretation *does* bring reconciliation and closure to it, as a correct analysis and interpretation should.

What is required now is for the proponents of the respective disciplines and viewpoints to leave behind, discard, expunge out of their consciousness, this tired and incorrect teaching that really does smack of an egocentric "earth-human religion". And adopt a far more expansive and recognitive attitude and mind-set toward all that emanates from Above. For we human beings surely did not create ourselves.

Fenton's intuitive awareness of that far greater reality, especially powerfully narrated in his marvellously guided work in Genesis, paints a picture that *should naturally awaken The Spirit within every reader*. If not to the same degree of knowing as he, then at the very least to the realisation that something really has been amiss for a very long time now in the standard Church position regarding the Creation process.

In reinforcement, then, unlike the lone Fenton who employed the intuitive faculty of his spirit to achieve his goal, the *"many scholars"* who ultimately contributed their particular level of "expertise" to The Jerusalem Bible clearly mainly utilised the inherently aspiritual, intellectual thought-processes for their assessment and interpretation. Especially so with The Book of Genesis. Were this not the case they would not have persisted with the use of the word ***day***, vis-a-vis , "the first day", "the second day" etc., to attempt to produce a 7-day time-frame for such a stupendous event as the Creation of all that we can see, and the far greater part of the whole that we cannot. Spiritually-correct insight would have permitted them to similarly divine the true nature of the happening, just as Fenton did.

15.2 Intellectual Volition versus Spiritual Volition

Whilst we may perhaps believe that both spirit and intellect might be identical in nature – or at least quite similar and thus ostensibly able to perform the same tasks and fulfil the same roles – that is not the case. Even though being an essential aid which we absolutely need to effectively carry out earthly work, the intellect is completely unsuited for higher tasks such as the divining of spiritual truths. Being an ordained tool for things of the material world, intellectual activity is necessarily and strongly tied to the activity of the brain.

Precisely because it is a very necessary aid, the intellect can and should be used to offer explanations of spiritual or non-material subjects and matters once the *spirit* has intuitively recognised the validity of such connections. The rightful place of *intellectual activity*, therefore, is that of transforming spiritual guidance for earthly activity into the corresponding deed on earth. Such activities run the full gamut of human work and will include most endeavours such as science, architecture, technology and societal infrastructure etc.

Since *intellectual activity* relates to the earthly deed, **intellectual volition** on the other hand, whilst obviously closely connected to the carrying out of the physical task, should be more an "inner force" wanting or desiring ennoblement of all that the intellect is capable of achieving on earth and in earthly life. Despite the fact that both terms might appear to mean the same thing, a high and ennobled *intellectual volition* does not at all mean that any associated task will *automatically* translate to a correspondingly ennobled or pure form at completion. Though of course it should.

Unfortunately, the **intellectual volition** which permeates the planet today may well be the least ennobled form it has ever been in the long and sorry history of mankind. For the most part it is very powerfully driven by crass materialism and the associated desire to acquire great wealth for its own sake, and therefore not necessarily for any kind of altruistic purpose or goal. This kind of *intellectual volition* thus *automatically* sows the seeds of its own destruction. This we may readily observe in the now collapsing, so-called, corporate ethos – to name just one.

Spiritual volition, by contrast, is that power which, when energised by The Spirit – the inner, animating core of all human beings – effectively determines its own life path and thereby its subsequent fate. By virtue of its nature as the "power-pack" and animating force within each of us, it possesses the free-will attribute to connect to ennobled activities, or to base, ignoble ones. And thus sets in train the appropriate "reciprocal returns" for itself. If used spiritually-correctly, our spiritual volition will strive, in the first instance, to seek connection with, and guidance from, the Origin of All Life! It will further strive to hold to *all the virtues* whilst we are on earth thereby anchoring *personal* **spiritual** *threads* to higher and lighter realms above the earth, to which we will thus be drawn after earthly death.

With both the *intellectual volition* and the *spiritual volition*, the key word **volition** – in its *motive-desire aspect* – can be used to debase or ennoble. One, the intellectual, even when concerned with earthly activity only, can still nevertheless weigh down the spirit if used for debased or dishonest activity and prevent the spirit from fulfilling its ordained role. The other, the spiritual, in the same way is able to *drive* the entity to paradise or to perdition if it so chooses. For it is vitally concerned with the very *life* of the individual itself. Notwithstanding the key role of the spirit, the necessary balance between the spiritual and intellectual aspects within man should be striven for, exactly as The Law of Balance ordains. Unfortunately, through ignoring the inner guidance of the spirit and concomitantly strengthening the use of his intellect, man has seriously transgressed that vital ordination. The subsequential global result is clear for all to see.

Thus the huge and fundamental difference between the two respective aspects of the word "volition" is perfectly stated in the Scripture:

> "Do not hoard up for yourselves treasure upon the earth, where moth and canker destroy, and where thieves may burrow through and steal; but store up your treasure in heaven, where neither moth nor rust destroy, and where thieves cannot dig through nor steal: for where your treasure is, there your heart will also be."
>
> (Matthew 6:19-20, Fenton.)

To emphasise Fenton's more correct analysis of Genesis, we reproduce from Chapter 4 the main points of the Biblical sequence of Creation.

Key Points

The Utterance of the stupendous Creation-Words – "**LET THERE BE LIGHT!**" – thus resulting in: **The First Creation – (The Spiritual Realms.)**

1. The Creation of the Heavens and the Earth of **The First Creation** – "By **Periods** God created *that which produced the Solar Systems: then that which produced the Earth.*"

(Genesis 1:1, Fenton.)

2. The **Creation** of day and night (in the Heavens.)

3. The division of the waters which were **under** the expanse (firmament) from the waters which were **above** the firmament (expanse.) The firmament/expanse then named the Heavens.

4. The commanding of the waters **below** the Heavens to be collected in one place, and for dry land to appear.

5. The **Creation** of flora.

6. The Creator sets two great lights which divide day and night for earth.

7. The **Creation** of fish and bird life.

8. The **Creation** of animal life.

9. Then, the great **Creation** of man **in His Image** – both male and female – and the Blessing to rule over all flora and fauna.

10. The **completion** of the Creations at the end of the **sixth Age**. The Creator rests at the **seventh Age** and blesses and hallows the seventh **day**.

Note Scripture: Genesis 2:1 (Fenton) "Thus the whole Host of the Heavens (as well as the Earth were completed.)" This is the completion of The First Creation (i.e. Spiritual Realms.) (Parentheses mine.)

And only then:

The Creation of the Worlds of Matter, including our universes, solar systems and earth – **as planned by its Creator.**

11. After the completion of **The First Creation (The Spiritual Realms)** including all that was then **created** (as described in Genesis 1:1-3), **The Creation of the Worlds of Matter** through a long process of evolution leading to the forming by God of earth-man from out of **the dust of the ground** who, following a suitable time of evolution, became the first human being – **the man with the Living Soul.**

(Genesis 2:19 All emphases mine.)

12. Earth-man gives name to every creature – **formed** from out of the **dust of the ground also.**

13. Even though God had **already created** "man" in His Own Image (both male and female) in **The First Creation**, and had subsequently **formed earth-man** from out of **the dust of the ground**, there was still no earth-woman. (Biblical tradition states that she was constructed from a rib of the man.)

So there are clear pointers illustrating a number of very different and very distinct happenings that occurred and, as we affirmed in Chapter 4, clearly contrary to the one single sequence that the main churches generally believe and accept as having ostensibly **created** man/earth-man. And, moreover, him only. Fenton's delineation reveals these separate, stupendous events in clear sub-titles.

1. **The First Creation of the Universe by God = Elohim.**

2. **Creation of Man under the Shadow of God.**

3. **The formation of Man from the Dust of the Ground by the Ever-living God.**

Therefore, if we once more take careful note of points 3, 4, 9, 11 and 13, and similarly note the above sub-titles 1, 2 and 3 from Fenton's translation, a vastly different and more stupendous picture arises than the present, general belief.

Again, as stated in Chapter 4, the basic sequence outlined here from Fenton's Bible concurs with many of the scientific findings of anthropology and astronomy. Taken in concert, both the scientific view and Fenton's translation actually trace a path of evolutionary development that is clearly consistent with rational logic. Moreover, it encompasses and co-joins both the spiritual-religious and scientific points of view.

Therewith are the long-contested arguments of Creation versus Evolution – Christian fundamentalism versus intellectual science – **perfectly reconciled and harmonised!**

The effectiveness or otherwise of any new Bible translation must ultimately be predicated on whether or not it actually achieves its goal. With regard to Genesis, specifically, that goal should be an interpretation that unequivocally reveals it to be as it actually happened, actually was and therefore as it really is and must be. Thus according to Divine Ordination consistent with the Perfection of The Laws that derive solely from The Divine Will. Translation by a group that fails to achieve this necessary degree of spiritual correctness inherently lives the sage observation about one of the signs of the "end-time":

Ten men will take counsel, and it will come to nought.

It can perhaps also be applied to the "collective counsel" exhibited by "devout followers" of the "religious leaders" of so many self-styled cults and groups of recent times. In the glare of global media exposure, many have come to nought in often tragic ways. Many more will eventually follow the same path into oblivion at this time of full accountability.

15.3 Fenton's Translation of The Bible

Complete and genuinely clarifying insights can therefore only derive from the ultimate knowledge contained within The Laws of Spiritual Truth. Fenton's wonderful insights, though not derived from the "complete" knowledge of The Spiritual Laws – *which were not available to him at the time* – nevertheless must have been especially strongly guided by, and assisted from, that Perfect Source. The theologians who did support and endorse his work obviously agreed with very much of what he translated.

Some key Academics, Christian and otherwise, to whom Fenton was indebted were Drs. Westcott and Hort, the Finnish Professor Tischendorf, Professor Alford, and Bishops Wordsworth and Bloomfield.

During its progress the work was approved by Professor J. S. Blackie of Edinburgh University; Dr.Tait, Archbishop of Canterbury; Dr. Benson, Archbishop of Canterbury; Prof. Oliver Wendell Holmes, of Boston U.S.A.; Prof. C.A.L. Totten, of Yale University, U.S.A.; The Very Rev. E. Plumptre, D.D., Dean of Wells; The Rev. H.S. Champneys, Rector of Epperstone; The Rev. J. Bowen, B.D., Rector of St. Lawrence, Pembroke; Keshub Chunder Sen., Calcutta, India; The Rev. H. Stretton, Vicar of Eastville, Lincs.; The Rev. Charles Garrett, Ex-President of the Wesleyan Conference; The Rev. J. Davis, D.D., Ontario, Canada - and numerous others.

Epilogue

The concepts and conclusions outlined in this book may represent a major challenge to some present-day cultural, philosophical, academic, medical, religious and spiritual beliefs. Yet, under the aegis of The Spiritual Laws, these same concepts are nevertheless inviolable.

"Lone voices in the wilderness" who dare to challenge the status quo inevitably clash with the current academic thought of their particular generation. However, the historic, opposite inevitability is that each generation of academics must re-learn a basic truth, especially with regard to The Spiritual truths contained within the great religions. That it is not the truth that lies with the masses, but the *untruth*. Historically, it is the lone voice or the small group that holds, in lonely constancy, to the kernel. Very often that lone voice or small group will not possess that level of education or erudition which the establishment deems necessary for the retention, understanding and dissemination of such "elevated concepts" as religious or spiritual truth.

Yet the very same "learned" from Christian-religious academia generally laud Paul the Apostle as a key intellectual thinker and scholar. That being the case – for we do not disagree insofar as Paul's access to, then, current knowledge and truth allowed – let us use Paul's sharp intellect and hear what he says to his followers about the "learned".

> "For, contemplate your vocation brothers: that not many philosophers, not many powerful, not many high-born – on the contrary, God has **chosen** the **foolish of the world**, so that He might **shame the philosophic**...
> Therefore none can boast in the presence of God."
>
> (1 Corinthians 1:26-29, Fenton.)

"...how many of you were wise in the ordinary sense of the word, how many were influential people, or came from noble families? No, it was to *shame the wise* that God *chose what is foolish by human reckoning*..."

(The same from The Jerusalem Bible, All emphases mine.)

Since I have no academic mandate from a "higher education facility" I will, for this work – which greatly derives from The Bible and Teachings of Jesus – therefore accept without boast, the greater mandate from Paul, the appointed Apostle of that time.

If I therefore appear to be just one more "lone voice in the wilderness", or one more disturbing "boat-rocker", then I count myself blessed and fortunate indeed for, historically, I stand in very good company. The guidance to write this book – presented to me via a strong inner urging – has been fulfilled. And my spirit is at greater peace through its completion. Whether it is believed, accepted, reviled, mocked or offered any other view, is the concern of the reader alone. I have simply completed what I was urged to undertake, and what I firmly believe I was meant to do.

The free-will choice of each individual will ultimately determine how it is received. As constantly stated throughout the book, all our life-path choices will always be determined by our personal, free-will decisions in any case. Thus the reader is free to accept or reject this work too.

To this end, it is my sincere hope that readers who persevered to this point, and whose spirits may have been agitated, unsettled, or seeking clarification about the current uncertain state of the world, may find the same "peace in knowing" – which I hope is *strongly* reflected in this book – that I have experienced for some years now.

And for those among them who may not have grasped the full import of the explanations contained here, I would certainly recommend at least a second reading.

For whilst this work is relatively comprehensive in terms of how it mainly relates to Spiritual Law and aspects of primarily Christian beliefs it is, nevertheless, only a "signpost". A "signpost" pointing the way to where **all** explanations of life and of Spiritual Truth can be found. Thus a "signpost" pointing the way to that ultimate Truth which explains, and is also ultimately contained within, The Spiritual Laws of Creation!

That Truth is a particularly special, **Spiritual Work** which we first encountered in the Chapter: "Science Supports The Judgement Process" and without which the further explanations of global issues, racial problems, the environment and many more subjects etc.. – but more especially The Spiritual Laws and concomitant logical Bible interpretation – could not have been offered here. It is thus that irrefutable Truth which allowed us to definitively state that, in the final analysis, "science really does support the ***Judgement Process***".

Dr Richard Steinpach's key analysis of cosmological science and the knowledge of Spiritual Law therewith tie those two aspects into a complete whole. The Three Volume Edition of that essential Work – from which he sourced the necessary spiritual knowledge to explain cosmological concepts baffling even to astronomers and scientists alike – is unequivocal testimony to **its** incontestable authority.

Dr. Steinpach's seminal writings bear unequivocal testimony to the *incontestable authority* of **The Source** from which we both derive the knowledge and insights for our respective publications.

That especial **Source** is precisely that which Jesus warned would come onto the Earth at the **End-Time** – **The All-Truth** [John 16] – that we of all humankind were to await and seek out at this very time. [*But of which it was also long-prophesied that only the few would find and recognise.*]

> "I have still much more to tell you; but you are not yet able to bear it. When, however, the **Spiritual of Truth Himself** comes, <u>He will instruct you in all the truth</u>:...
>
> <u>He Himself will honour me</u>;..."
>
> (John 16:12-14, Fenton. Emphases mine.)

Reader: Do not make the foolish mistake of believing that **The Spirit of Truth** here is some kind of filmy, amorphous wraith as the Christian Church *so very wrongly teaches.*
In final reiteration: There is the very sure 'Personal Pronoun': – **He!** And there is also the equally sure term: – **Himself!**

And, of course, the very telling sentence:
"**He Himself will honour me**;..."

Unfortunately for well-meaning Christians, the non-recognition of the true nature of **The Spirit of Truth** by global Christendom coupled with their ongoing and terrible distortions of crucial Bible Scripture effectively means that 2,000 million [2 billion] so-called 'believers' have *missed the moment* – exactly as was prophesied. i.e., *"He shall come like a thief in the night..."* — *"Only the few would know..."*

So, what, exactly, *is* this most especial Teaching of **The All-Truth** that we have constantly alluded to throughout this book.

That crucial Work for humankind is:

The Grail Message

"IN THE LIGHT OF TRUTH"

by

Abd–ru–shin

As the author of a Work that offers deeper knowledge about the *true* meaning of Bible Scripture [and therefore from which we, in *this* book, elucidate the same for Bible readers especially] the name – **Abd-ru-shin** – might, at first glance, seem rather 'out of place'. Perhaps more so for 'Western Christendom', for that *especial Arabic name* translates to English as:

Son of The Holy Spirit.

So: Why an Arabic name? If you have read *this* book to *this* point, you will have well-noted the necessarily strong emphasis on the knowledge of **The Laws of Creation** throughout, including one that is problematic for many Westerners particularly: i.e., **The Law of Rebirth.** [You will also have noted in the Chapter on the life of **Jesus** the true meaning of **The Holy Grail** – the Origin of the very Life-Force for literally everything in Creation – and therefore why the word **Grail** is included in the overall Title of the Work: **IN THE LIGHT OF TRUTH.**]

Notwithstanding the full gamut of reactions from non-believers around the *concept* of "Rebirth", – from curiousity, to disbelief and rejection, to sheer vitriolic hostility; it is, nonetheless, an ***absolute reality*** under inviolable **CREATION-LAW**!

In this case, therefore, **Abd-ru-shin** – in His *first incarnation of that Name* – was an **Arabian Prince** who lived in the same time-frame as **'Moses the Law-Giver'** and the Egyptian Pharaoh, **Ramses II 'The Great'** (c.1300-1224B.C.) He was well-known to both, but *especially to Moses*. For the logically-minded, *astute* reader, therein lies a *clue* to a ***stupendous connection***. To be *strongly associated* with two men who not only hold key places in human history but whose lives and activity influenced countless millions thereafter, obviously presupposes the probability that **Prince Abd-ru-shin** also held a key place then. And that is so!

So whilst there were many Pharaohs by the name of Ramses, only *one* was given the title: **The Great**! Once more for the *astute* reader, therefore; to be historically associated with *both* **Ramses the Great** *and* **Moses the Law-Giver** clearly reveals the importance of **Abd-ru-shin**.

The stupendous nature of the Work — **IN THE LIGHT OF TRUTH** — unequivocally testifies that sure fact to we of this present time.

Because there is no well-known historical record about **Abd-ru-shin**, it would be easy to simply dismiss this nonetheless *actual historical figure* as a fabrication.[2] However, in the context of the immutable **Laws of Creation**; just as we have unequivocally stated where the once-crucified body of **Jesus** lies [with the legs 'not broken'] – and the equally-sure fact that contrary to the collective opinions of hundreds of millions of believers He will not set

---

[2]The recent discovery of the so-called "heretic Pharaoh", Akhenaton, is a case in point. For daring to abolish Egypt's Priesthood and her many gods for a 'One God'; after his death his new temple city was destroyed, his image was effaced, and all references to him were expunged by succeeding Pharaohs. The Priesthood re-introduced the 'old gods' and Egypt sank into a dark age that ultimately led to her fall. Despite attempts to 'erase him completely', Akhenaton is now the most studied Pharaoh of all.

physical foot on earth again – so, too, can we state what will one day be revealed as sure and irrefutable evidence of *this Man's* life on earth.

Murdered by a knife-wielding assassin – probably on the orders of Ramses – before He could *completely fulfil* His Mission for humanity *then*, the earthly cloak of **Abd-ru-shin** for that particular incarnation was placed in a Pyramid-tomb, now long-buried under desert sands. At the appropriate time, His tomb will one day be revealed. Then, however, the Christian Church, particularly – but *all* religions and belief systems ultimately – will have to contend with the hieroglyphic inscriptions on that especial tomb.

For the very last line of His story *then* reveals the completion of His Mission for humanity in the *20th century* as **THE ONE** Who was to come:

IMANUEL — THE SON OF MAN!

THE "WILL OF GOD":

— THE "SPIRIT OF TRUTH" —

— for the writing of The ALL-TRUTH:

"IN THE LIGHT OF TRUTH!"

Hence such a close association with **Moses** the **Law-Giver**, and thus the continuation of His Name and Title – **Abd-ru-shin** — from that time. Being *able* to write such knowledge in the first place very obviously means that **He** carries that highest of knowledge *Living* **within Him**. His Origin is clearly revealed in His Work.

Within that crucial Work, however, He states – as the *primary* consideration for all – to:

"Heed the Word, not the Bringer!"

...As should always have been done, as well, with the Teachings of Jesus – Who brought the knowledge of Creation and Divine Law to Earth *in a form understandable to believers then* – and with all others who similarly sought to *genuinely enlighten* earthly humanity... However, in the emotional stupidity that characterises we humans generally, we sought, instead, to *focus* on the 'Bringer/s'. The practice of elevating *them* to become the ***focus*** of the particular religion – rather than on **the Truths** they sought to impart – has resulted in the mess of religious intolerance and bloodshed we are burdened with today.

Whilst the thrust of this Work fulfils its major purpose elucidating precisely *why* there must be a comprehensive cleansing and "culling" of the many, many millions of global humankind who in their perverse blindness place their cultures, religions and societal garbage before the great and pure Laws of Creation, that vital knowledge cannot stand alone in grand isolation. For the very Laws which humankind have transgressed for millennia without thought or belief of future consequences deriving from those transgressions, now reveal their *inviolability* more powerfully with each passing day.

Yet science and religion still holds to its standard mind-set of *seeing only what it wishes to see*. In the impending "sorting out" process for all of humanity and its works, we *will* learn that we were, ***by choice***, both *intransigent* **and** *blind*. We will also learn, unfortunately very severely now, that the "judging process" ***we humans*** have set in train and now rolling more intensively, ***was not*** – ***is not*** – visited upon us by **THE CREATOR**.

By placing His Perfect, precise and *Inviolable Laws* – which govern *all life* and to which *all* human decisions and processes *are subject* – into **His Creation**, we of humankind were gifted the perfect set of ***rules*** by which we *could* have produced an harmonious paradise on Earth. In their inherent Perfection these Laws are, in their perfect outworking, ***Absolute***, and are therefore ***Immutable***: Thus ***Unchangeable***!

The present, final result is **crystal-clear** for all to see. For we, alone, are responsible for the tragic and long-failing state of earthly humanity. **The Almighty Himself**, being Perfect Love – but also Perfect Justice – has no need to, *and therefore does not*, actually judge humanity. Through the decisions we make for ourselves, ***but under the aegis and outworking of His Perfect Laws***, we thus judge, ***and pass judgement upon***, ourselves – as individuals and as a collective, global humanity.

In particular, moreover, under that decisive Law which unequivocally states in both perfect **Love** and **Justice**:

"**For what a man sows, that will he also reap...**" [Gal.]

Since The Son of God warned that "...if the times were not cut short, not a man would be saved", and The Revelation itself indicates a hard mathematical outcome for the six thousand million plus presently alive on Earth: – "A third of a third of a third shall die." – **The Gift of Grace** may yet still offer a saving-grace mechanism for *some*.

The unnerving portent of those two indicators, *on their own*, show just how far the human race has *deviated* from the *correct path* we were *ordained* to travel, and how *serious* our collective transgressions over millennia *must actually have been* to now call in such destruction. Quite logically, therefore, only one outcome is certain. Complete destruction of *all they* who refuse, along with *all that* which refuses, to live by *true* **CREATION-LAW** — clearly explained for all of global humanity in the Work:

"IN THE LIGHT OF TRUTH!"

May you, reader, choose to seek out this most Exalted Knowledge, and therewith build within yourself *that* peace of spirit which must necessarily *accept*, yet objectively and compassionately *understand*, the increasingly disturbing and *seemingly* incomprehensible fate of suffering humankind on Earth today. Unfortunately, however, a fate brought about simply by our collective refusal to pay heed to **Creation-Law** – **Perfect**, **Immutable**, **Inviolable**, **Absolute** – in which we have our life and being.

Yet what of the many millions of deluded, often hate-filled, fundamentalists of every religious 'bent' who radically promote their particular belief as the so-called *only truth* for all? The necessary 'cleansing' that will finally *rid the world of them* will usher in – *for the few who are left* – the long-awaited **Millennium of Peace**.

For the 'spiritually asleep', and those who would mock and revile; two simple messages. One from **The Son of God, Jesus**, to one of His disciples who asked for leave to attend the funeral of a member of his earthly family — [Parenthetic additions mine]:

"**Let the [spiritually] dead bury their [spiritually] dead.**"

— and 2 — Watch the nightly global News!

On an *individual* basis we can ameliorate, *at least for ourselves*, some of the *harder aspects* of the prophesied end-time for global societies. — Therefore:

"And acting nobly, we shall not suffer... So then, as we have opportunity, let us do good to all..."

(Gal. 6:7-10, Fenton.)

The golden key to that more positive outcome will be best achieved by striving to understand the "Crucial Imperatives" – most especially that of:

THE TWO SONS OF GOD!

*   *   *   *   *

For all of **Creation** and **THE LAW** resides in **The Living Form** of:

*   *   *   *   *

THE TRIUNE GOD!

*   *   *   *   *

THE TWO SONS

— — and — —

* * * * *

THE LORD GOD!

* * * * *

Bibliography

1. *A Gate Opens*, Herbert Vollmann, Composite Volume 1985, Stiftung Gralsbotschaft Publishing Co., Stuttgart.

2. *"The Inconceivable – Here it Happens."* Dr Richard Steinpach. Gralswelt (Magazine) Stiftung Gralsbotschaft Publishing Co., Stuttgart.

3. *The Holy Bible in Modern English*, Ferrar Fenton, Destiny Publishers, Massachusetts U.S.A. 1966 Edition.

4. *The Holy Bible, Authorised (King James) Version*, Eyre and Spottiswoode (Publishers) Ltd., Great Britain.

5. *The Jerusalem Bible, Reader's Edition*, First published 1968, Darton, Longman and Todd Ltd., London.

6. *The Apocrypha of the Old Testament*, Revised Standard Version, Published by Thomas Nelson and Sons Ltd.

7. *The Language of God: A Scientist Presents Evidence for Belief.* Francis S. Collins, M.D.,Ph.D. Published by Simon and Schuster Ltd., 2006.

8. *The Wisdom of Israel. [The Wisdom of Spinoza]*, Published by Michael Joseph, London 1949.

9. *The Gospel of the Essenes*, The original Hebrew and Aramaic texts translated and edited by Edmund Bordeaux Szekely, Revised Edition, London, C. W. Daniel, 1976.

10. *A Wanderer In The Spirit Lands*, Franchezzo, Transcribed by A. Farnese, Progressive Thinker Publishing House, Chicago 1913.

11. *Cruden's Complete Concordance to the Old and New Testaments (and to the Apocrypha)*, Revised Edition, Guildford: Lutterworth Press, 1954.

12. *The Christian and Reincarnation*, Stephen Lampe, Millenium Press (UK) 1990.

13. *Building Future Societies*, Stephen Lampe, Millenium Press (UK) 1994.

14. *Heavenly Thoughts*, Karl May.

15. *Autobiography of a Yogi*, Paramahansa Yogananda, First published 1946, Random House.

16. *Man's Eternal Quest*, Paramahansa Yogananda, Collected Talks and Essays on Realizing God in Daily Life, Volume 1.

17. *Great Illustrated Dictionary Vol's I & II*, Readers Digest, First Edition, 1984, USA.

18. *The Concise Oxford Dictionary of Proverbs*, 1983 Edition, Oxford University Press, First Printing 1982, USA, New England Journal of Medicine.

19. *Reflections on Life After Life*, Raymond A. Moody, Bantam Books USA and Canada, 3rd Printing, 1978.

20. *The Soul – Whence and Whither*, Hazrat Inayat Khan, East-West Publication, 1984 Edition.

21. *Music Forms*, Geoffrey Hodson, The Theosophical Publishing House, Adyar, 1976.

22. *The Romeo Error*, Lyall Watson, London: Hodder and Stoughton, 1974.

23. *Ideas and Opinions*, Albert Einstein, Bonanza Books, New York, 1954.

24. *Philosophy History and Problems*, Third Edition, Samuel Enoch Stumpf, McGraw-Hill, USA 1983.

25. *The Nature Of The Gods*, Cicero, Penguin Classics, 1972 Edition, Translation by Horace C P Macgregor, Printed by Richard Clay (S E Asia) Pte. Ltd. Reprinted 1978, 1984.

26. *On the Speech of Neanderthal Man*, Philip Lieberman and Edmund S. Crelin, Linguistic Inquiry 2:203-222, Cambridge Mass., MIT Press.

27. *Sophie's World*, Jostein Gaardner, Phoenix House, Great Britain, 1996 Edition.

28. *The Atlas of the Universe*, Patrick Moore, Mitchell Beazley Publishers, London, 1981 Edition.

29. *Lifecloud: the origin of life in the universe*, Fred Hoyle and Chandra Wickramasinghe, 1978.

30. *The Life and Letters of Charles Darwin* (Editor – Frances Darwin), 2nd Edition, London: John Murray, 1887.

31. *The Mystery of Life's Origin: Reassessing Current Theories*, Charles B. Thaxton, Walter L. Bradley, Richard L. Olsen, Philosophical Library, 1984.

32. *The Sacred Balance: Rediscovering our place in nature*, David Suzuki, Allen and Unwin, Australia, 1997.

33. *North American Indian Chiefs*, General Editor: Karl Nagerfeld, Tiger Books International, London. 1995.

34. *Native American Myths and Legends*, Editorial Consultant, Colin F. Taylor, New York: Smithmark, 1994.

35. *The Handbook of Unusual Natural Phenomena (Eyewitness Accounts of Nature's Greatest Mysteries)*, William R. Corliss, Arlington House, Crown Publishers, New York.

36. *Earthquake Information Bulletin*, 10: 231-33, 1978, National Earthquake Information Centre (NEIC), Published by the Centre (Rockville Md) Serial Publication, Bi-monthly, 1970-1985.

37. *Earthquakes and the Urban Environment*, Volume II, G. Lennis Berlin, Published Boca Raton, Fla: CRC Press, c 1980.

38. *Conference Notes, U S Geological Survey Conference*, 10 Oct. 1976.

39. Time Magazine 25th June 2001 Edition (Feature Article: "How The Universe Will End")

40. Readers Digest Magazine, Aug 2004, (Feature Article: "How to Make a Universe", Bill Bryson.)

41. *British Medical Journal.*

42. *Science Journal.*

43. *Economist.*

44. *Independent.*

45. *As You Like It*, Shakespeare, Act 11.

46. *The Helmet and the Cross*, W. H. Canaway Century Publishers, London, 1986.

47. *National Geographic Star Chart*, 1983.

48. *Friends of the Earth.*

49. *ASH (Action on smoking and health).*

50. "Our World" The Savage Earth – BBC Series (screened 1998)

51. Discovery Channel, "Earthquakes" (screened through 2002)

52. Encarta – Microsoft.

53. "The Human Body", New Series Documentary, Part 1, Dr Robert Winston.

54. Brittanica CD '97

55. CNN.

56. "Larry King Live".

www.ingramcontent.com/pod-product-compliance
Lightning Source LLC
Chambersburg PA
CBHW071232160426
43196CB00009B/1033